CHILDREN'S REASONING AND THE MIND

Children's reasoning and the mind

edited by

Peter Mitchell
Nottingham University, UK

Kevin John Riggs
London Guildhall University, UK

Psychology Press
a member of the Taylor & Francis group

Copyright © 2000 by Psychology Press Ltd, a member of the Taylor & Francis group
    All rights reserved. No part of this book may be reproduced in any form, by photostat,
    microform, retrieval system, or any other means without the prior written permission
    of the publisher.

Psychology Press Ltd, Publishers
27 Church Road
Hove
East Sussex, BN3 2FA
UK

British Library Cataloguing in Publication Data

A catalogue record for this book is available from the British Library

ISBN 0-86377-854-2 (hbk)
ISBN 0-86377-855-0 (pbk)

Cover design by Jim Wilkie
Cover illustration taken from an original
by Nick Orsborn

Typeset by Graphicraft Limited, Hong Kong
Printed and bound in the UK by Biddles Ltd, Guildford and King's Lynn

For my wife, Rita

Contents

List of contributors

Eric Amsel, Department of Psychology, Weber State University, 1202 University Circle, Ogden, UT 84408-1202, USA

Sarah Beck, School of Psychology, University of Birmingham, Birmingham, B15 2TT, UK

William V. Fabricius, Department of Psychology, Arizona State University, Box 871104, Tempe, AZ 85287-1104, USA

Norman H. Freeman, Department of Psychology, University of Bristol, 8 Woodland Road, Bristol BS8 1TN, UK

Douglas Frye, Graduate School of Education, University of Pennsylvania, 3700 Walnut Street, Philadelphia, PA 19104-6216, USA

Tim P. German, Department of Psychology, University of Essex, Colchester, CO4 35Q, UK

Andreas Gschaider, Institut für Psychologie, Universität Salzburg, Hellbrunnerstrasse 34, A-5020, Salzburg, Austria

Paul L. Harris, Experimental Psychology, University of Oxford, South Parks Road, Oxford, OX1 3UD, UK

R. Peter Hobson, Developmental Psychopathology Research Unit, Adult Department, The Tavistock Clinic, 120 Belsize Lane, London, NW3 5BA, UK

Alison Imbens-Bailey, Department of Education, University of California, Moore Hall, Box 951521, Los Angeles, CA 90095, USA

Haruo Kikuno, Department of Early Childhood Education, Osaka University of Education, 4-698-1 Asahigaoka, Kashiwara, Osaka 582, Japan

Deanna Kuhn, Department of Psychology, Columbia University, Box 119, New York, NY 10027, USA

Hilary Leevers, Center for Molecular Behavioral Neuroscience, Aidekman Research Center, 197 University Avenue, Rutgers University, Newark, NJ 07102, USA

Alan M. Leslie, Center for Cognitive Science, Psychology Building, Busch Campus, Rutgers University, Piscataway, NJ 08855-1179, USA

Peter Mitchell, School of Psychology, University of Nottingham, University Park, Nottingham, NG7 2RD, UK

Robert W. Mitchell, Department of Psychology, Eastern Kentucky University, Richmond, KY 40475-3108, USA

Josef Perner, Institut für Psychologie, Universität Salzburg, Hellbrunnerstrasse 34, A-5020, Salzburg, Austria

Donald M. Peterson, School of Computer Science, University of Birmingham, Birmingham, B15 2TT, UK

Kevin J. Riggs, Department of Psychology, London Guildhall University, Calcutta House, Old Castle Street, London, E1 7NT, UK

Elizabeth J. Robinson, School of Psychology, University of Birmingham, Birmingham, B15 2TT, UK

Jarom Smalley, Department of Psychology, Weber State University, 1202 University Circle, Ogden, UT 84408-1202, USA

Eugene Subbotsky, Department of Psychology, Lancaster University, Lancaster, LA1 4YF, UK

Jill de Villiers, Department of Psychology, Smith College, Northampton, MA 01063, USA

Peter de Villiers, Department of Psychology, Smith College, Northampton, MA 01063, USA

Heinz Wimmer, Institut für Psychologie, Universität Salzburg, Hellbrunnerstrasse 34, A-5020, Salzburg, Austria

Philip David Zelazo, Department of Psychology, University of Toronto, 100 St. George Street, Toronto, M55 3G3, Canada

CHAPTER ONE

Making judgements about mental states: Processes and inferences

Kevin J. Riggs
London Guildhall University, UK

Peter Mitchell
University of Nottingham, UK

INTRODUCTION

In 1978, the primatologists David Premack and Guy Woodruff introduced the term 'theory of mind' (TOM) when asking whether the behaviour of chimpanzees could be explained by crediting them with an ability to impute mental states such as beliefs, desires and intentions. Since that paper there has been a vast amount of research by philosophers and psychologists, trying to understand the form of our understanding of mind and how it develops. Premack and Woodruff originally identified a theory of mind with a 'system of inferences', suggesting that the class of TOM (or mindreading) problems might represent a class of inferential, or reasoning problems. Rather surprisingly, much of the subsequent research has not been particularly concerned with the form these inferences might take, or with the reasoning processes that may feature in mental state ascription. The research question is not a simple one though, with the complexity of the problem becoming apparent when we focus in to reveal a number of further questions: Are these processes a form of simulation or are they more like rule governed algorithms? If it is simulation, then in what sense, and what form does it take? How does the development of executive functioning feature in these reasoning processes, and how are these processes acquired? These questions form the basis of, and, are reflected in, the title and the content of this volume.

HISTORY

Philosophers have long been interested in the basis of our knowledge of self and others. For philosophers the debate has been between the Theory theorists on the one hand and simulation theorists on the other. The Theory theorists claim that we perform mindreading through inference from a common sense folk psychological theory. This theory contains the principles and concepts necessary to predict people's mental states and explain their behaviour. Questions arise about what, how explicit, and how organised these principles are, but the general idea is that we make inferences from some sort of common sense knowledge, or theory, concerning the principles that govern people's behaviour.

A psychological investigation into these principles was made by Wimmer, Hogrefe, and Perner (1988) (see also Wimmer and Gschaider, chapter 12, this volume) who suggested that very young children are unable to infer the epistemic consequences of various kinds of informational access. For example, they argued that young children do not understand that seeing X leads to thinking X while not seeing X means remaining ignorant about X. Children aged 3 years in their study were able to judge correctly when a person did or did not have visual access to a container, but these same children failed to make judgements of knowledge on the basis of this. Instead, they judged knowledge in an unsystematic manner. Their argument ran into difficulty though, when it was found that children also make errors in reporting mental states in contexts where there was no need to make inferences on the basis of informational access. Moreover, Pratt and Bryant (1990) gathered data which suggested that children aged 3 years do not have such a serious difficulty linking information with states of knowledge.

The simulation theorists claim that we perform mindreading through use of the imagination and simulating the mental states of other people. We perform a thought experiment in which we feed 'pretend' inputs into our own cognitive system, let our system run off line, and so arrive, experimentally, at the other person's mental state. The status of mental simulation as a process for judging about other minds has been recognised by researchers interested in adult cognition for a few decades (Kahneman & Tversky, 1982). As with developmental studies, this research was frequently concerned with the circumstances in which biases in judgements occur—biases that stand to enlighten us about the character of the human aptitude for simulation. For example, adults are much more likely to dwell upon deviation from a routine than adherence to a routine when considering the counterfactual of what might have been following a tragic accident. If John had a car crash on the way home after deviating from his usual route, people are likely to say, 'If only he had taken his normal route.' If John had a car crash after staying on his usual route, people seldom say, 'If only he had gone a different way.' It seems adults are uncomfortable reasoning to a counterfactual that differs from their expectations of what normally happens. In the developmental sphere, Harris (1992) made an important contribution when he suggested a link between young children's pretence and their ability to reason counterfactually, to entertain hypothetical suppositions and to reason about states of mind. In his account, the qualities of pretence have a bearing on the characteristics of reasoning about the mind.

This debate between the Theory theorists and simulation theorists can thus be viewed as a tension between one side focusing on a type of knowledge (from which *inferences* are made) and the other side focusing on a type of process (or set of processes) involved in (among other things) mental state ascriptions. Recently, though, a number of theorists (see Carruthers & Smith, 1996, for a review) have argued that neither TOM knowledge nor simulation alone, can fully explain how we are able to understand and predict the behaviour of other people. These authors have stressed the need for a hybrid approach combining both TOM knowledge *and* simulation. Perner (1996, p. 103) for example has recently proposed that "... the future must lie in a mixture of simulation and theory use. However, what this mixture is and how it operates must be specified in some detail before any testable predictions can be derived".

We see then that both the Theory theorists and simulation theorists (and adherents of a mixture of the two) acknowledge the role of inferential processing in mindreading. However, the philosophical debate (as noted by Perner) has often been conducted at too abstract a level; lacking the detail from which testable observations can be made. More detailed theorising and psychological investigation is required, and it is to this end that the chapters in this volume progress our understanding of the processes that underlie mental state ascription.

The psychological study of TOM took off in the 1980s with a paper by Wimmer and Perner (1983). Their original formulation of the unexpected transfer task involved a character Maxi who put some chocolate in one location and left for school. While he was absent, the chocolate was moved to a second location before he set off to return home in search of the chocolate. The findings from this study were that sometime between their 3rd and 5th year, children develop the ability to ascribe false beliefs, and to predict behaviours symptomatic of false belief. Their paper generated a vast amount of empirical work for primatologists and psychologists, and at the same time refreshed the philosophical debate between the Theory and simulation theorists.

Philosophers—who traditionally paid little attention to how TOM knowledge or the processes involved in mindreading are acquired—soon realised that work from developmental psychology might be able to inform the debate concerning mindreading in adults. Of major concern to psychologists, and in the Piagetian tradition, was the question of the developmental stages the child passes through on the way to developing adult mindreading abilities. They researched the age at which children passed the false belief test; the relationship between belief and behaviour; children's understanding of true belief, desire and intention; the relationship between pretend play and mindreading; and the development of mindreading in children with autism (for reviews, see Lewis & Mitchell, 1994;

Mitchell, 1996). Many of these psychologists asked about the child's mindreading development without regard for the broader philosophical debate.

However, some researchers clearly had strong views on the relationship between empirical work in developmental psychology and wider philosophical arguments. Consistent with the Theory theory (and current thinking in developmental science) many took seriously the metaphor of 'child as scientist'. This metaphor draws a parallel between the development of theories in science and the development of theories in children; with children formulating and testing hypotheses, and postulating mental states as theoretical constructs to explain and predict behaviour. For many this view was coupled with an ontological argument concerning the child's conceptualisation of belief. This argument claims that 3-year-olds fail false belief tasks because they do not appropriately conceptualise beliefs as representations (and false beliefs as misrepresentations)—thus crucial to mindreading development is the development of the concept of representation. Combining the 'child as scientist' metaphor with the idea of a developing concept of representation, led many to claim that children who pass false belief tasks move successfully from being situation theorists (Perner, 1991), or copy theorists (Wellman, 1990), to representational theorists holding a representational theory of mind (Gopnik & Wellman, 1992). Although influential, both theoretically and experimentally (it initiated a body of research looking at the relationship between children's understanding of the concept of representation and mindreading), a number of concerns were raised about this view.

One problem is that the Theory theory says very little about the mechanisms responsible for development. Russell (1996) points out that if we view the child as developing from one type of theorist to another, it merely begs the question: What processes underlie theory development? Moreover, on their own, theories predict nothing—it is only from a Platonic perspective that theories have predictive power. From a cognitive perspective, prediction is a joint effort between a theory and the inferential capacities of its user (Peterson & Riggs, 1999). It is true that to pass the false belief task, a child needs to conceptualise belief appropriately (or be in possession of the 'right' theory). However, the child also needs the quite separate ability to *reason* to answers when asked questions about constructs in that theory. Experienced physicists might make mathematical errors in their calculations concerning, say, a satellite launch, but it does not imply that they do not understand Newton's laws of motion, or the concepts of 'mass' and 'acceleration'. Errors in performance do not necessarily point to errors in underlying (conceptual or theoretical) competence. In short, invoking the possession of a theory of mind is *insufficient* to explain the developing competence of mindreading in young children—inferential concerns must also be taken into consideration.

An account that acknowledged the distinction between inferential abilities and conceptual understanding was developed by Leslie (Leslie, 1994; Leslie & Thaiss, 1992) based on neuropsychological data from children with autism.

Being less concerned with stages of development, and more with cognitive architecture, he proposed that humans are born with a theory of mind mechanism (ToMM) responsible for reading mental states from behaviour. ToMM works in conjunction with a selection processor (SP) responsible for selecting premises to feed ToMM, and it also functions in 'non mental' inferences. He argued that 3-year-olds have an understanding of mental state concepts, but fail false belief tasks due to an underdeveloped SP feeding wrong information into ToMM. In contrast, Leslie supposes that children with autism fail false belief tasks specifically due to a damaged ToMM. Despite its merits, a problem with this account is that it says nothing about *developmental* mechanisms (beyond maturation of modules). Further, this view says little about the *type* of inferences that might be used in mental state ascription.

A somewhat different attempt to account for developmental change without invoking changes in conceptual understanding was made by Fodor (1992). He proposed that young children are equipped with the necessary concepts to reason about false beliefs, but are hampered by limitations in processing resources. He suggested that children are endowed with the ability to apply a couple of hypotheses:

H1.   Predict that the agent will act in a way that will satisfy his desires.
H2.   Predict that the agent will act in a way that would satisfy his desires if his beliefs were true.

Fodor proposed that if young children are able to make a unique prediction of a person's behaviour, then they would apply H1 by default because this route demands fewer processing resources than H2. In Wimmer and Perner's (1983) unexpected transfer test, it leads them to judge that Maxi will look for his chocolate where it currently is rather than where Maxi last saw it. If application of H1 does not lead to a unique behavioural prediction (e.g. if Mum divided the chocolate between two locations) then the child is alerted to the inadequacy of H1. This prompts him or her to use H2 which does allow a unique prediction: If his belief were true that his chocolate was in the drawer where he put it, then searching there would satisfy his desire. Hence, Fodor argued that the hierarchical form of the reasoning heuristics leads to a realist error by default. This supposedly explains the impediment to correct judgements rather than any fundamental inability to grasp the concept of belief.

Although Fodor's (1992) formulation is highly seductive, there are problems. Whilst it is able to explain the pattern of young children's judgements in an unexpected transfer test, it is not able to explain their difficulty with their own past false beliefs. Inferential heuristics of the kind Fodor describes are not needed for these tasks, yet children still experience the same kind of difficulty.

Recently, a growing body of researchers has risen to the task of speculating about the core reasoning processes that might be involved in making judgements about mental states. The research of these authors has been stimulated, in part, by the views first expressed by Harris and colleagues. Harris has perhaps been the most articulate psychologist advocating the view that simulation ability, rather than theoretical knowledge, lies at the heart of mindreading (Harris, 1992, p. 302): "skilled mindreading [. . .] calls for the imaginative resonance of the biographer, rather than the theoretical postulates of the scientist". From a developmental perspective, he added detail to the simulationist framework, and argued that passing TOM tasks requires certain cognitive processes to adjust what he termed 'default settings'. These default settings are (1) current reality and (2) intentional states of the self toward that reality. The processes involved in adjusting these settings requires the use of the imagination and are used in reasoning more generally as "part of a wide-ranging ability to think about and describe counterfactual substitutes for current reality". Until very recently, though, there has been little evidence in support of Harris's ideas. However, a number of articles have now appeared reporting the inferential capacities of young children and their relation to mindreading development. For example, Harris, German, and Mills (1996), Frye, Zelazo, and Palfai (1995) and Riggs, Peterson, Robinson, and Mitchell (1998) have all recently published data reporting, and commenting upon, this relationship and it is this body of work that motivated us to bring together the authors presented in this volume.

PREVIEW OF THE VOLUME

Two early chapters lay down the philosophical background against which much TOM research is set. Hobson (Chapter 2) and R.W. Mitchell (Chapter 3) review many classic arguments and problems from the philosophy of mind and cognitive science often associated with thinkers such as Wittgenstein and Strawson. These include the argument from analogy, the private language debate and the symbol grounding problem. This philosophical review serves to convey many of the complexities and perhaps less obvious issues that researchers might want to take on board when considering the development of reasoning about the mind. Mitchell comes to the view that mental state words refer to both first person experiences and causal factors in a behavioural context (or story). Presenting data from a series of studies on children's pretend play, he reports that children apply a behavioural rule for ascribing pretence to others, but in the case of their own pretend behaviour, their own personal experience seems to be more salient. Hobson argues that the early experience of coordinating attitudes promotes the grounding of symbols in the world of objects and events. Prior to this, symbolic activity might be somewhat detached from reality, as in pretence. Hence, Hobson discusses how early social experiences could invest symbolism with the property of representational aboutness, which is bound to be vital in the acquisition of a representational understanding of the mind.

Around half the chapters in the volume are concerned with the inferential abilities of young children and how these relate to the development of mindreading. Harris and Leevers (Chapter 4) present findings from work with 3-, 4-, and 5-year-olds in syllogistic and counterfactual reasoning tasks. They argue that setting aside what you know and reasoning with premises known to be false is something that young children are able to do without any formal schooling; even 2- and 3-year-olds are fairly competent at considering counterfactual antecedents and consequents. Even so, they argue that counterfactual reasoning performance may be an important factor in mental state reasoning performance between the ages of 3 and 5 years. They suggest that children might first start to reason counterfactually in instances where an initial state of affairs is transformed by some mishap into a negative outcome, as when muddy shoes dirty a clean floor. However, children may not be able to reason in tasks with neutral transformations until about 4 years of age, as often observed in false belief tasks when chocolate is moved from one location to another.

Riggs and Peterson (Chapter 5) present evidence that failure in false belief tasks is symptomatic of a broader difficulty with counterfactual conditional reasoning. They report a correlation between performance in false belief tasks and performance in structurally similar counterfactual reasoning tasks. Arguing from a simulation/Theory theory mix, they suggest that answers to questions in false belief tasks require children to construct a response using their imagination together with some rudimentary folk psychological principles. They end with a brief suggestion that the process of 'pretending' in counterfactual reasoning (and belief ascription) are very different from the process of pretend play. Picking up from the Riggs and Peterson chapter, Robinson and Beck (Chapter 6) assume that the processes involved in counterfactual reasoning and pretence are different and then systematically explore what factors might be responsible for children's errors in the former. In a clever series of experiments they present evidence (in more detail than Riggs and Peterson) that conditional questions about the future (e.g. "If I draw on this piece of paper . . . ?") are easier to answer for 3- and 4-year-olds than counterfactual conditionals about the past or present (e.g. "If I had not drawn on this piece of paper . . . ?"). Moreover, this difference in difficulty persists even if the future situation to be entertained runs counter to very firm expectations about reality, such as the possibility that water might run up rather than downhill.

Amsel and Smalley (Chapter 7), contrary to authors of the two previous chapters, argue that the cognitive processes involved in pretence are the very same that are involved in counterfactual reasoning. These processes involve creating and analysing false states of affairs and co-ordinating them with true ones. What supposedly differs across pretence and counterfactual thinking are the real world implications for these false states of affairs: In pretend play, false states are playful alternatives to true ones, but in counterfactual thinking they are "copied and edited versions of true ones which are to be seriously compared to and contrasted with true ones".

Frye (Chapter 8) and Zelazo (Chapter 9) both consider the role of reasoning in the development of mental state understanding. They present and report data consistent with their Cognitive complexity and control (CCC) theory. Frye argues that a domain specific, theoretical understanding is insufficient for mental state ascription—a domain general reasoning process must also be employed. According to CCC theory, pre-school children develop the ability to handle increasingly complex 'if–then' rules. Understanding proceeds from simple 'if–then' rules to more complex embedded conditionals such as 'if A, if B, then C' that Frye claims are required for reasoning about false beliefs. Zelazo locates CCC theory within a developmental process model of consciousness, called the Levels of Consciousness model. This model describes how recursive processes in consciousness underlie the development of action control. Increases in self reflection make possible the use of increasingly complex representations to guide responding in task situations involving inhibition to pre-potent objects. According to the model, children below 4 years of age have yet to acquire the level of consciousness required for success in false belief tasks.

De Villiers and de Villiers (Chapter 10) take a different approach by questioning the role of language in the development of an understanding of the mind. Several studies published recently have highlighted the correlation between linguistic abilities and TOM, both in typical and atypical development. However, previous authors have often been unable to make strong claims about the direction of causality or even to show which aspects of linguistic ability are responsible for the correlation. De Villiers and de Villiers report longitudinal data which point to the benefit of mastering certain forms of syntactic structure. They make a strong and compelling claim to the effect that the syntax of language provides a dynamic framework for reasoning about representational states.

Two chapters analyse the child as scientist metaphor. German and Leslie (Chapter 11) argue that the Theory theory remains largely silent on information processing issues. They explore the idea that certain mechanisms might allow children to initially attend to mental states, and subsequently allow success in false belief tasks. Using examples from existing literature and by presenting new evidence they illustrate the wider role these mechanisms might play in allowing learning about mental states. Wimmer and Gschaider (Chapter 12) argue that if we are to take seriously the 'child as scientist' metaphor and the idea that an understanding of persons is theoretical in nature, we must focus not only on the concepts in that theory, but also on the causal role they play in that theory. Citing both experimental and longitudinal data, they argue that children only acquire a conception of false belief, once they understand the informational/causal conditions that give rise to the belief.

Fabricius and Imbens-Bailey (Chapter 13) review the evidence from the class of false belief tasks and argue that the (often inconsistent) data can be explained if children's ideas about the mind are seen to stem from their own direct experiences of their own mental states. Arguing a form of simulationism, they suggest that young children have a phenomenological awareness of what it is like to 'know' and 'not know', which they then project onto others when asked about what they (the others) know or think. Arguing against the view that children shift to a RTM at 4 years of age, they question whether research to date has overestimated children's understanding of the representational nature of mental states and suggest further work with older children. Mitchell and Kikuno (Chapter 14) take the opposite view, by arguing that the reasoning involved in judging about other people's beliefs is essentially the same as that involved in judging one's own beliefs. They suggest that whilst reporting a prior belief and a prior event could involve precisely the same response output, these outputs actually arise from different routes of processing. Reporting a prior event supposedly requires mere recall, while reporting a prior belief (or any belief for that matter) entails construction, where recall of the prior event is entered as a premise into the inferential process. Clues to this effect are evident as varying response times to questions about events and beliefs. A broader implication of this account is that development is gradual rather than stage-like. The probability of the child entering the correct premise into the belief-inference is thought to change by a matter of degree with increasing age.

A number of chapters urge us to consider the wider developmental issues in understanding about the mind. Kuhn (Chapter 15) argues that TOM knowledge should be seen in a context of "the human activity of knowing". She reviews research on knowing in older children, adolescents and adults, in order to highlight the lifespan context in which TOM research is best situated. Under a heading of metaknowing, she defines three sub-areas—the metacognitive, the metastrategic and the epistemological, and identifies the roots of all three in early mindreading achievements, as well as commenting on their role in later scientific reasoning and critical thinking. Subbotsky (Chapter 16) questions whether children and adults exclusively employ the 'rational, logical, scientific' mode of causal reasoning so strongly associated with Western cultures. He presents data suggesting that children's early beliefs in magic and animism do not die out, but continue to 'co-exist' well into adulthood. He argues that the development of children's understanding of psychological causality (or belief–desire reasoning) might be explained in terms of competition between these two modes of reasoning, with the logical/rational becoming more dominant as the child grows older, but never actually replacing the earlier 'magical' one. Freeman (Chapter 17) argues that mentalistic reasoning is a life-span task intimately bound up with communication. Presenting data from children's developing understanding of pictorial communication, he makes a highly original and provocative argument that mentalistic reasoning continues to develop well into middle or late childhood.

Finally, Josef Perner (Chapter 18) provides an incisive and thoroughly enlightened commentary on the contributions. He has appointed himself not only to identify strengths and weaknesses in others' accounts but to formulate a lucid and cogent view on how we should regard the role of children's reasoning in the development of their understanding of the mind.

REFERENCES

Carruthers, P., & Smith, P. (1996). *Theories of theories of mind*. Cambridge: Cambridge University Press.

Fodor, J.A. (1992). A theory of the child's theory of mind. *Cognition, 44*, 283–296.

Frye, D., Zelazo, P.D., & Palfai, T. (1995). Theory of mind and rule based reasoning. *Cognitive Development, 10*, 483–527.

Gopnik, A., & Wellman, H.M. (1992). Why the child's theory of mind really is a theory. *Mind and Language, 7*, 145–171.

Harris, P.L. (1992). From simulation to folk psychology: The case for development. *Mind and Language, 7*, 120–144.

Harris, P.L., German, T.P., & Mills, P.E. (1996). Children's use of counterfactual thinking in causal reasoning. *Cognition, 61*, 233–259.

Kahneman, D., & Tversky, A. (1982). The simulation heuristic. In D. Kahneman, P. Slovic, & A. Tversky (Eds.), *Judgement under uncertainty: Heuristics and biases* (pp. 201–208). Cambridge: Cambridge University Press.

Leslie, A.M. (1994). Pretending and believing: Issues in the theory of ToMM. *Cognition, 50*, 211–238.

Leslie, A.M., & Thaiss, L. (1992). Domain specificity in conceptual development: Neuropsychological evidence from autism. *Cognition, 43*, 225–251.

Lewis, C., & Mitchell, P. (1994) *Children's early understanding of mind: Origins and development*. Hove, UK: Lawrence Erlbaum Associates Ltd.

Mitchell, P. (1996). *Acquiring a conception of mind: A review of psychological research and theory*. Hove, UK: Psychology Press.

Perner, J. (1991). *Understanding the representational mind*. London: MIT.

Perner, J. (1996). Simulation as explication of prediction-implicit knowledge about the mind: Arguments for a simulation-theory mix. In P. Carruthers & P. Smith (Eds.), *Theories of theories of mind* (pp. 90–104). Cambridge: Cambridge University Press.

Peterson, D.M., & Riggs, K.J. (1999). Adaptive modelling and mindreading. *Mind and Language, 14*, 80–112

Pratt, C., & Bryant, P. (1990). Young children understand that looking leads to knowing (so long as they are looking into a single barrel). *Child Development, 61*, 973–982.

Premack, D., & Woodruff, G. (1978). Does the chimpanzee have a theory of mind? *Behavioural and Brain Sciences, 1*, 515–526.

Riggs, K.J., Peterson, D.M., Robinson, E.J., & Mitchell, P. (1998). Are errors in false belief tasks symptomatic of a broader difficulty with counterfactuality? *Cognitive Development, 13*, 73–91.

Russell, J. (1996). *Agency: Its role in mental development*. Hove, UK: Lawrence Erlbaum Associates Ltd.

Wellman, H. (1990). *The child's theory of mind*. London: MIT.

Wimmer, H., & Perner, J. (1983). Beliefs about beliefs: Representation and constraining function of wrong beliefs in young children's understanding of deception. *Cognition, 13*, 103–128.

Wimmer, H., Hogrefe, G.J., & Perner, J. (1988). Children's understanding of informational access as a source of knowledge. *Child Development, 59*, 386–396.

CHAPTER TWO

The grounding of symbols: A social–developmental account

R. Peter Hobson
The Tavistock Clinic and University College, London, UK

INTRODUCTION

What are the nature and origins of human beings' capacity to symbolise? My aim in this chapter is to reflect upon certain aspects of the nature of symbolic functioning, in order to set the question of the origins and development of symbolising in an appropriate framework. There is little doubt that something we call symbolising is essential to uniquely human forms of thought, not least those forms of thought about thought itself. Therefore it seems fitting to dwell on what this something is, if we are interested in accounting for its place in the cognitive repertoire of young children.

The title of this chapter is intended to frame what follows, by making reference to a problem that has confronted cognitive scientists who have tried to explain how we think by means of symbolic representations: How is it that symbols are connected to the objects and events that they mean? Steven Harnad (1990) employs Searle's (1980) Chinese room analogy to illustrate how a computer could not understand the symbols it manipulates, and emphasises that we need to explain how symbol meaning is to be grounded in something other than just more meaningless symbols. Although I shall not attempt to delve into the deepest layers of this 'symbol grounding problem'—and in particular, I shall not try to suggest how 'representations' as such acquire meaning or aboutness—I do want to highlight social–developmental factors that I believe to be critical for establishing *symbolic* representations, and for forging 'the crucial connection between the symbols and their referents' (Harnad, loc. cit. p. 344). I shall be arguing for an 'outside-in' account of the emergence of symbolic functioning, beginning with a story of symbolising-in-the-world and arriving at an account of

11

how representations-in-the-head (whatever *they* are) come to acquire new properties in virtue of the fact that they represent symbols and can mediate thought. The account pivots on the significance of people's attitudes, and more specifically the interpersonal co-ordination of attitudes, in providing the basis for the development of symbols that are not only connected with what they mean, but also available for a person to *use* meaningfully in a flexible and creative manner.

In order to approach such issues from a developmental perspective, we need to pause for a moment to check our bearings. What *are* symbols, and how do they symbolise—what are we trying to explain? I shall consider this topic from a developmental perspective, and then try to anchor the rather abstract discussion by joining in the contemporary debate on the nature of symbolic play in young children.

THE NATURE OF SYMBOLS

We are immediately faced with a paradox. On the one hand, it is possible to speak of symbols 'doing' things like referring, or 'having' properties like semantic content. On the other hand, symbolic representations such as written or spoken words, or even drawings or photographs, do not actually 'do' or 'have' any symbolic functions unless and until they are recognised and employed to do so by symbol-using creatures. In order for symbols to be interpreted, for example, they need to be treated as a special kind of 'thing', namely, that kind of thing for which interpreting is appropriate treatment. In order for a symbol to refer to anything, or to have a sense or meaning, there needs to be in the background a creature who intends that the symbol refers to and connotes something, and who can recognise the symbol as embodying an intention-to-refer and intention-to-mean (Sinha, 1988). For example, squiggles on a piece of paper remain just that—squiggles—unless and until they are both intended and recognised as words.

Perhaps this is to express the matter too strongly. There is *a* sense in which we can speak of symbols or strings of symbols referring to things, as I shall discuss in a moment. My point is that this is only the case, insofar as we presuppose a great deal about what makes a symbol a symbol (as opposed to a squiggle) in the first place. Moreover, this is more than a matter of grounding the content of symbols and symbol-systems, so that symbols act as vehicles of *meaning and understanding*, it is also a matter of establishing the properties of symbols as symbols within the cognitive system, that is, as *vehicles* of meaning and understanding. Therefore there is much to be said for examining and attempting to explain symbolic systems in their own right, so to speak, provided one does not fall into the trap of presupposing what one needs to explain—how squiggles ever come to be treated as symbols, and for this very reason become symbols.

Let me give a simple example to illustrate the point. When is a cloud not merely a cloud, but also a symbol? Consider this short excerpt from Hamlet, Act III, Scene II:

Hamlet: Do you see yonder cloud, that's almost in shape of a camel?
Polonius: By th' mass, and 'tis like a camel indeed.
Hamlet: Methinks it is like a weasel.
Polonius: It is back'd like a weasel.
Hamlet: Or like a whale?
Polonius: Very like a whale.
Hamlet: Then I will come to my mother by and by.

Hamlet could have treated the cloud as a symbol for anything, and Polonius could have followed him through every twist and turn—but once their minds turned elsewhere, the cloud was no longer a symbol at all. Of course there are critical differences between this example and instances of symbolising in language, especially insofar as a cloud-symbol does not have a conventionally fixed meaning, and its figurative and physical properties limit the degree to which it can enter into systematic relations with other symbols. In these respects, Hamlet's cloud is more like a symbol within a child's creative play. Nevertheless, what is true for this example may be true for all symbolic representations—that nothing is symbolic, but thinking makes it so.

To return to my earlier theme—a creature's intention-to-refer is more accurately an intention-to-refer-for-someone; and a creature's recognition of another's intention-to-mean is more accurately the recognition of an intention-to-mean-for-someone. The 'someone' here (and of course this need not be a particular someone) is meant to cover all symbolising beings, and arguably, appropriate kinds of non-living machines. This elaboration is not a trivial matter, for it suggests that a symboliser needs to have an appropriate level of awareness of what it is to be a 'someone' who can be symbolised for, and therefore needs to have the appropriate means to arrive at such awareness. Elsewhere (Hobson, 1993a,b), I have argued that it is only on the basis of affectively patterned interpersonal relations that an organism *could* become aware of persons as beings with minds who are able to share experiences and to communicate by means of symbols, but this is a matter I must pass over for now.

There is still the matter of explaining what we mean when we say that symbols, or linguistic expressions or sentences, 'mean' or 'refer'. Here I shall quote from Strawson's (1956, pp. 29–30) essay 'On referring':

'Mentioning', or 'referring', is not something an expression does; it is something that someone can use an expression to do. Mentioning, or referring to, something is a characteristic of *a use* of an expression, just as 'being about' something, and truth-or-falsity, are characteristics of *a use* of a sentence . . . To give the meaning of an expression (in the sense in which I am using the word) is to give *general directions* for its use to refer to or mention particular objects or persons; to give the meaning of a sentence is to give *general directions* for its use in making true or false assertions.

The notion of 'meaning as use' is a familiar one, and the point to highlight for the present purposes is that rules, habits and conventions governing correct use are irreducibly social (Hamlyn, 1978, 1990). If we are casting back in development to the beginnings of symbolic representation, then we arrive at what Mead (1934) would have called the first significant symbols, those expressions for which a symboliser anticipates that the response the expression calls out in others is just the same response that the symbol calls out in oneself. According to this perspective, symbols are what they are and do what they do only because their meanings are grounded and fixed in patterns of communication and social usage. And following Mead's lead, I would want to emphasise that symbols are what they are, in virtue of being recognised to be what they are—and it is only through communication that such recognition is possible.

Mead's way of putting things in his 'social behaviorist' style returns us to the paradox with which we began. Thus far I have been emphasising what human beings (or human-like 'mechanisms') have to do in order to make symbols what they are. Yet here is Mead writing of the responses that are 'called out' by symbols, and once again we are faced with the plausible idea that symbols operate on the mind as well as in the mind. So on the one hand, we are drawn towards a seemingly non-mechanistic account in which the emphasis is on a symboliser's intentions to use and to interpret symbols in what begin as essentially social contexts, and on the other hand we are tempted by the prospect that symbols may act mechanistically in causing sequences of mental events. On pain of infinite regress, we have to explain how usage or interpretation could occur other than through the medium of further symbols; and on pain of solipsistic retreat, we have to explain how symbols are constitutive of a symboliser's *understanding* of the world.

Of course I cannot resolve this dilemma, but I would like to try to arrange the problems in a particular way.

For the purposes of the present discussion, I am going to assume that within the cognitive apparatus of human beings, there is such a thing as a symbol manipulator, or at least, that there is a level of description at which it is appropriate to focus upon symbol-manipulating psychological properties. In fact, however, it is very likely that the mechanisms which effect symbol manipulation draw upon psychological processes that are intrinsic to other functions, even if there has been additional specialisation of symbol manipulation per se. I am going to call the physical mechanism for symbol manipulation an S-cruncher, where S's are supposed to be representations of squiggles, in order to highlight how a 'dedicated symbol system' (Harnad, 1990) must involve a great deal more than an S-cruncher, if interpretation is to be intrinsic to the system. Of course, the squiggles that are represented as S's can be arbitrary signifiers in any modality, whether written, verbal, gestural or whatever. The paradox is that as far as the S-crunching mechanism is concerned, it only has to crunch representations of squiggles; but as far as the organism's cognitive function is concerned, it is crunching representations of symbols (Kaye, 1982, p. 139).

My position is as follows: In addition to the S-cruncher, persons (or arguably, machines) will need to have the means for two kinds of relatedness; non-symbolic sensori-motor-affective systems for relating to the non-personal world, and partially dissociable non-symbolic sensori-motor-affective systems for relating to other persons. In individuals with early childhood autism, and in all machines created thus far, there is a great deal missing or abnormal with certain of the mechanisms for person-relating, and more precisely, with the means to establish patterned inter-individual co-ordination of subjective states, including affective states or 'attitudes' that have directedness towards objects and events in the world. This severely compromises autistic children's and machines' capacity to understand what symbols are, and therefore to symbolise. Why? Because they lack the means to treat squiggles as symbols. The reason is that there is an interpersonal zone of symbol grounding just as there is an intrapsychic zone of symbol grounding, and interpersonal grounding is the means to intrapsychic grounding. Interpersonal grounding implicates mechanisms for intersubjective modes of relating.

I shall devote much of the remainder of this contribution to suggesting how this is the case, but before doing so I want to gather up a couple of loose ends about symbols. The first has to do with the causative power of symbols, and the second to do with what it means for symbols to be vehicles for the conception of objects and events. With regard to the first of these issues, I turn to Ogden and Richard's (1985, originally 1923, pp. 10–11) ancient but classic work on the Meaning of Meaning, in which they write as follows:

> Between a thought and a symbol causal relations hold. When we speak, the symbolism we employ is caused partly by the reference we are making and partly by social and psychological factors—the purpose for which we are making the reference, the proposed effect of our symbols on other persons, and our own attitude. When we hear what is said, the symbols both cause us to perform an act of reference and to assume an attitude which will, according to circumstances, be more or less similar to the act and the attitude of the speaker.

I believe that the last sentence from this quotation solves the symbol grounding problem, and I shall return to it later.

What of the relation between symbols and what they symbolise? Ogden and Richards emphasise that there is no direct relation between symbol and referent, for this relation is one that is mediated through the thought of the person who symbolises. Or as Langer (1957) expressed it, symbols are not proxy for their referents, but are vehicles for the conception of referents.

A given conception embodies a particular way of construing the referent. Any object or event can be conceived of in an infinite number of ways, and a conception is just one of these. Correspondingly in language, the connotation of a word is different from its denotation; sense is not reducible to reference (Frege, 1960). In whatever way a symbol is anchored, therefore, this must allow the symbol to capture a particular way of experiencing the referent. Moreover, as I have already indicated, 'ways of experiencing' and abilities to conceive of objects and events depend upon the relations that can exist between the experiencer or thinker and the objects and events thought about. This is where the modes of relating to the non-personal world come into the picture. To conceive of a cricket bat, for example, one has to have had experiences relevant to establishing the conceptions of solid objects, of hitting things, of playing a specific instrumental role in a game, and so on. Ultimately, a complex of sensori-motor-affective experiences will have been implicated in the underpinnings of such concepts—and any computer that is to understand what a cricket bat is will have to have the capacity of experiencing such things. So on the one hand, a symboliser who understands what symbols mean has to understand the referents in their own right, so to speak; but on the other hand, the symboliser also has to relate to symbols themselves in an appropriate way, in order for their content to be apprehended through the 'transparent' symbolic medium. This brings us back to the decontextualisation of symbols, what their content amounts to, and how this content is grounded.

I am going to build upon Ogden and Richard's suggestion about the causal efficacy of certain symbols, namely that they lead a symbol-hearer to assume an *attitude* which is more or less similar to the attitude of the speaker. From the perspective of language acquisition, for example, I believe that a child learning the correct use of spoken words is often learning to anchor these words in attitudes—or to put this another way, attitudes and the communication of attitudes are what ground symbols. At the same time, of course, insofar as this linking of vocal squiggles to attitudes is occurring, the attitudes in question are abstracted and decontextualised; symbols do not evoke full-blown attitudes and actions appropriate to their referents, but merely introduce the conceptions of those referents. In the process, they apply not to specific individuals or events, but to 'this sort of thing' (Langer, 1957). That is why symbolising constitutes such a highly generative form of abstracting, whereby specific notions can be articulated in relation to one another and free from all sorts of psychological clutter.

Why am I giving such emphasis to attitudes? (I should also be talking about actions, but I think that involves a partly separate story that I shall mostly leave to one side.) By the very nature of people's attitudes, the world is subsumed under qualitatively distinct 'descriptions' for the persons whose attitudes they are. If I am afraid of something, then that something falls under the description of 'something frightening'. The characterisation of the object-in-the-world accords with the ways in which the object becomes the focus of attitudes as well as actions. My suggestion is that in many cases, the grounding of symbols involves processes of identification through which a child perceives and identifies with someone else whose symbol use expresses attitudes and ways of construing aspects of a shared environment. The child then appropriates those symbols as vehicles for just those attitudes towards the world. It is here that the critical processes of abstraction and decontextualisation take place. I think such processes are operative not only when the child acquires any given symbol to mean this or that, but also and more fundamentally, when the child achieves the feat of coming to understand what it is to symbolise in the first place. It is in this latter respect, the business of learning what it means to use symbols, that the interpersonal co-ordination of attitudes plays a critical developmental role. And according to my thesis, it is only when a child has a (sufficient) knowledge of what it means to anchor meanings in symbols, that he or she will show elaborate symbolic play.

At this point I shall focus upon a specific domain of symbolic functioning, that of symbolic play, and consider how my account both links in with and differs from those of other contemporary theorists. After this I shall provide a single illustration from language-learning, by considering how personal pronouns are acquired.

SYMBOLISING IN PLAY

It is appropriate to begin with the account of Alan Leslie (1987, 1994), a leading cognitivist–computational developmental psychologist who was largely responsible for stimulating the current surge of theoretical interest in symbolic play. Leslie set himself the task of tracing the connection between a young child's capacity for pretend play, and his or her ability to understand mental states. Leslie has been concerned with play that exhibits the pretence forms of object substitution, attribution of pretend properties, and the invention of imaginary objects. That is, a child can know an object for what it is but may choose to treat it as if it were a different object, or the child might endow an object with properties it does not have, or the child can act as though an object exists when it does not.

Leslie considers infants to begin with the capacity to form *primary representations* that encode aspects of the world in an accurate, faithful, and literal way. Toward the end of infancy, however, through the operation of an innately determined *decoupling mechanism*, children acquire the ability to represent not only the world, but also these representations themselves: it is as if children were quoting someone else, lifting out the representation, without committing themselves to the truth of whatever the person said or thought. The block of wood "is a car", the doll "can speak", and so on. Importantly for my argument, Leslie has come to give increasing prominence to the 'attitude' component in his account, for example in stating that a metarepresentation 'represents the attitude an agent takes to a description of a particular aspect of reality' (Leslie & Roth, 1993, p. 88).

The pivot of Leslie's thesis is that children's ability to recognise the nature of mental states in themselves and others depends on the same innately derived cognitive capacity that underpins the ability to pretend. Leslie offers the hypothesis that autistic children have an absence or malfunction of the processes required to form metarepresentations. He suggests this as an explanation for their impairments in symbolic play and for their 'specific deficit in theory of mind' (p. 424; see also Leslie, 1991). In this way he links autistic children's deficient capacity for pretence and their limited understanding of people, and proposes that these impairments reflect a unitary, innately determined cognitive abnormality.

There have been a number of critical reviews of Leslie's thesis (Harris & Kavanaugh, 1993; Hobson, 1990; Jarrold, Carruthers, Smith, & Boucher, 1994; Perner, 1988), and I shall try to situate the present account in relation to these contemporary viewpoints.

At the outset, I should state my own view (Hobson, 1991a) that the emergence of the 'Theory of Mind Mechanism'—and with this, the origins of those processes that subserve symbolic functioning—is what we need to explain, not merely describe (important though this has been!). From a developmental perspective, I suggest, the critical achievement in coming to understand a basic set of propositional attitudes (e.g. I pretend that such-and-such) is to distil out the 'proposition' or representation *from* those attitudes which are initially experienced and apprehended in 'non-propositional' form. At the outset, too, it is worth acknowledging the force of the criticisms of Perner and others (Jarrold et al., 1994; Perner, 1991), who argue that 'decoupling' alone (i.e. copying primary representations so that they become secondary representations detached from reality) does not itself amount to creating metarepresentations (i.e. representations *of* representations), because the status of the copied representation depends on the way in which it is used. Hence we should follow Leslie (1994) in extending his account of M-representations to encompass an agent, an informational relation (the attitude), an aspect of the real situation, and an imaginary situation (the description), such that a given agent takes a given attitude to the status of a given description in relation to a given anchor.

Harris (1991; Harris & Kavanaugh, 1993) and Lillard (1993a,b, 1994) consider that young children conceive of pretending as a distinctive form of non-serious action rather than a distinctive mental stance. For example, Harris and Kavanaugh (1993) propose that instead of entailing awareness of the mental state of their play partner or themselves, young children interpret and accept a set of stipulations about the make-believe status of the current situation. These authors castigate Leslie for collapsing the distinction between adopting a propositional attitude and having a conception about that attitude, in that the ability to engage in pretence may not emerge at the same time as the ability to represent that someone, be it the self or other, is engaged in the mental state of pretending. Shortly, I shall disagree with these criticisms of Leslie (just as in Hobson, 1991a, I have disagreed with Harris' suggestion that children start to understand other people's mental states by a process of simulation or by drawing analogy from their own mental states), but I also want to note my agreement with Harris and Kavanaugh that (a) symbolic play starts with the individual applying a set of ideas to whatever props lend themselves to the play, and that (b) the evidence they provide does indicate that young children understand how objects can be used to represent the signified as having certain properties or relations, and this establishes that 2 year-olds' play *is* symbolic.

Perner (1991), too, sees early pretence not as involving the use of something to represent (symbolise) something else, but as an instance of (knowingly) *acting-as-if* the world were different than it really is, 'by associating oneself or another person with a particular alternative situation' (Perner, 1988, p. 142). In the context of explaining how 15-month-olds come to understand the invisible displacements of objects and means-ends relationships, as well as to play in new ways, Perner suggests that they become able to use multiple models to free themselves from being tied to current reality, and to conceive of the hypothetical (e.g. where an object might be). Noting that around $1\frac{1}{2}$ years of age, children interpret pictures and mirror images, Perner (1991, pp. 72–73) writes:

> Clearly, then, in the second year children come to understand representations. But at what level? My answer is that children have only an implicit understanding of representations, in that they can *use them as representations*—in particular, they can interpret them. Their understanding of representation is not explicit in the sense that they could model the representational relationship between picture and depicted or model the fact that a picture needs to be interpreted.

I believe that there are serious problems with suggesting that children conceive of pretending as a form of action, rather than something 'mental'. To start with, this presupposes that a clear distinction between the behavioural and the mental is applicable in our theorising about young children's understanding— and this leads to the suggestion that children classify actions and do not conceive of the mental dimension of what is happening. I am quite unclear about what a form of action means here (pretending is to acting-for-serious as . . . stroking is to holding, or what?). A possible answer, of course, is that in the minds of young children, pretending is acting in such a way that the pretender is re-presenting (or in the case of invented objects and events, is presenting) chosen meanings through the objects acted-upon. This amounts to the child understanding (or, if you like, representing) the 'represent*ing* relationship' between the pretender and the world, without yet having a full grasp of the relationship between the structure or activity of the pretender's mind and what is pretended (a point on which Lillard has provided much helpful empirical and theoretical work, e.g. Lillard, 1993a,b, 1996). The relationship between the symbol and what it signifies is not centre stage (c.f. Jarrold et al., 1994); but the (mental) relationship between pretender and what-is-pretended is understood sufficiently to constitute a background for the pretence. As Wellman and Hickling

(1993, p. 99) emphasise, 'the subjects, child and other, and not just the objective text, form an integral part of pretense'.

Let me try to argue the case from another direction, taking off first from Perner and then from Harris. In my view, Perner underestimates the difference between entertaining hypothetical or counterfactual views of a situation, and using multiple models in contexts such as those of understanding object permanence or means-end relationships. In the latter two situations, the models are used automatically in coming to a new understanding, whereas in the former (as in symbolic play), a model that is used hypothetically is knowingly employed *as* a not-for-serious version of a situation or event, and is recognised to be a construal-as. To understand construing-as, the child has to have sufficient distance from and appreciation of person-dependent 'meanings' that he or she can relate to these in a playful way, choosing, recognising, altering, adopting, and abandoning the meanings in application to objects that are registered to have their own person-independent 'for serious' meanings. The critical issue is this: What is the nature of the child's ability to 'decouple' or create secondary representations *in such a way that these forms of imaginative activity are possible?* Is Harris (1994, p. 236, my italics) correct in supposing that a child does not require '*any* assumptions about the mental life of the adult' to simulate nonexistent situations or to pretend? And why are children with autism who understand means-end relations severely limited in their creative symbolic play?

By and large, the present account is on Leslie's side over these issues. As Wellman and Hickling (1993) emphasise, even young children appear to betray through their knowing smiles and playful manner, as well as in their statements about the pretend, that they understand something essential about the attitude of pretending that something is the case. Despite the protestations by Harris and Kavanaugh (1993) that this is encompassed by their account of the child construing someone as acting on imaginary or substitute objects, their claim is that an understanding of action rather than an understanding of mental attitudes is of the essence. It is instructive to quote how Harris (1991, pp. 302–303) takes Leslie to task, thus:

> An adult acts out a piece of make-believe. To join in, the child needs to recognize what the other person is pretending to do, and also that what they are pretending is not for real. For example, the child needs to recognize that the other person is pretending to pour tea, but that there is no real tea. This may be a lot, but it does not require any insight into the mind of the person pouring the (pretend) tea. In the same way, a theatre-goer need only respond to the play *as if* it were real while acknowledging that it is not; he or she can ignore the mental processes by which the actors produce their performance. They are as irrelevant to an appreciation of the play as the mechanical processes by which the scenery is shifted. Thus, although adults might eventually consider the mental processes that lie behind a fine piece of acting, they need not do so as they watch the play. Similarly, a child can share another person's pretence without considering that person's mental state.

I agree that a person does not need to consider the mental state of someone who acts. The problem is that you can only appreciate a play if you know what acting (or theatre) is. True, that understanding becomes a background feature of the experience of watching a play, but you cannot watch a play as a play unless you understand what it is to simulate reality intentionally. The point is not that you need to invoke the mental processes underlying the performance of these actors and actresses now, but rather that you need to know what it means to 'make-believe' so that you can suspend play-inappropriate kinds of judgement and feeling even when the action on stage draws such reactions from you. Following Lillard (personal communication, October, 1997), I am happy to think of this as a willing suspension of reality (or suspension of a for-serious mode); but I would still argue that *this* involves a distancing of oneself-as-experiencer from that which would otherwise be experienced as reality, and that such distancing occurs through an understanding of the distinction between experiences or construals (i.e. mental events) and the objects of those experiences. For example, one can reflect on what one is doing in following a play—and critically, following a play *as a play* is a mental doing. So, too, the 'distinctive form of action' that symbolic play involves is much more than acting playfully, it is re-presenting playfully. It is not necessary for the child who plays to focus upon the mental aspect of introducing meanings, either in self or other; rather, it is an understanding of the 'representing relation' (a person-to-world relation, and one that entails attitudes employed in the application of meanings) that underpins the play. Thus one might follow Perner's suggestion that all the child has to do is to distinguish between the real and the hypothetical by modifying the representational status of the representation, except that the crux for such a change in status is to mark how the representation is to be related-to. To be sure, one is representing through performing certain kinds of action, and the child may not understand that one can represent without so doing—but the child does understand that it is (re)presenting.

I have commented or the false (and forced) dichotomy between attributing the child with an understanding of actions, *or* with an understanding of 'mental representations'. There is a related dichotomy that is also false: that symbols are either external or internal to the mind. The fact is that symbols are created in the external world, and representations of those symbols are established in the head. As Kaye (1982, p. 139) has pointed out, 'the mind works with representations *of* symbols (as well as of acts, objects, and so forth), rather than working *by* symbols'. The special kind of representation that Leslie has attempted to characterise is special in virtue of the fact that it allows the individual to mark representations as being employed a certain way (viz symbolically)—and as Leslie has emphasised, understanding the nature of this employment entails understanding enough of the attitude of the representer to that which is represented. It is not enough for Perner to state that the pretender 'associates' oneself or another person with the model of a particular alternative situation (also Leslie, 1994,

p. 218), because it is the nature and development of that association that requires explanation. As I have argued before (Hobson, 1991b), the way that representations are marked in Leslie's scheme, by something like quotation marks, is
even more appropriate than Leslie appreciates.

For I go one step further than Leslie in believing that not only do we need a
notion of *attitudes* in characterising the pretend relation, but that it is precisely in
virtue of the child's attunement to and increasing understanding of attitudes
(both those of the child itself and those of others) that the child comes to grasp
that meanings can be dissociated from that to which they are normally applied,
and can be applied to novel objects pretendingly. It is *because* children appreciate meanings or 'descriptions' as person-dependent (or in Leslie's terms, agent-
centred), that they become available for symbolic anchorage and amenable to
reflective thought. Children recognise that meanings are (as it were) held in
quotation marks in virtue of their being 'associated' with the attitudes of the
persons who employ them, just as linguistic utterances will later be held in
quotation marks in accordance with who says them (a parallel worth pursuing in
appreciating that only sometimes need one attend to the source of an utterance
or pretend, rather than the utterance or pretence content). In other words, I
believe that the story of coming to acquire M-representations (in Leslie's terms)
is a story that focuses on children's relatedness to other people's relatedness to
the world, and leads to the point at which they can relate to their own and
others' relatedness to meanings—and the free application of meanings in symbolic play is a prime example of this. In the case of such social-dependent
decoupling (and not all forms of decoupling are social-dependent in this way), I
think that it is not a matter of making a mistake in collapsing the distinction
between having a propositional attitude and knowing that one is having one—it
is a claim that knowing sufficient about what it means to have this kind of
propositional attitude *is* a condition for having it! For example, one can only
pretend that this is a that, if one has sufficient understanding of what it is for
someone to make this stand for that.

I want to introduce one complication to my account, which I fear may prove
the last straw for those whose patience has already been taxed. I am not sure that
what one might call the 'pretend attitude', and the question of whether young
children manifest expressions of awareness of such an attitude in play, is really
critical for deciding whether the children understand symbolising. The central
issue is that children come to be able to distinguish attitudes from the objects of
those attitudes, and what we see in their symbolic play is that they can make this
distinction in the area of pretence i.e. they can do so pretendingly. Now it is true
that pretence itself involves characteristic attitudes, and a child may manifest
awareness of those attitudes. It is also arguable that in development, picking up
playful attitudes (even in the first year of life e.g. Reddy, 1991) may serve a
formative role in the child becoming aware of the distinction between attitudes
and their objects. On the other hand, this may not be the case, and my account is

neutral on the matter. When it comes to the business of symbolising in play, the pretend-attitude merely establishes a context within which the application of person-dependent meanings takes place. Although it is certainly suggestive that the signs of playfulness appear to betray that children know what they are doing in symbolising, therefore, the playful attitude and the child's awareness of the playful attitude is not cental for the story of symbolising.

In summary, let me return to Ogden and Richards. Just as a symbol does not have a direct relation to its referent, so the symbol-referent relationship need not be explicitly articulated in the child's mind; what does need to be explicitly amenable to articulation, is the relation between the child and her 'decoupled meanings' *as* decoupled meanings. Thus when Perner suggests that an object used in pretence need not 'represent' what it is intended to be, I would respond that it does, but only insofar as the child needs to know that through the use of the object, he or she is representing (or presenting) the signified. And this does entail that the child has an important if partial understanding, which is not the same as a complete understanding, of what it is to represent. Perhaps I might add that if it is indeed the case that symbolising entails the recognition and appropriation of attitudes through identification with others, this may help one to address a problem that I used to share with Perner, namely a 'difficulty appreciating Piaget's reasons for insisting that mental representation is internalized imitation' (Perner, 1991, p. 56).

Finally, it is necessary to add a brief post-script on what is the difference between understanding pretence and understanding belief. Here I am on Perner's side (e.g. Perner, Baker, & Hutton, 1994), not on Leslie's, because I accept that it is not until around four years of age that children acquire a concept of belief, and that this amounts to the ability to represent representations of reality *as* representations of reality (to 'metarepresent', in Perner's terms). Where I would differ from Perner, is in the added emphasis that I would give to the 'of reality' part of this formulation; I think that the critical acquisition here is the concept of reality *as* reality, for example as reality versus appearance. In short, it is only when one has the *concept* of reality as 'the way things are', that is, reality as characterised in a supra-individual manner, that one can contrast this with the appearances that amount to a particular individual's potentially fallible 'take' on reality. So, too, it is only when one understands what it means to 'take as true *of reality*' that one understands what it is to be correct or incorrect in believing something to be true of reality (and I accept that younger children's understanding of belief falls short of this). The reason that this is important is that it affects the way we explain the acquisition of the concept of belief. It is interesting that Perner (1991) discusses how a general might need 'several scouts' to determine what is true on the battlefield, because I think one needs experience of conflicting and corroborating points of view to arrive at the notion of 'reality' itself— that characterisation of things that anyone would assent to if the person were in the appropriate position to judge i.e. a description that transcends any particular person's viewpoint. Perhaps it is not surprising, then, that I would also emphasise the necessary role of interpersonal communication in providing the foundations for such a concept Just as we need a social–developmental explanation for the kind of decoupling necessary for M-representing, so we need a social–developmental explanation for what is acquired in acquiring the concept of belief.

Thus one can claim that (a) 3-year-olds understand that they and others can apply person-dependent meanings to arbitrary signifiers, and in so doing demonstrate their understanding that people can construe-as, without (b) claiming that these same children understand what it means to construe-as-reality (e.g. to have a false belief; where this has reference to a notion of reality as being the-way-things-are-for-everyone, however things may appear to anyone in particular). Although for a long time 3-year-olds have been relating to what we call reality, and have understood the distinction between this 'for-serious' world and the 'for-pretend' world, they have not understood its status as a state of affairs (or as a characterisation of a state of affairs) that transcends any particular viewpoint, and that serves as the measure of any individual's correct or incorrect beliefs. Perhaps I should conclude by emphasising again that (c) even children who can understand construing-as, and have the ability to detect and confer what I have called person-dependent meanings, may not always orientate to what a particular person is construing, nor to the act of construing itself; rather, these children have in the background a grasp of what it is to apply symbolic meanings.

THE SOCIAL–DEVELOPMENTAL ORIGINS OF SYMBOLISING

Here, then, is the crux of my account (elaborated in Hobson, 1993a). Towards the end of the first year of life, against the background of person-to-person intersubjective exchanges but before understanding much about persons, infants register and react to the *directedness* of other people's attitudes and actions toward a shared world. Take the case of a 12-month-old perceiving another person to have a particular attitude towards some object on which the child's attention is focused, or the infant perceiving a person performing an action on something. Note we have two senses of aboutness here: the infant and the other person are situated 'about' the object in question (a fact that relates to the physical embodiment of infant, other person and object), and the participants' mental states or actions are directed towards and thus connected with ('about') the object-as-experienced. So for example, Walden and Ogan (1988) reported that infants of 10–13 months spent more time touching a toy towards which a parent had previously expressed positive feelings, than a toy in relation to which the parent had communicated a fearful attitude ('What a scary toy!'). Now suppose that in such situations, the infant identifies with the attitude manifest in the other person's bodily expressions or actions, so that the infant comes to assume the other's psychological stance towards the focus of the other's attitude.

If it were also the case that the infant understood her new psychological orientation to *be* a new and separate psychological orientation, and moreover one that was 'about' something other than herself, such movement to another person's mental stance would constitute a movement in thought. My claim will be that this configuration of interpersonal events is indeed the cradle of symbolic thought.

I believe the infant's emotional reactions to and appropriation of other people's attitudes towards the world are critical for disembedding the infant from an immediate, unreflective, 'concrete' apprehension of the environment; that is, they are critical for the development of symbolic functioning. The reason is that they constitute the route by which the infant comes to adopt, and in due course to recognise, multiple attitudes to the same things and events. If the same things can be the objects of different attitudes, then things are different from thoughts. More than this—attitudes (or thoughts) can be anchored in and communicated through vehicles (symbols). With insight into this around the middle of the second year of life, the child can knowingly confer novel attitudes (thoughts) onto familiar things in symbolic play, and can appreciate how she herself as well as others can capture and intentionally convey attitudes and thoughts in language. In other words, it is through an infant's experiences of her own attitudes to and with other people's attitudes to a visually-specified world, that she comes to appreciate two complementary facts of psychological life: objects can have multiple meanings-for-persons, and persons can hold multiple attitudes to given objects (including that special class of object called symbols!). Or to put this differently, objects can fall under different descriptions for people, and different descriptions can be applied in a way that is a function of the person whose descriptions they are. Understanding this depends on what I have referred to as social-dependent decoupling.

Infants also adopt others' attitudes towards their own attitudes and actions (Hobson, 1993b; Tomasello, 1993). As Mead (1934) described, significant symbols arise in conjunction with self-reflective awareness when the child takes the role of the other vis-à-vis itself. The child recognises that the gestures used by others to communicate to the self are also gestures that can be used by the self to communicate similar messages to others.

Symbolising in play entails that the child is aware of playfully applying a pretend description-for-me to an object that is recognised to have a distinct for-serious description. As we have noted, the child's playful knowing looks, as well as her ability to tune into the play of others, demonstrate her awareness that a pretend description-for-me may differ from a pretend description-for-other, and it is probably no coincidence that new levels of empathy and interpersonal role-taking, as well as new expressions of self-consciousness, emerge in concert with creative symbolic play at around 18 months of age in non-handicapped children.

Although there are complexities to the issue, I suspect it is also no coincidence that insight into the nature of symbols in play—and one *must* understand that one is symbolising in order to designate and thus to engage in truly symbolic play (Huttenlocher & Higgins, 1978)—occurs at around the same age as the 'vocabulary spurt' is often observed. At least in some cases, children seem to have grasped something—it might be related to naming (McShane, 1980), and I am inclined to think it has something to do with predication—which brings a new mastery of symbolic functioning, both in play and in language. As Plunkett, Sinha and colleagues have observed (Plunkett & Sinha, 1992; Plunkett, Sinha, Moller, & Strandsby, 1992), children can now exploit the symbolic relation between sound sequences and the objects and events which these signify in a more systematic fashion than previously. Words that had earlier been embedded in specific situations and routines, and bound to a range of communicative functions, have become decontextualised, and with this a new means of representation has emerged. Reference is an intersubjective achievement. Correspondingly, studies of communication and language suggest that even before infancy is over, very young children seek and are able to understand another person's interpretation of a situation (Bretherton, 1992). As I now turn to the linguistic forms of symbolising, I shall restrict myself to a special but also revealing facet of language acquisition—that concerned with personal pronouns.

PERSONAL PRONOUNS

I am going to dwell on how a young child comprehends and learns to use personal pronouns, 'I' and 'you', as well as the related terms 'my and mine', for the reason that the processes involved highlight the movement in psychological stance and attitude that I believe is critical for the grounding of symbols.

Let us take the word 'mine'. In order to produce a word like 'mine' in an appropriate context, a child must have witnessed someone saying 'Mine!' when the word expressed that *other* person's attitude of possessiveness and/or appropriation. That is, the child must have recognised that when the other person said 'Mine!', the anchorage of the word was in the speaker's own attitude-cum-action. It is only by identifying with that attitude, and then adopting the term 'Mine!' as expressive of that attitude, that the child could come to express her own possessive attitude with this same term. It is interesting that Charney (1980) reports how in nearly all of the young children she studied, the earliest uses of 'my' were produced while a child was acting on an object—searching for, grabbing, acting upon, or claiming it, usually when the object was *not* the child's—rather than expressing more permanent ownership. The pronouns 'I' and 'me' also appeared in contexts such as those of searching for, requesting, claiming or noticing an object rather than describing the child's own body. Here we witness how a particular set of symbols is grounded interpersonally and intrapersonally in attitudes that are expressed through those symbols. It is because of the young child's ability to perceive and identify with those attitudes in someone else, that she is able to appropriate the symbolic expression for those same attitudes in herself. At the same time, the symbols come to circumscribe and 'decontextualise' the meanings that those attitudes exemplify, in such a way that the symbols can serve as a medium for thought and communication without the requirement that the attitudes themselves are evoked in full force on each occasion of word use. And what happens when we hear the child using the word 'mine'? As Ogden and Richards (1985, p. 11) explained, the word 'cause(s) us to perform an act of reference and to assume an attitude which will, according to circumstances, be more or less similar to the act and the attitude of the speaker'. This is an essential component of what it means to interpret the symbol.

SUGGESTIVE EVIDENCE FROM DEVELOPMENTAL PSYCHOPATHOLOGY

Now if all this is the case, then we might wonder whether there are conditions in which children are handicapped in perceiving the relation between people's attitudes and the objects and events in the world toward which those attitudes are directed, and/or handicapped in identifying with those attitudes—with resulting limitations in symbolising. I shall consider early childhood autism and congenital blindness as two possible cases in point.

Autistic children appear to face difficulty in perceiving, responding to and identifying with attitudes *as* attitudes. They can see the directedness of actions, for example, but their affective engagement with the emotional attitudes of others is seriously impaired. I believe it is this that accounts for autistic children's profound impoverishment in symbolic play, the 'concreteness' of their thinking, the pragmatic deficits in their language, and the delay and limitation in their comprehension and use of personal pronouns. Each of these cognitive–linguistic phenomena may be understood to reflect the autistic child's embeddedness in a fixed, one-track, 'literal' interpretation of the world and of word meanings, and a failure to lift himself out of his *own* way of apprehending objects and events, such that he can appreciate and adopt a variety of person-anchored and context-sensitive perspectives.

As Wulff (1985) describes, an autistic child who is left to his or her own devices in a playroom full of toys is very likely to ignore the toys and continue rocking or hand-flapping, or will spin moveable parts rather than becoming engaged in a meaningful way; and those autistic children who play with toys usually do so in a stereotyped and uncreative manner (Mundy, Sigman, Ungerer, & Sherman, 1987; Sigman & Ungerer, 1984; Wing & Gould, 1979). In the domain of language, as Kanner (1943) observed in his original description of early childhood autism, autistic children who are not mute may 'echo' the speech of others, confuse the personal pronouns 'I' and 'you', make idiosyncratic utterances that can only be understood with reference to the contexts in which the child acquired the words, and display a literalness of speech that seems to show a restricted grasp of connotative meanings. For example Baltaxe (1977) has cited examples of how autistic adolescents report events as if they were still the hearer in the original dialogue, without accommodation to the listener role. Echolalia, confusions with personal pronouns, and 'situational phrases' may be interpreted in the same way, as language is anchored not in the speaker's psychological perspective, but instead in the context as experienced by the children themselves (Hobson, 1993a). Autistic children's concrete thinking and failure to understand metaphor provide further illustrations of this abnormality. When one autistic child was asked if he had lost his tongue, he anxiously started to search for it; whenever another was instructed to put something down, he always had to put it on the floor (Ricks & Wing, 1975; Wing, 1969, 1981).

Now even if it is accepted that such phenomena reflect a lack of role-taking and an embeddedness in 'meanings' that are not mediated through the psychological orientations of others—and I would stress that in the case of creative symbolic play, my suggestion is highly contentious—it is a completely open question whether such abnormality arises from autistic children's relative failure to perceive and identify with the attitudes of others.

True, there are several lines of evidence compatible with this claim. In the domain of non-verbal communication, autistic children appear to be specifically impaired in emotional expressiveness, emotion recognition and affective responsiveness to others (Dawson et al., 1990; Hobson, 1991b; Kasari, Sigman, Mundy, & Yirmiya, 1990; Ricks, 1975; Sigman, Kasari, Kwon, & Yirmiya, 1992). They have a specific abnormality in sharing experiences of things with other people in 'protodeclarative acts' (Loveland & Landry, 1986; Mundy, Sigman, Ungerer, & Sherman, 1986; Wetherby & Prutting, 1984), and they relatively rarely engage in social referencing (Sigman et al., 1992). They appear to have limited self-consciousness, as the 'role-taking' theory would predict: for example they rarely appear coy before their own mirror images (Dawson & McKissick, 1984; Spiker & Ricks, 1984), and rarely show self-conscious emotions such as pride or shame (Bosch, 1970; Kasari, Sigman, Baumgartner, & Stipek, 1993). They also have specific limitations in understanding both their own and other people's minds (Baron-Cohen, Tager-Flusberg, & Cohen, 1993; Hobson, 1993a).

In reviewing these observations on autistic children, one is struck by autistic children's difficulty in achieving distance from their own engagement with the world so that they can reflect on the 'multiple-meanings' potential both of objects and of language. Although it is possible that certain of autistic individuals' tendencies to one-track, concrete, literal, perseverative thinking and lack of planning might be a direct manifestation of impairments in frontal lobe functioning (Ozonoff, Pennington, & Rogers, 1991; Rogers & Pennington, 1991), it would seem equally plausible that primary deficits in intersubjective engagement are at the developmental roots of their limited capacities for thinking.

There is at least one glaring anomaly in what I have been suggesting: although it is the case that many autistic children remain mute, making it plausible to suppose that for reasons of their limited intersubjective experience, these children are unable to grasp what symbolic communication *is*, there are also many who do learn to communicate in elaborate language. It has also been reported that a number of autistic children can be prompted to symbolise in play (Jarrold, Boucher, & Smith, 1993; Lewis & Boucher, 1988), although such play lacks the spontaneity and generativity of non-autistic children's play. I think that the relatively intact syntactic structures of many autistic children's language may well attest to squiggle-processing abilities that are autonomous, but more importantly for the present purposes, we need to consider whether there are alternative routes to quasi-symbolic or partly symbolic functioning. Especially relevant here is evidence that autistic children can perceive, understand and sometimes imitate the *actions* of other people (Baron-Cohen, Leslie, & Frith, 1986; Hobson, 1995; Moore, Hobson, & Lee, 1997). In this way they are able to achieve a degree of mental coordination with others, and such coordination may contribute to anchoring some aspects of language. More generally, there are areas of correspondence between the experiences of autistic children and those of non-autistic language users. Accordingly, even for autistic children, certain symbols and combinations of symbols can acquire associative connections that suffice for instrumental comprehension and use. Having said this, it remains the case that autistic individuals' atypical and 'situational' uses of language, as well as their scant and laboured use of symbolic play materials, suggests that most autistic individuals do not fully share *our* modes of symbolising. The implications for their cognitive function are profound (Hobson, 1993a).

Yet to be sure, there are reasons for doubting the intersubjective theory of symbolising I have propounded. Earlier, I considered one contrasting theory. According to Leslie, children with autism have a specific deficit in the innate cognitive operation that leads to the 'decoupling' of representations. But suppose there are other kinds of children who have difficulty in perceiving how other people's attitudes are *directed* towards a world which is also the world experienced by the children themselves. This, too, would deprive such children of the kind of social 'triangulation' which I have suggested is the basis for symbolic thinking, self-reflective awareness, and context-sensitive language and thought. These considerations led colleagues and myself to study blind children —for if this is a condition in which we might look for autistic-like clinical features as the developmental outcome of a handicap which is *not* a missing innate 'decoupling mechanism', then we might have reason to prefer an account of such features which focuses on obstacles to achieving normal patterns of interpersonal relatedness. After all, blind children cannot *see* how people's attitudes are directed to a visually specified and shared external world. My thesis is that because of this, they have that much more difficulty in triangulating self, other, and the objects towards which attitudes are directed, and therefore more difficulty in recognising how 'meanings' are person-dependent and ascribable in symbolic play, and/or in anchoring meanings in symbols.

There is indeed evidence that congenitally blind children have specific impairments in symbolic play, confusions in the use of personal pronouns and other deictic expressions, and a tendency to be echolalic. One especially vivid case history is that of a bright and sociable 3-year-old girl described by Fraiberg and Adelson (1977), who could neither pretend that playdough was a cookie, nor understand personal pronouns. When an interviewer asked "Can I have a bite of the cookie, Kathie?", Kathie put the playdough in her own mouth and said: "This cookie different". It was not until she reached the age of 4 that Kathie began to represent herself in doll play and, in parallel with this, to master the use of personal pronouns.

Although Kathie's language was in many respects well-developed, so that it would be difficult to claim she had a global deficit in symbolic functioning, Andersen, Dunlea, and Kekelis (1984) report a study of blind children's language that appears to suggest a subtle but important lack of perspective-taking ability in these children's use of verbal symbols. Moreover, a study of 24 congenitally blind children recently completed by colleagues and myself (Brown, Hobson, Lee, & Stevenson, 1997) has revealed a high prevalence of 'autistic-like' features in the children, with around half the sample showing echolalia, personal pronoun difficulties and poor symbolic play. Why should blind children echo back the language that they hear, if not for reason of their failure to anchor themselves in the speech roles of others? If a form of 'psychological triangulation' among a child, another person and the world is what enables the child to perceive and adopt perspectives needed for flexible role-taking and symbolic play, then no wonder blind children have specific abnormalities in these respects—for as I have stressed, blind children cannot see how people's attitudes (both their own and those of others) are directed from people towards a shared, visually-specified world. They face serious but potentially surmountable problems in grasping what it is to have and to transpose attitudes both across individual people, as in speech-role-sensitive language, and across the objects at the focus of those attitudes, as in symbolic play.

If this account is valid, would we not expect that blind children should manifest specific limitations in adjusting to the mental states of others, including states such as those of having beliefs and false beliefs which require recognition of the psychological orientations of others? My colleagues and I have recently completed a controlled study of non-autistic congenitally blind children in which we employed two rather different tasks (Minter, Hobson, & Bishop, 1998). The first was modelled on that of Perner, Leekham, and Wimmer (1987), but took the form of asking 21 blind and 21 matched sighted children aged between 5 and 9 years (mean verbal mental age of each group almost 7 years) to feel a warm teapot and to guess its contents. They were then shown that it contained sand, not liquid. The children were asked two questions, in counterbalanced order: what they first felt was in the teapot, before the contents were poured out (the 'representational change' question), and what a peer who was coming in next would think was in the teapot when he/she felt it. The results were that nearly all the sighted children answered both questions correctly, but approximately half the blind children answered one or both of the questions incorrectly, basing their replies on their current awareness of the teapot's contents.

In a subsequent task based on the method of Wimmer and Perner (1983), but employing a method that depended on touch, children were asked to predict in which box a person would look for a pencil, when in the person's absence, the pencil was moved from one kind of box and hidden in another kind of box. In this case, all the sighted and also the majority of the blind children made a correct prediction, but a significant minority (20%) of the blind children failed to do so.

What struck us when conducting this task, was how careful we had to be in communicating to the blind children through language and touch, what we were asking about. At times it was also difficult to interpret their responses, and we had to set a number of responses aside from the analysed data because they were ambiguous. Therefore one needs to be cautious about concluding that some blind children lack *concepts* of 'belief' and so on. On the other hand, this study has revealed just the kinds of difficulty in psychological co-reference between the children and others, that may be significant for the development of 'theory of mind' and related abilities. Moreover, it proved to be the case that a number of congenitally blind children were impaired in evaluating the beliefs and expectations of others.

No doubt such evidence from blind as well as autistic children is going to need a lot of sifting and re-evaluation, but it would seem that studies in developmental psychopathology may point to certain of the conditions that are needed for an adequate grounding of symbols. I believe we shall find that non-inferential mechanisms for responsiveness to and identification with the attitudes of other person vis-à-vis the world are needed by anything or anyone who is to engage in the flexible and creative symbolising characteristic of human beings.

CONCLUSION

I have suggested that the factor of social experience will play an essential part in any account of the origins of the capacity to symbolise, as well as in any theoretical solution to the symbol grounding problem. I have stressed the 'attitude' component of interpersonal relations, for the reason that the developmental role of attitudes is most often neglected in accounts of symbolising. The first part of my thesis is that symbolic representations are connected to that which they represent, in virtue of the fact that they are the cognitive distillate of human beings' attitudes towards and psychological engagement with the world. As Vygotsky (1962, p. 8) stated, 'every idea contains a transmuted affective attitude toward the bit of reality to which it refers'. The second part of my thesis is that symbols function as symbols, in virtue of the fact that they are the cognitive distillate of human beings' attitudes towards and psychological engagement with *other people's* attitudes towards the world.

Any organism or machine that symbolises, not only has to interpret what individual symbols or complexes of symbols mean, but also has to recognise what it is to 'mean' through symbols. I have proposed that for the young child, symbols become decontextualised and recognised for what they are and for what they can do, through the child's social–communicative transactions in which she perceives and identifies with the attitudes and actions of another person, as these attitudes and actions are directed towards objects and events in a shared world. Symbolising is grounded in specific configurations of interpersonal-affective relations and in the self-reflective awareness that such relations promote.

When we come to consider particular symbols, these have meaning insofar as they are vehicles for conceptions of objects and events; only in a derivative sense do symbols themselves 'refer', and even in this sense they embody specific ways of characterising their referents.

Once acquired, symbols do have causal efficacy in evoking absent realities-as-experienced (Piaget & Inhelder, 1969), summoning the memory-traces of the attitudes and actions to which the symbols were linked at the time they were learned. They do not need further symbols for their interpretation. They inherit reference from two sources; firstly, from the directedness of the attitudes and actions which they encompass *qua* symbols; and secondly, from the communicative acts of intending-to-single-out for someone (where the someone may be the symboliser herself). Squiggles become symbols when they are intended as such and experienced as intended as such; but according to the present thesis, the requisite forms of communicative intention and experience can only occur if the symboliser has appropriate forms of affectively-patterned relations with other people who are perceived to express attitudes towards a shared world.

If this thesis is correct, then any organism or computer with the capacity to engage in symbolic pretence would need to be endowed with the kinds of attitude and communicative potential we can observe in interpersonally related and communicating human beings. Moreover, such an organism or computer would require a social–developmental grounding.

REFERENCES

Andersen, E.S., Dunlea, A., & Kekelis, L.S. (1984). Blind children's language: Resolving some differences. *Journal of Child Language, 11*, 645–664.

Baltaxe, C.A.M. (1977). Pragmatic deficits in the language of autistic adolescents. *Journal of Paediatric Psychology, 2*, 176–180.

Baron-Cohen, S., Leslie, A.M., & Frith, U. (1986). Mechanical, behavioural and intentional understanding of picture stories in autistic children. *British Journal of Developmental Psychology, 4*, 113–125.

Baron-Cohen, S., Tager-Flusberg, H., & Cohen, D.J. (Eds.) (1993). *Understanding other minds: Perspectives from autism.* Oxford: Oxford University Press.

Bosch, G. (1970). *Infantile autism.* New York: Springer-Verlag.

Bretherton, I. (1992). Social referencing, intentional communication, and the interfacing of minds in infancy. In S. Feinman (Ed.), *Social referencing and the social construction of reality in infancy* (pp. 57–77). New York: Plenum.

Brown, R., Hobson, R.P., Lee, A., & Stevenson, J. (1997). Are there 'autistic-like' features in congenitally blind children? *Journal of Child Psychology and Psychiatry, 38*, 693–703.

Charney, R. (1980). Speech roles and the development of personal pronouns. *Journal of Child Language, 7*, 509–528.

Dawson, G., Hill, D., Spencer, A., Galpert, L., & Watson, L. (1990). Affective exchanges between young autistic children and their mothers. *Journal of Abnormal Child Psychology, 18*, 335–345.

Dawson, G., & McKissick, F.C. (1984). Self-recognition in autistic children. *Journal of Autism and Developmental Disorders, 14*, 383–394.

Fraiberg, S., & Adelson, E. (1977). Self-representation in language and play. In S. Fraiberg (Ed.), *Insights from the blind* (pp. 248–270). London: Souvenir Press.

Frege, G. (1960). On sense and reference. In P. Geach & M. Black (Eds.), *Philosophical writings of Gottlob Frege* (pp. 56–78). Oxford: Blackwell.

Hamlyn, D.W. (1978). *Experience and the growth of understanding*. London: Routledge & Kegan Paul.

Hamlyn, D.W. (1990). *In and out of the black box*. Oxford: Blackwell.

Harnad, S. (1990). The symbol grounding problem. *Physica, 42*, 335–346.

Harris, P.L. (1991). The work of the imagination. In A. Whiten (Ed.), *Natural theories of mind*. (pp. 283–304). Oxford: Blackwell.

Harris, P.L. (1994). Understanding pretence. In C. Lewis & P. Mitchell (Eds.), *Children's early understanding of mind* (pp. 235–259). Hove, UK: Psychology Press.

Harris, P.L., & Kavanaugh, R.D. (1993). Young children's understanding of pretense. *Monographs of the Society for Research in Child Development, 58*, 1 (serial no. 231).

Hobson, R.P. (1990). On acquiring knowledge about people and the capacity to pretend: Response to Leslie (1987). *Psychological Review, 97*, 114–121.

Hobson, R.P. (1991a). Against the theory of 'Theory of Mind'. *British Journal of Developmental Psychology, 9*, 33–51.

Hobson, R.P. (1991b). Methodological issues for experiments on autistic individuals' perception and understanding of emotion. *Journal of Child Psychology and Psychiatry, 32*, 1135–1158.

Hobson, R.P. (1993a). *Autism and the development of mind*. Hove, UK: Lawrence Erlbaum Associates Ltd.

Hobson, R.P. (1993b). The emotional origins of interpersonal understanding. *Philosophical Psychology, 6*, 227–249.

Hobson, R.P. (1995). Apprehending attitudes and actions: Separable abilities in early development? *Development and Psychopathology, 7*, 171–182.

Huttenlocher, J., & Higgins, E.T. (1978). Issues in the study of symbolic development. W.A. Collins (Ed.), *Minnesota Symposia on Child Development*, (Vol. 11, pp. 98–140). Hillsdale, NJ: Lawrence Erlbaum Associates Inc.

Jarrold, C., Boucher, J., & Smith, P. (1993). Symbolic play in autism: A review. *Journal of Autism and Developmental Disorders, 23*, 281–307.

Jarrold, C., Carruthers, P., Smith, P.K., & Boucher, J. (1994). Pretend play: Is it metarepresentational? *Mind and Language, 9*, 445–468.

Kanner, L. (1943). Autistic disturbances of affective contact. *Nervous Child, 2*, 217–250.

Kasari, C., Sigman, M.D., Baumgartner, P., & Stipek, D.J. (1993). Pride and mastery in children with autism. *Journal of Child Psychology and Psychiatry, 34*, 353–362.

Kasari, C., Sigman, M., Mundy, P., & Yirmiya, N. (1990). Affective sharing in the context of joint attention interactions of normal, autistic and mentally retarded children. *Journal of Autism and Developmental Disorders, 20*, 87–100.

Kaye, K. (1982). *The mental and social life of babies*. London: Methuen.

Langer, S.K. (1957). *Philosophy in a new key*. Cambridge, MA: Harvard University Press.

Leslie, A.M. (1987). Pretense and representation: The origins of "theory of mind". *Psychological Review, 94*, 412–426.

Leslie, A.M. (1991). The theory of mind impairment in autism: Evidence for a modular mechanism of development? In A. Whiten (Ed.), *Natural theories of mind* (pp. 63–78). Oxford: Blackwell.

Leslie, A.M. (1994). Pretending and believing: Issues in the theory of TOMM. *Cognition, 50,* 211–238.

Leslie, A., & Roth, D. (1993). What autism teaches us about metarepresentation. In S. Baron-Cohen, H. Tager-Flusberg, & D.J. Cohen (Eds.), *Understanding other minds: Perspectives from autism* (pp. 83–111). Oxford: Oxford University Press.

Lewis, V., & Boucher, J. (1988). Spontaneous, instructed and elicited play in relatively able autistic children. *British Journal of Developmental Psychology, 6,* 325–339.

Lillard, A.S. (1993a). Pretend play skills and the child's theory of mind. *Child Development, 64,* 348–371.

Lillard, A.S. (1993b). Young children's conceptualisation of pretense: Action or mental representational state? *Child Development, 64,* 372–386.

Lillard, A. (1994). Making sense of pretense. In C. Lewis & P. Mitchell (Eds.), *Children's early understanding of mind* (pp. 211–234). Hove, UK: Psychology Press.

Lillard, A.S. (1996). Body or mind: Children's categorizing of pretense. *Child Development, 67,* 1717–1734.

Loveland, K.A., & Landry, S.H. (1986). Joint attention and language in autism and developmental language delay. *Journal of Autism and Developmental Disorders, 16,* 335–349.

McShane, J. (1980). *Learning to talk.* Cambridge: Cambridge University Press.

Mead, G.H. (1934). *Mind, Self and Society.* Chicago: University of Chicago Press.

Minter, M., Hobson, R.P., & Bishop, M. (1998). Congenital visual impairment and 'theory of mind'. *British Journal of Developmental Psychology, 16,* 183–196.

Moore, D., Hobson, R.P., & Lee, A. (1997). Components of person perception: An investigation with autistic, non-autistic retarded and typically developing children and adolescents. *British Journal of Developmental Psychology, 15,* 401–423.

Mundy, P., Sigman, M., Ungerer, J., & Sherman, T. (1986). Defining the social deficits of autism: The contribution of non-verbal communication measures. *Journal of Child Psychology and Psychiatry and Allied Disciplines, 27,* 657–669.

Mundy, P., Sigman, M., Ungerer, J., & Sherman, T. (1987). Nonverbal communication and play correlates of language development in autistic children. *Journal of Autism and Developmental Disorders, 17,* 349–364.

Ogden, C.K., & Richards, I.A. (1985, originally 1923). *The meaning of meaning.* London: Routledge.

Ozonoff, S., Pennington, B.F., & Rogers, S.J. (1991). Executive function deficits in high-functioning autistic individuals: Relationship to Theory of Mind. *Journal of Child Psychology and Psychiatry and Allied Disciplines, 32,* 1081–1105.

Perner, J., (1988). Developing semantics for theories of mind: From propositional attitudes to mental representation. In J.W. Astington, P.L. Harris, & D.R. Olson (Eds.), *Developing theories of mind* (pp. 141–172). Cambridge: Cambridge University Press.

Perner, J. (1991). *Understanding the representational mind.* Cambridge, MA: MIT Press.

Perner, J., Baker, S., & Hutton, D. (1994). Prelief: The conceptual origins of belief and pretense. In C. Lewis & P. Mitchell (Eds.), *Children's early understanding of mind* (pp. 261–286). Hove, UK: Psychology Press.

Perner, J., Leekam, S.R., & Wimmer, H. (1987). Three-year-olds' difficulty with false belief: The case for a conceptual deficit. *British Journal of Developmental Psychology, 5,* 125–137.

Piaget, J., & Inhelder, B. (1969). *The psychology of the child* (H. Weaver, Trans.). London: Routledge & Kegan Paul.

Plunkett, K., & Sinha, C.G. (1992). Connectionism and developmental theory. *British Journal of Developmental Psychology, 10,* 209–254.

Plunkett, K., Sinha, C.G., Moller, M.F., & Strandsby, O. (1992). Symbol grounding or the emergence of symbols? Vocabulary growth in children and a connectionist net. *Connection Science, 4,* 293–312.

Reddy, V. (1991). Playing with others' expectations: Teasing and mucking about in the first year. In A. Whiten (Ed.), *Natural theories of mind: Evolution, development and simulation of everyday mindreading* (pp. 143–158). Oxford: Blackwell.

Ricks, D.M. (1975). Vocal communication in pre-verbal normal and autistic children. In N. O'Connor (Ed.), *Language, cognitive deficits, and retardation* (pp. 75–80). London: Butterworths.

Ricks, D.M., & Wing, L. (1975). Language, communication and the use of symbols in normal and autistic children. *Journal of Autism and Childhood Schizophrenia, 5*, 191–221.

Rogers, S.J., & Pennington, B.F. (1991). A theoretical approach to the deficits in infantile autism. *Development and Psychopathology, 3*, 137–162.

Searle, J.R. (1980). Minds, brains, and programs. *Behavioral and Brain Sciences, 3*, 417–457.

Sigman, M., Kasari, C., Kwon, J.-H., & Yirmiya, N. (1992). Responses to the negative emotions of others by autistic, mentally retarded, and normal children. *Child Development, 63*, 796–807.

Sigman, M., & Ungerer, J.A. (1984). Attachment behaviors in autistic children. *Journal of Autism and Developmental Disorders, 14*, 231–243.

Sinha, C. (1988). *Language and representation: A socio-naturalistic approach to human development*. New York: Harvester-Wheatsheaf.

Spiker, D., & Ricks, M. (1984). Visual self-recognition in autistic children: Developmental relationships. *Child Development, 55*, 214–225.

Strawson, R.F. (1956). On referring. In A. Flew (Ed.), *Essays in conceptual analysis* (pp. 21–52). London: Macmillan.

Tomasello, M. (1993). On the interpersonal origins of self-concept. In U. Neisser (Ed.), *The perceived self* (pp. 174–184). Cambridge: Cambridge University Press.

Vygotsky, L.S. (1962). *Thought and language*. Cambridge, MA: MIT Press.

Walden, T.A., & Ogan, T.A. (1988). The development of social referencing. *Child Development, 59*, 1230–1240.

Wellman, H.M., & Hickling, A.K. (1993). Understanding pretense as pretense. Commentary on P.L. Harris & R.D. Kavanaugh. Young children's understanding of pretense. *Monographs of the Society for Research in Child Development, 58*, 1 (Serial no. 231).

Wetherby, A.M., & Prutting, C.A. (1984). Profiles of communicative and cognitive–social abilities in autistic children. *Journal of Speech and Hearing Research, 27*, 364–377.

Wimmer, H., & Perner, J. (1983). Beliefs about beliefs: Representation and constraining function of wrong beliefs in young children's understanding of deception. *Cognition, 13*, 103–128.

Wing, L. (1969). Perceptual and language development in autistic children. In M. Rutter (Ed.), *Infantile autism: Concepts, characteristics and treatment* (pp. 173–195). Edinburgh: Churchill Livingstone.

Wing, L. (1981). Asperger's syndrome: A clinical account. *Psychological Medicine, 11*, 115–129.

Wing, L., & Gould, J. (1979). Severe impairments of social interaction and associated abnormalities in children: Epidemiology and classification. *Journal of Autism and Developmental Disorders, 9*, 11–29.

Wulff, S.B. (1985). The symbolic and object play of children with autism: A review. *Journal of Autism and Developmental Disorders, 15*, 139–148.

CHAPTER THREE

A proposal for the development of a mental vocabulary, with special reference to pretence and false belief

Robert W. Mitchell
Eastern Kentucky University, Richmond, KT, USA

> Look at the blue of the sky and say to yourself "How blue the sky is!"—When you do it spontaneously—without philosophical intentions—the idea never crosses your mind that this impression of colour belongs only to *you.* (Wittgenstein, 1953/1965, #275).[3]

INTRODUCTION

An acquaintance of mine once informed me that as a child he did not wear glasses and consequently saw double. When he first experienced corrective lenses, suddenly everything was united. He was surprised that everything could be united, that everything could *not* be doubled, because he thought that everyone saw double. It never occurred to him that people were in any way different from himself in their perceptual experience. The problem of other people's minds was just not a problem for him—he assumed that everyone saw the world as he did.

Believing that people and other animals have experiences like one's own is understandable. Yet how do we know that they have experiences like our own? In answer to the questions "What gives us *so much as the idea* that living beings, things, can feel?" and "How could one so much as get the idea of ascribing a *sensation* to a *thing*?", the philosopher Wittgenstein (1953/1965, #283–284) responded "And now look at a wriggling fly and at once these difficulties vanish and pain seems able to get a foothold here, where before everything was, so to speak, too smooth for it".[3] My expectation is that the problem of other minds is not thought about extensively by most people, and the idea that people have minds like one's own is rarely questioned (though one may not know exactly what other people are thinking at any moment). Still, the philosophy concerning other minds has consequences for our understanding of children's theory of mind, which I discuss below. I begin by examining a tradition of (largely European) philosophy of mind concerned with the analogy to other minds, which provides (I believe) a useful starting point for discussion of the importance of behaviour, context, norms, language, theory, and stories for the development of a psychological vocabulary. I then provide a brief discussion of the sorts of evidence which can be used to come up with psychological terminology by English speakers, and apply this discussion when presenting a series of studies examining children's understanding of pretence and false belief.

THE ANALOGY TO OTHER MINDS

As it is classically presented, the problem of other minds is potentially solved by analogical argument. I have a body, which produces experiences (feelings and other mental states), which cause my behaviours; other people have a body very like mine in many ways, and produce behaviours very like mine in many ways. I know my own experiences, and can correlate these experiences with my behaviours. Therefore, when I perceive another person behaving as I do (in a similar situation) when I have particular experiences, I expect they have similar experiences. That is, I extrapolate from similarity in body, behaviour, and context to similarity in conscious experience (see, for example, Shorter, 1967).[1]

The argument via analogy to other minds has a variety of problems, one of which is that analogical reasoning cannot lead to certainty; it is only suggestive of similarity between two things. Given that one cannot verify that another has the conscious experiences that one presumes based on the analogy, one can never know directly, as one knows in one's own case, that the other has the same experience (Ryle, 1949, p. 58). Thus, the analogy has difficulties at the empirical end. However, philosophers have regularly constructed attacks on two other aspects of the analogy: that one knows one's own mind directly and one's own experiences privately, and that one can extrapolate from one's own unique mind to another's via similarity in behaviour. Once these attacks are rebuffed or redirected, the unverifiability of the analogy becomes a less vexing problem in that the analogy seems infrequently used in understanding other minds.

ONE'S OWN (AND ANOTHER'S) EXPERIENCES

The first assumption, that one knows one's own mind directly and one's own experiences privately, is subject to several objections. Perhaps the most important objection is that our experiences are often far less than we take them to be (Ryle, 1949, p. 61): "knowing what we are about does not entail an incessant actual monitoring or scrutiny of our doings and feelings, but only the propensity *inter alia* to avow them, when we are in the mood to do so". One's beliefs, knowledge and desires are often made known (and understandable) to oneself by what one says and does, both internally and externally, and by the context within which these sayings and doings occur. Knowing how an internal feeling is to be categorised sometimes depends on the particulars of conscious experience, but is frequently determined by context. For example, knowing that that feeling in the pit of my stomach is lust or fear may depend upon whether I am with an object of sexual desire or have suddenly seen a police car while speeding (see, for example, Ryle, 1949, p. 167). Similarly, one's own jealousy is not directly experienced, but rather is detected by taking into account how one feels (i.e. internal sensations) along with contextual and behavioural information (including what other people say); and, in acting on a belief, one need not be simultaneously conscious of the belief. Some philosophers have argued that using mental state terms to refer to internal experiences to which we have introspective access is inherently erroneous (Ryle, 1949, p. 5): "when we characterise people by mental predicates, we are not making untestable inferences to . . . processes occurring in streams of consciousness which we are debarred from visiting; we are describing the ways in which those people conduct parts of their predominantly public behaviour". The same argument holds for oneself (Ryle, 1949, p. 53). Although such a view of mental states seems inadequate (e.g. Place, 1954/1964), it causes us to make clear that many mental state terms are not descriptions of conscious mental states.

Other philosophical investigations raise questions about whether there can be evidence for conscious mental states (one's own or another's) and about the importance of language in understanding mental states (Wittgenstein, 1953/1965). In determining that something is the case, one commonly uses either criteria or symptoms (empirical correlations). For example, the criterion for a team's earning points in basketball is that a team member shot a basketball through that team's hoop during a basketball game, and a symptom is intense and extreme jubilation from fans for that team. But in the case of experiences, e.g. perceptions, we have neither criteria nor symptoms by which to discern them. This analysis leads Wittgenstein (#304) to the idea that language about sensation need not have a consistent referent: "if we construe the grammar of the expression of sensation on the model of 'object and name' the object drops out of consideration as irrelevant" because a sensation (the "object") has no independent means of recognition. For Wittgenstein, then, naming a sensation does not indicate that the sensation is an object. This idea does not mean that no experience or sensation exists; rather, "The conclusion was only that a nothing would serve just as well as a something about which nothing can be said. We have only rejected the grammar which tries to force itself on us here."[3]

Wittgenstein questions the use of language to *describe* internal states and be consistent in our naming them. Suppose that a man wanting to keep track of a particular sensation marked "E" in his diary whenever he experienced that sensation. Wittgenstein (#258) believes that this person can have no criterion of correctness, no way of knowing if the sensation marked by "E" is the same every time. Even though a sensation may feel the same as a previous sensation, there is no independent method of verification (presumably one compares a current perception to a corrigible memory of that perception). In writing or saying that one experiences the same sensation, "What I do is not . . . to identify my sensation by criteria: but to repeat an expression" (#290). Wittgenstein continues, playing questioner and critic:

> But isn't the beginning the sensation—which I describe?—Perhaps this word "describe" tricks us here. I say "I describe my state of mind" and "I describe my room". You need to call to mind the differences between the language-games.[3]

Words may not be descriptions of *experiences*, though our language suggests that they are; rather, they are often descriptions of the *objects* of experiences, which can be cross-validated (Glover, 1981). For Wittgenstein, "An 'inner process' stands in need of outward criteria" (#580), an experience requires criteria in order to be experienced (#509).[3]

One response to Wittgenstein's concern about criteria for one's own mentality is to state simply that no independent method of verification is needed, in that internal perceptions simply are given as such and may be just as corrigible as any externally oriented perception, though memory can serve as a check of sorts (Strawson, 1954/1966, pp. 46–49, 52–53). Another response is to wonder if we can in fact recognise (identify) the same internal state again and again. In some cases (e.g. persistent pain) one feels correct in identifying it; in others (e.g. an image of one's own face) one feels less inclined to believe that the internal image is exactly or essentially the same.

EXTRAPOLATION FROM ONE'S OWN CASE TO ANOTHER'S

The second problem about the analogy to other minds concerns extrapolating from one's own experience to that of another, given that one cannot directly compare experience across individuals and that one extrapolates from only one instance.

> The essential thing about private experience is really not that each person possesses his own exemplar, but that nobody knows whether other people also have *this* or something else. The assumption would thus be possible—though unverifiable—that one section of mankind had one sensation of red and another section another. . . . If I say of myself that it is only from my own case that I know

what the word "pain" means—must I not say the same of other people too? And how can I generalize the *one* case so irresponsibly? (Wittgenstein, 1953/1965, #272, 293).[3]

Wittgenstein does not intend to deny here that the other's experience is saliently present to us: "Just try—in a real case—to doubt someone else's fear or pain" (#303). This salience does not, however, mean that we know how the pain or fear feels to another, i.e. know directly their experience of it, even though we use the same words to describe an inner experience. Similarly, other scholars have suggested that mental state terms need not be transferable from self to other: "such terms as *think, believe, intend,* or *remember* do not refer to psychological states that are invariant to their holder, but rather are devices used by speakers to characterize the behavior of people or animals from the perspective *of the speaker*" (Olson, 1988, p. 416).

To make the problem of cross-person comparisons of consciousness salient, Wittgenstein imagines a scenario (#293) in which everyone had his or her own box containing something called a "beetle", and everyone could know what a beetle is only by looking in his or her own box. Everyone might have something different in his or her box, or might have nothing at all (presumably the "beetle" could be the air in the box, or nothing—a sleight of hand by Wittgenstein). So the term "beetle" would not refer to anything commensurate across individuals. Similarly, one's name for a particular inner state one experiences can be used across individuals, without being a name for the same (type of) experience across individuals (or, as the sleight of hand suggests, for any experience at all).

Thus, language (or at least naming) holds a special place in our understanding of mental states. In a sense, language creates mental states: "You learned the *concept* 'pain' when you learned language" (Wittgenstein, #384). Even when we conceive of mental states as inaccessible to others, we still talk about them, and can teach others to talk about them:

> What is it like to say something to oneself; what happens here?—How am I to explain it? Well, only as you might teach someone the meaning of the expression "to say something to oneself". And certainly we learn the meaning of that as children.—Only no one is going to say that the person who teaches it to us tells us 'what takes place'. . . . Rather it seems to us as though in this case the instructor *imparted* the meaning to the pupil—without telling him directly; but in the end the pupil is brought to the point of giving himself the correct ostensive definition. And this is where our illusion is. (Wittgenstein, 1953/1965, #361–362).[3]

The illusion is, apparently, in the idea that one can point to (i.e. provide an ostensive definition for) one's talk to oneself, or describe it to another (#370); the language implies that one can, but the language is (for Wittgenstein) all that there is: "The mental picture is the picture which is described when someone describes what he imagines" (#367), i.e. the mental picture is not of something inside.

RESPONSES

One can be sceptical about the idea that language functions to describe experience, but this scepticism should not lead one to claim that if language does not describe something, there is nothing there. "It is hard to *describe* what it feels like to have a headache or a toothache, but these *occur*" (Penelhum, 1956–1957/1964, p. 234). Just because something is unobservable to another does not make it inappropriate to describe that something in terms of things which *are* observable (Strawson, 1954/1966, pp. 45–46, 51–53), and something's being unobservable to someone does not indicate its nonexistence. True, many experiences may not be amenable to linguistic description, which is based on intersubjectively acceptable categories. But "only a prejudice against 'the inner' would lead anyone . . . to deny that I can sometimes say something by way of description of my experiences of having imagery, as well as describing to people what I am imagining" (Strawson, 1954/1966, pp. 52–53).

Many of our internal states are analogically comparable to things presumed to be mutually understandable (Strawson, 1954/1966, p. 53):

> It is . . . true that when we describe 'private' or 'inner' or 'hidden' experiences, our descriptions of them (like our descriptions of their status) are often *analogical*; and the analogies are provided by what we *do* observe (*i.e.*, hear, see, touch, etc.). This is in itself an important fact. It throws light once more on the conditions necessary for a common language. . . . [A] description is none the worse for being analogical, especially if it couldn't be anything else. Moreover, some of these analogies are *very good ones*. In particular the analogy between saying certain words to oneself and saying them out loud is very good. (One can even be unsure whether one has said them out loud or to oneself.) The analogy between mental pictures and pictures is, in familiar ways, less good.

Language allows us to talk about what is private by reference to what is public.

What results from Wittgenstein's (unreasonable) denial that reports of experiences describe anything is his concern to understand the origins of such reportings. For an answer, he looks to natural expressions and development of social interaction (#257). Imagine a child developing a name for pain; such naming requires more than having the sensation of pain.

> When one says "He gave a name to his sensation" one forgets that a great deal of stage-setting in the language is presupposed if the mere act of naming is to make sense. And when we speak of someone's having given a name to pain, what is presupposed is the existence of the grammar of the word "pain"; it shews [sic] the post where the word is stationed.

Language, then, is the network into which words are placed. However much a person has experiences, the question of how that person learns to use mental state terms (and if he or she uses these to refer to experiences) depends upon

others teaching a person language about intersubjectively observable phenomena, either analogically or directly (Strawson, 1954/1966). Wittgenstein (1953/
1965, #244) questions how this teaching occurs:

> But how is the connexion between the name and the thing named set up? This
> question is the same as: how does a human being learn the meaning of the names
> of sensations?—of the word "pain" for example. Here is one possibility: words are
> connected with the primitive, the natural, expressions of the sensation and used in
> their place. A child has hurt himself and he cries; and then adults talk to him and
> teach him exclamations and, later, sentences. They teach the child new pain-
> behaviour . . . the verbal expression of pain replaces crying and does not describe it.[3]

One might argue that this analysis obviates the need for analogy to other minds
because both you and I produce what are taken as natural expressions of internal
states (whether or not these internal states are similar across individuals, or even
exist), and the language of mental states can build upon these natural expressions, rather than upon any extrapolation from one's own experiences to another's (Malcolm, 1963/1966, p. 383). But the question remains unanswered:
why is one compelled to assume that one's own pain behaviour, for example, and
that of another, are about the same sort of thing? (As we shall see a bit later,
the compulsion derives in part from kinaesthetic–visual matching, which allows
not only for the coordination of one's own sensory modalities into a coherent
whole, but also creates a schema which can be applied to others.)

ASCRIBING EXPERIENCE AT ALL

That one has experiences, and that one must have a common language with
others (rather than a private language, or an impersonal language without terms
for experiences), prepare one to use something intersubjective (behaviour and
circumstances) as the basis for ascribing mental states to others (Strawson, 1954/
1966, p. 48). But the fact that one *has* experiences at all—that one ascribes
experiences *to oneself*—has implications about our understanding of other minds
which become clearer when one asks "Why are one's states of consciousness
ascribed at all, to *any* subject?" (Strawson, 1959/1963, p. 89).

> If, in identifying the things to which states of consciousness are to be ascribed,
> private experiences are to be all one has to go on, then, just for the very same
> reason as that for which there is, from one's own point of view, no question of
> telling that a private experience is one's own, there is no telling that a private
> experience is another's. All private experiences, all states of consciousness, will be
> mine, i.e. no one's. (Strawson, 1958/1964, p. 387; 1959/1963, p. 96)

The analogy to other minds argues that I know other subjects exist and have
experiences because "the subject of those experiences . . . stand[s] in the same

unique causal relation to body N [the other's body] as *my* experiences stand to body M [the analogizer's body]", but this analysis "requires me to have noted that *my* experiences stand in a special relation to the body M, when it is just the right to speak of *my* experiences at all that is in question" (Strawson, 1958/1964, p. 388).

> There is no sense in the idea of ascribing states of consciousness to oneself, or at all, unless the ascriber already knows how to ascribe at least some states of consciousness to others. So he cannot (or cannot generally) argue "from his own case" to conclusions about how to do this; for unless he already knows how to do this, he has no conception of *his own case*, or any *case* (i.e. any subject of experiences). Instead, he just has evidence that pain, etc., may be expected when a certain body is affected in certain ways and not when others are. (Strawson, 1958/1964, p. 393)

Thus, a primitive concept of a person is essential to the ascription of experience to any body, such that if one ascribes experience to oneself, one has the concept of person, and the concept of person implies that there are entities (like oneself) capable of having experiences ascribed to them, by oneself as well as by themselves (p. 395). Specifically, "the concept of a person is the concept of a type of entity such that *both* predicates ascribing states of consciousness *and* predicates ascribing corporeal characteristics, a physical situation, etc. are equally applicable to a single individual of that single type" (p. 388).

> To put it briefly: one can ascribe states of consciousness to oneself only if one can ascribe them to others; one can ascribe them to others only if one can identify other subjects of experience; and one cannot identify others if one can identify them *only* as subjects of experience, possessors of states of consciousness. (Strawson, 1958/1964, p. 387; 1959/1963, p. 96)

Because the concept of a person is essential to self-ascription, and self-ascription requires attributing states of consciousness to one's own body, "a necessary condition of states of consciousness being ascribed at all is that they should be ascribed to the *very same things* as certain corporeal characteristics, a certain physical situation, etc." (Strawson, 1958/1964, p. 389). Thus, any person is a simultaneous instance of M-predicates (material attributes), such as "weighs 150 pounds" and "has red hair", and P-predicates (psychological attributes), such as "is going for a walk", "is depressed", and "is talking to herself". These P-predicates are "unambiguously and adequately ascribable *both* on the basis of observation of the subject of the predicate *and* not on this basis (independently of observation of the subject): the second case is the case where the ascriber is also the subject" (Strawson, 1958/1964, p. 395). Note that our knowledge of some P-predicates is highly tied to someone's behaviour in context ("going for a walk"), whereas our knowledge of other P-predicates requires information from the person ("talking to herself"). Strawson's (1959/1963, p. 103) ideas answer

Wittgenstein's objections that there are no criteria for mental states, in that behaviours are "criteria of a logically adequate kind for the ascription of P-predicates".

Consistent with Strawson's view, people find it unproblematic to ascribe mental states to other humans as well as to many animals. For example, if subjects are presented with a story in which a human protagonist would be reasonably described as having emotions or thoughts based on the person's behaviour in context, they characterise him or her psychologically. Interestingly, they do the same if the humans in the story are replaced with animals (chimpanzees, monkeys, elephants, bears, otters, and dogs), even if such animals are generally viewed as not being particularly humanlike psychologically (Mitchell & Hamm, 1997). For example, in one study, subjects were presented with a brief story in which a male who had been stroking (or nuzzling) a female turned away and looked at his hand (or paw or foot) after his stroking was taken over by another male. These subjects agreed that the male, no matter whether human or not, was upset, jealous, thinking about what to do next, and angry. (All animals were rated highly at thinking about what to do next, although humans were rated higher than other animals on this attribute and, along with elephants and dogs, on trying to hide feelings.) Such attributions of mental states to animals may be more common in cultures which experience animals as difficult to control, and less common in cultures in which animals are easier to control (Mitchell, 1994a), and the same may be true for attributions to other humans.

Strawson's account neatly solves the problem of why we believe that there are other minds, by making it essential for the ascription of a mind to oneself. A quite similar, but more psychological, analysis is presented by Merleau-Ponty (1960/1964), who argues that recognition of one's own experience requires a structure or schema which is "relatively transferrable from one sensory domain to the other in the case of my own body, just as it could be transferred to the domain of the other" (p. 118). Specifically, "I can perceive, across the visual image of the other, that the other is an organism, that that organism is inhabited by a 'psyche,' because the visual image of the other is interpreted by the notion I myself have of my own body and thus appears as the visible envelopment of another 'corporeal schema.'" (p. 118). For Merleau-Ponty, the child's consciousness initially does not distinguish self from other, does not assign its consciousness to itself (much as Strawson argued), but eventually does so through imitation of others and recognition of self in the mirror (p. 119). The "corporeal schema" which Merleau-Ponty describes as ascribable to both self and other seems to imply an ability to match kinaesthetic experience within the self to visual experiences of self (in the mirror) and of others (in imitation) (see Mitchell, 1993). Although it has been claimed that "we know little about the impetus for . . . the notion of a self with internal experiences [which] may emerge as a powerful, unitary concept shortly before 2 years" (Smiley & Huttenlocher, 1989, p. 46), in fact kinaesthetic–visual matching, the corporeal schema, is the impetus.

After the child understands the corporeal schema, he begins to recognise a perspective on himself which is the same as that which others can have on him. Such perspective-taking becomes evident in the child's use of the word "I," for "there must be consciousness of the reciprocity of points of view in order that the word *I* may be used" (Merleau-Ponty, 1960/1964, p. 150; see Loveland, 1984). In addition, in Merleau-Ponty's view, the recognition of herself through imitation and the mirror-image leads the child to a Cartesian view of her own body, and consequently her subjective experience, as closed in on itself (p. 119).[2]

With Strawson's account, our expectations that others *have* experiences and mental states like ours are made understandable by taking possession of our own experiences. And Merleau-Ponty's elaboration suggests that animals which have kinaesthetic–visual matching (great apes and perhaps dolphins—see Mitchell, 1993, 1994b) would likely understand that others have mental states (whereas other animals might experience tactile–kinaesthetic invariants [Sheets-Johnstone, 1990] which are unascribed). Of course, expecting that others have mental states and looking to behaviour in context as essential for understanding others' mental states does not necessarily lead to correct interpretations, and it is perfectly possible for one to expect that others have mental states but to have a limited ability to attribute them (as may be, for example, with many great apes: Mitchell, 1993; see also Ayer, 1963). Indeed, some learning may be necessary for the human child, some links forged between particular behaviours and particular inner states (Smiley & Huttenlocher, 1989, pp. 46–47). "If there is any learning in [understanding people's minds], it seems more necessary to learn to check and refine our projections and attributions than to learn to make them. . . . The trick is to make them at the appropriate level of generality, and unfortunately *that* trick is not part of our initial, constitutional dispositional equipment" (Rorty, 1995, p. 215). Understanding *which* psychological experiences another (as well as oneself) is having depends upon knowing how to interpret behaviours and circumstances, a knowledge which seems dependent upon language. In addition, perhaps because humans are what humans know best, people make attributions of human psychological characteristics to nonhuman, nonliving "things" (e.g. ghosts, gods), which indicates that not all people require that behaviours and circumstances be humanly derived (Guthrie, 1993). Given that language is culturally inscribed, widely differing interpretations of behaviours and circumstances are possible (Howes, 1991; Lillard, 1998; Werner, 1940/1948).

LANGUAGE AND MENTAL STATE UNDERSTANDING

Although by Strawson's account Wittgenstein's doubts about the descriptive accuracy of language concerning some mental states are misplaced, his analysis is still interesting in its focus on inferences based on linguistic structure.

Wittgenstein (e.g. #297, 398–401) expresses doubts about the way mental images are talked about, not because he thinks imagistic experiences do not exist, but because our *knowledge* of them derives in part from linguistic structure. He likens images to pictures, and notes that pictures do not have the same properties as the real objects they represent. For example, "if water boils in a pot, steam comes out of the pot and also pictured steam comes out of the picture pot; But what if one insisted on saying that there must also be something boiling in the pictured pot?" (#297). What happens here is that the language confuses us: "You interpret a grammatical movement made by yourself as a quasi-physical phenomenon which you are observing" (#401). The grammar of talking about mental images forces us to talk about them as if we are talking about physical things (e.g. real pots), but these images are very different from physical things. That the language we use creates constraints for understanding particular ideas or things indicates to Wittgenstein that these differences in language uses are "language-games", because like a game the language proscribes and prescribes particular ways of interpreting. In other words, language itself gives us an idea of what we are using language to talk about in the first place.

Wittgenstein's counterintuitive analysis of the importance of language in understanding mental states has special relevance when people who do not have experiences can yet talk about them and respond to other's talk about them, e.g. in the case of blind persons talking about and understanding properties of vision (Landau & Gleitman, 1985). Clearly it is (1) the fact of a common language, of convention, that allows such talk and understanding, but (2) the knowledge derived from such talk, as well as the talk itself, depends on (a) recognition of empirical correlations between actions or experiences and terms and (b) recognition of similarity in syntactic arrangements of words which are directly understood and those which are not.

To understand these ideas, consider the position of a child learning words and sentences about the perceptions, emotions, intentions, and thinking of himself and other people. Each psychological term (e.g. "emotion"), as well as its subterms (e.g. "anger", "fear"), depend on different forms of evidence to be recognised (Ryle, 1949, p. 169; Rorty, 1995, pp. 209–210). The child must be able to recognise which behaviours in which circumstances the words label, the child must be told when he himself or others are experiencing particular states, and the persons telling the child must be aware of when the child is likely to be having a particular experience based on his behaviour and/or the circumstances (Asquith, 1997; Austin, 1946/1979, p. 110; Caporael & Heyes, 1997; Hall, Frank, & Ellison, 1994, p. 252; Russell, 1997).

But even with all this information, children do not immediately understand the meanings of mental state words, because often these can refer to more than one aspect of a context, behaviour, or experience. For example, although sighted children use terms like "look" and "see" to refer to visual perception, rather than to an amodal idea of perception, in fact "Their experiences must support either of these interpretations; i.e. every experience of 'perceive visually' . . . is also a case of 'perceive'" (Landau & Gleitman, 1985, p. 118). Indeed, 3-year-old and even older children do not always correctly label perceptual experiences ("look", "listen", "touch") of both self and others, often using globally terms for particular modalities (Landau & Gleitman, 1985; O'Neill, Astington, & Flavell, 1992; Pillow, 1993). These children may misunderstand how knowledge is gained through perception, but they might also simply be overextending terms which they eventually use correctly. It would seem that children would readily learn to recognise that they see with their eyes, or listen with their ears, whether or not they could codify that experience in language.

Still, although the development of a psychological vocabulary depends critically upon patterns in experiences, behaviours, their circumstances, and word use, these patterns may not be distinct enough to understand appropriate uses of psychological words: "no inevitable inductions about the meanings of verbs like *look* and *see* (or *know, think, pretend, lie, want, hope, need*, etc.) which involve mental states, goals, and apprehensions, could reasonably fall out of simple correlations between real-world events and the utterance of words" (Landau & Gleitman, 1985, p. 117). Rather, in learning to understand such words, "a child equipped with the capacity and inclination to examine the syntactic format of each sentence [is] in a position to distinguish among the common verbs . . . and could then extract certain linguistic environments" which constrain the possible inductions as to word meaning, such that "the internal syntactic distinctions among verbs hold promise for discoveries about the meanings of the predicates they encode" (pp. 117–118, 119). As Wittgenstein (1953/1965, #257) noted, the syntactic arrangements of words indicate some of their interpretation, show the child "the post where the word is stationed". Our language-games about mental states have particular constraints which may reveal how mental states are understood at all.

THEORIES AND STORIES

One could argue that almost all of our understanding of others' and our own psychology derives from language. Not only does the structure of language inform us of how experiences are understandable (even experiences we don't have), but language itself is used to develop models and hypotheses about experiences of ourselves and others. In this view, justification for the use of mental state terms has nothing to do with criteria and symptoms, but rather depends "on appeals to the simplicity, plausibility, and predictive adequacy of an explanatory system as a whole" (Chihara & Fodor, 1965/1966, p. 411). Chihara and Fodor (1965/1966, p. 413) continue:

> [I]n learning . . . language, we develop a number of intricately interrelated "mental concepts" which we use in dealing with, coming to terms with, understanding,

explaining, interpreting, etc., the behavior of other human beings (as well as our own). In the course of acquiring these mental concepts we develop a variety of beliefs involving them. Such beliefs result in a wide range of expectations about how people are likely to behave. Since only a portion of these beliefs are confirmed in the normal course, these beliefs and the conceptual systems which they articulate are both subject to correction and alteration as the consequence of our constant interaction with other people. . . . We . . . form complex conceptual connections which interrelate a wide variety of mental states. It is to such a conceptual system that we appeal when we attempt to explain someone's behavior by reference to his motives, intentions, beliefs, desires, or sensations.

Chihara and Fodor view understanding other minds as almost a scientific analysis of predictions, based on hypotheses and confirmation or disconfirmation. Their analysis is identical to that of modern-day scientists' interpretations of what children are doing in developing mental state vocabulary: "children's early understanding of desires and beliefs is part of a larger conceptual enterprise, an understanding of persons' actions, minds, and lives" (Bartsch & Wellman, 1995, p. 112; see also Wellman, 1986). One remarkable suggestion from this analysis is that language may allow a child to make inferences about experiences he or she has never experienced, as when a child might grasp the idea of dreaming by combining her notions of imagining and sleep (Chihara & Fodor, 1965/1966, p. 415). Thus, language itself can serve as a medium for understanding minds which differ from one's own.

Assuming that this "theory exploration" conception of the development of mental state vocabulary is true, and assuming that Strawson's analysis that self-ascription of experiences presumes (potential simultaneous) other-ascription is also correct, there are still a few problems. Developing any terminology requires a normative perspective, such that one must learn the conventions of use (Lewis, 1969). Thus, developing a psychological theory requires norms of interpretation, which presumes that the person to be interpreted is normal or that one can know what is normal for that person. (Correctly interpreting someone implies that one knows the appropriate vantage point.) Interpretation of another depends upon what is plausible given the evidence, and this plausibility depends upon a normative frame of reference within which the evidence is interpreted (Bennett & Feldman, 1981). At a simple level, this normative framework is supplied by words and sentences. For example, children learn that many intention terms normally name particular behaviours, as in eating, playing tennis, and going to the shops. Children at around 3 years of age develop the (normative) rule that if there is a matching between an intention and a behavioural outcome, then the behavioural outcome is intended (Poulin-Dubois & Shultz, 1988, p. 110). To understand more elaborate intentions, children must understand the pattern that sentences about behaviours form. They must understand stories, which can transform behavioural evidence into a particular framework for understanding. A story is "a communicational form that provides for the development, climax, and denouement of action in the context of a defined collection of actors, means, motives, and scenes" (Bennett & Feldman, 1981, p. 7). A story "simplifies the natural event, selects out a set of information about it, symbolizes the information in some way, and organizes it so that [listeners] can make an unambiguous interpretation and judge its validity" (pp. 66–67). A story requires that one fulfil normative expectations about the meanings of the behaviours in context represented in the story. My belief that a given psychological interpretation of another (or of myself) is *plausible* will depend upon these normative expectations. If my normative expectations are not satisfied, I may disbelieve the (perhaps accurate) psychological interpretation; if my normative expectations are satisfied, I may believe one psychological interpretation is correct when in fact another is (p. 68).

The significance of normative expectations for interpreting another's psychology is salient in court cases, where prosecution and defence present different stories about a defendant. When evidence is inconsistent with a story, lawyers often suggest that jurors

> place the evidence in the comparative context of what an ordinary person would do in the situation or what the evidence would mean to an ordinary person. [But because this] involves removing the evidence from a context provided by the witness and placing it in a context tailored to the juror's experience, it may result in inferences based narrowly on the juror's past experiences. (Bennett & Feldman, 1981, p. 130)

Note that what a juror does in thinking about what an ordinary person intended is not to take on the mental stance of another (as might be suggested by Harris, 1991), but rather to examine a story with certain taken-for-granted assumptions in mind, or to make inferences from an assumption or from the salient aspects of evidence. Because "Almost any act can be associated with diverse causes, effects, and meanings" (Bennett & Feldman, 1981, p. 66), how the act is interpreted is usually unconstrained by the act itself. By ignoring some particulars and emphasising others in a story, one can build a case that one intention is in progress when in fact the actions are consistent with an entirely different intention. The story can then be examined as to its plausibility. But differences among people in norms and social understandings may result in disagreements about a story's plausibility (Bennett & Feldman, 1981, p. 171). Thus, it is not surprising that divergent systems of explanation based on psychological terms, including even perceptual terms, have developed cross-culturally (Howes, 1991; Lillard, 1998; White & Kirkpatrick, 1985). It may be said that: "We have a good idea of the *sort* of thoughts a stranger has in (what we regard as) perceptually and emotionally laden circumstances, even though we may not be able to identify his beliefs with any precision" (Rorty, 1995, p. 214), *because* we have culturally based expectations about plausible thought-circumstance connections, rather than because we have accurate ideas about what specifically goes on inside a person. Given the ubiquitousness of stories about actions in so many examinations of children's understandings of false belief and other mental states (e.g. Wimmer & Perner, 1983), differences between children and adults in their psychological interpretations may well be based on differences in interpretations of what is plausible given a story.

If, in judging intentions, we must look for plausibility in a story to indicate truth, and plausibility is itself dependent upon normative expectations, then, in talking of another's intentions (and presumably other psychological states), the other's conscious knowledge of intention (and other states) is irrelevant to our understanding of and beliefs about his or her intentions and other states. As Wittgenstein noted, the states themselves become a something about which nothing can be (or is) said. Such ideas make one suspicious of theories (e.g. Gallup, 1983; Harris, 1991) which presume that people (and some animals) extrapolate from their conscious experience to those of others to interpret others psychologically (see Mitchell, 1997).

One could conclude that our language seduces us into believing that language about mental states is language about experiences, when often it is not. Thus, it is not surprising that people frequently report erroneous explanations for their own behaviours based on presumably conscious mental processes (Ryle, 1949, p. 162). For example, when asked to select one from four *identical* pairs of stockings, women tended to select the right-most stockings by almost 4 to 1; but when asked their reasons for choosing the stockings, the women never mentioned the position of the article as a factor in their selection and indeed all denied that position had any effect (Nisbett & Wilson, 1977). These people presumably offered perceptual aspects of the stockings as their reason for choosing one, but given that the stockings were identical such perceptions cannot have been the reason for their choice. Interestingly, "people's erroneous reports about their cognitive processes are not capricious or haphazard, but instead are regular and systematic" because their reports appear to be based on culturally explicit "rules [about psychological explanation,] implicit theories, presumed empirical covariation, or overlapping connotative networks" (Nisbett & Wilson, 1977, pp. 247, 248). As a result, "People's reports about their higher mental processes should be neither more nor less accurate, in general, th[a]n the predictions about such processes made by others" (p. 249). And (p. 249):

> When subjects were asked about their cognitive processes, . . . they did something that may have felt like introspection but which in fact may have been only a simple judgment of the extent to which input was a representative or plausible cause of output. It seems likely . . . that . . . ordinary people in their daily lives, do not even attempt to interrogate their memories about their cognitive processes when they are asked question about them. Rather, they may resort . . . to a pool of culturally supplied explanations for behavior of the sort in question or, failing in that, begin a search through a network of connotative relations until they find an explanation that may be adduced as psychologically implying the behavior.

In this interpretation, the analogy to other minds is not at all present in understanding other minds because, in essence, we don't understand our own or another's mind at all—we simply provide plausible storylines, causes, or reasons that explain our behaviour. Apparently, much of our psychological language has to do with providing culturally accepted causal explanations for our own and others' actions, where mental states are inferred causal factors, rather than with experienced mental states. If inference is involved in using mental state terms, the inference is often to logical categories of causation, not experiential ones. In this context, it is interesting that when asked what they were thinking about after watching puzzling things, 5-year-old children often stated "nothing" (Flavell, Green, & Flavell, 1995). It may be that children have to learn to come up with thoughts, generally not having any *conscious* internal responses to puzzling material. Young children can examine their conscious thoughts when they have them or are instructed to have them (see Lillard, 1993b; P. Mitchell, 1996), but that does not mean that their thoughts are always conscious. (The same seems true for adults, and I for one often find my conscious mind a blank!)

One could infer from these ideas that "one has no more certain knowledge of the workings of one's own mind than would an outsider with intimate knowledge of one's history and of the stimuli present at the time the cognitive process occurred" (Nisbett & Wilson, 1977, p. 257; see also Ryle, 1949, p. 179). Contrary to the explicit assumption in analyses of child language that psychological language develops to name or refer to internal states in self and other (see Bartsch & Wellman, 1995, pp. 32, 38), instead psychological talk may simply be about norms of language use in relation to behaviour in context. This viewpoint posits or implies that *all* we have are normative uses of psychological terminology, none of which refers to any occurrent experiences.

Note, however, that in much of the work of Nisbett and Wilson, the objective was not for people to describe their experiences, but to explain *why* they did or said something. Specifically, subjects were asked to infer their reasons for their actions. Even if children or adults sometimes inaccurately attribute conscious mental states to themselves, inaccurate use or overextension of a terminology does not indicate that the terminology has no reference.

The fact that discerning when it is appropriate to use psychological terminology (for oneself or another) requires taking a normative point of view need not indicate that children are oblivious to their own or another's psychological experience, for there is no reason to think that children cannot attend to regularities in their own experience which co-occur with linguistic norms and with regularities in their own and others' behaviours in circumstances, which regularities are themselves (vis-à-vis Strawson) evidence for one's own and others' mental states.

A child's learning of a language and her learning to name and diagnose her own psychological states, along with the norms that govern the kinds of attitudes appropriate to specific contexts, do not exist apart from one another but are fused: They occur simultaneously in the normal course of daily life. The interactions that form our own psychological dispositions also form our understanding of the standard psychological states of others. Words, self-diagnosis, the categorical frames for understanding others, and normative cultural expectations are all acquired simultaneously in the same act. (Rorty, 1995, p. 215)

But our psychological understanding of others (and ourselves) need not stop at normatively (culturally) prescribed interpretations. Rather, "Our relatively general projective 'takes' on the perceptions, emotions, and thoughts of others . . . specified through our common cultural formation . . . are then further articulated through the minutiae of interaction and negotiation" (Rorty, 1995, p. 220). By starting with norms of interpretation for language use about regularities in experience and behaviour in context and discovering the inadequacy of these norms, we can discover that others have points of view (norms) which differ from our own. For example, children who engage more with others in discussions of internal states, and who have more siblings to interact with, are better at false belief tasks and understanding others' mental states (Dunn & Brown, 1993; Dunn, Brown, & Beardsall, 1991; Perner, Ruffman, & Leekam, 1994), perhaps because they are able to develop multiple "norms" for interpretation (e.g. one for each sibling). Chihara and Fodor, as well as Wittgenstein, are right in talking about language as a network for interpretation. Similarly, a child's theory of mind is "a network of constructs embedded in an intricate web of causal-explanatory connections" (Bartsch & Wellman, 1995, p. 113). A consequence of using norms to interpret others' and one's own mental states (that is, using the framework that children must use in any culture) is that it may lead one to recognise different frames of reference. A blind child presumably begins to understand colour terms by assuming some sense to their use and eventually recognises that her colour terms are not making sense, yet can still gain knowledge about colour terms as well as understand that there is a perspective to which she does not have access (Landau & Gleitman, 1985). A consequence of our examination of norms and their violation is an elaborated understanding that the same psychological term can refer to experiences as well as to behaviour in context (Olson, 1988, p. 421). Beliefs, thoughts, ideas, anger, sights, and images, as well as believing, thinking, conceiving, feeling anger, seeing, and imagining, can refer to both experiences and causal factors inferred from behaviour in context or from a story.

IDEAS AND IMPLICATIONS

All of this discussion indicates that we should be looking for the normative patterns in behaviour, circumstances, and the language describing these patterns which children employ to decide upon the appropriate use of a given psychological term. I shall now elaborate several ideas and implications about understanding of mental states and mental state terms which seem, to me, to derive from the above sally through philosophy.

Knowledge that one *can* ascribe mental states to self and others develops in early childhood through kinaesthetic–visual matching (which allows for self-ascription of mental states and the potential simultaneous ascription of mental states to others via the "corporeal schema") as well as through language, and may be assisted by linguistic structure. Such knowledge does not mean that people want or know how to discuss their own and others' mental states, however; humans from many cultures have little desire to discuss their own or others' experienced mental states, even though they are clearly aware of the existence of these mental states (see Lillard, 1998, p. 13). Nonhuman animals such as great apes, and 18-month-old human infants, both of which have kinaesthetic–visual matching but little or no linguistic ability, are likely to understand *that* others have mental states like their own but to have limited understanding of how to discern which mental states are present in any given behaviour in context. Most other nonhuman animals are likely to have experiences without ascribing them to themselves; they may know that this body (what we would call their own) feels pain when poked, but they need not ascribe such feelings to anyone, much as they may act to avoid pain.

Some mental states are ascribed to others and to oneself on the basis of behaviour in context, either observed or in a story. The ascription of particular mental states to others or to oneself does not normally require mapping between one's own behaviour and that of others, or of thinking about what oneself would experience if one acted similarly in the same context (via the analogy to other minds), but rather requires understanding normative uses of language about behaviour in context and culturally plausible inferences from norms for interpreting behaviour, language, and stories. Consequently, given a story, adults can be expected to base their decisions about the protagonist's psychological states on plausibility of beliefs, knowledge, and intentions given what information and norms the interpreter has. Children may also base their decisions on plausibility, but may differ in what is believed to be plausible.

Experienced internal mental states, other than kinaesthesis and other direct perceptions, are mostly auditory and visual images. The kinds of information one can get by introspection are limited to perceptual experiences (kinaesthesis, pain, sensations emanating from changes in internal organs), quasi-perceptual experiences (visual and auditory images), or these experiences organised (e.g. into planned intentions, inner speech). Given that these internally experienced, typically private mental states need not be revealed in behaviour nor directly derivable from circumstances, they are the sorts of mental states easier to know about for the self than for another. (That is, it is easier to know that I myself am having an upset stomach than that you are having an upset stomach, unless of course you tell me directly by language or indirectly by behaviour.) Most of these internal states, experienced by the self, can be described by analogy to shared (normatively understood) perceptual experiences like vision or audition. However, describing another's individual experience of these states will be less accurate than for oneself, because the evidence for most of these experiences in others is not available.

Beliefs, knowledge, and thoughts (other than the just preceding experiences) are typically not experienced, but rather are used to describe behaviour in context, are inferred on the basis of behaviour, context, or storyline, or are understood to be causal in behaviour; language about these mental states is often based on their status as causal entities in theoretical interpretations (including stories) rather than as experiences. Thus, language about mental states is often not language about experiences. (Again, recognition that another has experiences like oneself is necessary for recognising that one's own experiences belong to oneself, but knowledge of particulars of an experience is typically available only to oneself.) The kinds of mental states which one can talk about using, to some degree, the same sort of evidence for *both* self and others concern beliefs, knowledge, emotions, perceptions of external objects, and thoughts (when not referring solely to experiences).

Because attribution of these mental states for self and other requires evidence which could be publicly observable, our interpretations of ourselves and others with these terms depend on inferences from stories about and observation of behaviour in context. Thus, one would expect little or no difference between self and other in interpretation of these mental states. By contrast, because what an individual is experiencing *is* evidence for herself, that individual's interpretation of these experiences is less influenced by inferences than is her interpretation of another's experiences, and thus one would expect her to be more accurate about her own experiences than about another's. Even for cases, such as visual perception, in which behavioural cues (such as direction of eye gaze) provide relatively accurate inferences about the other, a person is still likely to be more accurate about what he himself observed than about what another observed. However, accurately using the *names* for particular perceptual experiences may not come quickly, even for the self.

Intentions are a confusing blend between beliefs, knowledge, and thoughts on the one hand, and perceptions and quasi-perceptual states ("experiences") on the other. Intentions are the sort of thing which one might be conscious of or not (Poulin-Dubois & Shultz, 1988, p. 110). Intentions of others are primarily read from their behaviour in context (which can include what they say about themselves), whereas intentions of oneself can be based on plans (prior intentions) or from reading one's own behaviour in context (intentions in action; see Searle, 1983). Reading one's own behaviour differs from reading another's behaviour, in that the former is experienced predominantly kinaesthetically and potentially in the form of plans, whereas the latter is experienced predominantly visually.

PRETENCE

The philosophical discussion presented above is highly relevant to children's understanding of their own and others' pretence. Although it has been argued that understanding pretence of self and other should occur simultaneously (Leslie, 1988), self and other do not have comparable evidence about their own and others' pretence, and so it is unlikely that they will have comparable understandings. During pretence, children have more "direct access" to the visual experience of the other than to their own visual image, which is known "visually" only indirectly through kinaesthetic–visual matching (Mitchell, 1993). In addition, "when something in the world—like action . . . or the way things are—contradicts mental contents, or in any sense gives a different message than the mental contents, children appear to go with the external information" (Lillard, 1993b, p. 383), viewing it as more plausible than internal information because they have a realism bias (P. Mitchell, 1994). If this idea is correct and children are asked to judge whether their own and others' actions are pretend or not, then one would expect that children would focus on the other's actions in determining the other's pretence, but their own actions, being less visible, would be less used in determining their own pretence.

In adult usage, pretence typically depends upon someone having an intention to act similarly to the way another acts in a given situation (see Mitchell, 1990). Pretence focuses on intended actions: it is about creating imaginary worlds through actions and props (Hall, Frank, & Ellison, 1995; Lloyd & Goodwin, 1995), and adult uses of the word "pretend" are consistent with the characterisation "acting-as if" (Lillard, 1993a,b; P. Mitchell, 1996). Pretence is thus an intention term, such that determining one's own pretence depends upon recognising prior intentions, but determining another's pretence is usually based on his or her behaviour in context. Consequently, children should judge others as pretending to be another when their behaviour is similar to that other, but should judge themselves as pretending only when they are aware of a prior intention to behave similarly to that other. When children aged 4 and 5 years old shown a puppet (for example) hopping around were told that this puppet did not know what a kangaroo is and were asked if the puppet were pretending to be a kangaroo, they responded that the puppet *was* pretending to be a kangaroo (Lillard, 1993b), consistent with the prediction. Given that young children read a behavioural outcome consistent with an intention as intended (Poulin-Dubois & Shultz, 1988, p. 110), and that they tend to ignore verbal statements which are inconsistent with behaviour (Riggs & Robinson, 1995), they may view the similarity of the behaviour to the kangaroo as intended (and therefore pretence) and ignore the fact that the puppet does not know about kangaroos (which, given its behaviour as characterised by the experimenter, is implausible). About themselves as well children remember what is plausible, even if false (Pezdek, Finger, & Hodge, 1997), much as do adults (Bartlett, 1932/1972), for whom "introspection" is often retrospection (Ryle, 1949, p. 166).

Whether or not children understand their own pretence differently than others', as predicted above, is examined below. I collaborated with Melissa Neal and Wanda Gaskin on a series of studies based in large part on methods developed from Lillard (1993b), but modified to be appropriate for both self and other. I describe part of one study which examined children's understanding of their own ability to pretend, and part of another study which examined, using a variety of tasks, children's understanding of their own and others' false belief and pretence.

In the first study we examined this understanding in 42 children (not all of whom answered all questions): 6 school-children from 3.5 to 4.4 years of age, 22 school-children from 4.5 to 5.4 years of age, and 14 school-children from 5.5 to 6.5 years of age. Each child was asked if (and how or why not) he or she could pretend to be a known animal (a bee or a kangaroo) or an unknown creature (a vilnuk or a blorp). Most children (29/42) said that they couldn't pretend to be an animal they didn't know about for both nonexistent animals (χ^2 (1, $N = 39$) = 6.1, $P = .014$), but only a little more than half (23/39) said they could pretend to be an animal they knew about for both real animals (χ^2 (1, $N = 39$) = 1.26, $P = .262$). More interesting are the responses children offered to the how or why not question. One type of response indicated a lack of knowledge or ability as a reason for not being able to pretend to be an animal: children who were asked what the animal is or does, indicated that they didn't know the animal or what it does, or (in the case of the real animals) indicated that they did not have a skill ("I don't know how to fly") or body part ("I don't have a pouch") needed to pretend to be the animal. Another type of response indicated how the child would pretend to be the animal: the child either described the actions he or she would perform, or simply acted them out. Not surprisingly, children were more likely to offer a lack of knowledge or ability as an explanation for why they could not be a nonexistent animal (mean = 1.39 times per 2 questions) rather than a real animal (mean = 0.28), and were more likely to describe or act out the pretence for a real animal (mean = 1.41) than for a nonexistent animal (mean = 0.51; F (1, 36) = 43.06, $P < .0001$). Thus, children generally knew that they needed to know what an animal is to pretend to be it, and recognised that they could pretend to be an animal that they knew of. Children generally recognised "the impossibility of pretending to be a bear if one does not know what a bear is" (Shorter, 1952/1964, p. 162).

These findings about children's understanding of self pretence contrast with those for children's understanding of *others'* pretence described by Lillard (1993b), who found that children believed that a puppet who did not know what an animal is could still pretend to be that animal. The difference in findings probably comes from the child's recognising, when asked about the self, that he or she cannot produce an action that is similar to that of an animal of which he or she has no knowledge, but not recognising this when asked about the other because, after all, the other *is* providing evidence of an action similar to that of the animal described. In a sense, someone's knowing is read off from that person's behaviour (Bartsch & Wellman, 1989); given that the behaviour of the puppet matches the (implied) intention given to the puppet by the experiment, the child reads the behaviour as having the matching intention (Poulin-Dubois & Shultz, 1988, p. 110) and expects the other to have the knowledge appropriate to the intention. Note, however, that some children in our study said they *could* pretend to be blorps and vilnuks and explained how by imagining what the nonexistent animal probably did (e.g. "they have to eat") or might be like (e.g. "Blorps don't walk, they fly. They can stand and walk on their heads, and have 6 hands, on their head, feet, and ears."), or by acting out behaviours, presumably pretending to be blorps and vilnuks. These behaviours suggest that pretend can be, as Lillard noted, a word naming action-as-if, and also display some children's ease in imagining a similarity relation, and their lack of concern about an *elaborate* similarity relation existing between what they are pretending to be and their own actions. Pretending to be a blorp can simply be doing something and thinking of yourself as, or declaring yourself, a blorp! But overall children were concerned about knowing what something is in order to pretend to be that something, which suggests that they know that pretending to be something usually requires making oneself similar to that something. This finding argues against the idea that children have a more extended definition of pretence to include any similarity matching whether intentional or not, at least for their own pretence.

In the second study, we examined 50 children (not all of whom answered all questions): 22 aged 3.2 to 4.4 years, 14 aged 4.5 to 5.4 years, and 14 aged 5.5 to 6.6 years. These children were tested with two series of questions, offered at sessions at least one week apart, concerning their understanding of their own and others' false beliefs and pretence. Each series contains three types of false belief problems about self and other, and two sets of three types of pretence problems, one set concerning the self and the other set concerning another. (Orders of problems and questions within problems were varied and counterbalanced to avoid order effects.) One type of false belief task used the "deceptive box test", and the other two types used the "unexpected transfer test" (P. Mitchell, 1994, pp. 2–3). Of the latter types, one employed a story in which the experimenter *accidentally* knocked over two boxes, one of which contained the desired object (e.g. chocolate); not knowing which box the chocolate came from, the experimenter placed it in one of the two boxes (the wrong one) and closed both. The other unexpected transfer test used a story in which the desired object (e.g. an instant oatmeal packet) was *intentionally* moved from its box and placed elsewhere (e.g. in a cookie box) to hide it from the child and an adult confederate; this deception scenario was expected to make the transfer more salient (see Dalke, 1995). Both types of unexpected transfer tasks involved a story which indicated what the child and the confederate knew and didn't know about the location of the desired object; the deceptive box tasks were more direct, and required fewer inferences.

In addition to the false belief tasks, there were 6 pretence tasks per session (and thus 12 per child), with half about actions of the child him/herself and half about actions of the confederate. In one type of pretence task, the child (or the confederate) was asked to perform an action (e.g. reaching for an object), and then was asked what she or he was thinking about when performing the action. (The confederate always answered so as to indicate that she or he wasn't thinking about anything; the child typically answered "Nothing", "I don't know", or described something irrelevant.) The child (or confederate) was then asked if she or he was trying to look like a particular animal (a cat, dog, monkey, or squirrel) when performing the action (which is one that the animal might plausibly perform, and which the experimenter imitated); e.g. the child was asked "Were you trying to look like a cat when you reached for the pencil like this?" as the experimenter imitated the child's actions. The confederate always answered "No"; if the child answered "Yes", the experimenter asked if the child were trying to be a different animal, until the child said "No". Once the child answered "No", the experiment told the child or confederate, e.g. "Well, when you just did this (experimenter again imitated action), you looked just like a cat reaching for a ball. You know how when a cat wants something it will reach its paw forward, and I thought you looked just like a reaching cat". (If the task was about the confederate, he or she then left the area.) The experimenter then asked the child if he or she (or the confederate) was pretending to be the animal, and if the child thought that he or she (or the confederate) looked like the animal (these last two questions were counterbalanced across sessions).

A second type of pretence task is similar to the first type, except that non-existent animal names were used (crillbo, vilnuk, blorp, slack) and the child or confederate was not asked if he or she were *trying to look like* the animal. A third type of pretence task is also similar to the first type, except that the child (or confederate) was asked to perform actions more typically conventional of the animal (snake, fish, bird, rabbit) whose actions they are compared to, and the child was not asked if he or she thought that he or she (or the confederate) *looked like* the animal; instead, the child was told (e.g.) "you (or the confederate) weren't *trying* to look like a fish, but you *looked* like a fish", and was then asked if he or she (or the confederate) were pretending to be a fish when performing the action (in this case, opening and closing the mouth). The second type of pretence task was to allow comparison of real and nonexistent animals, and to discern if the experimenter's claim that the children's own actions (or the confederate's) look like those of the animal was enough for pretence to be inferred if the children didn't know what an animal looked like. The third type of pretence task was to see if children's success increased when the *intent* to make actions similar to those of an animal was explicitly denied even though the similarity was (presumably) more salient than in the first type of pretence task.

Thus, in these problems, the child was provided with stories and/or observations about the self, another, and/or objects, and was asked to make judgements about the self and another based on plausibility. If simply knowing about the discrepant object in the false belief tasks is what children focus on, without ascribing that knowledge only to themselves, then children should succeed equally on false belief tasks whether talking about the self or the other. If children ascribe knowledge of the discrepant object in false belief tasks only to themselves (and not to the other), then they should do better at false belief tasks about the other than on those about the self. If children find making inferences from stories difficult, they should do better on the deceptive box tasks than on the unexpected transfer tasks. And if either the similarity of the visible behaviour of the other to the designated animal implies an intention to pretend (even though the other denies this intention), and the child's recognition that she herself did *not* have a prior intention to pretend to be the animal designated, are both influential in the child's decisions, then children should do better on tasks about their own pretence than on tasks about the other's pretence.

Overall, for the 28 children (mean age 4 years, 10 months) who answered all 24 problems (6 each about self pretence, other pretence, self false belief, and other false belief), children were somewhat more likely to answer accurately false belief tasks about the other (mean = 3.75) than about the self (mean = 3.07), but they were much more likely to answer accurately pretence questions about the self (mean = 3.75) than about the other (mean = 1.86; F (1, 25) = 27.49, $P < .0001$). (Simple effects showed significant differences between self and other in false belief, F (1, 25) = 6.94, $P = .014$, and in pretence, F (1, 25) = 24.70, $P < .001$.) In addition, children understood the deceptive box tasks (1.4 correct for every 2 problems) better than they understood either of the unexpected transfer tasks (about 1 correct for every 2), regardless of whether these tasks were about self or other, but showed no differences in their responses to questions about whether one could pretend to be a real animal or a nonexistent animal. These findings suggest several ideas: Children utilise knowledge of the discrepant object in false belief tasks slightly more often in evaluating what they would think themselves than in evaluating what the other would think. They find stories more difficult to interpret than straightforward observations, even when these stories match salient scripts (like those for intentional deception). They ascribe pretence (or perhaps the intention to pretend) to another based on the proposed match between the other's behaviour and the animal's, but do not (usually) make the same ascription to themselves. These findings also suggest that children judge, as plausible, inferences from stories or observations which adults would regard as implausible.

One might conclude from these two studies that children understand their own pretence better than another's. However, given the salience of the confederate's visual appearance and the nonsalience of the child's own visual appearance in the pretence tasks, it could be that a child is not better at understanding her own pretence; rather, she is just more likely to believe that the other looked like what he was described as looking like than the child did herself, and knowing that someone looks like an animal (even if the animal is unknown) is enough to believe that they are pretending to be that animal. Thus, we examined those pretence problems in which the child was asked if he or she (or the confederate) looked like the animal he or she was purported to look like by the experimenter. In fact, a child was more likely to say that the confederate looked like (and pretended to be) the described animal than that the child him or herself looked like (and pretended to be) that animal. Thus, children may be more accurate about the self's pretence than about another's pretence because they are less likely to believe that their own actions look like those of a given animal than they are to believe that the other's actions look like those of that animal—i.e. the visual image of the other as like a particular animal is more salient than the (inferred) image of the self as like a particular animal. When the eight problems in which children were asked about both looking like and pretending to be an animal are examined (ignoring whether they were about the self or the confederate), children were consistent in their yes/no response to looking like and pretending to be an animal 77.6% of the time on average (ranging from 65.22 to 85.42% per problem). Thus, a significant predictor of the accuracy or inaccuracy of children's understanding about their own and another's pretending to be an animal is the children's beliefs about whether or not their own or another's actions look like those of that animal: if a person's actions look like an animal's actions, then that person is pretending to be that animal, and if a person's actions do not look like an animal's actions, then that person is not pretending to be that animal. (Still, there are other interpretations: it could be that children usually denied that they themselves looked like a particular animal because they knew that they weren't trying to look like that animal, whereas the confederate's behaviours' stated similarity to an animal matched a presumed intention to simulate which went against the claim that the confederate wasn't trying to look like that animal. Remember, children tend to ignore others' verbal statements in favour of realism—Riggs & Robinson, 1995.)

We have, therefore, examined whether visual access is an important factor in deciding whether someone, either oneself or another, is an important factor in deciding that someone is pretending by having children (as well as the confederate) perform requested actions while looking in a mirror. The 37 children (mean age = 5 years, 5 months) tested with a mirror show the same pattern as the children tested without a mirror: when children and confederates were requested to look in a mirror while performing actions, children who looked at themselves and the confederate in a mirror were still more likely to answer accurately about their own pretence (mean = 3.84 correct per 6 trials) than about the confederate's pretence (mean = 2.24 correct per 6 trials; paired t (36) = 5.126, $P < .0001$).

Our findings suggest that children think that, to pretend to be an animal, just looking like an animal is enough for another, but not for themselves. Indeed, few children appeared to have difficulty with the "simulative" aspect of pretend play (i.e. that pretence usually requires pretend actions be similar to other actions), and it is likely that the representational nature of pretence (i.e. that pretend A represents real A) comes to be understood based in part upon recognition of similarity (Mitchell, 1990, p. 216). In addition, children's using what they know themselves from observation or experience influences their responses in false belief and pretence tasks: in the false belief tasks, they tend to answer using their knowledge of what they observed for themselves more than for others, whereas in pretence tasks, they tend to use their knowledge of a lack of an intent to look like something as evidence against pretence for themselves more than for others.

Overall, the findings support several ideas developed from the review of the philosophical and psychological literature. Children seem ready and willing to apply psychological terms to others, but appear to misjudge when the terms are appropriate. They appear to judge what is plausible in a story based more on what they know than on information provided in the story when thinking about themselves, but apply the reverse when thinking about the other; consequently they answer inaccurately more false belief tasks about the self than about another, and they answer accurately more pretence tasks about the self than about another. Children seem to judge their own intentions based on whether or not they planned to act according to an intention, but judge the other's intentions based on conformity of his or her actions to a particular intention. The child's own conscious experiences seem to be more salient to the child than the implications of a storyline when interpreting him or herself, but the reverse is true when interpreting the other.

NOTES

1. Note that the analogy to other minds is about conscious experience, though of course non-analogical inferences can be made about common non-conscious processes. For example, while out driving I stop at a red light and I notice you stop at a red light. I could infer a belief in myself and in you that one must stop at red lights, but this belief need not be consciously experienced when either of us stops at the red light. So even though I can state some of my beliefs to myself, I do not necessarily use such consciously stated beliefs to determine that you have beliefs—our behaviour in context is to a great extent criterial of our beliefs. So in this case, I would not be applying an analogy from my mind to yours, but rather inferring in both cases that we shared the same belief, based on behaviour and context. Indeed, psychological terms often do not refer to an internal state which one recognises while having it, but to the having of the internal state whether experienced or not (which should become clearer as this chapter progresses).
2. Neonates' apparent ability for imitation suggests that the ascription of experience to self and other is present from birth, but there is much against the view that very young human infants have an ability for imitation. Although neonates have been observed to stick their tongue out when an adult sticks his or her tongue out toward them (Meltzoff & Moore, 1977), such actions are suspect as evidence of kinaesthetic–visual matching for several reasons (Anisfeld, 1991), including the fact that infants commonly stick their tongue out when looking at something interesting (Jones, 1996). Observations of other apparently imitative behaviours by neonates have not been replicated (Anisfeld, 1991). In addition, infants have at best 20/660 vision at birth and still only 20/100 vision by 6 months (Courage & Adams, 1990), which seem likely to make observation of the fine details of a human face difficult. Although it is useful to ground children's understanding of other minds in an early imitative ability (e.g. Gopnik & Meltzoff, 1993), such a grounding may not be necessary (Guillaume, 1926/1971).

3. Extracts from *Philosophical Investigations*, 3/E by Wittgenstein (trans. Anscombe). Copyright © 1953. Reprinted by permission of Prentice-Hall, Inc., Upper Saddle River, NJ.

ACKNOWLEDGEMENTS

I greatly appreciate the thoughtful and useful comments provided by Angel Lillard, Kevin Riggs, and Peter Mitchell; the assistance of Angel Lillard and Peter Mitchell in the development of some of the materials used in the studies of pretence and false belief; the work of Wanda Gaskin, Melissa Neal, Kelly Johnson, and Nicola Oakley in collecting data; and the patience of the students in my class "Understanding other minds", who responded enthusiastically in our attempts to master the sometimes obscure readings I assigned. The research on pretence and false belief was supported by an NSF EPSCoR grant, for which I am also grateful.

REFERENCES

Anisfeld, M. (1991). Neonatal imitation. *Developmental Review, 11*, 60–97.

Asquith, P.J. (1997). Why anthropomorphism is *not* metaphor: Crossing concepts and cultures in animal behavior studies. In R.W. Mitchell, N.S. Thompson, & H.L. Miles (Eds.), *Anthropomorphism, anecdotes and animals* (pp. 22–34). Albany: SUNY Press.

Austin, J.L. (1946/1979). Other minds. In *Philosophical papers* (3rd ed., pp. 76–116). Oxford: Oxford University Press.

Ayer, A.J. (1963). *The concept of a person and other essays*. New York: St. Martin's Press.

Bartlett, F.C. (1932/1972). *Remembering*. Cambridge: Cambridge University Press.

Bartsch, K., & Wellman, H.W. (1989). Young children's attribution of action to beliefs and desires. *Child Development, 60*, 946–964.

Bartsch, K., & Wellman, H.W. (1995). *Children talk about the mind*. New York: Oxford University Press.

Bennett, W.L., & Feldman, M.S. (1981). *Reconstructing reality in the courtroom*. New Brunswick, NJ: Rutgers University Press.

Caporael, L.R., & Heyes, C.M. (1997). Why anthropomorphize? Folk psychology and other stories. In R.W. Mitchell, N.S. Thompson, & H.L. Miles (Eds.), *Anthropomorphism, anecdotes and animals* (pp. 59–73). Albany: SUNY Press.

Chihara, C.S., & Fodor, J.A. (1965/1966). Operationalism and ordinary language: A critique of Wittgenstein. In G. Pilcher (Ed.), *Wittgenstein: The philosophical investigations* (pp. 384–419). Garden City, NJ: Anchor Books.

Courage, M.L., & Adams, R.J. (1990). The early development of visual acuity in the binocular and monocular peripheral fields. *Infant Behavior and Development, 13*, 123–128.

Dalke, D.E. (1995). Explaining young children's difficulty on the false belief task: Representational deficits or context-sensitive knowledge? *British Journal of Developmental Psychology, 13*, 209–222.

Dunn, J., & Brown, J. (1993). Early conversations about causality: Content, pragmatics and developmental change. *British Journal of Developmental Psychology, 11*, 107–123.

Dunn, J., Brown, J., & Beardsall, L. (1991). Family talk about feeling states and children's later understanding of others' emotions. *Child Development, 27*, 448–455.

Flavell, J.H., Green, F.L., & Flavell, E.R. (1995). Young children's knowledge about thinking. *Monographs of the Society for Research in Child Development, 60* (Serial No. 243).

Gallup, G.G., Jr. (1983). Toward a comparative psychology of mind. In R.L. Mellgren (Ed.), *Animal cognition and behavior* (pp. 473–510). Amsterdam: North-Holland Publishers.

Glover, J. (1981). Critical notice: *Mortal questions* (by Thomas Nagel). *Mind, 90,* 292–301.

Gopnik, A., & Meltzoff, A.N. (1994). Minds, bodies, and persons: Young children's understanding of the self and others as reflected in imitation and theory of mind research. In S.T. Parker, R.W. Mitchell, & M.L. Boccia (Eds.), *Self-awareness in animals and humans* (pp. 166–186). New York: Cambridge University Press.

Guillaume, P. (1926/1971). *Imitation in children* (2nd ed.). Chicago: University of Chicago Press.

Guthrie, S.E. (1993). *Faces in the clouds.* New York: Oxford University Press.

Hall, W.S., Frank, R., & Ellison, C. (1995). The development of pretend language: Toward an understanding of the child's theory of mind. *Journal of Psycholinguistic Research, 24,* 231–254.

Harris, P.L. (1991). The work of the imagination. In A. Whiten (Ed.), *Natural theories of mind* (pp. 283–304). Oxford: Basil Blackwell.

Howes, D. (1991). *The varieties of sensory experience.* Toronto: University of Toronto Press.

Jones, S.S. (1996). Imitation or exploration? Young infants' matching of adults' oral gestures. *Child Development, 67,* 1952–1969.

Landau, B., & Gleitman, L.R. (1985). *Language and experience: Evidence from the blind child.* Cambridge, MA: Harvard University Press.

Leslie, A.M. (1988). Some implications of pretense for mechanisms underlying the child's theory of mind. In J.W. Astington, P.L. Harris, & D.R. Olson (Eds.), *Developing theories of mind* (pp. 19–46). New York: Cambridge University Press.

Lewis, D.K. (1969). *Convention.* Cambridge, MA: Harvard University Press.

Lillard, A.S. (1993a). Pretend play skills and the child's theory of mind. *Child Development, 64,* 348–371.

Lillard, A.S. (1993b). Young children's conceptualization of pretense: Action or mental representational state? *Child Development, 64,* 372–386.

Lillard, A.S. (1998). Ethnopsychologies: Cultural variations in theories of mind. *Psychological Bulletin, 123,* 3–32.

Lloyd, B., & Goodwin, R. (1995). Let's pretend: Casting the characters and setting the scene. *British Journal of Developmental Psychology, 13,* 261–270.

Loveland, K.A. (1984). Learning about points of view: Spatial perspective and the acquisition of 'I/you'. *Journal of Child Language, 11,* 535–556.

Malcolm, N. (1963/1966). Knowledge of other minds. In G. Pilcher (Ed.), *Wittgenstein: The philosophical investigations* (pp. 371–383). Garden City, NJ: Anchor Books.

Meltzoff, A.N., & Moore, M.K. (1977). Imitation of facial and manual gestures by human neonates. *Science, 198,* 75–78.

Merleau-Ponty, M. (1960/1964). The child's relations with others. In *The primacy of perception* (pp. 96–155). Evanston, IL: Northwestern University Press.

Mitchell, P. (1994). Realism and early conception of mind: A synthesis of phylogenetic and ontogenetic issues. In C. Lewis & P. Mitchell (Eds.), *Children's early understanding of mind: Origins and development* (pp. 19–45). Hove, UK: Lawrence Erlbaum Associates Ltd.

Mitchell, P. (1996). *Acquiring a conception of mind.* Hove, UK: Psychology Press.

Mitchell, R.W. (1990). A theory of play. In M. Bekoff, & D. Jamieson (Eds.), *Interpretation and explanation in the study of animal behavior,* (Vol. 1, pp. 107–227). Boulder, CO: Westview Press.

Mitchell, R.W. (1993). Mental models of mirror-self-recognition: Two theories. *New Ideas in Psychology, 11,* 295–325.

Mitchell, R.W. (1994a). Review of *The biophilia hypothesis. Anthrozoös, 7,* 212–214.

Mitchell, R.W. (1994b). The evolution of primate cognition: Simulation, self-knowledge, and knowledge of other minds. In D. Quiatt & J. Itani (Eds.), *Hominid culture in primate perspective* (pp. 177–232). Boulder: University Press of Colorado.

Mitchell, R.W. (1997). Kinesthetic-visual matching and the self-concept as explanations of mirror-self-recognition. *Journal for the Theory of Social Behavior, 27,* 101–123.

Mitchell, R.W., & Hamm, M. (1997). The interpretation of animal psychology: Anthropomorphism or behavior reading? *Behaviour, 134,* 173–204.

Nisbett, R.E., & Wilson, T.D. (1977). Telling more than we can know: Verbal reports on mental processes. *Psychological Review, 84*, 231–259.

Olson, D.R. (1988). On the origins of beliefs and other intentional states in children. In J.W. Astington, P.L. Harris, & D.R. Olson (Eds.), *Developing theories of mind* (pp. 414–426). New York: Cambridge University Press.

O'Neill, D.K., Astington, J.W., & Flavell, J.H. (1992). Young children's understanding of the role that sensory experiences play in knowledge acquisition. *Child Development, 63*, 474–490.

Penelhum, T. (1956–1957/1964). The logic of pleasure. In D.F. Gustafson (Ed.), *Essays in philosophical psychology* (pp. 227–247). New York: Anchor Books.

Perner, J., Ruffman, T., & Leekam, S.R. (1994). Theory of mind is contagious: You catch it from your sibs. *Child Development, 65*, 1228–1238.

Pezdek, K., Finger, K., & Hodge, D. (1997). Planting false childhood memories: The role of event plausibility. *Psychological Science, 8*, 437–441.

Pillow, B.H. (1993). Preschool children's understanding of the relationship between modality of perceptual access and knowledge of perceptual properties. *British Journal of Developmental Psychology, 11*, 371–390.

Place, U.T. (1954/1964). The concept of heed. In D.F. Gustafson (Ed.), *Essays in philosophical psychology* (pp. 206–226). New York: Anchor Books.

Poulin-Dubois, D., & Shultz, T.R. (1988). The development of the understanding of human behavior: From agency to intentionality. In J.W. Astington, P.L. Harris, & D.R. Olson (Eds.), *Developing theories of mind* (pp.109–125). New York: Cambridge University Press.

Riggs, K.J., & Robinson, E.J. (1995). What people say and what they think: Children's judgements of false belief in relation to their recall of false messages. *British Journal of Developmental Psychology, 13*, 271–284.

Rorty, A.O. (1995). Understanding others. In L. Rosen (Ed.), *Other intentions* (pp. 203–223). Sante Fe, NM: School of American Social Research.

Russell, R.L. (1997). Anthropomorphism in mother-infant interaction: Cultural imperative or scientific acumen? In R.W. Mitchell, N.S. Thompson, & H.L. Miles (Eds.), *Anthropomorphism, anecdotes and animals* (pp. 116–122). Albany: SUNY Press.

Ryle, G. (1949). *The concept of mind*. New York: Barnes & Noble.

Searle, J. (1983). *Intentionality*. Cambridge, UK: Cambridge University Press.

Sheets-Johnstone, M. (1990). *The roots of thinking*. Philadephia: Temple University Press.

Shorter, J.M. (1952/1964). Imagination. In D.F. Gustafson (Ed.), *Essays in philosophical psychology* (pp. 154–170). New York: Anchor Books.

Shorter, J.M. (1967). Other minds. In P. Edwards (Ed.), *The encyclopedia of philosophy*, (Vol. 6, pp. 7–13). New York: Macmillan Publishing Co. & The Free Press.

Smiley, P., & Huttenlocher, J. (1989). Young children's acquisition of emotion concepts. In C. Saarni & P.L. Harris (Eds.), *Children's understanding of emotion* (pp. 27–49). New York: Cambridge University Press.

Strawson, P.F. (1954/1966). Review of Wittgenstein's *Philosophical investigations*. In G. Pilcher (Ed.), *Wittgenstein: The philosophical investigations*. Garden City, NJ: Anchor Books.

Strawson, P.F. (1958/1964). Persons. In D.F. Gustafson (Ed.), *Essays in philosophical psychology* (pp. 377–403). New York: Anchor Books.

Strawson, P.F. (1959/1963). *Individuals* (pp. 22–64). Garden City, NJ: Anchor Books.

Wellman, H.M. (1988). First steps in the child's theorizing about the mind. In J.W. Astington, P.L. Harris, & D.R. Olson (Eds.), *Developing theories of mind* (pp. 64–92). New York: Cambridge University Press.

Werner, H. (1940/1948). *Comparative psychology of mental development*. New York: Follett.

White, G.M., & Kirkpatrick, J. (Eds.) (1985). *Person, self, and experience: Exploring Pacific ethnopsychologies*. Berkeley: University of California Press.

Wimmer, H., & Perner, J. (1983). Beliefs about beliefs: Representation and constraining function of wrong beliefs in young children's understanding of deception. *Cognition, 12*, 103–128.

Wittgenstein, L. (1953/1965). *The philosophical investigations*. New York: The Macmillan Co.

CHAPTER FOUR

Reasoning from false premises

Paul L. Harris
University of Oxford, UK

Hilary J. Leevers
Rutgers University, Newark, NJ, USA

INTRODUCTION

In order to work out the implications of a given premise, it is often necessary to set aside doubts about its truth or likelihood. According to a long tradition of research, adults who have received little or no schooling find it difficult to set aside such doubts, and therefore often fail to grasp the implications of the premise as stated. Building on these findings, it has been proposed that the ability to adopt an "analytic mode"—to set real-world considerations aside, and to reason from the premises as stated—is not something that comes either naturally or early to human beings. Martin Braine formulated this conclusion as follows (1990, p. 136): "Artificially setting aside part of what you know is an academic game, and there is no reason to assume that our ancestors' life conditions would lead them to acquire much skill at that game."

In this chapter, we argue for a different position. We contend that subjects with little or no formal education, including young children, can reason analytically, in the sense that they are good at temporarily setting aside their real-world knowledge and reasoning from premises that they know to be false. They are able to do this in the case of syllogistic reasoning, when drawing causal conclusions about what would have happened if the antecedent circumstances had been different, and when considering false beliefs or unfulfilled desires. In our view, education does not bring about any sea-change in the way that counterfactual premises are handled. Instead, it helps the reasoner to decide more accurately what stance toward the premises is appropriate for a given context. To make our case, it will be useful to present a historical account of the way that research has evolved. We look back first to the pioneering work of Luria and his successors.

RESEARCH ON ADULTS IN THE SOVIET UNION
AND WESTERN AFRICA

In the 1930s, Luria and his close colleague Vygotsky realised that the Soviet Union offered a vast, natural laboratory in which to study their theoretical claims about the links between social and intellectual practices. During that period, members of the traditional peasantry were being recruited into agricultural collectives where they received a rudimentary education and learned how to read. Luria speculated that these social changes would have a major impact on the cognitive processes of the adults in question, and conducted two research expeditions to Uzbekistan to check these claims. A variety of perceptual, memory, and reasoning tests was used. We concentrate here on the tests that are especially pertinent to reasoning.

Luria presented adult subjects with two kinds of classical syllogism. One kind introduced material familiar to the subjects from their own practical experience, and then introduced a question about how that experience might transfer to new conditions. For example: "Cotton grows well where it is hot and dry. England is cold and damp. Can cotton grow there or not?" The second kind introduced material unfamiliar to the subjects, so that they could not rely on the transfer of their own experience. For example: "In the Far North, where there is snow, all bears are white. Novaya Zemlya is in the Far North. What colour are bears there?" The results revealed an interaction between the kind of syllogism and the educational level of the subject. Traditional, uneducated villagers performed reasonably accurately on the first kind of syllogism, those containing familiar material, but they performed poorly on the syllogisms with entirely unfamiliar material. In contrast, less traditional villagers, who had had some education and literacy training in the context of the collective, answered both kinds of syllogism quite accurately.

The traditional villagers displayed an interesting difficulty with the unfamiliar material, a difficulty which we shall refer to as the 'empirical bias' following a suggestion by Scribner (1977). Faced with such premises, they often balked at giving an answer at all, implying that they could not possibly provide one in the absence of empirical experience. "You should ask the people who live there" they might say. A different but related behaviour was to distort or elaborate upon the unfamiliar premise in order to render it consistent with prior experience. In either case, subjects refused to reason from a starting point that lay outside their own sphere of experience. By contrast, the less traditional villagers on the collective farms appeared to have learned that such reasoning was possible and, indeed, sometimes required.

For many years, Luria's findings remained unpublished. They cast the traditional peasantry in a negative light, and were deemed unacceptable in the political climate of the time. In fact, Luria was forced to abandon his programme of cross-cultural research, and turned instead to neuropsychology. Only in the 1970s, when the political climate had changed did he publish a synoptic report (Luria,

1971) and in due course an extended monograph (Luria, 1976). Meantime, his intriguing findings with respect to syllogistic reasoning had come to the attention of Michael Cole and his colleagues who gave equivalent reasoning problems to members of the Kpelle community in Liberia, West Africa (Cole, Gay, Glick, & Sharp, 1971). Notwithstanding the change of culture, these investigators confirmed that schooling was strongly associated with a reduction of the empirical bias. Moreover, manifestations of that bias—including refusals to go beyond personal experience and distortion of the premises—were expressed in Africa in much the same way as they had been in Uzbekistan.

Reviewing subsequent work with schooled and unschooled adults and children in many different cultures, Scribner (1977) reported a remarkably consistent pattern of results: people from non-literate societies performed at around chance levels; and within each culture there was a discrepancy between schooled and unschooled subjects of all ages, with even limited schooling greatly improving logical performance. Scribner also argued that traditional, uneducated subjects did not lack the ability to reason consequentially from a premise. Their conclusions did follow from the premises that they adopted, but these adopted premises were often a distortion or re-formulation of the premises that had actually been presented. Thus, their difficulty lay in accurately encoding the premises as a starting point for the reasoning process, rather than in the logical machinery that they subsequently applied. What these subjects lacked, according to Scribner, was an appreciation, which can be cultivated in the context of schooling, that certain types of reasoning must sometimes be confined to the premises as stated.

Scribner (1977) offered a plausible and persuasive explanation for this effect of schooling. Classroom problems are often divorced from real-world problems. For example, the learner may be asked to calculate what 8 kilos of corn will cost, if one kilo costs so many pennies or roubles. To make that calculation correctly, it is important that the specified price is accepted as a starting point for the calculation—even if it contradicts knowledge of the actual price. Thus, education cultivates the encoding and utilisation of the premises as stated, independent of their plausibility. In effect, the learner acquires a particular logical genre—one that sets empirical considerations aside, and focuses on the logical implications of a premise rather than its truth value.

RESEARCH ON PRE-SCHOOL CHILDREN USING FANTASY CONTENT

The findings of Luria on the one hand, and Cole and Scribner on the other, fitted well together, and given the stretch of time over which they were gathered, and the marked difference between the cultures in which they were collected, their agreement offered a convincing demonstration that uneducated subjects have difficulty in reasoning from false or unfamiliar premises. As we noted in the introduction, some authors have extrapolated from these findings to the more general conclusion that the adoption of the analytic mode in which empirical considerations are set aside is a special, academic skill, one that must be cultivated in the context of education, rather than a universal disposition.

A hint that this far-reaching conclusion might be wrong first emerged in a report by Hawkins, Pea, Glick, and Scribner (1984). Pre-school children aged 4 and 5 years were given syllogistic problems with three different types of initial premise: (i) congruent with children's empirical experience (e.g. "Bears have big teeth"); (ii) incongruent with their experience (e.g. "Everything that can fly has wheels"); or (iii) a fantasy statement that lay outside of their experience (e.g. "Every banga is purple"). All of these problems were of the simplest syllogistic form, modus ponens (e.g. "Pogs wear blue boots. Tom is a pog. Does Tom wear blue boots?"). As might be expected from the findings presented so far, children usually answered the congruent problems correctly and the incongruent problems incorrectly. Moreover, the empirical bias revealed itself on the incongruent problems: children answered them in ways that were consistent with what they knew rather than what was stated in the premises of the problem.

An unexpected and intriguing result was obtained with the fantasy material. Provided that the fantasy material was presented before the congruent or incongruent material, children performed very accurately. The authors concluded that children are naturally inclined to use an empirical strategy when they encounter problems with real-world relevance. Hence their correct replies with the congruent problems, and incorrect replies with the incongruent problems. Once use of the empirical strategy is established, it is applied to any later fantasy problems leading to unsystematic performance. On the other hand, when children receive the fantasy problems first, they reason accurately from the premises as stated.

An important implication of this result is that young children with little or no schooling are capable of answering correctly when presented with premises that lie outside their empirical experience. Their correct replies must be based on logical reasoning from the premises because an empirical solution is not possible with fantasy material. In line with this conclusion, children justified many of their correct responses by referring back to the premises. Note, however, that young children are unlikely to apply this logical strategy to fantasy material if they have been prompted to attempt an empirical strategy by the empirically relevant content (either congruent or incongruent) of earlier problems.

RESEARCH ON PRE-SCHOOL CHILDREN USING MAKE-BELIEVE PROMPTS

The findings of Hawkins and his colleagues raised the possibility that young children, even before they go to school, can adopt the analytic mode by reasoning with the premises as stated, rather than by having recourse to their empirical experience. Nevertheless, one could reasonably argue that their findings are less persuasive of such a capacity than they might be. To have any generality, the analytic mode ought to be applicable to premises that run directly counter to empirical experience and not just to premises that lie outside of that experience. Nothing in the findings reported by Hawkins and his colleagues indicates that pre-school children can deploy the analytic mode in that more stringent context. Recall that children in their study performed poorly with the incongruent premises. Thus, it is possible that children can manage the analytic mode if, and only if, they are offered fantasy content; once they are confronted by material with empirical relevance they abandon the analytic mode and reason empirically. However, it is also possible that children did well with the fantasy premises not because of their content *per se*, but because they prompted children to adopt a particular stance. More specifically, fantasy content might stimulate children's imagination, leading them to adopt a make-believe stance in which they simply pretend that the premises as stated are true. An exciting implication of this interpretation is that children might be able to apply such a make-believe stance to premises with empirical content—including incongruent content—provided they are given an effective prompt to do so.

Dias and Harris (1988) set out to explore this latter possibility. Children aged 4 and 6 years were presented with syllogistic problems including those with an incongruent, initial premise, for example: "All fishes live in trees. Tot is a fish. Does Tot live in the water?" Children's knowledge regarding the incongruent, initial premise was always checked in a pre-test to be sure that the premise contradicted what the children knew to be true. Half of the children received the problems in a normal, matter-of-fact intonation. The other half of the children had the problems presented as a kind of make-believe game, in a dramatic intonation, just as one might in telling a story, and as if they described a differ- ent planet ("Let's pretend that I am in another planet . . ."; Dias & Harris, 1988; Experiment 4). This make-believe presentation produced a clear change in chil- dren's pattern of responding. Within each age group, the make-believe presenta- tion led to more logical replies than the matter-of-fact presentation. Admittedly, the 6-year-olds were more accurate than the 4-year-olds. However, the more important finding was the impact of presentation on both age groups, as illus- trated in Fig. 4.1.

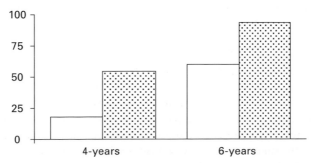

FIG. 4.1   Percentage of logical replies by age and presentation. □, matter of fact; ⊡, make- believe.

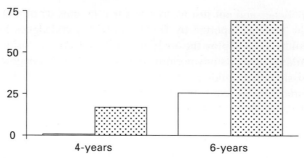

FIG. 4.2   Percentage of premise-oriented justifications by age and presentation. □, matter of fact; ⊡, make-believe.

Further evidence that the make-believe presentation encouraged use of the analytic mode was provided by children's justification of their answers. As shown in Fig. 4.2, children were more likely to give premise-oriented justifications for the make-believe presentation, in that they referred to what the interviewer had said rather than to their own knowledge. For example, they might say: "Because we're pretending that fishes live in trees" or "You said that fishes live in trees". This type of justification was less frequent for the standard, matter-of-fact presentation.

Taken together, these findings provide persuasive evidence that young children, even those with little or no formal schooling, can reason accurately from false premises. Returning to the two points raised earlier regarding the findings of Hawkins and his colleagues, we can draw the following conclusions. First, children can reason accurately not just with fantasy premises that lie outside of their experience but also with premises that run directly counter to their experience. Second, it is likely that children in the study of Hawkins et al. (1984) performed well on the initial fantasy problems not simply because of their content but also because the presentation of such content before any of the congruent or incongruent problems sparked off children's imagination, and led them to adopt a make-believe stance. The findings of Dias and Harris (1988) show that the same stance can be promoted not by the content of the premises but by various cues offered by the experimenter as the problem is introduced and presented. Under such circumstances, the make-believe stance can even be applied to counterfactual material.

The 4-year-olds tested in the experiment of Dias and Harris (1988) were recruited from nursery classes in which they had received little or no formal instruction in reading, writing or arithmetic. By implication, therefore, it is possible for children to suppress the empirical bias even in the absence of schooling. A follow-up study, carried out in Brazil reinforces this point (Dias, 1988; Experiment 6). The children were 5-year-olds but none of them had been to school at all. As in the experiment just described, children were either presented with the problems in a standard, matter-of-fact manner or they were given the problems accompanied by signals to treat them as a kind of make-believe game. The same pattern emerged as before. The make-believe prompts boosted the number of logical replies and also the number or premise-oriented justifications, as shown in Fig. 4.3.

In both the studies just described, children had been given more than one cue to spark their imagination. The experimenter used a dramatic, story-like intonation and also referred to a distant planet. In a follow-up study, we looked more closely at the various ways that 4-year-old children can be prompted to adopt a make-believe attitude (Dias & Harris, 1990; Experiment 1). Four- and five-year-olds were presented with incongruent syllogisms, with three different types of make-believe cue: the use of a story-telling intonation when presenting the problems; the introduction of the problems as referring to experiences on a different planet; and instructions to use imagery, that is, to "make a picture in your head" of the initial premise of each problem. Each cue could be either present or absent. As Fig. 4.4 shows, the presence of any one of the three cues increased the proportion of logical replies and premise-oriented justifications relative to the baseline presentation when none of the cues was present.

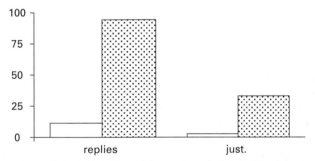

FIG. 4.3 Percentage of logical replies and premise-oriented justifications by presentation. □, matter of fact; ⊡, make-believe.

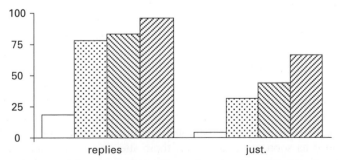

FIG. 4.4 Percentage of logical replies and premise-oriented justifications by presentation. □, baseline; ⊡, intonation; ⊠, planet; ⊘, imagery.

Our interpretation of these findings was that a variety of make-believe cues can prompt children to enter a make-believe world, in which real-world considerations are set aside. As a result, the empirical bias is reduced, and the initial premise is used as a starting-point for reasoning even though the children know it to be false. As Fig. 4.4 shows, the most direct make-believe prompt—the imagery cue—was particularly helpful in this respect, raising the percentage of correct replies from a baseline of 19% to 96%.

Despite its plausibility, there was one questionable feature of this interpretation. In some experiments, we had included premises with unknown facts. For example, children might be told: "All hyenas laugh. Rex is a hyena. Does Rex laugh?". To the extent that the initial premise falls outside children's experience (as ascertained by pre-testing) there ought to be no intrusion from empirical knowledge, and hence no benefit to be obtained from setting real-world considerations to one side. Nevertheless, even with this type of problem we found that the make-believe presentation led to an improved performance by 5- and 6-year-old school children in England (Dias & Harris, 1988; Experiment 1) and by 5-year-old children in Brazil who had never attended school (Dias, 1988; Experiment 6). Still, one might reasonably argue that children start off by trying to bring previous empirical experience to bear, even on facts that are new to them. This tendency might lead them to distort or re-code the premise in so far as they assimilate it to more familiar information. To the extent that make-believe prompts lead children to avoid such assimilation, and to concentrate on the premise exactly as stated, it would improve performance. Accordingly, despite this potentially problematic finding, we felt justified in concluding that children can adopt the analytic mode so long as they are prompted to adopt a make-believe stance to the initial premise. In the next section, we consider evidence that led us to reformulate this hypothesis.

PERSISTING EFFECTS OF INSTRUCTION

So far, we have reported that when children are given make-believe cues, their logical performance immediately afterwards is enhanced. In the next stage of our research, we asked whether this benefit is transient or persistent. It was evident from the cross-cultural findings of Luria, Cole and Scribner that schooling had brought about a stable change in the subjects that they had tested. Whatever change of stance schooling had induced in these subjects, they readily transferred it to new material. We asked if make-believe prompts would have a similar, persistent effect. From a theoretical point of view, we expected the effect to last for only a few minutes. We reasoned that if the prompts operate by encouraging children to adopt a make-believe stance then that stance is likely to be abandoned as soon as children turn their attention to new input and revert to normal reality-testing. To test this expectation, we examined the responses of 4-year-old children to two sets of incongruent (modus ponens) syllogistic

problems presented in two sessions approximately a week apart (Leevers &
Harris, 1999). At the start of the first session, half of the children were given a
minimal introduction to the problems whereas the other half were given instructions and a worked example encouraging them to concentrate upon the initial
premise of each problem and to use imagery. At the start of the second session,
both groups of children were given just the minimal introduction to the problems. As expected, the children without instruction displayed the empirical bias
in both sessions; they gave incorrect replies and justified these replies with
reference to empirical knowledge. Also consistent with previous results, the
children in the instructed group gave predominantly logical replies in the first
session, and justified these replies with reference to the information given in the
premises. Surprisingly, the instructed children continued to give logical replies
and premise-oriented justifications in the second session, a week after the
instructions had been given. In fact, there was no difference in the performance
of these children between the two sessions, both in the number of logical replies,
as shown in Fig. 4.5, and in the prevalence of premise-oriented rather than
knowledge-oriented justifications.

A later experiment, examining the performance of different subject groups
(children with autism, children with moderate learning disabilities, and normal
4-year-olds), also used a two-session design (Leevers, 1997; Experiment 6). We
will not focus on group differences here, but the design of the experiment allows
us to look further at long-term effects in reasoning. In the first session, children
answered a set of incongruent problems after either a minimal introduction or
after instruction with an example encouraging imagery. In the second session, 2
to 3 weeks later, children answered another set of incongruent problems, but in
this session the condition that children received was reversed: children who had
been given only a minimal introduction in the first session received instruction
whereas children who had received instruction in the first session received only
a minimal introduction. The pattern of results, illustrated in Fig. 4.6, confirmed
the persisting effect of instruction. Children who were not instructed in the first

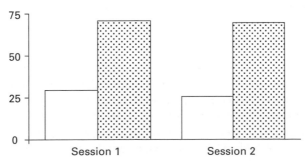

FIG. 4.5   Percentage of logical replies by instruction and session. □, not instructed; ⊡, instructed
in Session 1 only.

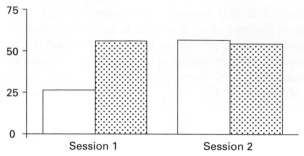

FIG. 4.6   Percentage of logical replies by order of instructions and session. □, not instructed—instructed; ⊡, instructed—not instructed.

session answered mostly empirically in that session but more logically following instruction in the second session (see white bars of Fig. 4.6). Children who received instruction in the first session produced a similar number of logical replies in both sessions (see tinted bars of Fig. 4.6). These results were mirrored in the extent to which children gave premise- rather than knowledge-oriented justifications, and extended our findings in two ways. First, the effects of instruction were found to last up to three weeks. Second, it seems that children did not simply adopt an initial approach to the problems and continue to use that same approach whenever they confronted similar problems; children who reasoned empirically in the first session without instruction, reasoned logically in the second session with instruction, thus showing a flexibility in approach and suggesting that the durable effects of instruction are limited to those which increase logical responding.

The consistent findings of long-term effects in children's reasoning led us to rethink the mechanism by which cues or instruction might enhance logical performance. Hitherto, all of the interventions that successfully prompted logical reasoning had included a make-believe element, and we had taken that element to be critical. Still, one might argue that the key feature of such cues is not that they incorporate a make-believe element but that they serve to clarify the experimenter's intention that the initial premise be temporarily accepted as true and used as a basis for reasoning. Conceivably, other cues—with no make-believe element—might also promote such acceptance. We tested this by giving 4-year-old children incongruent problems following one of four different instructions: a minimal introduction; instruction and an example encouraging the use of imagery; instruction and an example encouraging the use of imagery with an explanation that imagery is beneficial; and instruction and an example encouraging children simply to think about the initial premise of each problem (Leevers & Harris, 1999). Children were re-tested one week later following just a minimal introduction to the problems. As expected, the children in the two groups instructed to use imagery gave more logical relies in both sessions than

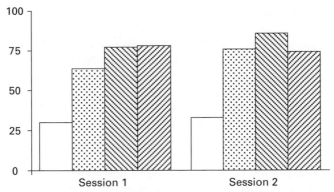

FIG. 4.7   Percentage of logical replies by instruction and session. □, uninstructed; ⊡, imagery; ⊠, imagery and explanation; ▨, thinking.

the children given just the minimal introduction to the problems. Interestingly, the children encouraged to think about the premises (but not instructed to use imagery) also gave more logical replies than the uninstructed children in both sessions and as many as the children instructed to use imagery. Figure 4.7 illustrates this pattern of results, which was also seen in the extent to which children favoured premise- as compared with knowledge-oriented justifications.

Thus, young pre-school children can be prompted to adopt an analytic approach to incongruent problems by further instruction encouraging them simply to think about the content of the initial premise, without any make-believe prompt. This result is consistent with the suggestion that the underlying benefit of conditions which prompt children to reason analytically is that they convey the need to accept the initial premise as a basis for reasoning. The reasoning context of the traditional experimental situation is pragmatically anomalous, with the experimenter stating untruths but with little indication of how these untruths should be handled (see Donaldson, 1978; Braine & Rumain, 1983). Encouraging children to think about the premises should convey to the children that the experimenter believes the premises to be important and relevant to the questions that she is asking (by the principle of relevance, Sperber & Wilson, 1987). Alternatively, using a make-believe presentation signals to the child that the information in the problems is not necessarily consistent with reality, but should be accepted for the sake of the story. Thus, either cue clarifies the experimenter's intention that the children should accept the premises as a basis for reasoning. Once children understand what is required of them, they remember that requirement and spontaneously conform to it in later reasoning tasks.

In summary, our historical review has traced a gradual, conceptual revolution. The early cross-cultural research more or less ruled out the possibility that young children with no schooling could reason accurately from an initial premise that lay outside their experience. However, the findings of Hawkins et al. (1984)

uncovered young children's competence with fantasy content. The findings of Dias and Harris (1988, 1990) then revealed that such competence could be found with false premises as well as fantasy premises, so long as make-believe prompts were used. Finally, Leevers (1997) showed that make-believe prompts were not critical to improved logical performance: prompts encouraging children to think about the premises could be equally beneficial, and the effects of both sorts of prompts are relatively persistent.

COUNTERFACTUAL, CAUSAL REASONING

We have argued that the poor performance of unschooled children with traditionally presented counterfactual problems does not stem from an inability to reason with false premises, but rather it reflects confusion over the task requirements in the pragmatically anomalous reasoning context of a reasoning task. If this is the case, we would expect unschooled children to be able to reason with false premises in a more pragmatically natural situation. One plausible context for this mode of thinking is causal reasoning.

In trying to explain an outcome, especially a mishap, we often ask ourselves what might have occurred had things been different. When we identify some prior condition or antecedent which—had it been in place—might have prevented the outcome, we can arrive at a causal judgement. This judgement is a natural example of reasoning from false premises: the prior condition, the consequences of which are being considered, did not actually occur. Consider an intriguing example introduced by Hart and Honoré (1959/1985) which illustrates this process. If a fire breaks out in an ordinary factory, we would not normally draw the conclusion that the presence of oxygen was a cause even if we know that it is a necessary, standing condition for fire to occur. Suppose, however, that a fire breaks out in a special laboratory environment where precautions are normally taken to exclude oxygen during experimental work. Under these circumstances, we might well attribute the fire to the unexpected and anomalous presence of oxygen.

How can we explain our different causal conclusions in these two cases? If we do indeed try to explain a mishap by considering how it might have been prevented, then, in the case of the fire in an ordinary factory, most of the alternative scenarios that we might consider will include the presence of oxygen, since in any normal environment it is virtually omnipresent. In the case of the fire in the special laboratory, by contrast, most of the alternative scenarios that we might consider will exclude the presence of oxygen, because that is standard practice for the laboratory in question. By implication, as we think about the laboratory fire—but not the factory fire—the presence of oxygen will emerge in our mind as a key factor in bringing about the mishap when it is viewed against the backdrop of the counterfactual but routine condition in which oxygen is not present. This example shows that our causal conclusions are frequently informed by a consideration of what might have happened had antecedent circumstances been different and, in addition, that the particular causal conclusion that we reach depends on the type of counterfactual antecedent that we bring to mind. Here, then, is a context in which we might probe whether young children invoke counterfactual possibilities and alter their causal judgement depending on which possibilities they bring to mind.

In an initial study, we asked whether young children can think about counterfactual antecedents at all (Kavanaugh, Goodrich, & Harris, 1995). We showed them a simple, causal outcome which was enacted for them with the help of puppets and props. For example, a puppet was placed in a bowl of water so that it got wet. Children were then asked what the outcome would have been had the antecedent conditions been different. They were asked to suppose that the puppet had been put into a bowl of popcorn or a bowl of milk—what would have happened then? Children from 2 to 3 years of age (with an average age of 33 months) were able to distinguish between antecedent conditions (immersion in a bowl of popcorn) that would not have caused the observed outcome of getting wet versus those that would have caused it anyway (immersion in a bowl of milk).

In a further study, we asked whether young children think about counterfactual antecedents not just when they are explicitly told about such an antecedent, as in the study by Kavanaugh et al. (1995), but also when asked to make a causal judgement (Harris, German, & Mills, 1996). We also asked whether children make a different causal judgement depending on the counterfactual antecedent that they bring to mind—as implied in the example described by Hart and Honoré. We presented 3- and 4-year-olds with simple stories involving a child protagonist who had a small accident. For example, in one story, the story character chose to go out wearing a yellow cardigan and ended up getting cold. Stories were presented in one of two versions. In the experimental version, the child chose a yellow cardigan rather than a coat to wear. In the control version, she chose a yellow cardigan rather than a green cardigan. Accordingly, in the experimental stories, the choice of the other option would have prevented the outcome, but in the control stories the outcome would have occurred even if the other option had been chosen. We anticipated therefore that if children considered what might have happened had the protagonist chosen differently, the failure to make that alternative choice would emerge as a salient causal factor in the experimental stories but not in the control stories.

To examine this prediction, children were given three stories of each type and following each story they were asked to say why the outcome had occurred (e.g. "Why did Sally get cold?") and what might have prevented it (e.g. "What should Sally have done instead so that she wouldn't get cold"). Figure 4.8 illustrates the frequency with which children referred to the option that the protagonist had rejected (e.g. "She should have worn the coat"; "She should have worn the other cardigan") when answering these two questions for the experimental and the control stories.

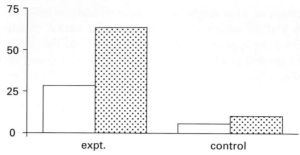

FIG. 4.8   Percentage of references to rejected option by question and type of story. □, why?; ⊡, prevention?

For both the *why* question and the *prevention* question children were much more likely to mention the rejected option with the experimental stories, for which it would have blocked the outcome, as compared to the control stories, for which it would probably have led to the same outcome. Thus, in analysing the outcome, children referred to a counterfactual condition—a course of action that the protagonist had not pursued—and they altered their causal judgement depending on the counterfactual alternative that they had been prompted to bring to mind. This pattern of performance mirrors that seen in a similar study with adults (Wells & Gavinski, 1989).

Still, one might argue that children's references to the rejected option were prompted by the story format because in each story the protagonist was described as choosing one possibility rather than another, such as the yellow cardigan rather than the coat. However, children's counterfactual explanations were not restricted to this explicitly mentioned alternative. The children also invoked other courses of action that the story character might have pursued but which had not been mentioned in the story. For example, they suggested that the character should have "put her anorak on" or "get by the fire". Figure 4.9 shows that children did spontaneously invoke such alternatives, especially in the control stories where either of the explicitly mentioned options would have led to the same mishap.

Two follow-up studies have extended and consolidated these findings. First, Hadwin and Bruins (1997) tested three groups of children—normal 5-year-olds, children with autism and children with learning disabilities (the latter two groups had a minimum verbal mental age of 4 years and a mean of around 6 years). Children were given experimental and control stories similar to those used by Harris et al. (1996), and asked what the protagonist could have done instead to avoid the mishap. All three groups mentioned the rejected alternative more often for the experimental stories than the control stories, paralleling the findings for the *prevention* question in Fig. 4.8. The reverse pattern emerged for references to other courses of action not explicitly mentioned in the story. All three groups mentioned them more often for the control stories than the experimental stories,

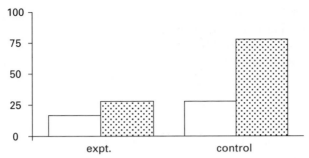

FIG. 4.9   Percentage of references to alternative action by question and type of story. ☐, why?; ⊡, prevention?

paralleling the findings for the *prevention* question in Fig. 4.9. Thus, the ability to invoke counterfactual alternatives is a robust capacity—one that remains un-affected by developmental pathology.

Second, German (in press) gave 5-year-olds stories with either a positive or a negative outcome, and asked them why the outcome had happened. The results for the negative stories were very similar to those obtained by Harris et al. (1996): children often invoked a rejected option as a causal factor when that rejected option would have led to a different and more positive outcome. This type of counterfactual explanation was advanced even though children were never invited to think about preventive measures, but simply asked why the outcome occurred. In the case of positive outcomes, by contrast, such counter-factual explanations were rare. By implication, children's causal analyses spon-taneously turn to preventive measures—thoughts of what might have happened instead—when they are confronted by negative outcomes.

These studies show that young children, including children with learning difficulties or with autism, explain why something has happened and how it might have been prevented by reference to counterfactual conditions—ante-cedents that might have obtained but did not. This disposition is more evident for negative outcomes than for positive outcomes. Nonetheless, even with this restriction, it is likely that children will have many occasions—unless they lead an extraordinarily charmed life—to reason from false premises when thinking about what might otherwise have happened.

Taken together, the findings on syllogistic and causal reasoning show that children can set aside part of what they know prior to any formal education. They can entertain a situation that they know not to be the case (e.g. that all fishes live in trees, or that Sally wore her coat) and work out its logical or causal implications. Moreover, they entertain such situations, whether they are expli-citly described (as in the experiments on syllogistic reasoning), implied (as in the experimental versions of the causal stories) or not referred to in any way by an interlocutor (as when children spontaneously invented alternative courses of action not mentioned in the causal stories). By implication, children are not just capable of setting aside part of what they know, they do so spontaneously with minimal prompting from others. If our analysis is correct, this skill emerges quite early—from about two or three years of age (Kavanaugh et al., 1995). Furthermore, once they have identified a context in which it is appropriate to accept and reason from a false premise, children continue this strategy at a later date. We may now consider the implications of these findings for children's understanding of belief.

THE UNDERSTANDING OF BELIEF

As recent experimental findings have made abundantly clear, between the ages of three and five, children become much more accurate in diagnosing people's beliefs, especially when the beliefs in question are false. This improvement is found whether they are asked to figure out another person's mistaken belief or to report on their own previously mistaken belief. In accurately diagnosing the content of such mistaken beliefs, older children set aside what they currently know to be the case and invoke some counterfactual situation—a situation that might have obtained, or even did obtain, but does not currently obtain. By contrast, younger children appear not to invoke such counterfactual situations. Instead of reporting on the other person's belief—or their own past belief—they invoke what is currently true, making what have been called "realist" errors.

Given this pattern of development, one of us speculated that: (1) children are improving between 3 and 5 years of age in their ability to invoke counterfactual situations and (2) this improvement accounts for the age change on the false belief task, and close cousins such as the appearance-reality task (Harris, 1991; p. 293). This 'counterfactual' hypothesis was contrasted with the standard emphasis on children's developing understanding of representation (Perner, 1991) as follows: ". . . the important step taken between 3 and 5 years . . . is not the discovery that the mind is a representational device, but rather the appreciation that mental states . . . can be directed at situations that the child rules out as part of reality as it stands. This discovery is part of a more wide-ranging ability to think about and describe counterfactual substitutes for current reality." (Harris, 1992, p. 131).

However, there are two potential objections to this counterfactual hypothesis. First, as the present chapter has shown, children of 2 and 3 years are fairly competent at considering counterfactual antecedents and consequences. Moreover, when 3- and 4-year-olds have been compared on counterfactual reasoning tasks (e.g. Harris et al., 1996), there is no obvious indication of any age change. Thus, one could reasonably conclude from these data that the competence for counterfactual reasoning emerges between 2 and 3 years of age, and undergoes no dramatic improvement from 3 to 4 years. If this conclusion is accepted, then it is difficult to ascribe the age change on the false belief tasks and its variants to an emerging ability to engage in counterfactual thinking.

A second potential stumbling-block for the counterfactual hypothesis comes from the pattern of findings obtained for children with autism. A high proportion of relatively high functioning autistic children fail the standard false belief task. On the other hand, as noted earlier, Hadwin and Bruins (1997) found that autistic children (with a verbal mental age of at least 4 years) readily invoke counterfactual alternatives when asked to speculate how a protagonist might have avoided a mishap.

Thus, whether we focus on normal children or on children with autism, it looks as if difficulties on false belief tasks are not paralleled by comparable difficulties with the invocation of counterfactual alternatives. By implication, the improvement between 3 and 5 years in false belief understanding must reflect some other aspect of the false belief task over and above its counterfactual component. However, recent findings indicate that for normal children, at least, this rejection of the counterfactual hypothesis would be premature. In a clever series of experiments, Riggs, Peterson, Robinson, and Mitchell (1998) found a close link between performance of 3- and 4-year-olds on counterfactual tasks and performance on false belief tasks, even when the contribution of age and verbal ability had been partialled out. In their experiments, the two tasks were designed to have a similar structure. For example, children watched as a puppet called Donald was put into a bag and went to sleep. As Donald slept, a ball of Play-doh belonging to him was rolled into a sausage shape by the experimenter. Children could then be asked a counterfactual question: "If I had not played with the dough what shape would it be?" or a false belief question: "What shape does Donald think the dough is?" Children tended to give similar replies to each type of question: incorrect, realist replies (i.e. long, sausage) or correct, counterfactual replies (i.e. round). The presence of incorrect replies was not due to any generalised difficulty in setting current reality aside because children correctly answered a memory check about the prior state of the dough and because most children answered correctly in a follow-up study where they were asked a hypothetical (rather than a counterfactual question) about the future consequences of rolling a ball of clay.

Clearly, the correlation between performance on carefully matched counterfactual and false belief tasks offers persuasive support for the counterfactual hypothesis—the proposal that the emergence of counterfactual thinking is critical for performance not just on counterfactual tasks but also on false belief tasks. Nonetheless, as described earlier, Harris et al. (1996) found that 3- and 4-year-old children were quite competent at considering counterfactual alternatives whereas Riggs et al. (1998) report a considerable number of errors on apparently similar tasks. How can we reconcile these two sets of findings—the evidence suggesting that 3- and 4-year-olds readily invoke counterfactual alternatives, and the evidence suggesting that they often make realist errors? A close scrutiny of the two sets of findings points to a potentially critical procedural difference. In their studies with 3- and 4-year-olds, Harris et al. (1996) created stories in which an initially ordinary or unblemished state was transformed into a negative state by some mishap. For example, a clean floor was dirtied by muddy footprints, a tower of bricks was knocked down by a stick, or a finger was pricked by a pin. Similarly, in the study of 2-year-olds carried out by Kavanaugh et al. (1995), children were questioned about the outcome of untoward transformations such as a doll's immersion in a bowl of liquid. Given these negative outcomes, children might have been especially prone to consider ways in which the mishap might have been avoided. By contrast, Riggs and his colleagues presented children with transformations that were neutral rather than negative: changes of location, shape or colour. Thus, children probably did not see the change as regrettable, and would not spontaneously have considered ways in which the outcome might have been blocked or prevented so as to maintain the prior state. In sum, Harris and his colleagues focused on situations likely to optimise counterfactual thinking whereas Riggs and his colleagues focused on situations in which such thoughts may have been prompted, if at all, only when children were explicitly asked to consider what might have happened instead.

This analysis leads not just to a reconciliation of the two sets of findings but to an interesting speculation for future research. In standard false belief tasks involving the unexpected transfer of an object from one container to another, the change does not amount to a regrettable mishap likely to prompt counterfactual thinking. Thus, the child who focuses on the actual location is not likely to spontaneously entertain thoughts about how the transposition might have been blocked or prevented. However, it would be possible to test children on location changes that do provoke such thoughts. Suppose that Maxi were to put some money for an ice-cream in his pocket and then go to the shop to buy it. Suppose further that there is a hole in his pocket and that just as he is going out of the house the money falls on to the front-door mat but Maxi does not notice. When he arrives in the shop, where will Maxi look for his money at first—on the mat back home or in his pocket? Our hypothesis is that children who fail the standard false belief task involving an unexpected displacement will be more likely to pass this task.

If we now turn to the findings for children with autism, a similar analysis may be appropriate. Hadwin and Bruins (1997) presented children with stories that ended with a negative outcome, and asked them how that outcome might have been prevented. Such a *prevention* question explicitly invites children to consider counterfactual possibilities in a context where counterfactual thinking is already prone to occur, namely a negative outcome. Accordingly, their study may have provided optimal conditions for counterfactual thinking. Children who can engage in counterfactual thinking under such conditions may nevertheless fail to recruit that mode of thought when left to their own devices as in the standard false belief task. If correct, this analysis makes two predictions: first, that the correlation between performance on counterfactual tasks and false belief tasks for normal children (Riggs et al., 1998) may well re-emerge for children with autism; and second, that autistic children should also perform better on false belief tasks if the story-line is one that prompts counterfactual thoughts about the unexpected change or displacement *not* having occurred.

In sum, despite initial indications to the contrary, the claim that children's developing understanding of belief is part of a wide-ranging ability to think about and describe counterfactual situations may well be on the right track. In future research, it will be important to identify the conditions under which young children spontaneously base their reasoning on a counterfactual supposition (Leevers, 1997; Mitchell & Kikuno, Chapter 14, this volume). Current evidence indicates that a negative outcome is one such condition (Hadwin & Bruins, 1997; Harris et al., 1996) but there may be others. If the counterfactual hypothesis is correct, these conditions should be those under which children diagnose a false belief with greater accuracy.

CONCLUSIONS

We have argued that counterfactual thinking is not an esoteric or fancy mode of thinking. Indeed, rather than accepting Braine's provocative claim that "artificially setting aside part of what you know is an academic game" that requires education and cultivation, we would assert instead that such a disposition is critical for the analysis of reality—it is important for making causal judgements and it is important for understanding mental states. Indeed, contrary to the thrust of Braine's remark, we might speculate that our ancestors' life conditions favoured just such an ability.

ACKNOWLEDGEMENT

This research was supported by a postgraduate award from the Medical Research Council, UK to HJL, and by a grant (R000 22 1174) from the Economic and Social Research Council, UK to PLH.

REFERENCES

Braine, M.D.S. (1990). The "natural logic" approach to reasoning. In W.F. Overton (Ed.), *Reasoning, necessity and logic: Developmental perspectives*, (pp. 135–157). Hillsdale, NJ: Lawrence Erlbaum Associates.

Braine, M.D.S., & Rumain, B. (1983). Logical reasoning. In P.H. Mussen (Series Ed.), J.H. Flavell, & E.M. Markman (Vol. Eds.), *Handbook of child psychology: Vol. 3. Cognitive development* (4th ed., pp. 263–340). New York: Wiley.

Cole, M., Gay, J., Glick, J., & Sharp, D.W. (1971). *The cultural context of learning and thinking.* New York: Basic Books.

Dias, M.G. (1988). *Logical reasoning.* Unpublished doctoral dissertation, University of Oxford, UK.

Dias, M.G., & Harris, P.L. (1988). The effect of make-believe play on deductive reasoning. *British Journal of Developmental Psychology*, 6, 207–221.

Dias, M.G., & Harris, P.L. (1990). The influence of the imagination on reasoning by young children. *British Journal of Developmental Psychology*, 8, 305–318.

Donaldson, M. (1978). *Children's minds*. London: Fontana Press.

German, T.P. (in press). Children's causal reasoning: counterfactual reasoning occurs for 'negative' outcomes only. *Developmental Science*.

Hadwin, J., & Bruins, J. (1997). *Imagining alternative outcomes: counterfactual reasoning in children with autism*. Unpublished paper, University of Essex, UK.

Harris, P.L. (1991). The work of the imagination. In A. Whiten (Ed.) *Natural theories of mind* (pp. 283–304). Oxford: Blackwell.

Harris, P.L., German, T., & Mills, M. (1996). Children's use of counterfactual reasoning in causal reasoning. *Cognition, 61*, 233–259.

Hart, H.L., & Honoré, A.M. (1959/1985). *Causation in the law* (2nd ed.). Oxford: Oxford University Press.

Hawkins, J., Pea, R.D., Glick, J., & Scribner, S. (1984). "Merds that laugh don't like mushrooms": Evidence for deductive reasoning by preschoolers. *Developmental Psychology, 20*, 584–594.

Kavanaugh, R.D., Goodrich, T., & Harris, P.L. (1995). *Counterfactual reasoning in two-year-olds*. Paper presented at the VIIth European Conference on Developmental Psychology, Kraków, Poland.

Leevers, H.J. (1997). *Children's logical reasoning*. Unpublished D.Phil., University of Oxford, UK.

Leevers, H.J., & Harris, P.L. (1999). Persisting effects of instruction on young children's syllogistic reasoning with incongruent and abstract premises. *Thinking and Reasoning, 5*, 145–173.

Luria, A.K. (1971). Towards the problem of the historical nature of psychological processes. *International Journal of Psychology, 6*, 259–272.

Luria, A.R. (1976). *Cognitive development: Its cultural and social foundations*. Cambridge, MA: Harvard University Press.

Perner, J. (1991). *Understanding the representational mind*. Cambridge, MA: Bradford Books, MIT Press.

Riggs, K.J., Peterson, D.M., Robinson, E.J., & Mitchell, P. (1998). Are errors in false belief tasks symptomatic of a broader difficulty with counterfactuality? *Cognitive Development, 13*, 73–90.

Scribner, S. (1977). Modes of thinking and ways of speaking: Culture and logic reconsidered. In P.N. Johnson & P.C. Wason (Eds.), *Thinking: Readings in cognitive science* (pp. 483–500). New York: Cambridge University Press.

Sperber, D.S. & Wilson, D. (1987). Précis of relevance: Communication and cognition. *Behavioural and Brain Sciences, 10*, 697–754.

Wells, G.L., & Gavinski, I. (1989). Mental simulation and causality. *Journal of Personality and Social Psychology, 56*, 161–169.

CHAPTER FIVE

Counterfactual thinking in pre-school children: Mental state and causal inferences

Kevin J. Riggs
London Guildhall University, UK

Donald M. Peterson
Birmingham University, UK

INTRODUCTION

A powerful feature of human thinking is the ability to reflect on how the world might have otherwise been, or how it might be under different circumstances rather than how it is immediately presented to us. We often want to answer questions about things which are not immediately accessible: situations in the future, situations in the past, situations that do not exist, inaccessible places or even other people's minds. In this chapter[1] we will look at the development of the ability to consider inaccessible things by focusing on counterfactual thinking in children of 3 and 4 years of age. By the age of 4 years, the ability to free themselves from the constraints of the immediate environment is already apparent in children's spontaneous speech, with the appearance of counterfactuals in their syntax (Kucjaz & Daly, 1979). Moreover, this seems not to be a purely linguistic development since the age at which counterfactuals appear in children's speech is not dependent on the complexity of the linguistic form available in the mother tongue (Slobin, 1966). Experimental work on counterfactual reasoning in children of this age has focused mainly on the ability of 4- and 5-year-olds to reason deductively with false premises (Dias & Harris, 1988, 1990; Harris & Leevers, Chapter 4, this volume). Very little is known about their ability to reason in a more natural, non-deductive manner. Recently however, Harris, German, and Mills (1996) found that young children could consider counterfactual scenarios when reasoning about cause and effect, for example, many 3-year-olds were able to answer questions such as 'What if Carol had taken her shoes off, would the floor be dirty?'

Over the past 15 years or so it has come to our attention that pre-school children undergo a dramatic development in their understanding of their own and other people's mental states. Specifically, between the 3rd and 5th year children develop the ability to ascribe false beliefs to both themselves and other people, and to predict and interpret behaviours symptomatic of false beliefs (Perner, 1991; Wellman, 1990; Wimmer & Hartl, 1991; Wimmer & Perner, 1983). Arguing from a simulationist perspective (or more accurately, a simulation/ theory theory mix; see Carruthers & Smith, 1996, and Davies & Stone 1995a,b) we suggest that the ability to ascribe false beliefs is symptomatic of a more general ability to imaginatively reason about inaccessible things. By looking at the development of counterfactual thinking in pre-school children we hope to shed new light on the debate concerning children's ability to engage in pretend play, their understanding of the relationship between belief and behaviour, and their ability to ascribe false beliefs.

Philosophers have long characterised counterfactuals as conditionals with antecedents that are known to be false. Although the antecedent is false, the consequent may turn out to be either true or false. If the consequent does remain true, then Goodman (1983) refers to this as a semi-factual and the proposition is often prefaced by 'even if' (e.g. even if Clinton had inhaled, he would still be President of the United States). In the studies reported below though, we focus on counterfactuals in which both the antecedent and consequent are false. What sort of questions can we ask people to get them to engage in counterfactual reasoning? Imagine John has a car and that yesterday it was dirty. He forgot to wash it this morning, therefore it remains in the same state as yesterday. Concerning this sequence of events we can ask counterfactual conditional questions with both negatively and positively worded antecedents. For example, (a) If John had washed the car, would it be clean now?, and (b) If John had *not* forgotten to wash the car, would it be clean now? Additionally, if we assume that this morning John did wash the car, we can again ask two counterfactual questions with different syntactic forms, (c) If John had forgotten to wash the car, would it be clean now?, and (d) If John had *not* washed the car, would it be clean now?

Although these questions have different syntactic forms, and are about two different event sequences, to answer correctly one has to engage in counterfactual conditional reasoning: reasoning with a known to be false antecedent (that the car had been washed in questions (a) and (b), and that the car had not been washed in questions (c) and (d)). Developmentally of course, young children might find questions with certain linguistic forms (or different rule-following complexity, see Zelazo, Chapter 9, this volume) easier to answer than others. However, the evidence presented below suggests that a major advance occurs in children's reasoning when they are able to reason conditionally with antecedents that are known to be false, irrespective of the syntactic form of the question, or the type of event sequence that the question asks about.

THE FALSE BELIEF TASK AS A
REASONING TASK

We now present the case for viewing the false belief tasks as a reasoning task. Initially we focus on the unexpected transfer task (Wimmer & Perner, 1983), with the deceptive box task receiving treatment later in the chapter. In the unexpected transfer task a typical sequence of events is as follows:

'Maxi and Mummy are in the kitchen. They put some chocolate in the fridge. Then Maxi goes away to play with his friend. Mummy decides to bake a cake. She takes the chocolate from the fridge, makes the cake, and puts the rest of the chocolate in the cupboard. Maxi is returning now from visiting his friend.' Children are then asked the test question: 'Where does Maxi think the chocolate is?'.

It is reasonable to assume that a necessary condition for success on these tasks is that the child conceptualises belief appropriately. One approach to explaining children's performance on these tasks consists in analysing this prerequisite in terms of mental representation (Gopnik & Astington, 1988; Perner, 1991). A belief is a representation of the world and a false belief a misrepresentation. If I believe you have a false belief, then I represent you misrepresenting the world (a meta-representation). In general, it has been argued that performance in false belief tasks depends on the child's understanding of these (meta) representational concepts. Furthermore, following the 'theory theory' according to which we understand behaviour through use of a domain-specific set of quasi-scientific principles, this understanding has been construed as a representational theory of mind, and it has been argued that successful performance in false belief tasks depends on the acquisition of such a theory (Gopnik & Wellman, 1992).

It could be argued that this account of development assumes a naive ontological view of beliefs. Although we speak of 'having a belief' much as we speak of having a marble in our pocket, it seems implausible to suppose that the majority of beliefs are resident in the mind in finished form. Rather, many of our beliefs are constructed on demand in response to a query. We may for example have no resident belief about whether cabbages are smaller than a football pitch. If asked whether they are, we answer 'yes' and in doing so state a belief. But we had no resident opinion on the matter until the question was posed; we were not host to a resident mental representation of the answer. What we had was the means of constructing a response, not the answer itself.

Likewise in the unexpected transfer task, we think it unlikely that the child has a *resident* belief about Maxi's belief. If the answer to the question were given in the story, we might (though not necessarily) see this as a task of retrieval from memory. But the story says nothing about what Maxi or anyone else believes. It is a story about a person who puts an object in one location, and is absent when the object is moved, not a narrative about mental states. The child has to work out what Maxi believes when the question is asked. It is reasonable to assume then that realist errors arise due to errors in reasoning, rather than a failure to understand the concepts of belief or representation.

To consider what type of reasoning is involved in the unexpected transfer task we initially filter out issues of mind and belief, and look at the structure of the story. We consider the knowledgebase that Maxi has (the facts of the story along with other relevant background information, such as, things generally stay where they are put) and also the knowledgebase of AR, a competent adult reasoner to whom the story might be told.

At the end of the story, Maxi is unaware that Mummy has baked a cake and moved the chocolate. If he is asked the question. 'Where is the chocolate?', he refers to his knowledgebase and—in the absence of evidence to the contrary— responds with the default answer 'In the fridge'. We now consider AR to whom the full story has been told. Unlike Maxi, AR *is* aware that the chocolate has been moved, and has this extra information in her knowledgebase. If we ask her the question 'Where is the chocolate?', she answers 'In the cupboard'. Because of this new overriding information (that the chocolate has been moved) AR updates her knowledgebase and answers accordingly. The default answer (in the fridge) is overridden, and she responds with the answer 'In the cupboard'. However, in the absence of this new information, the default answer (in the fridge) would be given.

We now ask AR the counterfactual question 'If Mummy had not baked a cake, where would the chocolate be?' The question contains the instruction to ignore information (the overriding fact) in her knowledgebase, and since this information relates to the chocolate's new location, the default answer (in the fridge) is given. To answer this question, AR engages in counterfactual reasoning: conditional reasoning requiring the cognitive effort to ignore a known fact.

We now come to the pivotal point in the present analysis. In making changes to her knowledgebase to answer the counterfactual question, AR has in effect modelled Maxi's process of answer derivation above. That is, the strategy used in adapting one's own knowledgebase to reason about an alternative situation serves also to model the epistemic perspective of another person. This suggests the use of knowledgebase adaption as part of a mindreading strategy for working out what Maxi believes, in response to the test question 'Where does Maxi think the chocolate is?' To do this, AR needs to identify the thing which Maxi does not know, implement an instruction to ignore this fact, ask herself the question 'Where is the chocolate?', and then attribute the answer to Maxi. Thus AR employs a process of knowledgebase adaption in order to model Maxi's knowledgebase. The answer to the belief question (in the fridge), is then attributed to Maxi.

On this view, the ability to ascribe false beliefs is part of a more general imaginative capacity to make known to be false adjustments to one's own knowledgebase in reasoning conditionally to a new conclusion. This general imaginative reasoning ability is used to make inferences about many inaccessible things, other people's false beliefs being just one of many applications.

There are two further points worth making. First, the reasoning employed is everyday practical reasoning, not deductive reasoning where the conclusions necessarily follow from their knowledgebases. In the reasoning of the sort described here, the answers derived are generally at best reasonable or probable, not certain. Second, the strategy outlined above is inherently hybrid involving both the use of theoretical knowledge and the ability to simulate (see Peterson & Riggs, 1999). In order to simulate Maxi's knowledgebase, we need to identify what Maxi is ignorant of. This requires the theoretical understanding that people can be ignorant of things that we are aware of, and also, that if a person is absent when a change takes place, that person may be unaware of the change. Finally, we attribute the result of the simulation to Maxi, this again requires the understanding that he may believe something which we know to be false. It is theory based understanding which urges us to run the simulation, and which allows us to make use of its end result.

EMPIRICAL SUPPORT

Findings consistent with the suggestion that performance in false belief tasks is symptomatic of the ability to reason counterfactually are reported in Riggs, Peterson, Robinson & Mitchell (1998). In that study, the authors compared performance on false belief tasks with tasks having the same logical structure but not requiring an understanding of the mentalistic notions of belief.

In study one, 32 children aged 3 and 4 years were tested on two stories, each with a false belief (FB) and a counterfactual reasoning (CR) question. The first story was a Chocolate Story of the sort used in Wimmer and Perner's original experiment', with the FB question 'Where does John think the chocolate is?', and the CR question 'If Mummy had not baked a cake, where would the chocolate be?'

The second story was a post office story: Sally and Peter were in their house but Peter wasn't feeling very well, so he went to bed. Sally then went to the shops to get some medicine (the doll was placed behind the experimenter's back). Whilst Sally was at the shops, the phone rang and the man from the post office asked Peter to come and help put out a fire. Peter got out of bed and went to the post office. At this point, children were asked if Sally knew where Peter was, and corrected if they answered wrongly. They were then told that Sally had finished shopping and asked the test question. In the CR condition the test question was, 'If there had been no fire, where would Peter be?' In the false belief condition the test question was 'Where does Sally think Peter is?' Half the children were asked the CR question in the chocolate story and the FB question in the post office story, and half were asked the FB question in the chocolate story and the CR question in the post office story.

The results were consistent with the counterfactual reasoning account. Twelve children answered correctly in both conditions and sixteen children answered incorrectly in both conditions. Only 4 children out of a sample of 32 answered differently across conditions. There was a significant correlation between performance on the CR and FB tasks ($\chi^2 = 18.5$, $\phi = 0.75$, $P < .001$).

In a second study, children were tested over two sessions. In session one, 44 children were given a FB and an CR task. In session two, 28 of the same children were again tested on another FB and CR task. This time four story formats were used and for each story there was again both a FB and a CR version. The children tested in session two were given the stories not given to them in session one. Within child the order of story version (CR or FB) remained constant over the two sessions. Between children, all conditions and story formats were counterbalanced. Verbal mental age was also assessed, to see what role this may have played in the original correlation. In session one, 14 children answered both the FB and CR questions correctly, and 19 children answered both questions incorrectly. Eight children answered the CR question correctly but the FB question incorrectly, and three children answered correctly on FB but incorrectly on CR. As in the first study there was a significant correlation between tasks ($\chi^2 = 11.59$, $\phi = 0.51$, $P < .05$). The children tested over two sessions, with verbal mental age partialled out, also showed a significant correlation between performance on the FB and CR tasks ($r = 0.72$, $N = 28$, $t = 5.26$, $P < .001$) making it unlikely that the reported correlation in the first study was due to general verbal ability.

The results from these two studies are consistent with the counterfactual reasoning hypothesis. Nearly half the children tested made realist errors on 'belief-free' analogues of the false belief task.[2] These findings offer an alternative to the view that realist errors in the false belief task are due to an underdeveloped representational theory of mind, and suggest that children's errors extend beyond acknowledgement of mental misrepresentation. Indeed, given the correlated performance on the counterfactual reasoning and false belief tasks —suggestive of the same underlying factor being responsible for both—the data support the idea the children's difficulty with false belief is symptomatic of a more general difficulty with counterfactual reasoning.

There are though a number of possible alternative explanations for why children made so many errors in the counterfactual reasoning tasks. It might be argued that the negative wording of the test question ('If Mum had *not* baked a cake . . . ?') was too confusing for 3-year-olds and they merely responded with what was visibly salient (although this does not explain why a correlation was obtained). Nevertheless, we went on to compare children's performance in counterfactual reasoning tasks with both negatively and positively worded antecedents of the test question.

Each child was given a counterfactual reasoning task with either positive or negative wording. One of the tasks was a colouring task in which children were asked to name the colour of a square (yellow) and a pen (blue). Children in the negative wording condition were told by the experimenter 'I know, I'll colour in this square'. The square was coloured in by the experimenter and then children were asked 'Now can you tell me, if I had not coloured in the square with my colouring pen, what colour would it be?' (correct answer yellow). In the test with positive wording the experimenter did not colour in the square but told children 'I could colour in things with my colouring pen, but I won't, I'll put it in my bag. Now can you tell me, if I had coloured in the square with my colouring pen, what colour would the square be?' (correct answer blue).

There was no difference in difficulty between the two tasks: 14 out of 28 answered correctly in the positive version, and 13/28 answered correctly in the negative version. From this study, we found no sign that children's difficulty with counterfactual reasoning is confined to counterfactual conditional questions with negatively worded antecedents.

There might though be a broader development which accounts for the reported correlation across the counterfactual reasoning and false belief tasks. It is well documented that children who fail false belief tasks consistently make *realist* errors: their answers coincide with how the world really is. Perhaps the correlation arose because the younger children lacked the cognitive control to inhibit a response to a visibly salient feature of the environment (Mitchell, 1994). To address this we tested children on two counterfactual reasoning tasks, but the characteristics of the environment to be ignored varied. In one task children had to ignore a currently visible aspect of the world, and in the other they had to ignore an action which had earlier occurred, but was not currently visible.

Forty-six children were tested and each child was given a 'counterfactual to present reality' task (present task) and a 'counterfactual to past action' task (past action task). There were two story types, a road story and a play story. The following describes the road story in both the past action and present versions. 'This is Sally and this is Sally's house. This is the shop where Sally works. Sally goes to work every day by going along this short straight road. Can you see there are two roads? Every morning Sally walks to her shop along the short straight road because it is much much quicker. (Sally was placed next to her house). Today though, the road is closed because the men are mending it'. (Two men were placed on the short road).

In the *past action* version, Sally was walked along the long road, placed in the shop, the men then finished mending the road and were removed from the scene. Children were then asked two questions in counterbalanced order: the test question 'If the men had not been mending the road, which road would Sally have walked along?' and a memory question 'Which road does Sally usually walk along every morning?'

In the *present* version, Sally was walked halfway along the road and remained there whilst the experimenter explained the men had now finished mending the road before removing them from the scene as in the other condition. Again children were asked a memory question and a test question, 'If the men had not been mending the road, which road would Sally be walking along?'

Only 6 children were excluded for answering memory questions incorrectly, leaving a sample of 40. Of these, 22 answered correctly in both tasks, and 7 answered incorrectly in both. There was no difference in difficulty between the two tasks, and performance across them was significantly correlated ($\chi^2 = 6.09$, $\phi = 0.38$, $P < .02$). The results from this study provide no support for the suggestion that realist errors in the Riggs et al. (1998) study arose because of an inability to inhibit a response to a *visibly* salient feature of the environment. In this task, the salience (in terms of visibility) of the 'incorrect response option' differed across conditions but no difference in difficulty was found between the two tasks. Moreover, given the *correlated* performance across the past action and present versions, the results suggest that the difficulty lies in the counterfactual reasoning required, not in inhibiting a response to a currently visible salient aspect of the world.

However, an alternative interpretation of the results is that children's difficulty does lie in inhibiting a response to a salient feature of the environment, but it is irrelevant whether it has a currently visible presence. Rather, children's problem might lie in inhibiting a prepotent response in terms of their own current state of knowledge about the world. To overcome inhibition to a prepotent object requires a certain amount of 'executive' control. Executive errors are made when behaviour is controlled by a salient feature of the environment and when children are unable to frame their thoughts in a sufficiently top down manner. In short, 3-year-olds have a problem with 'failing to suppress the salience of their own knowledge' (Russell, 1996, p. 225).

To test this, in a final experiment (see also Robinson & Beck, Chapter 6, this volume, for further discussion on this study) we attempted to keep the executive demands across two reasoning tasks constant, but varied the type of reasoning required in each. In one children had to engage in counterfactual conditional reasoning, and in the other they had to engage in conditional but not counterfactual reasoning. As an example of a conditional but not counterfactual question, we can ask: 'If I pour ink on my shoes, what colour will they be?' To answer this we clearly have to engage our imagination and reason conditionally. However, the answer does not require counterfactual thinking, because we do not have to reason with an antecedent that is known to be false. The question asks about a potential future action (the pouring of ink)—a proposition about which there is no current truth value. We label such questions future hypotheticals. However, answering correctly does involve inhibiting a prepotent response in terms of one's current state of knowledge, namely, the colour of the shoes. If children's errors in false belief and counterfactual reasoning tasks to date are 'executive' in nature, then counterfactual and future hypothetical tasks (requiring the same executive control) should also be of similar difficulty. If however, counterfactual reasoning and false belief tasks are difficult because of the counterfactual reasoning required, then future hypothetical tasks (not requiring counterfactual reasoning) should be easier than counterfactual reasoning tasks.

Each child was given two tasks, one involving the sorting of plasticine shapes and the other involving the sorting of items with and without pictures on them. Each child was asked a counterfactual question for one task and a future hypothetical question for the other. In the picture/no picture sorting task the child was shown a number of objects (badges, cards, erasers) sorted into two boxes: one containing objects with pictures on and a second containing objects without pictures. The experimenter then took a blank piece of paper from the second box, drew on it, and having asked the child where it should go, placed it in the box containing objects with pictures. In the counterfactual version children were asked 'If I had not drawn on the piece of paper, which box would it be in?'. In the future hypothetical version, they were asked 'If I rub out the drawing I just did, which box will the paper go in?'.

A total of 59 children were tested and after memory question exclusions the results were as follows: 30 children answered both questions correctly, 6 answered both incorrectly, 18 answered correctly in the open conditional task only, and 5 answered correctly in the counterfactual reasoning task only. Children found the future hypothetical question significantly easier than the counterfactual reasoning question (sign test, $P < .02$). The results from this study suggest that pre-school children find conditional reasoning relatively easy if questioned about a future hypothetical state.

In summary, these findings suggest that children's errors in counterfactual reasoning tasks reflect a specific difficulty with the counterfactual reasoning required, rather than a difficulty inhibiting a response to a visibly salient aspect of the environment, or more generally, inhibiting a prepotent response in terms of their own current state of knowledge.

OTHER FINDINGS IN THE LITERATURE

So far, we have argued that the unexpected transfer task is a reasoning task, and provided evidence to support the claim that errors occur because children are poor reasoners. There are though, a number of well documented findings reported in the literature suggesting that children have problems with false belief in tasks not requiring any reasoning. Two examples are (1) children's performance in deceptive box tasks and (2) tasks in which they are told of the protagonist's false belief but are asked instead to predict the protagonist's behaviour. There is also the problem of why children entertain seemingly counterfactual states in pretend play at 2 years of age, but fail counterfactual reasoning tasks at 3 years.

In deceptive box tasks, children are shown a container and asked what they think is inside. The box is opened to reveal an atypical content whereupon children are asked what they thought the box contained prior to opening. Many 3-year-olds make errors and report the actual content. It might be tempting to think of this as a memory task: children have to access in memory their previously held false belief. There are, however, grounds for doubting this assumption. Earlier we argued that many of our beliefs are not resident entities sitting in our heads in finished form. We may for example have no resident belief that $33412 + 3 = 33415$, until the question is asked whereupon we reason to an answer and state it as a belief. Likewise, in the deceptive box task, when children are asked, 'What do you think is in here?' we think it unlikely that they have any *resident* belief concerning the tube's contents. Children give the typical answer and in doing so state a belief—but it was not 'sitting' there before the question was asked and we see no reason to suppose that it continues to 'sit' there after the answer has been given. Consequently, when they are asked the *test question* 'When you first saw this tube, before we opened it, what did you think was inside?' children have to construct their answer in response to the query.

We suggest that in deceptive box tasks, to answer the test question we engage in knowledgebase adaption to model the epistemic perspective of our past 'ignorant' self. This requires suppression of information that we currently know (the *overriding* information that the box actually contains pencils) to simulate the knowledgebase of our past (ignorant) self. This knowledgebase contains the information that there is a Smarties box. We then derive an answer from this knowledgebase (it is a Smartie box therefore it *probably* contain Smarties) and attribute to ourselves this answer as a belief. As in the unexpected transfer task, this process requires the cognitive effort to ignore a known fact when answering a query. On this view then, the reasoning involved in ascribing false beliefs to other people is the same as ascribing false beliefs to our self. In neither case though do we simulate the mental state directly. We propose a 'derivation' rather than a 'copy theory' of simulation: it is the knowledgebase that we simulate directly, while the belief is derived.

It has been suggested (Astington, 1991) that the simulation view implies that it should be easier for children to determine their own (past) false beliefs than it is to determine those of other people. Children might first have knowledge of their own mental states and learn to apply these concepts to others by analogy from their own case. The ability to access own false belief might then develop before the ability to infer someone else's. Our version of the simulation account dissolves this implication, since the reasoning requirements of the two tasks are the same. In the unexpected transfer task we simulate another person's inference process, and in the deceptive box case we simulate that of our past self. Although limited, the evidence is consistent with our account, with the two tasks of apparently equal difficulty (Gopnik & Astington, 1998; Wimmer & Hartl, 1991).

Another finding that might be seen to pose a problem for our counterfactual reasoning account is reported in Wellman and Bartsch (1988). In their study, children were told both about the current state of the world, and the protagonist's false belief, but were asked instead to predict the protagonist's behaviour. For example, they were told 'Jane's kitten is in the playroom, but Jane thinks it is in the kitchen. Where will Jane look for her kitten?' Here children do not have to infer the protagonist's false belief, instead they have to make use of it to predict where the protagonist will look. Many children though still made realist errors and answered 'playroom'. However, we think it is a mistake to assume that *no* inference is required in this task. Children have to work out where Jane will go based on what Jane thinks and this involves conditional reasoning. We know that children of this age can reason conditionally if the antecedent is not known to be false, as shown above in the experiment with future hypotheticals. However, in the Wellman and Bartsch task children *are* asked to reason with something they know to be untrue. They are told that Jane believes the kitten is in the kitchen, however they themselves know that the kitten is really in the playroom. In other words, the children are asked to reason with an antecedent that is known to be false when predicting Jane's behaviour. Viewed this way, it is not surprising that children make realist errors in behaviour prediction tasks. Making explicit Jane's belief, is essentially no different from telling them to imagine that mum did not bake a cake. In both cases, they have to imagine something as true which they know to be false and work out what follows from it.

We now turn to pretend play. At around 2 years of age children start to engage in pretence: they might imagine an object is another object, for example, that a brick is a car or a banana is a telephone. In the Maxi task, the knowledgebase adaption described above also involves a sort of pretending: we temporarily pretend that things are not as we know them to be, and work out what follows from that. Children seem unable to do this until 3 or 4 years of age. Why then is there a developmental lag between these abilities, or to phrase the problem differently, are the two types of pretending the same?

In counterfactual reasoning, the pretend proposition or 'input' has three salient characteristics:

(1)   There is a crucial, non-arbitrary relation between the imagined proposition and the answer we give to the counterfactual reasoning question. We ask the question 'If Mum had not baked a cake, where would the chocolate be?' not 'If Mum had baked some bread, where would the chocolate be?' If we make substitutions such as this we may well alter the outcome of the reasoning process.

(2)   The imagined proposition is known to be false, and for this reason is

(3)   in conflict with the rest of the facts contained in our knowledgebase.

In pretend play the pretend input is very different and more akin to a statement of dramatic interpretation. When we say 'Charlton Heston is Ben Hur' we mean that the actor (CH) plays the part of Ben Hur in the film. When an actor holds up a piece of wood on stage and says 'This is my trusty sword', we are to understand that the prop is to be interpreted as such in the play. The same also holds for the child's statement 'The brick is a car' or 'The banana is a telephone': for the duration of the pretend episode the banana is to be interpreted as a telephone. As in counterfactual reasoning there are three important characteristics:

(1)   The choice of prop is *arbitrary*, not crucial. The same purpose is achieved by saying 'The pen is a telephone' or by replacing one actor for another to play the same character.

(2)   The statement 'Charlton Heston is Ben Hur' is not counterfactual—it describes a relation between an actor and a character in a story. The use of 'is' in the sentence 'Charlton Heston is Ben Hur' is not the 'is' of predication or identity, it is the 'is' of dramatic interpretation and is used to make a *true* statement about role assignment.

(3)   Since this statement of assignment is not counterfactual, it is not in contradiction with the other facts contained in our knowledgebase.

In short, there is a difference in status between pretending in pretend play and pretending in counterfactual reasoning. In counterfactual reasoning we *contradict* what is real for the purpose of experimental reasoning in trying to work out real world consequences. In drama, of which children's pretend play is an example, our pretend input serves to propose an interpretive fix on a real object for *use* as a prop in the telling of a story.

SUMMARY

In this brief chapter we have argued that the development of counterfactual reasoning in pre-school children may not only be an important factor in causal reasoning, but may also play a role in mindreading and social interaction. By 'side stepping' two major and influential narratives—the 'representational' narrative and the 'domain specific' narrative—we have presented preliminary evidence that a domain general reasoning ability (coupled with the child's own imaginative resources) plays an important part in belief ascription and behaviour prediction.

Findings from the other studies reported here (in particular with future hypotheticals) suggest that there is more to children's realist errors than mere 'reality seduction' or 'executive control' (though it would perhaps be premature to rule out an 'executive' explanation for why children fail counterfactual reasoning tasks, and future work is clearly needed, see Robinson & Beck, Chapter 6, this volume). Why children do fail counterfactual reasoning tasks is presently unknown. However, with the expansion of research in this area, from many of the authors in this volume, we might soon have an answer and hopefully a better understanding of the role that counterfactual reasoning plays in the cognitive development of the pre-school child.

NOTES

1. For a more technical treatment of the theoretical ideas presented here, see Peterson and Riggs (1999).
2. Harris et al., (1996) found that a *majority* of 3-year-olds were able to engage in counterfactual reasoning—a finding at odds with the data reported here. However,

Harris and Leevers (Chapter 4, this volume) offer an insightful explanation for the different response patterns across the two studies.

ACKNOWLEDGEMENTS

The empirical research reported here was supported by an Economic and Social Research Council grant (No. R000236230) to E.J. Robinson, D.M. Peterson, K.J. Riggs and P. Mitchell. The authors would like to thank Sarah Beck for her helpful comments and assistance in data collection.

REFERENCES

Astington, J.W. (1991). Intention in the child's theory of mind. In C. Moore, & D. Frye (Eds.), *Children's theories of mind* (pp. 157–172). Hillsdale, NJ: Lawrence Erlbaum Associates Inc.

Carruthers, P., & Smith, P. (1996). *Theories of theories of mind*. Cambridge: Cambridge University Press.

Davies, M., & Stone, T. (1995a). *Folk psychology: The theory of mind debate*. Oxford: Blackwell.

Davies, M., & Stone, T. (1995b). *Mental simulation: Evaluations and applications*. Oxford: Blackwell.

Dias, M.G., & Harris, P.L. (1988). The effect of make belief play on deductive reasoning. *British Journal of Developmental Psychology*, 6, 207–221.

Dias, M.G., & Harris, P.L. (1990). The influence of the imagination on reasoning by young children. *British Journal of Developmental Psychology*, 8, 305–315.

Goodman, N. (1983). *Fact, fiction and forecast* (4th ed.). Cambridge, MA: Harvard University Press.

Gopnik, A., & Astington, J.W. (1988). Children's understanding of representational change and its relation to the understanding of false belief and the appearance-reality distinction. *Child Development*, 59, 26–37.

Gopnik, A., & Wellman, H.M. (1992). Why the child's theory of mind really is a theory. *Mind and Language*, 7, 145–171.

Harris, P.L., German, T.P., & Mills, P.E. (1996). Children's use of counterfactual thinking in causal reasoning. *Cognition*, 61, 233–259.

Kuczaj, S.A., & Daly, M.J. (1979). The development of hypothetical reference in the speech of young children. *Journal of Child Language*, 6, 563–579.

Mitchell, P. (1994). Realism and early conception of mind: Phylogenetic and ontogenetic issues. In C. Lewis & P. Mitchell (Eds.), *Children's early understanding of mind: Origins and development* (pp. 19–45). Hove, UK: Lawrence Erlbaum Associates Ltd.

Perner, J. (1991). *Understanding the representational mind*. London: MIT.

Peterson, D.M., & Riggs, K.J. (1999). Adaptive modelling and mindreading. *Mind and Language*, 14, 80–112.

Riggs, K.J., Peterson, D.M., Robinson, E.J., & Mitchell, P. (1998). Are errors in false belief tasks symptomatic of a broader difficulty with counterfactuality? *Cognitive Development*, 13, 73–91.

Russell, J. (1996). *Agency: It's role in mental development*. Hove, UK: Lawrence Erlbaum Associates Ltd.

Slobin, D. (1966). Grammatical transformations and sentence comprehension in childhood and adulthood. *Journal of Verbal Learning and Verbal Behaviour*, 5, 219–227.

Wellman, H.M. (1990). *The child's theory of mind*. London: MIT.

Wellman, H.M., & Bartsch, K. (1988). Young children's reasoning about beliefs. *Cognition*, 30, 239–277.

Wimmer, H., & Hartl, M. (1991). Against the Cartesian view on mind: young children's difficulty with own false belief. *British Journal of Developmental Psychology*, 9, 125–138.

Wimmer, H., & Perner, J. (1983). Beliefs about beliefs: Representation and constraining function of wrong beliefs in young children's understanding of deception. *Cognition*, 13, 103–128.

CHAPTER SIX

What is difficult about counterfactual reasoning?

Elizabeth J. Robinson and Sarah Beck
University of Birmingham, UK

People's readiness to construct imaginary worlds has been a topic of great inter-est to researchers in adult cognition and in children's thinking. Research on adults has identified the circumstances which prompt people to think about what might have been, on the content of their imagined alternatives to reality, and on the cognitive mechanisms which underlie this activity (Byrne, 1997; Kahneman & Miller, 1986; Kahneman & Tversky, 1982; Roese, 1997; Roese & Olson, 1995). This research has highlighted just how central to human reasoning is the ability to consider what is actually the case in relation to how things could be or could have been. Adults do not only imagine alternative worlds, but also reflect on what actions could have produced them. Our causal reasoning seems to be integrally linked with our readiness to imagine alternative situations. Byrne (1997) suggests that without a capacity for such counterfactual thinking we may entertain little hope or ambition, have little sense of progress or perfectibility, and little sense of boredom or curiosity.

Most of the research on children's consideration of imaginary worlds has focused on their readiness to engage in pretend play, with the aim of specifying the cognitive mechanisms which allow them to engage in pretence and to com-ment upon what they are pretending (Custer, 1996; Harris & Kavanaugh, 1993; Leslie, 1987; Lillard, 1993; Perner, 1991; Perner, Baker, & Hutton, 1994). Much less attention has been paid to the development of the ability to reflect on how things could realistically have been different, or of the ability to imagine the consequences had certain actions been performed or not performed. This kind of counterfactual thinking is clearly not the same as pretence. Imagining that you are a princess is not the same as thinking "If only I had taken such and such a social opportunity I could have become a princess". It is this latter kind of thinking which is our concern in this chapter.

Harris (1995) reports what may be the earliest sign of something approaching this kind of counterfactual thinking. Two- and three-year-olds watched an event such as two toy horses galloping across a table, one stopping well before the edge but the other stopping just short of it. These children could identify correctly which horse "almost" or "nearly" fell off the table. That is, they could describe what actually happened in relation to what might have been. Older children can comment directly on what might have happened (Harris, German, & Mills, 1996; Riggs, Peterson, Robinson, & Mitchell, 1998). For example, in studies by Harris et al., 3- to 4-year-olds watched a number of episodes such as a doll making dirty footprints on the floor, and they judged whether the floor would be dirty had the doll taken her shoes off. In Harris et al.'s samples even the 3-year-olds performed above chance though the 4-year-olds did better. The episodes used by Riggs et al. (1998) were somewhat more complicated in that children had to identify exactly what the counterfactual situation would be had some different action been taken, rather than just judge that the current situation would have been avoided, or how it could have been avoided. For example in our tasks children saw a doll's picture being blown from a table to a tree, and were asked to indicate where the picture would be had the wind not blown. Our samples of 3- and 4-year-olds commonly made errors in tasks such as these, further details of which are given in the rest of this chapter. (See Harris & Leevers, Chapter 4, this volume, for further consideration of the relationship between our tasks and theirs.) On the basis of this evidence it seems that by around four to five years many or even most young children can not only construct pretend worlds which run alongside their knowledge of the true state of affairs, but can also consider the true state of affairs in relation to imaginary but realistic alternatives and can report imaginary but realistic alternatives to the true state of affairs.

Yet within this range of ways of considering alternative realities, a difference which seems trivial to adults turns out to be highly significant for young children. If we are considering why a cup of tea we have just made is not very tasty, we might ask "What if we warm the teapot next time?" This seems to be largely equivalent to asking "What if we had warmed the teapot?" insofar as both require the person to imagine the consequences of a particular action which was not carried out on this occasion. Three- and four-year-olds find the former type of question much easier to answer than the latter. In what follows we shall consider why this might be, and what the implications are for accounts of children's developing ability to consider alternative worlds.

COUNTERFACTUALS IN RELATION TO FUTURE HYPOTHETICALS

Study 1

In one experiment in which we compared answers to a counterfactual and a future hypothetical test question, each child was given two tasks, one involving the sorting of plasticine balls and sausages and the other involving the sorting of items with and without pictures on them. Each child was given a counterfactual variant of one task and a future hypothetical variant of the other. In the picture/ no picture sorting task the child was shown a sorting of items (rubbers, badges, cards) into two boxes, so that one box contained items which had pictures on, and a second box contained items with no pictures. The experimenter then took a blank piece of paper from this second box, drew on it, asked the child where the paper should now go, and on the child's advice placed it in the other box. Then the experimenter asked a counterfactual reasoning question, "If I had not drawn on the piece of paper, which box would it be in?" In a corresponding future hypothetical task, the experimenter drew on a blank piece of paper, placed it in the box containing things with pictures on, and then asked the child "If I rub out the drawing I just did, which box will the paper go in?" A sample of fifty-nine 3–4-year-olds took part in this study, and a further twenty-eight took part in a similar study (Riggs et al., 1998) in which the experimenter did not actually draw on the paper in the future hypothetical task, but asked the child "If I draw on this piece of paper, which box will it go into?" In both studies children were much more likely to answer correctly in the future hypothetical task than in the counterfactual one. Amongst our first sample of fifty-nine 3- and 4-year-olds, 30 performed correctly in both tasks, 6 were wrong in both, 18 were correct on the future hypothetical only and 5 on the counterfactual only (sign test, $P < .02$). Amongst our second sample of 28, the corresponding frequencies were 10, 1, 15 and 2 (sign test, $P < .01$).

An important implication of these results is their demonstration that errors on the counterfactual task were not due simply to a general difficulty inhibiting a response to current reality. There is evidence that children this age do have such difficulty in a range of tasks including judgements of shape (Taylor & Mitchell, 1997), acknowledgement of false belief (Mitchell & Lacohee, 1991; Robinson & Mitchell, 1995; Saltmarsh, Mitchell, & Robinson, 1995; but see Robinson, Riggs, & Samuel, 1996) and tasks in which the child must inhibit pointing to a desired object (Russell, Mauthner, Sharpe, & Tidswell, 1991; but see Samuels, Brooks, & Frye, 1996). This behaviour has been variously interpreted as a failure of executive control which presents as a tendency to make responses which are controlled by salient features of the environment (Russell, 1996); as a reality bias according to which "current reality is extremely likely to grab attention" (Mitchell, 1994, 1996); and as the consequence of an underdeveloped "Selection Processor" whose job is to select the appropriate information on which to base an inference (Leslie, 1994; Leslie & Roth, 1993; Leslie & Thaiss, 1992). There are significant differences between these various accounts, but for our present purposes they have in common the idea that young children are prone to respond with their own current view of reality when asked to do something else. Yet in both our counterfactual and future hypothetical tasks, the child had to avoid reporting current reality and had to imagine instead an alternative situation. Children seem to have particular difficulty handling counterfactual situations which is over and above this more general problem they have of inhibiting a response to current reality.

Wherein does this problem lie? In the future hypothetical the child does not have to imagine an alternative situation replacing current reality; the child does not have to imagine that a situation which she or he knows to be false, is actually true. Why is it that children find it particularly hard to imagine replacing reality with an alternative?

The first part of our search to find out took the following route. We began by checking whether the errors in a counterfactual task can accurately be described as "realist" errors. Do children positively choose the current state of affairs rather than just fail to choose the correct response? If they do, then it could be that for some reason any general difficulty inhibiting a response to reality is particularly marked when the child tries to conjure up a counterfactual situation. If that is the case, then we should be able to help the child by altering the balance between the relative availabilities of the true state of affairs and the counterfactual alternative.

ARE CHILDREN'S ERRORS REALIST ERRORS?

Can children who err in our counterfactual tasks justifiably be described as making realist errors? In our counterfactual tasks like the ones described above the only error the child can make is to choose the current state of affairs; errors are necessarily realist errors. Children might err because they fail to construct correctly the counterfactual alternative, rather than because they fail to inhibit a response to current reality. To find out we introduced a third location. With this modification we could also check another possibility: with a two-response choice task, some correct responses might be false positives given by children who realise that the correct answer is *not* the current state of affairs, but who cannot construct the correct counterfactual situation. These children would simply be avoiding the current situation, rather than positively choosing the correct counterfactual alternative. Finally, we took the opportunity to vary the wording of our test question to see whether we could make the task demands clearer to the children.

Study 2

Each child was given two counterfactual tasks, both of which involved a narrative which the child saw acted out with dolls. In one, Jenny paints a picture in the garden and leaves it on the garden table while she goes to school, when a wind blows it up into a tree. Each narrative was followed by a question about a counterfactual physical state, either "If the wind had not blown, where would Jenny's picture be?" or "Pretend the wind didn't blow, where would the picture be?".[1] Each child had the same question form for both his/her tasks. In one task the child had two possible response locations, the tree and the table for the painting story, and in the other task each child had three possible response locations. In the painting story, Jenny moved her picture from the table to a chair before she went to school, so the possible response locations were table, chair and tree. In addition each child was given a memory check question: "Can you remember, at the very beginning of the story, where was the picture?".

Our sample of forty-two 3- and 4-year-olds showed no difference in difficulty between the pretend and if–then wordings: 11/21 answered correctly with the pretend wording, compared with 12/21 for the other wording. From this result we have no grounds for arguing that children's difficulty with counterfactuality is due to failure to understand test questions with if–then wording. This is consistent with our finding that future hypothetical tasks with if–then test questions are relatively easy. The problem seems not to lie in the particular language used.

Given the lack of difference between the two test questions, we combined across the two forms of wording to look at the within child effect of 2 versus 3 response locations. There was no difference in the incidence of correct responses: out of 37 children who answered memory questions correctly in both tasks, 27 children answered correctly in the 2-choice task, and 27 did so in the 3-choice task. There was no sign, then, of false positives in the 2-choice task. Furthermore, of the 10 who made errors in the 3-choice task, all but 2 children chose the current state of affairs (e.g. the tree). Most errors were appropriately described as realist errors.

This result leads us to explore the possibility that children's difficulty handling counterfactual situations is due primarily to difficulty avoiding a response to current reality. We argued earlier that since children find it much harder to report a counterfactual alternative than a future hypothetical one, we cannot treat errors on counterfactual tasks simply as another symptom of a broad realist bias (Mitchell, 1994, 1996), or of poor executive control (Russell, 1996), or of an undeveloped Selection Processor (Leslie, 1994). We have to specify what is particularly hard about handling counterfactual alternatives to reality. Nevertheless, we may not need to identify a new variable. It could be that for some reason when they try to imagine a counterfactual alternative, children are particularly prone to get trapped in the current state of affairs. If so, we would still want to explain why, but at least we would have identified the source of the difficulty.

DO CHILDREN GET TRAPPED IN CURRENT REALITY?

Study 3

If children do tend to get trapped in the current state of affairs when asked to imagine a counterfactual alternative, then they should make fewer errors if the counterfactual situation they are asked to report is not an alternative to *current* reality, but an alternative to a *past* reality. Yet we found that children made just as many errors under these two circumstances. We compared performance in two tasks in which an identical action was performed—for example a boy Peter normally plays with his football in the garden before going to school, but on this occasion it rained in the night leaving the grass wet so he played inside with his construction toy instead. In one task the child was asked to entertain an alternative to the current situation: the boy was playing indoors when the question was asked "If it had not rained in the night, what would Peter be playing with?" In the other task, which we called a past action counterfactual, the child was asked to entertain an alternative to what had happened: the boy had left for school when the question was asked "If it had not rained in the night, what would Peter have played with?" The current state of affairs, the boy on his way to school, remained unchanged when the child imagined him playing with his football rather than his construction toy. We already know that children have no difficulty reporting a past state of affairs, rather than current reality, when they are asked a memory check question in a false belief or counterfactual physical state task. In our past action counterfactual task, then, children might be able to recover the past state of affairs and then readily imagine an alternative to that. The 3- and 4-year-olds in our sample made just as many errors in the two types of task. The results provide no evidence that a past reality exerts a less powerful influence on children's ability to handle a counterfactual than does a present reality. Children found it just as hard to entertain an alternative to something that had happened but was no longer visible, than to entertain an alternative to something that was currently visible. (See Riggs & Peterson, Chapter 5 this volume, for further details of this study.)

Children's difficulty handling counterfactual situations seems not to be due primarily to difficulty avoiding a response to current reality. Maybe avoiding a response to reality is not the main problem at all, but before drawing that conclusion we tested performance under further modified versions of our counterfactual task. Our aim was to try to alter the balance in the relative availability or salience of the true and counterfactual situations. If we could make the counterfactual alternative relatively more available than the true one, the task should become easier. In our first two modifications we attempted to make the true state of affairs less available than it is in the standard task in which the child sees a sequence of events and is then asked to report a counterfactual alternative.

MODIFYING THE CHILD'S INFORMATION ABOUT THE TRUE STATE OF AFFAIRS

First, we tried making current reality less salient by telling children about it rather than letting them see. It has been suggested that children may remain unsure about reality when they are only told about it, and as a consequence find it easier to consider alternatives to current reality (Zaitchik, 1991). Using false belief tasks, Zaitchik reported that children found it easier to acknowledge a doll's belief when the experimenter told them where an object was really located and where a story character had been falsely told it was located, than in a standard task in which children saw the object moved from one location to another in the doll's absence. This result was replicated by Robinson, Mitchell, and Nye (1995), though these authors make a different interpretation, the details of which are not relevant here. In the tasks we used here children saw an object removed from a container, so knew for sure that a change had taken place, but were only told which one of two possibilities then occurred. Hence children could have been unsure about current reality. This could have made it easier for them to inhibit a response to current reality and to reason correctly in response to the test question. Would children now find it easier to avoid reporting current reality instead of a counterfactual alternative?

In our second modification, children again saw an object removed from a container, but we left them ignorant about which of two possible objects replaced the original one. If children's knowledge of current reality was vague, unspecified, would they find it easier instead to report a counterfactual alternative?

Study 4

Eighty-four 3- and 4-year-olds entered one of three conditions: a reality unknown condition, a reality known (by seeing) condition and a reality known (by being told) condition.

Each child heard a story acted out with dolls. One of the stories, the fruit story, follows: Dad is getting Jane's lunch ready for Jane to take to school, while Jane is upstairs. Dad puts a banana in Jane's lunch-box, then leaves the room to go and get some more food. Jane comes into the room, and looks in the box, doesn't want a banana, removes it, and decides to choose another piece of fruit instead. She might choose an apple or she might choose an orange. (The experimenter places an orange and an apple on the table for the child to see.) The story then differed according to condition.

(1) Reality known (told): Jane decides to choose the apple, so she puts the apple in her box and closes the lid. (The experimenter places the apple in the box, but does not allow the child to see it, and the orange is removed without the child seeing it.)
(2) Reality known (see): As above, except the child sees the apple going into the box.
(3) Reality unknown: The experimenter says "We don't know which piece of fruit Jane is going to choose, but she is going to choose one. It might be the apple or it might be the orange, we don't know". (The experimenter places an item of fruit in the box without allowing the child to see.)

The child was then asked a counterfactual question: "If Jane had not come in, what would be inside the lunch box?". A reality check question followed: "What's in the lunch box now?". In all three conditions, then, children saw the original content of the lunch box, and saw the two possible subsequent contents, but the conditions differed in the information given about the choice between these possibilities—children either saw or were told which one had been chosen, or did not know.

First we checked whether our told and reality unknown conditions had left children in a state of uncertainty about which item was currently in the lunchbox. It could have been that in the reality unknown condition children simply made a guess between the two possibilities and then treated that confidently as 'reality'. We made our check by comparing answers to the counterfactual question with answers to the reality check question, amongst children who answered the counterfactual question wrongly. If we assume that errors to the counterfactual question were realist errors, then children who had a firm view of reality should have answered the reality check question and the counterfactual question in the same way. On the other hand, if they answered these two differently we can infer they were unsure about the current state of affairs.

The results showed clearly that children who were wrong on the counterfactual question were much more likely to answer the counterfactual and reality check questions differently if they were in the reality unknown condition than if they were in either of the other two conditions. There was, however, no difference between the see and tell conditions. We conclude from this result that children were indeed uncertain about the current state of affairs in the reality unknown condition, but were no more uncertain when they had been told about reality than when they had seen for themselves which item had been chosen. The suggestion mentioned earlier based on Zaitchik (1991) gains no support from these results.

Did children find it easier to inhibit a response to current reality when they were unsure about it, than when they knew which item was currently in the lunchbox? For the counterfactual questions, in the see condition, 15 out of 28 (54%) answered correctly; in the tell condition, 12 out of 28 (43%) did so and in the unknown condition, 11 out of 25 (44%) did so. There was no significant difference between conditions in the success rate, and certainly no sign that children performed better in the unknown condition. If anything the tendency was towards worse performance when current reality was unknown, and we come back to this later in the chapter. These results provide no support for the suggestion that children find it easier to resist responding with current reality when they are unsure what reality is.

MODIFYING THE AVAILABILITY OF THE COUNTERFACTUAL ALTERNATIVE

In our next two experiments we attempted to facilitate children's performance in counterfactual tasks by increasing the availability of the counterfactual alternative, without modifying the child's information about the current state of affairs.

Study 5

We compared performance on two types of task. In one, we expected that the counterfactual alternative would be highly available as a response, since it was the standard content of a container. In the other, the standard content was the current one and the counterfactual alternative was something unexpected. For example, the child was shown a video box, opened it to find a video inside, and then watched as Teddy replaced it with a fork. This action was labelled for the child as "swapping". In the other version, the child first saw a fork inside and Teddy swapped it for a video. In both tasks the test question was "What if Teddy hadn't swapped? What would be in there now?", followed by a check question, "What was in there before Teddy swapped?". We predicted that children would perform better when the correct answer was the typical content, a video in this example, since that would be more available than the atypical content. In contrast, a realist error should be more likely when the readily available answer was currently in the box.

This pattern of results could be obtained, though, if children just tend to say "video" when they see a video container, whatever sequence of events they have witnessed. We included a control condition to check for that possibility. In this, the initial and final contents of the container (video case in this example) were both atypical, but immediately prior to testing the child had seen the experimenter place a video in a different video case so the response "video" had been prompted to some extent. Despite this, no child offered "video" as a response to the counterfactual test question about the video container that first contained a ball and then a crayon.

Each child had one control task and one experimental task with a different container, either of the typical–atypical or atypical–typical kind. For the typical–atypical task, 6 children out of 20 answered correctly (30%), and for the atypical–typical task, 9 out of 21 did so (43%). There is no significant difference between these results, and they provide no sign that the typical–atypical task was the easier.

Study 6

We made a second attempt to make counterfactual reasoning easy by making the counterfactual alternative available by basing the procedure around a well-learned sequence—writing and posting a birthday card. Child and experimenter jointly wrote a birthday card to the experimenter's friend, but in one version of the task the experimenter omitted to put the card in the envelope so the empty envelope with the address and stamp were posted in the postbox and the card itself remained on a brightly coloured "writing area" on the table. Nine children commented on the error and had to be omitted from the analysis. The child was asked "What if we had put the card in the envelope, where would the card be now?" (answer—in the postbox). In the comparison version there was no omission from the normal sequence, and the test question was "What if we hadn't put the card in the envelope, where would the card be now?" (answer—on the table).

A control group of 24 children went through the card-writing sequence and were asked at four points "What do we do next?" to check on their familiarity with the activity. Performance was quite good in this group: 17 children answered at least 3 of the 4 questions correctly. It seems likely that for most of our children, leaving the card out of the envelope did constitute a deviation from a normal sequence of events, and the counterfactual alternative restored the situation to normal.

Research with adults suggests that deviations from *a priori* norms or expected behaviour commonly form the basis of counterfactuals, and the counterfactual content returns things back to the normal state of affairs (Kahneman & Miller, 1986; Roese, 1997). If there is any parallel between the kind of counterfactual reasoning which adults readily engage in spontaneously, and the kinds of counterfactual reasoning which young children find easy to carry out on request, then we would predict that children would perform better when the birthday card was not put in the envelope and children had to imagine the normal sequence of events, than when the sequence was completed normally and children had to imagine a deviation from normality.

Again our results were negative. Our sample of fifty-six 3- and 4-year-olds showed no significant difference in performance between the two versions of the card task: 20/33 (61%) answered correctly in the 'forget' version, and 12/23 (52%) did so in the 'remember' version.

INTERIM CONCLUSION

By comparing performance in a variety of tasks which required children to consider how things could be or could have been, we have shown that it makes no difference to task difficulty whether the counterfactual is to replace a current or past true event (study 3), whether the child has seen or been told about the true event (study 4), whether the child is sure or unsure about the true state of affairs (study 4), or whether the counterfactual situation represents the normal or an abnormal state of affairs (studies 5 and 6). The negative results of these experiments suggest that either we did not achieve our aim of modifying the balance in the relative availability to the child of the true and counterfactual situations, or modifying this balance makes it no easier for the child to report a counterfactual situation. We shall come back to this later, but first we need to be sure that we are correct to consider children's difficulty as particular to counterfactuals.

COUNTERNORMALS AND FUTURE HYPOTHETICALS

The results of study 1 demonstrated clearly that children found it relatively easy to report a future alternative to reality. As we pointed out, in the future hypothetical the child does not have to imagine the alternative situation replacing what is known to be true; the past and current states of affairs remain unaltered when an imagined future event is considered. We assume that this imagined replacement is what young children find difficult for some reason. But is it just the replacement of events which have actually happened which children find hard to imagine? What if a future event is so likely to happen that one can safely treat it as a future reality? For example, if I pour tea from my teapot I know for certain that it will run downwards towards the cup below rather than flow up towards my face. Would children find it hard to imagine this future certainty being replaced by an alternative? If so, we could describe children's difficulty with counterfactuals as extending to 'counternormals'. The 'facts' which children find it hard to counter would include not only currently visible events and past events, but even events which as yet have not occurred. One implication of such a result would be that children's background knowledge of the world's working constrains their ability to imagine alternatives, just as does their current or recent experience.

At the same time as examining that possibility, we made one last comparison between counterfactual tasks. Research with adults suggests that when adults try to imagine how a particular event could have been avoided, they tend to report controllable rather than uncontrollable events (Miller, Turnbull, & McFarland, 1990; Roese, 1997). So if an adult were to scald herself as she fills her cup with tea, she is unlikely to think "If only the tea had run uphill instead of downwards". If we can draw any analogy between task difficulty in children and content of spontaneous counterfactuals amongst adults, we would predict that children might find it particularly hard to imagine an impossible counterfactual situation like that one. (Note though that this prediction ignores the role of negative consequences, see Roese, 1997; see also Harris & Leevers, Chapter 4, this volume.)

Study 7

We began by confirming that nursery-age children expected water to run downwards. Then each of 83 children was given two tasks, a water task and a car task. Half the children received both tasks in counterfactual version, and the other half in future hypothetical version. In the water task, the child was shown a gutter sloping at 45° with a cup attached to each end and a line across the middle. From this midway point, children watched as the experimenter poured some water from a teapot down the pipe and allowed it to run into the lower cup. Children were then asked either a counterfactual question "What if the water had run the other way? Which cup would it be in now?" and the other half were asked a future hypothetical question "What if next time the water runs the other way? Which cup will it be in?".

The car task was similar, except that the gutter was replaced by a road with a garage (box) at either end, and the water was replaced with a toy car. The experimenter demonstrated that the car was self-propelled by running it along the floor and allowing the child to have a turn, and then allowed the car to drive down the road and into the lower garage. Children who had the counterfactual water question had an equivalent counterfactual question with the car: "What if the car had driven the other way? Which garage would it be in?". The future hypothetical question given to the other children was "What if next time the car drives the other way? Which garage will it be in?".

We were interested in whether or not the future hypothetical version of the water task was harder than the car task. If so, we would conclude that children's difficulty imagining alternatives to reality extends to future certainties. It would not be just counterfactuals which children find relatively hard, but also counternormals. We were also interested in whether or not the counterfactual version of the water task was harder than the car task. If so, this would be consistent with the adult literature mentioned above.

As it turned out, there was no difference in difficulty between the car and water tasks either in their counterfactual version or in their hypothetical version. In the hypothetical tasks performance on the two tasks was near ceiling, with 37 out of 40 children answering correctly in both tasks, and 1 child correct in the car task only. The counterfactual questions were significantly harder with 10 children out of 43 wrong on the water task and 10 wrong on the car task. Combining across car and water tasks the difference was significant: χ^2 ($N = 83$ df = 2) = 8.04, $P = .02$. Our children found future hypothetical reasoning easy even when it involved contradiction of an established norm. Implications of this finding are considered in the next section.

MENTAL REPRESENTATIONS AND THEORIES OF MIND

Earlier in the chapter we described children's problem as difficulty imagining that a situation which they know to be false, is in fact true. The results of experiments 2–7 give us no cause to change that description. What we can now suggest, though, is that the problem lies in the child's own mental representation of the true state of affairs, however the child has gained information about reality. It makes no difference whether the counterfactual situation is one which is likely to be true (a video in a video box), or whether the true situation is now past, or is known only indirectly via an utterance. To consider a counterfactual alongside the true state of affairs seems to stretch the mental resources of many preschool children to their limits.

This comes as no surprise if taken in the context of work on adult reasoning. Byrne (1997) considers the mental models which adults construct of factual situations (Johnson-Laird, 1983; but see Bonatti, 1994; Russell, 1996), and shows how the addition of counterfactual alternatives to these models increases the demands on working memory. According to Byrne (1997), counterfactual reasoning requires the reasoner to keep track both of what is true and of what is false but is temporarily supposed to be true. Byrne's account has no developmental component as it stands, but an implication of her account is that the demands on working memory of a counterfactual task could simply be too great for a young child, even though a matched future hypothetical can be within their capacity. One possibility is, then, that the only reason for the difference in difficulty between future hypotheticals and counterfactuals in the age group we tested, is that the former place greater demands on working memory, and that as children's working memory capacity increases, counterfactuals come within their capacity. We return to this suggestion shortly.

Drawing on results of Johnson-Laird and Byrne (1991), Byrne shows how the construction of a mental model which involves a counterfactual is particularly difficult when the true state of affairs is underspecified. In our reality unknown condition in study 4 this is exactly the sort of model we expected children to construct, with the aim of making the task relatively easy by reducing the availability of the true state of affairs. If we can apply Byrne's account to children's counterfactual reasoning, then our attempt to make things easy was misguided, and our prediction should have been that the reality unknown condition would be particularly difficult. Although effects were not significant, if anything the results were indeed in that direction.

We could create a reality unknown task which avoids imposing high demands on working memory. Suppose we modified the water task used in study 7, so that the child could not see whether water had actually been poured from the teapot or not, and the child was asked "What if I *did* pour the water, where would it be?" (in the lower cup) and/or "What if I *didn't* pour the water, where would it be?" (in the teapot). Now the child does not have to represent what might have happened in addition to what actually happened, because he or she has no representation of what actually happened (so long as he or she has not made a guess). A task like this should be relatively easy.

Our suggestion is then that the high demands of representing mentally a counterfactual situation which pose difficulties for adults, pose even greater difficulties for children. Adults would find our counterfactual tasks absurdly simple, since we provide the framework within which we want them to imagine an alternative to reality: the test question asks "What if such and such had not happened . . . ?". In research into adults' counterfactual reasoning, the participants are left to generate their own counterfactuals; they ask themselves the question "How could the current situation have been avoided?" and the interest is in the alternative sequences of events which they choose to construct.

Looked at in this way, it is not surprising that the predictions which we drew from the adult literature, concerning the birthday card task in study 6 and the water task in study 7, received no support. Our rationale for making the predictions was that counterfactuals which adults rarely produce spontaneously might be harder for children to produce on request. This rationale makes no sense if we consider the mental representation the child attempts to construct during our tasks. According to Byrne's (1997) analysis of the results with adults, the information which is explicitly represented in a person's mental model of the true state of affairs determines which counterfactual situations will be easy or hard to create. So, for example, actions which are exceptional will be represented explicitly, like posting an envelope without its birthday card inside, whereas actions which are routine will be represented only implicitly. Information about controllable actions will be represented explicitly whereas information about background assumptions like water running downhill will be represented only implicitly. By offering the child a particular alternative in our test question, we specify the mental representation which the child attempts to construct, and so the effects found with adults' spontaneous reasoning could not emerge when the alternative to be considered is explicitly offered.

We can also understand why telling children about the true state of affairs rather than letting them see for themselves made the counterfactual task no easier. So long as the child accepts the information about reality as true, we have no grounds for supposing that the information contained in the child's mental representation is different depending on the source of his or her knowledge.

Our analysis in terms of the mental representations which children have to construct if they are to handle a counterfactual situation is in line with an argument presented by Perner and colleagues in their early work on children's developing theory of mind. Perner, Leekam, & Wimmer (1987) identify children's difficulty with understanding about false beliefs as failure "to understand that another person will assign a conflicting truth value to a critical proposition which conflicts with the value they themselves assign" (p. 135). Although Perner (1991) applies his analysis to the higher level of children's understanding about mental or physical misrepresentation (such as false beliefs or symbols), we see no reason in principle why Perner's account could not be applied to the level of reasoning we consider here, that is to the child's own mental representation of a true situation and of alternatives which could realistically have occurred instead. If this suggestion is correct, then it follows from Perner et al.'s analysis that children's difficulty understanding false beliefs should extend to circumstances under which a false situation is not held as a belief, but is simply considered as a possibility by the child him- or herself. In both cases, the child has to assign a conflicting truth value to a particular proposition (or, to apply Byrne's framework, mental model). That is, children who fail to acknowledge false belief, should also have difficulty handling counterfactual situations of the kind we suggested to them in our physical state counterfactual tasks.

This leads us to an interesting twist in the argument put forward by Riggs et al. (1998). In that paper (see also Riggs & Peterson, Chapter 5 this volume) we reported significant correlations between performance on false belief tasks and on matched tasks similar to those used in studies 1–7 which required no understanding of belief but which seem to require similar counterfactual reasoning. For example in a standard test of false belief such as Wimmer and Perner's

(1983) story about Maxi and his chocolate, the child saw Mum move the chocolate from one location to another while she used some to make a cake in Maxi's absence. The child was then asked where Maxi thinks his chocolate is, or where he will look for his chocolate. In our comparison tasks the story was exactly the same, but the child was asked "If Mum had not baked a cake, where would the chocolate be?". Both kinds of task required the child to handle a counterfactual situation, but only in the false belief tasks was the counterfactual situation held to be true by someone. No understanding of representation was required for the tasks involving counterfactual physical states. Correlations between performance on the belief and physical state tasks remained significant with verbal mental age partialled out, and occurred both for narrative type tasks similar to the one just described and for tasks similar to Wimmer and Hartl's state change task (Wimmer & Hartl, 1991; Saltmarsh et al., 1995) which did not require the children to track an extended narrative.

We argued on the basis of these correlations that children's difficulty with false belief is not due simply to the absence of a representational theory of mind (Gopnik & Wellman, 1992; Perner, 1991; Wellman, 1990; Wimmer & Hartl, 1991; Zaitchik, 1990); children's difficulty with counterfactuality was not particular to circumstances which required handling of representations. Yet we now suggest that one of those representational deficit accounts, namely Perner's, may be perfectly able to handle our results. The other accounts which fall within the category of 'representational deficit' accounts place their main focus not on development of the ability to handle misrepresentation (and so counterfactuality), but rather on children's development of a theory which they use to understand and predict their own and other people's behaviour. Whereas for Riggs et al. (1998), and, we speculate, Perner, the immediate impediment to understanding false belief is the ability to handle counterfactual situations, for other representational deficit accounts such as Gopnik and Wellman (1992) or Gopnik and Meltzoff (1997) the immediate impediment seems to be the child's rudimentary theory of mind. At around 4–5 years, it is argued, children's theory undergoes a revolutionary change and the child comes to see that "all mental life partakes of the same representational character" (Gopnik & Wellman, 1992, p. 153). On the basis of such accounts there seems to be no reason why children who fail to understand about false beliefs (because their theory of mind is insufficiently developed), should not be able to handle counterfactual physical states like those specified in our counterfactual tasks. Yet our evidence suggests that they cannot.

We return now to our earlier prediction concerning the relationship between working memory and ability to handle counterfactuals. Gordon and Olson (1998) report a high correlation between children's performance on a false belief task, and their performance on a test of working memory. In this, children had both to count and label a series of objects, saying for example "One is a doll, two is a car, three is a spoon". Gordon and Olson point out that prediction of a relationship between computational resources and performance on theory of mind task would be common to most if not all developmental accounts, but they go on to consider how a developmental increase in such resources could allow not just improved theory of mind performance but formation of theory of mind concepts. They suggest that the concept of false belief is acquired once the child has the computational resources to hold in mind two representations and represent one of them as false. As with Perner et al.'s (1987) account, we see no reason in principle why this suggestion should not be applied to the child's handling of counterfactual physical states which are not held as beliefs.

An obvious follow-up to Gordon and Olson's (1998) study is to compare performance on their working memory task with that on our physical state counterfactual and future hypothetical tasks. Our expectations would be that the working memory demands of the future hypothetical are less than those of the counterfactual, and that the correlation between false belief and working memory reported by Gordon and Olson would be replicated with physical state counterfactuals and working memory.[2]

COUNTERFACTUALS, FUTURE HYPOTHETICALS AND CAUSES

Much of the argument in this chapter revolves around the difference in difficulty between future hypotheticals and counterfactuals. Children seem able to imagine how things could realistically be in the future much more readily than they can imagine how things could realistically have been different now. We now draw one final implication of this difference in difficulty. Both kinds of thinking imply an understanding of the causal sequence which led to the current state of affairs. The child who can imagine where the car will be if it runs the other way next time understands the causal relationship between direction of running and garage entered. Similarly, the child who can imagine where the car would have been now had it run the other way, understands the same causal relationship. There has been a good deal of discussion in the literature of the psychological link between counterfactual reasoning and causal reasoning (see summaries in Roese, 1997; Roese & Olson, 1995). Harris et al. (1996) consider the developmental relationship between handling counterfactuality and causal reasoning, raising the possibility that, consistent with Mackie (1974), counterfactuals provide the basis for picking out a causal agent.

Our results perhaps allow us to go further. If future hypothetical reasoning is developmentally prior to counterfactual reasoning, and if it implies the same understanding of causal relations, then we cannot make the strong argument that understanding of causality arises from or relies upon handling of counterfactuality. But then is it not more useful to be able to reflect on how to avoid falling into the same hole next time, than to reflect on how one could have avoided falling into it on this occasion?

NOTES

1. Note that the children did not enter a pretend world here. Contrast our task with one of Harris and Kavanaugh's (1993) tasks, in which 2-year-olds accepted the pretence that an empty teapot was full of tea, and that a block of wood was chocolate, and were able to judge that the "chocolate" was now wet having had "tea" tipped upon it. Being able to engage in such causal reasoning *within* the already accepted pretend framework does not necessarily imply the ability to reflect on the causal processes which could convert the true situation into the imaginary alternative: "If this teapot had tea in it, the block would be wet".

2. Data collected by Robinson and Caddick after the completion of this chapter are consistent with these predictions. Each of 33 children aged 3–4 years was given a narrative counterfactual physical state task, a narrative future hypothetical task, an "unexpected contents" false belief task, and Gordon and Olson's (1998) counting test of working memory. We replicated Gordon and Olson's finding of a correlation between performance on false belief and working memory tasks, and also found a highly significant correlation between the working memory task and the counterfactual task. Performance on the future hypothetical task was virtually at ceiling and substantially better than that on any of the other three tasks.

ACKNOWLEDGEMENT

The research reported in this chapter was funded by a grant awarded to E.J. Robinson, D.M. Peterson, K.J. Riggs, and P. Mitchell, by the Economic and Social Research Council, UK

REFERENCES

Bonatti, L. (1994). Why should we abandon the mental logic hypothesis? *Cognition, 50*, 17–39.

Byrne, R.M.J. (1997). Cognitive processes in counterfactual thinking about what might have been. *Psychology of Learning and Motivation, 37*, 105–154.

Custer, W.L. (1996). A comparison of young children's understanding of contradictory representations in pretense, memory and belief. *Child Development, 67*, 678–688.

Gopnik, A., & Meltzoff, A.N. (1997). *Words, thoughts and theories*. Cambridge, MA: Bradford Books, MIT Press.

Gopnik, A., & Wellman, H.M. (1992). Why the child's theory of mind really is a theory. *Mind and Language, 7*, 145–171.

Gordon, A.C.L., & Olson, D.R. (1998). The relation between acquisition of a theory of mind and the capacity to hold in mind. *Journal of Experimental Child Psychology, 68*, 70–83.

Harris, P.L. (1995, August). *On realizing what might have happened instead*. Paper presented at VIIth European Conference on Developmental Psychology, Krakow, Poland.

Harris, P.L., German, T., & Mills, P. (1996). Children's use of counterfactual thinking in causal reasoning. *Cognition, 61*, 233–259.

Harris, P.L., & Kavanaugh, R.D. (1993). Young children's understanding of pretence. *Monographs of the Society for Research in Child Development, 58, Serial no. 231*.

Johnson-Laird, P.N. (1983). *Mental models*. Cambridge: Cambridge University Press.

Johnson-Laird, P.N., & Byrne, R.M.J. (1991). *Deduction*. Hove, UK: Lawrence Erlbaum Associates Ltd.

Kahneman, D., & Miller, D. (1986). Norm theory: Comparing reality to its alternatives. *Psychological Review, 93*, 136–153.

Kahneman, D., & Tversky, A. (1982). The psychology of preferences. *Scientific American, 246*, 160–173.

Leslie, A.M. (1987). Pretense and representation: The origins of "theory of mind". *Psychological Review, 94*, 412–426.

Leslie, A.M. (1994). Pretending and believing: Issues in the theory of ToMM. *Cognition, 50*, 211–238.

Leslie, A.M., & Roth, D. (1993). What autism teaches us about metarepresentation. In S. Baron-Cohen, H. Tager-Flusberg, & D.J. Cohen (Eds.), *Understanding other minds: Perspectives from autism* (pp. 83–111). Oxford: Oxford University Press.

Leslie, A.M., & Thaiss, L. (1992). Domain specificity in conceptual development: Neuropsychological evidence from autism. *Cognition, 43*, 225–251.

Lillard, A.S. (1993). Young children's conceptualisation of pretense: Action or mental representational state? *Child Development, 64*, 372–386.

Mackie, J.L. (1974). *The cement of the universe: A study of causation*. Oxford: Oxford University Press.

Miller, D.T., Turnbull, W., & McFarland, C. (1990). Counterfactual thinking and social perception: Thinking about what might have been. In M.P. Zanna (Ed.), *Advances in Experimental Social Psychology, 23*, 305–331. New York: Academic Press.

Mitchell, P. (1994). Realism and early conception of mind: Phylogenetic and ontogenetic issues. In C. Lewis & P. Mitchell (Eds.), *Children's early understanding of mind: Origins and development* (pp. 19–45). Hove, UK: Lawrence Erlbaum Associates Ltd.

Mitchell, P. (1996). *Acquiring a conception of mind*. Hove, UK: Lawrence Erlbaum Associates Ltd.

Mitchell, P., & Lacohee, H. (1991). Children's early understanding of false belief. *Cognition, 39*, 107–127.

Perner, J. (1991). *Understanding the representational mind*. London: MIT.

Perner, J., Baker, S., & Hutton, D. (1994). Prelief: The conceptual origins of belief and pretence. In C. Lewis & P. Mitchell (Eds.), *Children's early understanding of mind* (pp. 261–286). Hove, UK: Lawrence Erlbaum Associates Ltd.

Perner, J., Leekam, S., & Wimmer, H. (1987). Three-year-olds' difficulty with false belief: The case for a conceptual deficit. *British Journal of Developmental Psychology, 5*, 125–137.

Riggs, K.J., Peterson, D.M., Robinson, E.J., & Mitchell, P. (1998). Are errors in false belief tasks symptomatic of a broader difficulty with counterfactuality. *Cognitive Development, 13*, 73–90.

Robinson, E.J., & Mitchell, P. (1995). Masking of children's early understanding of the representational mind: Backwards explanation versus prediction. *Child Development, 66*, 1022–1039.

Robinson, E.J., Mitchell, P., & Nye, R.M. (1995). Young children's treating of utterances as unreliable sources of knowledge. *Journal of Child Language, 22*, 663–685.

Robinson, E.J., Riggs, K.J., & Samuel, J. (1996). Children's memory for drawings based on a false belief. *Developmental Psychology, 32*, 1056–1064.

Roese, N.J. (1997). Counterfactual thinking. *Psychological Review, 121*, 133–148.

Roese, N.J., & Olson, J.M. (Eds.) (1995). *What might have been: The social psychology of counterfactual thinking*. Hillsdale, NJ: Lawrence Erlbaum Associates Inc.

Russell, J. (1996). *Agency: Its role in mental development*. Hove, UK: Lawrence Erlbaum Associates Ltd.

Russell, J., Mauthner, N., Sharpe, S., & Tidswell, T. (1991). The 'windows task' as a measure of strategic deception in preschoolers and autistic subjects. *British Journal of Developmental Psychology, 9*, 331–350.

Saltmarsh, R., Mitchell, P., & Robinson, E.J. (1995). Realism and children's early grasp of mental representation: Belief-based judgements in the state change task. *Cognition, 57*, 297–325.

Samuels, M., Brooks, P., & Frye, D. (1996). Strategic game playing in children through the "windows task". *British Journal of Developmental Psychology, 14*, 159–172.

Taylor, L.M., & Mitchell, P. (1997). Judgments of apparent shape contaminated by knowledge of reality: Viewing circles obliquely. *British Journal of Psychology, 88*, 653–670.

Wellman, H.M. (1990). *The child's theory of mind.* London: MIT.

Wimmer, H., & Hartl, M. (1991). Against the Cartesian view on mind: young children's difficulty with own false belief. *British Journal of Developmental Psychology, 9*, 125–138.

Wimmer, H., & Perner, J. (1983). Beliefs about beliefs: Representation and constraining function of wrong beliefs in young children's understanding of deception. *Cognition, 13*, 103–128.

Zaitchik, D. (1990). When representations conflict with reality: The preschooler's problem with false beliefs and "false" photographs. *Cognition, 35*, 41–68.

Zaitchik, D. (1991). Is only seeing really believing? Sources of the true belief in the false belief task. *Cognitive Development, 6*, 91–103.

CHAPTER SEVEN

Beyond really and truly: Children's counterfactual thinking about pretend and possible worlds

Eric Amsel and J. David Smalley
Weber State University, Ogden UT, USA

INTRODUCTION

By way of introduction to this chapter, consider the reasoning of two people. First imagine a child pretending that a banana is a telephone. The child holds the banana like a telephone, talks into it, and then hands it off to her mother saying, "You talk to Daddy!". Now think about a parent whose child is throwing a temper tantrum in a toy store. The exasperated parent considers ways in which the day could have been different so as to have avoided the scene now playing out in front of her (e.g. if only the parent had been more patient, if only the child had had a longer nap, if only the parent had just driven past the toy store).

At first glance, it would seem that the child who is playing pretend and the parent who is pondering possibilities are engaged in very different forms of reasoning. Maybe because playing pretend is a fanciful distortion of reality and pondering possibilities is a serious examination of reality (see Kahneman & Tversky, 1982, for an account of the 'simulation heuristic'), the two forms of reasoning appear to be different (Woolley, 1995). Moreover, if we are to believe Piaget (1970), pretence is, well, child's play, requiring no more demanding cognitive processes than the symbolic assimilation of the world to desired mental schemes. In contrast, pondering possibilities is a formal operational stage accomplishment involving thoughts about hypothetical rather than actual states of affairs.

One goal of this chapter is to convince the reader that, contrary to Piaget and others, playing pretend and pondering possibilities are close relatives in the reasoning family. The analogy is that the two forms of reasoning are like siblings,

121

who may be different but nonetheless share a common underlying (genetic) nature. We will argue that the cognitive processes underlying both playing pretend and pondering possibilities, the processes which give them their common underlying (computational) nature, are those associated with counterfactual thinking, defined as reasoning about states of affairs which are contrary to known facts (Roese, 1997). We will propose a simple counterfactual model of pretence which involves such counterfactual reasoning skills as representing true and false states of affairs, marking them as such, and reasoning on the basis of the false state of affairs. Evidence will be presented demonstrating the importance of children's capacity to coordinate separate representations of true and false states of affairs in their development of pretend play. A similar model of counterfactual reasoning that also focuses on the growth of the capacity to coordinate separate true and false representations will be proposed to explain the nature and development of children's ability to ponder possibilities.

As a part of the argument supporting our claim, a distinction will be drawn between children's lower-level processes involved in playing pretend and pondering possibilities (e.g. representing and managing relevant information) and higher-order understanding of such activities (e.g. conceptualising the mind as a representational and interpretative entity). The distinction introduces a second goal of the chapter, that of considering the proper relation between children's development of lower-level processing and higher-order understanding of mental phenomena. We will review traditional accounts of the development of children's understanding of mind (i.e. simulation theory and the Theory theory), which propose different views of the relation between the lower-level processing and higher-order understanding of mental phenomena. We will conclude the chapter with an alternative to the traditional views of the development of children's knowledge of the mind.

COUNTERFACTUAL REASONING AND PLAYING PRETEND

A central question regarding pretend play is how children do it without becoming confused. Pretending that a banana is a telephone, Leslie (1987) points out, is an activity that young children perform without dire consequences for their concept of bananas or telephones. Yet such dire consequences (what Leslie calls "representational abuse") seem to be an outcome of, or at least are not prohibited by, other accounts of pretence notably Piaget's (1962). Piaget's model proposes that a real and true state of affairs (an event or object) is symbolically assimilated by a scheme other than the one to which the state of affairs is habitually or typically assimilated. Thus, there is no mechanism stopping a child who pretends that a banana is a telephone from again assimilating bananas to her telephone scheme in contexts where a telephone is actually desired. The problem according to Leslie is that we cannot have a theory of pretence which supposes that children employ cognitive structures in the service of pretence that are the same ones used to understand the real world in non-pretend contexts.

As a solution to the problem, which has been widely acknowledged and accepted, Leslie (1987) proposed that children in pretend contexts (whether observing or participating) reason counterfactually; this is, they create a reality that is an alternative to the one known or believed to be true (Amsel et al., 1996; Bretherton & Beeghly, 1989; Harris, 1991; Harris & Kavanaugh, 1993; Lillard, 1993a; Perner, 1991; Woolley, 1995). So a child pretending a banana is a telephone reasons counterfactually by representing two identities for the same physical object: A true identity in the real world (i.e. a real banana) and a false identity in the pretend world (i.e. a pretend telephone). This resolves the problem of representational abuse because the child in a pretend context can now distinguish between and keep track of both states of affairs.

Beyond solving the problem of representational abuse, a counterfactual model of pretend play can explain the ease with which children pretend and their success at it. A child who failed to distinguish between or lost track of the false states of affairs in the pretend world and true states in the real one would behave in a manner which could hardly be appropriate in pretend contexts. For example, a child who loses track of the fact that she is really and truly holding a block while pretending that it is a cookie may bite down on the block when "eating the cookie" (Lillard, 1993a) or start building a house with the block, forgetting about the pretend scenario she was just playing. Generally speaking, children do not show such inappropriate behaviour in pretend contexts. Indeed, the evidence suggests that young children are competent at distinguishing between and keeping track of the true states of affairs in the real world and their false ones in the pretend world, even when false states in the pretend world change (Gopnik & Slaughter, 1991; Harris & Kavanaugh, 1993; Harris, Kavanaugh, & Meredith, 1994; Leslie, 1994; Walker-Andrews & Harris, 1993). Even evidence of periodic apparent confusion of pretend and real states of affairs (see reviews by Lillard, 1994; Woolley, 1995, 1997) does not deny that children are usually successful pretenders who act appropriately in most pretend contexts and show no signs of representational abuse (Lillard, 1993a; Woolley, 1995, 1997).

Despite wide acceptance for general aspects of Leslie's analysis, there is still much debate and discussion about *how* children reason counterfactually in pretend contexts; that is, how it is that they successfully distinguish between and keep track of true states of affairs in the real world and false ones in the pretend world. What follows is a review of two theoretical issues about the nature and development of children's counterfactual reasoning in pretend contexts. The first issue concerns *lower-level processing* of pretend information, specifically, the manner by which information regarding true and false states of affairs is represented and managed. On the one hand, some theories propose that information about true and false states of affairs are represented together by forming a single "counterfactual" proposition which encodes both types of states of affairs (Harris

& Kavanaugh, 1993; Leslie, 1987, 1994). This contrasts with other theories, which propose that information about true and false states of affairs in pretend contexts are represented separately and so need to be managed by other means because there is no proposition relating them (Lillard, 1993a, 1996; Perner, 1991). The second way of dividing the theoretical pie addresses children's *higher-order understanding* of pretence as a mental activity. The issue addresses when or if young children conceive of pretence in terms of the thoughts of a pretender. The issue pits those who deny that children ever conceive of pretence representationally, as a mental activity, for the purposes of understanding the goings-on in pretend contexts, against those who have sought to explain when and how children arrive at such a conceptual insight.

Lower-level processing of pretend information

At the level of representing and managing information in pretend contexts, some theorists suppose that children represent true and false states of affairs in pretend contexts by actually encoding each of the states and the relation between them in a counterfactual proposition. For example, according to Leslie (1987, 1988, 1994; Leslie & Roth, 1993), to pretend a banana is a comb, children would have to compute the M-representation *I pretend (of) the banana that "it is a comb"*. Similarly, for Harris (1991, 1994; Harris & Kavanaugh, 1993; Harris, Kavanaugh, & Meredith, 1994) the same child would form the "flagged" representation *"In this episode, this banana is a (make-believe) comb"*. While there are important differences between these mental structures, each of them specifies that, in a pretend context, true states of affairs are redefined as false ones. These structures are thought to guide children's understanding of, actions in, and memory for pretend contexts.

In contrast, other theorists deny that young children represent the relation between the true and false states of affairs as part of their counterfactual reasoning competence. Perner (1991; Perner, Baker, & Hutton, 1994) likens the cognitive demands of pretending to remembering, where true (or current) and false (or past) states of affairs are represented separately as distinct models, with young children needing only to monitor which state is being attended to, not form a relation between them. Lillard (1993a,b, 1994, 1996) suggests that the true and false states of affairs may be represented at different cognitive levels, with the true state of affairs "cognitively backgrounded" relative to the false state of affairs. Children may simply shift attention between the different representations in much the same way someone shifts attention between figures in a reversing figures stimulus. Since the true and false states of affairs are represented at different cognitive levels, each can influence young children's activities in pretend contexts, without children understanding the role of the mind, knowledge, or intention in pretending.

To assess whether young children in pretend contexts encode true and false states of affairs together as a counterfactual proposition or separately as distinct representations, Amsel et al. (1996) examined 3- and 4-year-olds' memory for each state of affairs. In study 1, sixteen 3- and nineteen 4-year-olds initially pretended that a banana was a comb and "combed" a white teddy bear, then immediately afterwards pretended that the banana was a spoon and "fed" a brown teddy bear. After the pretence was completed (and a 5 minute delay), children were asked two questions about the first pretend scenario: a question about the identity of the object in the real world (When you played with the white teddy bear, what did you really and truly have in your hand? Did you have a spoon, banana, stick, or comb?) and one about its identity in the pretend world (When you played with the white teddy bear, what did you pretend to have in your hand? Did you have a spoon, banana, stick, or comb?). After the last pair of questions was asked, children were asked to reconstruct their actions (Show me exactly what you did when you played with the white teddy bear) with an array of objects and the white teddy bear in front of them.

With regard to their memory for actions, a majority of children in each age group (63% of 3- and 87% of 4-year-olds) correctly remembered that they picked up a banana and "combed" the white teddy bear. Only two children (a 3- and a 4-year-old) confused the true identity of the object with its pretend identity by picking up the comb and "combing" the white teddy bear. Such errors would be expected if young children were confused about the contents of the real and pretend world (DiLalla & Watson, 1988) or believed that their mental representations correspond to reality (Woolley & Wellman, 1993).

If a counterfactual proposition formed in a pretend context was retrieved when remembering what had happened in that context, then children who correctly remembered their actions should also have identified the banana as the true identity of the object and the comb as its pretend identity. However, this was not the case. Overall, 3-year-olds correctly identified both identities only 19% of the time, whereas for 4-year-olds the corresponding figure was 61%. More generally, children's performance remembering actions and an object's identities in a pretend context appears to be unrelated: 77% of the children who correctly identified both identities of the object also successfully remembered their actions whereas a surprisingly similar 72% who never successfully remembered both identities correctly remembered their action. Thus, there were many children (largely 3-year-olds) who remembered picking up a banana and combing the white teddy bear but who could not correctly identify the banana as what they really had in their hand and the comb as what they pretended to have in their hand.

Three further findings additionally challenge the proposal that children form and retrieve a counterfactual proposition.

(1) Children's tendency to correctly remember one identity of the object was *unrelated* to their tendency to correctly remember the other identity. A positive relation was expected if children in object-substitution pretend contexts encode the true and pretend identities of the object together into a single counterfactual proposition: Either children successfully retrieve the proposition and correctly

remember both identities or they fail to successfully retrieve it and have to guess, probably incorrectly, which is the true and which is the pretend identity.

(2)   There was an unexpected *asymmetry* in young children's memory performance, with more 3-year-olds correctly naming the object's true than pretend identity. Again, such an asymmetry was not expected since it was supposed that children would either retrieve the counterfactual proposition and remember both identities or fail to retrieve it and likely remember neither one.

(3)   When children erred, they showed an unexpected *perseveration*, tending to give the same response to both questions. Indeed, on 66% of the trials on which an error was made identifying an object's true or pretend identity, children gave the same response to both questions. On 70% of these trials children responded that both identities of the object were the true identity (banana), on 26% of them they responded that both were the initial pretend identity (comb), and on 3% of the trials both were the final pretend identity (spoon). Such response perseveration was also found by Flavell, Flavell, and Green (1987), who characterised it as an "apparent tendency to select a single representation of an object and stick with it". These perseveration errors are difficult to explain if both identities are encoded together in the same counterfactual proposition.

These findings were replicated in study 2 of Amsel et al. (1996), in which 42 preschoolers (37–54 months) were asked to specify the true and pretend identities of an object used by an experimenter in a pretend scenario. In an extension of this work, Amsel, Foulkes, Gilmore, Smalley, and Volpe (1998) had twenty 3- and 4-year-olds pretend one object was another and then placed the object they played with in an opaque jar. Children were then asked whether the true and the pretend object were in the jar (in counterbalanced order). For example, children pretended a straw was a comb by "combing" the fur of a white teddy bear. The straw was placed in an opaque jar and children were asked whether there was a comb in the jar and whether there was a straw in the jar. Despite the different procedure and type of question posed in this study than in Amsel et al. (1996), children's performance still showed (1) non-contingency (correctly judging the presence of the true identity was unrelated to correctly identifying the absence of the pretend identity); (2) asymmetry (more children correctly identified the true identity of the object than the pretend identity); and (3) perseveration (children erred by claiming that both identities were in the jar, rather than by claiming that only the pretend identity was in the jar).

A model

The results of the study suggested that children do not reason counterfactually regarding pretend contexts by forming and retrieving a counterfactual proposition. This was made clear by the fact that children specified the true and pretend identities of an object noncontingently, asymmetrically, and they erred by persevering on one identity. The data were more consistent with those who claim that the two identities are represented separately, with the true identity of the object encoded into a representation of a true state of affairs and the pretend identity encoded into a distinct representation of a false one.

The evidence that 3-year-olds have difficulty remembering both identities can be explained by their poor cognitive management abilities (see Harris, 1993, for a related discussion). That is, rather than easily shifting between representations of the true and false states of affairs when they were both activated by questioning, young children tended to adopt Flavell et al.'s (1987) "select and stick with one representation" strategy. Moreover, children had a rich multi-modal experience (visual, proprioceptive, verbal) of the actual objects but not of the pretend (verbal) objects in otherwise mundane and effectively-neutral pretend play scenarios. As a result, children responded to both questions by reference to the better elaborated and more strongly activated representations of true states of affairs, failing to shift to the less salient representations of the false states.

Perhaps if the pretend context were such that the false state of affairs were more elaborated and strongly activated than the true one, children would have difficulty disengaging from pretend identity. Such a claim is supported by Lillard (1994) and Woolley (1995), who reviewed the literature and suggested that young children are susceptible to acting as if the pretend world is in fact real if they have a strong emotional response to the pretend world. For example, as the pretend monster or "bad guy" becomes better elaborated and more strongly activated than the mundane perceptions out of which it was created, children will be increasingly likely to fail to disengage from and to be frightened by their pretend creation. Thus, cases in which children appear to confuse fantasy and reality may be best interpreted as the result of limitation in children's management of the multiple representations formed during pretend play, rather than due to a profound conceptual or ontological confusion.

Children's actions in pretend contexts may serve as a means to concretise and externalise the problem of managing the separate representations of the true and false states of affairs. That is, actions in pretend contexts may serve to help children to monitor the relation between true states of affairs, which are being manipulated, and false ones, which are being simulated. Previous research has demonstrated an age-related decrease in preschoolers' preference for actual objects that are similar in form and function to pretend ones (Elder & Pederson, 1978; Jackowitz & Watson, 1980; Overton & Jackson, 1973; Pederson, Rook-Green, & Elder, 1981; Ungerer, Zelazo, Kearsley, & O'Leary, 1981). Such preferences may exist initially because young children have no other means to manage the multiple representations formed when pretending so they seek out objects that afford actions manipulating the true and simulating the false states of affairs.

Older children may rely less on a similarity between the true and false states of affairs in order to engage in pretence as they find mental means of managing the representations. Such an argument regarding children's progression away from relying on externalised and concretised information as a means of relating true (i.e. referent) and false (symbol) states of affairs has been demonstrated in children's production and comprehension of pantomimes. O'Reilly (1995) found that children's reasoning about pantomimes was supported by the use of concretised and externalised body part information (e.g. brushing teeth using a finger as a toothbrush) relative to the same actions with an imaginary object (e.g. brushing teeth with an imaginary toothbrush) for 3- but not 5-year-olds. Young pretenders' vocalisations may also serve as a concretised means for them to manage the separate representations of true and false states of affairs. Young children may use different voices when talking about the true and pretend world and make supportive sounds (e.g. saying "vroom" when pretending a block is a car) to aid them in selectively activating and/or attending to a target represented state of affairs.

A model of the proposed representations children formed during (object-substitution) pretence is presented in Fig. 7.1. Children encode the physical object's true and pretend identities as separate representations of the true and false states of affairs, depicted in Fig. 7.1 by different shapes for the representations. It is further proposed that the representations are unequally activated in memory, which is depicted by the different sizes for the representations in Fig. 7.1. Finally, the representations are related by actions performed in pretend contexts (depicted by an arrow). When asked to reconstruct their actions, children retrieve the entire structure, including the represented true identity of the object as the thing being manipulated and the represented pretend identity as the thing being simulated by actions. However, when asked about each object independently of the other and the action performed, the action link between the

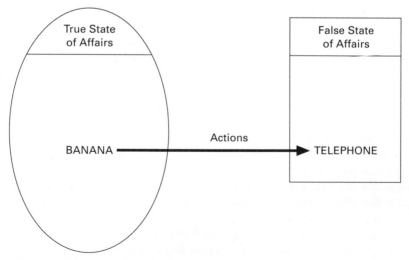

FIG. 7.1   A model of counterfactual reasoning about pretence.

models is not activated and young children are left to (unsuccessfully) attend selectively to the appropriate representation. Older children, it is assumed, can perform the appropriate mental management to correctly attend to the appropriate representation.

Higher-level understanding of pretence

Beyond the manner by which children process information in pretend contexts, the theories of how children reason counterfactually about pretence differ in how pretence is understood. As mentioned, the issue hinges on when or if children understand pretence representationally, as a mental activity in which pretenders represent false states of affairs. Three aspects of children's conceptualisation of pretence have been examined: their appreciation of (1) the role of knowledge in pretending; (2) the diversity of pretence; and (3) the difference between pretence and false belief.

Lillard (1993a, 1996) challenged the claim that children in pretend contexts appreciate that the same state of affairs is represented in multiple ways (Flavell et al., 1987; Forguson & Gopnik, 1988; Leslie, 1987). Lillard (1993a) argued that although children are aware and keep track of true and false states of affairs, that is not the same as saying that they understand pretence in terms of the representations that pretenders form. In experimental tests of these ideas, Lillard (1993b, 1996, 1998) found that a majority of pre-school-aged children assert that a protagonist who is hopping like a rabbit is pretending to be a rabbit despite the protagonist having been described as having no knowledge of or desire to act like rabbits. Young children miss critical points about the representational nature of pretence: Pretending involves knowledge of the pretend object and an intention to pretend. According to Lillard, rather than conceiving of pretence as based on intentionally created mental *representations* of false states of affairs, young children conceived of it in terms of the *actions* which simulate false states.

A number of researchers have attempted to detect any insight children may have about the role of knowledge in pretence on Lillard's task by (1) minimising the salience of protagonists' actions (Aronson, Golomb, & Kirkpatrick, 1997); (2) making mental state information more salient (Custer, 1996); or (3) both (Bruell & Woolley, 1998). The general finding is that children as young as 3 years of age understand that pretenders have thoughts of the false states of affairs they represent. Such evidence though, does not detract from the fact that children's representational understanding of pretence is fragile and can be easily overwhelmed in normal pretend contexts where actions and verbalisations are salient. The claim that children have at least a fragile understanding of pretence as representational (although see Lillard, 1996) is supported by evidence that they appreciate the diversity of pretence: that two people may be pretending that a particular true state of affairs are different false ones (Davis, Woolley, & Bruell, 1997; Hickling, Wellman, & Gottfried, 1997). For example, Hickling et al. found that 3-year-olds judge that a puppet will continue to believe that a glass contains pretend milk even though the child has since pretended that the milk was emptied out behind the puppet's back.

Thus, even young children appear to understand that the same true state of affairs may be responded to by pretenders as different false ones. However, this may be a relatively superficial appreciation which contrasts pretenders' *expectations* about what to do and say in response to different pretend stipulations for the same true state of affairs. This is in comparison with the conceptually deeper appreciation which contrasts pretenders' *interpretations* of same true states of affairs as different false ones. While expectations and interpretations both refer to a pretender's subjective state, the latter entails understanding pretenders as actively creating different pretend worlds, whereas the former involves understanding pretenders as merely responding as they should to distinct pretend stipulations.

Perner, Baker, and Hutton (1994) tested the claim that young children initially have, at best, a superficial understanding of the relation between pretenders and the false states of affairs they represent, if they have any understanding of it at all. They argued that young children appreciate that an agent may act with respect to false states of affairs but not understand the difference between *pretending* false states of affairs are true and *falsely believing* false states of affairs are true. As evidence, Perner et al. demonstrated that children younger than four years old could not distinguish between whether a protagonist was pretending or (falsely) believing to feed a rabbit, despite being told the protagonist saw or did not see the rabbit being removed from its cage prior to feeding it.

Thus, there appears to be growth in children's understanding of the relationship between a pretender and the false state of affairs being represented. Initially, children have little or perhaps no insight into the nature of the relationship. By four years, children appreciate that a pretender knows the false state of affairs is false, and later grasp more fully that the false state of affairs is a product of and so constrained by the pretender's knowledge base.

Representing pretend information and understanding pretend contexts

The distinction between lower-level processing and higher-order understanding of pretend contexts leaves open the question of the developmental relation between them. Theoretical accounts of the relation between changes in lower-level processing and higher-order understanding of pretence come from the two major theories of the development of a theory of mind. On the one hand, and consistent with the Theory theory, the emergence of a representational understanding of pretence may influence how information in pretend contexts is processed. The Theory theory proposes that young children form and revise intuitive theories (of mind in this case) which have the same function for children that formal theories have for scientists: as a basis to encode, explain, predict, and understand relevant phenomena (Gopnik & Meltzoff, 1997; Wellman & Gelman, 1992). The idea is that children's misunderstanding of a phenomenon (e.g. whether someone is pretending) can be traced back to their domain-specific theory of the phenomenon (e.g. non-representational theory of mind) rather than to them having a domain-general limitation (e.g. lacking a general reasoning capacity).[1] Thus, as a consequence of children replacing their behavioural understanding of pretence (i.e. pretence as acting "as if") with a representational one, they would acquire the means to better represent and manage information in pretend contexts.

On the other hand, and consistent with the simulation theory, developmental changes in children's higher-order understanding of pretence as a mental state may be irrelevant to and thus independent of changes in lower-level processes involved in encoding and managing true and false states of affairs. the simulation theory (cf. Harris, 1991, 1994) proposes that children and adults alike understand behaviour in a particular context by mentally simulating the context and "seeing" what they (and by implication others) would say, feel, and do in the same circumstances. Harris proposes that with the growth of children's information processing system (i.e. the central executive), they can run more complex simulations; from ones that alter only states of affairs (i.e. creating simulations of false states of affairs), to those that additionally alter children's attitude that the simulations are false (i.e. creating simulations of false states of affairs that are taken to be true for an agent). So the development of children's representations of information in pretend contexts and their discrimination of pretend from false belief contexts results from their being able to form more complex simulations, and their understanding of pretence has its source elsewhere.

To summarise, children reason counterfactually about pretence by forming distinct representations of true and false states of affairs. Although children have some difficulties managing these representations outside the immediate pretend context, their competence managing the representations within a pretend context may be related to the pretend information being largely externalised and concretised through actions and verbalisations. The actions and verbalisations allow children to monitor both and selectively attend to each of the multiple representations. It is interesting to note that another function of pretenders' externalising and concretising information is in order to share the pretence with others (Goncu, 1993). Perhaps because externalised and concretised information is so socially and psychologically significant for children's pretence, such information is taken by children to define what it means to pretend. Young children show only a fragile understanding of pretence as involving pretenders' reinterpretation of the true states of affairs as false ones.

The developmental changes in children's counterfactual reasoning about pretence involve changes not only in the lower-level processes for representing and managing the true and false states of affairs but also in the higher-order understanding of pretenders' relations to representations. Over age children rely less on externalised and concretised information as a means of managing the information represented from pretend contexts and acquire deeper insight into pretenders' thoughts about the representations they form. Ironically, by the time children achieve full control over and a stable representational understanding of pretence (i.e. at 6 or 7 years), their tendency to spontaneously engage in the activity begins to dwindle (Rubin, Fein, & Vandenberg, 1983).

COUNTERFACTUAL THINKING AND PONDERING POSSIBILITIES

Our interest in comparing the cognitive processes involved in playing pretend and pondering possibilities is that we think by mastering the former, children become better able to do the latter. They begin to competently 'play' with a particularly interesting set of false states of affairs—possible ones. By *possibilities* we mean unactualised states of affairs that are capable of happening, existing, or being true without contradicting proven facts, laws, or circumstances. Typically, possibilities are contrasted to *actualities* which are states of affairs that are known or believed to be real and true.

There are a number of ways in which children can reason about the relation between possibilities and actualities (Amsel, Foulkes, & Smalley, 1997). First, an actual state of affairs can be interpreted as one among a set of possible states. Exhaustively enumerating the set of possible states of affairs involves combinatorial reasoning, wherein all logically possible combinations of actual elements in a set (without regard to their order) are generated (Inhelder & Piaget, 1958; Pitt, 1983). Second, features of actual states of affairs in a context can be interpreted as possible conditions or causes in accounting for some other state of affairs in the context. Modal logical reasoning about possibility and necessity underlies the appreciation that multiply sufficient features are individually and in combination possible causes or conditions of some other state of affairs (Fay & Klahr, 1996; Piaget, 1987). Third, features of actual states of affairs in a context can be mentally altered, thereby creating a possible state of affairs with which actual ones can be compared and contrasted. Creating such a possible state of affairs and comparing and contrasting it to an actual one involves counterfactual reasoning (Amsel et al., 1991; Roese, 1997).

Counterfactual reasoning about possibilities

The parent pondering possibilities who was introduced at the beginning of this chapter, is perhaps best described as engaged in the third form of reasoning about possibilities, where possible states of affairs are created in order to be compared with and contrasted to actual ones. The parent is pondering those possible states of affairs as a means to understand why the child threw a temper tantrum and to prevent it in the future. By determining the event sequence which would have led to the child not throwing the temper tantrum, the events in the actual sequence that are causally relevant would be discovered. Of course this process of identifying alternative sequences which would undo the undesirable outcome is based on the parent's knowledge and experience with the child.[2] For example, having dressed the child differently would likely be dismissed by the parent as undoing the tantrum but having had a longer nap may be accepted. With a longer nap, the parent imagines, the child would have been better able to control herself in the late afternoon.

Counterfactual reasoning about possibilities and emotions

There are other uses of counterfactual reasoning about possibilities than making causal attributions. One line of research we have been pursuing concerns the development of counterfactual reasoning about possibilities in the domain of emotions (Amsel, Robbins, Tumarkin, Foulkes, Janit, & Smalley, 1999). What is the connection between emotions and counterfactual reasoning about possibilities? Our feelings about actual states of affairs are often influenced by states that could have but do not occur. For example, consider a contestant on the TV game show, "Let's Make a Deal". Contestants select one of two gift boxes and keep whatever they find inside. How a contestant feels about what is in the selected gift box is typically influenced by what is in the box they could have but did not select. On the one hand, if the contestant gets a refrigerator but could have had a brand new car, they feel sad, regretting the choice they made. Like the pondering parent, the contestant appreciates that a more desirable outcome could have been realised if another course of action had been followed. On the other hand, if the contestant gets a refrigerator but could have had a case of cat food, they are happy, satisfied that they chose the best gift possible. The contestant appreciates that if another course of action had been taken, a less desirable outcome would have been realised.

The influence of the possible gift on contestants' feelings about the actual gift is appreciated not only by the contestant but also by the audience. For both, a true state of affairs (i.e. the contestant opens the "selected" box and reacts to its contents) is represented. In addition, a false state of affairs (i.e. the contestant opening the "unselected" box) is represented, reasoned about (i.e. the reaction is imagined) and compared to the true state (i.e. the false state is judged to be more desirable, less desirable, or no different than the true state of affairs).

Amsel et al. (1999) assessed pre-schoolers' ability to reason counterfactually about possibilities in the domain of emotions; that is, whether false states of affairs are represented, reasoned about, and compared to true ones. In each of three studies, pre-school and college students judged their own or a protagonist's feelings about an actual state of affairs (i.e. a gift) before and after being presented with information about a possible one (i.e. the gift the protagonist could have but did not receive) which varied in desirability from the actual state. Study

1 examined whether pre-schoolers' judgements of protagonists' emotions would be influenced by information regarding counterfactual possibilities. Sixteen pre-schoolers (38–68 months, 8 females and 8 males) and seven college students (4 females and 3 males) were introduced to two protagonists (dolls of the same sex as the subject) who were each associated with two gift boxes. Participants were told that each protagonist selected one of the two gift boxes and, upon opening the selected box, the child participants were told that each protagonist found the same toy figurine whereas the adult participants were told that each protagonist found $5.00. Children and adults were then asked the *Initial Question* for each protagonist: "How happy is (naming one protagonist) with the gift she (he) received: not happy or sad, a little happy, pretty happy, or very happy?".

Next, each protagonist's unselected gift box was opened and found to contain either a high valued gift for one protagonist, whom we will designate as protagonist+ (stickers or $20.00), and a low valued gift for the other protagonist, designated as protagonist– (a block or $0.50). Children and adults were then asked the same *Counterfactual Question* for each protagonist: "How happy would (naming one protagonist) have been if she (he) had taken the other gift box: not happy or sad, a little happy, pretty happy, or very happy?".

The children and adults performed no differently in response to the Initial and Counterfactual Questions (Fig. 7.2). All participants recognised that the two protagonists were equally happy initially, but that protagonist+ would have been happier and that protagonist– would have been less happy with the gift they could have but did not receive, compared to the one that they did receive. From these data it seems that pre-schoolers have adults' abilities to represent a false state of affairs (i.e. the protagonists opening an "unselected" gift box) and reason about it (i.e. imagine the protagonists' feelings discovering what is inside).

At this point in the procedure, the participants had assessed the protagonists' feelings about the gift each actually received and the one they could have had. The issue of whether participants appreciate the influence of the possible gift on

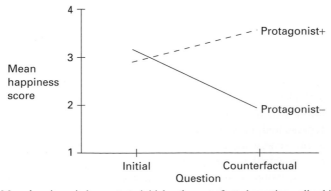

FIG. 7.2   Mean happiness judgements to initial and counterfactual questions, all subjects.

the protagonists' feelings about the actual one was assessed by asking the *Final Question* which was the same as the initial one: "How happy is (naming one protagonist) with the gift she (he) received: Not happy or sad, a little happy, pretty happy, or very happy?". Adults judged protagonist+ as less happy and protagonist– as happier in response to the Final Question compared to the Initial Question (Fig. 7.3) and so were influenced by the counterfactual information. As expected, protagonist+ was judged as less happy because she could have got $20 but only got $5, whereas protagonist– was judged as happier because she got $5 instead of only $0.50.

   In contrast, the pre-schoolers showed no change from the Initial to Final Question (Fig. 7.4), suggesting that they were uninfluenced by the information regarding the possible gift. This lack of influence occurred despite evidence that children were just like adults in knowing how the protagonists would have felt if they had received their possible gifts. Nevertheless, that knowledge had no influence on pre-schoolers' reassessment of protagonist happiness with their actual gift. The implication of these findings is that pre-schoolers represent and

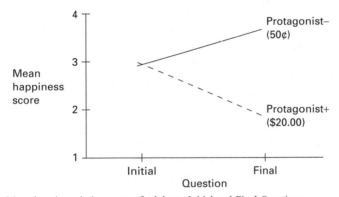

FIG. 7.3   Mean happiness judgements of adults to Initial and Final Questions.

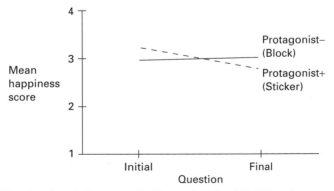

FIG. 7.4   Mean happiness judgements of children to Initial and Final Questions.

reason about false states of affairs in the same way that adults do, but they do not compare the true state of affairs to the false ones.

Two other studies in the Amsel et al. paper (1999) replicated the basic finding of study 1. In study 2, 26 pre-school and 24 college students rated protagonists' feelings about the contents of a selected box before and after learning about (1) the higher or lower value of the contents in the box that they could have but did not select (counterfactual information) or (2) the fact that the protagonists were satiated with or desired the contents (factual information). Children and adults were influenced in predicted ways by factual information: Compared to their initial judgement of protagonist happiness with contents, those described as satiated with it were judged as less happy and those described as desiring it were judged as happier. However, only adults were influenced as predicted by counterfactual information. Once again, children did not alter their assessment of protagonist happiness regarding the actual content depending on the value of the possible content.

In study 3, 10 pre-school and 10 college students blindly turned over one of two face-down playing cards, judged whether or not it 'beat' the experimenter's face-up card, and rated their feelings about the card they selected. On trials where the experimenter and the participant tied, the participants were asked to turn over and rate their feelings about the unselected card, which was either higher or lower than the card they actually turned over. Finally, subjects re-rated their feeling about the card they actually turned over. The results again replicated those of study 1: Compared to their feelings about the card they actually turned over which tied the experimenter's, children and adults judged that they would have been happier having turned over the "unselected" card when it would have won and less happy having turned over the "unselected" card when it would have lost. However only adults compared true states of affairs to false ones in predicted ways: Compared to their initial judgements, adults were happier about having tied after finding out that they would have lost the hand, and less happy about the tie after finding out that they would have won the hand. In contrast, the children's ratings of the selected card were the same before and after learning about the card they did not select.

Another model

Children do not have adults' appreciation of how an agent's (self or other) feelings about actual states of affairs depend on states that could have but do not occur. In this regard, children live in a different emotional world from adults— one in which counterfactual possibilities do not bear on how they feel about actualities. Why do pre-schoolers reason differently from adults about the influence of possibilities on emotions? It seems that pre-schoolers can successfully represent and reason about false states of affairs, but they do not compare the true states of affairs to false ones in predicted ways.

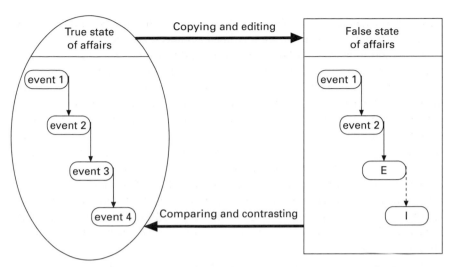

FIG. 7.5   A model of counterfactual reasoning about possibilities.

Figure 7.5 presents a model of counterfactual reasoning about possibilities in the domain of emotions to further unpack our claim about pre-schoolers' capability. Actual sequences of events leading up to an agent's (self or other) emotional reaction are marked as a true states of affairs, depicted in Fig. 7.5 by an event sequence (event 1 to event 4) within the representational structure labelled as "true state of affairs." A copied and edited version of the true state of affairs, in which a particular event node is altered, is represented as the false state of affairs. This is depicted in Fig. 7.5 as an event sequence, paralleling the true event sequence except for the altered event node (labeled "E" for "edited") within a representational structure labelled as "false state of affairs". The copying and editing function by which the true state of affairs became the false one is depicted as an arrow in Fig. 7.5. Beyond editing a change in an event sequence, the consequences of the edited change must be imagined, depicted here by a broken arrow to an event node labelled "I" for "imagined". The imagined event node can now be compared and contrasted with the corresponding event node in the true state of affairs such that the assessment of an actual state of affairs can be evaluated in light of a possible one. This process is depicted in Fig. 7.5 by an arrow going from a false state of affairs to a true one.

The data from Amsel et al. (1999) suggest that pre-schoolers are like adults in their competence to copy an actual sequence of events, edit it by altering a specific event, and then imagine the consequences of the edited change on an agent's emotional reaction. However, pre-schoolers are unlike adults in bringing such possible states of affairs to bear when evaluating (i.e. comparing and contrasting with) true ones: Adults' but not children's assessments of true states of affairs were affected in predicted ways by false ones. Thus, there seems to be an asymmetry in children's similarity to adults in their ability to reason counterfactually about possibilities. On the one hand, children and adults are similar in their creation of states of affairs which could have but did not occur and imagining the consequences of those possible states; that is, in their reasoning about possibilities, given actualities. On the other hand, children and adults are dissimilar in their use of information about the states of affairs which could have occurred to evaluate the actual ones; that is, in their reasoning about actualities, given possibilities.

Extending this analysis of children's counterfactual reasoning about possibilities in the domain of emotions are the results from Harris, German, and Mills (1996), who examined young children's counterfactual reasoning about possibilities in the domain of causality. In studies 1 and 2, Harris et al. found that a majority of 3- and 4-year-olds could answer questions about *preventing* a negative outcome. In these studies, children were told of an event sequence (i.e. a protagonist paints the floor red with a paint brush) that has an undesirable outcome (the floor is dirty). They were asked then to imagine the consequence for the outcome (i.e. the floor would still be dirty or would not have gotten dirty) of mentally altering a causally-relevant event (i.e. the protagonist not having painted) or a causally-irrelevant event (the protagonist using his fingers to paint). Children showed a great deal of competence to think counterfactually about the conditions under which negative outcomes could have been avoided. The finding supports the claim that children copy and edit true states of affairs, altering particular events, and then imagine whether the altered events can 'undo' negative outcomes. Put differently, the data from Harris et al. suggest that children can readily reason about false states of affairs, given true ones.

In study 3, Harris et al. additionally examined whether children can reason counterfactually to attribute the causal conditions in a real event sequence rather than to identify preventative conditions in an imagined event sequence. To test children's ability to reason counterfactually about causation children were asked to identify the causes of an undesirable outcome (i.e. inky fingers) befalling a protagonist. Children wcre told that the protagonist had acted in a certain way (i.e. selecting a black pen with which to draw) after rejecting a course of action which would have led to the same outcome (i.e. drawing with a blue pen: control condition) or after rejecting a course of action which would have led to a desirable outcome (i.e. drawing with a pencil: experimental condition). The experimental condition *invites* children to reason counterfactually about the role of the protagonist's course of action in producing the undesired outcome whereas the control condition *blocks* such reasoning. Children answered the causal question by reference to the protagonist's failure to adopt an appropriate course of action, specifically identifying the rejected option in the experimental condition (e.g. failure to use a pencil) more frequently than in the control condition. Harris et al. claim that their study 3 finding replicates with children the results of Wells and Gavanski's (1989)[3] study with adults. In each study, the differential impact of the experimental condition over the control on children's and adults' causal judgements was cited as evidence of the influence of counterfactual reasoning about possible states of affairs (i.e. unselected options which undo outcomes) on the evaluation of actual ones (i.e. attributing events as causal).

The findings suggest that children are influenced by possibilities in their assessments of actualities in the domain of causality, which contrasts with Amsel et al.'s finding that children are not so influenced in the domain of emotions. While such domain-specificity in the development of children's counterfactual reasoning about possibilities may well yet turn out to be the case, the present data, we claim, are insufficient basis to make such a claim. Specifically, we are sceptical of Harris et al.'s finding as evidence of children's sophistication in reasoning counterfactually about causality because the central finding reported by Harris et al. is different and less compelling than Wells and Gavanski's finding to which it was compared; a finding which is now under a great deal of criticism. First, with regard to the nature of the effect, Harris et al. and Wells and Gavanski found that the experimental condition influenced children and adults alike to arrive at different causal attributions than did the control condition. However, the causal attributions were framed in terms of what the protagonist *hadn't done*[4] (i.e. the alternative actions such as not having used a pencil) for Harris et al.'s children, whereas they were framed in terms of what the protagonist *had done*[5] (i.e. the decision of the protagonist such as ordering the meal with wine) for Wells and Gavanski's adults. While this difference may be an artifact of the different tasks, procedures, or coding systems used in the two studies, it may also be the case that possibilities have a different influence on children's than on adults' causal reasoning. Second, with respect to how compelling the findings are, Wells and Gavanski found that adults made reference to what the protagonist had done as the cause of the undesirable outcome approximately 67% of the time overall (about 86% of the time in the experimental and 48% of the time in the control condition). In contrast, Harris et al. found that children made reference to what the protagonist had not done as the cause of the undesirable outcome only about 39% of the time overall.[6] This difference, too, may be an artifact of differences in the tasks, but may reflect that adults are more strongly influenced by possibilities than children. Finally, social psychologists have criticised Wells and Gavanski's claims about the role of counterfactual reasoning on causal attribution, suggesting instead that counterfactual reasoning leads to judgements of how to prevent undesired outcomes and typically not to causes of such outcomes (Mandel & Lehman, 1996; N'gbala & Branscombe, 1995). Such an argument may be too strong given the centrality of the role of counterfactual reasoning as a tool for performing causal analysis in law (Amsel et al., 1991). Nonetheless, the criticism suggests that Wells and Gavanski's findings may not be sufficient evidence of the role of counterfactual reasoning in causal attributions, undermining Harris et al.'s appeal to the parallel between the respective findings as evidence of children's counterfactual reasoning competence.

In summary, young children have little difficulty in reasoning about possible states of affairs, given actual ones, whether the possibilities reasoned about are alternatives to actual causal sequences (e.g. what would have happened if things were different?) or emotional reactions (e.g. how would an agent have felt if things were different?). However, young children's ability to reason about actualities in light of possibilities is very much in question. There is no evidence that young children's assessment of actual emotional reactions is influenced in an adult-like way by possible ones (Amsel et al., 1999); such an influence first appears in early elementary school (Amsel et al., 1998). Moreover, there is only weak evidence that young children's assessment of the causal status of events in an event sequence is influenced *in an adult-like way* by possible ones (Harris et al., 1996). While more research is needed, it would nonetheless appear that the source of developmental change in children's counterfactual reasoning about possibilities lies in their ability to bring information about possibilities to bear on their evaluation of actualities; that is, to compare and contrast true states of affairs with false ones.

The growth of the ability to reason counterfactually about possibilities may be explained by one of the two developmental accounts previously discussed for pretence. On one hand, and consistent with the Theory theory, children's higher-order understanding of mental activities may lead to changes in their lower-level processing of such information. The higher-order understanding in this case may be an appreciation of what Chandler and Lalonde (1996) describe as an "inter-pretative" theory of mind, where children understand the active nature of mind to construe situations. Chandler and Lalonde point out that standard theory of mind tasks assess whether children appreciate that the same state of affairs can give rise to unique representations in different agents (or in the same agent at different times) due to the different agents' (or the same agent's changing) relations (e.g. spatial, temporal, history, or quality) to the state of affairs. Chandler and Lalonde further point out that children sometimes have to make sense of situations where the same actual state of affairs is interpreted differently by different agents, even though the agents' *relationship* to the state is identical. Such situations call for an understanding of mind as more than just representational; it calls for an understanding of mind as interpretative. For example, an interpretative mind is implicated in cases where agents who otherwise have the same relation to a state of affairs, react with different emotions[7] or make different causal attributions. Consistent with an interpretative theory of mind, children may appreciate that the differing emotional reactions and causal attributions are the product of a feature associated with the thoughts of the agents rather than with the state of affairs itself or the relation between the agents and state of affairs. From this perspect-ive, it is only when they understand the mind as interpretative that they will acquire the lower-level cognitive processes required for computing how two agents' different emotional reactions or causal attributions may be due to each evaluating an actual state of affairs in light of different possible ones.

On the other hand, and consistent with simulation theory, the acquisition of a higher-order theory of a constructive mind may be irrelevant to and so independent of changes in lower-level processes involved in children's managing representations of actual and possible states of affairs. As previously noted, Harris proposes that over age children can run more complex simulations. Perhaps they also become better able to compare and contrast simulations with actual sequences, thereby being able not only to create representations of false states of affairs and treat them as true, but also to bring them to bear when evaluating actual sequences.

SUMMARY, CONCLUSIONS, AND IMPLICATIONS

So in what ways are the processes of playing pretend and pondering possibilities related? We make two broad arguments. The first argument, outlined in the introduction, is that counterfactual thinking underlies both activities. Each form of mental activity involves the creation and analysis of false states of affairs, and coordination of the false states with true ones. When children play pretend and ponder possibilities they create false states of affairs out of true ones as alternatives to them. What differs between the false states of affairs created for each activity are the real world implications assumed for each: False states of affairs created as pretend worlds are assumed to have no real world significance, whereas those created as possible worlds are assumed to have such significance. Put differently, when playing pretend, false states of affairs are created from true ones as playful alternatives to them, but when pondering possibilities, the false states of affairs are copied and edited versions of true ones which are to be seriously compared to and contrasted with true ones.

Once children create a false state of affairs, whether as a pretend or possible world, they seem to be able to use all their available inference tools to create new false information. For example, children may draw on the same causal knowledge to determine the consequences of an alternative event sequence (Amsel et al., 1999; Harris et al., 1996) or of a pretend action (Harris & Kavanaugh, 1993). Finally, the false states of affairs are coordinated with true ones. In the case of playing pretend, that coordination involves keeping the false states of affairs separate from true ones, whereas in the case of pondering possibilities the coordination involves bringing the false states of affairs to bear on true ones. Thus, although the manner by which representations of false states of affairs are created and coordinated with true ones are different when playing pretend and pondering possibilities, the two involve similar kinds of cognitive processes.

The second argument regarding the similarity of playing pretend and pondering possibilities is the source of developmental change in each activity. Young children appear to be able to form representations of false states of affairs early on, at least by the time that the word "no" is used to express denial, typically before their second birthday (Bloom & Lahey, 1978). But in contrast to contexts in which children deny representations of false states of affairs in favour of true ones, those in which children play pretend and ponder possibilities involve managing the true and false states of affairs. It is managing the multiple representations which gives young children the most difficulty in each activity and is the source of development of each. Just as young children have more difficulty compared to older children appropriately shifting between the representations of true and false states of affairs when playing pretend, so do they have difficulty bringing representations of false states of affairs to bear on true ones when pondering possibilities. Children seem to work out the former management problem (pretence) earlier than the latter (possibilities), at least for the tasks examined here.

It remains unclear exactly how children overcome their difficulties managing the represented true and false states of affairs when playing pretend or pondering possibilities. Two accounts have been reviewed here: the Theory theory and simulation theory. The Theory theory supposes that changes in children's higher-order understanding of mind alters their lower-level management of true and false states of affairs. Understanding the mind as representational enables children to encode an agent in pretend contexts thinking of true states of affairs as false ones. Understanding the mind as interpretative enables children to bring false states of affairs to bear on true ones. In the alternative simulation theory, change in higher-order understanding of mind is denied to have any role in the development of children's ability to create simulations, whether they be of a pretend or possible world. The development of children's ability to appropriately simulate pretend and possible worlds, which reflects more complex forms of counterfactual thinking, may involve the growth of general cognitive capacities and control systems (i.e. the central cognitive executive).

We offer, as a concluding statement, a third account of the development of counterfactual reasoning about pretence and possibilities, in the form of an interaction between changes in higher-order conceptual understanding and lower-level information processing. That is, as children develop more powerful cognitive capacities and control systems, more complex forms of counterfactual thinking become possible and will occur under the right circumstances. But such a form of reasoning is not always strategic, that is, under the child's own control. Nonetheless, the occurrence of such thoughts may serve as a basis for children's conceptual reorganisation of their theory of mind. For example, on certain occasions, children may appreciate that an agent's thoughts about a false state of affairs is a way to judge whether or not the agent is playing (pretending) or is serious (holding a false belief) Later on, the child may appreciate the role of different possibilities entertained by agents for why they arrived at different conclusions about the same state of affairs. While each insight may not generalise beyond the conditions of the particular context, it was enabled by the child's developing information processing system. A younger child would simply not have the lower-level processing power necessary for the particular insight.

Nonetheless, the insight may be the kind of interesting case which is the basis for a conceptual reorganisation. Once the new theory is in place, the once haphazard strategy for managing true and false states of affairs may become more strategic and under the control of the child. Contrary to simulation theory, this proposal supposes that conceptual reorganisations may serve an important role in the development of counterfactual reasoning: from successful counterfactual reasoning about pretence (based on the acquisition of a representational theory of mind) to possibilities (based on the acquisition of an interpretative theory of mind). Contrary to the Theory theory, the present proposal claims conceptual development of children is unlike that for scientists, since only for the former is conceptual development tied intimately to the growth of the cognitive system. Future research will determine whether the present proposal belongs to the pretend or possible world. In either case, our point has been to show just how similar it is to reason about these worlds.

NOTES

1. It is acknowledged that the Theory theory does *not* imply that the only source of developmental change is children's domain-specific theories (Gopnik & Meltzoff, 1997). However, these other sources of developmental change cannot be seen as substantially constraining the theories that children form since these other sources and not the theories would be implicated as the reason for children's misunderstandings.
2. There are a number of proposals regarding how the truth of propositions about counterfactual possibilities are evaluated (Sosa, 1981), each of which agree that real-world knowledge is relevant.
3. Wells and Gavanski found that adults come to different conclusions regarding the cause of an undesirable outcome (e.g. a person dying) associated with a protagonist acting a certain way (e.g. protagonist ordering a wine-based dinner for a person who was allergic but who ate it anyway), depending on whether the protagonist considered but rejected another course of action which would have either prevented the undesirable outcome (experimental condition: considered but did not order a non-wine-based meal) or not have prevented it (control condition: considered but did not order another wine-based meal).
4. The causal question came before a prevention question in which children were asked what the protagonist should have done instead so that the undesirable outcome would not have occurred. Harris et al. note, knowledge that the prevention question was coming may have influenced the use of "alternative action" responses to the causal question. Indeed, a close examination of the first time the causal question was asked (prior to the prevention question ever being asked) showed only a minority of children (6 out of 32) reporting a cause in terms of an alternative action that the protagonist could have taken.
5. The causal question was counterbalanced with and shown to be uninfluenced by a prevention question.
6. About 17% of all the children's responses referred specifically to the protagonist's unselected actions (e.g. not using a pencil), which accounted for 29% of all responses in the experimental condition and 5% in the control condition. About 22% of all the

children's responses referred to other alternative actions (e.g. not using a crayon), which accounted for 16% of all responses in the experimental condition and 28% in the control condition.

7. Even young children may appreciate that agents have different *expectations* and so respond differently to the same situation, as discussed in the case of children pretending. But this reflects the agents' differing relation to the state of affairs thereby disqualifying it as an example of an interpretative theory of mind. A better example of what is meant are two people coming to the scene of the same car accident with the same expectation of the victim's level of injury. Nonetheless, one observer may feel happy for the victim because she could have easily died in the car accident and one feels sad for her because she could have easily avoided the car accident.

ACKNOWLEDGEMENTS

Collection of the data described in this chapter was partially supported by a Weber State University Research, Scholarship & Professional Growth grant to the first author. We would like to thank Judi Amsel, Michael Chandler, Nick DeLeeuw, Tamara Ferguson, Paul Harris, Chris Lalonde, Angeline Lillard, Bill McVaugh, Peter Mitchell, Kevin Riggs, and Cecilia Wainryb for many very helpful comments and discussions.

REFERENCES

Amsel, E., Bobadilla, W., Coch, D., & Remy, R. (1996). Young children's memory for the true and pretend identities of objects used in object-substitution pretense. *Developmental Psychology, 32,* 479–491.

Amsel, E., Foulkes, S., Gilmore, B., Smalley, J., & Volpe, H. (1998, July). Preschoolers' reasoning about pretend and possible worlds. In E. Amsel & E. Robinson (Chairs), *The development of counterfactual reasoning.* Symposium conducted at the biennial meeting of the International Society for the Study of Behavioral Development, Berne, Switzerland.

Amsel, E., Foulkes, S., & Smalley, J.D. (1997, April). *The development of reasoning about three types of possibilities.* Paper presented at the Annual Meeting of the Rocky Mountain Psychological Association. Reno, NV.

Amsel, E., Langer, R., & Loutzenhiser, L. (1991). Do lawyers reason differently from psychologists? A comparative design for studying expertise. In R.J. Sternberg & P. Frensch (Eds.), *Complex problem solving: Mechanisms and processes* (pp. 233–250). Hillsdale, NJ: Lawrence Erlbaum Associates Inc.

Amsel, E., Robbins, M., Tumarkin, T., Foulkes, S., Janit, A., & Smalley, J.D. (1999). *The development of children's counterfactual thinking about emotions.* Manuscript submitted for publication.

Aronson, J.N., Golomb, C., & Kirkpatrick, L. (June, 1997). *Bridging the gap between implicit and explicit representation and exploring the effects of training on preschoolers' understanding of pretense.* Paper presented at the 26th Annual Symposium of the Jean Piaget Society. Santa Monica, CA.

Bloom, L., & Lahey, M. (1978). *Language development and language disorders.* New York: John Wiley & Sons.

Bretherton, I., & Beeghly, M. (1989). Pretense: Acting "as if". In J.J. Lockman & L. Hazen (Eds.), *Action in social context* (pp. 239–271). New York: Plenum Press.

Bruell, M.J., & Woolley, J.D. (1998). Young children's understanding of diversity in pretense. *Cognitive Development, 13,* 257–277.

Chandler, M., & Lalonde, C. (1996). Shifting to an interpretative theory of mind: 5- to 7-year-olds' changing conceptions of mental life. In A.J. Sameroff & M.M. Haith (Eds.), *The five to seven year shift: The age of reason and responsibility* (pp. 111–139). Chicago, IL: The University of Chicago Press.

Custer, W.L. (1996). A comparison of young children's understanding of contradictory mental representations in pretense, memory, and belief. *Child Development, 67,* 678–688.

Davis, D.L., Woolley, J.D., & Bruell, M.J. (1997). *Young children's representation of pretense as a mental representation.* Unpublished manuscript, University of Texas at Austin.

DiLalla L.F., & Watson, M. (1988). Differentiation of fantasy and reality: Preschoolers' reactions to interruptions in their pretend play. *Developmental Psychology, 24,* 268–291.

Elder, J.L., & Pederson, D.R. (1978). Preschool children's use of objects in symbolic play. *Child Development, 49,* 500–504.

Fay, A., & Klahr, D. (1996). Knowing about guessing and guessing about knowing: Preschoolers' understanding of indeterminacy. *Child Development, 67,* 689–716.

Flavell, J., Flavell, E., & Green, F. (1989). Young children's knowledge of the apparent-real and pretend-real distinction. *Developmental Psychology, 23,* 816–822.

Forguson, L., & Gopnik, A. (1988). The ontogeny of common sense. In J.W. Astington, P.L. Harris, & D.R. Olson (Eds.), *Developing theories of mind* (pp. 226–243). New York: Cambridge University Press.

Gopnik, A., & Meltzoff, A. (1997). *Words, thoughts, and theories.* Cambridge, MA: MIT Press.

Gopnik, A., & Slaughter, V. (1991). Young children's understanding of changes in their mental states. *Child Development, 62,* 89–109.

Goncu, A. (1993). Development of intersubjectivity in social pretend play. *Human Development, 36,* 185–198.

Harris, P.L. (1991). The work of the imagination. In A. Whiten (Ed.), *Natural theories of mind* (pp. 283–304). Oxford, UK: Basil Blackwell.

Harris, P. (1993). Pretending and planning. In S. Baron-Cohen, H. Tager-Flusberg, & D.J. Cohen (Eds.), *Understanding other minds: Perspectives from autism* (pp. 112–137). New York: Oxford University Press.

Harris, P.L. (1994). Understanding pretence. In C. Lewis & P. Mitchell (Eds.), *Origins of an understanding of mind* (pp. 235–260). Hove, UK: Lawrence Erlbaum Associates Ltd.

Harris, P.L., German, T., & Mills, P. (1996). Children use of counterfactual thinking in causal reasoning. *Cognition, 61,* 233–259.

Harris, P.L., & Kavanaugh, R.D. (1993). *Young children's understanding of pretense.* Monographs of the Society for Research in Child Development, 58 (1, Serial No. 231).

Harris, P.L., Kavanaugh, R.D., & Meredith, M.C. (1994). Young children's comprehension of pretend episodes: The integration of successive actions. *Child Development, 65,* 16–30.

Hickling, A.K., Wellman, H.M., & Gottfried, G.M. (1997). Preschoolers' understanding of others' mental attitudes toward pretend happenings. *The British Journal of Developmental Psychology 15,* 339–354.

Jackowitz, E.R., & Watson, M.W. (1980). The development of object transformations in early pretend play. *Developmental Psychology, 16,* 543–549.

Kahneman, D., & Tversky, A. (1982). The simulation heuristic. In D. Kahneman, P. Slovic, & A. Tversky (Eds.), *Judgment under uncertainty: Heuristics and biases* (pp. 201–208). New York: Cambridge University Press.

Inhelder, B., & Piaget, J. (1958). *The growth of logical thinking from childhood to adolescence.* New York: Basic Books.

Leslie, A. (1987). Pretense and representation: The origins of "theory of mind". *Psychological Review, 94,* 412–426.

Leslie, A. (1988). Some implications of pretense for mechanisms underlying the child's theory of mind. In J.W. Astington, P.L. Harris, & D.R. Olson (Eds.), *Developing theories of mind* (pp. 19–46). New York: Cambridge University Press.

Leslie, A. (1994). Pretending and believing: Issues in the theory of ToMM. *Cognition, 50,* 211–238.

Leslie, A., & Roth, D. (1993). What autism teaches use about metarepresentation. In S. Baron-Cohen, H. Tager-Flusberg, & D.J. Cohen (Eds.), *Understanding other minds: Perspectives from autism* (pp. 112–137). New York: Oxford University Press.

Lillard, A. (1993a). Pretend play skills and the child's theory of mind. *Child Development, 64*, 348–371.

Lillard, A. (1993b). Young children's conceptualization of pretense: Action or mental representational state? *Child Development, 64*, 372–386.

Lillard, A. (1994). Making sense of pretence. In C. Lewis & P. Mitchell (Eds.), *Children's early understanding of mind* (pp. 211–234). Hove, UK: Lawrence Erlbaum Associates Ltd.

Lillard, A. (1996). Body or mind: Children's categorizing of pretense. *Child Development, 67*, 1717–1734.

Lillard, A. (1998). Wanting to be it: Children's understanding of intentions underlying pretense. *Child Development, 69*, 979–991.

Mandel, D.R., & Lehman, D.R. (1996). Counterfactual thinking and ascriptions of cause and preventability. *Journal of Personality and Social Psychology, 71*, 450–463.

N'gbala, A., & Branscombe, N. (1995). Mental simulation of causal attribution: When simulating an event does not affect fault assignment. *Journal of Experimental Social Psychology, 31*, 139–162.

O'Reilly, A.W. (1995). Using representations. Comprehension and production of actions with imagined objects. *Child Development, 66*, 999–1010.

Overton, W.F., & Jackson, J.P. (1973). The representation of imagined objects in action sequences: A developmental study. *Child Development, 44*, 306–314.

Pederson, D.R., Rook-Green, A., & Elder, J.L. (1981). The role of action in the development of pretend play in young children. *Developmental Psychology, 17*, 756–759.

Perner, J. (1988). Developing semantics for theories of mind: From propositional attitudes to mental representations. In J.W. Astington, P.L. Harris, & D.R. Olson (Eds.), *Developing theories of mind* (pp. 141–158). New York: Cambridge University Press.

Perner, J. (1991). *Understanding the representational mind*. Cambridge, MA: MIT Press.

Perner J., Baker, S., & Hutton, D. (1994). Prelief: The conceptual origin of beliefs and pretence. In C. Lewis & P. Mitchell (Eds.), *Children's early understanding of mind* (pp. 261–286). Hove, UK: Lawrence Erlbaum Associates Ltd.

Piaget, J. (1962). *Plays, dreams, and imitation in childhood*. New York: Norton.

Piaget, J. (1970). Piaget's theory. In P.H. Mussen (Ed.), *Carmichael's manual of child psychology* (Vol. 1, pp. 703–732). New York: John Wiley & Sons.

Piaget, J. (1987). *Possibility and necessity*. Minneapolis, MI: University of Minnesota Press.

Pitt, R.B. (1983). Development of general problem-solving schema in adolescence and early adulthood. *Journal of Experimental Psychology: General, 4*, 547–584.

Roese, N. (1997). Counterfactual thinking. *Psychological Bulletin, 121*, 133–148.

Rubin, K.H., Fein, G.G., & Vandenberg, B. (1983). Play. In P.H. Mussen (Series Ed.), E.M. Hetherington (Vol. Ed.), *Handbook of child development* (Vol. 4, pp. 693–774). New York: John Wiley & Sons.

Sosa, E. (1981). Introduction. In E. Sosa (Ed.), *Causation and conditionals* (pp. 1–14). Oxford: Oxford University Press.

Ungerer, J., Zelazo, P.R., Kearsley, R.B., & O'Leary, K. (1981). Developmental changes in the representation of objects in symbolic play from 18 to 34 months of age. *Child Development, 52*, 186–195.

Walker-Andrews, A.S., & Harris, P.L. (1993). Young children's comprehension of pretend causal sequence. *Developmental Psychology, 29*, 915–921.

Wellman, H., & Gelman, S. (1992). Cognitive development: Foundational theories for core domains. *Annual Reviews in Psychology, 43*, 337–375.

Wells, G., & Gavanski, I. (1989). Mental simulation of causality. *Journal of Social and Personality Psychology, 56*, 161–169.

Woolley, J.D., & Wellman, H.M. (1993). Origin and truth: Young children's understanding of imaginary representations. *Child Development, 64*, 1–17.

Woolley, J.D. (1995). The fictional mind: Young children's understanding of imagination, pretense, and dreams. *Developmental Review, 15*, 172–211.

Woolley, J.D. (1997). Thinking about fantasy: Are children fundamentally different thinkers and believers from adults? *Child Development, 68*, 991–1011.

CHAPTER EIGHT

Theory of mind, domain specificity, and reasoning

Douglas Frye
University of Pennsylvania, USA

INTRODUCTION

Theory of mind has often been characterised as being domain specific, in the sense formulated by Fodor (1983) and applied to development by Carey (1985). This claim means something like the principles and evidence we use in understanding mental states are different from those employed in other domains (e.g. naïve physics, biology) and, as a consequence, the developments in this domain are independent of changes in the others. The possibility that theory of mind is domain specific has been argued cogently by the "Theory theory" view (Gopnik & Wellman, 1994), which explains the development of mental state understanding as a succession in theories that the child forms, and by modularity accounts (Baron-Cohen, 1994; Leslie, 1994b), which identify mental state understanding with one or a number of innate mental modules.

An odd aspect of the view that theory of mind is domain specific is that it is one Fodor's (1983) own approach to modularity would explicitly disclaim. Fodor divides psychological processes into the two broad categories of input systems and central systems. Input systems correspond basically to perceptual processes. The central systems are what are involved in thought and problem solving. Fodor states that he distinguishes between "what the input systems compute and what the organism (consciously or subdoxastically) *believes*" (p. 102, emphasis in the original) and that "Even if input systems are domain specific, there must be some cognitive systems that are not" (p. 102).

It is of interest to see how Fodor reaches these conclusions. In this formulation, domain specificity depends on the sorts of determinations a system can make. So, for example, there may a domain specific input system that handles the perception of colour. Fodor additionally argues that the input systems are

149

modular. The most important feature of modularity is information encapsulation. In the colour example, in other words, the information that is used to perceive colour is restricted to that module and is not influenced by information from other modules. A quick illustration of the effects of encapsulation is that having knowledge of a perceptual illusion typically does not alter the illusion. It is because input systems are domain specific and encapsulated that the central systems cannot be. When we see the world, the central systems must operate across different input systems (they are not domain specific) and they must bring in information from other sources including memory (they are not encapsulated).

Fodor introduces an analogy to scientific reasoning to indicate why the central systems cannot be domain specific or encapsulated. He points out that in testing scientific hypotheses, and even more so in forming them, it is impossible to stay rigidly within domains. He says (1983, p. 105) that:

> . . . the facts relevant to the confirmation of a scientific hypothesis may be drawn from anywhere in the field of previously established empirical (or, of course, demonstrative) truths. Crudely: everything that the scientist knows is, in principle, relevant to determining what else he ought to believe. In principle, our botany constrains our astronomy, if only we could think of ways to make them connect.

The reason that information cannot be restricted to domains is that we do not know in advance what is going to be related to what. The possibility that what is known in one domain can affect what is known in another is needed for scientific theorising, and it is similarly needed for the individual's understanding of the world (or "nondemonstrative inference in the service of individual fixation of belief", Fodor, 1983, p. 105).

These arguments have implications for the entire enterprise of domain specific explanation in cognitive development. They are particularly relevant to theory of mind. When the relation of mental state understanding to other knowledge domains is considered, it becomes apparent that one will influence another. The older child's understanding that Maxi will look in the wrong cupboard for the chocolate clearly depends on the mental state accomplishment of being able to infer Maxi's false belief (Wimmer & Perner, 1983). However, the inference also depends on understanding the basic physical aspects of the situation. The child must know that objects can be moved, that they have a persistent existence, and that when they are moved they tend to stay in the new place. This non-theory-of-mind knowledge is necessary to piece together Maxi's false belief. Were the child's understanding of the mechanics of objects different, then the understanding of the mental states in this situation would be different as well. An outlandish example can illustrate the point. Assume that 3-year-olds still made the AB error. They would presumably predict that Maxi will look where the object originally was, but only because that is where they think it is too! It is clear that unless they can accurately keep track of where the object is, they are unlikely to discover that someone can be mistaken about its location.

One way to avoid the problem posed by interdependent domains is to move mental state understanding from the central to the input systems or, in other words, make it more of a matter of perception. Baron-Cohen (1994) appears to take this line when he proposes modules like the intentionality detector (ID), which computers others' intentions on the basis of the direction of their movements. It is not clear that modules like these can successfully carry out their designated tasks for the very reasons Fodor identifies. Assigning an intention on the basis of the direction of movements will tend to over-ascribe intentionality to every change in direction we or our hands happen to take (Gergely & Csibra, 1994). Moreover, there are times when we act intentionally by doing nothing at all, as in the case when we could have prevented something from happening but did not. These intentions can only be detected against an expectation of what should have happened. In other words, outside knowledge must be brought to bear at the central systems level. It will not be available in the immediate situation itself.

Another complication arises when theory of mind is assumed to be domain specific. It seems conceivable that mental state understanding is domain specific when other people's mental states are being considered. Even if encapsulated input systems are not sufficient to reveal those mental states, intuitively it still seems possible to identify a body of knowledge that encompasses our understanding of what other people are thinking, feeling, wanting, and the like. However, one of the consistent findings of theory of mind research is self–other equivalence. The most notable example is representational change (Gopnik & Astington, 1988; Wimmer & Hartl, 1991) which shows that 3-year-olds who lack an understanding of other people's false beliefs also do not acknowledge their own. Wellman and Woolley (1990) show that still younger children do not understand others' beliefs, even when those beliefs are not false. These younger children presumably would also not recognise that they themselves hold beliefs. Equivalence indicates that the domain of theory of mind must include the understanding of others' beliefs and our own. However, if own belief is included, it is difficult to see where the boundaries of the domain would be, because our beliefs can be about physics, biology or anything else. To the extent that belief is involved in all of our own thoughts, what is the contrasting domain?

An alternative way of stating this point is that it will be a mistake to equate mental state understanding with any particular subject matter or content. In this regard, theory of mind is quite unlike naïve physics or biology. These domains are identified by their content, theory of mind is not. Understanding a mental state like belief does not simply involve understanding the content of the belief, it demands recognising the connection between the mental state and that content. The propositional attitudes (e.g. I think that it is raining outside) illustrate this point because they construe mental state understanding as an attitude taken by an agent towards a statement. Attempting to make theory of mind domain specific collapses these distinctions. It creates the misleading impression that mental state understanding is another knowledge domain on a par with naïve physics or biology. It also loses the critical insight that mental state understanding involves a set of relations that takes those domains as content.

The arguments that knowledge requires central systems processes and that theory of mind ranges over other domains suggest that a non-denominational ability may be involved in the basic change in mental state understanding between 3 and 5 years. Perner's (1991) metarepresentation proposal was one of the first along these lines. The emergence of metarepresentation, or the representation of representation as representation, at about 4 years makes understanding false belief possible because the child becomes able to grasp that someone else can misrepresent a situation. The account has the proper characteristics. It is cast in terms of a central systems process because it treats representation as a system. It cuts across domains, as the 'meta' prefix suggests, because it concerns representation rather than what is being represented or, in other words, the system rather than the content.

Since Perner's original account, several other suggestions for the general process involved in the onset of theory of mind have been made. They include how much information the child is able to "hold in mind" (Gordon & Olson, 1998; Olson, 1993), the number of simultaneous relations the child can form (Halford, 1993; Halford, Wilson, & Phillips, 1998), and the complexity of reasoning the child can sustain (Frye, Zelazo, & Palfai, 1992, 1995; Zelazo & Frye, 1997). These suggested processes bear a resemblance to simulation (Harris, 1992) except that they have application beyond reasoning about others' points of view. They differ from the familiar Theory theory framework in that they reject complete domain specificity, and they propose that changes in theory of mind occur not just because of changes in the child's theory but because of developments in the child's psychological capabilities.

COGNITIVE COMPLEXITY AND CONTROL THEORY

The explanatory value of reasoning complexity for theory of mind is taken up in Cognitive Complexity and Control theory. This account identifies a series of changes in reasoning during late infancy and pre-school, one of which is thought to be crucial for the improvement in theory of mind at about four years (Frye et al., 1992, 1995; Zelazo & Frye, 1997). The emphasis on reasoning in the account is very much akin to the role Fodor assigns to non-demonstrative inference as a prototypic central systems process. Unlike it, the CCC account proposes that there are genuine developmental changes in reasoning, a possibility that Fodor (1980) would presumably deny.[1] The effects of these changes are predicted to be important beyond theory of mind because reasoning or inference rules apply across multiple domains. Thus, the reasoning account will foresee broader

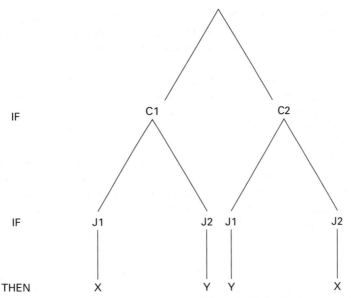

FIG. 8.1 Tree structure illustrating the complexity of the embedded rules judgements in which setting conditions (C1, C2) control the application of judgements (J1, J2) that produce conflicting outcomes (X, Y) across related perspectives or contexts.

non-denominational consequences than metarepresentation, for example, because the latter is restricted to representational systems (e.g. people, cameras, drawings).

Although CCC theory identifies several changes in reasoning during the pre-school period, the specific one the theory holds is important for the advance in mental state understanding at four years is formation of higher-order or embedded rules. The account claims that embedded inference rules are essential to understand the mental states—e.g. false belief—that become intelligible at this time. The need for these rules can be seen in the reasoning required to understand particular mental states. For example, understanding false belief requires, according to the account, that some aspect of an object (e.g. its location or identity) can be seen from two separate perspectives (e.g. the child's and Maxi's) and those perspectives produce incompatible judgements about that aspect of the object. Consequently, children become able to infer false belief when they can switch judgements flexibly in line with whichever perspective is being asked about.

The theory proposes that children become able to switch judgements in these situations by embedding one set of judgements within another, as illustrated in Fig. 8.1. Judgements here are governed by if–then rules or their logical equivalents. Increases in complexity correspond to increases in the degree of embedding. The developmental change that alters theory of mind occurs when the child is able to reflect upon the judgements that he or she can make, and become aware of the conflict. (I think one thing while Maxi will think another.)

By embedding one judgement within another, the child is able to use a higher-order, if–if–then rule to select the judgement (e.g. "If me, if looking for chocolate, then here" and "If Maxi, if looking for chocolate, then there") that is appropriate to each question. The added 'if', or the setting condition (self or Maxi), allows the child to select which location (here or there) should be inferred for the object in question. Thus, the higher-order rule controls the application of the individual (incompatible) judgements, forming them into an integrated system.

There are three features of this account that should be commented on: complexity, bias, and judgements. The account maintains that embedded rules are needed to infer mental states of a particular complexity. That complexity can be seen in the tree diagram shown in Fig. 8.1. Basically, to require embedded rules, the inference problem must have the potential of four outcomes (the four leaves of the inverted tree) and there must be a conflict in at least two of the outcomes that spans the width of the tree. Flavell (1988) early on identified the extensive role conflict appears to play in theory of mind and other problems in this period. The current account assigns a similar importance to conflict, but is different in that conflict is only thought to cause difficulty when it is coupled with the currently specified level of complexity.

Complexity provides a means to explain the relative difficulty of different theory of mind problems. It does *not* indicate that young pre-schoolers lack all understanding of mental states. The account specifies that 5-year-olds can employ embedded rules and hence can understand false belief. In contrast, 3-year-olds are assumed only to be able to apply simple if–then rules. In the sorts of problems typically given in theory of mind studies, this capacity roughly means that they can solve problems with the complexity of two potential outcomes. So, for example, 3-year-olds are able to solve a 'standard belief' problem in which they are told that a character thinks an object is in one of two locations and are asked where the character will search (Wellman & Bartsch, 1988). The children are not told the actual location of the object in this problem, so a simple if–then rule is all that is needed to encode the single piece of information of where the character thinks the object is. The account is also in accord with the findings that 3-year-olds can solve 'true belief' tasks (Wimmer & Perner, 1983); for example, the child and Maxi both see the chocolate being moved from one cupboard to another. Here, there are not two different perspectives, so the tree in Fig. 8.1 collapses and a pair of simple if–then rules is enough to specify correctly where the object was before and where it is now.

Three-year-olds' performance will also be characterised by bias according to the CCC account (Frye et al., 1995, p. 504; Frye, Zelazo, Brooks, & Samuels, 1996, p. 130; Zelazo & Frye, 1997, pp. 129, 141). Bias gives an explanation of young children's characteristic errors. When 3-year-olds are confronted with a too complex problem like that of false belief, they nonetheless try to solve it with the abilities at their disposal. Specifically, when given an if–if–then problem, they reduce it to an if–then problem and solve that (see Halford et al., 1998, for a similar account). In the instance of false belief, this formulation means that they will lose the setting condition or perspective and be faced with the problem of where to search to find the object. The straightforward conclusion on the basis of past experience is to search where the object is. This conclusion will result in a reality bias that P. Mitchell (Mitchell & Kikuno, Chapter 14, this volume) rightly identifies as an informative property of 3-year-olds' lack of success on theory of mind problems, but mistakenly says is absent from CCC theory.

As the preceding discussion shows, bias is not an additional, independent term in the account. Bias is thought to arise because of the child's previous experience. It will occur when the child has been exposed to similar situations in the past (see the discussion of causality below), but it can also be induced experimentally (e.g. in the dimensional change card sort; Zelazo & Jacques, 1997). Bias also illustrates that setting conditions typically function to allow a change in judgements or the making of an exception. It is because the child is accustomed to making a judgement in a stereotypic fashion (someone will search for an object where it is) that a setting condition is needed to reach a new conclusion. Another way of stating this point is that embedded rules are not sufficient to support a combining of perspectives (or, more generally, dimensions) in the sense of the classic Piagetian conservation and matrix classification problems. Embedded rules are developmentally prior in that they only allow the child to *ignore* a familiar or predominant perspective (self) in order to make a judgement from another, less familiar one (Maxi).

Finally, it needs to be mentioned that the term 'judgement' is meant to be active in the account. Children are thought to be making actual judgements in the theory of mind problems, and that in part is why reasoning is involved. P. Mitchell (Mitchell & Kikuno, this volume) raises the interesting example of Wellman and Bartsch's (1988) explicit false belief task in which children are shown the location of the object and directly told Maxi's false belief about it. The mystery of this task is that 3-year-olds do not solve it in spite of being provided with Maxi's belief. (See the later 'Example evidence' section for a similar example in which 3-year-olds misjudge causality in spite of being given the correct rule.) In the explicit false belief task, the children nonetheless make a judgement, even though they should only attend to Maxi's stated belief. Without setting conditions, they apply the if–then rules that they have, as was outlined before, and infer where to find the object. Because the location of the object is known, it generates the usual reality errors. This same point indicates why making the location of the object less salient, by describing it rather than showing it, improves 3-year-olds' performance (Zaitchik, 1991).

EXTENSIONS TO THE ACCOUNT

To be a useful account of the 3- to 5-year transition in theory of mind, this part of CCC theory must not only apply to false belief, but also to the developments that are closely related to it. At least two of those developments are appearance-reality and representational change (Gopnik & Astington, 1988). The two perspectives here do not map to different people because both tasks involve the child's own judgements. The tasks still have a complexity comparable to false belief, however, because they encompass two different judgements and a before–after dimension. Thus, in appearance-reality, the child initially sees the appearance and reality of, say, the rock-sponge as being a rock, but after touching it must reach the conflicting judgement that it really is a sponge. Representational change also involves two different judgements (Saltmarsh, Mitchell, & Robinson, 1995; Samuels, Brooks, & Frye, 1997) and a before–after change. The sequence of events is the same except that after learning what the object actually is, children must state the conflicting answer of what they originally thought it was. As usual, 3-year-olds are assumed to apply simple if–then rules to these problems and to make judgements in response to the questions. As a consequence, they tend to give the same answer to the questions of what the object is and what it appears to be or what they had thought it was.

It has also been suggested that theory of mind should be related to executive function (Frye et al., 1995; Ozonoff, Pennington, & Rogers, 1991; Russell, Mauthner, Sharpe, & Tidswell, 1991), and subsequent research has verified this relation (Carlson, 1997; Hughes, 1998). CCC theory was designed to bear on critical elements of executive function as the 'Control' term in the name indicates. It is most relevant to the executive functions of planning and deliberative action. It classifies the majority of theory of mind tasks as inference problems because they require the child to infer a mental state from a given set of circumstances. These are thought to be matched by an equally complex set of action problems that require the child to manipulate circumstances in order to produce a target mental state.

The most familiar example within theory of mind is inferring false belief versus deception, or intentionally acting to give someone a false belief (Brooks, Frye, & Samuels, 1997; Carlson, Moses, & Hix, 1998; Wimmer & Perner, 1983). CCC theory suggests that the relation between false belief and deception can be attributed to their joint dependence on if–if–then rules, with the difference being that the consequent must be inferred in false belief compared to one of the antecedents in deception. In false belief, the child is given a person and a particular situation, and must infer the resultant mental state. In deception, the child is given the person and the target mental state, and must infer what situation will produce the target. The same rules are involved in both. Dependence on the same rules would also explain why false belief is related to other executive function accomplishments that, for example, involve control of the child's own actions rather than the manipulation of others' mental states. These points are described more fully elsewhere (Frye, 1998; Zelazo, Carter, Reznick, & Frye, 1997).

EXAMPLE EVIDENCE

The current account is interactional in the sense that both non-denominational and domain-specific processes are thought to be involved in the acquisition of theory of mind (see also Amsel & Smalley, Chapter 7, this volume). Judgements constitute the more domain-specific aspect. They will differ, and in particular the evidence used to make them will differ, depending on what is being reasoned about. These differences will occur even within theory of mind because different mental states will require different judgements. For instance, the evidence used to infer what someone thinks or believes will be very different from the evidence used to judge what someone wants or desires. The judgements needed outside of theory of mind will be different again still. In spite of the differences in judgements, if theory of mind also depends on a non-denominational reasoning process, then the effects of that process should be just as apparent in other developments during this period. The dimensional change card sort (Zelazo & Jacques, 1997) has proved to be very productive in demonstrating these related developments. Causal reasoning serves as another example that can help to illustrate the similarities that occur in bias and in the effect complexity has on bias.

Understanding physical causality is no less important to the child than theory of mind. Causality forms the basis for any understanding of the physical world. The effects of a change in reasoning as outlined in the CCC approach should be evident in this domain. They should be detectable in specific causal problems that reflect the same complexity as false belief and the other 3- to 5-year theory of mind developments—i.e. causal problems that encompass four possible outcomes, at least two of which are in conflict. To test this possibility, we constructed a device meeting these requirements. The physical causality analog had children reason about an enclosed ramp that worked in two distinct configurations. It had two holes at the top in which a marble could be placed and two holes at the bottom from which it could roll out (see Frye et al., 1997, for a photograph). In one configuration, marbles rolled across the ramp from either input hole; whereas in the other, they rolled straight down from either input. The child had to infer the causal sequence to predict where the marble would emerge. Making the predictions led to incompatible judgements because a marble put in either hole at the top could come out of either hole at the bottom depending on the configuration of the apparatus.

The device yielded the expected 3- to 5-year age difference (Frye et al., 1995). The 3-year-olds were typically only able to predict for one configuration of the ramp and did not change their predictions when the configuration switched. They were not able to predict accurately even though they were first shown the entire workings of the device and subsequently told the correct rule on *every* trial. In contrast, the 5-year-olds' causal predictions were virtually perfect for both configurations of the ramp. Performance on this task was correlated with false belief understanding, and remained so after the effects of age were removed. Taken together, the results confirm an age-related change in both causal prediction and false belief understanding during this period, and indicate that individual children's performance was associated for the two.

The results exhibit the expected effect of complexity. Accurate predictions for both configurations of the ramp require if–if–then rules with setting conditions—e.g. "if in the straight configuration, if placed in left, then emerge left" and "if in across configuration, if placed in left, then emerge right". Simple if–then rules are not sufficient to predict accurately in both configurations. The complexity interpretation is further enhanced by the finding that 3-year-olds can make accurate predictions when only simple if–then rules are required. They succeed when the device is modified so that there is only one input hole present (Frye et al., 1997). This change reduces the possible states that can be considered to two, and removes the need for an input conditional in the rules. As a consequence, correct predictions (e.g. for a single input hole on the left) can be made with the simple if–then rules of "if straight, then emerge left" and "if across, then emerge right". The 3-year-olds' success shows that complexity, and not just switching responses or inhibition, is what is crucial, because they could switch with the less complex task.

The ramp causality task exhibits an additional similarity to theory of mind. The 3-year-olds displayed a bias. They entered the study with the expectation that the marble should roll straight down the ramp. Even when they began with the across configuration, they tended to predict the marble would emerge directly below where it was put. This bias is comparable to the 3-year-olds' reality bias in false belief. Given the chance, 3-year-olds tend to judge someone will look for an object where it is, regardless of whether the person has seen it there before. Both biases are likely to be the result of previous experience. Marbles typically do roll straight down inclined planes and an object's real location is usually a good guide to where to search for it. The causality results provide another important finding, however. The 3-year-olds did not show a bias in the simplified ramp task. They were able to make predictions for the across trials when only one input hole was involved. This pattern indicates that bias interacts with complexity. It is only when children are presented with a problem that is more complex than their reasoning allows that they default to a simpler solution, one that previous experience has often shown to be accurate.

CHALLENGES FOR THE ACCOUNT

The preceding findings looked for a similar developmental pattern between two content areas, theory of mind and physical causality, that were deliberately chosen to be unlike. The observed similarities speak for a non-denominational reasoning process being involved in both. The connection across widely separated domains seems to promise that it would not be difficult to find analogous connections for more closely related ones. Nonetheless, the doubts that have been raised about the utility of a non-denominational process have often come from theory of mind research, usually in regards to mental states besides belief. The two most obvious examples are pretence and desire. Leslie (1994a) has employed the evidence of early understanding of pretence to argue against Perner's non-denominational process of metarepresentation, but the age discrepancy is equally problematic for CCC theory. Similarly, Bartsch and Wellman (1995) have raised the possibility that early success on desire may have troubling implications for CCC theory.

Leslie (1987) points out that infants typically begin to engage in pretence sometime between 18 and 24 months. Pretence takes many forms at 2 years but it can include making sense of someone else pretending to use a banana as a telephone or pretending that an empty cup contains water. Leslie accords full propositional attitude status to the child's understanding of these episodes. He credits them with recognising the role of the agent, attitude, and object of the attitude in an M-representation. Interestingly, he accepts self-other equivalence and contends that there should not be a developmental gap between the understanding of own and other's pretence. Furthermore, his theory (Leslie, 1994a) incorporates a selection processor that develops over the course of the pre-school period and might accommodate general problem solving rules akin to the ones in CCC theory. These rules are different, however, in that they are additional to a theory of mind module that is independently responsible for computing mental states including belief. Improvements in the selection processor increasingly allow children older than 2 years to overcome complicated task demands to display their already existing understanding of mental states.

If Leslie is right about very young children's understanding of pretence, and in particular the representations that underlie that understanding, then the assigned roles of both Perner's (1991) metarepresentation and CCC theory's embedded rules at four years come too late. Counterclaims to this rich an interpretation of early pretence already exist. Lillard (1993a; see also Mitchell, Chapter 3, this volume) has made the case that early pretence may be based on action rather than mental representation. The early forms of pretence do seem to be tied to characteristic actions. When the child recognises that someone is pretending a banana is a telephone, it is done in the context of someone holding the banana up and talking into it. Moreover, action at first appears to be all that is considered in determinations of pretence. Lillard (1993b) told children a story about a character who was hopping up and down like a rabbit but did not know what a rabbit was. She found that until about 5 years of age (see also Perner, Baker, & Hutton, 1994) children conclude that the character is pretending to be a rabbit. This result indicates that although children can make some judgements about pretence early on, they cannot do so in reference to what adults consider to be a necessary precondition to pretending.

This pattern is in agreement with CCC theory because the theory expects a change in the complexity of the child's understanding of pretence. The early understanding of pretence is based on action. Or, an even better characterisation might be to acknowledge that it is based on intentional action. Children near the age of two years are adept at inferring the goals of people's actions (Frye, 1991; Meltzoff, 1995), and this period ought to be characterised by the use of means and goals to analyse others' behaviour (Frye, 1992). If so, pretend actions could be identified as those in which it is absolutely clear that the action cannot accomplish its goal (e.g. when someone pretends to drink water from an empty cup). This analysis has the advantages that it is general, so it will not be the action itself that defines it as an instance of pretence, but the relation of the action to the circumstances. It nonetheless preserves the idea that action is required because young children will need to see the action to judge that it is out of place. It finally indicates that young children should not distinguish pretend actions from mistaken ones (Perner et al., 1994), because both fit the description of being actions that are overtly inconsistent with their circumstances.

Using these grounds to conclude that an action is pretence should only require simple if–then rules because all that is being compared is the action and the circumstance in which it is being performed. A more complicated understanding of pretence becomes possible with setting conditions. One such instance occurs when pretence is put in the format of the appearance-reality task in which the child must make sequential judgements of what the object is being pretended to be and what it really is (Flavell, Flavell, & Green, 1987; Frye et al., 1995). Although children appear to succeed on pretend-reality before appearance-reality, both tasks produce a 3- to 4-year age difference indicating that a developmental change occurs. The same considerations may apply to Lillard's discovery. When hopping up and down is being done for no apparent reason, it can be identified as an instance of pretence. However, a setting condition or additional if-statement is needed to code that the actor must be acquainted with rabbits. Should children not be able to add the setting condition, then they will not be able to restrict the judgement of pretence only to those specific instances in which the actor knows about the topic of the pretence.

The story for desire is much the same. Wellman and Woolley (1990) found that older 2-year-olds have an impressive understanding of desire. They can state what someone wants, and recognise the specificity of the desire because they know that the desire will not be fulfilled by some other favourable outcome. Bartsch and Wellman (1995) point out that 3-year-olds seem to be able to reason about conflicts in desires. They can correctly state that a person had one desire previously and has a quite different desire now (Gopnik & Slaughter, 1991). They also appear to understand that one person can like something whereas another person dislikes it (Flavell, Flavell, Green, & Moses, 1990). This constellation of findings would suggest an earlier understanding of desire that would violate the timing of the developmental changes expected by CCC theory.

A careful evaluation of the desire results suggests they do not contradict CCC theory. Recognising the specificity of another's desire is a matter of simple if–then rules because all that is being compared is the person's goal and the actual outcome. The conflict cases are more interesting; however, they also would not require embedded rules according to the account. Judging someone's past and present desire is analogous to judging someone's understanding of a past and present state of the world or, in other words, it is on a par with true belief. As long as it is only one person and both judgements are about desire, then the complexity account would hold that there is a single before–after dimension involved, which 3-year-olds ought to be able to comprehend. The simultaneous conflict in desires is similar. Here, there are two people but no time dimension. Each desire can be unambiguously associated with one character and the other (much like the simple ramp causality task in which one outcome is associated unambiguously with each output hole). Again, a pair of simple rules ought to be sufficient for 3-year-olds to determine that "if it is this person, it's this desire" and "if that person, that desire."

This *post hoc* analysis would be strengthened if it could be shown that there were desire problems that required embedded rules and that these problems fit the 3- to 5-year age change. Moore et al. (1995) found just such a development. They had children engage in a simple competitive game in which the child and another person originally needed the same playing card. The child's desires then changed upon receiving this card. Three-year-olds did not seem to understand that they and the other player now wanted different things. Embedded rules are needed for this problem because, just like false belief, it involves both a time dimension and two different actors. The problem has the complexity of four potential outcomes—the two actors by the two cards—and the two final outcomes are in direct conflict. Nguyen and Frye (1999) found a comparable age change in desire understanding for a non-competitive social situation. Berger, Nguyen, and Frye (1998) have shown that the same effect can be obtained with one character's desires towards the physical world, demonstrating that the results are not unique to social situations.

These more recent results for pretence and desire affirm the interaction between domain specific and non-denominational processes described in CCC theory. Different mental states require different judgements. Each is inferred on the basis of different evidence. What is relevant to deciding what someone believes is different from what is relevant to deciding what the person wants. Nonetheless, these judgements are bounded by non-denominational reasoning processes. The change at 4 years of adding setting conditions to form embedded rules makes it possible to solve new mental state inference problems of a certain complexity. As the pretence and desire results illustrate, the domain specific and non-denominational interaction leads to a pattern in which one mental state does not precede the development of another, but rather that related changes can be identified across various mental states.

COUNTERFACTUALITY AND CCC THEORY

Finding similar changes across different mental states, and across causality and executive function, offers positive evidence that a change in a non-denominational reasoning process is an integral part of these developments. Another straightforward form of evidence would be to investigate the change in reasoning *per se*. It should be possible to verify that a shift in reasoning occurs during the pre-school period. The change should be evident apart from the understanding of mental states. Nonetheless, it should be related to the improvement seen in the child's understanding of mental states.

Riggs, Peterson, Robinson, and Mitchell (1998) have isolated such a change and demonstrated that it is related to theory of mind. In one of their studies, they presented pre-schoolers with various Maxi or change-in-object-location stories. One story described a character at work on a painting, the character then went off to school, and subsequently the wind blew the painting to a new location. As usual, the events make it possible to ask a false belief question about where the character thinks the painting is, but it also makes it possible to ask a counterfactural reasoning question about where the painting would be if the wind had not blown. Pre-schoolers strongly tended to be either right on both problems or wrong on both. In a separate study, children who answered the counterfactual question incorrectly could use a simple conditional to reason correctly in a future hypothetical of, roughly, "if this action is done, then what will happen".

The Riggs et al. (1998) results come as a part of a renewed interest in counterfactual reasoning stimulated by Harris and his colleagues (see Harris, 1993; Harris & Leevers, Chapter 4, this volume). They have studied how pre-schoolers are able to overcome the challenge of reasoning about situations that run counter to the state of the world. The problems are presented as elementary syllogisms—e.g. "All cats bark. Rex is a cat. Does Rex bark?". Pre-schoolers and slightly older children have difficulty with these problems, often giving answers that agree with the state of the world rather than the problem's counterfactual premise. Dias and Harris (1988) have collected convincing evidence, however, that 4- to 6-year-olds' reasoning can be much improved if they are encouraged to take a make-belief stance towards the problems. Indeed, a wide variety of manipulations—use of imagery, reading the problem with a storybook intonation, situating it on a different planet—are effective (Dias & Harris, 1990), and remain effective over a period of at least several weeks (Harris & Leevers, Chapter 4, this volume).

The pattern for counterfactual reasoning is compatible with CCC theory (for an example in moral reasoning see Zelazo, Helwig, & Lau, 1996). Both the Riggs et al. and Harris problems have the complexity and bias expected by the theory. Both types of problems stand in contrast to a line of reasoning in the real world that is familiar to the child. In the Harris syllogism, for instance, cats could bark or meow in the real world with the correct conditional rule being "if cat, then meow". In the counterfactual situation, two alternatives are also possible, cats could bark or meow, but now the opposite or conflicting inference is correct, "if cat, then bark". Embedded or higher-order rules, as shown in Fig. 8.1, are necessary to remove the conflict. The conflicting inferences must be subsumed under another rule that makes it possible to choose between them. Setting conditions in if–if–then rules permit the choice. A likely rule would be "if this story, if a cat, then barks". The original syllogism itself fits this frame, "if all cats bark, if Rex is a cat, then Rex barks", although the empirical evidence is not currently available to decide if children process the syllogism in just this fashion.

The CCC account also illuminates additional findings from the research. Riggs et al. (1998) found that children could solve an if–then future hypothetical ("if this is done, then what will happen") before they could solve a Maxi-like counterfactual ("if this had not happened, then what would be the case"). This difference coincides with CCC theory because the future hypothetical is a simple if–then conditional that is not in conflict with the current situation. In fact, the future hypothetical must be compatible with the current situation for the action to be possible to carry out. The counterfactual, in contrast, requires the child to ignore what has occurred (the current situation), assume a different set of circumstances, and reason from them to a conclusion that conflicts with the current situation.

The Harris findings are also interpretable. The make-believe manipulation is very likely effective because it explicitly helps children form a setting condition to partition the conflicting inferences. The different inferences can be isolated with the added conditional. The improvement should not be limited to imagery alone because the setting condition could as easily be formed around the conditional of "if in this story". Furthermore, the effects ought to persist because the children are not just adopting a make-believe stance, but are being given practical experience in a successful form of reasoning.

Although the CCC account can interpret the current findings on counterfactual reasoning, its value as a theory depends on whether it makes unique predictions for further findings. The most obvious prediction is for an age effect. If 3-year-olds have difficulty forming embedded rules, then in spite of giving them experience with a make-believe stance their performance in the Harris syllogisms should remain significantly worse than 4- and 5-year-olds. This manipulation has apparently not been tested with children younger than four years. The CCC approach would also anticipate broader effects than the term "counterfactual" would suggest. Indeed, counterfactuality may be a misnomer. The account would expect that young children should have difficulty, not when a premise conflicts with reality, but when it conflicts with the child's experience. Instead of just a reality bias, violating the conventional and the familiar will also lead to trouble (see also Riggs & Peterson, this volume). So, for instance, the premise "All adults crawl around the house"—which is probably true because all adults are likely at one time or another to crawl around looking for something—would be difficult according to CCC theory even though it is not strictly counterfactual, only countertypical. Finally, the account would stipulate that countertypicality will interact with complexity. It predicts that being countertypical alone is not sufficient. Countertypicality will surpass the understanding of 3-year-olds when it is present in problems, like the temporal sequence of events in the Maxi-type stories, that have a complexity requiring embedded rules.

CONCLUSION

Theory of mind's lack of encapsulation and its dependence on a set of relations rather than a particular content make it a poor candidate for domain specificity. Interestingly, Fodor's *Modularity of Mind* (1983), which occasioned the domain specific approaches to mental state understanding, may argue credibly against the form they have taken. There is now converging empirical evidence for the involvement of a non-denominational process in the development of children's theory of mind. In line with that evidence, CCC theory characterises mental state understanding as an interaction between domain specific judgements and a non-denominational reasoning process that incorporates embedded rules at about four years. The effects of the change in reasoning can be seen in the core theory of mind developments, executive function, and the understanding of physical causality. The latest findings suggest that, opposed to commonly held assumptions, it is also apparent in pretence and the understanding of desire. The new research that focuses directly on the nature of reasoning in the pre-school period seems also to be having the added effect of showing the importance of non-denominational reasoning in theory of mind.

NOTE

1. Fodor's (1992) recent account of children's theory of mind cites the 1983 *Modularity* book, but it is interesting to speculate how well it conforms to the arguments of the book, or at least to the present rendering of them. The 1992 explanation is designed to show that there is no fundamental change in children's theory of mind with age. Performance changes between three and four years because of the heuristics that the child adopts to reason about beliefs and desires. Beliefs and desires in this account are a part of an "innate, modularized database" (p. 284). Hence, contrary to the assertions made here, Fodor treats these entities as domain specific and presumably relies on the perceptual system to derive them. The apparent change in theory of mind between three and four years occurs because there is an age-related change in the computational resources the child has available, which in turn favours the application of a more reliable belief–desire heuristic. The increase in computational resources, like the present approach, is a non-denominational change, but it is unlikely Fodor would want to identify it as a change in the central system itself. Whether a change in resources stops short of a change in how (and consequently what) the system computes is not easily determined without a detailed account of the cognitive model that Fodor is proposing.

ACKNOWLEDGEMENTS

Thanks are extended to P.D. Zelazo for his contributions to this chapter. I am indebted to Aileen Tang for the "All adults crawl around the house" example.

REFERENCES

Baron-Cohen, S. (1994). How to build a baby that can read minds: Cognitive mechanisms in mindreading. *Cahiers de Pyschologie Cognitive*, *83*, 513–552.

Bartsch, K., & Wellman, H.M. (1995). *Children talk about the mind*. New York: Oxford University Press.

Berger, S., Nguyen, L., & Frye, D. (1998, May). *The effect of conflict and context on young children's understanding of desire*. Poster presented at the meetings of the American Psychological Society, Washington, DC.

Brooks, P.J., Frye, D., & Samuels, M.C. (1997). *The comprehension and production of deception for self and other*. Manuscript submitted for publication.

Carey, S. (1985). *Conceptual change in childhood*. Cambridge, MA: MIT Press.

Carlson, S.M. (1997, April). *Individual differences in inhibitory control and children's theory of mind*. Meetings of the Society for Research in Child Development, Washington, DC.

Carlson, S.M., Moses, L.J., & Hix, H.R. (1998). The role of inhibitory processes in young children's difficulties with deception and false belief. *Child Development*, *69*, 672–691.

Dias, M.G., & Harris, P.L. (1988). The effect of make-believe play on deductive reasoning. *British Journal of Developmental Psychology*, *6*, 207–221.

Dias, M.G., & Harris, P.L. (1990). The influence of the imagination on reasoning by young children. *British Journal of Developmental Psychology*, *8*, 305–318.

Flavell, J.H. (1988). The development of children's knowledge about the mind: From cognitive connections to mental representations. In J.W. Astington, P.L. Harris, & D.R. Olson (Eds.), *Developing theories of mind* (pp. 244–267). Cambridge: Cambridge University Press.

Flavell, J.H., Flavell, E.R., & Green, F.L. (1987). Young children's knowledge about the apparent-real and pretend-real distinctions. *Developmental Psychology*, *23*, 816–822.

Flavell, J.H., Flavell, E.R., Green, F.L., & Moses, L.J. (1990). Young children's understanding of fact belief versus value beliefs. *Child Development*, *61*, 915–928.

Fodor, J.A. (1980). On the impossibility of acquiring "more powerful" structures. In M. Piatelli-Palmarini (Ed.), *Language and learning: The debate between Jean Piaget and Noam Chomsky* (pp. 142–161). Cambridge, MA: Harvard University Press.

Fodor, J.A. (1983). *The modularity of mind*. Cambridge, MA: MIT Press.

Fodor, J.A. (1992). A theory of the child's theory of mind. *Cognition*, *44*,

Frye, D. (1991). The origins of intention in infancy. In D. Frye & C. Moore (Eds.), *Children's theories of mind* (pp. 15–38). Hillsdale, NJ: Lawrence Erlbaum Associates Inc.

Frye, D. (1992). Causes and precursors of children's theories of mind. In D. Hay & A. Angold (Eds.), *Precursors, causes, and psychopathology* (pp. 145–168). Chichester: John Wiley & Sons.

Frye, D. (1999). The development of intention: The relation of executive function to theory of mind. In P.D. Zelazo, J. Astington, & D. Olson (Eds.), *Theories of mind in action: Development and evolution of social understanding and self control* (pp. 119–132). Mahwah, NJ: Lawrence Erlbaum Associates, Inc.

Frye, D., Zelazo, P.D., & Brooks, P.J., & Samuels, M.C. (1996). Inference and action in early causal reasoning. *Developmental Psychology*, *32*, 120–131.

Frye, D., Zelazo, P.D., & Palfai, T. (1992). *The cognitive basis of children's theory of mind*. Unpublished manuscript.

Frye, D., Zelazo, P.D., & Palfai, T. (1995). Theory of mind and rule-based reasoning. *Cognitive Development*, *10*, 483–527.

Gergely, G., & Csibra, G. (1994). On the ascription of intentional content. *Cahiers de Pyschologie Cognitive, 83*, 584–589.

Gopnik, A., & Astington, J.W. (1988). Children's understanding of representational change and its relation to the understanding of false belief and the appearance-reality distinction. *Child Development, 59*, 26–37.

Gopnik, A., & Slaughter, V. (1991). Young children's understanding of the changes in their mental states. *Child Development, 62*, 98–110.

Gopnik, A., & Wellman, H. (1994). The theory theory. In L.A. Hirschfeld & S.A. Gelman (Eds.), *Mapping the mind: Domain specificity in cognition and culture* (pp. 257–293). New York: Cambridge University Press.

Gordon, A.C.L., & Olson, D. (1998). The relation between acquisition of a theory of mind and the capacity to hold in mind. *Journal of Experimental Child Psychology, 68*, 70–83.

Halford, G. (1993). *Children's understanding: The development of mental models.* Hillsdale, NJ: Lawrence Erlbaum Associates Inc.

Halford, G., Wilson, W.H., & Phillips, S. (1998). Processing capacity defined by relational complexity: Implications for comparative, developmental, and cognitive psychology. *Behavioral and Brain Sciences, 21*, 803–864.

Harris, P.L. (1992). From simulation to folk psychology: The case for development. *Mind and Language, 7*, 120–144.

Harris, P.L. (1993). Thinking about what is not the case. *International Journal of Psychology, 28*, 693–707.

Hughes, C. (1998). Executive function in preschoolers: Links with theory of mind and verbal ability. *British Journal of Developmental Psychology, 16*, 233–253.

Leslie, A.M. (1987). Pretense and representation: The origins of "theory of mind". *Psychological Review, 94*, 412–426.

Leslie, A.M. (1994a). Pretending and believing: Issues in the theory of ToMM. *Cognition, 50*, 211–238.

Leslie, A.M. (1994b). ToMM, ToBy, and Agency: Core architecture and domain specificity. In L.A. Hirschfeld & S.A. Gelman (Eds.), *Mapping the mind: Domain specificity in cognition and culture* (pp. 257–293). New York: Cambridge University Press.

Lillard, A.S. (1993a). Pretend play skills and the child's theory of mind. *Child Development, 64*, 348–371.

Lillard, A.S. (1993b). Young children's conceptualization of pretence: Action or mental representational state? *Child Development, 64*, 372–386.

Meltzoff, A.N. (1995). Understanding the intentions of others: Re-enactment of intended acts by 18-month-old children. *Developmental Psychology, 31*, 838–850.

Moore, C., Jarrold, C., Russell, J., Lumb, A., Sapp, F., & MacCullum, F. (1995). Conflicting desire and the child's theory of mind. *Cognitive Development, 10*, 467–482.

Nguyen, L., & Frye, D. (1999). Children's theory of mind: Understanding desire, belief, and emotion with social referents. *Social Developments, 8*, 70–92.

Olson, D.R. (1993). The development of representations: The origins of mental life. *Canadian Psychology, 34*, 293–304.

Ozonoff, S., Pennington, B.F., & Rogers, S.J. (1991). Executive function deficits in high-functioning autistic individuals: Relationship to theory of mind. *Journal of Child Psychology and Psychiatry, 32*, 1081–1105.

Perner, J. (1991). *Understanding the representational mind.* Cambridge, MA: MIT Press.

Perner, J., Baker, S., & Hutton, D. (1994). The conceptual origins of belief and pretence. In C. Lewis & P. Mitchell (Eds.), *Children's early understanding of mind: Origins and development* (pp. 261–286). Hove, UK: Lawrence Erlbaum Associates Ltd.

Riggs, K.J., Peterson, E.J., Robinson, E.J., & Mitchell, P. (1998). Are errors in false belief symptomatic of a broader difficulty with counterfactuality? *Cognitive Development, 13*, 73–90.

Russell, J., Mauthner, N., Sharpe, S., & Tidswell, T. (1991). The 'windows task' as a measure of strategic deception in preschoolers and autistic subjects. *British Journal of Developmental Psychology*, *9*, 331–349.

Saltmarsh, R., Mitchell, P., & Robinson, E. (1995). Realism and children's early grasp of mental representation: Belief-based judgments in the state change task. *Cognition*, *57*, 297–325.

Samuels, M., Brooks, P., & Frye, D. (1997). *The developing relation between past beliefs and states of the world in the preschool years*. Manuscript submitted for publication.

Wellman, H.M., & Bartsch, K. (1988). Young children's reasoning about beliefs. *Cognition*, *30*, 239–277.

Wellman, H.M. & Woolley, J.D. (1990). From simple desires to ordinary beliefs: The early development of everyday psychology. *Cognition*, *35*, 245–275.

Wimmer, H., & Hartl, M. (1991). Against the Cartesian view of mind: Young children's difficulty with own false beliefs. *British Journal of Developmental Psychology*, *9*, 125–138.

Wimmer, H., & Perner, J. (1983). Beliefs about beliefs: Representation and constraining function of wrong beliefs in young children's understanding of deception. *Cognition*, *13*, 103–128.

Zaitchik, D. (1991). Is only seeing really believing? Sources of the true belief in the false belief task. *Cognitive Development*, *6*, 91–103.

Zelazo, P.D., Carter, A., Reznick, J.S., & Frye, D. (1997). Early development of executive function: A problem-solving framework. *Review of General Psychology*, *1*, 198–226.

Zelazo, P.D., & Frye, D. (1997). Cognitive complexity and control: A theory of the development of deliberate reasoning and intentional action. In M. Stamenov (Ed.), *Language structure, discourse, and the access to consciousness* (pp. 113–153). Amsterdam & Philadelphia: John Benjamins.

Zelazo, P.D., Helwig, C.C., & Lau, A. (1996). Intention, act, and outcome in behavioral prediction and moral judgment. *Child Development*, *67*, 2478–2492.

Zelazo, P.D., & Jacques, S. (1997). Children's rule use: Representation, reflection, and cognitive control. In R. Vasta (Ed.), *Annals of Child Development* (Vol. 12, pp. 119–176). London: Jessica Kingsley Press.

CHAPTER NINE

Self-reflection and the development of consciously controlled processing

Philip David Zelazo
University of Toronto, Canada

INTRODUCTION

It is often supposed that one function of consciousness, or at least the function of one aspect of consciousness (which Block, 1995, refers to as "access consciousness"), is to permit the use of representations to control action. This supposition makes sense from an evolutionary standpoint (because it grants consciousness direct consequences for behaviour), but it is also buoyed by a fair bit of empirical support. Action control (including, in human beings beyond a certain age, control of speech) is indeed a key behavioural correlate of representations that are likely conscious. Of course, insofar as we rely on verbal report in order to determine whether or not a representation is conscious, then it would seem that consciousness is actually *defined* as having the function of control (at least the control of speech). However, we escape from this circle of definition when we ask about the relation between the reportability of a representation and the extent to which that representation can be used to control actions other than speech. The question, then, becomes one of specifying the conditions under which complete versus partial access obtains (i.e. access to both action and speech vs. access to speech alone), and providing an account of consciousness that explains why only partial access occurs under certain conditions.

Recent demonstrations of specifically age-related abulic dissociations between reporting rules and using them (Zelazo, Frye, & Rapus, 1996) provide support for one answer to this question concerning the function of consciousness. Based on our research, as well as reviews of the literature on the development of action control, we have proposed a process model of consciousness and its development, called the Levels of Consciousness (LOC) model (Zelazo & Jacques,

1996; Zelazo & Zelazo, 1998), which describes how recursive processes in consciousness underlie the development of action control. According to the model, partial access occurs because the control of action under conditions of interference (from prepotent representational or response-based tendencies) requires a higher level of consciousness than does the control of speech in the absence of interference.

AGE-RELATED CHANGES IN ACTION CONTROL: A BRIEF REVIEW

A growing body of research has demonstrated convincingly that there are systematic, age-related changes in action control from infancy through the preschool years (for reviews, see Zelazo, Carter, Reznick, & Frye, 1997; Zelazo & Jacques, 1996). Action control can be defined as the use of explicit representations to guide responding. Because tests of action control typically involve competition among different underlying processes, one of which is correct and one of which is prepotent (see Zelazo et al., 1997, for a discussion of this paradigm and its limitations), failures of action control at all ages are often manifested as perseveration, or responding that is consistent with the prepotent process. However, the specific situations in which perseveration occurs, and ultimately, the specific psychological processes that are likely to be involved, vary as a function of age.

In infancy, action control is perhaps most clearly assessed via delayed response tasks, in which an object is conspicuously hidden at one of several locations (Hunter, 1917). In order to retrieve the object, infants are required to use a representation of the object's location to guide their search. One particularly well-studied variant of the delayed response task is Piaget's (1936/1952) A-not-B search task (see Marcovitch & Zelazo, in press, for a recent meta-analysis). In the standard A-not-B task, an object is hidden at one of two locations (location A) for one or more trials, and is subsequently hidden at the other location (B). Nine-month-old infants often search at A when the object is hidden at B. In more complicated versions of the task (e.g. the multi-step multi-location search task; Zelazo, Reznick, & Spinazzola, 1998), even 24-month-olds are susceptible to this type of perseveration in reaching to the initial, pre-switch location.

In slightly older children, with whom verbal instructions are appropriate, the rule use paradigm (Zelazo & Jacques, 1996) provides a straightforward assessment of action control. If we assume (rather uncontroversially) that people are conscious of information that they can verbally report, then rule use can be seen as a clear case of the use of a conscious, action-oriented plan to guide behaviour. Rules are statements (usually, if–then statements) that specify relations between antecedent conditions and actions to be executed or inferences to be made. In any rule-use task, participants are presented with rules that they must remember and consult in order to determine how to act.

The ability to use a single rule systematically to control behaviour seems to be acquired sometime during the third year of life. Our research on the use of arbitrary rules to sort cards (Jacques, 1995; Zelazo, Reznick, & Piñon, 1995), indicates that 2.5-year-olds can represent and follow a single rule (e.g. "If I show you something that goes inside the house, put it here."). Card sorting by an ad hoc rule provides a clear demonstration of rule use because systematic responding is under-determined by non-linguistic aspects of the task. However, although 2.5-year-olds can use a single rule, they have difficulty using two rules simultaneously. Children in the study by Zelazo et al. (1995) were told two rules (e.g. "If inside, then here; if outside, then there.") and asked to use them to sort a series of 10 test cards (e.g. a snowman, a refrigerator). Although they rarely put all the cards into the same place, when they made an error, it usually involved putting a card in the place in which they had put a card on the previous trial. Thus, they might put the snowman in the correct box, but then assimilate the refrigerator to that same rule. Indeed, 71% of children's errors were perseverative in this sense, which is significantly more than the 50% that would be expected if children were sorting randomly. These results indicate that 2.5-year-olds represented the rules and actually started to use them, but were susceptible to perseverative errors and ultimately failed to sort systematically.

Three-year-olds rarely perseverate in tasks requiring the use of two rules (Zelazo & Reznick, 1991). However, they frequently have difficulty switching between two incompatible pairs of rules. In the dimensional change card sort (see Fig. 9.1), children are asked to sort a series of test cards according to one dimension (e.g. for colour, they are told, "Put the blue ones here; put the red ones there.") and then, after sorting several cards, they are told to stop playing the first game and switch to another game (e.g. shape, for which they are told, "Put the flowers here; put the boats there."). Regardless of which dimension is presented first, 3-year-olds typically continue to sort the cards by that dimension despite being told the new rules on every trial and despite having sorted cards by the new dimension on other occasions (Frye, Zelazo, & Palfai, 1995).

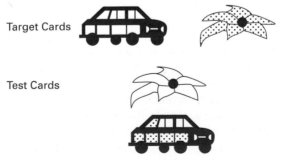

FIG. 9.1 Stimuli from the dimensional change card sort, a rule-use task in which children are told explicit rules and required to use them to sort test cards with target cards.

Perseveration in 3- to 4-year-olds has also been documented in a variety of other tasks that are formally analogous to the dimensional change card sort, including tasks assessing causal reasoning (Frye, Zelazo, Brooks, & Samuels, 1996), behavioural prediction (Zelazo, Helwig, & Lau, 1996), modified Simon Says (Reed, Pien, & Rothbart, 1984; see also Diamond & Taylor, 1996), and a Stroop-like task (Gerstadt, Hong, & Diamond, 1994). On all of these tasks, 5-year-olds typically perform well (see Zelazo & Jacques, 1996, for review and discussion of children's performance on a wide range of tasks).

A THEORETICAL ACCOUNT OF AGE-RELATED CHANGES IN ACTION CONTROL: THE COGNITIVE COMPLEXITY AND CONTROL (CCC) THEORY

Although perseveration has been documented in children at all ages, the situations in which perseveration occurs become increasingly complex as children get older. Complexity, therefore, provides a useful metric for predicting task difficulty across domains (cf. Halford, Wilson, & Phillips, 1998). The Cognitive Complexity and Control (CCC) theory of the development of deliberate reasoning and intentional action (Frye, Zelazo, & Palfai, 1995; Zelazo & Frye, 1997) was developed, in part, to explain why task complexity predicts task difficulty. According to the CCC theory, there are age-related changes in the complexity of the situations that elicit perseveration because there are age-related changes in the complexity of the representations that can be used by children to control their behaviour. The complexity of children's representations is measured in terms of the relations among explicit representations of actions and events (e.g. stimuli, goal states, etc.). At the end of the first year, children are able to represent a goal and use it to guide their responding. Later action control usually involves the use of if–then rules, which are formulated in potentially silent self-directed speech, as when we tell ourselves. "If I see a mailbox, then I need to mail this letter". These rules represent a conditionally specified instrumental behaviour or means. The reason that our action-oriented representations are conditional, or rule-based, is that we act only when it is appropriate to do so (i.e. when certain antecedent conditions are satisfied). It should be noted, however, that our rules continue to be further conditioned by the representation of a goal (e.g. I might mail a letter because ultimately, I wish to communicate with a friend).

Once children start using rules to control their behaviour (made possible by the acquisition of language; Bowerman, 1986; Nelson, 1997; Reilly, 1986), there are systematic, age-related changes in the complexity of the rule systems that children can represent: During the third year of life, and certainly by 30 months of age, children can represent a single explicit rule, such as, "if red, then here". However, at 30 months of age, children cannot represent a contrastive relation between two or more rules, which is necessary in order to consider carefully which of the two antecedent conditions is satisfied. Failure to represent a contrastive relation between two rules makes it difficult to switch flexibly between them in a single situation, resulting in perseveration on one of the rules.

By 36 months, children can reflect on two different rules and represent a contrastive relation between them. That is, they can integrate two separate rules into a single system. However, it is not until 4 or 5 years that they can represent a higher-order relation between two incompatible pairs of rules, which is required to select between rule pairs (e.g. "If colour, then if red, then here."). In the absence of a higher-order rule, they will perseverate on the first, or otherwise prepotent, pair of rules when asked to switch between rule pairs in a single unchanged situation.

The tree-structure in Fig. 9.2 illustrates the way in which one rule can be embedded under another and controlled by it. A rule such as A, which links antecedent 1 (a_1) to consequent 1 (c_1) is incompatible with rule C, which links a_1 to c_2. Rule A is controlled by a higher-order rule (rule E) that can be used to select rules A and B, as opposed to rules C and D. To use rule E, one must consider both the setting condition (s_1 or s_2) and the lower-order antecedent conditions (a_1 or a_2), in order to determine which consequence follows (c_1 or c_2). For cxample, in the dimensional change card sort, it is necessary to use a higher-order rule such as, "If playing colour, then if red, then it goes here". According to the CCC theory, 2-year-olds can apprehend one rule, 3-year-olds a pair of rules at a time, at 5-year-olds can consider two pairs of rules or perspectives in contradistinction.

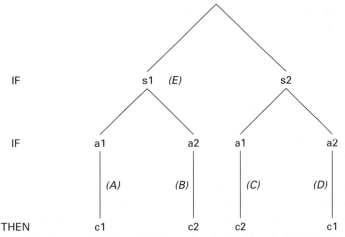

FIG. 9.2   Hierarchical tree structure showing how one rule can be embedded under another and controlled by it. Note: s_1 and s_2: setting conditions; a_1 and a_2: antecedent conditions; c_1 and c_2: consequences.

AGE-RELATED ABULIC DISSOCIATIONS

Research on perseveration in specific situations at specific ages has been directed at determining how best to describe the processes contributing to children's inflexibility. It is in the context of this research that age-related abulic
dissociations between representations and the use of those representations have
been documented.

As Zelazo, Reznick, and Piñon (1995) noted, action control entails both the
manipulation and maintenance of representations, on the one hand, and the use
of representations to control responses, on the other. Perseverative responses
could, therefore, be due to inflexibility either at the level of representations or at
the level of responses or both. Representational inflexibility occurs when performance fails because one has difficulty inhibiting an incorrect representation
and establishing a correct one. Failures of response control occur when one fails
to inhibit an incorrect response despite establishing and maintaining a correct
representation. Several lines of evidence support the suggestion that infants'
perseveration on search tasks is due to a failure of response control (Zelazo,
Reznick, & Spinazzola, 1998). For example, infants are considerably less likely
to perseverate when looking rather than reaching is used as a dependent measure
(Hofstadter & Reznick, 1996). Moreover, Piaget (1937/1954, p. 51) and others
(Diamond, 1985) have noted that infants sometimes reach perseveratively for an
object even while looking at the correct location, suggesting that they perseverate
on an inappropriate pattern of responding despite knowing what to do.

Similar abulic dissociations between knowledge and the use of that knowledge have been demonstrated in older children in the context of rule use tasks.
For example, although 2.5-year-olds failed to use a pair of rules in the study by
Zelazo and Reznick (1991), they performed quite well on a knowledge task in
which they were asked questions such as, "Does this [a snowman] go inside the
house or outside?". A later study (Zelazo, Reznick, & Piñon, 1995, Exp. 1)
found that 2.5-year-olds had difficulty even when (1) cards were labelled at the
superordinate level (i.e. in terms of the rule; e.g. as "something found inside"),
(2) children were reminded of the rules, and (3) children were rewarded for
responding correctly. However, the clearest demonstration of an abulic dissociation comes from Zelazo, Frye, and Rapus (1996), who gave children the dimensional change card sort. Three-year-olds who perseverated and continued to sort
by the first dimension were then asked questions to determine whether they
understood what they were supposed to be doing. For example, children who
were supposed to be sorting by shape, were asked, "Where do the boats go in the
shape game? And where do the rabbits go?" Almost invariably, children answered
these knowledge questions correctly, either by pointing to the correct box or by
naming it (Exp. 4). Nonetheless, when they were told to sort the cards according
to these rules ("Okay, good, now play the shape game: Where does this rabbit
go?"), nearly all of them perseverated. The children answered an explicit question

about the new rules, showing that they knew these rules, but then they immediately persisted in using the old ones.

Abulic dissociations are theoretically important because they imply that it is overly simple to suggest that children either are, or are not, conscious of the representations to be used. Children are clearly conscious of the relevant representations in some sense, but this consciousness fails to permit control. In the clearest case, involving the dimensional change card sort, children respond verbally to explicit questions about the rules that they fail to use. Thus, under some circumstances, children cannot use their *conscious* knowledge to guide their behaviour; they exhibit one kind of access consciousness (control of speech) but not another (control of sorting). From a functionalist perspective, dissociations indicate that partial access consciousness is a phenomenon that occurs naturally in the course of development. What is needed is a developmental model of consciousness that can account for this phenomenon.

According to the CCC theory, consciousness alone will not suffice to permit the control of action under conditions of interference from prepotent representational or response-based tendencies. Increases in reflection are required for children to reconcile conflicting explicit approaches to a problem and select appropriately between them. The LOC framework moves the CCC theory towards a process model of the role of reflection and rule use in the control of thought and action by showing how the contents of consciousness interact with other psychological processes, such as working memory. One general implication of this work is that consciousness itself develops through a series of levels or degrees of recursion. The idea of levels of consciousness accounts for the phenomenon of abulic dissociations and also provides a metric for measuring psychological distance at different ages and in different situations (e.g. Sigel, 1993).

THE LEVELS OF CONSCIOUSNESS (LOC) FRAMEWORK

According to the Levels of Consciousness (LOC) framework, consciousness can operate on multiple 'levels' that correspond to degrees of recursion or reflection. Developmentally, children become capable of increasingly higher levels of consciousness (although they may operate at different levels of consciousness in different situations). The least reflective level of consciousness, called minimal consciousness (Zelazo, 1996), is meant to be the simplest, but still conceptually coherent, kind of consciousness that we might grant even to newborn babies. On the positive side, Zelazo (1996) argued that minimal consciousness is necessarily characterised by intentionality in Brentano's (1874/1973) sense (i.e. if one is conscious, then one is necessarily conscious *of* something).[1] Minimal consciousness is *representational* in this sense. Minimal consciousness can also be called *conative* in that it motivates approach and avoidance behaviour. However, the phenomenon of minimal consciousness is most striking for what it is not: It is unreflective, present-oriented, and it makes no reference to an explicit sense of Self that contains or explains subjective experience. While minimally conscious, one is conscious of *what* one sees (the object of one's experience), but one is not conscious of *seeing* what one sees, let alone that *one* (as an agent) is seeing what one sees. And of course, one cannot subsequently remember seeing what one saw.

Perhaps it is obvious from this description that minimal consciousness is precisely the kind of consciousness that ought to underlie so-called implicit information processing, as when we drive a car without full awareness of what we are doing (Armstrong, 1980), or when we learn to respond to regularities in the environment but are unable to describe the regularities (Berry & Broadbent, 1984; Lewicki, Czyzewska, & Hoffman, 1987). It is often suggested that implicit processing is completely unconscious (for example, see Benjamin Libet's comments following Zelazo & Zelazo, 1998; Gray, 1998), but even in the simplest case, where behavioural routines are elicited directly and automatically, they are elicited as a function of consciousness of *something*—say, immediate environmental stimuli. Implicit processing does not occur in a zombie-like fashion; it is simply unreflective and unavailable for subsequent recollection (Zelazo, 1996).

Because several fundamental aspects of consciousness are assumed to be present even at birth (and therefore correspond to theoretical primitives in the LOC model), the problem of the first emergence of consciousness is temporarily side-stepped (although it awaits us farther down the ontogenetic ladder). However, by assuming minimal consciousness at birth, it becomes possible to account for the development of increasingly sophisticated forms of consciousness using very few theoretical tools.

In addition to minimal consciousness, the LOC model assumes the existence (at birth) of long-term memory (LTM), which has both a semantic and a procedural component (see Fig. 9.3). The semantic component stores knowledge that is (at least potentially) declarative, whereas the procedural component stores sensorimotor schemata (i.e. habits).

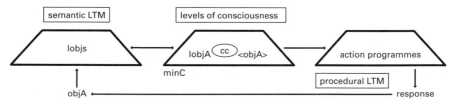

FIG. 9.3   A process model of minimal consciousness. (Adapted from *Children's rule use: Representation, reflection, and cognitive control* by P.D. Zelazo & S. Jacques, 1996, in R. Vasta [Ed.], *Annals of Child Development*, Vol. 12, p. 163, London: Jessica Kingsley Press.) An object in the environment (objA) triggers an intentional representation of that object (IobjA) that is stored in semantic long term memory (LTM); this IobjA, which is causally connected (cc) to objA, becomes the content of minimal consciousness (minC), by way of which it triggers an associated action programme stored in procedural LTM. Reprinted with permission.

Consider how an infant can act on the basis of minimal consciousness (i.e. in the absence of any reflection). An object in the environment (abbreviated ObjA) triggers a description that is stored in semantic LTM. This particular description (or intentional object; abbreviated IobjA), to which ObjA is assimilated, can then become the content of minimal consciousness, by way of which it, in turn, triggers an associated action programme that is stored in procedural LTM. It should be noted that all objects are represented under a description (Davidson, 1980); that is to say, within the system, there exist only intentional objects, objects that have 'aspectual shape' because they are interpreted from a particular (and hence, necessarily limited) perspective (Searle, 1990). The infant is aware of only one thing: the intentional object; the object as a thing in itself is *noumenal* (in Kantian, 1781/1927, terminology), and necessarily beyond the reach of phenomenal awareness. Thus, a rattle might be experienced by a (minimally conscious) baby as 'small thing'. This description might trigger the stereotypical motor schema of putting the rattle into his or her mouth. Indeed, behaviour at this minimally conscious level is necessarily stereotypical. Sensori-motor schemata can be refined and coordinated into higher-order units, as Baldwin (1894/1968) and Piaget (1936/1952) pointed out (see also Cohen, 1998), but the infant would not represent these schemata explicitly. The infant would only be aware of the stimulus (under a description) that triggers the schema, and even this minimal awareness would be fleeting and unrecoverable.

The empirical base of the LOC model as it applies to infancy has been reviewed by Zelazo and Zelazo (1998) and will not be reiterated here. This review revealed that there is a fair amount of support for the positive claims entailed by this characterisation of consciousness in early infancy. Thus, for example, research on learning and memory in the neonatal period has established conclusively that newborn babies have the ability to create mental representations that are modifiable through experience and that have conative properties (insofar as they motivate approach and avoidance behaviour; for reviews, see DeCasper & Spence, 1991; Slater & Morison, 1991; Zelazo, Weiss, & Tarquinio, 1991). The negative claims are more difficult to establish, but for further discussion, the reader is referred to Zelazo (1996) and Zelazo and Zelazo (1998).

On this account, the attribution of minimal consciousness manages to account for infant behaviour until about the end of the first year, when a large number of new abilities appear with high-interval synchrony (cf. Fischer, 1980), suggesting some sort of underlying central determinant. As is now well known, within the span of a few months, infants speak their first words, use objects in a functional way, point proto-declaratively, search for hidden objects, and display deferred imitation, social referencing, and joint attention, among many other major developmental milestones (see Frye, 1981; Kagan, 1972; Moore & Corkum, 1994; Zelazo, 1982, for reviews). Table 9.1 provides a list of important behaviours that typically emerge at the end of the first year of life.

TABLE 9.1
Developmental milestones that typically
occur at the end of the first year of life

Naming
Functional play
Proto-declarative pointing
Flexible search for hidden objects
Deferred imitation
Social referencing
Joint attention
Separation protest
Stranger anxiety
Walking

According to the model, these changes herald the first new form of consciousness (see Fig. 9.4). When the contents of minimal consciousness are fed back into minimal consciousness, then the contents of minimal consciousness become available to the infant, in what we call recursive consciousness (abbreviated recC, in Fig. 9.4). Recursive consciousness permits the infant to retain the subjective, phenomenal character of experience in a kind of 'remembered present' (cf. Edelman, 1989) because it allows the infant to label his or her intentional objects. The minimally conscious experience is labelled when it is identified with a description via a first-order integrative relation (abbreviated Rel1, an identity relation; cf. Olson & Campbell, 1993).

Proto-declarative pointing indicates, "[That thing, whatever it is] *is* that", just as the word 'dog', used ostensively, implies, "[That dog] *is* dog". Phenomenally, when we label something, we are aware of one thing, but there are two things, the label and the experience that is labelled. The argument here is that indeed

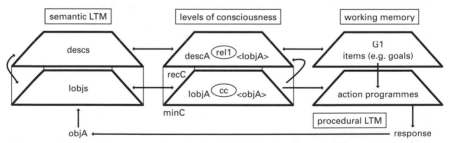

FIG. 9.4   Model of recursive consciousness. (Adapted from *Children's rule use: Representation, reflection, and cognitive control* by P.D. Zelazo, & S. Jacques, 1996, in R. Vasta [Ed.], *Annals of Child Development*, Vol. 12, p. 163.) When the entire contents of minimal consciousness (minC) are fed back into minC via a recursive process, a higher level of consciousness is achieved, namely recursive consciousness (recC). The contents of recC can be related (Rel1) to a corresponding description (descA) or label, which can then be deposited into working memory where it can serve as a goal (G1) to trigger an action programme (stored in procedural LTM). Reprinted with permission.

there *must* be two things in order for one of them, the experience, to become an object of consciousness in anything like the usual sense of the term. Recursion yields experience of consciousness (note the non-trivial redundancy of this expression) because it allows minimal consciousness to take the contents of minimal consciousness as its object.

In the absence of a label, the contents of consciousness are fleeting and unrecoverable; immediately replaced by new stimulation; limited only to minimal consciousness (which is often confused with un-consciousness). However, because a label can be decoupled from the experience that is labelled, the label provides a potentially enduring trace of that experience. Recursive consciousness therefore allows a label to be deposited into long-term memory for subsequent retrieval, but also, more importantly for our purpose, into working memory, which is understood here simply to be a short-term buffer for maintaining contents of consciousness in an activated state and treating them as if they were "presentations" despite the fact that they are "representations" (Baddeley, 1992; Goldman-Rakic, 1990). According to the model, recursive consciousness (at least) of a representation is a necessary precondition for the maintenance of that representation in working memory.

The contents of working memory can serve as goals (abbreviated G1; e.g. representations of hidden objects) to trigger action programmes indirectly so that the infant is not restricted to responses that are triggered directly by the (minimally conscious) perception of an immediately present stimulus. The maintenance of a goal in working memory thus permits the use of recursively conscious representations to guide responding (i.e. it permits the simplest form of action control), which arguably makes its appearance in infant behaviour towards the end of the first year of life (Diamond, 1985; Reznick, Fueser, & Bosquet, 1998). It is at this point, when the infant is capable of recursive consciousness and able to keep an (absent) object in mind as a goal, that the new behaviours at end of the first year become possible (see Zelazo & Zelazo, 1998, for discussion). At this point, when presented with a stimulus, such as a rattle or an object hidden at a new location, the infant is able to act mediately, in light of a less salient representation of that stimulus, rather than immediately, according to a prepotent action programme. For example, the recursively conscious baby may shake the rattle appropriately (Zelazo & Kearsley, 1980) or search successfully without perseverating. In terms of the model, an ObjA triggers IobjA, which then becomes the content of minC. Now, instead of triggering an associated action programme directly, IobjA is fed back into consciousness where it is related to a descA from semantic LTM. This descA is deposited in working memory where it serves as a goal (G1) and can trigger an action programme even in the absence of ojbA, and even if the IobjA would otherwise trigger a different, prepotent action programme.

Insofar as the LOC model emphasises the importance of a second-order process for the experience of awareness, it resembles a higher-order thought theory of consciousness (Armstrong, 1980; Carruthers, 1996; Rosenthal, 1986). However, it differs from these theories in two crucial ways. First, higher-order thought theories claim that consciousness consists in a belief about one's psychological states (i.e. a psychological state is conscious when one believes that one is in that state). In contrast, recursion in the LOC model is simply a functional process that permits the contents of minimal consciousness to become an object of consciousness considered in relation to a label; it entails no belief regarding psychological states (and indeed, according to the model, still higher levels of consciousness are required for such a belief; discussed later). Second, in the LOC model, RecC is only the first of several levels of consciousness.

As we ascend levels of consciousness, which are really just the same single function of minimal consciousness depicted in different psychological moments, or functional phases (but with very different consequences at each phase), we move away from an impetus to action, away from the "exigencies of a situation" (Dewey, 1960, p. 104). Reflective processing, with its potential consequences for the use of working memory and the control of action, is interposed between a stimulus in the environment and a response to that stimulus. Thus, levels of consciousness vary in what has been called *psychological distance* (DeLoache, 1993; Sigel, 1993; see also Dewey, 1931/1985). More reflective levels are psychologically more distant.

Now, although a year-old infant behaves in a way that is considerably more controlled than, say, a 6-month-old, there is no convincing evidence that children are self-conscious until the end of the second year of life, at which point they use personal pronouns, recognise themselves in mirrors, exhibit self-conscious emotions like shame, and so on (for reviews see Kagan, 1981; Lewis & Brooks-Gunn, 1979). Recall Kagan's (1981) description of the way in which 2-year-olds respond when shown a complex series of steps in the context of an imitative routine. Kagan found that infants at this age sometimes exhibited signs of distress, as if they knew that the series of steps was beyond the range of their behavioural repertoire, and was not among the means that they had at their disposal. This is the crucial thing: At about this age, children consider, for the first time, their own capabilities (against the background of a goal to imitate the experimenter). And knowledge of one's own behavioural potential in a situation (i.e. knowledge of a means to an end) *just is* knowledge of a rule, because all deliberate actions are conditionally specified (Zelazo & Jacques, 1996). Thus, according to the LOC model, the onset of self consciousness at about two years of age is what allows children to use a single rule to guide their behaviour. As shown in Fig. 9.5, a 2-year-old can take as an object of consciousness a natural language self-description (abbreviated SdescA) of his or her knowledge in the form of a single rule (abbreviated R1).

Recall that when 2.5-year-olds (30-month-olds) are presented with a pair of ad hoc rules for sorting, they start to use these rules, but tend to perseverate on one of them (Zelazo et al., 1995). If children were able to distance themselves

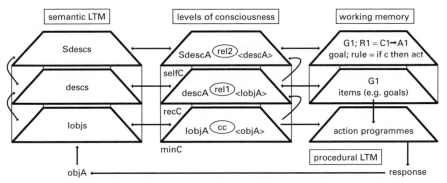

FIG. 9.5   Model of self consciousness. (Adapted from *Children's rule use: Representation, reflection, and cognitive control* by P.D. Zelazo & S. Jacques, 1996, in R. Vasta [Ed.], *Annals of Child Development*, Vol. 12, p. 163.) See text for definitions. Reprinted with permission.

from their knowledge, and consider one rule in relation to the other, then they would recognise the need to choose carefully between the rules and avoid assimilating test cards to only one of them. According to the LOC model, children are unable to do this until they reach a higher level of consciousness, called *reflective consciousness* 1 (abbreviated refC1; see Fig. 9.6). Most 3-year-olds can reflect upon a self description (SdescA) corresponding to one rule (R1) and consider it in a contrastive relation (abbreviated Rel2) to another self description (SdescB) of another rule (R2). Both of these rules can then be deposited into working memory where they can be used contrastively to control the elicitation of action programmes (in light of a goal, G1). A comparison of Figs. 9.6 and 9.2 reveals that levels of consciousness vary in a way that is directly proportional to

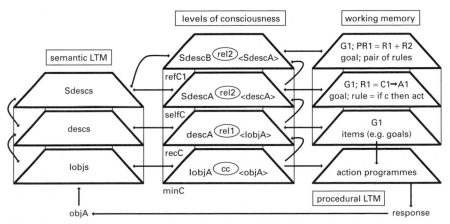

FIG. 9.6   Model of reflective consciousness 1. (Adapted from *Children's rule use: Representation, reflection, and cognitive control* by P.D. Zelazo & S. Jacques, 1996, in R. Vasta [Ed.], *Annals of Child Development*, Vol. 12, p. 163.) See text for definitions. Reprinted with permission.

the degrees of embedding illustrated in the tree structure in Fig. 9.2. Each level of embedding in the tree structure requires a new degree of recursion and therefore demands a new level of consciousness.

The next major age-related increase in children's level of consciousness allows them to select appropriately between two incompatible perspectives on a single situation, as in the dimensional change card sort. Recall that in this card sort, 3-year-olds perseverate when they are told to switch between rule pairs (Frye et al., 1995). They know the post-switch rules, which is why they can answer knowledge questions about them (Zelazo et al., 1996), but they do not know that they know them, which is why they cannot make a deliberate decision to use them in contradistinction to the colour rules (which are now prepotent).

According to the CCC theory, although 3-year-olds can represent a pair of rules, they cannot reflect on their representation of a pair of rules and consequently cannot represent a higher-order relation between two incompatible pairs of rules. It is not until 4 or 5 years of age that most children switch flexibly on the dimensional change card sort, and in terms of the LOC model, children at this age attain a higher level of reflective consciousness, depicted in Fig. 9.7.

At this level, *reflective consciousness 2* (RefC2), the entire contents of reflective consciousness 1 (RefC1) can be considered in relation to a self-description (Sdesc) of comparable complexity. By reflecting on their representations of two pairs of rules for responding to a single situation, they are able to appreciate a higher-order rule for determining which pair of rules to use. This system of rules (abbreviated ER1 in Fig. 9.7), which corresponds to the entire hierarchical system of rules depicted in Fig. 9.2, can then be put into working memory where it

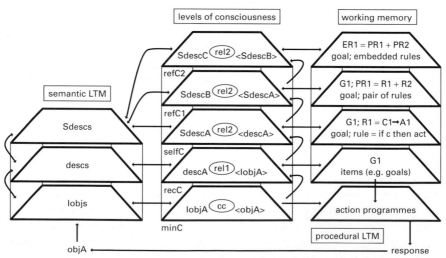

FIG. 9.7   Model of reflective consciousness 2. (Adapted from *Children's rule use: Representation, reflection, and cognitive control* by P.D. Zelazo & S. Jacques, 1996, in R. Vasta [Ed.], *Annals of Child Development*, Vol. 12, p. 163.) See text for definitions. Reprinted with permission.

can serve to control behaviour.[2] The close connection between reflective consciousness 2 and action control is well demonstrated by research showing that rule use is related to performance on tasks that require children to remember and reason about their own mistaken beliefs (Frye et al., 1995; Hughes, 1998). For example, Frye et al. (1995) found that performance on the dimensional change card sort was related to performance on several theory-of-mind tasks, even with age partialled out. The theory-of-mind tasks included an appearance-reality task (Flavell, Green, & Flavell, 1986), a false belief task (Perner, Leekham, & Wimmer, 1987), and a representational change task (Gopnik & Astington, 1988). On all of these tasks, children need to understand how two incompatible perspectives are related. The acquisition of RefC2 would allow children to form a higher-order rule that integrates the two perspectives (e.g. past and present self-perspectives in the representational change task) into a single coherent system and makes it possible to select the perspective from which to reason in response to a given question. (In the absence of the higher-order rule, they would respond from the prepotent perspective.)

According to the LOC model, there are a number of major transitions in children's level of consciousness. For each transition, a few general processes are recapitulated. Specifically, an increase in recursion permits children to appreciate a representation of a particular level of complexity, and this representation permits children to exercise a new degree of control over their environment and behaviour. However, these representations are subject to limitations that cannot be overcome until yet another level of consciousness is achieved. Although these representations are clearly conscious, and can be reported, they will not control action under conditions of interference (from prepotent tendencies) until a higher level of consciousness is attained and incompatible representations can be integrated into a single system of representations. In the absence of such an integration, the particular representation that will be selected and stored in working memory is determined by relatively local considerations, such as the way in which the question is asked, or what children have done previously in that (self-described) same situation.

COMPARISON WITH OTHER APPROACHES

In its emphasis on consciousness, the LOC model resembles a number of other recent proposals in the literature. For example, Clements and Perner (1994) found that 3-year-olds looked to the correct location in a change-of-location false belief task even though they failed to predict that a character would search there (i.e. on the basis of a false belief). The authors interpreted children's looking as evidence of an implicit understanding of belief. However, in other research contexts (e.g. research on the A-not-B error; Diamond, 1991), looking to the correct location (while reaching perseveratively) has been taken to indicate explicit knowledge (i.e. the contents of working memory) that fails to control responding. Indeed, from the current perspective, accurate looking may well reveal explicit knowledge that children cannot (in the absence of further reflection on this knowledge) bring to bear in response to particular questions or in particular contexts (perhaps due to interference from competing explicit knowledge). The application of their explicit knowledge might, in this case, be highly context dependent; it might depend on the way in which a question is asked, or perhaps, the dependent measure that is used. Thus, for example, children may have explicit knowledge about the association between the character and the initial location, and they may also have explicit knowledge about the object's new location. Which piece of explicit knowledge is expressed by children will depend on the type of measure that is employed. The fact that the character was only seen at the first location may be enough to established a tendency to look there. At the same time, children may be predisposed (on the basis of extra-experimental experience) to respond to the Action Prediction Question (i.e. the false-belief question) in terms of reality. In any case, from the perspective of the LOC model, the distinction between implicit and explicit knowledge is perhaps overly simple.

Karmiloff-Smith's (1992) Representational Redescription (RR) model moves beyond a simple distinction between conscious and unconscious processes by introducing the notion of explicit representations that are not conscious (for a commentary on this model, see Zelazo, 1994). According to this model, knowledge is originally represented in an implicit, procedural format (Level I), but, with sufficient practice, behavioural mastery of these procedures is achieved and the knowledge is automatically redescribed into a more abstract, explicit format (Level E1). This representational format reveals the structure of the procedures, but is still not conscious: Consciousness comes with yet additional levels of redescription or 'explicitation', which occur "spontaneously as part of an internal drive toward the creation of intra-domain and inter-domain relationships" (1992, p. 18). Level E2 is conscious but not verbalisable, whereas Level E3 is conscious and verbalisable. In contrast to the RR model, which relies on domain-specific experience, the LOC model describes domain-general and age-related constraints on children's highest level of consciousness. Moreover, the LOC model aims to illustrate how each level of consciousness functions in the intentional control of behaviour (e.g. via the selection of explicit rules).

The differences between the RR model and the LOC model can also be seen by considering how they explain (or would explain) 3-year-olds' perseveration on the dimensional change card sort. According to the LOC model, 3-year-olds approach the problem at level RefC1 rather than level RefC2, as described earlier. In contrast, the RR model would account for children's rigidity by proposing that their knowledge of the rules was less than fully explicit (due to lack of experience, not age). For example, children's knowledge might be represented at Levels E1 or E2, but not E3. However, 3-year-olds perseverate on this task even though they can respond verbally to explicit questions about the new, post-switch rules. This finding would seem to indicate that 3-year-olds persistently select inappropriate rules despite conscious, verbalisable knowledge of both the pre- and post-switch rules.

CONCLUSION

The LOC model is designed both generally to explain action control and its development, and also specifically to account for partial access consciousness, which is observed in age-related abulic dissociations. Several major changes in action control from birth until the end of the pre-school years are explained by increases in self-reflection, which are modelled by additions of recursive processes to an initial state of minimal consciousness. These increases in reflection make possible the use of increasingly complex representations to guide responding, as outlined in the CCC theory (Frye et al., 1995; Zelazo & Frye, 1997). For example, the cognitive metamorphosis at the end of the first year of life is accommodated in the model by the addition of a single recursive process to minimal consciousness. This recursion permits the decoupling of a description from the thing described and allows behaviour to be controlled mediately by the description (maintained in working memory) rather than immediately by the presentation of environmental stimulation. From infancy through early childhood there are continuing developments in reflective awareness that produce corresponding changes in controlled behaviour. Thus, the acquisition of self consciousness, as manifested in tasks assessing self recognition, has direct consequences for children's action control. Additionally, the emergence of reflective consciousness 2 at about four or five years of age quite naturally captures the major changes that have been observed in children's theory of mind (see Astington, 1993, for a review), as well as the finding that changes in theory of mind are correlated with changes in action control (Frye et al., 1995; Hughes, 1998).

Like the CCC Theory, the LOC model emphasises the importance of language to both consciousness and action control. Language is important not only because description (labelling) is crucially involved in the subjective experience of consciousness (i.e. in recursive consciousness), but also because it plays an instrumental role in regulating behaviour (cf. Luria, 1961; Vygotsky, 1978; see Zelazo & Jacques, 1996, for a comparison with Luria's work). Self-descriptions of knowledge are formulated as rules and maintained in working memory so that they can control responding regardless of changes in environmental stimulation.

Although it is a developmental model, the LOC model has implications for our characterisation of consciousness in general. In contrast to other process models of consciousness (Block, 1995; Edelman, 1989; Moscovitch, 1989; Schacter, 1989), in which consciousness is taken to be a unitary, or at most a binary, phenomenon, the LOC model offers an expanded conception of consciousness and provides a metric for measuring the level at which consciousness is operating in specific situations. This metric should be useful in a wide variety of investigations, because although the model emphasises age-related constraints on the highest level of consciousness that children can attain, levels of consciousness clearly fluctuate even in adults.

NOTES

1. It should be noted that for Brentano, intentionality was the criterion of 'the mental', as opposed to the merely physical, and he evidently understood mentality to be coextensive with consciousness (see his description of 'presentations', p. 78 ff).
2. Incidentally, it might be noted that the contents of working memory are obviously not identical to the occurrent contents of consciousness. For example, when we rehearse a telephone number, all seven digits remain in an activated state (i.e. in working memory) even though we are only aware of a subset of them at any given instant.

ACKNOWLEDGEMENTS

Philip David Zelazo, Department of Psychology, University of Toronto. Preparation of this chapter was supported in part by a grant from NSERC of Canada to P.D. Zelazo. I would like to thank D. Frye and P.R. Zelazo for their valuable contributions to the ideas contained in this chapter.

REFERENCES

Armstrong, D.M. (1980). *The nature of mind and other essays*. Ithaca, NY: Cornell University Press.
Astington, J.W. (1993). *The child's discovery of the mind*. Cambridge, MA: Harvard University Press.
Baddeley, A.D. (1992). Working memory. *Science, 255*, 556–559.
Baldwin, J.M. (1894/1968). *Mental development in the child and the race (3rd Ed.)*. New York: Augustus M. Kelley.
Berry, D.C., & Broadbent, D.E. (1984). On the relationship between task performance and associated verbalizable knowledge. *Quarterly Journal of Experimental Psychology, 36A*, 209–231.
Block, N. (1995). On a confusion about a function of consciousness. *Behavioral and Brain Sciences, 18*, 227–246.
Bowerman, M. (1986). First steps in acquiring conditionals. In E.C. Traugott, A. ter Meulen, J.S. Reilly, & C.A. Ferguson (Eds.), *On conditionals* (pp. 285–307). Cambridge: Cambridge University Press.
Brentano, F. (1874/1973). *Psychology from an empirical standpoint*. (O. Kraus, Ed.; A.C. Rancurello, D.B. Terrell, & L.L. McAlister, Trans.). London: Routledge & Kegan Paul.
Carruthers, P.K. (1996). *Language, thought, and consciousness: An essay in philosophical psychology*. New York: Cambridge University Press.
Clements, W.A., & Perner, J. (1994). Implicit understanding of belief. *Cognitive Development, 9*, 377–395.
Cohen, L.B. (1998). An information processing approach to infant perception and cognition. In F. Simion & G. Butterworth (Eds.), *Development of sensory, motor, and cognitive capacities in early infancy: From perception to cognition*. Hove, UK: Psychology Press.
Davidson, D. (1980). *Essays on actions and events*. Oxford: Oxford University Press.
DeCasper, A., & Spence, M.J. (1991). Auditorily mediated behavior during the perinatal period: A cognitive view. In M.J.S. Weiss & P.R. Zelazo (Eds.), *Newborn attention: Biological constraints and the influence of experience* (pp. 142–176). Norwood, NJ: Ablex.

DeLoache, J. (1993). Distancing and dual representation. In R.R. Cocking & K.A. Renninger (Eds.), *The development and meaning of psychological distance* (pp. 91–107). Hillsdale, NJ: Lawrence Erlbaum Associates Inc.

Dewey, J. (1960). *On experience, nature, and freedom* (R.J. Bernstein, Ed.). New York: The Liberal Arts Press.

Dewey, J. (1985). Context and thought. In J.A. Boydston (Ed.), & A. Sharpe (Textual Ed.), *John Dewey: The later works, 1925–1953* (Vol. 6, 1931–1932, pp. 3–21). Carbondale, IL: Southern Illinois University Press. (Original work published in 1931.)

Diamond, A. (1985). Development of the ability to use recall to guide action, as indicated by infants' performance on AB. *Child Development, 56,* 868–883.

Diamond, A. (1991). Neuropsychological insights into the meaning of object concept development. In S. Carey, & R. Gelman (Eds.), *The epigenesis of mind: Essays on biology and cognition* (pp. 67–110). Hillsdale, NJ: Lawrence Erlbaum Associates Inc.

Diamond, A., & Taylor, C. (1996). Development of an aspect of executive control: Development of the abilities to remember what I said and to "Do as I say, not as I do". *Developmental Psychobiology, 29,* 315–334.

Edelman, G. (1989). *The remembered present: A biological theory of consciousness.* New York: Basic Books.

Fischer, K.W. (1980). A theory of cognitive development: The control and construction of hierarchies of skills. *Psychological Review, 87,* 477–531.

Flavell, J.H., Green, F.L., & Flavell, E.R. (1986). Development of knowledge about the appearance-reality distinction. *Monographs of the Society for Research in Child Development, 51* (1, Serial No. 212).

Frye, D. (1981). Developmental changes in strategies of social interaction. In M.E. Lamb & L.R. Sherrod (Eds.), *Infant social cognition* (pp. 315–331). Hillsdale, NJ: Lawrence Erlbaum Associates Inc.

Frye, D., Zelazo, P.D., Brooks, P., & Samuels, M. (1996). Inference and action in early causal reasoning. *Developmental Psychology, 32,* 120–131.

Frye, D., Zelazo, P.D., & Palfai, T. (1995). Theory of mind and rule-based reasoning. *Cognitive Development, 10,* 483–527.

Gerstadt, C.L., Hong, Y.J., & Diamond, A. (1994). The relationship between cognition and action: Performance of children $3\frac{1}{2}$–7 years old on a Stroop-like day-night test. *Cognition, 53,* 129–153.

Goldman-Rakic, P.S. (1990). The prefrontal contribution to working memory and conscious experience. In J.C. Eccles & O. Creutzfeldt (Eds.), *The principles of design and operation of the brain* (pp. 389–407). New York: Springer-Verlag.

Gopnik, A., & Astington, J.W. (1988). Children's understanding of representational change and its relation to the understanding of false belief and the appearance-reality distinction. *Child Development, 59,* 26–37.

Gray, J.A. (1998). Abnormal contents of consciousness: The transition from automatic to controlled processing. In H.H. Jasper, L. Descarries, V.F. Castellucci, & S. Rossignol (Eds.), *Consciousness: At the frontiers of neuroscience, Advances in Neurology* (Vol. 77, pp. 195–208). New York: Lippincott-Raven Press.

Halford, G.S., Wilson, W.H., & Phillips, S. (1998). Processing capacity defined by relational complexity: implications for comparative, developmental, and cognitive psychology. *Behavioral and Brain Sciences, 21,* 803–831.

Hofstadter, M., & Reznick, J.S. (1996). Response modality affects human infant delayed-response performance. *Child Development, 67,* 646–658.

Hughes, C. (1998). Executive function in preschoolers: Links with theory of mind and verbal ability. *British Journal of Developmental Psychology, 16,* 233–252.

Hunter, W.S. (1917). Delayed reaction in a child. *Psychological Review, 24,* 74–87.

Jacques, S. (1995). *The development of rule use during the preschool period.* Unpublished master's thesis, University of Toronto, Ontario, Canada.

James, W. (1890/1950). *The principles of psychology* (2 vols.). New York: Dover.

Kagan, J. (1972). Do infants think? *Scientific American, 226,* 74–82.

Kagan, J. (1981). *The second year.* Cambridge, MA: Harvard.

Kant, I. (1781/1927). *Critique of pure reason.* (F.M. Muller, Trans.). New York: Macmillan.

Karmiloff-Smith, A. (1992). *Beyond modularity.* Cambridge, MA: MIT Press.

Lewicki, P., Czyzewska, M., & Hoffman, H. (1987). Unconscious acquisition of complex procedural knowledge. *Journal of Experimental Psychology: Learning, Memory, & cognition, 13,* 523–530.

Lewis, M., & Brooks-Gunn, J. (1979). *Social cognition and the acquisition of self.* New York: Plenum Press.

Luria, A.R. (1961). *The role of speech in the regulation of normal and abnormal behaviour.* New York: Pergamon Press.

Marcovitch, S., & Zelazo, P.D. (in press). The A-not-B error: Results from a logistic meta-analysis. *Child Development.*

Moore, C., & Corkum, V. (1994). Social understanding at the end of the first year of life. *Developmental Review, 14,* 349–372.

Moscovitch, M. (1989). Confabulation and the frontal systems: Strategic versus associative retrieval in neuropsychological theories of memory. In H.L. Roediger & F.I.M. Craik (Eds.), *Varieties of memory and consciousness: Essays in honour of Endel Tulving* (pp. 133–160). Hillsdale, NJ: Lawrence Erlbaum Associates Inc.

Nelson, K. (1997). *Language in cognitive development: The emergence of the mediated mind.* New York: Cambridge University Press.

Olson, D., & Campbell, R. (1993). Constructing representations. In C. Pratt & A. Garton (Eds.), *The development and use of systems of representation* (pp. 11–26). New York: John Wiley & Sons.

Perner, J., Leekham, S., & Wimmer, H. (1987). Three-year-olds' difficulty with false belief: The case for a conceptual deficit. *British Journal of Developmental Psychology, 5,* 125–137.

Piaget, J. (1936/1952). *The origins of intelligence in children.* (M. Cook, Trans.). New York: Vintage.

Piaget, J. (1937/1954). *The construction of reality in the child.* (M. Cook, Trans.). New York: Ballantine.

Reed, M.A., Pien, D.L., & Rothbart, M.K. (1984). Inhibitory self-control in preschool children. *Merrill-Palmer Quarterly, 30,* 131–147.

Reilly, J.S. (1986). The acquisition of temporals and conditionals. In E.C. Traugott, A. ter Meulen, J.S. Reilly, & C.A. Ferguson (Eds.), *On conditionals* (pp. 309–331). Cambridge: Cambridge University Press.

Reznick, J.S., Feuser, J.J., & Bosquet, M. (1998). Self-corrected reaching in a three-location delayed-response search task. *Psychological Science, 9,* 66–70.

Rosenthal, D. (1986). Two concepts of consciousness. *Philosophical Studies, 49,* 329–335.

Schacter, D. (1989). On the relation between memory and consciousness: Dissociable interactions and conscious experience. In H.L. Roediger & F.I.M. Craik (Eds.), *Varieties of memory and consciousness; Essays in honour of Endel Tulving* (pp. 355–389). Hillsdale, NJ: Lawrence Erlbaum Associates Inc.

Searle, J. (1990). Consciousness, explanatory inversion, and cognitive science, *Behavioral and Brain Sciences, 13,* 585–642.

Sigel, I. (1993). The centrality of a distancing model for the development of representational competence. In R.R. Cocking & K.A. Renninger (Eds.), *The development and meaning of psychological distance* (pp. 91–107). Hillsdale, NJ: Lawrence Erlbaum Associates Inc.

Slater, A., & Morison, V. (1991). Visual attention and memory at birth. In M.J.S. Weiss & P.R. Zelazo (Eds.), *Newborn attention: Biological constraints and the influence of experience* (pp. 256–277). Norwood, NJ: Ablex.

Vygotsky, L.S. (1978). *Mind in society: The development of higher psychological processes.* Cambridge, MA: Harvard University Press.

Zelazo, P.D. (1994). From the decline of development to the ascent of consciousness. *Behavioral and Brain Sciences, 17,* 731–732.

Zelazo, P.D. (1996). Towards a characterization of minimal consciousness. *New Ideas in Psychology, 14,* 63–80.

Zelazo, P.D., Carter, A., Reznick, J.S., & Frye, D. (1997). Early development of executive function: A problem-solving framework. *Review of General Psychology, 1,* 198–226.

Zelazo, P.D., & Frye, D. (1997). Cognitive complexity and control: A theory of the development of deliberate reasoning and intentional action. In M. Stamenov (Ed.), *Language structure, discourse, and the access to consciousness* (pp. 113–153). Amsterdam & Philadelphia: John Benjamins.

Zelazo, P.D., Frye, D., & Rapus, T. (1996). An age-related dissociation between knowing rules and using them. *Cognitive Development, 11,* 37–63.

Zelazo, P.D., Helwig, C.C., & Lau, A. (1996). Intention, act, and outcome in behavioral prediction and moral judgement. *Child Development, 67,* 2478–2492.

Zelazo, P.D., & Jacques, S. (1996). Children's rule use: Representation, reflection, and cognitive control. In R. Vasta (Ed.), *Annals of Child Development, Vol. 12.* (pp. 119–176). London: Jessica Kingsley Press.

Zelazo, P.D., & Reznick, J.S. (1991). Age-related asynchrony of knowledge and action. *Child Development, 62,* 719–735.

Zelazo, P.D., Reznick, J.S., & Piñon, D.E. (1995). Response control and the execution of verbal rules. *Developmental Psychology, 31,* 508–517.

Zelazo, P.D., Reznick, J.S., & Spinazzola, J. (1998). Representational flexibility and response control in a multi-step, multi-location search task. *Developmental Psychology, 34,* 203–214.

Zelazo, P.R. (1982). The year-old infant: A period of major cognitive change. In T. Bever (Ed.), *Regressions in mental development: Basic phenomena and theoretical alternatives* (pp. 47–79). Hillsdale, NJ: Lawrence Erlbaum Associates Inc.

Zelazo, P.R., & Kearsley, R. (1980). The emergence of functional play in infants: Evidence for a major cognitive transition. *Journal of Applied Developmental Psychology, 1,* 95–117.

Zelazo, P.R., Weiss, M.J., & Tarquinio, N. (1991). Habituation and recovery of neonatal orienting to auditory stimuli. In M.J.S. Weiss & P.R. Zelazo (Eds.), *Newborn attention: Biological constraints and the influence of experience* (pp. 120–141). Norwood, NJ: Ablex.

Zelazo, P.R., & Zelazo, P.D. (1998). The emergence of consciousness. In H.H. Jasper, L. Descarries, V.F. Castellucci, & S. Rossignol (Eds.), *Consciousness: At the frontiers of neuroscience. Advances in Neurology* (Vol. 77, pp. 149–165). New York: Lippincott-Raven Press.

CHAPTER TEN

Linguistic determinism and the understanding of false beliefs

Jill G. de Villiers and Peter A. de Villiers
Smith College, Northampton, MA, USA

INTRODUCTION

We intend in this chapter to put forward a radical proposition about the relationship between language and the understanding of false beliefs. We begin by contrasting the roles that language acquisition might play with respect to the development of theory of mind reasoning, separating out the language-for-the-task from the social constructivist view of language as one of several facilitators of social cognition, and both of these from the strongest position that certain linguistic structures make available a representational format for false beliefs. We then present empirical data from a longitudinal study of normally developing pre-school children and from our work with language-delayed oral deaf children, to test among the rival hypotheses for the role of language in the development of false belief reasoning. The empirical data make a surprisingly coherent story, though many pieces remain to be worked into the puzzle. The empirical story is at least suggestive enough that it forces us to examine the strongest theoretical position seriously, and ask, is it viable?

OVERVIEW OF GENERAL THEORETICAL POSITIONS ON LANGUAGE OF MIND

Coincident development in language and theory of mind

Several researchers have noted that mastery of false belief reasoning tasks is closely related to measures of language ability, in both normally developing and autistic children (Happe, 1995; Tager-Flusberg, 1994, 1996; Tager-Flusberg &

Sullivan, 1994). For example, Jenkins and Astington (1996) found that general false belief understanding, summed across four standard tests of false belief reasoning, was significantly correlated with measures of syntactic and semantic maturity on the Test of Early Language Development (TELD), even when the effects of age were partialled out. More specifically, the sophisticated use of sentence forms involving mental state verbs and their complements coincides roughly in time with the child's successful performance on standard false belief tasks (Astington & Jenkins, 1995; Bartsch & Wellman, 1995; de Villiers, 1995b; Tager-Flusberg, 1996). The usual proposal to account for this relationship is that the understanding of beliefs and states of mind is prerequisite for correctly using the linguistic forms that express those concepts—the standard orthodoxy of cognitive determinism of language development (Cromer, 1991; Tager-Flusberg, 1994). Hence in many cases the emergence of children's talk about mental states, using verbs such as "want", "need", "think", "know", and "remember" has been taken as a marker of their growing underlying conceptual understanding of a variety of mental states in themselves and others (Bartsch & Wellman, 1995; Bretherton & Beeghly, 1982; Shatz, Wellman, & Silber, 1983; Wellman, 1990).

However, there has recently been increased interest in examining which particular aspects of language may be fundamentally involved in theory of mind development and in specifying more clearly the precise nature of the relation between language and theory of mind. As stated by Bartsch and Wellman (1995, p. 209): "We will make little progress in understanding how theory of mind is acquired unless we investigate more closely how development of a theory of mind relates to development of language."

What aspects of language might be involved?

As Astington and Jenkins (1995) point out, in exploring this issue researchers have focused on several different features of language. Thus several have suggested that an understanding of people's mental states—their intentions, desires, beliefs and states of knowledge or ignorance—is both a prerequisite for and emerges out of the *pragmatics* of conversational communication (de Gelder, 1987; Harris, 1996; Peterson & Siegal, 1995). Reading an interactor's communicative intentions is a fundamental component of conversation, as is the adjustment of one's own utterances to fit the listener's states of knowledge and belief (Grice, 1975; Sperber & Wilson, 1987). Breakdowns in communication serve to focus attention on differences in the assumptions and beliefs of the interactors.

Others have focused on the *semantics* of mental terms and the emergence of these lexical items in the language of the child to refer to both their own and others' mental states. Olson (1988) argued that theory of mind development requires a language for talking about the mind, a metalanguage based on the semantic understanding of terms such as "think" and "know". Bartsch and

Wellman (1995) believe that children's use of these words provides a window on the child's growing understanding of the concepts that underlie them. Similarly, Gopnik and Meltzoff (1997) propose that conceptual and semantic development may go hand in hand: at particular periods of development when the child is actively engaged in solving specific conceptual problems (such as those to do with theory of mind) their attention may be drawn to learning words that are relevant to those problems.

Still others have argued that there is a relation between theory of mind understanding and language at the *syntactic* level. Feldman (1988) sees the link at the level of the topic–comment structure of languages and the process of linguistic recursion by which comments are turned into topics. She argues that a similar recursion rule is needed for the child to be able to reflect on their own and others' mental attitudes in a mature theory of mind. Thus the mastery of recursion underlies both the linguistic advances of the child and their emerging thinking about thinking during the third and fourth year of life. Both de Villiers (1995a,b) and Tager-Flusberg (1995, 1997) have noted that verbs of communication (e.g. "say" and "tell") and mental state (e.g. "think", "believe", and "know") are the two primary classes of verbs that take embedded sentential complements. The syntactic process of complementation allows for the embedding of one propositional argument under another proposition, as is needed for the expression of propositional attitudes such as beliefs and states of knowledge. Furthermore, in these sentential complement structures a false proposition can be embedded under a verb of mental state and the whole sentence nevertheless remain true, so the syntax of complementation may be uniquely suited to the conceptual representation of false beliefs.

What role does language play in theory of mind development?

The nature of the relation between language and theory of mind development has also been conceptualised in several different ways (Astington & Jenkins, 1995).

Conceptual understandings of the mind develop first and are the basis onto which language maps. For a long time the dominant view has been that cognitive development leads the way, with a conceptual understanding of mental states emerging out of the interaction between maturing cognitive capacities and social awareness from interaction with others. More cognitive theories of ToM development have differentially stressed innate modules and the role of maturation (Leslie, 1994), the cognitive development of different levels of representation (Perner, 1991a,b), or more general cognitive skills such as working memory (Freeman, 1994; Mitchell & Lacohée, 1991; Olson, 1993) and executive function (Frye, Zelazo, & Palfai, 1995; Russell, 1996). More social theories have stressed the child's active participation in social interaction and the interpersonal context as the basis for the emergence of both concepts about other minds and language about the mind (Hobson, 1994; Shatz, 1994).

Conceptual understandings of the mind develop first but the child's underlying competence may be masked in theory of mind tests by linguistic complexity and pragmatic features of the language of the task (Freeman, Lewis, & Doherty, 1991; Siegal & Peterson, 1994).   This is a "weak" hypothesis about the role of language in theory of mind development. Language is seen as simply one of several possible performance variables (such as working memory limitations) that may constrain or limit the child's task performance. Language acquisition plays no fundamental or causal role in the conceptual changes taking place in the child's theory of mind: at best it has an indirect or peripheral effect through its impact on performance.

Many of the standard tests of reasoning about mental states involve the child in following and integrating a verbal narrative, often supported by pictorial or dramatic representation of the events. These are followed by questions posed by the tester. The language in which the false belief questions are posed has a significant effect on whether 3- to 4-year-old pre-schoolers pass the standard tasks or not.

For example, key questions assessing the child's understanding of false beliefs are sometimes put in the form of multi-clause sentences with "think" and an embedded complement clause, such as: "Where does Johnny think his candy is?" or "Before she looks inside, what will Sarah think is in the box?".

Obviously to answer these questions correctly, the child must have acquired sufficient language to comprehend such embedded complement structures with verbs like "think" and "know", and there is bound to be a strong relationship between their language skills and their performance on these tests.

More subtly, the wording of the question may communicate particular conversational presuppositions about how it should be answered. So in the usual task in which an object's location is changed, Siegal and Beattie (1991) changed the test question to "Where will Jane look *first* for her kitten?". Simply inserting the word "first" in this way significantly increases the percentage of 3-year-olds who answer correctly in terms of the character's false belief (see also Leslie, 1994). This is because the conversational pragmatics now communicate to the child that the question should not be taken to mean "Where will Jane find her kitten?" or "Where should Jane look for her kitten?". Rather the insertion of "first" indicates to the child that Jane may be wrong at first but still look in the "right" place eventually.

Even when the language of the task does not itself involve an understanding of complex language about the mind, the child's language skills can be a major constraint on their performance. Thus Lewis (1994) has demonstrated that children's ability to recount the narrative in standard false belief tests, and so to organise their memory for the events in verbal form, contributes to successful performance on the subsequent false belief reasoning questions posed by the tester.

Language facilitates social cognition and development of a theory of mind by focusing attention on the mental explanation of behaviour (Bartsch & Wellman, 1995; Dunn et al., 1991).   It is possible that access to language about mental events scaffolds the child's understanding in a more expedient way than observation of social interaction alone. Human children do not need to learn simply by observation, because the people around them structure that understanding through talk. Dunn et al. (1991) demonstrated a relationship between the amount of talk about feelings and causation of behaviour in various families and the children's understanding about beliefs, emotions, and desires seven months later. Astington and Jenkins (1995) consider as one explanation of their data the "social constructivist" view that ToM is mediated by talk within the family. Similarly, Peterson and Siegal (1995) in a study of deaf children's ToM development, entertain the idea that "communicative fluency" is what engenders the social relationships necessary to build a ToM. Adults and other children use language to refer to such states of desire and belief from the time the child is quite young, and provide a discourse about other persons that might serve as a vital experience in the child's conception of others' minds. In the extreme, language could merely *highlight* pretence, desire, and false belief events without explicitly representing them. Imagine a mother sits down with her child and in front of his eyes, pours salt into her tea. She might groan and say, "Oh no! I wanted the sugar!" or, "OOPS! I made a mistake!". It seems plausible to suggest that language provides a marking that highlights unusual behaviour that has no surface explanation, i.e. behaviour that requires the development of a "folk psychology" of intention, desire and belief, thus children as young as three and four are brought more rapidly to that understanding. On this account, there is nothing particularly special about the structure or the content of language, as long as it serves to draw the child's attention to the odd event. However, the facts suggest that the child does not just hear exclamations of distress, but rather begins to learn the way we talk about such events in our culture.

The language of complementation provides a representational structure for embedded propositions.   In the example above, the language event provides a marking but not an explicit representation of the mother's false belief, which would still need to be inferred and represented, as something like: "Mother thought *she was pouring sugar in her tea*". But we have been driven to ask: in what form is that representation, and could language facilitate that representation more directly? If one believes that the representation of false beliefs is not propositional at all, perhaps being mediated by identification or empathy, then linguistic complementation would play no specific role in enhancing it (see Gopnik, 1993, for discussion of alternatives). However, we continue to find the representational position more persuasive, or at least less disruptive of our other philosophical commitments.

We have argued that a child who becomes capable of the language of complementation, namely embedded propositions, might have available a new *representational capacity* for propositional attitudes. That is, perhaps the complex syntax that is used for describing mental events makes possible the representational changes that allow for understanding false beliefs. The language for discussing mental events provides the child with a formal means of embedding propositions, and thus provides a necessary ingredient for representing false beliefs. This theory would impute a much more significant role to language development than is currently discussed.

Consider some special properties of sentences involving mental states that might provide this representational means. Sentences involving mental states require an embedded proposition called a *complement* in linguistics: He thought *it was a lion*. Complements appear under verbs of desire (*want*), communication (*say, ask*) and mental state (*know, think, forget*). Some of these verbs can take a simple NP (She wants *a ride*) but they can also take a whole embedded proposition (We forgot *that he lost the key*). Complements provide a way to discuss lying or mistakes: He said *he had salad for lunch* (but he really had pizza); He thought *he left the door open*.

Notice that the overall sentence can be true, though the embedded complement can refer to a proposition that is false, e.g. in this latter case he shut the door. Thus complementation provides a means of representing someone's mental world, and that mental world could be distinct from our mental world. On this account it is not just that language provides the discourse within which children reach an understanding of mind, it is critical that it also provides structures of the right semantic complexity and power for the representation of false beliefs.

De Villiers (1995b) speculated about the stages of development necessary for the child to reach false belief understanding, and traced its development to the emergence in language of complements that express mental state and communication verbs, summarised in the following model:

Step 1: the child masters the basic sentence forms: a simple sentence is mapped onto a simple event. The child encounters true sentences that match reality.

Step 2: the child first encounters discrepancy between sentences and reality: the child learns to recognise pretence as well as mistakes.

Step 3: the child masters the first embedded structures under verbs of communication/mental state/desire: child acquires the fundamental syntax of embedding but makes no accommodation of meaning within that structure. That is, the complement retains its truth value as a simple sentence independent of the matrix verb. So, if the child hears a sentence such as "Jim said he ate the broccoli", the child thinks it is true *both* that Jim said something, and that he ate the broccoli.

Step 4: the child first notices occasions with verbs of communication that suggest the complement can be false when embedded e.g. reports of lying, mistakes. For example, the child notices that what Jim *said* he ate is not what he really ate. Because statements are overt and can be compared to reality, the semantic accommodation is made evident.

Step 5: the discovery about semantic accommodation mastered with the complements of verbs of communication can now be extended to verbs of mental states, e.g. beliefs. The child can then understand a statement such as "Jim thought he ate broccoli", to imply that Jim had a false belief. The "thought" is not overt, so it must be inferred from actions or statements, but the analogy with communication structures allows the sentence to be understood, thus the possibility of other minds with thoughts that do not map onto one's own reality is given expression.

This model attributes a significant role to the child's exposure to sentences and events containing acts of mis-speaking (lying, mistakes) as the stepping stone to the mastery of sentence complements, which then become available for representing the invisible thoughts and beliefs of others. The position taken in this model is a variety of linguistic determinism: linguistic complementation allows the representation of "propositional attitudes" such as needed in a theory of mind framed in a language of thought. The model tries to capture how the development might be bootstrapped by linguistic structures in domains less opaque than mental states.

De Villiers (1999) elaborates the claim that young children below the age of about three and a half years misrepresent the structure of embedded complements such as: "He said he drank milk". We have consistently found that children younger than about age four years do not represent complement structures, even about communication verbs, in a completely adult fashion. In particular, children have a difficulty with questions such as: "What did he say he drank?", if the character said he drank something other than what he really drank. The strong tendency is for young children to respond as if they were answering instead the question: "What did he drink?" (see also Riggs & Robinson, 1995; Wimmer & Hartl, 1991). Having tried several alternative linguistic and non-linguistic interpretations of the problem, it is clear that it cannot be reduced to one in which children simply don't process the matrix verb, nor can it be written off as a purely cognitive limitation. De Villiers concludes that the problem is a linguistic one: that young children have an "under-articulated" clause structure that lacks some crucial feature, namely, whatever it is that allows the embedded proposition to be false without disturbing the overall truth value. Interestingly, only embedded complements have the property that they can be false yet the sentence that contains them can still be true. In all other instances where propositions combine to make sentences, if any of the propositions is false then so is the whole.[1] Compare: "He fell after he drank milk". If he drank cider, the sentence is false. "He fell and drank milk". If he drank cider, the sentence is false. "He liked that milk he drank". If he drank cider, the sentence is false. But: "He said he drank milk". If he drank cider, the sentence is still true. The lower clause is embedded in the first, it is crucially not an independent clause such as a conjoined sentence. The claim is that only complements of mental and communication verbs can be "false" propositions (vis-à-vis the "real world", i.e. our point of view) and not upset the truth of the entire sentence. This special property of dependence "opens up" possible worlds, that is worlds different than the world in which the proposition is false. The special semantics of complements allow the possibility of talking about a fundamental distinction between things in the world and things as they are represented in someone's mind.

There must be some feature in the clause to distinguish these cases from other clauses—adjuncts, matrix clauses—whose truth is judged with respect to "the real world". In essence we subordinate the truth value of the complement to the truth of the matrix clause. In linguistic theory, factive complements are usually considered to have some unique marking, but on the current analysis it is the non-factive complements of mental and communicative verbs that have the more distinctive characteristic. Where might such a feature be marked? In current linguistic treatments (Chomsky, 1981, 1995) all clauses are headed by a "functional category"[2] CP, that is normally the site for complementisers (*that, which, where, how, for*) in embedded clauses and also for wh-questions and perhaps other Operators in matrix (main) clauses. In one recent treatment (Rizzi, 1996) the CP is multiplied into several functional sites to accommodate e.g. focus, topic and wh-questions. Other linguists prefer the idea of a single structural position with features that must be checked for particular semantic and functional purposes (Kratzer, 1997). Whatever the correct formulation, de Villiers (1997) suggests that there is some feature in the CP subcategorised for a particular verb that says that the proposition in its complement *can* be false. This feature must take one value in the CP of mental and communicative verbs, and a different value in the matrix CP, the CP of factive verbs, or in the CP of relative clauses attached to head nouns, which are obligatorily true if the sentence is true. The complements of mental and communicative verbs are marked by this feature as intensional clauses, i.e. their propositions describe "possible worlds" with truth relativised to those worlds. Until the point that this feature is established in the child's grammar, the child has no way to express anything but "real world" semantics.[3] The "possible world" semantics expand the child's repertoire of linguistic representations, and via those representations, new ways of reasoning become a possibility.

When young children lack that feature in CP, or have it "set" to the default form, then they will not be able to represent reports of lies or mistakes. When children can finally represent that feature, it is only the first of a series of features in an articulated CP feature set that eventually must accommodate at least tense perspective (cf. Hollebrandse, 1999), speaker beliefs / referential opacity (de Villiers & Fitneva, 1996) and factivity (de Villiers, Curran, Philip, & DeMunn, 1997). In other words, it is argued that the full articulation of linguistic *structure* eventually accommodates all the other special *semantic* features of certain propositional attitude reports.

Do other linguistic forms connect to mental state knowledge?

The question then returns to the representation of other propositional attitudes, such as those of *desire: want, like, need,* and those of pretence: *imagine, pretend.* For instance, several researchers have reported earlier understanding of other's desires before false beliefs (Gopnik, 1993). The structures necessary in language to represent desire do not typically involve a full, tensed *that* clause in English (see also Perner, 1991a), but rather a *to*-clause that represent an event that is "irrealis" rather than true/false: "He wanted to go home" or a simple NP: "He likes apples".

In fact, these kinds of structures enter children's language well before full tensed complements (Bloom, Rispoli, Gartner, & Hafitz, 1989). Whether or not those language forms play any particular role in the ability to represent those propositional attitudes about another person remains to be investigated. A similar point may be made about some forms of pretence, in that the linguistic forms for *pretend* also can involve a to-complement that is irrealis: "She pretended to be a dog". However, pretend can also take a *that* tensed complement in striking similarity to the structures for mental verbs of false belief: "We pretended that the rug was a desert island".

Now clearly, there are important differences still to be explored concerning the parallelisms of pretence and false belief representations. Perhaps some of the controversy over the age at which children genuinely understand pretence has to do with the kind of underlying representation, paralleling the two linguistic forms (Lillard, 1993; Perner, Baker, & Hutton, 1994). However, Custer (1996) reports an experiment in which all else is held constant about the scenario except for the use of the verb *think* versus *pretend* versus *remember*, all with that-complements, and found that 3-year-old children did show better performance based on the verbs *pretend* and *remember*. The conclusion Custer reaches is that only *think* involves a genuine conflict with reality. Since we have not yet worked on pretence, we leave these issues for the future to resolve.

Finally, there is the interesting work on counterfactuals discussed by Riggs and Peterson (Chapter 5, this volume). Do counterfactuals provide an alternative encoding of the structures necessary for the representation of mental state knowledge, one that need not involve the use of mental verbs such as *think, know*? From the linguistic standpoint, counterfactuals are not found in young children's speech until after at least age four or so (Cromer, 1968, 1971; Kuczaj & Daley, 1979), and are probably understood later than mental verbs with complements.

Even if they do provide the appropriate semantic structures for representing false belief reasoning, it is less clear that the linguistic forms could be the bootstrap for false belief representation.

EMPIRICAL DATA TO DISTINGUISH THE POSITIONS

We next discuss the empirical data we have gathered on the relationship between language and theory of mind that attempts to tease apart the four positions outlined above. These data come from two sources: work on normally developing pre-school children, and work on language-delayed orally-taught deaf children, who provide us with a most important means of teasing out cognitive and linguistic developments that are usually intertwined.

Longitudinal study of normally-hearing pre-school children

De Villiers and Pyers (1997) report the initial results of a longitudinal study of children aged 3 to 4 years old which tested the order of development of key language and false belief achievements. The 3-year-olds were tested four times over the course of one year with varying versions of the same tasks, and what follows summarises the analysis of data from the first three rounds of data collection from the first cohort of 19 children (collected in October, January, and May of one year). The tasks used were a collection of standard false belief tasks and language tasks.

False belief tasks

(a) *Unexpected contents task* (Perner, Leekam, & Wimmer, 1987). On each round of testing we asked about a different familiar container: a CRAYOLA crayon box, a Playdough container, a Cheerios cereal box, and a small milk carton, and asked both about the child's own prior belief (Gopnik & Astington, 1988) and their friend's likely belief, for a total of two points.[4]

(b) *Unseen displacement* (Wimmer & Perner, 1983). In this type of task, a child is told a story which is acted out in front of her, and in the story a character comes to hold a false belief about the whereabouts of an object. The child must then predict where the character will first look for that object.[5] The problem lies in interpreting this answer, because chance is 50/50 for identifying the right place, given that only two places are usually highlighted in the story via the memory check questions. We therefore also ask the question "why will he look there?" and gave a point for a suitable explanation for the character looking in the wrong location. This explanation did not have to use mentalistic vocabulary, so saying "because he put it there" counted as a perfectly adequate answer. An answer that did not count as adequate might be saying "because the Dad moved it". Thus this task gave a total of two points.[6]

(c) *Explaining action* (Bartsch & Wellman, 1989).   The third false belief task used was a combination of the above two scenarios in which a puppet is deceived. While the puppet is asleep, the child is shown a familiar box, say an egg carton with eggs, and the eggs are removed from the container and hidden in another unmarked box. The puppet is then woken up and the child is told "You know what he likes to do when he wakes up? He likes to eat eggs!". The puppet is then made to manipulate the (empty) egg box and the child is asked, "Why is he looking in there?" and "Why isn't he looking in that (other) box?". Mental explanations are again not necessary for points on this task: saying, "because they were in there" is coded as a satisfactory explanation. These three false belief tasks thus each had a maximum score of 2, for a total of 6 each round. The "passing" criterion was set at 5 or 6 out of 6.

Language tasks

(a) *Memory for complements in described mistakes*:   Previous work had shown that children have difficulty in answering such questions when the lower or embedded proposition is false (de Villiers, 1995a,b). On each round, children received 12 sets of photographs or drawn pictures of brief stories in which a character was described as making a mistake, telling a lie, or having a false belief. Half the scenarios involved acts of thinking (verbs *think*, *believe*) and half involving acts of communication (verbs *say* and *tell*). For half of the events, the question asked for a report of the contents of the character's belief/statement, e.g.:

> He thought he found his ring, but it was really a bottle cap.
>   What did he think?
> She said she found a monster under her chair, but it was really the neighbour's dog.
>   What did she say?

For the other half, the question asked for a report on the object of the character's believed or stated action, which required simply a noun rather than the whole propositional content:

> This girl saw something funny at a tag sale and paid a dollar for it. She thought it was a toy bird but it was really a funny hat.
>   What did she think she bought?

Memory for complements had a total possible score of 12 and the criterion for passing was set at 10 or more out of 12. Notice that we regard this task as a relatively pure measure of the child's understanding of the linguistic representation, unconfounded by the ability to make the appropriate false belief attribution.

In this task we provide the attribution, and the child just has to be able to represent it in memory and repeat it. Oddly enough, this does not just involve parroting; instead children seem to "fix" the sentence to have a true complement if they have not reached the point of allowing false complements under a verb.

(b) *Spontaneous speech.*   In Rounds 2 and 3 the spontaneous speech of the children was transcribed from a variety of situations inside the test sessions, for example while playing computer adventure games with us, and after watching silent videos of odd mistakes, when the children often described similar things that happened to them.

Analysis

We derived MLU scores, and we also used the Index of Productive Syntax (IPSyn) (Scarborough, 1990) to derive a quantitative measure of the grammatical complexity of the children's language. The IPSyn codes the emergence in children's spontaneous language of a set of grammatical types that were selected on the basis of the considerable normative research on syntactic development in pre-schoolers over the past 30 years. The IPSyn demonstrates good reliability for child language corpora of as few as 50 utterances, and is more discriminating of normal syntactic development between the ages of 24 and 48 months than is mean length of utterance (MLU). Furthermore, the IPSyn captures persistent syntactic differences between normal and language-delayed pre-schoolers in longitudinal studies (Rescorla & Schwartz, 1988). From the IPSyn scoring we created several subtotals such as the total Sentence Structure score (SS), the total complex sentences (total complex IPSyn), the total score for complements (IPSyn comps), and the total complex minus complements (IPSyn complex no comps). These last two scores allowed us to separate the critical feature of sentential complements with mental/communication verbs from other forms of complex sentence that play no role in our theoretical argument, such as relative clauses and if–then clauses. In this way we hoped to separate out the general role of language as a facilitator, or as an index of general maturity, from the more specific role we attribute to the appropriate representation of complements.

Several different analyses were conducted to explore the relationship among the language and theory of mind tasks. The most crude is of course intercorrelations among performance on individual tasks. Table 10.1 shows the intercorrelations at Round 2, when there was the greatest variance on all tasks.[7] At this point the average age of the children in the study was 3 years 8 months, with a range of 3;4 to 4;1. There are higher values for the correlations between the false belief tasks and the IPSyn complement measure rather than the more general language measures. As expected, the language measures also correlated with each other, so more refined analyses are needed to separate the contributions.

TABLE 10.1

Pearson product moment correlations between measures of language acquisition and performance on the three types of false belief tasks at Round 2

	Unseen object displacement	Unexpected contents	Explaining actions
IPSyn complements	.68***	.50*	.58**
IPSyn No Comps	.33	.13	.17
MLU	.45*	.28	.12
Memory for complements	.50*	.61**	.31

$* P < .05; ** P < .01; *** P < .001$ (two-tailed).

If it is true that the false belief tasks have as a prerequisite the representation of false complements in language, then we expect growth in the ability to represent complements among children who fail false belief tasks. However, children who pass false belief tasks should show no continued growth in this aspect of complementation. Figure 10.1 shows changes across rounds in the success on language (memory for complements) task as a function of passing or failing the false belief tasks. The results partially support that argument, at least for rounds 2 and 3. The converse, namely that children who pass complement tasks might still be developing the consistent use of them for false belief reasoning, is supported by the growth patterns in Fig. 10.2. However, children who fail on complement representation should show no growth in false belief ability, as also confirmed in Fig. 10.2.[8]

A further analysis used simple regressions to try to predict false belief at Round 3 on the basis of language at Round 2. The outcome variable was passing (5 or 6) or failing (< 5) on Round 3 false belief tasks and the predictor variable in language was memory for complements at Round 2. A respectable 32.1%

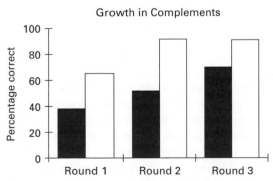

FIG. 10.1   Development in memory for complements in children who fail or pass false belief tasks (■, failers; □, passers).

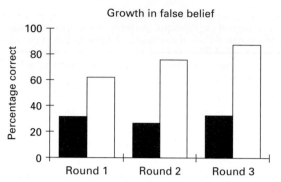

FIG. 10.2   Development in false belief understanding in children who fail or pass memory for complements (■, failers; □, passers).

$(P < .01)$ of the variance is accounted for with this direction of analysis. The opposite analysis is to attempt to predict complement syntax (memory for complements) at Round 3 on the basis of false belief measures at Round 2. The outcome measure used was passing (10 to 12 out of 12) or failing (< 10) on memory for complements and the predictor variables were the subscores on false beliefs: prediction, contents, explanation. However, the percentage of variance accounted for was only 9.5% (n.s.). The fact that the results are asymmetrical in this way lends credence to the argument that mastery of complements is prerequisite for false belief.

The final analysis goes one step further to investigate whether the mastery of complements can be teased out as a variable beyond the contribution made by general language development. For our theory, the critical mastery is complementation, not overall length of utterance or other kinds of complexity. For these analyses we used the measures derived from the spontaneous speech analyses, that separated out the score on complements from other kinds of complex syntax as well as gross developmental indices such as MLU. The "memory for complement" measure does not allow that separation, so only the spontaneous measures can contribute to that question. Of course these speech measures have significant intercorrelations—a child who develops complementation and uses it frequently will also have a high MLU and undoubtedly other signs of complex syntax such as relative clauses or if–then clauses. Stepwise regression allows a test of which language measures contribute most strongly.

We first tried to predict "passing" false belief at Round 2 on the basis of language measures in that same round. It revealed that the most significant predictor variable was production of sentential complements (IPSyn comps) (47% of variance, $P < .001$). No other language measure added significantly to the variance accounted for by this complement measure. The entire set of language measures at Round 2 predict 55% of the variance in false belief on that round. But it would be more convincing if we could predict not simultaneous, but future performance in false belief. So we then performed a stepwise regression to predict "passing" false belief at Round 3 on the basis of language measures at Round 2. Once again, the analysis revealed that the most significant predictor variable was the production of sentential complements (IPSyn comps) at Round 2 (29% of variance, $P < .01$). The whole set of language measures at Round 2 predict 38% of the variance in later false belief, thus the other measures add only slightly to the predictive power of complements.

Consider a major criticism of the interpretation of the empirical findings of the longitudinal study. It could be argued that the language measures of complementation themselves involved false-belief understanding, but that some tasks were sufficiently simple (e.g. memory for complements just involved remembering what was said) that they inevitably preceded success on the more demanding tasks of false belief reasoning. Thus, our direction of effects are trivially true: easier tasks precede harder tasks, but the same thing is involved in all of them, namely, the representation of false beliefs. On that view, either conceptual development is independent of linguistic development, or is facilitated by language via one of the weaker mechanisms suggested above. In partial defence, we do find evidence that the spontaneous use of complements in speech is predictive of false belief reasoning. This covers communication verbs as well as verbs of mental state, so the complements used do not necessarily involve reference to either true or false beliefs, but sometimes just to acts of speech. We have argued above (and de Villiers, 1999) that we cannot be sure that complementation in child language is *genuine* until the second clause *can* be false, but the individual tokens we count in spontaneous speech do not have to be false, and neither do they have to be about mental events.

We will return to interpretation after exploring another source of evidence, namely our work with deaf children. We hope to demonstrate with these data that the critic who dismisses the significance of the coincidental development of complements and false belief reasoning in normally developing children should find it troubling that deaf children should be delayed in ToM, if language is not causally relevant. Those theories that might attribute the intercorrelations of language and false belief reasoning to some more general underlying cognitive change in development, such as the maturation of an innate ToM module (Leslie, 1994), would not predict a delay in nonverbally-tapped false belief reasoning in intellectually normal but language-delayed children.

Empirical data on standard and non-standard ToM tasks from language-delayed deaf children

Most profoundly deaf children have hearing parents, many of whom decide to raise them in an oral environment, and send them to school to learn English and lip-reading. Even with the best and earliest intervention with hearing aids and special teaching, the first few years of language development for such a child are known to be significantly delayed compared to the normal case (Mogford, 1993; Paul & Quigley, 1993). However, with some variation, orally-taught deaf children test in the normal range on non-verbal tests of intelligence, at least up to age 6 (Marschark, 1993). Furthermore, although caregiver–child interaction can be disrupted for deaf children with hearing parents (Lederberg, 1993; Meadow, Greenberg, Erting, & Carmichael, 1981; Montanini-Manfredi, 1993); deaf children can also be socially active, tuned in to the family and their peers, and even inventors of rich systems of gestures to convey simple and even embedded propositions (de Villiers, Bibeau, Ramos, & Gatty, 1993; Goldin-Meadow, 1982; Goldin-Meadow & Mylander, 1984). So unlike autistic children, deaf children are interested in and motivated by social interaction and actively seek it out. This is not to claim that oral deaf children are completely unimpaired in the area of social functioning. Several researchers have reported more egocentrism and delayed role-taking abilities in situations in which the deaf child needs to predict the feelings of others (Greenberg & Kusché, 1989, 1993). Greenberg and Kusché (1993) show that these deficits are primarily predicted by the language skills of the children, and are much less noticeable in nonverbal, game-like tasks. Thus any subtle social deficits in deaf children seem to be causally tied to their development of language and communicative skills. Much of the socio-emotional development of the deaf child depends on the development between the child and the caregiver of fluent and easy communication, in whatever modality. However, with an orally-taught deaf child not exposed to Sign, the limited speech, vocabulary and syntax typically present at age 4 years is insufficient to support elaborate mind-talk, especially reference to other's beliefs. It is not yet clear that the subtleties expressed in mind-talk can be accomplished with a non-conventional gesture system, unless the listener has rich contextual support.

For all these reasons, it becomes very interesting to study the development of ToM in oral profoundly deaf subjects, who can be argued to be normally developing both cognitively and socially in non-verbal realms, but lack access to talk and expression about the states of mind of other persons. If we are wrong in attaching importance to language as a catalyst for developing false belief understanding, then deaf children will succeed at these tasks on the basis of their nonverbal understanding of social interaction, which might be acute, given their dependence on it rather than language for predicting other's behaviour. Indeed, it could be that such an essential ingredient for proper social interaction is a "robust" module of mind, buffered against the vagaries of cultural and biological accidents, and hence accessible by a variety of developmental routes, much like language itself.

Since we wished to test the hypothesis that access to a rich language is a necessary ingredient in establishing the mature ToM on a normal timetable, we needed to demonstrate that young oral deaf children have limited access to language of sufficient complexity to capture false belief statements, and that they fail traditional, language-based false belief tasks. However, that failure could be due to the lack of language for the tasks. We needed in addition to find tasks to demonstrate tested understanding of ToM without the associated use of language. We needed to show first that these tasks were equivalent in difficulty and representational demands for normally-developing 3- to 5-year-olds. We then endeavoured to test whether oral deaf children would fail these same non-verbal tasks of false belief or knowledge inference.

In Gale, de Villiers, de Villiers, and Pyers (1996) we report the results of an initial series of studies that begin to tease out these possibilities with orally-taught deaf children. We are engaged in a much larger enterprise that examines the language and theory of mind abilities in other groups of deaf children exposed to American Sign Language at different ages, but that data collection is in its very early stages and we will not discuss it here.[9]

The children that serve as the subjects in our work must meet certain criteria to be included, such as having a normal non-verbal IQ, showing active social interaction, and being moderately to profoundly deaf. As a result of the latter, the subjects have varying degrees of delay in language acquisition, with especially delayed complex syntax (such as complementation), but also reduced vocabulary.

Consider first how such children fare on standard theory of mind tasks, adapted to accommodate their difficulties in speech comprehension, and compared to their language competencies. Gale et al. (1996) used the following tasks:

Unseen displacement. A standard unseen displacement story was modified for use with the 23 deaf subjects aged between 4 and 9 years. Two modifications in the way the task was administered made the procedure more accessible to the deaf children. First, our pilot testing with oral deaf children revealed that acting out the events with dolls while telling the story was very distracting for deaf children trying to follow the narrative by lip-reading, whether the narrative was simultaneous with or sequential to the actions. Therefore, an artist depicted each event in the scenario in watercolour pictures which were placed in a three-ring binder in the form of a flip-up book. The narrative was told with the book held just below the experimenter's chin, a procedure familiar to the deaf children from the way their teachers read them picture book stories.[10] Second, as in the longitudinal study with hearing children, the word "first" was inserted into the crucial question about where the character would look for the moved object—namely, "where will the boy *first* look for his cake?". As in our studies with hearing children, control questions were asked before the crucial "where look" question to make sure that the child remembered where the object had first been placed and then where it had been moved to.

False belief reasoning—unexpected object in a familiar container. In the standard unexpected contents task using a Crayola crayon box the deaf children were asked about their own prior belief and a friend's likely false belief about the contents of the box.

For the *unseen change in object location* story we consider only the data from the 20 deaf children who could answer the "memory check" questions. Only 11 of the 20 children (55%) correctly answered the false belief question by indicating that the boy would first look in the cupboard where he had put the cake, not in the refrigerator where the cake now was.

For the *unexpected contents task* the children each received a score out of two, one point for correctly reporting their own initial false belief and one point for giving the same answer for their friend's likely false belief. Only 8 of the 21 children (38.1%) answered both of the questions correctly. Ten children (47.6%) correctly reported their own previous false belief and 12 children (57.1%) correctly answered the question about their friend's initial false belief.

The average age of passers on the tasks was 7.41 years (unseen displacement), and 7.25 years (unexpected contents), that is, 3 years older than the normally hearing pre-school children who we tested on precisely the same tasks. This would suggest that language delay can have a significant impact on false belief reasoning, but we must also demonstrate that the deaf children's language was predictive of their performance on the false belief tasks.

Language tasks: Explanation of action—elicited language about the mind.   To elicit language that might include language about mental states, the 18 deaf children above the pre-school level[11] were shown several short videotape clips taken from Charlie Chaplin silent films and from Loony Tunes cartoons. All of the videos were shown without sound. Each video clip included events involving mistakes or deception that could be satisfactorily explained only by referring to the characters' desires, lack of knowledge, or false beliefs.

For example, in one Tom and Jerry cartoon, Tom the cat ties Jerry the mouse onto his fishing line and casts him into a pond as bait. Unseen by the cat, the mouse swims underwater to a dock on which a big dog is asleep in the sun. Carefully he ties the fishing line to the dog's back leg and then tugs on the line to fool Tom into thinking that he has caught a fish. As the cat excitedly reels in the "fish" (still underwater and so unseen by him), Jerry hands him a club with which to stun it. Tom wades into the pond and begins beating the underwater "fish" with the club, only to have it emerge from the water as a large, irate dog.

After viewing a video clip twice, the child was asked to describe the events: "Tell me all about what happened". Following this spontaneous narrative, one or two digitised still pictures from the video were shown to the child, one at a time. These pictures captured key moments in the scenario at which inferring the character's cognitive state was essential for understanding the events. For each such picture the experimenter pointed at the key character in the event and asked the child: "What is happening in the story here?". If this open-ended picture description did not elicit a mental explanation of the action(s), E again pointed at the pictured character and asked two increasingly specific prompt questions: "Why did/is X . . . (action)?", and "What is happening in his head when he . . . (action)?".

Each child saw 8 video clips and 12 still pictures. The testing session was videotaped and the children's spontaneous and prompted utterances were transcribed for later analysis.

Relationship between language and verbal false belief reasoning.   The children's spontaneous and prompted explanations of the characters' actions on the video clips were transcribed and scored for whether they contained references to cognitive states such as beliefs, thoughts, knowledge, or ignorance, or to other mental states such as desires and emotions. Points were assigned on the basis of the spontaneity and developmental sophistication of the explanations given. Thus a child received three points for producing at least one spontaneous explanation referring to the character's cognitive state, two points if cognitive state explanations were only given following prompts, and only one point if they made reference to desires or simple emotions but not to thoughts or knowledge (see Bartsch & Wellman, 1995, for developmental data). Giving a cognitive explanation of action in this task of necessity involved producing an embedded complement construction.

The children's performance on the two standard false belief tasks was combined into a verbal false belief reasoning score and then correlated with the explanation of action score, the children's age and degree of hearing loss, and with their PPVT-R verbal mental age (which served as a more general measure of language ability). Producing complex sentences with cognitive state verbs like think and know was by far the strongest predictor of the children's false belief reasoning on the standard verbal tests. The correlation between the verbal explanation of action scores and verbal false belief reasoning was + .70 (df = 16; $P < .001$); however, none of the other three variables—age, hearing loss or PPVT—was significantly related to performance on the standard false belief tests. Furthermore, the correlation between explanation of action and false belief reasoning remained significant even when the effects of the other three variables were partialled out (partial $r = + .59$, $P < .01$).[12]

These data suggest that it is the language of these deaf children that is responsible for their delays in standard false belief performance. However, the standard tasks themselves place demands on the children for language comprehension: how can we be sure that it is not language-for-the-task that is responsible for these tight interconnections? To address this issue, we have undertaken studies using non-verbal (or less-verbal) procedures to tap false belief reasoning with oral deaf children, to see if their performance is enhanced if language demands are lessened. In this case, it is possible that deaf children could show appropriate age performance, if language development is only relevant as a task demand.

The critical data come from the oral deaf children with language delay. However, we have first demonstrated that normally developing pre-school children show roughly equivalent performance on the non-verbal or less verbal tasks that we discuss below, compared to their performance on standard verbal false belief tasks (de Villiers, de Villiers, Pyers, Frey, & Gale, in preparation; Gale et al., 1996). They have not shown us earlier or better mastery on the nonverbal procedures.

Sticker-finding game.   In Gale et al. (1996) we describe a task we call the sticker-finding game, a modification of the procedure used by Povinelli and deBlois (1992) with 3- and 4-year-olds (and with chimpanzees). Its basic purpose is to see whether children can understand that seeing leads to knowing, and that knowledge leads to good advice. It is thus not strictly a false-belief task, more of a seeing-knowing task, but as we report in Gale et al. (1996), it is highly correlated with performance on the standard false belief tasks, and is mastered at the same age (around age 4;4 in our sample of pre-schoolers). The child plays a game in which she must find stickers hidden by the experimenter in a series of boxes, and clues are given by pointing. However, the people who give the clues are either a confederate of the experimenter who has watched where the sticker was hidden (the knower), or a confederate who has been blindfolded and therefore cannot know (the guesser). Obviously the child should go with the reliable advice given by the knower, but she has to figure out the contingencies herself by observing and extrapolating points-of-view.

Only 11 of the 23 deaf children (47.8%) succeeded in choosing the knower's box significantly more often than expected by chance over the course of 10 test trials. Ten of these children fulfilled both criteria that we set for success: at least seven of the last eight trials correct and a run of at least six consecutive trials correct. The average age of these passers was virtually identical to the age of deaf passers on the standard theory of mind tests, that is, 7.31 years. Scores on the standard verbal tasks and the mostly non-verbal game were highly correlated (r (18) = + .60, $P < .01$). As for the verbal false belief tasks, correlational analyses revealed that having the language to explain actions in terms of cognitive states was the strongest predictor of performance on the sticker-hiding game ($r = + .61$, df = 16; $P < .01$).

Thus Gale et al. (1996) demonstrated that oral deaf children were equivalently delayed in their mastery of verbal and non-verbal theory of mind tasks tapping their reasoning about their own and others' cognitive states. This argues against an explanation of the delayed theory of mind performance of deaf children merely in terms of the language-of-the-tasks. Nevertheless, the degree of delay in the individual deaf children's theory of mind reasoning was closely related to their language ability, particularly their production of complex language about the mind.

The above studies still have several limitations. In particular, the non-verbal task was really a test of the children's reasoning about the relationship between seeing and knowing, rather than more closely tied to the understanding of expectations and false beliefs being tested in the standard verbal tasks (though it is clear for both hearing pre-schoolers and the deaf children that there is a close relationship in development of the concepts of knowledge/ignorance and true/false belief). Second, the explanation of action measure that was used in Gale et al. (1996) might be considered as much a highly verbal measure of theory of mind reasoning as it is a measure of language development (see Bartsch & Wellman, 1995, for the use of linguistic expression as a measure of theory of mind development). So it is not surprising that the explanation of action measure should emerge as the strongest predictor of performance on the standard verbal false belief tasks, though perhaps a little more surprising that it should also be so predictive of the non-verbal sticker-hiding game.

So we carried out a further study of 27 oral deaf children using a different less-verbal procedure more closely related to the standard unexpected contents test of false belief and a more linguistic analysis of syntax development (the IPSyn scale for spontaneous speech that was used in de Villiers & Pyers, 1997).

What face? Surprised or not surprised.   This relatively non-verbal procedure is basically a version of the unexpected contents concept, involving a familiar container that leads one to expect it to contain certain items. The trick of it as a non-verbal procedure is that rather than verbally reporting what someone thinks is in the box, the child must predict whether a character is surprised or not when they see the unusual contents. They do this by choosing the right facial expression to stick on the character's blank face.[13] The character has either seen the unexpected item being placed in the container (so will not be surprised), or has seen only the closed container (surprised).

A pre-test established that the children knew the facial expression corresponding to surprise, or more specifically, our artist's rendition of it. Next came a warm-up or "training" phase in which the general idea of the procedure was demonstrated to the child. This consisted of two multi-picture sequences involving characters who were either "surprised" or "not surprised" by an event or object depending on whether they had seen it before or not. Other than the utterances specified below, the picture sequences were not accompanied by a full spoken narrative, relying on the pictures to tell the overall story. In the warm-up phase the children were given the chance to complete the character's face as directed, and were given corrective feedback if they chose the inappropriate expression.

There followed a series of six test picture sequences, in the first picture of each a character was shown finding or manipulating an object (e.g. finding a coin on the ground). After the picture was placed in front of the child E pointed to the focal object and made sure that the child knew what it was called. In picture 2 the character emptied the usual contents out of a familiar container, i.e. one that predisposed the viewer to expect particular contents (e.g. a Crayola crayon box, an egg carton, or a Bandaid [plasters] tin). Again, after picture 2 was placed in front of the child E pointed to the contents being emptied out and made sure that the child knew what they were called. In picture 3 the character put the object from the first picture into the familiar container. Two different

FIG. 10.3   An illustrated pair of parallel stories from the "what face?" task.

versions of pictures 2 and 3 were drawn. In each of these a friend of the character is shown: in one version (the "not surprised" condition) they are closely watching the character's actions as the usual contents of the container are removed and the unusual contents are substituted, but in the second version (the "surprised" condition) they are engaged in another activity, turned away from the action, and do not see the substitution. In picture 4 the friend is shown with the closed familiar container, about to open it. Motivation for obtaining either contents is supported by objects present with the container. So in the Crayola crayon box picture sequence there is a colouring book and a lockable treasure chest shown on the table with the crayon box in picture 4. Thus the pictured person could either be wanting a crayon or the key that the box now contains. Finally in picture 5 the friend opens the box and its unusual contents are revealed. In this picture the friend is drawn with only an outlined blank face. The child was asked to choose which face to put on the last picture (see Fig. 10.3). On the first two test trials, before asking which face should be placed on the picture, E pointed at the friend in pictures 2 and 3 (when the object substitution took place) and said: "S/he saw" or "S/he did not see". However, on the remaining four test trials, E simply pointed back at the friend in pictures 2 and 3, then pointed to the final picture and said: "What face? Is s/he surprised or not surprised?".

In the test phase each child saw three picture sequences in which the key character did not see the object substitution and thus the "surprised" face should be chosen and three sequences in which the friend watched the substitution and so the "not surprised" face should be chosen. No correcting feedback was given on any of these six trials.

How do normally developing pre-schoolers fare on this task? De Villiers et al. (in preparation) tested twenty-eight 3- and 4-year-old children on this task and on standard false belief tasks. A score of five or six out of six was taken as a passing score ($P = .10$, binomial test), for the "what face" task. According to this criterion, ten out of eighteen of the 4-year-olds and two out of ten 3-year-olds passed the task. On the standard verbal tasks, children who correctly answered both questions on an unexpected contents task (own belief and other's belief) and also answered correctly about where the character would first look in two displaced object stories, counted as passing, i.e. scoring 4 out of 4. Table 10.2 shows the average ages of the passers and failers on the standard verbal false belief tasks and the less verbal "what face?" task. There was a significant average age difference between passers and failers on the "what face?" task, but not on the standard verbal tasks.

The less verbal task seems to have been a little harder for the pre-schoolers than the standard verbal tasks. Fifteen of the twenty-eight pre-schoolers (53.6%) passed the standard tasks, but only twelve of them (42.9%) passed the "what face?" task. Furthermore, whereas three children passed the verbal false belief tasks without passing the less verbal surprise task, for no children was the reverse true. Nevertheless, children's total score on the standard false belief

TABLE 10.2

Mean age and number of pre-schoolers passing or failing the verbal and less verbal theory of mind reasoning tasks. Also shown are the results of *t*-tests on the difference between the ages of passers and failers

	Passers	*Failers*	
Standard verbal false belief tasks	4.33 (*n* = 15)	4.05 (*n* = 13)	$t(26) = 1.49$, ns
"What face?" surprise task	4.46 (*n* = 12)	4.01 (*n* = 16)	$t(26) = 2.63$, $P < .02$

tasks was significantly correlated with their score on the "what face?" task (r (26) = + .61, $P < .001$).

Having demonstrated that the "what face" task is roughly equivalent to more verbal standard theory of mind tasks for normally hearing pre-schoolers, we can now ask how language-delayed deaf children perform on this task. De Villiers et al. (in preparation) tested 27 moderately to profoundly deaf children in the elementary grades of a prominent oral school for the deaf. None of them had been formally exposed to sign languages in their education. Their ages varied from 5:2 to 10:1, with a median of 7:0 years.

All of the children received three unseen object displacement stories in which they were asked both where the crucial character would first look for the moved object and why s/he would first look there. The stories were administered in the same picture-book format described in the Gale et al. (1996) experiment. The deaf children received one point for each of the "where will s/he look?" questions that they correctly answered. Verbal false belief reasoning scores therefore varied between 0 and 3, with 3 correct answers considered "passing" the verbal tasks. In this group of oral deaf children, 14 of the 24 children (58.3%) who passed the "memory control" questions passed all of the "where look" questions.

The "what face?" task was administered and scored in the same way as for the normally hearing pre-school subjects. Two of the deaf children could not correctly identify the "surprised" and "not surprised" faces in the pre-test, so only the data from the other 25 children are considered. Taking as the criterion for passing the task 5 or 6 correct choices out of 6 sequences, 8 of the 25 deaf children (32%) mastered the "what face?" task. All of them had scored 3 out of 3 on the questions following the standard unseen object displacement stories. So the less verbal "what face?" task was harder for the deaf children than the standard verbal unseen displacement test of false belief understanding. Six children who answered correctly all of the "where look" questions did not pass the "what face?" task.[14] However, across all the children there was a close relationship between performance on the verbal false belief tasks and performance on the less verbal "what face?" procedure: a significant Pearson product moment correlation was obtained between scores on the "what face?" procedure and scores on the standard unseen object displacement stories ($r = + .58$, $P < .02$).

Analysis.   We can again ask whether the deaf children's language ability was related to their performance on the false belief tasks of all varieties, and whether we can tease apart general language ability from the specific mastery of mental state complements. The relationship between language and theory of mind performance was examined for the 23 deaf children who met the following criteria: they had passed the memory control questions for all of the unseen object displacement stories; they had correctly identified the "surprised" and "not surprised" faces in the pre-test of the "what face?" task; and they had produced at least 50 utterances during the testing sessions and while chatting about things happening in the school to allow scoring of their spontaneous speech.

Measures of the children's *syntax production* were determined from the language samples. These samples varied in size from 51 to 111 utterances, with a mean of 67. The Index of Productive Syntax (IPSyn) was used to derive a quantitative measure of the grammatical complexity of the children's language (Scarborough, 1990), paralleling the work of de Villiers and Pyers (1997) described above. Our IPSyn scoring of the language samples from the deaf children focused on the sentence structure subscale. We concentrated on this subscale for two reasons. First, it does not rely on subtle morphological features of English. Oral deaf children are particularly inconsistent in supplying inflectional morphemes in their speech even when their sentence-structuring syntax is well developed, and even the accurate transcription of such morphemes in oral deaf speech is problematic. Second, it enabled us to separate out the critical feature of syntax that we were interested in, namely the production of sentential complement structures with verbs of communication or mental state. Thus we derived two separate scores for each deaf child from the sentence structure (SS) subscale of the IPSyn: productive use of sentential complements (IPSyn SS-Comps), a score varying from 0 to 4; and the remainder of the sentence structure items (IPSyn SS-Other), a score varying from 0 to 36. Pearson product-moment correlations revealed that the children's IPSyn SS-Comps and IPSyn SS-Other scores were strongly correlated with each other (r (21) = + .75, $P < .001$); and each of the IPSyn SS scores was significantly correlated with the PPVT-R. However, none of the other background variables—age, non-verbal IQ, and hearing loss— was significantly related to any of the language measures.

Table 10.3 shows the correlations between the children's performance on the theory of mind tasks and several possible predictors of that performance. All of the language measures were significantly related to the children's theory of mind performance, though the strongest relationships were with the production of sentential complements with verbs of communication and mental state (the IPSyn SS-Comps). Of the other background variables, only age showed any significant relationship with theory of mind performance—correlating with scores on the "what face?" surprise procedure.

Multiple regression analyses allowed us to test the independent effects of the predictor variables on theory of mind performance, carried out for each of two

TABLE 10.3

Pearson product moment correlations between predictor variables and performance on the verbal and less verbal ("what face?") theory of mind tasks for 23 oral deaf children

	Verbal false belief ("Where look?")	"What face?" surprise task
IPSyn SS-Comps (embedded complements)	.73***	.74***
IPSyn SS-Other (minus complements)	.66***	.58**
PPVT-R verbal MA	.55**	.57**
TONI-2 nonverbal IQ	.15	.16
Hearing loss (aided)	-.32	.01
Age	.16	.43*

df = 21; * $P < .05$; ** $P < .01$; *** $P < .001$ (two-tailed).

dependent measures: (1) total verbal false belief reasoning score on the three standard stories ("where look?" questions only); and (2) score out of six on the "what face?" scenarios. Six predictor variables were entered into each regression: IPSyn SS-Comps, IPSyn SS-Other, PPVT-R verbal mental age (i.e. vocabulary), TONI-2 non-verbal IQ, aided hearing loss, and age. The results for each of the regression analyses are shown in Table 10.4.

TABLE 10.4

Multiple regression analyses of language and background measures as predictors of performance on the standard verbal false belief stories and the less verbal "what face?" procedure

	Verbal false belief ("Where look?")	"What face?" surprise task
Multiple regression	$R^2 = 62.2\%$ $F (6, 16) = 4.39$ $P < .01*$	$R^2 = 67.0\%$ $F (6, 16) = 5.42$ $P < .005$
Significant predictors	IPSyn SS-Comps $t = 2.34, P = .032$	IPSyn SS-Comps $t = 2.73, P = .015$ Age $t = 2.31, P = .035$
Non-significant variables	IPSyn SS-Other PPVT-R verbal MA Nonverbal IQ Aided hearing loss Age	IPSyn SS-Other PPVT-R verbal MA Nonverbal IQ Aided hearing loss

* Values of P are all two-tailed.

For the verbal false belief reasoning tasks, the children's IPSyn complement score emerged as the only significant independent predictor of performance, separable from the contribution of the more general language measures and background variables like IQ, hearing loss and age. For the less verbal "what face?" task, both the IPSyn complement score and age made significant independent contributions to the variance in the children's performance on the theory of mind task.

Summary of empirical data

In sum, we have demonstrated the following:

(1) A predictive relationship over time for normally developing hearing preschoolers between control of complement syntax in comprehension and production and performance on standard false belief tasks, with syntax at an earlier age predicting later theory of mind performance (not vice versa).
(2) Oral deaf children with normal IQ and active social intelligence are significantly delayed in both standard verbal false belief tasks and much less verbal theory of mind tasks. Performance on both verbal and non-verbal tasks are delayed to the same degree and highly intercorrelated, so it is not just the language of the tasks that leads to delay.
(3) Both verbal false belief reasoning and non-verbal ToM reasoning in deaf children are best predicted by complement production with verbs of communication or mental state, not just by general language ability.

THE CONTINUITY OBJECTION

Before we consider the theoretical ramifications of the empirical data, we must digress briefly to consider the objection to the strongest position based on the continuity of development in both linguistic and cognitive domains. This objection goes as follows: the acquisition of theory of mind is a continuous process, not an all-or-none development, as is the acquisition of complementation. How can one trigger or provide computational resources for the other if both are continuous developments, not breakthroughs?

We fully accept that development is most likely continuous and context- and resource-dependent. However, it might also be true that there is a point when something is achieved reliably, and that point is reached sooner for the language representation than the false belief tasks. We consider the point of reliable performance to constitute some "permanent" change in the representation, that presumably makes it impervious to further assaults of resource or context changes or limitations. In the false belief literature that change is usually referred to as the acquisition of the "theory"; in the language acquisition literature, researchers would agree that the structure has been acquired. In both domains however, there are persuasive advocates of the position that the skill/structure/capacity can be seen much earlier, and that the earliest point at which it is achieved should be regarded as the point of acquisition, with subsequent ups and downs being regarded as the usual vagaries of performance, or computational limitations. We have not studied the onset points of either false belief or of complementation, because we are concerned that "chance" performance is so often near 50% on all these standard tasks that we may be seriously misled into mistaking success for mastery. For example, consider the graph of change in Fig. 10.4, from de Villiers and Pyers (1997).

Obviously at the first point of testing, the children are occasionally getting some questions right in the battery of false belief tasks, and some questions right in the complement comprehension task. However, their performance does not stabilise for months thereafter, so we feel more confident setting the usual statistical criteria for successful performance and judging them to "pass" when that point is exceeded. Unless one does a study with sufficient exemplars at each testing point, it is very hard to determine the appropriate criteria, and errors of attribution are very likely to be made. Nevertheless, the question is an open one for empirical inquiry, and the rich anecdotal literature would seem to bear out the claim that children get "glimmers" of success in both linguistic and cognitive domains for several months prior to reliable mastery on the standard tasks. That does not alter the significance of the findings that we report here, though it leaves room for other interpretations of direction-of-effect for *normally developing*

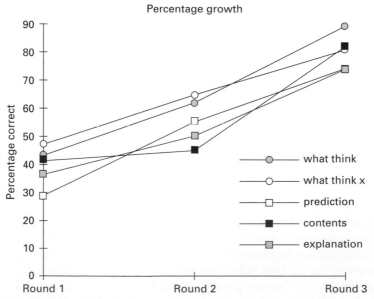

FIG. 10.4   Percentage growth over three rounds of the longitudinal study across false belief and memory for complements task.

children. What those other interpretations do not explain is the delay in false belief understanding in *language-delayed deaf* children.

In language acquisition there are also serious arguments for the Continuity Hypothesis, namely, that children's grammars are the same as adult grammars in all essential respects. Learnability considerations in language acquisition lead to an assumption that since children cannot learn grammars from the inadequate environment and exposure (the so-called "poverty of the stimulus"), their grammars must be present fully formed from the beginning. What the child's task is then is to learn (no, actually *fix*) the parameter settings that define her particular language (see Cook & Newsom, 1996; Hyams, 1986). On this account it is also unthinkable to propose that children have less-than-adequate complementation until they are approaching four years of age, since their grammars must contain all the relevant structures from the beginning. In extensive work on the development of complex syntax in children speaking several different languages, we (de Villiers, 1995a,b, 1996; Roeper & de Villiers, 1994) have argued that there is developmental change in grammar throughout the age period three to six years, and especially that the domain of complementation and clause combining is an area fraught with lexical specificity—of both verbs and connectives—that could not be fixed prior to learning a particular language. Penner (1996) draws a similar conclusion about the acquisition of Swiss German, following an extensive diary study of one child. That is, it is not necessarily the case that we must attribute the apparent delay in acquisition of the structures to insufficient computational power, or a cognitive system that is inadequately developed. Instead, it could be that the evidence necessary to fix the subtle properties of clauses embedded under and adjoined to verbs has to be amassed over a prolonged period of time, and awaits just the right combinations of context, intention and clearly structured talk. This is traditionally called learning, though it is learning of a highly constrained sort.

THEORETICAL VARIANTS OF THE STRONG POSITION

The data presented above, while far from conclusive, are compatible with the position that says that acquiring the language of complementation is prerequisite for being able to reason about false beliefs. It behoves us therefore to examine the theoretical position carefully. How could it be true? There are several alternative positions within this claim of linguistic determinism, and we need to unpack them to see which ones are plausible. The following set may not be exhaustive, but even sorting through these possibilities will take considerable theoretical and empirical work, involving considerable innovation.

First take the arguments on behalf of a separate, propositionally based language of thought. Fodor makes several relevant claims in his 1975 *The language of thought*:

(1) Thinking requires a language of thought. Imagistic representations are not sufficient to serve as a medium of propositional attitudes, though they may stand for "referents". Pictures are not the kind of things that have truth value, but thoughts must have.

(2) That inner language of thought cannot be, for example, English, because it is prerequisite for the acquisition of a natural language that you have a language of thought in which to entertain and form concepts in advance of learning the words and expressions of your language. So natural language is parasitic on a language of thought that is as rich in its conceptual and representational power as a natural language.

(3) Therefore, natural language cannot add to the representational power of the inner language of thought.

Taking this proposal seriously, let us examine the possible variants of how the representation of complements in natural language might relate to the representation of false beliefs within a language-of-thought. These fall naturally into two classes: one which stands in contradiction to (3) above, because natural language does add to the representational power of the language-of-thought, and a second class that does not contradict (3) because it just credits language with improving computational efficiency. These are important theoretical distinctions, but we do not wish to take a stand in favour of any of the alternatives until there are clearer empirical ways to tease them apart.

Class 1. The linguistic development of complementation makes possible a new form of representation in the language of thought

(1) Development in language triggers the corresponding representational structure in cognition. This possibility is the most vague, but has the virtue that it preserves the distinction between the representational structures in natural language and those in some more abstract, propositional language of thought. On this account, the structure exists already in an innate language of thought but is dormant until triggered by the equivalent development in natural language. This is a possibility that sounds attractive, as it preserves the idea that our representational structures are present without learning (Fodor, 1975, 1992). But like many triggering notions, it is hard to get beyond the surface of the metaphor. Notice, however, that the prediction of this alternative is that an adult who lost the grammatical structures in their natural language, say in aphasia, might be able to preserve the equivalent representational structures in the language-of-thought. This possibility is ruled out by most of the remaining hypotheses.

(2) The cognitive component is parasitic on the results of the specialised linguistic system of representation: it borrows the output. This position might be dismissable out of hand if it is agreed that ToM is a module (Leslie, 1994)

and that under modularity, each system is supposed to have its own fast, encapsulated processing of a specific type of stimulus input (Fodor, 1983). However, there is no agreement yet on either conjecture. If ToM uses general-purpose cognition, then there may be less restriction. Why could language-of-thought not use the resources of any developed module? The perception of 3-D forms is meant to be modular, though surely our reasoning makes use of the products of that perception. Furthermore, there are domains in which the specialisation of the procedures is such that it does not make sense to duplicate its representational capacity elsewhere: take for example, visual imagery, and the claim of a visuo-spatial "scratchpad" that could feed its output to other modules (Kosslyn, 1994). A good argument can be made that the semantic specificity and detail needed to represent propositional attitudes can only be done within a linguistic system (Segal, 1997): if so, why duplicate the functions and structures, since they are needed for natural language anyway?

(3) Reasoning in this case is bound to language: there is no separate "language of thought" for false belief reasoning. Suppose the language of thought *in this instance* is the logical form substrate of natural language, that is, give up *for this function* on a separate language-of-thought, and conclude that language is the medium necessary for false belief reasoning. Fodor dismisses the idea that thought *in general* is reducible to natural language for obvious reasons rehearsed in elementary psychology and philosophy classes: animals and infants can be shown to do things that we count as thinking, these forms of thought cannot just be imagistic but must be propositional, because images cannot have truth value. However, the possibility arises that certain specific forms of thought, perhaps those involved in false belief reasoning, do use natural language as the representational system. After all, infants and animals do seem to be capable of very clever thinking, but as yet no-one has proven that they understand others' false beliefs. It is a revolutionary thought to have language as the medium for thought in just this instance, but perhaps one should not rule it out.

Class 2. The linguistic representation of complementation facilitates computation in the language of thought

(1) By providing mnemonic structures via natural language that reduce the load on processing capacity. In addition to the claims (1)–(3) above that natural language could not add to the representational capacity of the language-of-thought, Fodor argues that even so, natural language could serve to enhance thinking *performance*, because it could serve as a mnemonic advantage to collect together heterogeneous examples under a symbol for the purposes of using them in higher computations.

So if one agrees with Fodor, advantage of linguistic complementation can be regarded as a useful mnemonic device for computational efficiency. Fodor (1992) has claimed that the child who acquires a theory of mind does nothing of the sort: she just gets rid of some awkward performance limitations to reveal what she knew all along. For Fodor, then, this role of language would be akin to several other performance "enhancers": the child should get better under any of a number of conditions, even without the role that language plays. Many such performance enhancers have been demonstrated: reducing the salience of "reality" as a distracter (Zaitchik, 1991) providing other mnemonics (Mitchell & Lacohée, 1991), improving the child's investment in the answer (Chandler & Hala, 1995), highlighting and engaging the child in the trickery (Avis & Harris, 1990; Sullivan & Winner, 1991), lessening the response demands by measuring initial direction of gaze (Clements & Perner, 1995). None of these studies measured the language status of their subjects, so we do not know if these devices are sufficient on their own, or just close a gap between mastery of complementation and mastery of false beliefs. We have not yet attempted ways to improve the performance of our oral deaf subjects, so the question must remain open.

(2) By providing mnemonic structures via natural language that make possible a quantum step up in processing capacity. This version sets a higher premium on what is achieved via the linguistic representation. It is not just computational efficiency, but a major step up in the ability to do the computation at all. For instance, it may be equivalent to the computational power achieved by gathering multiple instances together under a single symbol, which can then participate in higher order processes. One can imagine instances in which the multiplication and duplication of machinery and computation in the absence of such a symbol is so great that it strains the resources beyond capacity to attempt them.[15] The position is not incompatible with Fodor (1975) though it may well be with Fodor (1992), because the change in performance is so radical that we would be unable to distinguish it from a change in capacity. And, nothing else would do: no other lessening of performance limitations would be enough to open the door.

These alternatives may not be easily distinguished using the population of normally developing young children that has traditionally provided the empirical data for previous research on theory of mind developments. Our ongoing work with deaf children promises to allow us to separate more definitively among some of these alternatives: however, they may not all be empirically distinguishable.

CONCLUSION

Our empirical results have pointed us down a path for which we had some unique preparation: we have done most of our work in psycholinguistics. One of us had done detailed work on deaf children's language; the other, on how children handle complementation in the late pre-school years. Perhaps it was inevitable that we should attribute causal powers to the phenomena we know the best.

We have been careful not to make the more general claim that "a theory of mind depends on language". We are specifically referring to the false belief understanding critical for the classical tasks of unseen displacement and unexpected contents. Some theory of mind developments seem to emerge at different times, and each task deserves a critical analysis of its representational requirements (Astington, 1992; Gopnik, 1993; Leslie, 1994; Perner, 1991b; Wellman, 1990). In addition, it is clear that conceptual developments in theory of mind may also facilitate later language developments. Thus, it has become strikingly evident in much recent work that developments in theory of mind, including false belief understanding, may be a prerequisite for understanding in complex linguistic tasks such as using the subjunctive in relative clauses (Pérez-Leroux, 1997), substitution in referentially opaque contexts (de Villiers & Fitneva, 1996) and interpretation of embedded tense (Hollebrandse, 1999). The overall process is undoubtedly one of mutual facilitation between language and theory of mind, but the critical piece for us is the relationship between mastery of the fundamental syntax of complementation and false belief understanding. The direction of that effect is the focus of our empirical interest.

NOTES

1. Conditional and counterfactual sentences complicate the simplified picture here, as do performative utterances of various kinds whose truth value is not evident.
2. Functional categories are distinct from lexical categories (NP, VP, PP) in that they play mostly grammatical roles in sentences, such as IP for tense, CP for questions and sentence connectives (see Cook & Newsom, 1996; de Villiers, de Villiers, & Hoban, 1992).
3. Except in pretence, which must be considered as a separate case that does not violate truth conditions in the same way. To go into the details of how pretence differs from false belief would take us far beyond the present discussion, and is explicitly addressed in other contributions in this volume.
4. We explicitly marked the child's prior belief with the following question form, "Before, when you were sitting over there, what did you think was in the box?".
5. As suggested by Siegal and Beattie (1991) we used the form of the question "where will the boy *first* look for the cake?".
6. It has since been pointed out to us that the scale created by this analysis has some unfortunate properties, since the child can only gain the second point by gaining the first. We have changed the scoring in our subsequent work to count as "passing" only if the child gets both points. However, since we wish to report on the earlier work in de Villiers and Pyers (1997) we have left the coding in place for this report. We checked and found that new coding would not in fact affect the coded status (pass/fail) of any of our subjects, because this is a sum across several tasks.
7. In Round 1, performance was at floor with only one child passing false beliefs at all, so there could not be correlations of any significance there, and by round 3, the majority had passed.
8. In both Figs 10.2 and 10.3, the groups constituting the "failers" are not made up of the same children over rounds.

9. There are two other published studies of false belief reasoning in deaf children from total communication backgrounds (simultaneous signing and speech)—Peterson and Siegal (1995) and Steeds, Rowe, and Dowker (1997). Both of these studies showed significant delays in ToM reasoning in their subjects though they differ in the degree of delay. However, both studies used only standard verbal ToM tasks and neither had any measures of the language levels of the children in either of their communication modalities.

10. We have confirmed that the narrated picture book format is essentially equivalent to the acted out dolls house scenario for hearing pre-schoolers in terms of their understanding of the key character's false belief.

11. The five pre-school deaf children in this study were only using one and two-word sentences, so we did not attempt to elicit spontaneous speech from them.

12. Tager-Flusberg and Sullivan (1994) similarly reported high correlations between explanations of actions by reference to desires and cognitions and hearing pre-schoolers' performance on standard false belief tasks.

13. The version we used was modified from one first proposed by Ron Frey in unpublished dissertation research at the Ontario Institute for the Study of Education in Toronto.

14. Note that the "what face?" task requires the child not only to compute that the character has a false belief, but then make an additional inference about emotional state based on that belief. This may be harder than computing action based on belief, which is what is required for the "where look" task (Tager-Flusberg, personal communication).

15. Bickerton (1995) comes close to arguing this with respect to the power of language in thought in the evolutionary process.

ACKNOWLEDGEMENTS

The research reported here and writing this chapter was supported by NIH grant no. R01 HD32442 and NIH grant no. R01 DC02872 to the authors.

REFERENCES

Astington, J.W., & Jenkins, J.M. (1995). *Language and theory of mind: A theoretical review and a longitudinal study*. Paper presented at the biennial meeting of the Society for Research in Child Development, Indianapolis, IN.

Avis, J., & Harris, P. (1991). Understanding reasoning among Baka children: Evidence for a universal conception of mind. *Child Development, 62*, 460–467.

Bartsch, K., & Wellman, H.M. (1989). Young children's attribution of action to beliefs and desires. *Child Development, 60*, 946–964.

Bartsch, K., & Wellman, H.M. (1995). *Children talk about the mind*. New York: Oxford University Press.

Bickerton, D. (1995). *Language and human behavior*. Seattle, WA: University of Washington Press.

Bloom, L., Rispoli, M., Gartner, B., & Hafitz, J. (1989). Acquisition of complementation. *Journal of Child Language, 16*, 101–120.

Bretherton, I., & Beeghly, M. (1982). Talking about internal states: The acquisition of an explicit theory of mind. *Developmental Psychology, 18*, 906–921.

Chandler, M., & Hala, S. (1994). The role of personal involvement in the assessment of early false belief skills. In C. Lewis & P. Mitchell (Eds.), *Children's early understanding of mind: origins and development* (pp. 403–425). Hove, UK: Lawrence Erlbaum Associates Ltd.

Chomsky, N. (1981). *Lectures on government and binding*. Dordrecht: Foris.

Chomsky, N. (1995). *The minimalist program*. Cambridge, MA: MIT press.

Clements, W.A., & Perner, J. (1994). Implicit understanding of belief. *Cognitive Development, 9*, 377–395.

Cook, V., & Newson, M. (1996). *Chomsky's universal grammar* (2nd Ed.). Oxford: Blackwell.

Cromer, R. (1968) *The development of temporal reference during the acquisition of language*. Unpublished Ph.D. diss., Harvard University.

Cromer, R. (1971). The development of the ability to decenter in time. *British Journal of Psychology, 62*, 353–365.

Cromer, R. (1991). *Language and thought in normal and handicapped children*. Oxford: Blackwell.

Custer, W.L. (1996). A comparison of young children's understanding of contradictory representations in pretense, memory and belief. *Child Development, 67*, 678–688.

de Gelder, B. (1987). On not having a theory of mind. *Cognition, 27*, 285–290.

de Villiers, J.G. (1995a). Questioning minds and answering machines. In D. MacLaughlin & S. McEwen (Eds.), *Proceedings of the 19th Boston University Conference on Language Development* (pp. 20–36). Cascadilla Press.

de Villiers, J.G. (1995b). *Steps in the mastery of sentence complements*. Paper presented at the biennial meeting of the Society for Research in Child Development, Indianapolis, IN.

de Villiers, J.G. (1996). Defining the open and closed program for acquisition: The case of wh-questions. In M. Rice (Ed.), *Towards a genetics of language* (pp. 145–184). Hillsdale, NJ: Lawrence Erlbaum Associates Inc.

de Villiers, J.G. (1999). On acquiring the structural representations for false complements. In B. Hollebrandse (Ed.), *New perspectives on language acquisition* (pp. 125–136). University of Massachusetts Occasional Papers in Linguistics, GLSA, Amherst, MA.

de Villiers, J.G., Bibeau, L., Ramos, E., & Gatty, J. (1993). Gestural communication in oral deaf mother-child pairs. *Journal of Applied Psycholinguistics, 14*, 319–347.

de Villiers, J.G., Curran, L., Philip, W., & DeMunn, H. (1997, November). *Acquisition of the quantificational properties of mental predicates*. Paper presented at 22nd annual Boston University Conference on Language Development.

de Villiers, J.G., de Villiers, P.A., & Hoban, E. (1994). The central problem of functional categories in the English syntax of oral deaf children. In H. Tager-Flusberg (Ed.), *Constraints on language acquisition: Studies of atypical children* (pp. 9–47). Hillsdale, NJ: Lawrence Erlbaum Associates Inc.

de Villiers, J.G., & Fitneva, S. (1996). *Referential transparency for opaque containers*. Unpublished manuscript, Smith College.

de Villiers, J.G., & Pyers, J. (1997). Complementing cognition: The relationship between language and theory of mind. In *Proceedings of the 21st annual Boston University Conference on Language Development*. Somerville, MA: Cascadilla Press.

Dunn, J., Brown, J., Slomkowski, C., Tesla, C., & Youngblade, L. (1991). Young children's understanding of other people's feelings and beliefs: Individual differences and their antecedents. *Child Development, 62*, 1352–1366.

Feldman, C.F. (1988). Early forms of thought about thoughts: Some simple linguistic expressions of mental state. In J.W. Astington, P.L. Harris, & D.R. Olson (Eds.), *Developing theories of mind* (pp. 126–137). Cambridge: Cambridge University Press.

Fodor, J.A. (1975). *The language of thought*. New York: Crowell.

Fodor, J.A. (1983). *The modularity of mind*. Cambridge, MA: MIT Press.

Fodor, J.A. (1992). Discussion: A theory of the child's theory of mind. *Cognition, 44*, 283–296.

Freeman, N.H. (1994). Associations and dissociations in theories of mind. In C. Lewis & P. Mitchell (Eds.), *Children's early understanding of mind: Origins and development* (pp. 95–111). Hove, UK: Lawrence Erlbaum Associates Ltd.

Freeman, N.H., Lewis, C., & Doherty, M. (1991). Preschoolers' grasp of a desire for knowledge in false-belief reasoning: Practical intelligence and verbal report. *British Journal of Developmental Psychology, 9*, 139–157.

Frye, D., Zelazo, P.D., & Palfai, T. (1995). Theory of mind and rule-based reasoning. *Cognitive Development, 10,* 483–527.

Gale, E., de Villiers, P., de Villiers, J., & Pyers, J. (1996). Language and theory of mind in oral deaf children. In A. Stringfellow, D. Cahana-Amitay, E. Hughes, & A. Zukowski (Eds.), *Proceedings of the 20th annual Boston University Conference on Language Development* (Vol. 1, pp. 213–224). Somerville, MA: Cascadilla Press.

Goldin-Meadow, S. (1982). The resilience of recursion. In E. Wanner & L. Gleitman (Eds.). *Language acquisition: the state of the art* (pp. 51–77). New York: Cambridge University Press.

Goldin-Meadow, S., & Mylander, C. (1984). Gestural communication in deaf children: The effects and non-effects of parental input on early language development. *Monographs of the Society for Research in Child Development, 49,* 143–151.

Gopnik, A. (1993). How we know our minds: The illusion of first person knowledge of intentionality. *Behavioral and Brain Sciences, 16,* 1–14.

Gopnik, A., & Astington, J.W. (1988). Children's understanding of representational change and its relation to understanding of false belief and the appearance-reality distinction. *Child Development, 59,* 26–37.

Gopnik, A., & Meltzoff, A.N. (1997). *Words, thoughts, and theories.* Cambridge, MA: MIT Press.

Greenberg, M.T., & Kusché, C.A. (1989). Cognitive, personal and social development of deaf children and adolescents. In M.C. Wang, M.C. Reynolds, & H.J. Walberg (Eds.), *Handbook of special education, Vol. 3: Low incidence conditions* (pp. 95–129).

Greenberg, M.T., & Kusché, C.A. (1993). *Promoting social and emotional development in deaf children: The paths project.* Seattle, WA: University of Washington Press.

Grice, H.P. (1975). Logic and conversation. In R. Cole & J. Morgan (Eds.), *Syntax and semantics: Speech acts* (pp. 41–58). New York: Academic Press.

Happe, F.G. (1995). The role of age and verbal ability in the theory of mind task performance of subjects with autism. *Child Development, 66,* 843–855.

Harris, P.L. (1996). Desires, beliefs and language. In P. Carruthers & P.K. Smith (Eds.), *Theories of theories of mind* (pp. xx–xx). Cambridge: Cambridge University Press.

Hobson, R.P. (1994). Perceiving attitudes, conceiving minds. In C. Lewis & P. Mitchell (Eds.), *Children's early understanding of mind: Origins and development* (pp. 71–93). Hove, UK: Lawrence Erlbaum Associates Ltd.

Hollebrandse, B. (1999). Acquisition of sequence of tense. In B. Hollebrandse (Ed.), *New perspectives on language acquisition* (pp. 137–154). University of Massachusetts Occasional Papers in Linguistics, GLSA, Amherst, MA.

Hyams, N. (1986). *Language acquisition and the theory of parameters.* Dordrecht: Reidel.

Jenkins, J., & Astington, J. (1996). Cognitive factors and family structure associated with theory of mind development in young children. *Developmental Psychology, 32,* 70–78.

Kosslyn, S. (1994). Computational theory of imagery. In M.W. Eysenck (Ed.) *The Blackwell dictionary of cognitive psychology.* Oxford: Blackwell.

Kratzer, A. (1997). *Course lectures in semantics.* University of Massachusetts, Amherst.

Kuczaj, S.A. II, & Daley, M.J. (1979). The development of hypothetical reference in the speech of young children. *Journal of Child Language, 6,* 563–580.

Lederberg, A.R. (1993). The impact of child deafness on social relationships. In M. Marschark & D. Clark (Eds.), *Psychological perspectives on deafness* (pp. 93–119). Hillsdale, NJ: Lawrence Erlbaum Associates Inc.

Leslie, A.M. (1994). *Pretending* and *believing*: Issues in the theory of ToMM. *Cognition, 50,* 211–238.

Lewis, C. (1994). Episodes, events, and narratives in the child's understanding of mind. In C. Lewis & P. Mitchell (Eds.), *Children's early understanding of mind: Origins and development* (pp. 457–480). Hove, UK: Lawrence Erlbaum Associates Ltd.

Lillard, A. (1993). Young child's conceptualization of pretence: action or mental representational state? *Child Development, 64,* 348–371.

Marschark, M. (1993). *Psychological development of deaf children*. New York: Oxford University Press.

Meadow, K.P., Greenberg, M.T., Erting, C., & Carmichael, H. (1981). Interactions of deaf mothers and deaf preschool children: Comparisons with three other groups of deaf and hearing dyads. *American Annals of the Deaf, 126*, 454–468.

Mitchell, P., & Lacohée, H. (1991). Children's early understanding of false belief. *Cognition, 39*, 107–127.

Mogford, K. (1993). Oral language acquisition in the prelinguistically deaf. In D. Bishop & K. Mogford (Eds.), *Language development in exceptional circumstances* (pp. 110–131). Hillsdale, NJ: Lawrence Erlbaum Associates Inc.

Montanini-Manfredi, M. (1993). The emotional development of deaf children. In M. Marschark & D. Clark (Eds.), *Psychological perspectives on deafness* (pp. 49–63). Hillsdale, NJ: Lawrence Erlbaum Associates Inc.

Olson, D.R. (1988). On the origins of beliefs and other intentional states in children. In J.W. Astington, P.L. Harris, & D.R. Olson (Eds.), *Developing theories of mind* (pp. 414–426). Cambridge: Cambridge University Press.

Olson, D.R. (1989). Making up your mind. *Canadian Psychology, 30*, 617–627.

Olson, D.R. (1993). The development of representations: The origins of mental life. *Canadian Psychology, 34*, 1–14.

Paul, P.V., & Quigley, S.P. (1993). *Language and deafness* (2nd Ed.). San Diego, CA: Singular Publishing Group.

Penner, Z. (1996). *Continuity constraints on the acquisition of the complementizer system: A case study of Bernese Swiss German*. Unpublished manuscript, University Of Bern, Switzerland.

Pérez-Leroux, A.T. (1997). *The acquisition of mood selection in Spanish relative clauses*. Unpublished manuscript, The Pennsylvania State University.

Perner, J. (1991a). On representing that: the asymmetry between belief and desire in children's theory of mind. In D. Frye & C. Moore (Eds.), *Children's theories of mind*. Hillsdale, NJ: Lawrence Erlbaum Associates Inc.

Perner, J. (1991b). *Understanding the representational mind*. Cambridge, MA: MIT Press.

Perner, J., Baker, S., & Hutton, D. (1994). Prelief: the conceptual origins of belief and pretence. In C. Lewis & P. Mitchell (Eds.), *Children's early understanding of mind: Origins and development* (pp. 261–286). Hove, UK: Lawrence Erlbaum Associates Ltd.

Perner, J., Leekam, S., & Wimmer, H. (1987). Three-year-olds' difficulty with false belief: The case for a conceptual deficit. *British Journal of Developmental Psychology, 5*, 125–137.

Peterson, C.C., & Siegal, M. (1995). Deafness, conversation and theory of mind. *Journal of Child Psychology and Psychiatry, 36*, 459–474.

Povinelli, D.J., & deBlois, S. (1992). Young children's (*Homo sapiens*) understanding of knowledge formation in themselves and others. *Journal of Comparative Psychology, 106*, 228–238.

Rescorla, L., & Schwartz, E. (1988). *Outcome of specific expressive language delay*. Paper presented to the International Conference on Infant Studies, Washington, DC.

Riggs, K.J., & Robinson, E.J. (1995). What people say and what they think: children's judgements of false belief in relation to their recall of false messages. *British Journal of Developmental Psychology, 13*, 271–284.

Rizzi, L. (1996). *The fine structure of the left periphery*. Unpublished manuscript, University of Geneva.

Roeper, T., & de Villiers, J.G. (1994). Lexical links in the Wh-chain. In B. Lust, G. Hermon, & J. Kornfilt (Eds.), *Syntactic theory and first language acquisition: Cross linguistic perspectives. Volume II: Binding, dependencies and learnability* (pp. 357–390). Hillsdale, NJ: Lawrence Erlbaum Associates Inc.

Russell, J. (1996). *Agency: Its role in mental development*. Hove, UK: Lawrence Erlbaum Associates Ltd.

Scarborough, H.S. (1990). Index of productive syntax. *Applied Psycholinguistics, 11*, 1–22.

Segal, G. (1997). *Representing representations*. Unpublished paper, University College, London.

Shatz, M., Wellman, H., & Silber, S. (1983). The acquisition of mental verbs: A systematic investigation of first references to mental state. *Cognition, 14*, 301–321.

Siegal, M., & Beattie, K. (1991). Where to look first for children's knowledge of false belief. *Cognition, 38*, 1–12.

Siegal, M., & Peterson, C.C. (1994). Children's theory of mind and the conversational territory of cognitive development. In C. Lewis & P. Mitchell (Eds.), *Children's early understanding of mind: Origins and development* (pp. 427–455). Hove, UK: Lawrence Erlbaum Associates Ltd.

Sperber, D., & Wilson, D. (1986). *Relevance: Communication and cognition*. Cambridge, MA: Harvard University Press.

Steeds, L., Rowe, K., & Dowker, A. (1997). Deaf children's understanding of beliefs and desires. *Journal of Deaf Studies and Deaf Education, 2*, 185–195.

Sullivan, K., & Winner, E. (1991). When 3-year olds understand ignorance, false belief and representational change. *British Journal of Developmental Psychology, 9*, 159–171.

Tager-Flusberg, H. (1994). What language reveals about the understanding of minds in children with autism. In S. Baron-Cohen, H. Tager-Flusberg, & D.J. Cohen (Eds.), *Understanding other minds: Perspectives from autism* (pp. 138–157). Oxford: Oxford University Press.

Tager-Flusberg, H. (1995). *Language and the acquisition of a theory of mind: Evidence from autism and Williams syndrome*. Paper presented at the biennial meeting of the Society for Research in Child Development, Indianapolis, IN.

Tager-Flusberg, H. (1996). *Relationships between language and thought: Cognition verbs and theory of mind*. Paper presented at the meeting of the International Association for the Study of Child Language, Istanbul, Turkey.

Tager-Flusberg, H. (1997). The role of theory of mind in language acquisition: Contributions from the study of autism. In L. Adamson & M.A. Romski (Eds.), *Research on communication and language disorders: Contributions to theories of language development*. Baltimore, MD: Paul Brookes Publishing.

Tager-Flusberg, H., & Sullivan, K. (1994). Predicting and explaining behavior: A comparison of autistic, mentally retarded and normal children. *Journal of Child Psychology and Psychiatry, 35*, 1059–1075.

Wellman, H.M. (1990). *The child's theory of mind*. Cambridge, MA: MIT Press.

Wimmer, H., & Hartl, M. (1991). Against the Cartesian view on mind: young children's difficulty with own false beliefs. *British Journal of Developmental Psychology, 9*, 125–138.

Wimmer, H., & Perner, J. (1983). Beliefs about beliefs: representation and constraining function of wrong beliefs in young children's understanding of deception. *Cognition, 13*, 103–128.

Zaitchik, D. (1990). When representations conflict with reality: The preschooler's problem with false beliefs and "false" photographs. *Cognition, 35*, 41–68.

CHAPTER ELEVEN

Attending to and learning about mental states

Tim P. German
Department of Psychology University of Essex, UK

Alan M. Leslie
Center for Cognitive Science, Rutgers University, USA

OVERVIEW

A current view in the 'theory of mind' literature is that children acquire know-ledge about the mind between the ages of 2 and 5 years by going through a process of conceptual 'discovery'. Most theorists who make this assumption couch this discovery process in terms of the child actively constructing a kind of 'scientific theory' (Gopnik, 1993, 1996a,b; Gopnik & Meltzoff, 1997; Gopnik & Wellman, 1992, 1994; Perner, 1988, 1991, 1995). To date, none of these theor-ists have provided an account of (i) how even a single mental state concept might be 'discovered' this way, (ii) how any of the proposed sequences of theories might be 'constructed', (iii) what the critical evidence is that children are exposed to at different points in the sequence, or (iv) how children are able to identify and assess this 'evidence' as critically relevant to the process of theory discovery. In general, although a 'theory' is an information structure, theory-theorists seem unaware of the information processing issues raised by their proposals.

We explore an alternative approach that rejects the assumption that concept possession depends upon discovering theories. Instead, we give a central role to an elementary ability to attend to mental states. We examine how the elementary ability to attend to *beliefs* becomes gradually more flexible and promotes in-creasing success on false belief problems. Using examples from the literature, together with new evidence on children's reasoning about different mental states, we illustrate the larger role that these specialised attentional mechanisms play in allowing learning about mental states to take place.

INTRODUCTION

In making sense of the actions, reactions and interactions of other agents, appeal to abstract concepts such as BELIEF, DESIRE and PRETEND, comes so naturally as to appear trivial.[1] Indeed, this knowledge and ability sometimes goes under the name of mere 'common-sense' or 'intuitive' psychology, and one might be forgiven for thinking therefore, that there must be other, more rigorous, more scientific models of mind or brain that provide better or more successful interpretations, predictions, and explanations of behaviour. But as Pinker (1997, p. 63) reminds us:

> intuitive psychology is still the most useful and complete science of behaviour there is . . . this part of common sense has so much power and precision in predicting, controlling and explaining everyday behaviour, compared to any alternative ever considered.

It is striking to reflect that the best efforts of several generations of the brightest research scientists have done so little to improve upon the ideas that are grasped effortlessly by every untutored 4-year-old, mostly before they can add two and two.

The theorist attempting to explain how this common-sense knowledge is acquired is faced with many puzzles. Leslie (1994a) describes the 'fundamental problem of theory of mind' as follows: given that beliefs, desires and pretends can be neither seen, heard nor felt, how does the young brain succeed in learning about them? In this chapter, we review two principal kinds of answer provoked by this question. One answer suggests that 'theory of mind' knowledge is acquired by discovering a succession of explicit 'theories' about mental states, through the operation of 'theory'-formation processes akin to those involved in 'real' science formation. The second kind of answer suggests that innate mechanisms provide an initial representational competence—a small, core set of primitive mental state concepts that allow the child to attend to instances of a basic set of mental states, and thus *to learn about them.*

The role of 'theory' in 'theory of mind' has been greatly exaggerated, or so we believe. One unfortunate consequence has been to downplay the role of performance factors in 'theory of mind' development. We will argue that it is necessary to understand the role of performance as well as competence factors, and will outline several strands of recent evidence that highlight the need to develop information processing models of how conceptual competence is deployed and how this deployment develops.

The theory-theory account of common-sense psychology

According to the theory-theorists, children 'discover', over the pre-school period, a succession of 'theories' about the mind (Forguson & Gopnik, 1988; Gopnik, 1993, 1996a, b; Gopnik & Meltzoff, 1997; Gopnik & Wellman, 1992, 1994;

Perner, 1988, 1991, 1993, 1995; Perner, Baker, & Hutton, 1994; Wellman, 1990). The culmination of this process, at about age four, is the 'adult theory' that reveals the *representational nature of beliefs*. The emergence of the representational 'theory' is marked by the child succeeding at standard false belief tasks (Baron-Cohen, Leslie, & Frith, 1985; Perner, Leekham, & Wimmer, 1987; Wimmer & Perner, 1983). Children begin to predict that a protagonist, who has hidden an object in a particular location then been absent while it was moved elsewhere, will subsequently search for it where she *thinks* it is, rather than where it really is. Younger children typically fail this task by predicting search at the object's current location. The theory-theory explains the shift in performance between age three and four by a change in the child's conceptual competence, which, in turn, is explained by a shift in the underlying 'theory' the child holds with regard to the nature of mental states. The younger child fails because she operates with the wrong 'theory' of belief which dictates that she employ a deficient BELIEF concept. The older child, having grasped the adult 'theory', now employs the adult concept which bestows the ability to solve the false belief task.

'Theory' plays the central role in 'theory-theory' because which concepts you possess depends upon which theories you grasp. The theory-theorist is thus committed to offering a characterisation of the content of each of the theories (said to be) acquired by the child in the course of 'theory of mind' development. The theory-theorist also needs to address the question of how the successive theories are acquired, and thus how children discover concepts such as BELIEF, DESIRE and PRETEND. It will be our contention that, to date, no plausible characterisation of theory contents nor serious account of 'theory' formation has emerged.

Two versions of the theory-theory can be identified. Though they have much in common, and many of the arguments raised here will apply to both, it is worth outlining the principal differences between these versions. Perner (1988, 1991, 1995; Perner et al., 1994) is concerned primarily with accounting for the shift in children's reasoning about the mind between ages 3 and 4. He makes specific proposals about the nature of both the 3-year-old theory, and about the content of 4-year-olds' representational theory of belief. Though Perner (1995, p. 264) sees the shift between the two as involving theory change:

my view lies in the tradition of the theory-formation view of conceptual change.

Perner (1995, p. 264) distances himself from making any strong claims with respect to how the conceptual changes are realised:

The use of the word *theory* is to emphasize that concepts develop within groups of theoretically related concepts. Its purpose is not to model children's intellectual growth on the way in which scientists at the forefront of human knowledge break new ground.

For Perner, then, 'theory-theory' is primarily the view that concept possession, and thus concept change, depends upon grasping the 'theory' that defines the concept. He remains sceptical about whether the process through which a child forms a 'theory' is really the same as the process through which a scientist forms a theory.

By contrast, Gopnik and her colleagues (Gopnik, 1993, 1996a, b; Gopnik & Meltzoff, 1997; Gopnik & Wellman, 1992, 1994) have no such qualms (but see Wellman, 1990, p. 130 for a dissenting view). These writers (Gopnik, 1996a, p. 169) propose a deeper explanatory role for the 'child as scientist'[2] than mere analogy:

> there are quite distinctive and special cognitive processes that are responsible both for scientific progress and for particular kinds of development in children.

Gopnik's position also differs from Perner's in terms of the specific nature of the successive theories of mind that children are said to discover. First, children adopt a 'belief as copy' theory at age 3 (Gopnik & Wellman, 1992, 1994; Wellman, 1990), rather than the 'situation theory' (or 'theory of prelief') proposed by Perner (1991, 1995; Perner et al., 1994). Secondly, Gopnik (and Wellman) is far less explicit than Perner about what the content of the 4-year-old's 'representational theory of belief' is supposed to be. In fact, it is hard even to determine whether Gopnik's (and Wellman's) 'representational theory of belief' is the same or a different 'representation theory of belief' that Perner attributes to the 4-year-old. Thirdly, the two versions have somewhat different views on the extent to which later 'theories' of mind replace earlier versions rather than simply extend them (see for example Perner, 1991, chapter 10 versus Gopnik, 1993).

In the following sections, we outline some of the more important details of these two versions of theory-theory. Following this, we discuss some general problems with theory-theories, as well as some more specific problems that arise for each version. Finally, we outline an alternative to theory-theory, along with several strands of evidence in its favour.

Understanding semantic evaluation and the representational theory of mind (RTM)

Perner's focus over the last several years has been on the specific conceptual shift that the child makes between age three and four, that results in the child becoming able to solve the false belief task (Perner, 1988, 1991, 1993, 1995; Perner et al., 1987; Perner et al., 1994; Wimmer & Perner, 1983). Perner has described the key conceptual achievement that enables an understanding of false beliefs as the child grasping the defining feature of representation. That is, as Perner (1995, p. 248) stated, the child 'must have mastered the distinction between what something represents (refers to, makes a claim about) and how it represents (conceives of) it as being'. In the case of the false belief task, this distinction is between the target of Sally's belief (the current location of the marble) and the way that Sally represents this target as being (a non-factual 'situation' where the marble remains in the basket).[3]

Children must have, at minimum, mastered the above distinction in a very particular way to have what Perner (1995, p. 248) describes as 'a representational understanding of mind'. For Perner, it is *not* enough for the child merely to have an *ability* to honour this distinction as she represents people's mental states. An ability merely to honour this distinction while representing pretence was built into the metarepresentational mechanisms proposed by Leslie (1987) and roundly criticised by Perner (1991) as entirely inadequate for genuine metarepresentation, for the sort of metarepresentation required for understanding belief. For Perner's metarepresentation, the child must have explicit knowledge that there is such a distinction and that it is precisely this distinction that the concept BELIEF expresses. We can make the difference between Leslie and Perner a little clearer by considering an example that does not have the confusing feature that we are discussing a mental entity (BELIEF) that designates a mental entity (belief). We can all agree that having the concept WATER is having a concept that expresses the property of *being* H_2O. The equivalent of Leslie's position is that you have the concept WATER just in so far as your concept WATER in practice represents things that have the property of *being* H_2O. You are not required to know what H_2O is nor that H_2O is the property that WATER expresses. That is, you are not required to know the chemical theory of water (or any other theory) in order to have the concept WATER. The equivalent of Perner's position, is that you cannot have the concept WATER unless and until you understand that water is really H_2O—coming to possess the concept WATER is discovering the theory that water is really H_2O. Our hunch is that most human beings, past and present, possess the concepts WATER and BELIEF without understanding either chemical theory or the representational theory of mind, respectively.

As well as explicit claims about the 4-year-old's theory of mind, Perner has specified in some detail the 'theory' held by the younger child. He has described this variously as a 'propositional attitude' theory (Perner, 1988), a 'situation' theory (Perner, 1991, 1993) and most recently a 'prelief' theory (Perner, 1995; Perner et al., 1994). In a recent defence of his position (Perner, 1995), younger children are characterised as able to relate an agent (in a particular mental state) to a 'situation'.[4] The child herself might evaluate the 'situation' as true or false, in Perner's notation, child represents: [Agent—attitude → 'proposition'], and child represents the proposition (P) as being true or false. The additional insight gained by 4-year-olds is to recognise that situations are *also evaluated by the agents holding attitudes to them* and *might be evaluated differently by different agents*. Perner captures this in his notation as: [Agent—attitude→(P), Agent—semantically evaluates as true→(P), P is false].

The understanding attributed to the 3-year-old is sufficient, according to Perner, to explain young children's success at reasoning about concepts such as DESIRE (Hadwin & Perner, 1991; Wellman & Woolley, 1990). A desire is represented as the agent desiring a state of affairs: [Agent—wants → (P)], and if the child evaluates the state of affairs as true then the desire is understood to be fulfilled, while if the state of affairs is evaluated as false the desire is understood as unfulfilled.

Perner also claims that 3-year-old children, with this conceptual repertoire, can understand something (though not all) of the 'belief component' of adult belief-desire psychology. This is evidenced by their appreciation of pretend play, understood by the younger child as an agent acting according to propositions that the child evaluates as false. The child can achieve this understanding, according to Perner, because she is able to relate the agent to the proposition and evaluate the proposition as false [Agent—attitude → (P), P is false]. But, because she cannot understand that the agent also semantically evaluates the proposition (and may evaluate it differently from the child), she cannot distinguish this pretend action from an inappropriate action caused by a false belief. Accordingly, Perner suggests that the younger child's understanding of the epistemic component of belief-desire psychology takes the form of an undifferentiated understanding of belief and pretend, so called PRELIEF, and hence Perner's use of the phrase 'prelief theorist' alongside 'situation theorist', to describe children at this stage. Elsewhere (Perner et al., 1994: footnote p. 284), he states that understanding the mind via the concept PRELIEF is to be read as compatible with his ideas that younger children are *situation theorists* (Perner, 1991). Perner has also talked of the younger child's competence as involving 'understanding propositional attitudes' (Perner, 1988, though see endnote no. 4, p. 169).

Perner seems torn between two contradictory views of early pretence understanding. He is tempted in places (Perner, 1988, 1991) to attribute to the young child a purely behaviourist 'theory' of pretence as merely a form of action. At other times, he is willing to attribute an early understanding of pretence (or 'prelief') as a propositional attitude in which an agent pretends a fictitious something (e.g. "that's a telephone") about a real something else (e.g. about a real banana). But here the child's processing 'merely honours' the fact that the agent pretends this of that and does not represent explicitly what pretending (or 'prelieving') really is, namely a relation in which an agent semantically evaluates a mental representation that expresses a proposition.

We can easily agree with the second of the above views of early pretence understanding. Our only difference on this score is that we think (a) that nothing more than 'honouring' is required in order to understand belief, and (b) that young children have two distinct concepts, PRETEND and BELIEVE, instead of a single undifferentiated concept, PRELIEF.

The 'child as scientist'?

The key claim made by proponents of the 'child as scientist' version of the theory-theory, is that the very same theory-formation abilities responsible for our cultural scientific progress are at the heart of children's acquisition of knowledge about the mind and knowledge in other domains (Gopnik, 1993, 1996a, b; Gopnik & Meltzoff, 1997; Gopnik & Wellman, 1992, 1994). As Gopnik (1996a, p. 169) puts it:

> theories and theory changes, in particular, are responsible for the changes in children's understanding of mind.

According to this version of theory-theory, children are equipped with innate 'starting-state' theories which are modified and revised by innate theory formation mechanisms, with such modification argued to start as early as birth (Gopnik 1996a, b; Gopnik & Meltzoff, 1997). Children's performance on various mental state reasoning problems, on this view, is to be accounted for in terms of the properties of successive theories. Again, a key assumption is that the concepts you have depend upon the theories you grasp. The child employs different concepts at different stages in development because new theories replace older theories. There are even 'transitional' periods in the individual's life that are akin to periods in the history of our culture during which a scientific 'paradigm' shifts. Gopnik and Wellman (1992, p. 156) put it thus:

> Recent evidence suggests that during the period from three to four many children are in a state of transition between the two theories, similar, say to the fifty years between the publication of *De Revolutionibus* and Kepler's discovery of elliptical orbits.

Gopnik and Wellman (1992, 1994) describe a succession of theories of the mind employed by children between age 2 and age 5. The 2-year-old theory recognises fewer, simpler, different concepts than do later theories; DESIRE and PERCEPTION are 'drives toward' objects and 'awarenesses of' objects respectively: 'in neither case need the child conceive of a complex propositional relationship between these mental states and the world' (Gopnik & Wellman, 1992, p. 150). The 2-year-old theory is revised such that a successor theory (e.g. at age three) recognises new concepts, for example a version of BELIEF modelled on earlier understanding of perception: 'belief, like perception and desire, involves rather direct causal links between object and believers' (ibid., p. 151). There is still more conceptual change required however, because this early 3-year-old concept of BELIEF does not allow for false contents.

It is only after children acquire a 'quite different view of mind' (ibid., p. 152), at around age 4 or 5, that their concepts resemble the adult versions: 'perceiving becomes perceiving that and desiring becomes desiring that, we might even add, that believing becomes believing that' (ibid., p. 153). The key achievement, as we saw with Perner's position, is the mastery of the concept of *mis*representation allowing success at the false belief task. Only then is the child credited with having constructed a 'representational theory of mind'.

Contrary to the claims of Gopnik (1993), the 'copy theory' of belief cannot be the same as the 'situation theory' or the 'prelief' concept proposed by Perner (1988, 1991, 1995; see above). The child who understands beliefs only as copies of the world has a different understanding than a child who can conceive of agents as holding attitudes to 'situations' that might be evaluated by the child as either true or false (Perner, 1995). If a child were to understand beliefs as *only being true*, then, together with Perner (1991), one must ask, why is this not simply the concept, KNOWING?

As Fodor (1992) points out, Wellman's own data appear to show that 3-year-old children are not limited to a 'copy theory of belief', i.e. to the concept, KNOW; for example, in his 'Not Own' belief task (Wellman & Bartsch, 1988), young children understand that Billy might think his puppy is in the garage and will look for it there when the child herself guesses it is in the shed, and knows that she would look in the shed. These beliefs cannot *both* be copies of reality (see also Perner, 1991, pp. 275–276).

Wellman also has data that contradict the 'drive theory of desire' that he attributes to 2-year-old children. Children in Wellman and Woolley (1990) were required to understand that Billy, for example, wants to find a puppy so that he can take it to school. They found that the children were capable of predicting that Billy will cease searching and go to school with his puppy when he finds his puppy, but not when he finds nothing and not when he finds a different pet. Wellman's theory characterises the 2-year-old's 'theory' of desire as a drive toward a physical object. Wellman proposes this 'drive theory' to reconcile the data showing very early understanding of desire with his larger assumption that children younger than 4 years cannot understand propositional attitudes. Wellman's move is to attribute to the young child only mental state notions that relate agents to physical objects and not to states of affairs. This is because he assumes that a state of affairs would have to be represented by the child as a proposition (see for example, Wellman & Woolley, 1990, p. 249). Thus, to attribute mental state notions that relate agents to states of affairs would be, Wellman thinks, to attribute propositional attitudes to young children, something he rules out on a priori grounds. He hopes to avoid this result by attributing to young children mental state notions in which agents relate only to physical objects, presumably because physical objects can be represented by single concepts rather than by propositions.

But the 2-year-olds in Wellman's experiment correctly predict that Billy will go to school when he finds his puppy, a prediction based on understanding Billy's desire to find his puppy *in order that he can take it to school*. The children have understood that Billy's finding the 'object' satisfies a sub-goal of a larger goal. But this larger goal is expressible only as a state of affairs. Therefore, the child cannot be limited to conceiving of desire as 'an internal longing for an external object', if 'object' means physical object as opposed to state of affairs, because 'he will take his pet to school' is not a physical object, but a state of affairs. Wellman's own data therefore contradict his 'drive theory of desire' (see also German, 1995a; Leslie, 1994b; Perner, 1991).

Problems with the theory-theory

Both versions of the theory-theory claim that *conceptual change* in the domain of common-sense psychology are responsible for the pattern of performance on theory of mind tasks over the first few years of life. But precisely what kinds of conceptual changes are hypothesised to occur? What specific mechanisms are proposed to realise theory change?

The 'child as scientist' view advocated by Gopnik and colleagues appears at first blush to offer an answer to this question; the mechanisms that come into play are the same mechanisms that are responsible for theory changes in science. But nothing is known about the mechanisms of conceptual change in science. Gopnik's 'mechanisms' are simply a reiteration of familiar, but still mysterious, processes like 'testing predictions', 'evaluating evidence', the 'positing of hypotheses' and so on, the stuff of popular conceptions of science. However, she makes no new proposals about where new concepts come from, how the concepts that feature in hypotheses under test get to be there in the first place, how 'evidence' leads to new 'theories', and so on. Apparently, Gopnik believes that addressing these information processing questions is unnecessary (Gopnik, 1993).

Interestingly, there are other accounts of conceptual change in the literature in regard to domains other than theory of mind. Carey and colleagues (Carey, 1985, 1988, 1991, 1995; Carey & Spelke, 1994, 1996; Johnson & Carey, 1998) have suggested that conceptual change is involved in the restructuring of children's knowledge about living things between the ages of 4 and 10 years, changes in children's intuitive theory of matter between ages 6 and 12 years, intuitive cosmology (Vosniadu & Brewer, 1992), as well as the construction of certain numerical concepts such as zero, infinity, negative numbers and fractions during the later elementary school period (Gelman, 1991). Although Gopnik sees the work of these authors as supporting the general theory-theory line on 'theory of mind' (Gopnik, 1996a, p. 169, 1996b, p. 485; Gopnik & Wellman, 1992, p. 145, 1994, p. 257), there are important differences between the approach taken by Gopnik and these other uses of the theory-theory framework.

First, the principal claims about conceptual change in these other domains are seen as descriptive rather than explanatory (see, for example, Carey, 1988, p. 141); the issue for Carey is the extent to which it might be useful to describe changes in a child's knowledge in a given domain as changes in an intuitive 'theory'. The relationship between the concepts and structure of the 'theory' at one point in time (T_1) and the 'theory' at a later point in time (T_2) can be described as involving conceptual changes of specific types. For example, *differentiation* where a concept recognised in T_1 is split into two concepts in T_2, *coalescence* where more than one T_1 concept is aggregated to just one concept in T_2, concepts can change in their peripheral/core feature structure, such that changes to a concept core are regarded as a conceptual change, and, finally, conceptual change can result in the creation of new ontological categories (Chi, 1992). Perhaps this kind of description can be offered for the putative 'theories' in the domain of theory of mind: BELIEF and PRETEND might be differentiated from PRELIEF (Perner, 1995), or there may be a shift from understanding pretend in terms of peripheral or characteristic features (action) to understanding the core or defining feature of mental representation (Lillard, 1993).

However, where putative mechanisms of change have been discussed (Carey & Spelke, 1994), they have been argued to involve complex processes such as the creation of mappings across domains, physical analogies, thought experiments and limiting case analyses. Johnson and Carey (1998) also discuss, in general terms, the types of abilities upon which conceptual change might be based. They suggest, in addition to the above, processes such as meta-cognitively aware uses of analogy, comprehension monitoring and abstract same/different comparisons. There are still no details of what these theory formation mechanisms might look like, but a key point is that such abilities seem themselves to develop after the pre-school period during early school age, and to be impaired in those with mental retardation (Campione, Brown, & Ferrara, 1982).

By contrast, as we indicated above, proponents of the theory-theory in the domain of theory of mind have not addressed the question of underlying mechanisms. Moreover, it is unlikely that the kinds of processes that have been proposed for theory change in other domains could account for conceptual change in theory of mind. Theory of mind acquisition proceeds uniformly, routinely, effortlessly, in the first few years of life, is very largely independent of IQ (Leslie, 1987), and does not require formal instruction. All of these differences between 'theory of mind' knowledge and common-sense knowledge in other domains (such as intuitive biology, theory of matter and number) have led even proponents of conceptual change in other domains to doubt that the theory-theory approach is appropriate to explain the acquisition of common-sense psychology (see for example Carey & Spelke, 1996; see also German & Samuels, in preparation, for further discussion of these issues).

Turning to Perner's account, recall that there is no commitment to the 'child as scientist' as anything other than analogy. For Perner, the process of acquisition does not have to mirror what a professional scientist does; instead, the role of theory-theory is to give an account for the nature of concepts and concept acquisition. The child comes to possess knowledge of a domain that is theory-like in the following sense: she has to discover the nature of the things in the domain—she has to discover what these things really are. In particular, for the 'theory of mind' domain, the child must discover what beliefs (and other mental states) really are, namely, *representations*. This gives Perner's approach greater explanatory depth than the Gopnik–Wellman version of theory-theory. By insisting that the child must develop a 'theory' of what beliefs really are, he is able to account for why grasping *that* 'theory' results in the possession of a particular concept, namely, BELIEF, and to establish criteria whereby we may judge whether or not the child in fact possesses the concept.

Perner's views are also distinguished from those of Gopnik–Wellman because he has been at pains to specify what the 'theory' is that he is attributing to the child. Clearly, if, as according to theory-theory, the key to understanding development is that the child is supposed to grasp and hold a certain 'theory', then we are entitled to be told exactly what this 'theory' is that the child grasps and holds. Neither Gopnik nor Wellman ever tell us what the child's 'representational theory' of belief is. But Perner does. According to Perner (1995), the 4-year-old child comes to understand that when John believes a certain proposition *p*, John is semantically evaluating a mental representation which expresses *p*. As Roth & Leslie (1998) point out, stating the child's 'theory' inevitably means using other concepts. And because the 'theory' stated is something that the child is said to grasp, this means that the child must possess those concepts too. Therefore, in order to acquire the concept, BELIEF, the 4-year-old, according to Perner, must acquire the prior concepts, SEMANTIC, EVALUATE, MENTAL, REPRESENTATION, EXPRESS and PROPOSITION. The natural next question is, how are *these* concepts acquired?

Perner expresses a leaning toward the view that 'theory of mind' is acquired through 'interaction with the environment' (1995, p. 263). We have no doubt that 'interaction with the environment' plays an important role; in fact, we regard this essentially as a truism. The question is, what role precisely? It is not at all easy to imagine how the six concepts comprising the child's 'representational theory of belief' are acquired through 'interaction with the environment'.

In summary, current theory-theory views suffer from a number of shortcomings which invite a more sceptical attitude than is usually given them in the field. Although future development of theory-theory may overcome some of these problems, our feeling is that the entire approach is flawed. The heart of this flaw, in our view, is the assumption that possession of abstract concepts *must* depend upon possession of abstract knowledge.

INFORMATION PROCESSING AND THE THEORY OF MIND MECHANISM

We turn now to consider an alternative to the conceptual change framework for the acquisition of knowledge in this domain. We believe that understanding children's developing theory of mind means specifying the mechanisms that will allow the child firstly to *attend to* and subsequently to *learn about* mental states. Without the ability to attend to the relevant properties in the environment, there is no way that the child will learn about states such as *beliefs*, *desires* and *pretends*. These assumptions underlie a model of 'theory of mind' acquisition developed over the years by Leslie and colleagues (Baron-Cohen, 1995; Frith, 1989; German & Leslie, unpublished a, b; Leslie, 1987, 1988, 1991, 1994a,b; Leslie & German, 1995; Leslie & Roth, 1993; Leslie & Thaiss, 1992; Roth & Leslie, 1991, 1998). A central postulate of this model is the existence of the Theory of Mind Mechanism (ToMM), a brain mechanism specialised for attending to mental states. The theory of ToMM is a two factor theory, encompassing a critical distinction between mechanisms underlying the child's conceptual competence and the performance demands that are made by particular 'theory of mind' problems, such as the false belief task.

Competence

As far as competence is concerned, ToMM equips the child with an innate, specialised representational system that employs the basic attitude concepts, BELIEF, DESIRE and PRETEND. These attitude concepts feature in representational structures called 'metarepresentations' (or 'M-representations'), which provide the cognitive system with agent-centred descriptions of behaviour, additionally specifying an *agent*, a 'propositional' *content* and an *anchor* to an aspect of the real world. Two well worn examples of M-representations appear in (1) and (2):

(1) Mother PRETENDS (that) "it is a telephone" (is true of) the banana
(2) Sally BELIEVES (that) "it is in the basket" (is true of) the marble

In example (1), Mother is the agent, who holds the attitude of pretending toward the truth of the proposition 'it is a telephone', while her attitude is anchored in a particular banana in the world. In (2), the agent (Sally) is represented as holding the attitude of believing toward the truth of the content ("it is in the basket") with respect to a particular object (the marble).

The ToMM theory does not, however, claim that the child is equipped with a 'theory' of either pretending or believing. Nor is the child expected to be highly proficient immediately in deploying his conceptual competence when reasoning about these mental states. ToMM provides only the *basis* for acquiring knowledge about mental states. The initial concepts supplied by ToMM allow the child, at least on some occasions, to interpret behaviour in terms of these underlying mental states; the child, by attending to instances of mental states, can begin to learn particular facts about them. Note that this contrasts sharply with the main claim of the conceptual change view, namely, that the meaning of concepts such as BELIEF and DESIRE is given by a 'theory' to which the child subscribes or grasps. On the ToMM view, it is an open empirical question whether or not the child has some innate 'theory' of this or that mental state; but no such 'theory' is required to ground the M-representation. The child can, for example, simply recognise instances of pretending without knowing what pretending *really is*.

Performance factors in theory of mind tasks

ToMM is initially limited in its effectiveness when 'theory of mind' problems require non-default answers (Leslie, 1991; Leslie & Roth, 1993; Leslie & Thaiss, 1992; Roth, 1993; Roth & Leslie, 1998). Beliefs, by their nature, are normatively true; their contents ought to match reality because that is what beliefs are for (Dennett, 1981; Fodor, 1992; Leslie, 1994a; Leslie & Thaiss, 1992). By default, a belief reasoner should attribute beliefs with contents that are true. In false belief tasks, the default must be over-ridden, and the correct non-factual content must be selected instead. According to the ToMM theory, over-riding the default requires inhibition followed by identification or selection of an alternate content. This inhibition/selection process is handled by a mechanism that co-operates closely with or is part of ToMM, and which has been called the Selection Processor (SP). The SP mechanism develops gradually, becoming increasingly effective over the pre-school years, and beyond. Its gradual increase in efficiency leads to a gradual extension of the child's ability to reason about beliefs, making it progressively easier for children to attend to beliefs that have false contents. In this way, selection processing leverages the child's initial competence.

There is increasing evidence, collected by researchers working within the framework of providing a *task analysis* of 'theory of mind' problems, that information processing demands play an important role in determining the likelihood that children at a given age (and therefore with SP abilities at a given level) will perform well at tasks assessing mental state reasoning (Freeman & Lacohée, 1995; German, 1995a, b; German & Leslie, 1999a, b; Leslie & Polizzi, 1998; Mitchell & Lacohée, 1991; Moore et al., 1995; Riggs, Peterson, Robinson, & Mitchell, 1998; Roth & Leslie, 1991, 1998; Saltmarsh, Mitchell, & Robinson, 1995; Surian & Leslie, 1999; Wellman & Bartsch, 1988; Zaitchik, 1991). In the following sections, we outline some of this evidence consistent with a two factor approach to the development of theory of mind problem-solving ability.

Reasoning about pretend and desire. The flip side to the idea that some 'theory of mind' problems make processing demands that the child cannot meet is the idea that other 'theory of mind' problems make trivial demands. Consider a typical pretend play scenario. Leslie and Happé (1989; see also Leslie, 1987, 1988) argue that children are supported in their task of reading the contents of the protagonist's mental states by the efforts made, on the part of the participants in pretence, to communicate those pretend contents. Shared pretend play is always accompanied by specific communicative displays: 'knowing' looks and smiles, exaggerated intonations, gestures, and actions, explicit verbalisations, and so on (Leslie, 1987; Piaget, 1962). Success at inferring the content of an agent's pretend, and indeed inferring *that the agent is pretending*, may depend on this communicative display.

Perner et al. (1994), arguing that children are utilising the concept 'PRELIEF' rather than BELIEF and PRETEND, found that 3-year-old children were unable to distinguish whether an actor, putting food in a rabbit hutch (when no rabbit was there), was doing so because the actor *pretended* it or *really believed* it until they were aged about four. However, children in this study were deprived of the cues they might normally use in order to recognise the communicative act of pretending; the character behaves precisely the same way in both the 'pretend' and 'false belief' versions of the scenarios. Therefore, the inference required (from the protagonist's knowledge), is the same in each case. On the view we have been advocating here, where pretenders take no steps to reduce the difficulty of the inferences required by the young child to infer pretence, it is unsurprising that children might be confused between these two cases in the task presented in Perner et al. (1994). It is doubly unsurprising that children who fail to recognise the false belief in a standard false belief task should also fail to distinguish the (unrecognised) false belief from pretence under the same conditions of testing. The only chance a 3-year-old has of doing this is in a 'modified' false belief task where they enjoy greater success with identifying the false belief. Freeman and Lacohée (1995) using a modified 'Smarties' task found 3-year-olds who successfully identified their own false belief were also able to distinguish it from pretending. Interestingly, those children who failed even the modified false belief task were more likely to judge that their claimed knowledge was in fact pretence, suggesting that these children had some inkling that their claim to knowledge was suspect.

An information processing perspective can also account for the early emergence of children's reasoning with the concept desire relative to the concept belief. There is no need to assume, as the theory-theory does, that DESIRE is recognised as a concept in the 2-year-old's innate 'theory of mind' whereas BELIEF is a concept in a later discovered 'theory'. Considering the tasks typically used in assessing understanding of desire versus belief, one can identify task structural differences. While the contents of desire need to be inferred just as do the contents of belief, there is no 'default' content-type that needs to be inhibited prior to the selection procedure. Therefore reasoning about differing desires should stress the SP mechanisms considerably less than reasoning about non-default beliefs. However, might it be possible to arrange circumstances such that an inhibition requirement is introduced into a desire reasoning task?

Moore et al. (1995) did exactly this, by arranging a desire task that closely matched the structure of the false belief task. Children were playing a game with a competitor and initially, both competitors required a certain event to occur to progress (say, that a card turned over should be red)—thus both child and competitor *wanted a red card*. Events were arranged such that children themselves achieved this interim goal and now could only progress if the card turned over were to be blue, while the competitor was left requiring a red card. Now the child's desire (blue card) has changed, while the competitor's desire remains the same (red card). Children were simply asked what colour card the competitor wanted next. Note that this situation is analogous to the false belief task, where the child and the protagonist start out with one belief (marble in the basket) and the child's belief (but not the protagonist's) is updated (marble in the box). The results showed that 3-year-old children failed this task, predicting that the competitor would have the same desire as the child. Performance was in fact comparable to performance on the standard false belief task. This result is compatible then, with the view that differences in performance in children's reasoning about different mental states can be accounted for in terms of differing information processing demands associated with different task structures (Leslie, 1994a).

Leslie and Polizzi (1998) used a different method of creating an inhibitory process with desire reasoning. Following an idea of Cassidy's (1995), Leslie and Polizzi used a desire that demands what they called 'target-shifting'. The task is to figure which of two locations a protagonist wants when they want the location that does *not* have property X. To identify the NOT(X) location, one must first identify the X location then shift to the alternate. Leslie and Polizzi hypothesised that the brain would have to inhibit its attention to the X location in order to disengage from it and shift to the alternate target. A similar process is hypothesised to occur in selection processing during a false belief task. First, by default, the brain attributes a true belief to a protagonist and thereby identifies a target of belief, then it inhibits attention to that default target and shifts to the alternate target identified by the non-factual content of the false belief. Leslie and Polizzi used a target-shifting desire to probe the existence of the postulated target-shifting (i.e. false) belief. The reasoning was that the combination of two target-shifts would produce a very difficult interaction in which the brain has to return to a previously inhibited target. In one scenario, a sick kitten is in box A. Sally does not want to give her fish to the sick kitten in case she makes it worse. When Sally goes out of the room, the kitten moves from box A to box B. Sally then comes back to her fish. In addition to control questions, the child is asked two standard questions, *Think*: 'Where does Sally think the kitten is?', and Prediction: 'Where will Sally put the fish?'. A group of 4-year-old children who were 100% correct on the Think question, were only 38% correct on the Prediction question.

What makes this last result particularly interesting is, first, performance of 4-year-olds on a target-shifting desire coupled with a *true* belief was near ceiling and, second, all the children who failed prediction in the false belief task had just seconds earlier passed the *Think* question. So the result cannot be accounted for simply by assuming (a) that solving target-shifting desire is hard for 4-year-olds (it is not), and (b) because 4-year-olds are barely able to pass false belief, any further difficulty pushes them over the edge (these children had *already* solved the false belief and only had to remember the solution for a second or two). So 'vanilla' information processing assumptions will not account for this finding. It needs an interacting-inhibitions SP model such as those discussed by Leslie and Polizzi (1998). Even when the false belief calculation is over, the default belief target remains inhibited, making it difficult for the brain to return to when required by a target-shifting desire.

Reducing difficulty with false belief.   Information processing factors play an important role in explaining performance on the false belief task. Several investigations have shown that younger children's performance at the false belief task can be improved by modifying task structure. The SP theory makes specific predictions about the kinds of manipulations that ought to work. We review a few examples here.

One information processing variable assumed to be handled by SP is the task of inhibiting the default attribution of belief contents that reflect the current (true) state of affairs so that the typical error in false belief tasks can be avoided. Consequently, if the need for inhibition is reduced, for example by reducing the salience of the to be inhibited content, children ought to fare better at the task. Zaitchik (1991) and Wellman and Bartsch (1988) employ procedures of this kind. In Zaitchik (1991), children in an 'evidence' condition, who do not get to see that the object has changed location, but are merely told that it has, outperform children given a standard task. The need for SP is lessened here because children are not sure, in the evidence condition, which content is true. In the 'Not Own' belief task (Wellman & Bartsch, 1988), children are told about two possible locations for an object, and asked which location they think is correct. Children are told that a protagonist believes the object to be in the other location, and are asked where the protagonist will look. Again, presumably because children are not sure which location is correct, the need for inhibition is reduced and children pass.

One possible objection that theory-theorists might make to these findings is that children may succeed because they are not required to attribute a belief that they know to be false. German (1995b), addressed this issue using a version of the 'disappear' false belief task (Wimmer & Perner, 1983: Fodor, 1992). In the original disappear condition, the object, rather than being displaced to a second location, is destroyed so there is no 'true' location at which the protagonist can search. Wimmer and Perner's (1983) attempt at this manipulation was partially successful, but ran into the problem that children were unconvinced by the disappear event; Wimmer and Perner had simply removed the bait and placed it 'behind the scenes', with the result that children predicted that the character would look for the supposedly 'destroyed' object behind the scenes. German (1995b) showed in one experiment that destroying the object (chocolate) by eating it also improves performance, but only marginally, because even here children tend to predict search in the Experimenter's mouth or tummy, probably owing to their limited understanding of digestion (Carey, 1985). In a second experiment, children were presented with disappear conditions presented via cartoon pictures, in order to overcome the problem of destroying an object in real space. Children performed significantly better when presented with a story in which the object is carried off 'far away' by a dog. Although the children do not know exactly where the object is, they do know it is *not* where the protagonist thinks it is.

One potential problem with this finding is that children might succeed by 'guessing' on the basis of an association between the object and the initial hiding place, without taking into account the agent's belief (see for example comments in Perner, 1995, p. 259). A '*seeing*' control (Leslie, 1994a), where the protagonist sees the transfer and therefore should not look in the empty box is one possible check of the 'association strategy'—if this strategy were used then children should also point to the empty box in the *seeing* condition. But there are pragmatic problems in asking children to predict where a character, who has seen an object destroyed, will look for it. Instead, German (1995b), ran additional conditions in which the object was transferred to an intervening location before it disappeared. Children adopting a 'guessing' strategy should split their responses equally between the two locations visited by the object. Instead, children answered correctly on the basis of the protagonists' belief.

A key point as far as these studies is concerned is that unlike Wellman and Bartsch (1988) and Zaitchik (1991), children were required to attribute a *belief they knew to be false*. Reducing the load on the mechanisms responsible for inhibition of the true belief content thus can lead to improved performance in the false belief task.

Different processing routes for Self and Other in the false belief task? Recently, we have begun to explore whether different processing routes are employed when children reason about their own, rather than another person's mental states (German, 1995a; German & Leslie, 1999b). Within the competence-performance framework, it is plausible that reasoning about Self and about Other in 'theory of mind' tasks may differ. For example, a belief held for Self might be explicitly recalled at a later time, provided certain cues to recall are available, whereas for Other, direct recall of the belief contents is impossible; the past belief must be reconstructed from information about the timing of events and the Other individual's exposure to them. Conceptual shift explanations of the acquisition of 'theory of mind', by contrast, have tended to argue that there should be no differences between reasoning about Self and reasoning about Other. The child's performance is constrained by conceptual factors, not how information is processed; understanding the representational nature of belief provides the difficulty in false belief tasks, irrespective of whether the belief is one's own or that of another individual (Gopnik, 1993; Gopnik &

Astington, 1988; Wimmer & Hartl, 1991). Much of the evidence assessing the relative difficulty of belief reasoning for Self versus Other, collected using the deceptive box paradigm (or 'Smarties' task; Hogrefe, Wimmer & Perner, 1986; Perner et al., 1987) has indeed supported this view (Gopnik & Astington, 1988; Riggs & Robinson, 1995a, b; Wimmer & Hartl, 1991).

However, there are good reasons to suppose that the deceptive box task may not be best suited to discovering Self–Other differences should they exist. The false belief that the child is required to identify has been entertained by the child for a very short time and therefore is likely to provide a very small 'target' for direct recall. Moreover, there is no reason why the child at that time should have represented the belief she had as a belief she is having; therefore when asked even a few moments later, after the original belief has been corrected, the child might instead have to reconstruct what belief she should have had under the then prevailing circumstances. The processing route for calculating belief content for Self in this task is thus very similar to the task of calculating the content of the belief that another person should have under those circumstances (see for example Wimmer & Hartl, 1991, p. 127), and is likely to make similar demands on SP.

German (German, 1995a; German & Leslie, 1999b) removed these problems by asking children to explain their own incorrect search action. In one experiment, 3-year-old children (mean 3–6) were required to play the part of 'Sally' in a false belief task. Children were videotaped as they were given a bait object, asked to hide it, and then left the scene long enough for a confederate to move it to a second location. On their return, they searched the wrong location. Children were then shown the video recordings of either themselves, or of another child, going through this procedure. At the critical moment when the incorrect search took place, the video recording was paused and children were asked to explain their own (or the other child's) action, and questioned about their belief at the time of the search. Note that the structure of this task provides children who were asked about their own belief with the opportunity of 'directly' recalling the belief content, which has been entertained for minutes rather than seconds (as in the standard deceptive box task), rendering that content more salient. By contrast, children asked about the belief of another person would still be required to reconstruct the content from the available evidence, with the usual demands on SP.[5] The results showed that children asked about Self were more likely to offer false belief based explanations (46%) and more likely to attribute to themselves a false belief (88%) than were children asked about the beliefs of another (12% and 42% respectively).[6]

These results were replicated and extended in a second experiment, which showed that the Self–Other effect could be obtained without the use of 'video evidence' of the incorrect search, by making use of a different deception procedure. Children themselves transferred a target object (a sticker) from one box to another, before the boxes were both hidden. An intervening task was then administered before a pair of identical 'clone' boxes were removed from the hiding place, such that when the child searched the box identical to the resting place of the sticker, they were incorrect. Children again were more likely to explain their own incorrect search in terms of their false belief (60%), and were more likely to remember their incorrect belief (80%), than were children asked about another agent (a hand puppet) enacting the same incorrect search (25% and 30% respectively).

These results suggest that children's performance when asked about their own past false beliefs can exceed the performance observed when they are asked about the false beliefs of another. The conceptual deficit view cannot explain these findings because there is no *conceptual* difference between false belief for Self and false belief for Other (Gopnik, 1993; Gopnik & Astington, 1988; Wimmer & Hartl, 1991). However, children are able to recall their own previous belief even when false, if it is made salient enough; otherwise, they must reconstruct the belief from the prevailing circumstances, with the usual selection processing problems. Obviously, only the latter route is available for Other. Standard deceptive box procedures do not seem to allow this difference in strategy, perhaps because the belief is held so transiently (Morton, 1997). There is other evidence that retrieval variables affect the ease with which children succeed at the deceptive box task for their own belief (Freeman & Lacohée, 1995; Mitchell & Lacohée, 1991). Interestingly, we know of no evidence that the same memory procedures help children calculate the beliefs of others. This is consistent with the view that these manipulations help by bolstering a *recall* strategy for Self; where no recall strategy is available (as in the case of Other), these memory manipulations will not work.

Task demands outside the context of mental state reasoning.   Also consistent with the performance perspective on children's reasoning and the mind are recent results suggesting that tasks with *no mental state content at all*, but which involve inhibition /selection demands, are problematic for children to the same extent as are tasks involving the attribution of false belief.

Riggs et al. (1998) show that 3-year-old children fail a task where they are required to make an inference on the basis of a counterfactual state of affairs. Children were shown, for example, that round things were to be sorted into one pot, while long and thin things were to be placed into another pot. Children were shown a round lump of dough and it was put into the 'round things' pot. The experimenter then took the dough, squashed it into a long and thin shape and asked the children where it should go now. It was placed in the 'long things' pot and children were then asked where the object would be if the experimenter hadn't played with it. Note that this task requires children to inhibit the current shape of the object and select a counterfactual alternative description in order to pass the task. They performed at levels similar to their performance at false belief, and performance on the two tasks was also correlated, suggesting common performance demands.

Roth and Leslie (1998) provide another example of a task that 3-year-olds find difficult, despite its involving no mental state content. This task, called the 'screen task' was designed to match the Sally-Anne task in important structural details. Children are presented with an opaque screen. In front of this screen are placed a box and a basket, and a marble is placed inside the basket. All these items are then moved behind the opaque screen, and an identical box and basket are placed in corresponding positions in front of the screen. An identical marble is placed in the basket in front of the screen, left there for a few moments and subsequently moved to the box in front of the screen. The child is asked: 'Behind the screen, where is the marble?'. This task, it was hypothesised, would stress SP to some extent; children were faced with a question (about the situation behind the screen) that can be answered only by inhibiting the similar and salient state of affairs in front of the screen. Four-year-old children performed similarly on the screen task and a standard false belief task. Younger children, by contrast, were found to perform poorly at both the screen and standard false belief tasks, and the two tasks were correlated.

CONCLUSIONS

We have outlined two main approaches to the puzzle of how we acquire a 'theory of mind'. We have criticised theory-theory approaches that assume that children 'discover' a set of 'theories' about the nature of mental states. Children's performance on 'theory of mind' tasks is attributed to the sophistication of the 'theories' they possess. Children fail the false belief task, for example, when their 'theory' of belief does not stipulate that beliefs are representations. Theory-theories have yet to address the information processing questions that their claims raise, for example, how new concepts and 'theories' are devised by young, very ordinary children, how 'evidence' is identified, and how 'environmental interaction' leads to specific abstract formulations.

The ToMM competence theory suggests that children are equipped with a set of innate concepts that simply allow children to attend to mental states, and thus to learn about them. Concept possession is not assumed to depend upon possession of a package of knowledge or 'theory', and mental state concepts are not assumed to depend upon a package of knowledge other than the M-representation itself. Children are not initially expert in deploying their conceptual repertoire, their task is just beginning. To become effective reasoners about mental states, they need to draw on problem solving capacities that develop only gradually over the pre-school period. Children's proficiency at reasoning about pretending and desiring is likely to be influenced by the relatively low performance demands inherent in tasks assessing these mental states, while the standard false belief task is solved rather later, after children develop the resources to deal effectively with the inhibition and selection difficulties involved in these tasks. Only through carefully teasing apart competence and performance issues, will progress be made in understanding 'theory of mind' development.

NOTES

1. We use uppercase when we refer to concepts and lower case when we refer to the property 'in the world' that the concept designates. Thus, DOG is our mental representation, or concept, that designates the property *being a dog*. One of the potentially confusing things about 'theory of mind' is that both the concepts and the properties they designate are 'in the mind'. While on notation, we try to remember to place the 'theories' that are attributed by scientists to children in scare quotes to distinguish them from the theories that scientists devise: so, for example, Gopnik has devised a theory that children have 'theories'.
2. Gopnik (1996) has also argued for the symmetrical view of 'the scientist as child'.
3. Perner (1995) identifies this distinction with one made by Goodman (1976), and retreats from his (1991, pp. 19–20) terminology where he claimed that children must grasp the distinction between *sense* and *referent* (Perner, 1995, footnote 5).
4. Perner borrows this use of the term 'situation' from Barwise and Perry (1983) where it means roughly what others mean by the term 'proposition'—something that can be true or false—as opposed to what is usually meant by the term, a (non-intentional) state of affairs. Here, we use 'situation' and 'proposition' interchangeably.
5. It might be argued that the availability of evidence of incorrect search might help the child to reason 'back' to the false belief, but Moses and Flavell (1990) provide data suggesting that such extra evidence (i) only helps with belief attribution at the expense of failed control questions and (ii) does not result in a high proportion of belief based explanations for another's incorrect search ($\approx$ 12%).
6. The belief based explanation referred variously to the child's lack of knowledge, lack of perceptual access to the transfer events, memory of leaving the object in the initial location, as well as explicit mention of false belief.

ACKNOWLEDGEMENTS

We would like to thank Peter Mitchell and Kevin Riggs for helpful comments on an earlier version of this chapter.

REFERENCES

Baron-Cohen, S. (1995). *Mindblindness*. Cambridge, MA: Bradford Books, MIT Press.
Baron-Cohen, S., Leslie, A.M., & Frith, U. (1985). Does the autistic child have a theory of mind? *Cognition, 21*, 37–46.
Barwise, J., & Perry, J. (1983). *Situations and attitudes*. Cambridge, MA: MIT Press.
Campione, J., Brown, A, & Ferrera, R. (1982). Mental retardation and intelligence. In R.J. Sternberg (Ed.), *Handbook of human intelligence*. Cambridge: Cambridge University Press.
Carey, S. (1985). *Conceptual change in childhood*. Cambridge, MA: Bradford Books, MIT Press.
Carey, S. (1988). Conceptual differences between children and adults. *Mind and Language, 3*, 167–183.
Carey, S. (1991). Knowledge acquisition: Enrichment or conceptual change? In S. Carey & R. Gelman (Eds.), *The epigenesis of mind: Essays in biology and cognition*. Hillsdale, NJ: Lawrence Erlbaum Associates Inc.

Carey, S. (1995). On the origins of causal understanding. In D. Sperber, D. Premack, & A. Premack (Eds.), *Causal cognition*. Oxford: Clarendon Press.

Carey, S., & Spelke, L. (1994). Domain-specific knowledge and conceptual change. In L. Hirschfeld & S. Gelman (Eds.), *Mapping the mind: Domain specificity in culture and cognition*. New York: Cambridge University Press.

Carey, S., & Spelke, L. (1996). Science and core knowledge. *Philosophy of Science*, *63*, 515–533.

Cassidy, K.W. (1995, April). *Use of a desire heuristic in a theory of mind task*. Poster presented at the Biennial Meeting of the Society for Research in Child Development, Indianapolis, USA.

Chi, M.T.H. (1992). Conceptual change within and across ontological categories: Examples from learning and discovery in science. In R. Giere (Ed.), *Cognitive models of science: Minnesota studies in the philosophy of science*. Minneapolis, MN: University of Minnesota Press.

Dennett, D.C. (1981). Three kinds of intentional psychology. In R. Healey (Ed.), *Reduction, time and reality*, (pp. 37–61). Cambridge: Cambridge University Press.

Fodor, J.A. (1992). A theory of the child's theory of mind. *Cognition*, *44*, 283–296.

Forguson, L., & Gopnik, A. (1988). The ontogeny of common sense. In J. Astington, P.L. Harris, & D. Olson (Eds.), *Developing theories of mind* (pp. 226–243). Cambridge: Cambridge University Press.

Freeman, N., & Lacohée, H. (1995). Making explicit 3-year-olds' implicit competence with their own false beliefs. *Cognition*, *56*, 31–60.

Frith, U. (1989). *Autism: Explaining the enigma*. Oxford: Blackwell.

Gelman, R. (1991). Epigenetic foundations of knowledge structures: Initial and transcendent constructions. In S. Carey & R. Gelman (Eds.), *The epigenesis of mind: Essays in biology and cognition*. Hillsdale, NJ: Lawrence Erlbaum Associates Inc.

German, T.P. (1995a). *Children's explanation of action: Desires versus beliefs in theory of mind*. Unpublished Ph.D. thesis, University of London.

German, T.P. (1995b, April). *Testing Fodor's theory of the child's theory of mind*. Poster presented at the biennial meeting of the Society for Research in Child Development, Indianapolis, IN, March, 1995.

German, T.P., & Leslie, A.M. (1999a). Children's inferences from KNOWING to PRETENDING and THINKING. Manuscript, Department of Psychology, University of Essex. Paper submitted for publication.

German, T.P., & Leslie, A.M. (1999b). Self–other differences in false belief: Recall versus reconstruction. Manuscript, Department of Psychology, University of Essex. Paper submitted for publication.

Goodman, N. (1976). *Languages of art*. Indianapolis, IN: Hackett Publishing Co.

Gopnik, A. (1993a). How we know our minds: The illusion of first-person knowledge of intentionality. *Behavioral and Brain Sciences*, *16*, 1–14.

Gopnik, A. (1993b). Theories and illusions. *Behavioral and Brain Sciences*, *16*, 90–100.

Gopnik, A. (1996a). Theories and modules; creation myths, developmental realities, and Neurath's boat. In P. Carruthers & P.K. Smith (Eds.). *Theories of theories of mind* (pp. 169–183). Cambridge, Cambridge University Press.

Gopnik, A. (1996b). The scientist as child. *Philosophy of Science*, *63*, 485–514.

Gopnik, A., & Astington, J. (1988). Children's understanding of representational change and its relation to the understanding of false belief and the appearance-reality distinction. *Child Development*, *59*, 26–37.

Gopnik, A., & Meltzoff, A. (1997). *Words, thoughts and theories*. Cambridge, MA: MIT Press.

Gopnik, A., & Wellman, H. (1992). Why the child's theory of mind really *is* a theory. *Mind and Language*, *7*, 145–171.

Gopnik, A., & Wellman, H. (1994). The 'theory theory'. In L. Hirschfeld & S. Gelman (Eds.), *Mapping the mind: Domain specificity in culture and cognition* (pp. 257–293). New York: Cambridge University Press.

Hadwin, J., & Perner, J. (1991). Pleased and surprised: Children's cognitive theory of emotion. *British Journal of Developmental Psychology, 9*, 215–234.

Harris, P.L. (1996). Desires, beliefs and language. In P. Carruthers & P.K. Smith (Eds.), *Theories of theories of mind* (pp. 200–220). Cambridge, Cambridge University Press.

Hogrefe, G., Wimmer, H., & Perner, J. (1986). Ignorance versus false belief: A developmental lag in attribution of epistemic states. *Child Development, 57*, 567–582.

Johnson, S., & Carey, S. (1998). Knowledge enrichment and conceptual change in folkbiology: Evidence from Williams Syndrome. *Cognitive Psychology, 37*, 156–200.

Leslie, A.M. (1987). Pretence and representation: The origins of 'theory of mind'. *Psychological Review, 94*, 412–426.

Leslie, A.M. (1988). Some implications of pretense for mechanisms underlying the child's theory of mind. In J. Astington, P.L. Harris, & D. Olson (Eds.), *Developing theories of mind* (pp. 19–46). Cambridge: Cambridge University Press.

Leslie, A.M. (1991). The theory of mind impairment in autism: Evidence for a modular mechanism of development? In A. Whiten (Ed.), *Natural theories of mind: Evolution, development and simulation of everyday mindreading* (pp. 63–78). Oxford: Blackwell.

Leslie, A.M. (1994a). Pretending and believing: Issues in the theory of ToMM. *Cognition, 50*, 211–238.

Leslie, A.M. (1994b). ToMM, ToBy and agency: Core architecture and domain specificity. In L. Hirschfeld & S. Gelman (Eds.), *Mapping the mind: Domain specificity in culture and cognition* (pp. 119–148). New York: Cambridge University Press.

Leslie, A.M., & German, T.P. (1995). Knowledge and ability in 'theory of mind': One-eyed overview of a debate. In T. Stone, & M. Davies (Eds.), *Mental simulation: Evaluations and applications* (pp. 123–150). Oxford: Blackwell.

Leslie, A.M., & Happé, F.G. (1993). Autism and ostensive communication: The relevance of metarepresentation. *Development and Psychopathology, 1*, 205–212.

Leslie, A.M., & Polizzi, P. (1998). Inhibitory processing in the false belief task: Two conjectures. *Developmental Science, 1*, 247–253.

Leslie, A.M., & Roth, D. (1993). What autism teaches us about metarepresentation. In S. Baron-Cohen, H. Tager-Flusberg, & D. Cohen (Eds.), *Understanding other minds: Perspectives from autism* (pp. 83–111). Oxford: Oxford University Press.

Leslie, A.M., & Thaiss, L. (1992). Domain specificity in conceptual development: Neuropsychological evidence from autism. *Cognition, 43*, 225–251.

Lillard, A.S. (1993). Young children's conceptualization of pretense: Action or mental representational state? *Child Development, 64*, 372–386.

Lillard, A.S. (1996). Body or mind: Children's categorization of pretense. *Child Development, 64*, 348–371.

Mitchell, P., & Lacohée, H. (1991). Children's early understanding of false belief. *Cognition, 39*, 107–127.

Moore, C., Jarrold, C., Russell, J., Lumb, A., Sapp, F., & MacCallum, F. (1995). Conflicting desire and the child's theory of mind. *Cognitive Development, 10*, 467–482.

Morton, J. (1997). Free associations with EPS and memory. *The Quarterly Journal of Experimental Psychology, 50A*, 924–941.

Moses, L.J., & Flavell, J.H. (1990). Inferring false beliefs from actions and reactions. *Child Development, 61*, 929–945.

Perner, J. (1988). Developing semantics for theories of mind: From propositional attitudes to mental representation. In J. Astington, P.L. Harris, & D. Olson (Eds.), *Developing theories of mind* (pp. 141–172). Cambridge: Cambridge University Press.

Perner, J. (1991). *Understanding the representational mind*. Cambridge, MA: MIT Press.

Perner, J. (1993). The theory of mind deficit in autism: Rethinking the metarepresentational theory. In S. Baron-Cohen, H. Tager-Flusberg, & D. Cohen (Eds.), *Understanding other minds: Perspectives from autism* (pp. 112–137). Oxford: Oxford University Press.

Perner, J. (1995). The many faces of belief: Reflections on Fodor's and the child's theory of mind. *Cognition, 57,* 241–269.

Perner, J., Baker, S., & Hutton, D. (1994). Prelief: the conceptual origins of belief and pretense. In C. Lewis & P. Mitchell (Eds.), *Children's early understanding of mind: Origins and development* (pp. 261–286). Hove, UK: Lawrence Erlbaum Associates Ltd.

Perner, J., Leekham, S., & Wimmer, H. (1987). Three-year-old's difficulty with false belief: The case for conceptual deficit. *British Journal of Developmental Psychology, 5,* 125–137.

Piaget, J. (1929). *The child's conception of the world.* London: Routledge & Kegan Paul.

Piaget, J. (1962). *Play, dreams and imitation in childhood.* London: Routledge & Kegan Paul.

Pinker, S. (1997). *How the mind works.* New York: Norton.

Riggs, K.J., & Robinson, E.J. (1995a). What people say and what they think: Children's judgements of false belief in relation to their recall of false messages. *British Journal of Developmental Psychology, 13,* 271–284.

Riggs, K.J., & Robinson, E.J. (1995b). Children's memory for actions based on a false belief. *Journal of Experimental Child Psychology, 60,* 229–244.

Riggs, K.J., Peterson, D.M., Robinson, E.J., & Mitchell, P. (1998). Are errors in false belief tasks symptomatic of a broader difficulty with counterfactuality? *Cognitive Development, 13,* 73–91.

Roth, D. (1993). *Beliefs about false beliefs: Understanding mental states in normal and abnormal development.* Unpublished Ph.D. Thesis, Tel Aviv University.

Roth, D., & Leslie, A.M. (1991). The recognition of attitude conveyed by utterance: A study of preschool and autistic children. *British Journal of Developmental Psychology, 9,* 315–330.

Roth, D., & Leslie, A.M. (1998). Solving belief problems: Towards a task analysis. *Cognition, 66,* 1–31.

Saltmarsh, R., Mitchell, P., & Robinson, E.J. (1995). Realism and children's early grasp of mental representation: Belief-based judgements in the state-change task. *Cognition, 57,* 297–325.

Surian, L., & Leslie, A.M. (1999). Competence and performance in false belief understanding: A comparison of autistic and normal three-year-old children. *British Journal of Developmental Psychology, 17,* 141–155.

Vosniadu, S., & Brewer, W.F. (1992). Mental models of the Earth: A study of conceptual change in childhood. *Cognitive Psychology, 24,* 535–585.

Wellman, H.M. (1990). *The child's theory of mind.* Cambridge, MA: Bradford Books, MIT Press.

Wellman, H.M., & Bartsch, K. (1988). Young children's reasoning about beliefs. *Cognition, 30,* 239–277.

Wellman, H.M., & Woolley, J.D. (1990). From simple desires to everyday beliefs: The early development of everyday psychology. *Cognition, 35,* 245–275.

Wimmer, H., & Hartl, M. (1991). Against the Cartesian view on mind: Young children's difficulty with own false belief. *British Journal of Developmental Psychology, 9,* 125–138.

Wimmer, H., & Perner, J. (1983). Beliefs about beliefs: representation and constraining function of wrong beliefs in children's understanding of deception. *Cognition, 53,* 45–57.

Zaitchik, D. (1991). Is only seeing really believing? Sources of true belief in the false belief task. *Cognitive Development, 6,* 91–103.

CHAPTER TWELVE

Children's understanding of belief: Why is it important to understand what happened?

Heinz Wimmer and Andreas Gschaider
University of Salzburg, Austria

In this chapter we try to show that the mature concept of belief entails more than what usually is examined in developmental "theory of mind" studies. In particular we will argue that the concept of belief entails that the wrong thought which we took to be reality was caused in such a way that left no possibility other than to take it to be reality. In other words, we not only understand what we wrongly believed to be the case, but also that we did so for good reasons. In the case of false beliefs about simply situational facts (like what something is or where it is), these good reasons are important as they save our view of ourselves as healthy persons who are not hallucinating, and they also save our view of an orderly world where objects do not change their identity or their place in unpredictable ways. Understanding the causation of wrong thoughts about what is the case is also responsible for the fact that at times we find false beliefs so funny or tragic.

For the first author the issue of children's understanding of the causation of knowledge and belief has some tradition and what is proposed here is actually a reformulation of the theoretical stance originally formulated more than 10 years ago in Wimmer, Hogrefe, and Sodian (1988). The old formulation was that for mastering the false belief tasks developed in Salzburg (Hogrefe, Wimmer, & Perner, 1986; Wimmer & Perner, 1983), the child has to infer what another person believes from the misleading informational circumstances the other person was exposed to. The main hypothesis was that children below the age of 4 years or so lack the conceptual basis for the inference, namely an understanding of the causal relationship between informational circumstances on the one hand and resulting epistemic states on the other.

253

This informational causation account was a minority position at the first theory of mind conferences in Toronto and Oxford—only Alan Leslie shared the opposition bench (Leslie, 1988). The majority of researchers viewed young children's false belief problem and similarly their problem with the appearance-reality distinction as due to a more profound conceptual failure, namely as a failure to understand representational relationships in general and in particular the representational nature of mind states (e.g. Flavell, 1988; Perner, 1988; Wellman, 1988). The informational causation position came under empirical attack from various quarters, when it was shown that young children's difficulty with false belief also existed when no inference problem was present. This was the case, for example, for the own-false belief tasks used by Gopnik and Astington (1988), where the child was tricked into a false belief and immediately afterwards was unable to recall it. An attempt to get rid of this piece of counterevidence was unsuccessful and, in fact, strengthened the original finding (Wimmer & Hartl, 1991). This led us to declare defeat and to conclude that the representation deficit position is right and our own causation deficit position wrong. However, there was an additional finding (see later) in the Wimmer and Hartl study that suggested that children's understanding of the causal role of informational causation was involved in their ability to recall a belief. Further studies by Wimmer and Weichbold (1994) and by Wimmer and Mayringer (1998) added to the evidence for an empirical connection between children's ability to attribute a false belief and their understanding of the causal role of the misleading circumstances. The present reformulation of the original Wimmer et al. (1988) position tries to make theoretical sense of these empirical observations. The theoretical move is actually rather simple. Instead of seeing the false belief problem of young children as an inference problem based on the lack of a conceptual basis of understanding informational causation, we make the stronger claim that there can be no mature concept of belief as long as there is no conceptual understanding of informational causation, because the concept of belief entails such a causal component.

WHAT DOES IT MEAN TO UNDERSTAND "BELIEVE"?

The terms "believe" and "think" are used in everyday parlance with different meanings. The meaning we are concerned with is the one where a person mistakenly takes a situational fact simply as given, as reality so to say, when in fact it is a false thought. This, in a certain sense, is the strongest contrast between reality as it is and reality as it was thought to be. This meaning is also the one which is at stake in the developmental studies concerned with children's understanding of false belief. Two aspects of this meaning are important and get little theoretical and empirical attention. We try to explicate them with the help of an episode experienced by the first author (the "I" in the following section refers to H.W.).

Episode. When recently walking through Budapest, I suddenly discovered my purse no longer being in the trouser pocket. Warned about pickpockets, I expected the worst, but an immediate search discovered the purse in the rucksack. With the relief came the insight: After buying a T-shirt, I mindlessly must have put the purse together with the shirt into the rucksack and what I had felt in my pocket all along was not the purse but the handkerchief.

Thought was reality. The first important aspect highlighted by this episode is that—before discovery—"the purse is in the pocket" was not experienced as a thought at all but was reality. In other words there was no thinking about where the purse is. It was in the pocket in the same way as the rucksack was on my back and the shoes were on my feet. Understanding the experience as a case of false belief and describing the experience as "I thought the purse is in the pocket" captures this aspect of the experience, namely that "the purse is in the pocket" was reality and not a guess or a vague expectation.

Causation by misleading circumstances. In the moment of discovery the given fact "the purse is in the pocket" turned into a false belief and the concept of belief preserves what it was, namely simple reality, but also what had happened, namely that misleading circumstances were at work. In other words, I had good reasons to take "the purse is in the pocket" as reality: The purse was in the pocket before the displacement and feeling the handkerchief in the very pocket where the purse was, supported the thought that the purse is still in the pocket. Furthermore, the additional assumption of inattentiveness, when slipping the purse together with the T-shirt into the rucksack, is quite plausible. These reasons are important for mental hygiene. If I would have been unable to come up with my list of good reasons, hallucination or magical powers would follow. So there are not just epistemic reasons for establishing good reasons for wrong thoughts but also deep emotional ones that go to the heart of the self and the world.

Note that there is an intrinsic connection between "taken a false thought to be reality" and "having good reasons for that". If you cannot come up with reasons that are good in the sense that they fully determined what you were thinking about the critical fact, then you cannot claim to have experienced the thought to be reality. Of course, this analysis applies primarily to simple situational facts like what something is and where something is and not for the belief in the existence of God. However, let us also note that the two features we have highlighted are critical entailments of the everyday concept of belief. This becomes obvious when we ask ourselves what distinguishes a false belief from a false guess. In the latter case there is also a false thought and the thought is referring to a certain situational fact. However, in contrast to a false belief, the thought in the case of a false guess was not taken to be reality when it was conceived. Quite differently, there is typically uncertainty when a guess is formed. And when it turns out to be false then there obviously can be no good reasons for having guessed so.

In essence, our analysis shows that the relation between false belief and false guess is exactly analogous to the one between knowledge and true guess. In this respect, it is interesting to note that the developmental study of children's acquisition of the concept of knowledge had focused on the difference between knowledge and true guess (see Perner, 1991, chapter 7 for review) and so took notice of the importance of having or of not having "good reasons" for taking something to be true. In contrast, to the first author's dismay, the importance of "good reasons" for the concept of false belief has received little attention, neither in the conceptual analysis of the concept (for example, Perner, 1991) nor in the empirical developmental study of it. The field was more or less captured by one critical feature of the concept of belief, namely by the fact that thoughts can be false. As our analysis shows, this is only one aspect and it does not distinguish between false belief and false guess.

Our exemplary false belief episode highlighted "taken to be reality for good reasons" with respect to the self-experience of a false belief. These aspects are also present in understanding false beliefs of other persons. Take our understanding of the fate of Oedipus: When he meets Iocaste there is the attraction of the woman and no chance to know her true identity. Or less tragically: When the Count in "La Nozze di Figaro" is trying to get hold of Susanna in the garden, he is led by the dress of a veiled woman, who turns out to be his wife. We experience these stories as tragic or funny as they are intended to be. We are doing so, because we understand that the other takes as reality something that is not the case and we understand why the other has to do so. For example, the Count is not guessing or mad and hallucinating when he is after Susanna in the garden. This would not be particularly funny. The episode is funny only because we understand that circumstances were at work—actually they were set up by the two cunning women—that left the Count no other chance than to take his wife to be Susanna and make a fool of himself.

DEVELOPMENTAL ISSUES

From the analysis of the belief concept it follows that of particular importance is children's understanding of what had happened, in other words, the question is when and how children begin to understand the causal role of informational conditions in the formation of thoughts. First, we summarise the results of several studies done in our laboratory, which were concerned with children's ability to explain false beliefs or misguided actions. Second, we present the developmental history of one closely watched child (Theo Wimmer) with respect to this causal understanding of knowledge and belief.

Studies on children's belief explanation

A study which is rather close to our exemplary false belief episode was done by Wimmer and Hartl (1991) as a follow-up to a study by Gopnik and Astington (1998). In this study quite similar to our episode, children (3-, 4-, and 5-year-olds) were tricked into a wrong expectation and then were asked what had happened. In particular, what they had thought and why they had thought so. The specifics were this. Children were shown a well-known container, for example, a Milka box (similar to the English Smarties box but with good chocolate) and were asked what is in it. Because children experienced *only one* such situation we can be pretty sure that children considered as simple fact that chocolate was in the box. Then the experimenter with mock surprise revealed the true content, for example, a pencil. After the box was closed again, children were asked what they initially had thought ("In the beginning, when I took the box out of my bag, what did you think is in here?") followed by the justification question ("Why did you think there is chocolate in here?") Obviously it is the justification question which is of particular interest here. This question was posed to all children. In the case of the many 3-year-olds who responded with the actual content to the belief question obviously a reminder had first to be given: "But in the beginning, you thought there is chocolate in here, didn't you" Then the justification question followed.

The results were quite clear-cut: Those children who responded correctly to the question what they had thought, were with very few exceptions also able to explain why they had thought so. The most frequent justification was: "Because it is a Milka box". In contrast, those children who had been unable to respond correctly to the belief question, rather infrequently were able to justify their initial response (after being reminded). The other important finding was the developmental progression. Only a minority of the 3-year-olds (about 30%) were able to identify and justify their belief, whereas nearly all the 5-year-olds showed this ability.

Let us assume that our 3-year-olds in fact did not understand the role of the misleading conditions as suggested by their inability to justify their "wrong saying". If this is the case then the last possibility to explain what has happened is lost. This is so because other possible explanations for "wrong saying" are also ruled out. For example, the child is aware that he or she had no intention to say something wrong or to play pretence and, therefore, these causes of "wrong saying" do not apply. So for this child there is no way to assimilate the "wrong saying" into any causal framework. What should follow is that the child quickly suppresses the incomprehensible event. This is exactly what was observed in Wimmer and Hartl's study. About a third of the 3-year-olds (Experiment 1) simply denied in the response to the reminder that they had ever said "chocolate is in here". These denials of having said something wrong were not due to embarrassment, because they also occurred when children observed another person being tricked and expressing a wrong expectation (Wimmer & Hartl, 1991; Experiment 3). The majority of the 3-year-olds in the observer role were unable to recall what the other person had said and in response to the reminder many of them denied that the other person ever had said something wrong. However, we also note that any embarrassment in the case of the self would also indicate a failure to understand the causal role of the misleading conditions. Obviously one should not be embarrassed when one understands that there was no chance other than to have a wrong expectation.

Our interpretation of children's difficulty with own false beliefs as being due to a lack of causal understanding is not the only one. Alternative interpretations of the "thought amnesia" phenomenon by Freeman and Lacohée (1994) and Mitchell (Chapter 3, this volume) are less radical and assume that the 3-year-old child does not have a conceptual difficulty, but only a memory problem. Freeman and Lacohée suggest that 3-year-olds have a problem with memory search and need helpful retrieval cues to recall their belief. Similarly, Mitchell proposes that "thought recall" is a reconstruction and inference process and that 3-year-olds have a problem with these processes. Both accounts despite their merits strike us as somewhat implausible on simple grounds. If a child has the full concept of belief as these researchers assume, then recognising that what one took to be reality was in fact a wrong belief is an outstanding experience both cognitively and emotionally. Such an experience should not be lost immediately. However, exactly such an immediate loss must be assumed by Freeman and Lacohée (1955) and by Mitchell (Chapter 3, this volume) because in the own false belief studies the time lapse between asking the expectation question ("What's in here?") and asking the belief question ("What did you think is in here?") is rather short, about half a minute or so. We have little doubts that with powerful cues (and luck) one may get 3-year-olds to repeat what they have said. This, however, does not necessarily imply that they understand their "wrong saying" as manifestation of a false belief.

Three other studies from our laboratory examined children's ability to explain the false belief or the misled action of another person (Gschaider, 1998; Wimmer & Mayringer, 1998; Wimmer & Weichbold, 1994). The overall findings with respect to children's emerging ability to understand the causal role of the misleading informational conditions were similar to the mentioned findings of the Wimmer and Hartl (1991) study. Of particular interest is the recent MA thesis work by Gschaider (1998). In this study every attempt was made to highlight the importance of the misleading circumstances by contrasting the misled story figure with a non-misled figure (inspired by Robinson & Mitchell's 1995 procedure). For example, in one of the stories the misled Peter was absent when the ice-cream man surprisingly decided to move from the playground to the train station, whereas the non-misled Susi was present during this change. With the intention to meet the ice-cream man Peter was shown on the way to the playground, whereas Susi was shown on the way to the train station. Children then were asked the action explanation questions: "Why does Peter go to the playground to meet the ice-cream man?", followed by the belief explanation question: "Why does Peter think that the ice-cream man is still on the playground?".

The children participating in this study were younger 3-year-olds (3;0–3;6), older 3-year-olds (3;6–3;11), 4-year-olds and 5-year-olds with 16 children in each age range. Several findings are important. The major developmental pro-gression was observed between the younger and the older 3-year-olds. Of the younger 3-year-olds only three children were able after somewhat extended questioning to come up with a correct action explanation and these explanations always were of the sort "Peter *thinks* the ice-cream man is there" or "Peter *doesn't know* where the ice-cream man is". In no case could they follow up this type of action explanation with a correct belief explanation. We interpret this pattern as a kind of reformulation of the action description into a belief or ignorance statement. In essence, not a single child among the young 3-year-olds was able to link the misled action or the false belief to the misleading condi-tions. In contrast, about half of the older 3-year-olds could do so, and the 5-year-olds were perfect. In addition, there was the observation that in contrast to the younger children the 5-year-olds in their responses to the action explanation question nearly always used epistemic terms (e.g. "Peter thinks the ice-cream man is still there") and without exception either spontaneously or in response to the following belief explanation question then referred to the misleading condi-tions (e.g. "Because he had to go home" [before the ice-cream man left the playground]). We interpret this pattern as indication that for the 5-year-olds the role of the misleading conditions was already implied by the use of the mental terms and the role of the misleading conditions was only explicated on further demand. In contrast, the younger children according to this interpretation did not have a concept of "believe" that entails the right sort of causation, there-fore, they preferred to immediately explain the wrong action by the misleading conditions.

In summary, this review of findings both from own false belief and other false belief explanation studies suggests a close developmental association be-tween recall of a wrong thought (in case of the self) or attribution of a wrong thought (in case of the other person) and the ability to causally link the wrong thought to the informational conditions which were responsible. Of course, one limitation of this research is that children's understanding of the causal role of informational conditions was always assessed in direct connection with the assessment of thought recall or thought attribution.

A methodological alternative to these cross-sectional group studies is the longitudinal detailed observation of how single children progress to an under-standing of false belief. That this alternative may provide interesting develop-mental data was shown by Shatz's (1994) remarkable observations of how her grandson Ricky in the age from 15 to 36 months acquired mental terms, and by Bartsch and Wellman's (1995) analysis of mental term acquisition based on CHILDES. In the following we add observations from Theo Wimmer, who in the age range from 12 to 48 months was closely watched by his father (the first author) for the occurrence of utterances with epistemic content. These diary data allow us to see in detail a possible developmental pathway with respect to the acquisition of the concept of belief. The "I" in this section refers to the first author.

A longitudinal single case observation

Early epistemic sensitivity.   The first use of the term "think"—actually Theo used the German equivalent for "believe" (i.e "glauben")—was observed at the age of 2 years and 2 months, when Theo used "think", apparently when experiencing uncertainty about what is the case. The observation was this. Theo one early morning walked into his parents' bedroom as he used to do and looked at the bed, where I was visible, whereas his mother was completely covered by the blanket. This led to the comment: "Mommy—I think—there in is".

Some days before this utterance, Theo began to use "I don't know" quite frequently. For example, when after recognising an indicative smell, I asked him "Is there something big or little in your napkin?" he appropriately responded with "I don't know". Two months later at the age of 2;4 we noted the first affirmative use of "to know". After visiting the house of his babysitter, he said in the evening: "I now know where Andrea (his babysitter) is living".

Also around this age, a false utterance with a plausible motive was noted. It occurred when his mother wanted to go with him to the bathroom to brush his teeth. This led him to say: "I already have brushed teeth—with daddy". Of course, the utterance may have been simply intended to avoid teeth-brushing and less to instil a false belief, but nevertheless.

In summary, we interpret these observations—in particular the use of "think" and "know"—as indications of a sort of epistemic sensitivity: A sense of uncertainty in the case of the "think" utterance, maybe a feeling of having the right answer in the case of the positive "know" utterance and a feeling of having no answer in the case of "I don't know". However, the use of "think" was an isolated one and was not observed again for quite some time. Also: Theo at this young age apparently paid no attention to the informational circumstances resulting in uncertainty or leading to knowledge. A relevant observation at the age of 2;5 was this. One evening when we were coming back from a walk, the car of a friend was standing in front of our house and Theo inferred: "Christine is here". The repeated question "How do you know that?" led to no answer although an answer of the type "her car is here" would not have posed a difficulty. Furthermore, Theo at that age was able to respond appropriately to why-questions as exemplified by the following dialogue:

Theo: "not slippers on"
I: "why not?"
Theo: "go into big bed" (he is not allowed to get into his parents' bed with slippers on).

Working out the role of informational circumstances for knowledge.   The first positive evidence that Theo could link informational circumstances to knowledge was observed at the age of 2;11. We were sitting at the table waiting for lunch. Theo, surprisingly for Andrea, his babysitter, who had prepared lunch, told me that we would get apple-strudel. Andrea asked him: "How do you know that?" (Actually the direct translation of the German phrase is "Wherefrom do you know that?") There was a long pause, but then he came up with the answer: "Because I've looked in the stove". This first explanatory use of informational circumstances was preceded by a phase of interest in what somebody is seeing. An episode from the age of 2;9 was that his tiny toy elephant had to see what Theo was eating by being placed onto the edge of the plate.

However, Theo's first correct answer to a "How do you know that?" question at the age of 2;11 was an isolated occurrence. More frequent occurrences of such answers were noted from the age of 3;6 onwards and at the age of 3;8 Theo's first spontaneous "How do you know?" question was observed. It occurred when he claimed that his friend Johnny doesn't have a bathtub and I claimed that Johnny does have one. My claim led him to ask "How do you know that?". This question was also asked on other occasions. One was that I claimed "Today we will have fine weather" or when I—sitting with him in the bathtub—said: "One gets sick from drinking soapy water". This latter claim led him to ask: "How do you know, that one gets sick? Have you tried it?". Another dialogue about reasons for knowing occurred when his mother said "Tomorrow there will be the devils run (Krampuslauf) in the city". Theo (age 3;9) asked "Wherefrom do you know that?" and Julia responded with "I read it in the newspaper" whereupon Theo commented: "The newspaper is made in the city. They have it in the newspaper what's going on in the city".

Quite impressive was an early utterance at the age of 3;0, when Theo formulated a general rule relating information to knowledge. After having asked his mother for the name when finding a piece of glucose, he said: "You know what, when you don't tell it (the name) to me, then I don't know it and when you tell me, then I know it".

In summary, these observations suggest a rather protracted acquisition of understanding the role of informational circumstances. Theo started with an interest in seeing and not seeing towards the end of the third year and ended with spontaneous questions for justifications of a claim one year later. However, it appears that the knowledge concept, at least in his early answers to "how do you know?" questions, is one rather closely tied to being able to respond correctly to a fact or a name question.

Understanding false beliefs.   The first case of identifying a false belief was observed at the age of 3;8. When sitting with him in the bathtub, I had asked Theo about the colour of the body-paint in one of the containers and he responded according to the colour of the misplaced lid on the container (sitting in the bathtub I was unable to write down the answer). After opening the container I asked him "But what did you think?" and he correctly repeated his initial answer and with some difficulty he also managed to respond appropriately to "Why did you think there is yellow colour in here?" by pointing to the lid. Two months before this episode, at the age of 3;6, Theo already had used the term "think" to refer to something I thought was a false belief. Theo's utterance was "Do you know, why I had waked you up? I thought there were ghosts". However, to my question "Were there really ghosts?" he disappointingly answered "yes".

Although the first instance of false belief understanding was observed for the self, nearly at the same age (3;8) Theo also gave evidence for understanding the false belief of other persons. He had watched a TV programme where children in the night took a moving curtain hanging in a tree to be a ghost. After the programme I asked him "What did the children think?" and "What was it really?" and he responded correctly to both questions.

With respect to these first observations it is important to note that Theo did not spontaneously comment on the false beliefs involved. However, at the age of 3;9 Theo also showed a kind of spontaneous belief understanding when he commented on creating a false belief: "I make myself a moustache (using father's razor foam), so that the ladies in the city think I'm a man".

In summary, we would interpret these observations of false belief understanding not as indications of a fully established belief concept, but as first occurrences of conceptually working through belief episodes. The impression particularly in the misleading container situation was that Theo was more or less forced to work through the experience by the questions posed to him. An interesting aspect is that Theo was always able to justify why he had thought something wrong. This is in remarkable agreement with Wimmer and Hartl's (1991) finding mentioned above. In Theo's case (apart from the theory of his father) this co-occurrence of "false thought identification" and "false thought justification" is not so astonishing because 2 months before the belief episodes, he already showed a good understanding of sources of knowledge by answering "how do you know?" questions.

A more general conclusion from the single case observation is the embeddedness of belief understanding into other aspects of the child's emergent thinking about epistemological matters. We were particularly impressed by what we called early epistemic sensitivity, that is, Theo's early use of "think" in a situation where he obviously was uncertain and his use of "know" when he had learned a new fact. This early epistemic sensitivity may have little to do with a clear conceptual distinction between thought and fact, but nevertheless it clearly indicates a kind of self-reflective awareness of differing epistemic states. Furthermore, this sensitivity for "being uncertain" in the case of "think" or for "having the right answer" or for "having no right answer" in the case of "know" and "don't know" may be the building-block for adopting the everyday concept of thought. We note that O'Neill (1996) has also used the term "sensitivity" to characterise her finding that 2-year-olds are responsive in their communicative attempts to the differing knowledge states of their parents.

In correspondence with the present observation about Theo's use of the term "think" is Shatz's (1994) observation that Ricky used "think" quite early to refer to possibilities and to modulate assertions and that only at the end of the observation period at around 36 months was "think" used to refer to false beliefs. This latter use occurred obviously earlier for Ricky than for Theo. The children studied by Bartsch and Wellman (1995) in their analysis of the CHILDES data exhibited the first advanced belief contrastives between 3;1 (Abe) and 3;9 (Adam) years of age.

The other impressive finding from the single case observation was the gradual understanding of what we call informational causation, which started with an interest into what one sees and what one doesn't see at the end of the third year to spontaneous "how do you know?" questions about one year later. This understanding of circumstances leading to knowledge preceded the first observations of false belief understanding and it is tempting to theoretically assume that first an understanding of informational causation has to be acquired before false belief understanding becomes possible. Of course, a precondition relationship follows from our position that the full everyday concept of false belief entails causation by misleading circumstances. However, some experimental data (Bartsch & Wellman, 1989) suggest that a partial understanding of false belief situations may be possible without an understanding of informational causation, that is, that the child may only register the occurrence of a wrong thought without understanding why.

CONCLUSION

The starting point of our argument was a conceptual analysis suggesting that we as adults experience a false belief as a wrong thought that was taken to be reality because it was caused in such a way that left no possibility other than to take it to be reality. We showed that this causal component of the everyday belief concept distinguishes a false belief from a false guess in the same way as it distinguishes a piece of knowledge from a true guess. We further showed that this causal component of the belief concept is important not only cognitively but also emotionally. In the case of the self it rules out hallucination and in the case of the other it is responsible for the tragic or the funny aspects of false belief episodes. Our complaint was that the study of children's acquisition of belief understanding has largely neglected the causal component of the belief concept and has focused more or less exclusively on children's ability to report (for the self) or attribute (for the other) a false thought.

The review of studies from our laboratory where children were asked to explain a misled action or to justify a given false belief supported our theoretical emphasis on the importance of causal understanding. For example, those children in Wimmer and Hartl's (1991) study who were able to identify what they took to be reality as a false thought most often were also able to identify the "good reasons" for their thought. The important suggestion from Gschaider's (1998) work on children's explanations of misguided actions was that for 5-year-olds the use of the term "think" already implied causation by misleading circumstances. However, more direct developmental evidence on the causal entailment of children's belief concept is needed. Such evidence may be provided by examining children's contrastive use of the terms "think" and (wrong) "guess".

The longitudinal single case study provided support for the position that the self-experience of false belief episodes presupposes an understanding of what had happened. In all of the observed instances of false beliefs, Theo was able to point out what had caused the belief. The case study further provided evidence for early epistemic sensitivity as evidenced by the use of "think" in a situation of uncertainty and as evidenced by the early use of "know" and "don't know". An important conclusion was that the understanding of the causal role of informational circumstances for knowledge and ignorance was fully established before the first instances of false belief understanding were observed. This is in agreement with earlier work on the relationship between knowledge/ignorance attribution and false belief attribution (Hogrefe, Wimmer, & Perner, 1986).

The case study suggested that it might be theoretically useful to distinguish two broad phases in children's understanding of belief. In a first one children solve a false belief task by conceptually working through the episode. For example, in a self-experienced false belief episode they may be asked what has happened or they ask themselves such questions. By doing so they may come up with correct answers. The first instances of Theo's false belief understanding may have been of this type. The conceptual prerequisites are that children have the concept of thought (not of belief) and an understanding of the causal role of informational circumstances. These prerequisites allow them to link a false statement to a false thought and a false thought to misleading circumstances. Working through several such episodes in a causal manner may provide the basis for abstracting the common components of such episodes and form the concept of belief as "a false thought taken to be reality because of misleading circumstances". The characteristic of the second phase would be that children in false belief episodes apply the already established concept.

One difference between the two phases has to do with the consequences of being unable to find the misleading informational conditions for a false thought. If this happens in the first phase then children may suppress the thought as incomprehensible as quite a number of children in Wimmer and Hartl's study did. In contrast, a child with an established belief concept may also be unable to find the causal antecedents of a false thought, but given the established belief concept this child will readily identify the false thought as belief and accept the default assumption that causal antecedents were present.

As a final point we would suggest that children's understanding of the causal role of informational conditions may offer a natural solution to one of the conceptual intricacies of the belief concept that led Perner (1991) among others to postulate that children must acquire or already have acquired a general concept of representation when they form the concept of belief. According to Perner's analysis such a concept of representation requires a distinction between the reference and the meaning of a representation, be this representation a sentence, a picture, or a thought. For example, in the Smarties box episode the child has to understand that the thought "Smarties are in here" refers to the content of the present box in front of him (which contains a pencil), whereas the meaning of the thought refers to, say, a usual Smarties box. The question is whether this theoretical analysis has psychological reality. Our suggestion is that all that is going on is an attempt to causally understand what had happened. If the child is able to understand that this box in front of him caused the thought "Smarties are in here" (because it is a Smarties box and he had no chance to look inside) then the reference-meaning dissociation is solved in a simple way: The wrong meaning of thought is determined by the specific misleading circumstances around this particular Smarties box and the reference of the thought is obvious anyway. So in our analysis there is a causal solution to the reference-meaning dissociation.

In conclusion, if one takes seriously that children's attempt to understand mental phenomena is a theoretical enterprise as suggested by the "theory" approach then it certainly is wise to focus on their causal understanding, because there is little doubt that causal relationships are at the heart of any good theory. One part of the causal understanding of mind phenomena is the understanding of the causal role of informational circumstances in the genesis of thoughts. This understanding is not easy because informational circumstances—such as what one sees and what one does not see—work silently.

REFERENCES

Bartsch, K., & Wellman, H.M. (1989). Young children's attribution of actions to beliefs and desires. *Child Development, 60*, 946–964.

Bartsch, K., & Wellman, H.M. (1995). *Children talk about the mind.* New York: Oxford University Press.

Flavell, J.H. (1988). The development of children's knowledge about the mind: From cognitive connections to mental representations. In W.J. Astington, P.L. Harris, & D.R. Olson (Eds.), *Developing theories of mind* (pp. 244–267). New York: Cambridge University Press.

Freeman, N., & Lacohée, H. (1995). Making explicit 3-year-olds' implicit competence with their own false beliefs. *Cognition, 56*, 31–60.

Gopnik, A., & Astington, W.J. (1988). Children's understanding of representational change and its relation to the understanding of false belief and the appearance–reality distinction. *Child Development, 59*, 26–37.

Gschaider, A. (1998). *Zum alltagspsychologischen Konzept des falschen Glaubens bei Vorschulkindern: Verstehen und Erklären von Handlungen, die auf falschem Glauben einer Person basieren* (About the folk psychological concept of false belief: Understanding and explanation of actions based on false belief of others). MA thesis, University of Salzburg, Austria.

Hogrefe, G.J., Wimmer, H., & Perner, J. (1986). Ignorance versus false belief: A developmental lag in attribution of epistemic states. *Child Development, 57*, 567–582.

Leslie, A.M. (1988). Some implications of pretense for mechanisms underlying the child's theory of mind. In W.J. Astington, P.L. Harris, & D.R. Olson (Eds.), *Developing theories of mind* (pp. 19–46). New York: Cambridge University Press.

O'Neill, D.K. (1996). Two-year-old children's sensitivity to a parent's knowledge state when making requests. *Child Development, 67*, 659–677.

Perner, J. (1991). *Understanding the representational mind*. Cambridge, MA: MIT Press.

Robinson, E.J., & Mitchell, P. (1994). Young children's false-belief reasoning: Interpretation of messages is no easier than the classic task. *Developmental Psychology, 30*, 67–72.

Shatz, M. (1994). *A toddler's life: Becoming a person*. New York: Oxford University Press.

Wellman, H.M. (1988). First steps in the child's theorizing about the mind. In W.J. Astington, P.L. Harris, & D.R. Olson (Eds.), *Developing theories of mind* (pp. 64–92). New York: Cambridge University Press.

Wimmer, H., & Hartl, M. (1991). The Cartesian view and the theory of mind: Developmental evidence from understanding false belief in self and other. *British Journal of Developmental Psychology, 9*, 125–138.

Wimmer, H., Hogrefe, G.J., & Sodian, B. (1988). A second stage in children's conception of mental life: Understanding sources of information. In W.J. Astington, P.L. Harris, & D.R. Olson (Eds.), *Developing theories of mind* (pp. 173–192). New York: Cambridge University Press.

Wimmer, H., & Mayringer, H. (1998). False belief understanding in young children. Explanations do not develop before predictions. *International Journal of Behavioural Development, 22*, 403–422.

Wimmer, H., & Perner, J. (1983). Beliefs about beliefs: Representation and constraining function of wrong beliefs of young children's understanding of deception. *Cognition, 13*, 103–128.

Wimmer, H., & Weichbold, V. (1994). Children's theory of mind: Fodor's heuristics examined. *Cognition, 53*, 45–57.

CHAPTER THIRTEEN

False beliefs about false beliefs

William V. Fabricius
Arizona State University, USA

Alison Imbens-Bailey
University of California, Los Angeles, USA

INTRODUCTION

In this chapter we re-examine what 3- to 5-year-olds may or may not understand about the mind. We begin by examining a dilemma that has arisen among studies of 3-year-olds' ability to attribute false belief to others. To anticipate, we conclude that evidence that 3-year-olds are able to pass certain modified tests of false belief can be explained without having to assume that they understand the representational nature of mental states. Instead we argue that it is only necessary to assume that 3-year-olds (1) represent people as thinking about things and as either knowing or not knowing the true state of affairs, and (2) project their own feelings of knowing onto others in reasoning about what others know. We also argue that previous research may have overestimated 4- and 5-year-olds' understanding because traditional tests of false belief allow children to answer correctly by reasoning only about absence or presence of knowledge in themselves and others. Our alternative explanations of 3- to 5-year-olds' understanding of mental states are based on studies suggesting what younger children already know about the mind, and on studies suggesting what older children still have to learn.

THE 3-YEAR-OLD DILEMMA

The dilemma is this: 3-year-olds have performed correctly on tests of false belief under certain conditions (Saltmarsh, Mitchell, & Robinson, 1995; Zaitchik, 1991), but the explanations given of 3-year-olds' performance in these studies do not account for the difficulty they have on a more traditional test of false belief

(Wimmer & Perner, 1983). Zaitchik presented children with two new conditions (Seen and Unseen). In the Seen condition the child is shown the location of a toy in a box by a Big Bird puppet. Big Bird then tells the child that he will trick a frog puppet by telling him that the toy is in another box. The child is asked where the frog puppet will then think the toy is located. Three-year-olds respond incorrectly, stating that the frog will know where the object really is. In contrast, in the Unseen condition 3-year-olds tend to answer correctly. In this condition the child does not initially see the toy's true location. He or she is only told where the toy is by Big Bird. Big Bird then goes on to describe how he will trick frog as before. Zaitchik's explanation focused on whether or not the child himself saw the true belief, that is, the actual location of the object. The explanation is as follows: When 3-year-olds see the true belief (as in the Seen condition) they will be unable to attribute a false belief to another because they are so certain of the true belief themselves. It is only when they do not see the true belief (Unseen condition) that they will be able to attribute a false belief to another.

However, Zaitchik's argument that the 3-year-old child's own feelings of certainty about the true state of affairs will derail his or her ability to attribute false belief does not explain Saltmarsh et al.'s (1995) findings with 3-year-olds. They presented a new condition to contrast with the traditional unexpected contents or Smarties task (Gopnik & Astington, 1988). In the Smarties task children are shown a Smarties tube and asked to state what they think it contains— namely Smarties sweets. They are then shown that it really contains a pencil. When asked to say what they first thought was in the tube 3-year-olds incorrectly answer "pencil" and provide the same answer when asked to guess what a naïve individual will think the tube contains. In their variation on the Smarties task, Saltmarsh et al. used a Smarties tube that at first really did contain Smarties. They showed the Smarties tube to both the child and the puppet Daffy and asked them to say what it contains. Both answered Smarties. Daffy then left the room and, as the child watched, the Smarties were removed and replaced by a pencil. Daffy then returned and the child was asked what Daffy thinks is in the tube now. Three-year-olds often correctly answered Smarties, apparently attributing a false belief to Daffy. Thus, in contrast to Zaitchik's findings, in this task the child had seen the true belief (the current contents of the tube, namely a pencil) but succeeds in attributing a false belief anyway. Saltmarsh et al.'s explanation did not focus on whether the child had seen the true belief. Instead, it focused on whether the child had seen the false belief (the previous contents of the tube, namely Smarties). They reasoned that when the 3-year-old sees the false belief, as in the Daffy task, he or she will be able to attribute that belief to another because it is salient enough to overcome reality; when he doesn't see the false belief, as in the traditional Smarties task, he won't.

Table 13.1 summarises these findings and explanations. While both explanations can account for 3-year-olds' performance on the Smarties task, Zaitchik's explanation cannot account for Saltmarsh et al.'s Daffy task, and Saltmarsh et al.'s explanation cannot account for Zaitchik's Unseen condition. However,

TABLE 13.1

Patterns of 3-year-olds' attributions of false belief to another as a function of whether they had seen the state of affairs corresponding to the true belief and the false belief in five tasks

	What the child sees		Does the child attribute
Task	True belief	False belief	a false belief
Unseen[a]	−	−	Yes
Seen[a]	+	−	No
Smarties[b]	+	−	No
Daffy[c]	+	+	Yes
Maxi[d]	+	+	No

[a] Zaitchik (1991); [b] Gopnik & Astington (1988); [c] Saltmarsh et al. (1995); [d] Wimmer & Perner (1983).

Robinson (1994) has pointed out that the two explanations can be combined into a single saliency rule that predicts success when either true belief is attenuated in the child's mind, or false belief is elevated, as follows: If the child does not see the true belief, then he or she will be able to attribute false beliefs (à la Zaitchik), but if the child does see the true belief, then he will need to see the false belief in order to attribute it (à la Saltmarsh et al.).

Nevertheless, we are still left with a dilemma, because while this combined rule can explain Zaitchik's two conditions and the Daffy and Smarties tasks, it cannot explain 3-year-olds' failure on the traditional unexpected transfer or Maxi task (Wimmer & Perner, 1983). In the Maxi task, Maxi is initially seen placing his chocolate in a cupboard and then leaving the kitchen. In his absence his mother comes in and moves the chocolate to a different cupboard. The child is asked to say where Maxi will look for his chocolate (or where he will think it is) once he returns to the kitchen. Here the child has seen the false belief (chocolate in the initial location) but still fails to attribute it to Maxi.

Table 13.1 shows that there is no pattern of the child's seeing the true beliefs and/or false beliefs that can account for 3-year-olds' attributions of false belief. We think this means that the various explanations are incomplete because they only take into consideration what the child sees.[1] Just focusing on what the child himself has seen or has not seen does not explain his attributions of knowledge to the other. Instead we need to focus on how the 3-year-old child reasons about what the other knows.

RECONSIDERATION OF 3-YEAR-OLDS' UNDERSTANDING OF MENTAL STATES

Our alternate explanation of 3-year-olds' pattern of success and failure in the studies above has three components. First, 3-year-olds are able to introspect their mental states of knowing or not knowing. In two studies of spontaneous language use by children 14–42 months of age, Imbens-Bailey, Prost, and Fabricius (1997) found that typically there is a year's delay between the onset of self versus other reference in the use of verbs of desire and belief. Children used the first person forms earlier despite the fact that they heard both forms from their parents and used the second person forms themselves with other verbs (i.e. perception verbs and action verbs). These findings contrast with those of Bartsch and Wellman (1995), and were taken to show that young children initially have privileged first-person experience of these mental states. In other words, children's references to their own desires and beliefs seem to stem from direct introspection on those mental states. Furthermore, there was some evidence that children's first expressions of belief tended to be in reference to their own genuine lack of knowledge (i.e. "I don't know").

Second, 3-year-olds assume that others know the state of affairs when they themselves do. They most likely lack any other way to determine what others know because they don't know that seeing leads to knowing (Wimmer, Hogrefe, & Perner, 1988). Introspection alone would not be enough to teach them that seeing is sufficient for knowing. They would only ever directly experience instances of seeing followed by experiences of knowing. Extracting a correlation reflecting a sufficiency relationship between seeing and knowing from an ongoing context of other antecedents of knowing and consequences of seeing, would require them to draw inductive inferences from patterns of co-occurrences of seeing and knowing in the past. That the relationship between seeing and knowing is not immediately given by introspection is shown by 3-year-olds' unawareness of it, and by their willingness to say, for example, that Maxi who has not seen what happened will nevertheless know about it. In this vacuum of explanations of how we know, we suggest that 3-year-olds simply reason that others know the state of affairs when they themselves do.

Third, 3-year-olds have no conceptions of mental states as representations of the state of affairs (Perner, 1991). The way that 3-year-olds understand people, themselves included, is that they either know the state of affairs or they don't. They don't understand that people carry around in their heads a representation of the state of affairs, be it a belief or a memory or a pretence, as we will consider later. They do conceive of themselves and others as being able to think *about* something, however (Perner, 1989). Relatedly, Lyon and Flavell (1994) argue that for 3-year-olds remembering something means simply to be thinking about it here and now. They argue that 3-year-olds do not understand remembering as the retention of knowledge (namely, the representation that something is true) over time.

Thus our answer to the question, "How do 3-year-olds consider what the other knows?" is that they do not represent the other as having a representational belief that some proposition about the state of affairs is true. Three-year-olds can only represent the other as thinking about something and as knowing or not knowing the state of affairs, and they accomplish the latter by projecting their own feelings of knowing onto the other.

First let us apply this to the Daffy task. Daffy is just thinking about the Smarties, so when he comes back and the child is asked "What does Daffy think is in there now?" the 3-year-old says "Smarties" just because that is what Daffy is thinking about. Our interpretation is that the 3-year-old does not think of Daffy as representing the Smarties in the last location in which he had known them to be (the Smarties tube).

This interpretation is consistent with how 3-year-olds respond in the Maxi task. The two tasks (Daffy and Maxi) are in fact structurally similar. In each, the character initially knows what is inside a container or in a particular location, and then goes away and has to remember that fact while the contents are removed. However, 3-year-olds say that Daffy, who has never seen the contents, will remember what is inside the container, while Maxi, who has in fact put the contents in the original location himself, will not. Three-year-olds do not think of Maxi as representing the chocolate as still in the original place, though on the surface that appears to be what they think Daffy does. Our interpretation of this conundrum is that the child does not conceive of either Maxi or Daffy as representing the chocolate or Smarties in any location or container at all. Maxi and Daffy are just thinking about the sweets themselves. So why does the child suppose that Maxi will actually look in the correct place (where the chocolate now is)? We explain this by assuming that the child has projected his or her own feeling of knowing about the chocolate onto Maxi. If Maxi is thinking about the chocolate, and also knows the true state of affairs about it (because the child herself does), then the 3-year-old can think Maxi will look for the chocolate where it really is without having to understand Maxi as representing that location as part of a belief about the chocolate.

But why doesn't the child also project her feeling of knowing onto Daffy and say Daffy will think a pencil is in the Smarties tube? Because, we think, the questions are different in the Maxi and Daffy tasks. In one case the child is asked "*What* does Daffy think is in there?" and in this case she reports what she takes to be the content of Daffy's thoughts (Smarties). In the other case she is asked, "*Where* will Maxi look (or Where does Maxi think it is)?" The 3-year-old only understands that Maxi is thinking about the chocolate, not that he is representing it in any particular location. This doesn't tell her where Maxi will look, so in this case she projects her own feeling of knowing onto Maxi and predicts that Maxi will look in the actual location.

By modifying the Maxi and Daffy tasks to include equivalent questions about the whereabouts of the sweets, it should be possible to get similar responses from 3-year-olds in each task. The Daffy task could be modified by transferring the Smarties to a second container and asking both the original question, "What does Daffy think is in (the Smarties tube)?" and a second question, "Where will Daffy look for the Smarties?". Similarly, the Maxi task could be modified by asking both the original question about where Maxi will look, or where he will think the chocolate is, and a second question, "What does Maxi think is in here (the original location)?". In each case 3-year-olds should say that what the character thinks is in the original container are the sweets, but at the same time that the character will look for the sweets in the actual location. Evidence that 3-year-olds answer both correctly and incorrectly about another's false belief would suggest that they do not conceive of the other as having a representational belief about the state of affairs.

Projection of feeling of knowing is also important in our interpretation of the Seen and Unseen conditions in the Zaitchik study. Here a frog puppet comes in and Big Bird tries to trick him by telling him that a toy is in a different location than it really is. In the Seen condition the 3-year-old knows the location of the toy because she has seen it ahead of time. So she projects this feeling of knowing about the state of affairs onto the frog and judges that the frog will know where the toy really is, despite what Big Bird says. In the "Unseen" condition, the child has not seen if the toy really is where Big Bird told him it was. Then she hears Big Bird tell the frog it is somewhere else. Big Bird is lying to somebody, so in this condition as Zaitchik argues, the child is likely to be somewhat less certain about where the toy really is. So when Big Bird tells the frog where it is, the child may be tempted to believe him. Thus the child will likely have some degree of feeling of knowing that the toy is where Big Bird told frog it was, and when asked where frog will think it is, the child will then be able to project this feeling of knowing onto the frog and predict he will also think the toy is where Big Bird says it is. The 3-year-old does not think of the frog as representing that the toy is in one location or the other, she just considers that the frog knows what she herself knows.

This new interpretation also offers a coherent explanation in the Smarties task for what 3-year-olds predict another will think, and what they report they themselves thought. Our explanation can best be understood within the context of two tasks contrasted in the Saltmarsh et al. (1995) study. They contrasted a version of the Smarties task (their standard false belief task) with what we have called the Daffy task (their false belief state change task). The procedures of both tasks were parallel, in particular Daffy was present at the beginning, stated he thought that the tube contained Smarties, and then left. Three-year-olds were more likely in the Daffy task than in the Smarties task to say Daffy[2] would still think Smarties were in the tube after they themselves found out a pencil was in there. We had said above in our explanation of the Daffy task that in the 3-year-old's mind Daffy was just thinking about the Smarties. We now need to elaborate this explanation.

We suspect that the 3-year-old simply projects onto Daffy what he himself remembers having thought about during the task. If so there should be some reason why the child himself (and by projection Daffy) was thinking more about Smarties in the Daffy task than the Smarties task. There is actually a three-event sequence in both tasks that should provoke the child to think more about Smarties in the Daffy task than the Smarties task. In the Daffy task, first the child sees the Smarties tube, and thinks about Smarties. Second, the tube is opened and the Smarties are revealed, which prolongs the child thinking about Smarties. Finally, a pencil is put in the tube, directing the child's thoughts to the pencil. We can refer to the three events as the *appearance* event, the *previous reality* event, and the *current reality* event. In the Daffy task, the child thinks about Smarties during the first two events, while in the Smarties task the child thinks about Smarties less often, namely only during the appearance event, because during the previous reality and current reality events it is a pencil that is revealed and put back in the tube. Thus our suggestion that the 3-year-old simply projects onto Daffy what he himself remembers having thought about is consistent with how often children answered correctly that Daffy would think that Smarties were in the tube in response to the false belief question. In the Smarties task children said Daffy would think Smarties less often (25%, averaged across all four experiments in Saltmarsh et al.), than in the Daffy task (45%, averaged across Experiments 2 and 3). This correspondence between the number of events in which Smarties occurred and the frequency with which children reported Smarties as the content of Daffy's thoughts is replicated across the two additional tasks Saltmarsh et al. used. In their "true belief state change" task, Smarties occurred during both the appearance and previous reality events as they did in the Daffy task, and children said Daffy would think Smarties just as frequently (58%, averaging across Experiments 1 and 3) as they said he would in the Daffy task (45%), even though the question here referred to Daffy's true belief and so might well have been easier. And finally in the "false belief state change with atypical content" task, Smarties occurred only during the appearance event as they did in the Smarties task, and children said Daffy would think Smarties just as frequently (about 25%, averaging across ages in Experiment 4) as they said he would in the Smarties task (25%).[3]

RECONSIDERATION OF 4-YEAR-OLDS' UNDERSTANDING OF MENTAL STATES

This leads us to consider what 4-year-olds know. They pass the Maxi and Smarties tasks, but their immature understanding of mental representation in other areas of cognition, including memory, pretence, and inference suggests to us that they may not have a representational understanding of belief.

While recent findings (Lyon & Flavell, 1994) indicate 3-year-olds understand memory more as "thinking about" than as "thinking (remembering) that" something is true, there is research suggesting the same may be true of 5- to 6-year-olds. This is shown in their ratings of the amount of memory involved in various mental activities (Fabricius, Schwanenflugel, & Schick, 1995), and in their understanding of how prospective memory retrieval cues work (Fabricius & Wellman, 1983). Five- to six-year-olds' ratings of memory in various mental activities such as "Telling your friend everything you had for lunch", and

"Listening to what your friend is saying in a noisy cafeteria" matched adult ratings of the amount of thinking or conscious attention involved, not adult ratings of memory (Fabricius et al., 1995). Thus "memory" for them meant "thinking about" something. It was only by about eight years of age that children's ratings closely resembled those of adults. This is consistent with young children's' understanding of prospective memory retrieval cues. When asked where a story character should put a note to help himself remember to go to a different class-room to get a book before he leaves school, many 6- to 7-year-olds said he should put it with the book (Fabricius & Wellman, 1983). Thus, they assumed that the person will keep thinking about the task to-be-remembered so that they will just go look at the cue at the proper time. They did not understand that the cue would really work by retrieving a representational mental state (memory) that the person was currently not having and which is different from the current situation in which the person finds himself.

The fact that 5- to 6-year-olds seem to conceive of remembering something as simply thinking about it, and that they think that a prospective memory retrieval cue works because the person goes to look at it when it is time to remember should cast doubt on what it is exactly that the 4-year-old understands when he says that Maxi will remember where he last saw the chocolate. The Maxi task is essentially a type of metamemory task. The child is asked in effect whether Maxi will remember that the chocolate is in the initial location. Clearly one difference between the Maxi task and the memory rating and retrieval cue tasks is that the Maxi task is relatively simple and concrete as opposed to rating the amount of memory involved in various mental activities or judging several different cue locations. So the Maxi task seems simpler and thus perhaps brings out earlier understanding. But the Maxi task is also more difficult in the sense that the memory involved is a false belief that contradicts current reality. From that point of view the other tasks that simply ask about remembering something true should be easier. If the 4-year-old understands that Maxi constructs and maintains and later acts upon a representation (memory) of the state of affairs that differs from the actual state of affairs, then why should children one to two years older have such difficulty understanding that people can construct and maintain representations (memories) of the state of affairs that do not differ from the actual state of affairs? In other words, why should the 4-year-old understand memory when it involves a false belief but not in other cases where it does not?

The data from both the Maxi task and these memory tasks may simply be telling us the same thing, that 4-year-olds are still not understanding representa-tional mental states. Four-year-olds have learned that seeing leads to knowing (Wimmer et al., 1988), and so they are less likely than 3-year-olds to simply transfer their knowledge onto the other. But they are still only reasoning about whether someone knows the actual state of affairs or not. They know that Maxi has not seen the chocolate in the new location, and consequently he doesn't know that it is there. He knew before where it was, but not now. So in the

4-year-old's mind, if Maxi doesn't know where the chocolate is, he will simply look in the wrong place for it. But the task is set up so that there is only one place for him to look where he will be wrong, and that is in the initial location. This suggests a modification of the Maxi task for 4-year-olds: Provide a third possible location for the chocolate by having it temporarily transferred to an intermediate location after Maxi leaves (so as to legitimise that location in the child's mind as a possible place for the chocolate to be). This would mean that there would now be two places for Maxi to look and not find the chocolate, the initial location where a false belief would give him reason to look, and the intermediate location where it was temporarily located before being moved to the final location. We suspect that many 4-year-olds would think that Maxi will think that the chocolate is in the intermediate location (which would throw into doubt those who pick the initial location). This would be evidence that 4-year-olds think Maxi's behaviour is driven not by memory for the previous state of affairs, but by ignorance of the current state of affairs.[4]

This view of 4-year-olds can also account for their performance on the Smarties task. In our view, 4-year-olds think that the other person will not know what is inside the Smarties tube because he cannot see the pencil inside. So they reason he will be wrong when he is asked to say what he thinks is in there. He will say "Smarties" just because that is a wrong answer. A modification of the Smarties task that would test whether in fact 4-year-olds are reasoning about false beliefs would be to use the "false belief state change with atypical content" task (Saltmarsh et al., 1995), but to use it to predict another's knowledge (which Saltmarsh et al. did not do). In this modification, the child would be shown a Smarties tube and asked what it contains. After replying "Smarties", the child would be shown it contains a pencil. While the child watches, the pencil would be removed and replaced with a key. When asked to predict what another will think is in there, we predict that she will reason that since the other person can't see the key, the other person will not know what is in there and will be wrong. But now the 4-year-old can predict the other will be wrong in one of two ways, one way by saying "pencil" (what used to be in there) and one way by saying "Smarties" (what she herself said). If we are wrong and the 4-year-old does in fact understand false belief, then she should only predict that the other will say Smarties, and not pencil, because there is no reason for the other to believe that a pencil is in the tube.

In other words, we are saying that in the traditional Smarties task 4-year-olds predict that the other will "think" that Smarties are in the tube not in the sense that the other will "believe" it because he has some way of knowing, but in the sense that he will "guess" wrong because he doesn't know what is really in there. If they attributed a false belief to the other, as opposed to simply an incorrect guess, they would have to know where the belief came from. In the Smarties task, the false belief arises from an inference made about the contents of the tube based on the pictures of Smarties on the outside. But there is evidence that 4-year-olds do not understand that inference can give rise to beliefs. This comes from the "inference neglect" task (Sodian & Wimmer, 1987). In this task, the child reports his own inferentially-gained true belief, but denies that an observer will gain the same knowledge. The child and observer both see that a bag contains only marbles. They are then told something will be taken from the bag (unseen by them) and placed in a second, empty bag. When asked if he knows what is now in the second bag the 4-year-old says he does, marbles. But he says that the observer will not know because, Sodian and Wimmer argue, he reasons that the observer has not seen in the bag and he fails to understand that the knowledge could have been gained by inference. We argue that the same thing happens in the Smarties task, except that there the child does not have the response option of saying the other will not know. The processing demands in the inference neglect task do not seem to be too difficult. Ruffman (1994) showed that 4-year-olds can remember and use the premise information in such tasks.

But the question arises in the inference neglect task, how does the 4-year-old know himself that the second bag contains marbles? This poses a problem for the Theory theory account (Gopnik & Wellman, 1994) of children's understanding of false belief. In the inference neglect task, the child reports his own inferentially-gained belief, but denies that an observer will gain the same knowledge. According to the Theory theory account, the child does not have direct introspective access to his own inferentially-gained belief (Gopnik, 1993; Wimmer & Hartl, 1991). Instead his judgement that he has a belief is embedded in his theory about what causes beliefs (Montgomery, 1997). In other words, he reasons in a theoretical fashion something along the lines of, "I saw that the first bag contained only marbles, and since something from the first bag was put into the second bag, I can conclude that the second bag has marbles in it". He is supposed to have engaged in analogous inferential reasoning in the Smarties task, which accounts for his being no more accurate in reporting what he himself had thought was in the tube than in predicting what another will think (Wimmer & Hartl, 1991). But reasoning about himself in the inference neglect task should also enable him to reason similarly about the observer, who has seen everything he himself has. But he doesn't. While it has been pointed out (Stich & Nichols, 1992) that 4-year-olds' failure on inference neglect tasks is a problem for simulation theory accounts of children's understanding of mental states, it is no less a problem for Theory theory accounts. It suggests that the child does not have a theoretical concept of his own belief in this situation if he cannot also apply it to the observer. In the inference neglect task the 4-year-old still acts as if he only understands that he knows the state of affairs while the observer does not, not as if he understands that both of them will have drawn an inference (representation) about the state of affairs.

Finally, recent evidence of 4-year-olds' understanding of the mental state of pretence is consistent with the negative picture we have drawn of their understanding of mental states. In several studies, Lillard has found that before age 6, most children do not understand that pretending requires mentally representing a state of affairs that is different from the real state of affairs. For example, she showed children a troll that was hopping, and explained that the troll did not think that it was hopping like a kangaroo (Lillard, 1993). Children were asked whether the troll was nevertheless pretending to be a kangaroo, and 60% of 4- and 5-year-olds said that it was. More recently, Lillard has found that 60% of 4- and 5-year-olds deny any mental aspects to pretence: They think that one does not need a mind or a brain to pretend (Lillard, 1996; Lillard & Sobel, 1999; Sobel & Lillard, 1998), that one can be pretending to be something even when one is not trying to pretend and does not want to pretend (Lillard, 1998), and, most dramatically, that inanimate objects can pretend (Lillard, Zeljo, Curenton, & Seja, in press). While most 6-year-olds do answer correctly on these kinds of questions, not all do, and deeper understanding of pretence as a mental representation continues developing even after age 8. Less than half of 8-year-olds understand that pretenders keep in mind the representation of the pretend state of affairs while they are pretending (Lillard, 1996). The majority thinks that pretenders use their minds when deciding to pretend, but not while they are pretending.

It is difficult to understand why pretence should be so hard to understand if by age 4 children generally understand false belief. Understanding that the mind is representational, and that one can form a belief about the state of affairs that differs from the actual state of affairs, and furthermore that one would be led to act upon that belief so that one's actions would not be in accord with one's self interests seems, if anything, to be more difficult than understanding that one holds in mind a representation of a pretend state of affairs while one is deliberately acting out of character. But the data show the opposite. Lillard (in press) examined the relative onset, among 3- to 5-year-olds, of (1) false belief understanding (as measured by the Maxi and Smarties tasks), (2) understanding of the mental representational aspects of pretence, and (3) tendency to engage in more extended bouts of pretend play. Children tended to pass the false belief tasks before the pretence understanding tasks, and to pass the pretence understanding tasks before they engaged in more extended bouts of pretend play. Lillard points out that the common hypothesis has been exactly the opposite, that engagement in pretence leads the child to become aware of the mental representational aspects of pretence, which in turn helps the child understand false beliefs. For example, Perner (1991) has argued that while early pretence does not reflect understanding of representational mental states it does become a representational concept by age 4, while Leslie (1987, 1988) has argued that even very young children have a representational understanding of pretence for both the self and others. Finally, Lillard (in press) found that only the pretence understanding tasks and not the false belief tasks predicted children's engagement in bouts of pretence. We take these findings to be further evidence that the false belief tasks can be answered correctly for the wrong reasons, and thereby overestimate 4-year-olds' understanding of mental representations.

SUMMARY

We have argued that in spite of current trends to credit younger children with early understanding of false belief there is much evidence that even 4- and 5-year-old children are unlikely to have grasped the representational nature of mental states. Specifically, we suggest that precocious performance on tests of false belief can be explained by processes that can be traced to much younger children; namely, their awareness that they think about things and their feelings of knowing and not knowing, which they then project onto others when asked about what others know and think. This approach proved fruitful in providing a coherent explanation of the inconsistent performance of 3-year-olds across different false belief tasks. We also argue that it seems unlikely that 4-year-olds understand belief as a mental representation when they themselves and older children continue to fail on tasks (pretence, memory, and inference) that also require an understanding of the representational nature of the mind. Finally we have suggested modified false belief tasks that should indicate whether 4-year-olds' typical success on traditional false belief tasks is due to their simply taking into account whether or not someone has had perceptual access to and therefore knows the state of affairs. The shift to understanding the mind as representational is currently characterised as occurring quite suddenly between 3 and 5 years of age, but given the developmental picture we have portrayed here it may likely prove more gradual and prolonged.

NOTES

1. Saltmarsh et al. (1995) suggest an additional factor to explain why the Maxi task does not appear to be as easy as it should be given that the child has seen the chocolate in its original location. They suggest that the narrative form of the story involving puppet characters may negate the advantage accruing from seeing the false belief.
2. In different tasks various questions were asked about Daffy's thoughts and the child's own thoughts, and no differences were ever found. For convenience we refer only to reports of Daffy's thoughts.
3. In the "false belief state change with atypical content" task, all three events were represented by different objects (appearance = Smarties; previous reality = pencil; current reality = key), allowing, we would suggest, separate measures of how likely children were to remember having thought about each of the events. In this task, in response to the false belief question, children reported the appearance event (Smarties) about 25% of the time, the previous reality event (pencil) about 25% of the time, and the current reality event (key) about 50% of the time. These various percentages sum to predict quite closely children's responses in the other tasks where one object occurs for two events. In the Daffy and "true belief state change" tasks, Smarties occurred for both the appearance and the previous reality events, so if children remembered thinking about either event they would report Smarties. Thus, based on the sum of the separate measures of each event in the "false belief state change with atypical content" task (appearance = 25% plus previous reality = 25%), they should report Smarties

50% of the time in each task. Children in fact reported Smarties 45% of the time in the former task, and 58% in the latter, averaging 51.5%. In the Smarties task, children would report pencil if they remembered thinking about either the previous reality event or the current reality event. Thus they should report pencil 75% of the time (previous reality = 25% plus current reality = 50%), which is what they did. Thus our explanation appears to account not only for children's correct responses across tasks, but also for the distribution of their errors.

4. We have found only two other studies that employed a third location, but neither of them in the way suggested here. In Wimmer and Perner (1983) the chocolate was never placed (temporarily) in the third location, and children virtually ignored it even though in the competitive condition they would have had a reason to refer to it had any reality bias crept into their judgements. In Wimmer and Weichbold (1994) the chocolate was divided in half and placed in both the second and third locations when it was moved from the place Maxi left it, thus still maintaining only the two original types of location (where it really is and where Maxi would falsely believe it is).

REFERENCES

Bartsch, K., & Wellman, H.M. (1995). *Children talk about the mind.* New York: Oxford.

Fabricius, W.V., Schwanenflugel, P.J., & Schick, K. (1995). *Conceptual change and theory of mind: Development of the concept of memory from kindergarten to adulthood.* Poster presented at the meetings of the Society for Research in Child Development, Indianapolis, IN.

Fabricius, W.V., & Wellman, H.M. (1983). Children's understanding of retrieval cue utilization. *Developmental Psychology, 19,* 15–21.

Gopnik, A. (1993). How we know our minds: The illusion of first-person knowledge of intentionality. *Behavioral and Brain Sciences, 16,* 1–14.

Gopnik, A., & Astington, J.W. (1988). Children's understanding of representational change and its relation to the understanding of false belief and the appearence-reality distinction. *Child Development, 59,* 26–37.

Gopnik, A., & Wellman, H.M. (1994). The theory theory. In L.A. Hirschfield & S.A. Gelman (Eds.), *Mapping the mind: Domain specificity in cognition and culture* (pp. 257–293). New York: Cambridge University Press.

Imbens-Bailey, A.L., Prost, J.H., & Fabricius, W.V. (1997). *Perception, desire, and belief in me and you: Young children's reference to mental states in self and other.* Unpublished Manuscript, University of California, Los Angeles.

Leslie, A.M. (1987). Pretense and representation: The origins of "Theory of Mind". *Psychological Review, 94,* 412–426.

Leslie, A.M. (1988). Some implications of pretense for mechanisms underlying the child's theory of mind. In J.W. Astington, P.L. Harris, & D.R. Olson (Eds.), *Developing theories of mind* (pp. 19–46). New York: Cambridge University Press.

Lillard, A.S. (1993). Young children's conceptualization of pretense: Action or mental representational state? *Child Development, 64,* 372–386.

Lillard, A.S. (1996). Body or mind: Children's categorizing of pretense. *Child Development, 67,* 1717–1734.

Lillard, A.S. (1998). Wanting to be it: Children's understanding of pretense intentions. *Child Development, 61,* 981–993.

Lillard, A.S. (in press). Pretending, understanding pretense, and understanding minds. In S. Reifel (Ed.), *Play and Culture Studies* (Vol. 3). Norwood, NJ: Ablex.

Lillard, A.S., & Sobel, D. (1999). Lion Kings vs. puppies: children's ideas of what it takes to pretend. *Developmental Science, 2,* 75–80.

Lillard, A.S., Zeljo, A., Curenton, S., & Seja, A. (in press). Young children's understanding of the animacy constraint on pretense. *Merrill-Palmer Quarterly.*

Lyon, T.D., & Flavell, J.H. (1994). Young children's understanding of "remember" and "forget". *Child Development, 65,* 1357–1371.

Montgomery, D.E. (1997). Wittgenstein's private language argument and children's understanding of the mind. *Developmental Review, 17,* 291–320.

Perner, J. (1989). Is "thinking" belief? Reply to Wellman and Bartsch. *Cognition, 33,* 315–319.

Perner, J. (1991). *Understanding the representational mind.* Cambridge, MA: Bradford/MIT Press.

Perner, J., Leekam, S., & Wimmer, H. (1987). Three-year-olds difficulty with false belief: The case for a conceptual deficit. *British Journal of Developmental Psychology, 5,* 125–137.

Robinson, E.J. (1994). What people say, what they think, and what really is the case: Children's understanding of utterances as sources of knowledge. In C. Lewis & P. Mitchell (Eds.), *Children's early understanding of mind* (pp. 355–384). Hove, UK: Lawrence Erlbaum Associates Ltd.

Ruffman, T.K. (1994). *Do children understand the mind by means of simulation or a theory? Evidence from their understanding of inference.* Unpublished manuscript, Laboratory of Experimental Psychology, University of Sussex.

Saltmarsh, R., Mitchell, P., & Robinson, E. (1995). Realism and children's early grasp of mental representation: Belief-based judgements in the State Change task. *Cognition, 57,* 297–325.

Sobel, D., & Lillard, A.S. (1998, May). *Does the word "pretend" interfere with children's understanding of pretense?* Paper presented at the annual meeting of the American Psychological Society, Washington, DC.

Sodian, B., & Wimmer, H. (1987). Children's understanding of inference as a source of knowledge. *Child Development, 58,* 424–433.

Stich, S.P., & Nichols, S. (1992). Folk psychology: Simulation or tacit theory? *Mind and Language, 7,* 35–71.

Wimmer, H., & Hartl, M. (1991). The Cartesian view and the theory view of mind: Developmental evidence from understanding false belief in self and other. *British Journal of Developmental Psychology, 9,* 125–128.

Wimmer, H., Hogrefe, G.J., & Perner, J. (1988). Children's understanding of informational access as a source of knowledge. *Child Development, 59,* 386–396.

Wimmer, H., & Perner, J. (1983). Beliefs about beliefs: Representation and constraining functions of wrong beliefs in young children's understanding of deception. *Cognition, 13,* 103–128.

Wimmer, H., & Weichbold, V. (1994). Children's theory of mind: Fodor's heuristics examined. *Cognition, 53,* 45–57.

Zaitchik, D. (1991). Is only seeing really believing?: Sources of the true belief in the false belief task. *Cognitive Development, 6,* 91–103.

CHAPTER FOURTEEN

Belief as construction: Inference and processing bias

Peter Mitchell
School of Psychology, University of Nottingham, UK

Haruo Kikuno
Department of Early Childhood Education,
Osaka University of Education, Japan

INTRODUCTION

One view of the development of a theory of mind that deserves special credit for its level of elaboration has been formulated by Wellman (1990). He suggested that a basic folk theory of mind takes the form of simple belief-desire psychology, which provides a conceptual framework to predict and explain human action. This is the notion that people usually act to satisfy their desires, in conjunction with the understanding that their beliefs about the state of reality feed into this. Hence, if an individual holds a false belief, then paradoxically, they might even act in a way that thwarts their desire. Wellman claims it is possible to demonstrate that children understand the role of desire in behaviour from about age 2 years, but that it is not until about age 4 years that children acquire an understanding of belief that could feed into their system of folk psychology. Superficially, there seems to be a fundamental problem with this account because it appears not adequately to explain why young children have difficulty acknowledging their own prior false belief in a Smarties deceptive box task (Gopnik & Astington, 1988). In this task, they are not required to explain action but simply need to give an explicit acknowledgement of what they had thought. Neither does the concept of desire seem to be an issue that could obscure a nascent ability to acknowledge belief, given that children would probably have desired there to be Smarties, not pencils, inside the box.

The more fundamental problem with Wellman's (1990) theory, as with other conceptual shift accounts, is that it never adequately explains how the conceptual revolution could occur that culminates in the construction of a concept of belief. It is not explained adequately what kind of experiences and processes combine to trigger a conceptual revolution. Neither is it explained why the acquisition of a concept of belief should be revolutionary.

A useful research heuristic would be to build upon the idea of a simple belief-desire folk psychology, but to consider development in terms of efficiency in identifying the appropriate content of belief for input into the belief-desire process. In other words, it might be that children younger and older than 4 years are alike in feeding information relevant to belief in to their belief-desire framework. The difference between age groups might be that those above age 4 stand a better chance of identifying the correct content of belief. In one sense, this departs from Wellman in a rather subtle way, given that we are in agreement in assuming that the belief-desire psychology does not function effectively during early childhood due to a problem in the department of belief input. In another respect, the accounts are radically different. Wellman seems to assume that when children give an incorrect judgement, this stems from an absence of a proper conception of belief, while we subscribe to the view that there is a belief input, but an inappropriate one. To suggest that children understand about beliefs but still give an incorrect judgement in a test of false belief seems contradictory on the face of things and further elaboration is required.

STATE CHANGE

The interesting characteristics of the state change task (Wimmer & Hartl, 1991) will cast some light on the matter. Wimmer and Hartl presented a Smarties tube and asked children what they thought was inside. After children replied with "Smarties", the experimenter opened the tube to reveal that there were Smarties inside, as expected. As the child watched, the experimenter then removed the Smarties altogether and replaced them with pencils. Finally, the experimenter asked children what they had thought was inside the tube first of all, and over 80% of them replied correctly with "Smarties". The predominance of correct judgements contrasted sharply with children's frequent errors in a standard deceptive box task, in which the Smarties tube contained pencils all along such that the child's initial expectation about the content was disconfirmed. In that, children tended to judge wrongly that they had thought the tube contained pencils.

Wimmer and Hartl (1991) subscribe to a conceptual shift view, and accordingly interpreted their striking result in those terms. They suggested that children's correct judgements in state change were actually false positives. If children had not yet experienced the conceptual revolution that equipped them with a concept of belief, then they would necessarily be unable to understand a sentence that contained reference to thought. Superficially, that might lead one to think that any question that makes reference to thought would render children silent on the grounds that they are unable to reply. However, as we all know, children are disposed to enter into conversation even if they are unfamiliar with many of the words uttered to them. If children did not have that trait, then presumably they would remain mute and reluctant to engage in interaction, with the consequence that enculturation would be seriously tardy or impossible. It seems that what children might do instead, is attend to words or concepts that they do know and then do the best they can to reply despite their partial comprehension. Even though young children understand hardly anything, it is very seldom for them to admit such or indeed to behave as if such were the case.

Returning to state change, if children did not understand in particular about thought and the word *think*, then presumably they would gloss "What did you think was inside?" as "What was inside?". In consequence, they would reply with "Smarties" and "pencils" in the state change and deceptive box tasks respectively. If an adult were asked "What was inside?" in these two tasks, that is how he or she would answer. Hence, in a state change, Wimmer and Hartl (1991) seem to suppose that although children above and below 4 years judge that they had thought there were Smarties inside, the older child is reporting the prior belief as a belief, while the younger one is merely reporting a prior reality. This is revealed by the possibility that the younger child can only give a correct judgement when the question is about true belief, because it is only then that they can give what would be deemed a correct judgement whilst actually report- ing reality. Apart from being an ingenious interpretation in favour of the concep- tual deficit account, Wimmer and Hartl's explanation helps to eliminate suggestions that incorrect judgements in a standard deceptive box procedure stem from artifacts of the task demands. For example, children evidently do not have a problem with past tense and misinterpret the question to be referring to the current content, otherwise they would report the current content in both the deceptive box and the state change.

It now seems, however, that Wimmer and Hartl's (1991) explanation for their state change result is fundamentally wrong. Such is suggested by the recent findings reported by Saltmarsh and colleagues (Saltmarsh & Mitchell, 1998; Saltmarsh, Mitchell, & Robinson, 1995). Saltmarsh included a confederate in the state change procedure in the form of a Daffy puppet. Daffy and the child participant were both shown a Smarties tube and both were asked what they thought was inside. After both had replied with "Smarties" the experimenter revealed that Smarties were indeed inside. The experimenter then cleared these away and replaced them with pencils. Finally, children were asked what they had thought was inside and also what Daffy had thought was inside. It was common for children to answer both questions correctly with "Smarties", which Wimmer and Hartl would interpret as false positives; as usual, in a standard deceptive box task, children typically answered wrongly with "pencils". How- ever, the introduction of Daffy allowed a modification to the procedure that was capable of refuting Wimmer and Hartl's interpretation. Instead of asking children what Daffy thought was inside the box, the experimenter asked them what Daffy thinks is inside right now. It so happened that Daffy had been absent when the box was opened and the Smarties replaced with a pencil, so an adult would judge that Daffy thought the box contained Smarties.

Interestingly, many young children also judged correctly that Daffy thought right now that the box contained Smarties, and thereby succeeded in acknowledging his *false* belief. Indeed, it was just as common for children to acknowledge Daffy's current false belief, as it was for them to acknowledge Daffy's past true belief. In sharp contrast, when the box had contained pencils all along, children typically failed to acknowledge either Daffy's current or his past false belief. At its simplest, it seems possible to modify a state change procedure such that children can succeed equally in acknowledging another person's or their own belief, no matter whether the belief to be acknowledged is true or false. State change seems to help children give a judgement of belief as belief. That is the only plausible and parsimonious way of explaining their success through state change in acknowledging a *false* belief.

There is a further reason for thinking that Wimmer and Hartl's (1991) interpretation of the state change result is wrong. Saltmarsh et al. (1995) showed children a Smarties tube and asked them what they thought was inside. After the child responded with "Smarties", the experimenter opened the lid to reveal a pencil, which she then exchanged for a spoon as the child watched. Finally, children were asked either what was inside or what they had thought was inside. This task combines elements of the deceptive box with those of the state change. On one hand, the box was seen to contain something atypical initially, as in a standard deceptive box, but this was then exchanged for another item, as in state change. If Wimmer and Hartl's account were correct, then children would gloss "What did you think was inside?" as "What was inside?" which would be revealed by their incorrect response of "pencil". However, whilst it was very common for children to reply correctly with "pencil" when asked "What was inside?", it was uncommon for them to respond with "pencil" when asked "What did you think was inside?". When asked the latter, the modal response was "spoon", which was the current content. Hence, it seems children were not glossing a question asking what they had thought as concerning what had been the case factually, so a better explanation for correct judgements in the standard state change task is required.

HINDSIGHT: ADULTS ALSO SHOW BIAS IN JUDGING FALSE BELIEF?

Let us return to the idea that children below and above the age of four years are equipped with simple belief-desire reasoning. Let us further suppose that they do understand beliefs as beliefs and utilise this understanding in their belief-desire psychology, but have some difficulty identifying the correct belief *content*. If so, then it seems that their belief input to the belief-desire process is susceptible to bias. What would be the character of this bias? At least superficially, it seems appropriate to describe their realist errors on a standard test of their own prior false belief as a hindsight bias. With hindsight, children know that the tube contained Smarties, and it seems they find it hard to suppress that knowledge when judging what they had actually thought. In other words, it seems they find it hard to imagine what they would have thought was inside the tube as if they had not known the true content as pencils. To stress the point, perhaps children are judging that they held the belief of *pencils* as a belief, in which case the form of their fledgling folk psychology is functioning, but they are prone to errors of content. Conversely, if the content errors in children's belief judgments were a sign that they had not yet negotiated a radical conceptual shift, then we would be committed to suggesting the following: Presumably, the rather gross hindsight bias that is descriptive of children's difficulty acknowledging their own prior false belief would be peculiar to the period of development that precedes the fourth birthday.

It is very well known in wider psychological circles, however, that hindsight bias is a characteristic of adult reasoning (Fischhoff, 1975). In his classic study, Fischhoff told participants about a battle between British and Ghurkha armies that took place a couple of centuries ago in India. Participants were informed of factors that might give one side the edge over the other, such as the quality of equipment, tactics, numerical superiority and knowledge of the terrain. On the basis of this information, participants had to rate which army they thought stood the best chance of winning. They were also told of the actual "outcome", but were instructed to put this out of their mind in arriving at a judgement. It turned out that despite the instructions, participants were substantially influenced by what they knew of the "outcome". Participants who were told that the British actually won, judged on balance that they thought the British would win, while participants who were told that the Ghurkhas won judged on balance that they thought the Ghurkhas would win! It seems that once the participants knew the outcome, it somehow became obvious and inevitable and hence they had succumbed to a hindsight bias.

Adults also show a similar kind of bias in their estimations of another person's belief, such that they seem reluctant to attribute a false belief (Mitchell, Robinson, Isaacs, & Nye, 1996). In Mitchell et al.'s study, participants watched a video in which Kevin looked into a jug and saw orange juice inside. He left the scene and returned later with Rebecca, who announced that there is milk in the jug. Under one condition, observing participants were told that Rebecca had replaced the orange juice with milk, while under another condition, they were given no additional information. Finally, participants had to judge what Kevin thought was in the jug. There is no right or wrong answer, so participants simply had to make a decision on how Kevin would prioritise the conflicting information.

The results demonstrated that participants were biased to ascribe a true belief to Kevin. If they the participants knew that Rebecca's utterance was true, then they tended to judge that Kevin would believe it, whereas if they were allowed to assume that her utterance was false, then they tended to judge that Kevin would retain his belief that there is juice in the jug based on what he had seen previously.

This is not so much a hindsight bias, of course, because the participants were not blinded by what they now knew when trying to recall what they used to think. Rather, their knowledge of reality was contaminating their judgement of belief. Fischhoff (1975) had found a similar kind of generalised bias in his classic study. Participants' knowledge of outcome also biased them to judge that other people, who did not know the outcome of the battle between the British and Ghurkhas, would also be inclined to think that the actual outcome was most likely. Given that adults are susceptible to something that seems like a hindsight bias but which is actually more general, it would be rather astonishing if children were not susceptible to the same. It would thus seem useful and parsimonious to consider the possibility that a tendency to report reality when asked about belief reflects this bias, irrespective of whether that tendency is apparent in individuals above or below the age of 4 years.

The bias theory and conceptual change theory make different predictions. The bias theory predicts that because children are captivated by reality when making a judgement about belief, then it should be possible to alter the probability of whether or not they give a correct judgement, depending on how salient reality is, and whether or not the belief to be acknowledged is supported by some anchor in reality. The conceptual change theory, in contrast, makes no such predictions because the view is that children are not captivated by reality at all but merely report reality by default in the absence of a concept of belief. In that case, not only do the state change results reported by Saltmarsh et al. (1995) pose a problem for the conceptual change theory, given that children can be helped to acknowledge false belief, they actually offer direct support for the bias theory. In state change, the belief that the child is asked to acknowledge, whether their own prior true belief or another individual's current false belief, has an instantiation in reality. A defining feature of state change is that in the initial part of the procedure, the belief that will later have to be acknowledged (e.g. Smarties) is seen to have a counterpart in reality. Hence, the salience of this belief is likely to be elevated to a point where it is no longer highly probable that the child will report current reality when queried about belief.

Independent evidence in favour of the same view derives from Mitchell and Lacohée's (1991; Freeman & Lacohée, 1995) picture posting experiment. Children were presented with a deceptive box task but on stating their initial belief that the tube contained Smarties, were asked to select and then post a picture from a set of alternatives. The authors suggested that the posted picture should serve as a counterpart to belief which in turn should make it more accessible when the child was required to judge what he or she thought was in the box after having seen that it really contained pencils. As predicted, the posting manipulation yielded facilitation in these studies.

COGNITIVE AVAILABILITY

If children's difficulty acknowledging false belief does reflect a bias towards reality, then that bias should be prone to influence, as suggested by the results of the state change and posting experiments. If it has anything to do with hindsight bias as defined broadly, then it should show susceptibility to influence in a similar kind of way. A framework worth exploring in connection with this is the "availability heuristic" presented by Kahneman (1973). He suggests that information which readily springs to mind is likely to be captivating in some way, such that it biases the judgement process. For example, Kahneman asked participants under one condition to estimate what percentage of people in any one year die from each of various natural causes, including cancer, heart failure and other disease. In this condition, participants had to give several percentage figures to cover each of the listed natural causes. When these percentages were added together, to form a general estimation of deaths from natural causes, the figure was reliably greater than for participants tested under another condition who also estimated the percentage of deaths from natural causes but not asked to provide such a break down. Kahneman interpreted this intriguing effect in the following way. He suggested that when participants were encouraged to focus on the component elements of "death by natural causes", these assumed a greater salience than was the case when summed together under a generic heading, perhaps because each cause was individually elaborated mentally. Their greater salience led participants to assign a relatively large percentage estimation to them, such that the whole was significantly less than the sum of its parts!

A somewhat similar bias, but not hitherto interpreted explicitly in terms of the availability heuristic, was reported by Markovits, Quinn, Fleury, and Venet (1997). They began by asking children to state what kinds of things have motors. A common response was "car" but a rare response was "fridge". Children were then presented with syllogisms:

(1) If it is a car, then it has a motor
(2) If it is a fridge, then it has a motor
A mystery object has a motor. Is it a car/fridge?

When asked "Is it a car?" most children aged around 8 years wrongly answered affirmatively, when they should have stated that they were uncertain. When asked "Is it a fridge?" most children correctly answered that they were not sure on the grounds that it could be a car. In this task, children had to recognise that knowing that a thing had a motor was not sufficient to decide exactly what kind of object it was. An impediment to this was their captivating presumption that motors and cars go together not quite but almost exclusively. When told that a mystery object has a motor, it seems the children could readily imagine it being a car but not much else, and hence were content to judge effectively that the information (it has a motor) was sufficient for a positive judgement that it is a car. In contrast, when asked if the thing is a fridge, participants easily resisted replying in the positive by invoking "car" as a counter-example. In brief, children's judgements were biased by information that was cognitively available and salient. It is not that children are unable to acknowledge a state of uncertainty in the face of insufficient information, but rather that their judgement to this effect is prone to bias with respect to cognitive availability.

BIAS IN RECALL

Returning to the ability to acknowledge representation, we suggest that even young children are able to make judgements of belief as belief, but are prone to bias. What form might this take? Is it a bias in reasoning or a bias in recall? In acknowledging one's own prior false belief, that seems on the face of things not to require any reasoning at all but merely recall. Still, it is possible that recall is prone to bias. A classic example of such is reported by Loftus (1979). She found that certain question wordings can lead participants to import fictitious detail when recalling a specified event. In a famous study, participants watched a movie showing a car accident and then were asked if there was any broken glass on the road following the smash/collision. When the question included the word *smash*, many participants judged that there was broken glass (in fact there was not). When the question included the word *collision*, many participants correctly judged that there was no broken glass.

The bias is also apparent when the information to be recalled is not factual but personal opinion or prediction. Conway (1990) asked participants to predict what grade they would attain in an exam they were about to take. Several weeks later, after the results had been published, participants were unexpectedly asked to recall what their predictions had been. Those who actually attained a higher score than expected tended to recall having predicted a higher score, while those who actually attained a lower score than expected tended to recall having predicted a lower score. Once again, this seems like a classic case of hindsight, demonstrating that recall of various forms of information is susceptible to bias.

Despite that, difficulty acknowledging false belief does not reduce to bias in the recall of information, as illustrated by the distinctive pattern of children's answers to questions presented in the unexpected transfer test. In this, mother takes the chocolate from the green drawer where Maxi left it, and moves it to the blue one in Maxi's absence. Observing child participants are then asked to predict where Maxi will look for the chocolate on his return. Many of those younger than about 4 years of age wrongly judge that he will look in the chocolate's current location, which is the blue drawer. This cannot be explained purely as bias in recall, however, since most children show no signs of difficulty judging correctly that Maxi had put the chocolate in the green drawer. In other words, they easily recall the central premise necessary for making an inference of false belief, yet still fail.

If difficulty acknowledging false belief does stem from bias, evidently the bias has to take the form of something more than just a weak memory. In this respect, the bias would have to be akin to the "knew it all along" of hindsight. The idea of hindsight is not that participants have a general distortion of memory, but in particular one that accommodates comfortably with the smug view of oneself as a smart and perceptive individual. If people were forced to admit to themselves that after all they were a little stupid and not very perceptive, then perhaps that would arouse an intolerable level of cognitive dissonance. In other words, hindsight bias might be seen as something that stems from the fear of suffering a loss of face if one is seen to be in error. However, this is not the best way to construe hindsight and in any case, it could not possibly account for children's difficulty with false belief. As mentioned, Fischhoff (1975) found that participants showed bias to judge that other people would be led towards thinking what was actually true, a bias which could not in principle stem from personal pride or fear of loss of face. In children aged 3 years something similar happens. In another aspect of Wimmer and Hartl's (1991) study, children were asked to recall not what they had thought was inside a Smarties tube but what Kasperl, a notoriously stupid puppet, had thought. Children had just as much difficulty recalling Kasperl's prior false belief as they did their own. It seems, therefore, that children and adults have a bias towards reality as they know it when invited to judge about belief in particular. This is a bias that is like hindsight but is not hindsight in the strictest sense because face-saving is not essential for it to occur.

So far the argument to unfold is that young children understand that beliefs are not necessarily isomorphic with reality, but nonetheless that children are contaminated by their own knowledge of reality when making a judgement of belief. We are also assuming that judgements of belief are not merely susceptible to general biases, as in the recall of factual information, but are also prone to a special bias towards the captivating effect of what is known or assumed to be true of reality. Perhaps judgements of belief require a certain amount of mental processing, not just recall, and it is during this process that the bias occurs. The possibility that processing is needed is obvious in the case of an unexpected transfer test, and other authors have made a similar argument to this effect. The possibility that children's acknowledgement of their own prior false belief requires similar processing is not so obvious and requires justification. We shall proceed first by considering what others have said about biases in processing others' beliefs.

PROCESSING ACCOUNTS

Fodor's (1992) argument is that young children do understand beliefs as beliefs but that an acknowledgement of false belief is especially taxing and prone to error that stems from limited processing resources early in development. He supposes that children routinely operate on the principle that people hold true beliefs, which they use as a basis for prediction of their behaviour. If a unique behavioural prediction is not possible from the assumption of true belief, then children's processing will be diverted along the route of inferring the behavioural implications of false belief. The trouble with Fodor's account is that it does not explain why children have difficulty acknowledging their own prior false beliefs or why they report reality when explicitly asked what another person thinks; unfortunately, his account is confined to children's apparent difficulty with behavioural predictions.

Another processing account has been formulated by Frye, Zelazo, and Palfai (1995). They found that children's performance on a variety of tests of false belief correlates with their performance on a child-based version of the Wisconsin Card Sort test. Children had to sort a pile of cards according to one categorical dimension, such as shape, and then had to sort according to a different dimension, such as colour. The children who were inflexible in shifting sorting category tended to be the same who reported reality when questioned about belief. The authors interpreted this striking correlation in the following way. They suggested that the shift between conceptual perspectives necessary for a judgement of false belief is akin to the shift between sorting principles in the card task, and noted that the requisite flexibility in thought deserves to be called *reasoning*, though a form of reasoning that is not identified in any explicit sense.

A problem with Frye et al.'s (1995) account is that it seems unable to explain the systematic character of children's difficulty with false belief. It is not just that children judge at random, but specifically that they are inclined to report reality when questioned about belief. Hence, it is not just that children seem to have difficulty switching between their own conceptual perspective and another individual's but specifically that they tend to report reality. A related problem is that they do not explain why children still have difficulty acknowledging false belief even when told explicitly what that belief is. For example, Wellman and Bartsch (1988) told children explicitly that Sam believes his puppy is under the porch, though it is really in the garage. Children then had to predict where Sam would look, and many still judged that Sam would look in the garage. Indeed, Flavell, Green, and Flavell (1993) found that many young children even made a realist error in a similar context when asked a "think" question. All they had to do was echo the false belief as stated by the experimenter, but they still reported reality! At the very least, some further elaboration of Frye et al.'s account would be needed to explain this.

Perhaps the way forward is to postulate that in some sense children, and perhaps everyone else for that matter, are predisposed not to take belief on face value but to engage in a form of processing and construction. This normally has to be true anyway, given that the beliefs of other people are not directly accessible but have to be inferred. For example, we infer that owing to Maxi's restricted informational history, he falls victim to false belief. In the case of Wellman and Bartsch's (1988; and also Flavell et al., 1993) study, Sam's belief is not directly accessible to them but has to be derived from the experimenter's or the protagonist's message. In no sense is Sam's belief directly accessible, so even in this case there still has to be an element of construction. The most controversial issue, however, surrounds children's difficulty acknowledging their own prior false belief. The common sense explanation is that children need only *recall* what they had thought, with the implication that construction is not involved. Is it possible that this common sense view is wrong after all, and that construction is involved in the acknowledgement of one's own prior belief also?

In the study by Conway (1990), in which participants had to report their predicted exam grades, they were being asked to state their prior *belief* of what they expected to attain, albeit a belief that was not held firmly. It is probable that participants simply could not remember exactly what they had said and had to engage in a process of reconstruction. That very process seems to have been contaminated by their subsequent discovery of their actual grading. Although children aged 3 years make a very severe error, perhaps it is nonetheless an error of the same kind. Perhaps they are predisposed to engage in construction when questioned about belief, whether that belief is their own or another person's, and the construction process is afflicted by a bias toward reality. Hence, our hypothesis is that when children make a judgement about their own prior belief, this is not just a matter of recall, contrary to Wimmer and Hartl (1991), but entails a process of construction. From the hypothesis, we predict that if children were presented with a true belief state change and asked "What did you think was inside?", they would take longer to answer than if asked "What was inside?". This is because the *think* question will provoke construction while the neutral question will only require recall, and we assume that construction will take more time to process than recall.

RESPONSE TIME AS A CLUE TO PROCESSING COMPLEXITY

The hypothesis concerning response time provides a reminder about the specific differences in the account based on Wimmer and Hartl (1991) and that based on Saltmarsh et al. (1995). In Fig. 14.1a, we see that relatively few processing steps are involved if the question "What did you think was inside?" was construed as "What was inside?". In Fig. 14.1b, we see that the comprehension of the question would be filtered through the child's conception of mind which would treat

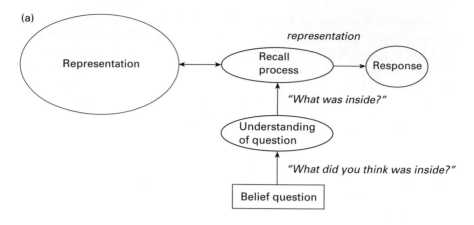

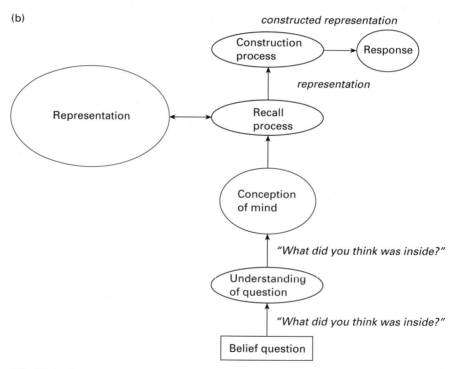

FIG. 14.1   (a) Wimmer and Hartl's (1991) assumption; (b) Saltmarsh et al.'s (1995) assumption.

the recall not as an end in itself, but as a premise to be entered into an additional stage that involves construction. The construction is of a representation based on a premise. In contrast, there is no constructed representation in Wimmer and Hartl's model: that is purely concerned with the recall of a representation.

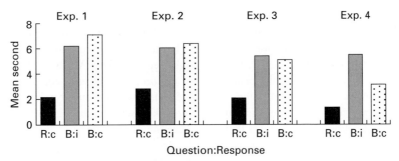

FIG. 14.2   Response time of the unexpected transfer task. R:c is the RT of children correct on the reality question; B:i is the RT of children incorrect on the belief question; B:c is the RT of children correct on the belief question.

Precisely the same argument applies to the unexpected transfer test, and fortuitously we have data on response time from four experiments carried out for quite different reasons which need not be considered here. Children were asked to recall where Maxi had put the chocolate initially and also had to predict where he would look for it. If Wimmer and Hartl's argument were correct, then it is likely that those who made a realist error in response to the belief question were doing little more than recalling the chocolate's current location and so should show a response time similar to that in answer to the question asking where Maxi put the chocolate initially. This account would predict a much longer response time for those who answer the belief question correctly on the grounds that this would be based on the more elaborate mentalistic processing. In contrast, our account predicts long response times for answers to the belief question whether correct or incorrect. We suggest that both kinds of answer require the child to construct a representation: They differ not in form but content due to the wrong premise having been entered when a realist error is made. Hence, we predict longer response time for answers to the belief question, whether correct or incorrect, relative to the recall question. As Fig. 14.2 shows, the results were highly consistent across the four experiments in supporting our prediction but in failing to provide any support for the prediction based on Wimmer and Hartl.

THE BASIS OF A REALIST BIAS

At this point, however, we encounter the same problem faced by Frye et al. (1995). Namely, to say that children's difficulty with false belief stems from errors in construction does not explain in particular why children are inclined to report reality. It is not sufficient to say just that children's construction of belief is prone to error: we need to posit that the processing is prone to a realist bias in particular. This raises at least two questions: (1) why should there be a realist bias?; and (2) what is the evidence for a realist bias? A detailed speculation on the function of a realist bias is presented elsewhere (Mitchell, 1994, 1996), so we shall concentrate here on the status of the evidence in support of a realist bias.

One source of evidence for a realist bias is the very finding that when young children are asked about belief, they typically report reality. When the salience of reality is manipulated, the proportion of children who give a correct judgement changes also (Mitchell, 1996, for a review). A sceptic might point out that the evidence for a realist bias is intrinsically linked with children's difficulty or success in acknowledging false belief. Hence, the phenomenon to be explained and the data put forward in support of an explanation amount to one and the same, meaning that we are left with a circular argument. The circle can be broken if we are able to present evidence for a realist bias that is pertinent to, but not the same as, children's difficulty with false belief.

Relevant evidence arises from Riggs, Peterson, Robinson and Mitchell (1998; see Riggs & Peterson, Chapter 5, this volume). They presented questions about counterfactual states in an unexpected transfer test. For example, children were asked "If mother had not baked a cake, where would the chocolate be?". Those who wrongly replied by pointing to the chocolate's current location tended to be the same who judged that Maxi would look in the current location; those who correctly replied by pointing to the chocolate's prior location tended to be the same who correctly judged that Maxi would look in the place he left his chocolate. The authors concluded that young children have difficulty constructing a counterfactual alternative, whether or not that is held as a belief. What is common to belief and counterfactuality, is that children had to construct an alternative to the present state. This is the element that seemed to be responsible for errors, not whether that counterfactual construction was then subsumed within a belief. When children had the task of making a construction that was relevant to, but not isomorphic with, the state of reality, they exhibited a realist bias. Hence, a realist bias seems substantive and not just an inherent aspect of judging about beliefs.

Further evidence of the substantive quality of a realist bias arises from errors in perceptual judgements. Mitchell and Taylor (1999) asked children to judge the shape of a circular disc oriented at a slant. Because of the slant, the disc appeared elliptical. Thouless (1931) had already demonstrated that adults tend to exaggerate the circularity of the shape and Taylor and Mitchell (1997) developed that early work to show that simply knowing that the thing under inspection is a slanted circle is sufficient for participants to exaggerate circularity. Participants viewed the disc in a darkened chamber through a view hole. The disc was the only thing visible therein, owning to the luminous material in its composition. Under one condition, participants had no information about the object and thus were allowed to believe that it was an ellipse, as its appearance suggested. Under another condition, participants had seen previously that the disc was in fact a slanted circle. Under a further condition, the object that participants viewed really was an ellipse presented squarely to the line of sight, and participants were privy to that fact. The participants then had to replicate the shape as they saw it on a computer screen. The results showed that participants only exaggerated circularity when they knew that the target was a slanted circle, suggesting that their knowledge of its identity was sufficient for the error to occur.

The error we have just described could be construed as a realist bias that has some relevance to difficulty acknowledging false belief. It seems participants' knowledge of reality contaminated their reconstruction of appearance by a matter of degree. It is also the case in young children that when asked about the appearance of an object, they tend to report its real identity (Flavell et al., 1983). Moreover, children who make that error tend to be the same who report reality when questioned about their own or another person's belief (Gopnik & Astington, 1988). Hence, we might say that a realist bias features in judgements of belief and this generalises to judgements of appearance also. Having said that, Gopnik and Astington do not interpret errors in judgements of appearance as a bias but as a lack of a concept of representation.

The value of the slanted disc task is that the concept of representation seems not to be at stake; participants are just asked to reconstruct a shape as they see it. If, however, the realist bias affects judgements of appearance as it affects judgements of belief, then there is reason to expect the degree of exaggeration in the disc task to be related with failure in acknowledging belief. Mitchell and Taylor (1999) presented the disc task to children aged 3–5 years, along with tests of false belief and appearance-reality. They found a significant correlation, in the sense that children who passed a test of false belief or appearance-reality tended to be the ones who were less prone to exaggerate circularity. The correlation was fairly small but reliable. The simple interpretation seems to be that children (and perhaps adults) are susceptible to bias when constructing or reconstructing reality, irrespective of whether that construction is attributed as a belief.

FACILITATING THE PROCESSING OF CORRECT BELIEF CONTENT

In summary, we propose that the following principles should be considered when contemplating how children process belief. Principle 1: When children perceive a question to be about belief they are led to construct a representation. When children perceive the question to be about reality/episode they are led to recall a current/prior representation. Principle 2: When children construct a representation, they are making an inference on the basis of what they assume to be the appropriate premise. However, there is a risk that what children assume to be reality will captivate their attention, in which case they will enter this as the premise and thus make the wrong inference.

Figure 14.3 illustrates the constellation of elements that might influence which premise is most salient when the child is constructing a belief-based response in

(a)

(b)

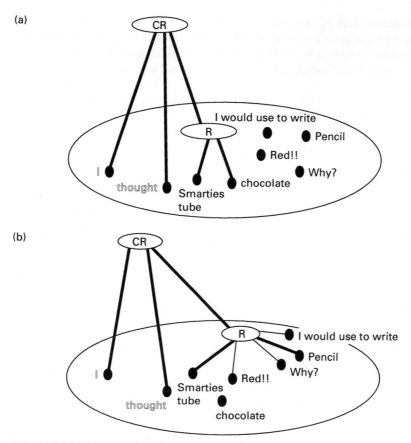

FIG. 14.3   (a) Correct constructed representation which young children would reconstruct; (b) wrong constructed representation which younger children would reconstruct.

a deceptive box task. If the elements of the atypical object are more elaborated, then they might present themselves more readily for the process of construction. If children make a realist error, then we are assuming by definition that this is because the premise underlying this representational content was more elaborated. So the wrong representational content is assumed to be more salient and stable than the correct representational content. Effectively, we are supposing that the bias to reality is a product of the degree of elaboration: that things which are assumed to be real are elaborated more than things assumed not to be real. And a candidate premise that has been elaborated extensively is more likely to be selected for the process of construction than one not elaborated.

In the light of this discussion, it follows that if we wished to give the child a better chance of making a correct judgement of belief, our efforts would be misplaced if they were aimed at making the *belief* more salient. We are assuming that beliefs are already salient, and that it is the requisite premise for correct belief content which might not be so salient. Indeed, it might be that manipulations reported in the published literature which yield facilitation do not help the child to acknowledge belief as such, but help them to identify the correct content of belief.

Having conceptualised the problem thus, it provides a framework for devising ways of assisting the child to give correct judgements. One of the simplest and most obvious manipulations would be to help the child elaborate on their encoding of the various facets of the premise to be entered into the belief inference. Accordingly, we tested 81 children aged 3 and 4 years in a modified version of the deceptive box task. Each child performed on two deceptive box tasks, both presented under the same condition. The design included four between-subjects conditions:

(1) Typical–atypical elaboration. The experimenter encouraged the participant to reflect on details of both the object that is typically inside the box and also on details of the atypical item that happened to be in the box on this particular occasion.
(2) Typical elaboration. The experimenter encouraged the child to reflect on details of the typical object only.
(3) Atypical elaboration. The experimenter encouraged reflection on the atypical object only.
(4) No elaboration. This was similar to a standard procedure.

Figure 14.4 shows the average number of trials, out of two, on which children gave correct judgements. It is apparent from Fig. 14.4 that when the typical content is elaborated, this helps children to give a correct judgement. This is consistent with the possibility that the elaboration assisted children to select the typical object as the appropriate premise to enter into the belief inference. It is

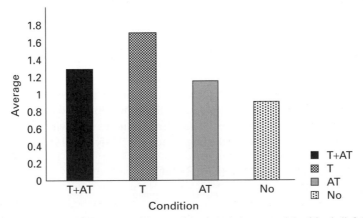

FIG. 14.4   Facilitated effect of elaboration on the acknowledgement of the false belief. T + A is the Typical–Atypical elaboration condition; T is the Typical elaboration condition; A is the Atypical elaboration condition; No is the No elaboration condition.

also notable from Fig. 14.4 that performance under the other conditions is fairly uniform. We might have expected performance to deteriorate under the condition in which the atypical object was elaborated, but this was not the case. Perhaps the natural salience of the atypical object that derives from its very presence in the box means that its salience has assumed a ceiling level that cannot be elevated any further with additional elaboration.

The interpretation we place on the finding presented in Fig. 14.4 raises the question of why older children do not require help in elaborating on the typical object to succeed in entering this as the correct premise in belief inference. It might be that older children spontaneously elaborate on their representations of objects more readily than younger children (Kail, 1990). Our suggestion, then, is that both younger and older children might be capable of recalling the premise for making an inference of belief, but the recall in itself might not be sufficient for that premise to be entered into the inference. The salience of the recalled premise could be a further factor in the equation. Owing to the possibility that older children routinely engage in greater elaboration, perhaps they would not be hampered by a detrimental imbalance of premise salience.

CONCLUSION

Wellman (1990) proposed a belief-desire psychology and in the light of this he outlined a way of explaining young children's errors in acknowledging belief by suggesting their folk psychology might actually take a somewhat different form. He suggested that young children might give much greater weight to desire than belief. We have suggested an alternative that differentiates between younger and older children, not in the form of their mentalism but in how they handle content. In the first instance, we are assuming that a judgement of belief entails a process that necessarily amounts to more than mere recall. This hypothesised process depends upon an inference, and whether or not the appropriate premise is entered rests upon a selection that the child has to make. It might well be the case that the correct selection is substantially easier for an older than a younger child, all other things being equal. Because we assume the form is much the same for an older and younger child, we also assume that with a belief problem of given content, a younger child could succeed. The bottom line is that if a judgement of belief requires some kind of reasoning process, then success is very likely to depend on the content as well as the form of the problem. After all, this would only be to echo the message from studies involving adult participants on more formal tasks of reasoning (Cheng & Holyoak, 1985).

REFERENCES

Cheng, P.W., & Holyoak, K. (1985). Pragmatic reasoning schemas. *Cognitive Psychology, 17*, 391–416.

Conway, M. (1990). On bias in autobiographical recall: Retrospective adjustments following disconfirmed expectations. *Journal of Social Psychology, 130*, 183–189.

Fischhoff, B. (1975). Hindsight is not equal to foresight: The effect of outcome knowledge on judgment under uncertainty. *Journal of Experimental Psychology: Human Perception and Performance, 1,* 288–299.

Flavell, J.H., Flavell, E.R., & Green, F.L. (1983). Development of the appearance-reality distinction. *Cognitive Psychology, 15,* 95–120.

Flavell, J.H., Green, F.L., & Flavell, J.H. (1993). Children's understanding of the stream of consciousness. *Child Development, 64,* 387–398.

Fodor, J.A. (1992). A theory of the child's theory of mind. *Cognition, 44,* 283–296.

Freeman, N.H., & Lacohée, H. (1995). Making explicit 3-year-olds' implicit competence with their own false beliefs, *Cognition, 56,* 31–60.

Frye, D., Zelazo, P., & Palfai, T. (1995). Theory of Mind and rule-based reasoning. *Cognitive Development, 10,* 438–528.

Gopnik, A., & Astington, J.W. (1988). Children's understanding of representational change, and its relation to the understanding of false belief and the appearance-reality distinction. *Child Development, 59,* 26–37.

Kahneman, D. (1973). *Attention and effort.* Englewood Cliffs, NJ: Prentice Hall.

Kail, E. (1990). *The development of memory in children.* New York: W.H. Freeman and Co.

Loftus, E.F. (1979). *Eyewitness testimony.* Cambridge, MA: Harvard University Press.

Markovits, H., Quinn, S., Fleury, M.-L., & Venet, M. (1997). *The development of conditional reasoning and the structure of semantic memory.* Paper presented at Society for Research in Child Development Biennial Meeting, April 1997, Washington, DC.

Mitchell, P. (1994). Realism and early conception of mind: A synthesis of phylogenetic and ontogenetic issues. In C. Lewis & P. Mitchell (Eds.), *Children's early understanding of mind: Origins and development* (pp. 19–45). Hove: Lawrence Erlbaum Associates Ltd.

Mitchell, P. (1996). *Acquiring a conception of mind: A review of psychological research and theory.* Hove, UK: Psychology Press.

Mitchell, P., & Lacohée, H. (1991). Children's early understanding of false belief. *Cognition, 39,* 107–127.

Mitchell, P., & Taylor, L.M. (1999). Shape constancy and theory of mind: Is there a link? *Cognition, 70,* 167–190.

Mitchell, P., Robinson, E.J., Isaacs, J.E., & Nye, R.M. (1996). Contamination in reasoning about false belief: An instance of realist bias in adults but not children. *Cognition, 59,* 1–21.

Riggs, K.J., Peterson, D.M., Robinson, E.J., & Mitchell, P. (1998). Are errors in false belief tasks symptomatic of a broader difficulty with counterfactuality? *Cognitive Development, 13,* 73–90.

Saltmarsh, R., & Mitchell, P. (1998). Young children's difficulty acknowledging false belief: Realism and deception, *Journal of Experimental Child Psychology, 69,* 3–21.

Saltmarsh, R., Mitchell, P., & Robinson, E.J. (1995). Realism and children's early grasp of mental representation: Belief-based judgments in the state change task. *Cognition, 57,* 297–325.

Taylor, L.M., & Mitchell, P. (1997). Judgments of apparent shape contaminated by knowledge of reality: Viewing circles obliquely. *British Journal of Psychology, 88,* 653–670.

Thouless, R.H. (1931). Phenomenal regression to the real object, II. *British Journal of Psychology, 22,* 1–30.

Wellman, H.M. (1990). *The child's theory of mind.* Cambridge: MIT Press.

Wellman, H.M., & Bartsch, K. (1988). Young children's reasoning about beliefs. *Cognition, 30,* 239–277.

Wimmer, H., & Hartl, M. (1991). Against the Cartesian view on mind: Young children's difficulty with own false beliefs. *British Journal of Developmental Psychology, 9,* 125–138.

CHAPTER FIFTEEN

Theory of mind, metacognition, and reasoning: A life-span perspective

Deanna Kuhn
Teachers College, Columbia University, USA

Theory of mind has certainly captured the interest and imagination of researchers in the field of cognitive development, to an extent rivalled by few topics in the history of the field. There is a sense that this topic finally focuses our attention on fundamental matters. How do children construct an understanding of their world, with other human beings the most salient component of this world? Yet theory of mind has been approached by most of its recent investigators both as a specialist's topic and as an entirely new domain of inquiry. At the same time, at least implicit in much of the discussion surrounding the topic has been a sense that characteristics of broad significance to the developing intellect are at stake. Indeed we would expect this to be the case. If an understanding of false belief is the major conceptual achievement that many have claimed it to be, this achievement should be evident in contexts and respects other than the already paradigmatic false belief task.

In this volume, we see the results of conceptual and empirical efforts to extend the false-belief research paradigm and the theory-of-mind conceptual framework to connect to other theoretical constructs and lines of empirical inquiry in developmental psychology. In the present chapter, I make the case that theory of mind as an area of inquiry would benefit if it were situated in a larger context that highlighted its conceptual connections and implications, as well as historical roots. Under a heading of meta-knowing, I distinguish and describe three separate dimensions—the metacognitive, the metastrategic, and the epistemological, and identify roots of all three in early theory-of-mind achievements.

These meta-knowing competencies figure prominently in other areas of cognitive development that have been the object of extensive research. Two of these, addressed in the present chapter, are scientific and argumentive reasoning. Study of the development of scientific reasoning, I argue, has been hampered by unclear definition of exactly what it consists of and, consequently, the kinds of competencies that constitute its developmental origins. Identifying key achievements in the early development of epistemological and theory-of-mind understanding as a foundation on which the development of scientific reasoning rests provides a framework for conceptualising and studying its subsequent development.

Theory-of-mind research also stands to benefit from being situated in a life-span context. Connections can be identified between the challenges that confront young children in thinking about their own and others' thought and these same challenges in more complex forms that limit the thinking effectiveness of adults. The early theory-of-mind achievements that have been the focus of so much recent work mark the beginning, not the culmination, of a developmental course that extends well into adulthood, and, significantly, most often is never completed. In reviewing research on the thinking of older children, adolescents, and adults, as well as young children, I endeavour in this chapter to highlight the life-span context in which theory-of-mind research is best situated. Linking early theory-of-mind achievements to the later and diverse developments that they prepare the way for makes their significance all the clearer.

THE DEVELOPMENTAL ORIGINS OF META-KNOWING

Meta-knowing is a broad, umbrella term used here to encompass any cognition that has cognition—either one's own or others'—as its object. The major distinction in types of meta-knowing to be drawn in this chapter is based on one of the most widely employed dichotomies in cognitive psychology—the dichotomy between procedural knowing (knowing how) and declarative knowing (knowing that). Meta-knowing, I claim, differs depending on the kind of first-order knowing that is its object. Knowing about procedural knowing (as a process) I address under the heading of *metastrategic knowing*. Knowing about declarative knowing (as a product) I address under the heading of *metacognitive knowing*. One further subdivision reflects the fact that metacognitive knowing can be either specific and situational, i.e. pertaining to a particular piece of knowledge, or general and more abstract, i.e. about knowledge and knowing in general. The latter I examine under the heading of *epistemological meta-knowing*, which in turn can be either personal (pertaining to one's own knowing) or impersonal (applicable to anyone's knowing).

How does meta-knowing arise? Many of the questions and issues that have arisen in studying the development of first-order cognition—particularly questions of mechanism—are encountered in a parallel way in examining second-order, meta-knowing. We have learned enough about cognitive development to reject, for example, the view that mental representations are direct copies internalised from the physical or social environment. Yet, as socioculturalists (Cole, 1996; Rogoff, 1998) have persuasively demonstrated, the constructivist alternative does not imply that a child constructs an understanding of self and world as a solitary enterprise in a social vacuum. Children's participation in a social culture transforms their experience in powerful ways. Still, recognising the power of culture is not sufficient to explain the process by which the child constructs meaning through participation in it. In the words of Astington and Olson (1995, p. 187): "Social understanding cannot . . . proceed via 'participation' without appeal to concepts". Analysis must include the meaning-making activity of the participants in this collective experience.

The capacity for mental representation of meaning develops early in life, certainly by the second year, as reflected by such traditional indicators as pretend play (Leslie, 1987) and deferred imitation (Piaget & Inhelder, 1951). Not long after, there is evidence that the content of these mental representations becomes recursive, i.e. includes mental phenomena themselves. By age 3, children are able to verbalise their awareness that the world includes not only material entities but also non-material ones such as desires, intentions, thoughts, and ideas, that are the product of human mental life (Flavell & Miller, 1998). They are able to distinguish mental entities from physical ones, for example thinking about a dog from looking at one (Estes, Wellman, & Woolley, 1989). Given explicit enough cues, they will acknowledge that another person is engaged in thinking (Flavell, Green, & Flavell, 1995). In everyday conversation children by age 3 make reference to their own knowledge states, using verbs such as *think* and *know* (Olson & Astington, 1986) and may even express awareness of absence of knowledge, as in "I don't know which" (Feldman, 1988, p. 134). Although appearing slightly later (Fabricius & Imbens-Bailey, Chapter 13 this volume), reference to others' mental states of knowledge, intention, or desire also becomes common, as in "He wants the biggest one for himself" or "She knows where it is and won't tell".

How has the child achieved this capacity to make mental experience its own object—to think about thinking? As in the achievement of first-order mental representations, both social participation and constructive meaning-making are implicated. As well as multiple processes, multiple sources of knowledge are involved, as the child constructs meaning based on both his or her own inner experience and the selves that others make visible in social interaction. An early contributor to this achievement is the joint attention to objects and events that emerges among infants and their caretakers and out of which the infant comes to recognise meaning-making and intention on the part of the other (Tomasello, Kruger, & Ratner, 1993). As children's experience, and hence awareness, of their own mental activities increases, the desire to communicate these to others may emerge, as for example when a child tells her mother a story she has invented, which then becomes a topic of conversation (Feldman, 1988). At the same time, a parent scaffolds the child's understanding by making reference to the mental states of parent, child, and others, hence making the child more aware of mental states as a topic of conversation and hence thought. Leslie (1987) argues for the special role of pretend play in contributing to the child's understanding of mental life, because it entails the same suspension of truth and reality requirements that characterise mental states such as belief and desire.

Those involved in the current study of theory of mind have drawn a distinction between "simulation" (Harris, 1992) and "theory" (Gopnik & Wellman, 1992; Montgomery, 1992) accounts of the mechanism responsible for children's developing theories of mind, the child generalising from his or her own inner life in the simulation account and constructing a theory based on social data in the theory account. But there is no reason to think that a choice must be made between the two mechanisms. Both self and others serve as sources of knowledge about both self and others. Projecting my own experience helps me to understand others, but also I come to know myself more fully—including what I think and feel—by how others react to and understand me.

I turn now to the content of thinking about thinking, once this second-order representational capacity has been achieved. What do children know or believe about their own and others' thinking? We begin with *metacognitive* knowledge, that is, one's beliefs about one's own and others' declarative knowledge—what self or other knows and how it is known. What does such meta-knowledge consist of and how does it evolve?

METACOGNITIVE KNOWING

By the end of their second year of life, children spend significant time engaged in pretend play—a form of mental representation which, as we noted earlier, entails the suspension of reality. One might anticipate, then, that 3-year-olds' metacognitive understanding of mental life would include the recognition that mental representations need not correspond to reality. This turns out, however, not to be the case. Although they routinely engage in pretend play, young preschool children are unwilling to accept that anyone could hold a belief that deviates from what they themselves take to be a true state of affairs. Although Leslie's (1987) conjecture may be correct that the experience of pretend play facilitates the eventual understanding that mental representations need not mirror reality, young children apparently do not have the reflective awareness of their own or others' mental states of pretence that would lead them to make this inference. They acknowledge that what another person *imagines* (e.g. an elephant in the room) need not reflect reality (Woolley, 1995), but this recognition does not extend to one's own or another's beliefs. Pretence, as Leslie (1987) notes, involves a temporary mental suspension of reality without obvious cause or consequence. Beliefs, in contrast, are assertions about the way the world really is. As such, they presumably derive from experiences in the world and in turn lead the believer to act in the world in ways consistent with these beliefs. In other words, unlike pretence, beliefs have causes and consequences that link them to the external world.

A good deal of evidence now exists suggesting that children below the age of about four regard the universe of assertions that people make, and the beliefs that these assertions reflect, as descriptive of and isomorphic to an external reality. An account of an event differs from the event itself only in that one exists on a representational plane while the other is perceived directly. In other words, the world is a simple one in which things happen and we can tell about them. There are no inaccurate renderings of events.

The most familiar source of evidence for this characterisation is young children's poor performance in the now classic false belief task. Three-year-olds believe that a newcomer will share their own accurate knowledge that a candy container in fact holds pencils (Perner, 1991; Wimmer & Perner, 1983). It is impossible that the other person could hold a belief that the child knows to be false. Less widely cited is the finding that this refusal to attribute false knowledge to another extends beyond the realm of factual knowledge to values, social conventions, and moral rules that the child takes to be valid or true claims. In a study by Flavell, Mumme, Green, and Flavell (1992), pre-school children were told, for example, about a girl Robin who thinks that it is okay to put her feet on the dinner table and then immediately asked, "Does Robin think that it is okay to put her feet on the dinner table?". Strikingly, a large majority of 3-year-olds responded negatively to such questions, as well as to parallel questions about whether someone could hold non-normative beliefs regarding moral rules (breaking a toy), values (eating grass), and facts (whether cats can read books). Performance improved, but remained below ceiling, among 4-year-olds.

Findings in related kinds of tasks support the claim that young children treat mental representations as in necessary correspondence with an external reality. Once the true state of affairs has been revealed to them, 3-year-olds deny their own earlier false beliefs (e.g. that they originally had thought the container held candy; Gopnik & Astington, 1988). Also, they deny that another child possesses knowledge that they lack regarding the contents of a box immediately after witnessing the other child being given this information verbally or visually (Wimmer, Hogrefe, & Perner, 1988). Apparently, the other's knowledge cannot deviate from the child's own. Wimmer et al. (1988) speculate that the child transforms questions about representations, such as "Do you [does he] know what's in the box?", to simpler questions about reality, i.e. "What's in the box?". The child can thus answer the "you" form correctly, by just reading off his or her own knowledge state. In the third-person form, however, the transformed question yields an incorrect answer.

Beginning at about age 4 (and largely completed by age 5), children come to recognise assertions as the expression of someone's belief—a milestone, I would claim, in their cognitive development, that lays the way for the later achievements examined in this chapter. Perner (1991) characterises this acquisition in formal terms as the ability to metarepresent, i.e. to mentally model the human representational function. Accordingly, the child comes to recognise that as expressions of humans' representational capacity, assertions do not necessarily correspond to reality. We do not know why this achievement occurs at exactly this time, but evidently the child accrues enough experience with human knowing (of both self and others) to link the products of knowing—beliefs and assertions—to the generative process that gives rise to them. Their source is a human representational system that is recognised as having intent and volition to represent what it wishes to represent. Accordingly, an assertion's closest link becomes to this source—the subject that is doing the representing, rather than the object being represented.

If assertions do not necessarily correspond to reality, they become susceptible to evaluation via à vis a reality from which they are now distinguished. Although such evaluation in its rudimentary form entails no more than a simple comparison of an assertion to reality and declaration of it as true or false, it is a critical step in the development of metacognitive knowing. It is also notable as the origin of what will become scientific thinking, as well as what has long been referred to as critical thinking (one traditional definition of which is in fact the evaluation of assertions). Evaluating assertions implies at least some distinction between an assertion and external evidence bearing on it—assertion and evidence must exist as distinct entities if one is to be evaluated in light of the other. The resulting potential for disconfirmation is a hallmark of science. We return later to the relation of metacognition to these traditional forms of higher-order reasoning.

Evolving more directly from the recognition of assertions as belief states susceptible to evaluation is attention to the *source* of an assertion—the basis for claiming it to be true. If assertions mirror reality, the source from which a particular assertion arises is of little consequence. All sources offer equally authentic knowledge. As soon as assertions become potentially false, however, their sources take on new significance. A concern with the sources of assertions takes us to the heart of metacognitive knowing: Is an individual aware that and why one knows some piece of declarative knowledge? Can the individual justify, accurately, to self or others, how and why he or she knows?

Several studies have documented the metacognitive challenge entailed in maintaining awareness of the source of one's claim—the evidence that led to making it—as knowledge distinct from the claim itself. Gopnik and Graf (1988) and O'Neill and Gopnik (1991), for example, found pre-school children unable to indicate whether they had just learned the contents of a drawer from seeing them or being told about them. Similarly, Taylor and colleagues (Esbensen, Taylor, & Stoess, 1997; Taylor, Esbensen, & Bennett, 1994) reported pre-schoolers as showing little ability to distinguish *when* they had acquired a particular piece of factual knowledge—whether it had just been taught to them or was something they had "always known" (as most of them claimed regarding a newly learned fact).

With respect to developmental mechanism, it bears emphasis once again that these achievements do not arise solely from the child's internal cognitive constructive efforts. As highlighted in work such as that by Dunn et al. (1991), equally important is the scaffolding provided by adults in natural settings, reflected for example in a parent's explanation of a sibling's false belief—"He didn't know you wanted it". The dual processes of social participation and cognitive construction that begin in infancy gradually increase in complexity and support the achievements of the pre-school period.

A number of studies have shown these pre-school achievements to be amenable to acceleration by various forms of scaffolding. To the extent tasks are situated in everyday contexts (Dunn et al., 1991), or familiar, purposive experimental settings, for example hiding and deceiving in a game context (Chandler, Fritz, & Hala, 1989; Hala & Chandler, 1996), performance is enhanced. Similarly, performance in the standard false-belief task is enhanced if the child is provided some representational depiction of the earlier (now falsified) knowledge state, such as a photograph (Freeman & Lacohée, 1995; Mitchell & Lacohée, 1991), if the new (correct) knowledge state is made less visually salient (Zaitchik, 1991), if the child is asked to explain rather than predict an action deriving from false belief (Robinson & Mitchell, 1995), or if the child is given direct experience regarding the changeability of belief states (Slaughter & Gopnik, 1996).

It would thus be a mistake to see a particular age level or competency as marking a singular turning point in what is better conceptualised as a gradual evolution. It would similarly be a mistake to see the evolution in metacognitive knowing as complete once the child reaches the age of 4 or 5. Four-year-olds who succeed in recognising another's failed search for an object as a product of the other's false belief have not achieved the most sophisticated understanding of the mental processes and products involved in knowing that we might hope for. Knowing at this point is explained by the knower's having perceptual exposure to the salient information. Knowing means seeing that it is so. Even inference is not fully understood as a source of others' knowledge (Sodian & Wimmer, 1987). Accordingly, false beliefs can only be the product of a lack of exposure or exposure to misinformation. The holder of a false belief has not seen the reality that is there to be seen.

Still to develop is the understanding that different minds can arrive at genuinely different and legitimate understandings following exposure to exactly the same information. Studies by several researchers have shown that 4- and 5-year-olds who are fully competent in reporting false beliefs attributable to incorrect information nonetheless do not make appropriate judgements regarding the mental representations of observers exposed to misleading or ambiguous stimuli (Carpendale & Chandler, 1996; Pillow & Henrichon, 1996; Taylor, Cartwright,

& Bowden, 1991), tending instead to assume that the other will interpret the stimulus in the same way they do. Even at age 8 they may not understand the difficulty in predicting others' responses to ambiguous stimuli (Carpendale & Chandler, 1996). Although children of this age have no difficulty in accepting that people can have different tastes and values (Flavell et al., 1992), and even emotional reactions to the same object or event (Taylor et al., 1991), they do not yet accept that different people can hold genuinely different beliefs regarding this object or event, except in the case where one party's belief is misinformed and incorrect. Children at this age evidently lack the "interpretive" or "construct- ive" theory of mind (Carpendale & Chandler, 1996; Wellman, 1988) that would lead them to understand conflicting representations of the same event as legit- imate products of individuals' unique meaning-making efforts—to understand that because interpretive mental processes vary across individuals, their products may also differ. This achievement is a stepping stone in the development of epistemological understanding, which we turn to later in the chapter.

METASTRATEGIC KNOWING

We turn now to metastrategic knowing—knowing about mental processes, as opposed to products. As noted earlier, the distinction rests on the first-order distinction between procedural (knowing how) and declarative (knowing that) knowledge. What do children come to know about their cognitive processes and what impact does this knowledge have on performance? The findings described in the preceding section lead to a prediction that young children are unlikely to have much awareness (let alone monitoring or management) of their own (or others') cognitive processes. For them, as we saw, mental representations reflect the external world more than they do the mental activity of the representer. As such, this mental activity does not assume great significance in its own right and is unlikely to be the object of the child's attention.

Recent research by Flavell and colleagues (1997; Flavell et al., 1995) con- firms this prediction. Although their responses make it clear that they understand thinking as internal mental activity, pre-school children show limited awareness of its occurrence or content, in themselves or others. They may not acknowledge that a person engaged in making a decision is thinking, and, despite explicit cues, are poor at judging what the person has been thinking about. When they themselves are asked to "not think about anything", in contrast to older children and adults who realise the difficulty of the task, they are likely to report having been successful. They also demonstrate limited awareness of the contents of their own thought. When asked, for example, to think about the room in their house where their toothbrush is kept and asked immediately afterward what they had been thinking about, 5-year-olds failed to mention either bathrooms or tooth- brushes (Flavell et al., 1995).

Flavell's recent work grows out of the earliest empirical research in devel- opmental psychology to examine meta-knowing—a literature focused on metamemory, originating with Flavell himself (1979; Flavell & Wellman, 1977; Kreutzer, Leonard, & Flavell, 1975), Brown (1975, 1978, 1987) and several others. This work, conducted largely in the 1970s and 1980s, has been reviewed in a number of places (Brown, Bransford, Ferrara, & Campione, 1983; Flavell & Wellman, 1977; Schneider, 1985), and will not be described in detail here. The major findings and their historical significance can be easily summarised.

The work focuses on children's knowledge and use of strategies, such as rehearsal or categorisation, to aid their performance in traditional memory tasks such as recalling a list of words. The ability to behave strategically is itself relevant to the present concerns since it implies some competence in the management of one's cognitive functions. It was initially thought that pre-school children were incapable of using strategies to aid their memory performance, but it has since been shown that they can do so if the task is simple (e.g. remembering where a toy was hidden) and the context supportive (DeLoache, Cassidy, & Brown, 1985). In this respect, the findings parallel those described in the preceding section with respect to false belief and other theory-of-mind tasks. Like those achievements, the development of strategies that enhance cognitive performance is gradual and context-sensitive, rather than sudden.

In contrast to evidence of early metacognitive achievements described in the previous section, no marked achievements in strategic memory performance or metamemory appear during the pre-school years. Early studies reported some success in teaching memory strategies to young children (Brown, 1975, 1978). The more significant finding, however, is that such teaching rarely generalises to new situations (Brown, 1997). Unless they are prompted to do so, children tend not to apply strategies spontaneously in contexts where they would be useful. Improvements in this respect occur during the middle childhood years, but even by the end of childhood performance is far from optimum. Such findings have led to the conclusion that children have poor metastrategic awareness and understanding of their memory processes (Brown et al., 1983; Flavell & Wellman, 1977; Schneider, 1985). Studies that have directly assessed children's knowledge about memory support this conclusion. Pre-schoolers display some elementary knowledge, e.g. that increasing the number of items makes a memory test harder (Kreutzer et al., 1975), but not before middle childhood do children understand, for example, that a memory strategy such as categorisation aids recall (Moynahan, 1978).

There has not been much research on metastrategic competence outside of the well-studied memory paradigm. An exception is a smaller literature on comprehension monitoring (Flavell, Speer, Green, & August, 1981; Markman, 1977, 1979; Pressley & Ghatala, 1990). Significantly, its implications parallel those from the meta-memory research. In a now classic set of studies, Markman (1977, 1979) found that children asked to read a short passage containing blatant contradictions do not report them, even when asked explicitly whether what they have read makes sense. Evidently, they do not engage in metastrategic monitoring of their processing of information, to achieve an awareness of whether it has been successful (or at least show no evidence of such awareness in their verbal reports). As in the meta-memory research, modest improvements can be observed through the school years, but weakness remains evident even in older children. Only if they were alerted in advance that something in the passage might not make sense, Markman (1979) found, did the performance of sixth graders exceed that of third graders, and even then their performance was far from perfect.

These findings, then, point to a more wide-ranging metastrategic deficit in children, one not limited to memory skills. Children apply cognitive skills to meet task demands, but even if capable of doing so, do not spontaneously apply metastrategies that would enable them to evaluate their performance—a first step toward the use of metastrategic understanding as a means to regulate and improve performance. Although there does not exist a substantial enough data base across diverse kinds of cognitive tasks and settings to make this judgement conclusively, little if any evidence exists to refute it. It is also a conclusion consistent, certainly, with a good deal of educational literature on children's rote learning rather than deep understanding of what they are taught (Gardner, 1991; Perkins, 1992).

This brief review of research pertaining to children's metastrategic knowledge of their own cognitive processes leaves us in a different place than the earlier review of research on children's developing metacognitive understanding of the beliefs that are the products of their own and others' knowing activities. The early and rapid progress that was noted in children's achieving an understanding of human representational activity is not matched in their achievement of awareness, understanding, or management of their own cognitive processes. In the next section we explore what connections might be made between the two bodies of findings and whether there is a more extended developmental framework in which they can be viewed.

LINKING METASTRATEGIC AND METACOGNITIVE KNOWING

Toward this end, I turn to a line of research I have pursued for a number of years (Kuhn, Amsel, & O'Loughlin, 1988; Kuhn, Garcia-Mila, Zohar, & Anderson, 1995; Kuhn & Phelps, 1982; Kuhn, Schauble, & Garcia-Mila, 1992) that I believe highlights connections between metastrategic and metacognitive knowing, as well as situates them in a life-span developmental framework. The latter is accomplished by addressing a key developmental question: In what directions and toward what ends are these developing competencies headed? Also, in what ways are they supported by and in what ways do they support other developing competencies? This developmental framework is critical in establishing the broader significance of the cognitive skills researchers study.

The work I describe here is based on a task suitable across a wide spectrum of the life span, making it possible to examine performance in an extended developmental framework. The task involves the kinds of inferential reasoning that people of all ages engage in commonly, even if not self-consciously or explicitly. Young adolescent and adult participants engage in the task over multiple sessions, during which they gradually coordinate their existing theories with an accumulating base of new evidence that they access and interpret (Kuhn et al., 1995). Their objective is to identify the causal and non-causal factors influencing an outcome in a multivariable context. The method allows us to follow over time both their evolving knowledge base (as their theories change in the face of new evidence) and changes in the strategies by means of which they acquire that knowledge. The task can be situated in the context of several different literatures in cognitive and developmental psychology—as a task of inductive causal inference, scientific, argumentative, or critical thinking (Kuhn, 1996), as well as learning and knowledge acquisition.

Because the method is a microgenetic one in which change over time is observed, the data address fundamental issues regarding the nature of the change process. Findings by other investigators who have used a microgenetic method to examine change converge with our own in showing that individuals approach a task with a repertoire of strategies that they apply variably over time, even when the task environment remains constant (for review see Kuhn, 1995; Siegler, 1996). Such findings lead to a revised conception of change. In contrast to the traditional conception of a single transition in which a new strategy replaces an old one, with the focus on the challenge of mastering the new strategy, the newer portrayal of change features continuing shifts in the frequencies of usage of multiple strategies, with the diminished usage and eventual relinquishment of less adequate strategies a developmental challenge at least equal to that of mastering new, more adequate ones.

This revised model of strategy change has major implications with respect to the role of metastrategic factors. Rather than the traditional focus on metastrategic understanding of a particular strategy (such as categorisation in meta-memory research) as a factor influencing performance, the major metastrategic task becomes the very different one of *strategy selection*, from the repertoire of strategies the individual has available that are applicable to the task. If the strategies an individual selects shift over repeated encounters with the task, as microgenetic research documents they do (Kuhn, 1995; Siegler, 1996), this is the change that needs to be explained in a model of the change process. Strategy selection is a metastrategic, not a strategic, function—hence, the burden of explanation shifts to the metastrategic level. Other solutions are possible, e.g. that strategy selection is accomplished by a non-metastrategic process such as competition among strategies based on associative strength (Siegler & Jenkins, 1989), but metastrategic operations are at the least a leading contender in accounting for strategy selection.

Since our task allows participants to freely choose strategies for both investigating the data base we make available and drawing inferences from their observations, it is ideal for studying strategy selection, especially since our data confirm that virtually all participants have available a variety of both investigative and inference strategies that they apply variably over time. At the same time as it calls on metastrategic skill in the selection and monitoring of strategies, the task requires metacognitive skill in justifying knowledge claims. Individuals are not required to make any inferences (they are free to say that they don't know or can't yet tell), but they are asked to justify each of the inferences they do make. Although we find age-related improvement, it is here that we see in adolescents and adults metacognitive weaknesses that parallel those observed among pre-schoolers. Like pre-schoolers, many older individuals blur the distinction between theory-based and evidence-based sources of their beliefs. Rather than seeing their theories as belief states subject to disconfirmation and representing theory and evidence as distinct entities to be reconciled with one another, they merge the two into a single representation of "the way things are", with little apparent awareness of the sources of their belief.

When supportive evidence accumulates, individuals may become more convinced of the correctness of their beliefs, but even less metacognitively aware of the source of this certainty. They are certain *that* they know, but not *how* they know. They frequently substitute theory-based justifications in response to questions about the implications of evidence, suggesting an indifference to the sources of claims. Evidence serves merely to *illustrate* what one knows to be true, with evidence-based and theory-based justifications functioning as interchangeable supports for a claim.

In cases in which evidence discrepant with a theory accumulates over time, rather than compare theory and evidence, individuals often ignore or distort the evidence or draw on fragments of this evidence to *support* the theory, disregarding the rest and using the allegedly supportive evidence to illustrate what from their perspective is true. Theories do change in response to discrepant evidence, but often with the individual manifesting little awareness of the process. Like young children in the theory-of-mind research described earlier, the older participants in our studies are likely to deny they ever held a belief different from the one they are now professing.

A common pattern across all ages, we found, is the use of a valid strategy to interpret theory-compatible evidence with respect to one feature and an invalid strategy to interpret theory-discrepant evidence with respect to another feature, even though the evidence with respect to the two features is identical. Weak metacognitive awareness of the basis for one's beliefs and metastrategic inconsistency in the application of inference strategies thus reinforce one another.

META-KNOWING AND THE ORIGINS OF SCIENTIFIC REASONING

Where precisely are the developmental origins of the scientific reasoning competencies highlighted in the preceding section to be found? The answer, I believe, brings us remarkably close to early theory-of-mind achievements involving awareness of the sources of one's knowledge. In recent work Susan Pearsall and I (Kuhn & Pearsall, in press) examined developmental origins of the metacognitive ability to differentiate theory and evidence as a basis for one's knowledge claims. Do young children appreciate whether they are claiming something to be true because it makes sense as a way for things to be or on the basis of specific evidence of its correctness? We showed pre-schoolers a sequence of pictures in which, for example, two runners compete in a race. Certain cues suggest a theory as to why one will win, e.g. one has fancy running shoes. The final picture in the sequence provides evidence of the outcome, e.g. one of the runners holds a trophy and exhibits a wide grin. When children are subsequently asked to indicate the outcome and to justify this knowledge, younger children show a fragile distinction between the two kinds of justification—"How do you know?" and "Why is it so?", i.e. the evidence for their conclusion (the outcome cue in this case) versus their explanation for it (the initial theory-generating cue). The two jointly support a single representation of a state of affairs that "makes sense", with the respective cues treated as interchangeable contributors to this knowledge state. In the race example, young children often answered the "How do you know [he won]?" question not with evidence (e.g. "He's holding the trophy") but with a theory of why this state of affairs makes sense (e.g. "Because he has fast running shoes"). In another instance in which a boy is shown first climbing a tree and then down on the ground holding his knee, the "How do you know [that he fell]?" question was often answered, "Because he wasn't holding on carefully". These confusions between theory and evidence diminish sharply among 6-year-olds, who are more likely to distinguish the evidence for their claim from a theory that explains it. The question "How do you know?" becomes a meaningful one, distinct from the question of whether this knowledge claim is a plausible one.

It is in the achievement of this epistemological distinction, we maintain, that the origins of subsequent development in scientific thinking are to be found. In its most generic form, scientific thinking can be described as the coordination of theory and evidence. This coordination entails representation of theory and evidence as distinct entities and the evaluation of one in light of the other. Theory and evidence may be congruent in pointing to a common conclusion, but if they are not clearly differentiated it is not possible to evaluate one in light of the other, i.e. to construe relations between them. The research described earlier involving older children and adults suggests the continuing difficulties that the task poses even into adulthood.

Both young intuitive scientists and mature, professional scientists make use of both theory and evidence in their thinking. This is not where the difference between them lies. Rather, the difference is that in the case of the mature scientist, the coordination of theory and evidence is carried out under a high degree of conscious control (and therefore explicit, consistent, and demanding criteria). Accordingly, the development in scientific thinking that has been thought to occur across the childhood and adolescent years can be characterised as the achievement of increasing cognitive control over the coordination of theory and evidence. This achievement, note, is metacognitive in nature, since it entails mental operations on entities that are themselves mental operations.

The findings of our study point to the years between 4 and 6 as ones of concentrated change in the development of an epistemological understanding of foundational status for scientific thinking. To understand that beliefs are claims to be evaluated in relation to evidence that is distinguishable from the claim itself and bears on it is a prerequisite for genuinely scientific thought. Among children in the age range examined, the two sources of knowledge are not sufficiently differentiated and understood as belonging to different epistemological categories. In other words, pre-school children's limited epistemological understanding, and in particular their lack of concern regarding the sources of knowledge, leads them to make a fundamental category mistake, something like the category mistakes that Chi (1992) describes as common in children's conceptual development.

An alternative account with regard to the developmental origins of scientific thinking is found in a study by Ruffman, Perner, Olson, and Doherty (1993). Children in the age range of 5–7 were successful in coordinating theory and evidence of very simple forms, in the sense that they could draw appropriate inferences from evidence (e.g. dolls who choose red food over green food) to theory (the dolls prefer red food to green) or from theory to evidence (in the form of a prediction of the dolls' food choice). This remained the case even when the child's own belief was that the theory was false.

What is the competence that Ruffman et al. (1993) identify as in place by this age? Their discussion suggests that it is the ability to identify correspondences between theories and data—to reason from one to the other. The study does appear to demonstrate the ability of most 5–7-year-olds to do this. The fact is, however, that such an ability can be observed at far earlier ages than those examined by Ruffman et al. Indeed, the ability to draw inferences from empirical data or to make predictions from implicit theories—to identify correspondences between theories and data—can be observed as early as the sensorimotor level (witness Piaget's infant who makes the inference that movement of his leg causes the movement of the attached rattles). In the social domain, Wellman (1988) and others have traced the very early development of attributions of intention and desire (theories) to explain one's own or other's behaviour. Such theories develop even earlier in the physical domain, e.g. the theory that glass objects break when dropped as an explanation or prediction of data that correspond to this theory. What is new, developmentally speaking, in the late preschool years is the ability to reason appropriately about such correspondences when one's own belief is counter to the theory. This is the achievement discussed earlier that is assessed by the false-belief task in the theory-of-mind literature (the actor's search of that location to obtain candy can be explained—or predicted—by his belief that the container contains candy, even though I know better). This achievement, however, is not the focus of Ruffman et al.'s analysis.

The particular correspondences between theories and patterns of evidence that a child is able to identify, and therefore to use as a basis for inference or prediction, increase in complexity with development. What needs to be recognised, however, especially as it is somewhat counterintuitive to anyone who has mastered the epistemological distinction in question, is the one thing the identification of correspondences between theories and patterns of evidence does not entail, and that is a firm differentiation between the two. Theory and evidence can "fit together" into a coherent depiction of a state of affairs, in the sense of being consistent with and implying one another, in the absence of a recognition of their differing epistemological status. Indeed, this is precisely what the data from our study show, supporting the claim that appreciation of the epistemological distinction between theory and evidence is a foundational achievement in the development of scientific thinking. Only with a firm distinction between them can one engage in the genuine coordination of theory and evidence—the consciously controlled evaluation of one in the light of the other—that I have depicted as the essence of scientific thinking.

Sodian, Zaitchik, and Carey (1991) take a different tack in identifying early forms of scientific thinking. Their focus is on the ability to design informative experiments, which has been found to be less than optimal in research on the scientific thinking skills of older children, adolescents, and even adults (Klahr, Fay, & Dunbar, 1993; Kuhn et al., 1988, 1995). Although the performance of 6-year-olds in their study was weak, by age 7, Sodian et al. (1991) found a majority of children able to choose the more informative of two tests to find out if a mouse was a large or small one, by placing food in a box overnight. Two boxes were available, one with a large opening (able to accommodate a large or small mouse) and one with a small opening (big enough for only the small mouse to pass through).

Although Sodian et al. do not identify this aspect of their work, their design also invokes the contrast between a determinant and indeterminant outcome. Fay and Klahr (1996), and before them Pieraut-Le Bonniec (1980), have conducted extensive studies of children's ability to recognise indeterminacy, which is difficult for pre-school children and develops gradually in the years from early to middle childhood. The ability to recognise indeterminate evidence and to prefer evidence that is determinate when it is available are central to the development of investigative strategies important to scientific thinking, although Sodian et al. do not focus on this aspect of their work.

Sodian et al. focus instead on their findings as illustrating their subjects' differentiation of theory and evidence, a claim we do not find convincing. Their task requires the child to choose the more informative of two potential forms of evidence. The distinction between what is the theory (big mouse or small mouse) and what is the evidence (big or small opening) is never in question. Their study does show children's capacity to behave strategically, in making a choice that involves the recognition of the superiority of determinate over indeterminate evidence. Strategic behaviour of various sorts, however, has been well-documented among children as young as 2 or 3 (Brown, 1997). More specifically, the ability to seek appropriate evidence capable of disconfirming a theory (by establishing its lack of correspondence with evidence) can be demonstrated in this same age range, as witnessed, for example, by the 2-year-old who knows that opening the closet door is capable of disconfirming her claim that it is the whooshing sound of a ghost inside her closet hat is keeping her awake. It will nonetheless be a number of years before this 2-year-old comes to appreciate the epistemological status of evidence as standing apart from a theory and bearing on it—the understanding addressed by the present study. For now, there exists either a state of affairs that can be represented as "ghost in the closet" or one that must be represented as "no ghost in the closet" and various strategic manoeuvres that may have the effect of transforming the depiction of reality from one state to the other.

The studies by Ruffman et al. (1993) and Sodian et al. (1991), this analysis suggests, examine strategic and inferential competencies that evolve in a gradual manner from the earliest years of life and, like even more rudimentary skills of observation or categorisation, support the development of scientific thinking, without being either specific or central to it. In contrast, our interest in pursuing the question of developmental origins centred on whether the early childhood years are characterised by any cognitive achievements specific and central to the development of scientific thinking, in the sense of defining its essence. The epistemological achievement identified in our work we have claimed is indeed in this sense essential and foundational. Skilled, consciously controlled coordination of theory and evidence cannot occur in the absence of firm boundaries between them. It remains to stress again, however, that although attention to the sources of one's knowledge—knowing how one knows—is arguably central to scientific thinking, it is, as the present chapter makes clear, by no means unique to it.

EPISTEMOLOGICAL META-KNOWING

Before proceeding to conclusions regarding meta-knowing in a life-span framework, it remains to examine the evolution of the third branch of meta-knowing, the epistemological. Beyond specific understandings of their own or others' cognition in particular contexts, how do individuals conceptualise knowing and knowledge more broadly? This is meta-knowing of an abstract, theoretical (Schraw & Moshman, 1995) sort, although it also extends to one's personal theories about the self's knowing capacities and dispositions (Dweck, 1991). Although a fair amount of research has accumulated regarding the development of epistemological theories, it has remained curiously isolated from other cognitive development research, and in particular unconnected to research on metacognitive and metastrategic knowing reviewed earlier in this chapter, especially the theory-of-mind work to which it is most directly related. A possible explanation is that theory-of-mind research has been largely confined to children only up to the age of about 6, whereas work on the development of epistemological thinking has focused on adolescents and adults. With a few isolated exceptions (Mansfield & Clinchy, 1997; Mitchell et al., 1996; Nelson et al., 1998; Schwanenflugel, Fabricius, & Noyes, 1996), no connecting research exists covering the period from middle childhood to early adolescence.

The conceptual connection between the two bodies of work is nonetheless clear. The understanding of assertions as belief states we identified earlier as providing an essential foundation for further developments in epistemological understanding. With this attainment, assertions are recognised as emanating from, and therefore connected to, the human activity of knowing. Nonetheless, the initial *absolutist* epistemological stance—the norm in childhood and into adolescence and even adulthood (Chandler, Boyes, & Ball, 1990; King & Kitchener, 1994; Kuhn, 1991; Perry, 1970)—does not accord a pivotal role to the knower as a constructor of knowledge. Rather, the locus of knowledge remains in the external world, where it awaits discovery by human knowledge seekers. A child by 4 or 5 appreciates knowing as connected to and generated by a knowing agent to a sufficient extent to understand that beliefs may deviate from a single, true reality. Yet much slower to be achieved, if indeed it is achieved at all, is a truly constructivist theory of mind that recognises the primacy of humans as knowledge constructors capable of generating a multiplicity of valid representations of reality.

The transition from a realist pre-epistemological unawareness of belief states to the initial epistemological stance of absolutism is nonetheless a profound one. It is a transition from simply knowing that something is true to evaluating whether it might be. To carry out such evaluation, absolutists rely on the concept of a certain truth, one that is known or potentially knowable through either direct apprehension or the authority of experts. Belief states can be judged as correct or incorrect in relation to this truth.

People can spend entire lifetimes within the protective wraps of either a pre-absolutist stance in which assertions are equated with reality or, more commonly, the absolutist stance in which disagreements are resolvable by appeal to direct observation or authority. In the modern world, however, it is difficult to avoid exposure to conflicting assertions that cannot readily be reconciled by appeal to observation or authority. As a result, most people progress beyond absolutism, venturing onto the slippery slope that will carry them to a *multiplist* epistemological stance, which becomes prevalent at adolescence. A critical event leading to the first step down the slope toward multiplism is likely to be exposure to the fact that experts disagree about important issues. If even experts cannot be counted on to provide certain answers, one resolution is to relinquish the idea of certainty itself, and this is exactly the path the multiplist takes. As the next inductive leap along this path, if experts with all of their knowledge and authority disagree with one another, why should their views be accepted as any more valid than anyone else's? A better assumption is that anyone's opinion has the same status and deserves the same treatment as anyone else's. Beliefs or opinions are the possessions of their owners, freely chosen according to the owner's tastes and wishes, and accordingly not subject to criticism. In the words of one of the adolescents in our research (Kuhn, 1991), "You can't prove an opinion to be wrong because an opinion is something somebody holds for themselves". Hence—in a conceptual slight-of-hand that represents the final step down the slippery slope—because everyone has a right to their opinion, all opinions are equally right.

In contrast to the absolutist stance, which is difficult to maintain in pure form, people often remain multiplists for life. Only a minority progress to an *evaluative* epistemology, in which all opinions are not equal and knowing is understood as a process that entails judgement, evaluation, and argument. Evaluative epistemologists have reconciled the idea that people have a right to their views with the understanding that some views can nonetheless be more right than others. They see the weighing of alternative claims in a process of reasoned debate as the path to informed opinion, and they understand that arguments can be evaluated and compared based on their merit (Kuhn, 1991).

A weakness of research on epistemological understanding has been the lack of a clear theoretical framework for conceptualising, and developing means of assessing, the developmental progression just sketched, despite broad agreement among different investigators regarding its nature. Details of the levels and stages described by different investigators have made it difficult to identify a core of what it is that is developing. My own conception of the core dimension underlying and driving this progression is the coordination of the subjective and objective components of knowing. The absolutist sees knowledge in largely objective terms, as located in the external world and knowable with certainty. The multiplist becomes aware of the subjective component of knowing, but to such an extent that it overpowers and obliterates any objective standard that would provide a basis for comparison or evaluation of opinions. Only the evaluativist is successful in integrating and coordinating the two, by acknowledging uncertainty without forsaking evaluation. This conception is compatible with that proposed by Hofer and Pintrich (1997) in a recent summary and review of the literature on the development of epistemological thinking. Endorsing the broad three-level (absolutist, multiplist, evaluativist) progression described here, they identify four dimensions of this progression, pertaining to the simplicity of knowledge (from simple to complex), the certainty of knowledge (from certain to uncertain), the source of knowledge (from external to internal), and the justification of knowledge (from external to internal and evaluative).

Schemes for the empirical assessment of epistemological thinking have ranged from a complex 7-level multidimensional coding system developed by King and Kitchener (1994), to the more skeletal coding scheme we have favoured in our research (so as to retain clarity as to the construct being assessed). Again, however, at this point the commonalities are more important than the differences in the coding schemes used by various researchers (see Hofer & Pintrich, 1997, for review), especially since the upper levels in the most complex, 7-level scheme by King and Kitchener appear relatively rarely as empirical realities except in highly educated samples.

In empirical research, my co-workers and I have relied on two schemes for distinguishing absolutist, multiplist, and evaluative levels of epistemological thinking. One is based on individuals' answers to questions regarding their own versus experts' judgements regarding the causes of complex social problems such as school failure, crime, and unemployment (Kuhn, 1991). We classify as absolutists those who believe that such questions have certain answers. Those who maintain that the causes of such phenomena cannot be known with certainty we classify as either multiplists, if they maintain that their own theories are just as likely to be right as those of experts who have studied the problem for a long time, or as evaluativists, if they see the expert's study of the problem as productive of understanding more likely to be correct than the average person's.

The second coding scheme is based on understandings of how to interpret conflicting claims (Kuhn, Weinstock, & Flaton, 1994; Leadbeater & Kuhn, 1989). In one scenario we have presented, two historians produce conflicting accounts of an historical event. Progression in epistemological understanding can be observed from a rudimentary pre-absolutist level in which the individual does not acknowledge discrepancies between the accounts (equating the account with the event itself) to the absolutist stance in which discrepancies are understood simply as omissions or incomplete renderings of a factual reality, then to a multiplist stance in which differences are unreconcilable since accounts become entirely subjective renderings, and finally to the evaluative stance in which differences are understood as ones of perspective, emphasis, and interpretation, with multiple accounts nonetheless susceptible to comparison and evaluation. For absolutists, then, only one account can be correct, whereas multiplists claim both can be right, since they are equally valid subjective opinions, and evaluativists claim both can be right but that one may be superior to the other (because it is better supported or argued).

Although epistemological thinking is of interest in its own right, it assumes greater significance to the extent it has implications for other aspects of intellectual functioning. Were such implications absent, epistemology reduces to simply another domain of knowledge, equivalent in significance to botany or geography or any other intellectual domain in which people may acquire some degree of knowledge or expertise. Although much remains to be learned in this respect, a number of recent studies have established that connections do exist between level of epistemological understanding and cognitive performance across a range of tasks and populations. In other words, epistemological understanding is not encapsulated knowledge. Schwanenflugel et al. (1996), for example, report a relation between children's differentiation of verbs that denote mental states varying in certainty (e.g. guess, think, know), which they interpret as reflecting growing appreciation of the constructivist nature of knowing, and their perform-ance on Markman's comprehension monitoring task. Carey and Smith (1993) and Sodian and Schrempp (1997) report relations between children's and adoles-cents' levels of epistemological understanding and their performance on scient-ific reasoning tasks. In my work on argumentative reasoning (Kuhn, 1991), I have found associations between levels of epistemological understanding and argumentative reasoning skill among adolescents and adults. Kardash and Scholes (1996) also report relations between epistemological understanding and reasoning about conflicting views. Such associations document the relevance of epistemo-logical understanding to intellectual functioning, in particular to higher-order thinking and reasoning. Unless one sees the point of intellectual debate, there is little incentive to expend the effort entailed to engage in it. Put simply by one of the multiplists in our studies, "I feel it's not worth it to argue because everyone has their opinion". In such cases, educators can undertake to teach cognitive skills, but the reasons to apply them will be missing.

META-KNOWING IN DEVELOPMENTAL PERSPECTIVE

We are now in a position to bring together the diverse array of phenomena that have been considered in this chapter. Again, I propose as a conceptual umbrella for doing so, the development of meta-knowing, defining this development as the achievement of increasing awareness, understanding, and control of one's own cognitive functions, as well as awareness and understanding of these func-tions as they occur in others. Young children's dawning awareness of their own and others' mental functions lies at one end of a developmental progression that eventuates in complex meta-knowing capabilities not realised before adulthood, if they are realised at all. Linking these diverse attainments within a develop-mental framework makes it possible to investigate ways in which earlier attain-ments prepare the way for later ones.

Competence in meta-knowing thus warrants attention as a critical endpoint and goal of childhood and adolescent cognitive development. This is even more the case since meta-knowing capacities inform cognitive performance (as well as being informed by it). Indeed, meta-knowing is strongly implicated in some of the most consequential intellectual skills that ordinary individuals may attain. To be competent and motivated to "know how you know" puts one in charge of one's own knowing—of deciding what to believe and why, of determining how new information should be interpreted and reconciled with one's current beliefs, and of updating and revising those beliefs as one deems warranted. In the absence of this control, beliefs are vulnerable to the twin hazards of rigidity and fluidity. They come into contact with external evidence only in an unstable manner, often with radical accommodations of one to the other. In contrast, with such control, thinking is sensitive to new evidence but not dominated by it. To achieve this control of their own thinking is arguably the most important way in which people both individually and collectively take control of their lives.

One other link that remains important to make explicit is that between the development of meta-knowing as discussed here and the cognitive skills commonly discussed in educational literature under the headings of higher-order or critical thinking. The latter have been the object of continuing attention and received wide endorsement as an overarching goal of education, at all levels from pre-school to post-graduate. Typically, however, they are discussed as first-order cognitive skills, rather than as second-order meta-knowing competencies (for exceptions, see Kuhn, 1991; Kuhn & Lao, 1998; Kuhn, Shaw, & Felton, 1997; Perkins, 1992). Proficiency in the execution of cognitive skills is by no means to be ignored, but repeatedly educational assessments of various kinds have shown students' most significant deficits to lie not in executing such skills under direct instruction but in applying these skills in appropriate contexts in the absence of explicit instruction to do so. As has already been argued in this chapter, metastrategic and metacognitive competencies are strongly implicated in such deficits. Attention to these competencies, including epistemological understanding, has the potential to inform educators' efforts to enhance students' thinking.

In sum, viewed in the terms proposed in this chapter, competencies in meta-knowing assume broad significance in people's lives, both individually and collectively. This portrayal stands in sharp contrast to the more circumscribed ways in which metacognitive and metastrategic skills have been examined in much of the existing literature that has been reviewed here. It is interesting, then, that even though the field did not follow his lead, Flavell (1979, p. 910), in a seminal paper highlighting metacognitive development as a promising new area of inquiry, conceptualised it in extremely broad terms, going even beyond what has been discussed here to incorporate personal life management as a domain in which meta-knowing skills are strongly implicated:

> In many real-life situations, the monitoring problem is not to determine how well you understand what a message means but to determine how much you ought to believe it or do what it says to do. I am thinking of the persuasive appeals the young receive from all quarters to smoke, drink, take drugs, commit aggressive or criminal acts, have casual sex without contraceptives, have or not have the casual babies that often result, quit school, and become unthinking followers of this year's flaky cults, sects, and movements . . . Perhaps it is stretching the meanings of metacognition and cognitive monitoring too far to include the critical appraisal

of message source, quality of appeal, and probable consequences needed to cope with these inputs sensibly, but I do not think so. It is at least conceivable that the ideas currently brewing in this area could someday be parlayed into a method of teaching children (and adults) to make wise and thoughtful life decisions as well as to comprehend and learn better in formal educational settings.

Flavell's wide-ranging conception of meta-knowing in this influential paper brings us a long way from the early theory-of-mind achievements that are the common focus of this volume. Yet it has been the aim of this chapter to establish just these connections. Becoming able to think about one's own and others' thought— the origins of which theory-of-mind research has highlighted—has profound, wide-ranging, and long-lasting consequences. It is an achievement that is realised only in small, gradual steps. Yet its profound consequences make attention to both developmental origins and process well worthwhile.

REFERENCES

Astington, J., & Olson, D. (1995). The cognitive revolution in children's understanding of mind. *Human Development, 38*, 179–189.

Brown, A. (1975). The development of memory: Knowing, knowing about knowing, and knowing how to know. In H. Reese (Ed.), *Advances in child development and behavior* (Vol. 10, pp. 103–152). New York: Academic Press.

Brown, A. (1978). Knowing when, where, and how to remember: A problem of metacognition. In R. Glaser (Ed.), *Advances in instructional psychology* (Vol. 1, pp. 77–165). Hillsdale, NJ: Lawrence Erlbaum Associates Inc.

Brown, A. (1987). Metacognition, executive control, self-regulation, and other more mysterious mechanisms. In F. Weinert & R. Kluwe (Eds.), *Metacognition, motivation, and understanding* (pp. 65–116). Hillsdale, NJ: Lawrence Erlbaum Associates Inc.

Brown, A. (1997). Transforming schools into communities of thinking and learning about serious matters. *American Psychologist, 52*, 399–413.

Brown, A., Bransford, J., Ferrara, R., & Campione, J. (1983). Learning, remembering, and understanding. In P. Mussen (Series Ed.), J. Flavell, & E. Markman (Vol. Eds.), *Handbook of child psychology: Vol 3. Cognitive development* (pp. 77–166). (4th Ed.). New York: John Wiley & Sons.

Carey, S., & Smith, C. (1993). On understanding the nature of scientific knowledge. *Educational Psychologist, 28*, 235–251.

Carpendale, J., & Chandler, M. (1996). On the distinction between false belief understanding and subscribing to an interpretive theory of mind. *Child Development, 67*, 1686–1706.

Chandler, M., Boyes, M., & Ball, L. (1990). Relativism and stations of epistemic doubt. *Journal of Experimental Child Psychology, 50*, 370–395.

Chandler, M., Fritz, A., & Hala, S. (1989). Small-scale deceit: Deception as a marker of two-, three-, and four-year-olds' early theories of mind. *Child Development, 60*, 1263–1277.

Chi, M. (1992). Conceptual change within and across ontological categories: Examples from learning and discovery in science. In R. Giere (Ed.), *Cognitive models of science* (pp. 129–187). Minneapolis: University of Minnesota Press.

Cole, M. (1996). *Cultural psychology: A once and future discipline*. Cambridge, MA: Harvard University Press.

DeLoache, J., Cassidy, D., & Brown, A. (1985). Precursors of mnemonic strategies in very young children's memory. *Child Development, 56*, 125–137.

Dunn, J., Brown, J., Slomkowski, C., Tesla, C., & Youngblade, L. (1991). Young children's under-standing of other people's feelings and beliefs: Individual differences and their antecedents. *Child Development, 62*, 1352–1366.

Dweck, C. (1991). Self-theories and goals: Their role in motivation, personality and development. In R. Dienstbier (Ed.), *Nebraska symposium on motivation, 1990* (Vol. 36, pp. 199–235). Lincoln: University of Nebraska Press.

Esbensen, B., Taylor, M., & Stoess, C. (1997). Children's behavioral understanding of knowledge acquisition. *Cognitive Development, 12*, 53–84.

Estes, D., Wellman, H., & Woolley, J. (1989). Children's understanding of mental phenomena. In H. Reese (Ed.), *Advances in child development and behavior* (pp. 41–87). New York: Academic Press.

Fay, A., & Klahr, D. (1996). Knowing about guessing and guessing about knowing: Preschoolers' understanding of indeterminacy. *Child Development, 67*, 689–716.

Feldman, C. (1988). Early forms of thought about thoughts: Some simple linguistic expressions of mental state. In J. Astington, P. Harris, & D. Olson (Eds.), *Developing theories of mind* (pp. 126–137). Cambridge: Cambridge University Press.

Flavell, J. (1979). Metacognition and cognitive monitoring: A new area of cognitive-developmental inquiry. *American Psychologist, 34*, 906–911.

Flavell, J. (1997). *Recent convergences between metacognitive and theory-of-mind research within children*. Presented in the symposium "Constructing metacognitive knowledge" (G. Schraw, chair) at the biennial meeting of the Society for Research in Child Development, Washington DC.

Flavell, J., Green, F., & Flavell, E. (1995). *Young children's knowledge about thinking. Society for Research in Child Development Monographs, 60*, Serial no. 243.

Flavell, J., & Miller, P. (1998). Social cognition. In W. Damon (Series ed.), D. Kuhn, & R. Siegler (Vol. eds.), *Handbook of child psychology: Vol 2. Cognition, language, and perception.* (5th Ed., pp. 851–898). New York: John Wiley & Sons.

Flavell, J., Mumme, D., Green, F., & Flavell, E. (1992). Young children's understanding of differ-ent types of beliefs. *Child Development, 63*, 960–977.

Flavell, J., Speer, J., Green, F., & August, D. (1981). The development of comprehension monitoring and knowledge about communication. *Society for Research in Child Development Monographs, 46* (Serial No. 192).

Flavell, J., & Wellman, H. (1977). Metamemory. In R. Kail & J. Hagen (Eds.), Perspectives on the development of memory and cognition (pp. 3–33). Hillsdale, NJ: Lawrence Erlbaum Associates Inc.

Freeman, N., & Lacohée, H. (1995). Making explicit 3-year-olds implicit competence with their own false beliefs. *Cognition, 56*, 31–60.

Gardner, H. (1991). *The unschooled mind: How children think and how schools should teach.* New York: Basic Books.

Gopnik, A., & Astington, J. (1988). Children's understanding of representational change and its relation to the understanding of false belief and the appearance-reality distinction. *Child Devel-opment, 59*, 26–37.

Gopnik, A., & Graf, P. (1988). Knowing how you know: Young children's ability to identify and remember the sources of their beliefs. *Child Development, 59*, 1366–1371.

Gopnik, A., & Wellman, H. (1992). Why the child's theory of mind really is a theory. *Mind and Language, 7*, 145–171.

Hala, S., & Chandler, M. (1996). The role of strategic planning in accessing false-belief under-standing. *Child Development, 67*, 2948–2966.

Harris, P. (1992). From simulation to folk psychology: The case for development. *Mind and Lan-guage, 7*, 120–144.

Hofer, B., & Pintrich, P. (1997). The development of epistemological theories: Beliefs about know-ledge and knowing and their relation to learning. *Review of Educational Research, 67*, 88–140.

Kardash, C., & Scholes, R. (1996). Effects of preexisting beliefs, epistemological beliefs, and need for cognition on interpretation of controversial issues. *Journal of Educational Psychology, 88*, 260–271.

King, P., & Kitchener, K. (1994). *Developing reflective judgment: Understanding and promoting intellectual growth and critical thinking in adolescents and adults.* San Francisco: Jossey-Bass.

Klahr, D., Fay, A., & Dunbar, K. (1993). Heuristics for scientific experimentation: A developmental study. *Cognitive Psychology, 25*, 111–146.

Kreutzer, M., Leonard, C., & Flavell, J. (1975). An interview study of children's knowledge about memory. *Society for Research in Child Development Monographs, 40* (Serial No. 159).

Kuhn, D. (1991). *The skills of argument.* New York: Cambridge University Press.

Kuhn, D. (1995). Microgenetic study of change: What has it told us? *Psychological Science, 6*, 133–139.

Kuhn, D. (1996). Is good thinking scientific thinking? In D. Olson & N. Torrance (Eds.), *Modes of thought: Explorations in culture and cognition* (pp. 261–281). Cambridge: Cambridge University Press.

Kuhn, D., Amsel, E., & O'Loughlin, M. (1988). *The development of scientific thinking skills.* Orlando, FL: Academic Press.

Kuhn, D., Garcia-Mila, M., Zohar, A., & Andersen, C. (1995). *Strategies of knowledge acquisition. Society for Research in Child Development Monographs, 60*(40), Serial no. 245.

Kuhn, D., & Lao, J. (1998). Contemplation and conceptual change: Integrating perspectives from social and cognitive psychology. *Developmental Review, 18*, 125–154.

Kuhn, D., & Pearsall, S. (in press). Developmental origins of scientific thinking *Journal of Cognitive Development.*

Kuhn, D., & Phelps, E. (1982). The development of problem-solving strategies. In H. Reese (Ed.), *Advances in child development and behavior*, Vol. 17 (pp. 1–43). New York: Academic Press.

Kuhn, D., Schauble, L., & Garcia-Mila, M. (1992). Cross-domain development of scientific reasoning. *Cognition and Instruction, 9*, 285–332.

Kuhn, D., Shaw, V., & Felton, M. (1997). Effects of dyadic interaction on argumentive reasoning. *Cognition and Instruction, 15*, 287–315.

Kuhn, D., Weinstock, M., & Flaton, R. (1994). Historical reasoning as theory-evidence coordination. In M. Carretero & J. Voss (Eds.), *Cognitive and instructional processes in history and the social sciences* (pp. 377–401). Hillsdale, NJ: Lawrence Erlbaum Associates Inc.

Leadbeater, B., & Kuhn, D. (1989). Interpreting discrepant narratives: Hermeneutics and adult cognition. In J. Sinnott (Ed.), *Everyday problem-solving: theory and application* (pp. 175–190). New York: Praeger.

Leslie, A. (1987). Pretense and representation: The origins of "theory of mind." *Psychological Review, 94*, 412–426.

Mansfield, A., & Clinchy, B. (1997). *Toward the integration of objectivity and subjectivity: A longitudinal study of epistemological development between the ages of 9 and 13.* Research display presented at the biennial meeting of the Society for Research in Child Development, Washington DC.

Markman, E. (1977). Realizing that you don't understand: A preliminary investigation. *Child Development, 48*, 986–992.

Markman, E. (1979). Realizing that you don't understand: Elementary school children's awareness of inconsistencies. *Child Development, 50*, 643–655.

Mitchell, P., & Lacohée, H. (1991). Children's understanding of false belief. *Cognition, 39*, 107–128.

Montgomery, D. (1992). Young children's theory of knowing: The development of a folk epistemology. *Developmental Review, 12*, 410–430.

Moynahan, E. (1978). Assessment and selection of paired associate strategies: A developmental study. *Journal of Experimental Child Psychology, 26*, 257–266.

Nelson, K., Plesa, D., & Henseler, S. (1998). Children's theory of mind: An experiential interpretation. *Human Development, 41*, 7–29.

O'Neill, D., & Gopnik, A. (1991). Young children's ability to identify the sources of their beliefs.
Developmental Psychology, 27, 390–397.

Olson, D., & Astington, J. (1993). Thinking about thinking: Learning how to take statements and
hold beliefs. *Educational Psychologist, 28*, 7–23.

Perkins, D. (1992). *Smart schools: Better thinking and learning for every child*. New York: Free
Press.

Perner, J. (1991). *Understanding the representational mind*. Cambridge, MA: MIT Press.

Perry, W. (1970). *Forms of intellectual and ethical development in the college years*. New York:
Holt, Rinehart & Winston.

Piaget, J., & Inhelder, B. (1951). *Play, dreams, and imitation in childhood*. New York: Norton.

Pieraut-Le Bonniec, G. (1980). *The development of modal reasoning*. New York: Academic Press.

Pillow, B., & Henrichon, A. (1996). There's more to the picture than meets the eye: Young children's difficulty understanding biased interpretation. *Child Development, 67*, 803–819.

Pressley, M., & Ghatala, E. (1990). Self-regulated learning: Monitoring learning from text. *Educational Psychologist, 25*, 19–34.

Robinson, E., & Mitchell, P. (1995). Masking of children's early understanding of the representational mind: Backwards explanation versus prediction. *Child Development, 66*, 1022–1039.

Rogoff, B. (1998). Cognition as a collaborative process. In W. Damon (Series Ed.), D. Kuhn, &
R. Siegler (Vol. Eds.), *Handbook of child psychology: Vol 2. Cognition, language, and perception*.
(5th ed.) (pp. 679–744). New York: John Wiley & Sons.

Ruffman, T., Perner, J., Olson, D., & Doherty, M. (1993). Reflecting on scientific thinking: Children's understanding of the hypothesis-evidence relation. *Child Development, 64*, 1617–1636.

Schneider, W. (1985). Developmental trends in the metamemory-memory behavior relationship:
An integrative review. In D. Forrest-Pressley, G., MacKinnon, & T. Waller (Eds.), *Cognition,
metacognition, and human performance* (Vol. 1, pp. 57–109). Orlando, FL: Academic Press.

Schraw, G., & Moshman, D. (1995). Metacognitive theories. *Educational Psychology Review, 7*,
351–371.

Schwanenflugel, P., Fabricius, W., & Noyes, C. (1996). Developing organization of mental verbs:
Evidence for the development of a constructivist theory of mind in middle childhood. *Cognitive
Development, 11*, 265–294.

Siegler, R. (1996). *Emerging minds: The process of change in children's thinking*. New York:
Oxford University Press.

Siegler, R., & Jenkins, E. (1989). *How children discover new strategies*. Hillsdale, NJ: Lawrence
Erlbaum Associates Inc.

Slaughter, V., & Gopnik, A. (1996). Conceptual coherence in the child's theory of mind: Training
children to understand belief. *Child Development, 67*, 2967–2988.

Sodian, B., & Schrempp, I. (1997). *Metaconceptual knowledge and the development of scientific
reasoning skills*. Paper presented at the annual meeting of the American Educational Research
Association, Chicago IL.

Sodian, B., & Wimmer, H. (1987). Children's understanding of inference as a source of knowledge. *Child Development, 58*, 424–433.

Sodian, B., Zaitchik, D., & Carey, S. (1991). Young children's differentiation of hypothethical
beliefs from evidence. *Child Development, 62*, 753–766.

Taylor, M., Cartwright, B., & Bowden, T. (1991). Perspective taking and theory of mind: Do
children predict interpretive diversity as a function of differences in observers' knowledge?
Child Development, 62, 1334–1351.

Taylor, M., Esbensen, B., & Bennett, R. (1994). Children's understanding of knowledge acquisition: The tendency for children to report they have always known what they have just learned.
Child Development, 65, 1581–1604.

Tomasello, M., Kruger, A., & Ratner, H. (1993). Cultural learning. *Behavioral and Brain Sciences*, *16*, 495–552.

Wellman, H. (1988). First steps in the child's theorizing about the mind. In J. Astington, P. Harris, & D. Olson (Eds.), *Developing theories of mind* (pp. 64–92). Cambridge: Cambridge University Press.

Wimmer, H., Hogrefe, G., & Perner, J. (1988). Children's understanding of informational access as a source of knowledge. *Child Development*, *59*, 386–396.

Wimmer, H., & Perner, J. (1983). Beliefs about beliefs: Representation and constraining function of wrong beliefs in young children's understanding of deception. *Cognition*, *13*, 103–128.

Woolley, J. (1995). Young children's understanding of fictional versus epistemic mental representations: Imagination and belief. *Child Development*, *66*, 1011–1021.

Zaitchik, D. (1991). Is only seeing really believing? Sources of the true belief in the false belief task. *Cognitive Development*, *6*, 91–103.

CHAPTER SIXTEEN

Causal reasoning and behaviour in children and adults in a technologically advanced society: Are we still prepared to believe in magic and animism?

Eugene Subbotsky
Psychology Department, Lancaster University, UK

INTRODUCTION

As a result of the growing fascination of psychology in the 20th century with a scientific model of reality, the human mind came to be viewed as an 'organically rational' construct whose fundamental features and the final point of development are based on the picture of the universe created by science over the last three centuries. Even the mind of a child has increasingly been presented as a mind of a 'little scientist' who is capable of grasping fundamental rational structures of the world nearly from birth (Bower, 1974; Gelman & Baillargeon, 1983). 'Rationalisation' of this kind can indeed be helpful, especially with regard to some studies of cognitive development in infancy, but it can create a distorted image of the human mind if developed in a general model destined to present the 'true' vision of the mind.

Indeed, the fact is that a contemporary Western individual is not an exclusively rational being and that he or she, living in the world created by science, dwells in the worlds of dreams, art, fantasies, play, and social myths. This means that if the individual is to encounter a certain phenomenon with no established scientific explanation, he or she may be prepared to explain the phenomenon in a number of ways, only some of which are compatible with the vision of modern science (Jahoda, 1969).

This 'metaphysical openness' of the contemporary human individual to heterogeneous interpretations is particularly evident in the case of unusual phenomena. Indeed, even if we admit that multiple descriptions of encounters with UFOs or the Loch Ness monster are nothing but sheer fantasies, it would be highly unlikely to assume that these fantasies have been created 'from thin air'. Rather, it would be more plausible to assume that there had been certain external events really observed by the reporters and that it was these events that were subsequently interpreted as apparitions of the extraterrestrial objects or survivors of the world of dinosaurs. It is impossible to deny that, along with those who welcome scientific interpretation of these phenomena (i.e. viewing UFOs as normal cosmic objects or as luminous phenomena generated by man-made geophysical variables; see Sheaffer, 1986) there exist a vast number of people preferring to view these phenomena in parascientific and occult terms (i.e. UFOs as 'chariots of Gods' and ghosts as apparitions from the four-dimensional world; see Kaku, 1994; Lehmann & Mayers, 1985; Rucker, 1984). It is also clear that modes of thinking alternative to scientific are still thriving in various religious practices, as well as in some forms of psychotherapy which consciously refuse to accept fundamental requirements of the traditional scientific approach.

The problem that arises in connection with this heterogeneity of the human mind in developmental perspectives is how it can be reconciled with the widespread view that children's early beliefs in magic and animism with age die out and are replaced by the strong belief in the universal nature of physical causality. The aim of this chapter is to investigate to what extent this view, originally advocated by Piaget, really reflects the whole complexity of the development of causal thinking.

Another important aspect of analysis which appears in connection with studying causal thinking is the development of children's and adults' 'theories of mind'. It was found that children younger than 4 years are limited in their understanding of how the mind works. For instance, in the so called 'false belief task' children often attribute their own knowledge of reality to the characters who obviously could not have that knowledge (Wimmer & Perner, 1983), and even to themselves in the past when they clearly did not have that knowledge (Gopnik & Astington, 1988). These limitations (traditionally called the failure to understand false belief, and the 'realist error' in judging about the mind) triggered a vast area of studies (Lewis & Mitchell, 1994; Perner, 1991). In these studies the ways that children older than 4, and even adults (Mitchell, Robinson, Isaacs, & Nye, 1996) acquire the capacity to understand false beliefs have been thoroughly analysed.

Yet, the rationalist view of the human mind has found its way in this area of studies too. This is evident in the fact that it was children's view on the cognitive operational function of the mind (i.e. the capacity to act on the basis of limited and insufficient information, and to hold false beliefs) that was the focus of these studies. Clearly, the mind has other functions and properties, which children and adults have to take into consideration in order to adapt themselves to the social world. One of these properties is that the mind is a kind of reality which is fundamentally different from the reality of physical objects. It follows from this that it is not possible to cause changes in the physical world by mental efforts only. In this regard, if children at a certain age abandon beliefs in magical and animistic causality, this would also mean that they develop the 'theory of mind', within which the reality of mind is divorced from physical reality and viewed as something principally 'nonphysical' and 'immaterial'. The questions that arise in this context are as follows: to which extent do children of advanced ages and adults hold the dualistic view on the human mind? Do they completely abandon the earlier beliefs that it is possible to affect physical objects by just 'thinking hard' or imagining something to happen? Is it possible for older children and adults to believe that the mind of another person can be 'transparent' for his or her own mind, and that 'mindreading' is possible?

STUDIES OF CHILDREN'S CAUSAL THINKING: FROM MAGIC TO PHYSICAL CAUSALITY

A causal connection between events A and B occurs if A is a necessary and sufficient condition for B to emerge, and precedes B in time. The causal connection can be psychological or physical. Psychological causality occurs when a cause (A) for the event (B) is a subject himself or herself. Within this type of causality further distinctions can be made between psychophysical, magical, artificial and social types of causation. In the case of psychophysical causation a subject's thought causes a motion of his or her body. In the case of magical causation a subject's thought (or symbolic action) causes an event in the physical world. In the case of artificial causation a subject's physical activity causes some changes in the world of nature, directly or 'by association' (i.e. windmills are viewed as creating wind). Finally, if a subject's action (physical or verbal) causes changes in another subject's behaviour, than social causation occurs.

In contrast, physical causality means that causal connection exists between two physical events; it can be further divided in two separate classes: spontaneous physical causality (the event A is 'causa finalis', i.e. it produces an effect B but cannot be viewed as an effect of some other cause), and natural physical causality (the cause A is in its turn an effect of some previous cause, and so on).

One of the earliest and most elaborate theories of the development of causal thinking in children belongs to Piaget (1930, 1986), who distinguished six stages in this development. In the first two stages (from 0 to 3 months of age) the infant is incapable of perceiving his or her universe as something separate from him or her. There are no stable objects or any types of causal relations within this universe. In the third stage of the development of intelligence (3 to 7 months of age) actions appear that can be viewed as the beginning of causal thinking: infants develop some appreciation of the connection that exists between their intentions (efforts) and the movements of their bodies. For instance, when the infant hears the sound of a rattle after accidentally pulling a string, he or she tries to reproduce the effect by repeating the motion of his or her hand alone. This kind of causal perception looks like a magical one, although Piaget often refers to it as to magic-phenomenalistic causality (Piaget, 1930, 1986). Belief in this type of causal relations persists throughout the fourth and fifth stages and gradually gives way to the more 'objective' physical causality. Yet, it is not until the sixth stage (about 2 years of age) that children develop the appreciation of physical causality which takes form of the capacities to (1) reconstruct the cause of an event by just observing the effect of it, and (2) anticipate the effect of a certain cause even if this effect has never been observed before.

However, in their verbal judgements, children of 4 and 5 years of age sometimes retreat to magic-phenomenalistic causality (Piaget, 1930, 1986). For instance, they often reason in a way as if motion of celestial bodies was caused by their own movements, or that certain natural phenomena (like wind or the flow of rivers) are created by human activities. It is only at the age of 7–8 years that children start to give physical causal explanations to natural phenomena.

A specific aspect of children's causal judgements is animism (Piaget, 1930, 1986). At the beginning, children attribute life and consciousness to nearly all inanimate objects, later—to objects which possess the capacity of spontaneous motion (wind, rivers), and at the last stage life is attributed exclusively to people and animals. Characteristically, children are more reluctant to attribute animistic capacities to human artifacts (such as machines) than to natural phenomena (Piaget, 1930).

As can be seen from this sketch, the Piagetian view on the development of causal thinking in children is teleological; the development is portrayed as gradually approaching a certain point, in which children's early forms of causal reasoning (such as magical, animistic, artificial) give way to the almost universal rule of physical causality. No wonder then, that subsequent post-Piagetian research on causal thinking in children was predominantly focused on studying children's judgements of physical causality (for a thorough review of the studies see White, 1995). There is yet a special area of studies which stands apart from this main trend: this is studying children's growing understanding of 'theories of mind' and psychological causality.

As has already been pointed out, a main focus of interest within the 'theory of mind' approach was on how children come to the understanding of causes of other people's behaviour. In contrast to Piaget who stressed children's representation about physical objects' 'behaviour', the advocates of the 'theory of mind' approach went a step further and became interested in children's 'representations about representations'. In a sense, a typical task on false belief (Wimmer &

Perner, 1983) can be viewed as stemming from the Piagetian 'three mountains task' on egocentrism, yet it develops the Piagetian task from a task on the perceptual point of view into a task on metarepresentation of knowledge and thinking. When and how do children start to acknowledge that what causes other people's behaviour depends on the people's situational knowledge, and not on some universal laws of nature? This question opens a new area in children's causal thinking, which is thinking about causes of behaviour in subjects who possess will, beliefs, motivations, drives, attitudes and other subjective states. In predicting how people would behave, children have to take into consideration the existing 'state of events', plus the characters' beliefs (knowledge, feelings, attitudes, memories) about this state of events. In other words, in this area of studies children's knowledge of psychological, rather than physical, causality is in focus.

According to the 'causal attribution theory' (Kelley, 1972), a prerequisite for a capacity to make judgements about people's actions is the distinction between externally and internally motivated actions: the former are based on external control (a threat of punishment or an anticipation of reward), while the latter are driven by internal forces (such as altruism or curiosity). Whenever the external motivation of an individual action is absent, an observer concludes that the individual is driven by internal incentives; if, however, the external motivation is obviously involved, the observer tends to ignore the role of the internal motivation (the so called 'discounting principle'). Children's use of the discounting principle, which is often viewed as an indicator of their ability to distinguish between external and internal motivation, became a focus of some experimental studies.

Thus, Karniol and Ross (1979) presented children of 7–9 years with stories in which a character (a boy) played with a toy either 'just for pleasure' or after having been given the object by his mother and promised a reward for playing with the object. When asked in which case the character 'really liked playing with the toy', first graders judged the character's motivation using the additive principle (the second character liked it more than the first one), while older children used the discounting principle (the first character liked the toy more than the second). These, and other data reported in this study suggested that children as young as 9 years old are capable of distinguishing between external and internal motives. Smith, Gelfand, Hartmann, and Partlow (1979) examined whether 7–8-year-olds can distinguish between these types of motives in their own behaviour. They offered children rewards for performing some tasks. In the course of the performance each child was given an opportunity to share part of his or her reward with another child. Some children were reinforced socially for being or not being helpful (praised or reprimanded—group A), others were reinforced by money (group B), still others received no reinforcement (group C). It was found that, when explaining why they shared their money with other children, children from groups A and C saw the incentive of their prosocial behaviour in internal motivation ('I wanted to help', 'I like helping'), while children from group B preferred to view their prosocial behaviour as determined externally. This shows that the children applied the discounting principle to their own actions.

In an attempt to simplify the methodology of studying causal attribution in children, Kassin and Gibbons (1981) showed 5- and 7-year-old children a cartoon in which two triangles of different colours were moving from the opposite sides towards a house, with one of the triangles being pushed by a square from behind. Children were asked to tell which of the two triangles 'was trying harder' to get to the house. Children of both younger and older groups gave similar answers with 80% of children from both age groups pointing to the object which was moving independently. This made the authors conclude that even 5-year-olds can appreciate spontaneous causality as something which acts 'from inside the object' by refusing to attribute this type of causality to the triangle that was moved by the external force.

A characteristic feature of children's growing understanding of psychological causality is that with age they increasingly attribute this kind of causality to animate objects only, while the attribution of spontaneous causality to inanimate objects is on a decline.

As mentioned earlier, if an object possesses spontaneous causality it means that the object has a source of activity within itself; this capacity is usually identified with life, psyche and consciousness. In contrast to natural physical causality which is always set in an infinite chain of cause–effect relationships, spontaneous physical causality is 'causa finalis' and has an 'agency' acting within itself. In developmental psychology, children's beliefs in spontaneous physical causality are known as beliefs in the 'animism of objects'. The problem targeted in many studies of animistic beliefs was to identify to what kinds of objects and to what extent children of various ages attribute life and consciousness.

In one of the early experimental studies in this area (Raspe, 1924) children of 7 to 11 years of age were asked to explain some unknown psychological phenomena (like the phenomenon of the successive light contrast). While often referring to irrelevant events as the causes of the phenomena, most children did not show any animistic judgements. These results were later confirmed in the study by Huang (1930), who demonstrated various unknown physical phenomena to 4–11-year-old children and found very few animistic, magical or artificial explanations. He interpreted this result as a demonstration of the fact that Piaget had strongly underestimated pre-school children's capacity to judge in natural physical causal terms. Yet, the discrepancy between the data of Huang and those of Piaget could also be explained by the fact that the phenomena Huang demonstrated were within the limits of the children's everyday experience, whereas Piaget asked his subjects questions about natural phenomena which go far beyond those limits. This explanation received support in subsequent experiments (Venger, 1958; Zaporojetz & Lukov, 1941).

Other authors employed Piaget's questionnaire to investigate children's developing ideas about animate and inanimate objects. Thus, Laurendeau and Pinard (1962), using a questionnaire based on Piagetian methodology in their study, confirmed the data earlier reported by Piaget. They found that children who were at zero stage attributed life and consciousness to all kinds of objects, including inanimate and immobile ones, children at the first stage attributed life to moving objects only, and it was not until children reached stage three that they became able to identify life exclusively with plants and animals.

In a modified Piagetian interview, Schwartz (1980) read sentences with anomalous structure (in which nouns that usually refer to animate objects were applied to inanimate objects) to children of 4 to 9 years of age. The children were also tested by the above mentioned Laurendeau and Pinard's questionnaire. It was found that children who were at zero level on this questionnaire frequently ignored the anomalies in sentence structure, whereas children at stage three made more corrective remarks than did children of lower stages. The data showed that there was a link between children's understanding of spontaneous causality and their sensitivity towards the correct usage of animistic nouns in speech.

Some scholars have tried to explain the contradictions that exist between various studies about 'animistic attitudes' in children by differences in methodologies applied. They argue that if a clinical interview method is applied in which children are asked to give physical explanations of various natural phenomena, children of 4–5 years of age usually show a high proportion of animistic answers; however, they are more reluctant to judge in the animistic way if given tests on non-verbal classification (Beveridge & Davis, 1983; Hagleitner, 1983; Williamson, Kelley, & Waters, 1982).

In a study by Bullock (1985) 3-year-old children performed poorly on the test on non-verbal classification between pictures of animate and inanimate objects. However, when children were shown cartoons in which animate and inanimate objects were pictured as being in motion, 69% of 3-year-old children proved to be capable of correctly attributing life to the appropriate objects. This suggests that 3-year-old children's failure to distinguish between living and non-living objects, shown in some studies, could indeed be explained by the inadequacy of methodologies employed.

Of special interest there are the studies which employed behavioural, rather than verbal, indices of children's capacity to discriminate between living and non-living objects. In the study by Golinkoff, Barding, Carlson, and Sexton (1984), children of 11, 17 and 23 months of age observed three types of events: (1) events that were initiated by children's mothers (i.e. a mother manipulating some toys in front of the child), (2) those initiated by a strange adult (i.e. the experimenter switched on a toy car), and (3) events which appeared to be initiated spontaneously (i.e. a toy chicken suddenly sets into motion). It turned out that, in order to make the event recur, 11-month-old infants relied on their body movements, thus showing behaviour typical for children in Piaget's stage four of sensorimotor development, 17-month-old infants addressed their mothers for help in all three situations, and only 2-year-old children acted appropriately in the circumstances—i.e. asked for their mother's help in situations (1) and (2), but acted on the object independently in (3). This suggests that at the age of 2 years children are capable of distinguishing between animate and inanimate self-propelled objects and understanding that some events can be caused spontaneously without people having a role in this. Characteristically, it is at this age that children become aware of the fact that some objects are not 'self-propelled': thus, in Golinkoff et al.'s (1984) study most 2-year-olds were surprised when shown a chair which suddenly started moving without an obvious external cause. All this brings about considerable corrections to the traditional claim that young children tend to view physical objects in animistic terms.

SCIENTIFIC AND NON-SCIENTIFIC MODES OF THINKING IN A DEVELOPMENTAL PERSPECTIVE

Although the studies reviewed made substantial corrections to the Piagetian picture of the development of causal thinking in children, most of them conform to the teleological model of this development proposed by Piaget. This model suggests that during the development of causal thinking in children their initial animistic view of physical objects changes and physical objects are gradually freed from any sort of spontaneity; this creates in children the notion of the so-called 'physical world', or 'the world of nature'. This also means that an adult person regards physical causality (with all the implications that this involves) as the only one possible in the world of natural objects, while other types of causal thinking (like psychological, magical, or spontaneous-physical causality) are viewed as existing only in the area of dreams and fairy tales. It is quite obvious that in this model the development of an individual mind mirrors the historic development of causal beliefs, according to which the onset of scientific thinking in technologically advanced societies exterminates the alternative ways of thinking, forcing them to search for an exile in such areas as fine arts, superstitions and religious practices.

However, this model (which will be referred to as the 'replacement model') leaves unexplained some facts of ordinary life, as well as some data reported in psychological research. In everyday life we constantly observe all sorts of superstitions and widely spread beliefs in various mysterious phenomena which escape scientific explanations (Jahoda, 1969). In psychological studies, it was shown that contemporary pre-school children endow fairy tale characters (like monsters or witches) with special capacities, and they are fearful of monsters despite the fact that their existence is openly denied (see Harris et al., 1991; Jersild, 1943). Johnson and Harris (1994) demonstrated that 3–5-year-old children can distinguish magical transformations of objects from ordinary ones, yet they show considerable credulity towards magic in their actions. Similar data were reported by

Rosengren, Kalish, Hickling, and Gelman (1994) and Rosengren and Hickling (1994), who showed that many 4-year-old children view magic as a plausible explanation for a certain kind of event. Even adults proved to be prepared to follow the rules of contagious and sympathetic magic in making their emotional preferences. Thus, Rozin, Millman, and Nemeroff (1986) showed that adult subjects avoided drinks that have briefly contacted a sterilised, dead cockroach, and rejected acceptable foods (e.g. fudge) shaped into a form of a disgusting object (dog faeces). The authors interpreted these and similar data as the proof that the laws of contagion (once in contact, always in contact), and similarity (the image equals the object), which underlie operation of magical beliefs in traditional cultures (Frazer, 1922; Mauss, 1972) still operate in the minds of contemporary individuals. It was also shown that adults, as well as children, make errors of overattribution of certain animate properties to inappropriate objects (Inagaki & Sugiyama, 1988), and quite often personalise complex devices like computers (Scheibe & Erwin, 1979). In this context, it has been even argued that it is useless to view the issue of attributing human agency to non-human entities as a problem of ontology; rather it should be viewed as a matter of social conventions and descriptive practices (Edwards, 1994).

All this makes it reasonable to assume that animism and magical thinking do not disappear from the mind of an individual in the course of intellectual development; rather, the modes of causal thinking which are alternative to scientific, retain their significance in the minds of older children and adults but are referred to only in special circumstances, in which a scientific explanation is impossible or difficult to offer. The questions which arise in connection with this assumption (that will be referred to as the 'coexistence model' of development of the mind) are as follows (1) what kind of situations elicit non-scientific explanations in children of advanced ages and adults?; (2) are these explanations strong enough to affect subjects' actions, and not their verbal judgements only?; and (3) in what way do non-scientific explanations coexist peacefully with scientific ones in the mind of an individual? In order to examine these questions, a series of experiments has been undertaken.

CHILDREN'S PERCEPTION OF UNUSUAL PHENOMENA

To answer the question whether children of advanced ages can still hold beliefs in spontaneous physical causality (which is a characteristic feature of animism) and be engaged in magical thinking, a procedure was developed in which the same phenomenon could be assimilated in two alternative ways: either on the basis of natural causal beliefs or on the basis of beliefs in animism and magic (Subbotsky, 1985). The phenomena in question were presented in two different forms: in the form of a story, and in the form of real physical events. It was assumed that children's preparedness to engage in either scientific or non-scientific thinking would depend on 'the level of functioning'. Specifically, it was predicted that in their verbal judgements children would be more inclined to give scientifically based explanations, thus conforming to expectations which dominate in technologically advanced societies, while in their practical actions they would rely on magical and animistic beliefs, if following these beliefs could bring the children to more attractive outcomes than those the children could hope for if they stuck to scientific explanations.

In the first of these experiments children were asked questions about whether drawings of various objects could turn spontaneously into the objects depicted on them, and then told a story of a girl who had been given as a present a magic box which could transform pictures of objects into real objects once 'magic words' were said. At first the girl did not believe that, but when later she tried the box, she became convinced of its magical properties. Children were asked whether they believed that the events described in the story could happen in real life.

Next, children were put in a real situation described in the story: they were given the wooden box, a few pictures of various objects (like that of a ring, a cigarette lighter, a wasp, etc.) and reminded of the 'magic words'. Each child was then left alone in a room and his or her behaviour was secretly observed.

The results showed that the majority of 4-, 5- and 6-year-old children rejected the idea that magic would work in real life; yet, when put in a real life situation, 80 to 90% of children of all age groups engaged in magical practice and tried to convert pictures of attractive objects into real objects with the help of magic words. In a post-experimental interview the children showed disappointment with the fact that magic had not worked, thus indicating that they really expected their magical actions to work and not just engaged in a pretend activity.

In another experiment children of the same age were told a story about a 'magic table' which could bring to life toy animals made of plasticine. The children were also asked questions about the possibility of an inanimate object coming to life (like "can a rhinoceros made from playdough be transformed into a living one?"). Most 4-year-olds and all 5- and 6-year-olds denied that it was possible in real life, and even after they heard the story about a girl who witnessed this transformation, the majority of children insisted this was "just a fairy tale".

Yet, when confronted with a real life situation (in which a figure of a plasticine lion was put on a specially designed table and started to move in a bizarre way), most of the children of all age groups displayed behaviour showing that they actually believed in the possibility of a spontaneous transformation of an inanimate object into a living one. Some of the children ran away from the room, while others used a 'magic wand' with which they had been provided in advance to be able 'to stop magic working' and to protect themselves against the lion in case it would start coming to life.

These experiments showed that children's beliefs in the possibility of affecting physical objects by means of a 'magic spell' (magical causality) and in the fact that inanimate physical objects could possess mental activity (animism) were still alive and acting over the children's behaviour. These results ran against the common assumption that at the age of six years children's magical and animistic views about ordinary physical objects die out and remain only in children's judgements about phenomena which are beyond the reach of children's practical experience (Piaget, 1986).

However, in these experiments the linear (replacement) model of the development of causal thinking was questioned only with regard to children's actual behaviour in special conditions, in which disregarding magical causality or animistic beliefs meant running the risk of losing some attractive opportunities or putting him/herself in danger. Children's verbal judgements generally conformed to this model, and the majority of children overtly denied that magical causality or the conversion of inanimate objects into living ones were possible. The question arises whether this denial was the result of children's disbelief in magical causality and animism (as the 'replacement model' of development would prompt one to think), or whether it was just an 'artifact' of the way the questions were presented to children. Indeed, when questions about the possibility of magic and animism are asked in an abstract way, through just describing certain imaginative situations to children,[1] the children may be encouraged to perceive those situations as unreal. Besides, when asked directly by an adult experimenter whether they believed in the possibility of magic and animism, children may be reluctant to openly acknowledge those beliefs simply because those beliefs are denied by Western scientific education. This made it necessary to continue the analysis of the conditions under which children and adults are tested on their verbal magical beliefs

CHILDREN'S AND ADULTS' JUDGEMENTS AND BEHAVIOURS IN SCIENTIFIC AND NON-SCIENTIFIC CONTEXTS

In order to examine whether children of advanced ages can still show causal beliefs alternative to scientific ones in their verbal judgements, an experiment was conducted (Subbotsky, 1997).[2]

In Condition 1 of this experiment (disconnected device) a subject was shown a phenomenon which looked like a magical one (a disappearance of a half of a postage stamp in an empty box after an unknown sound and light producing device was switched on for some time). The procedure was as follows. The subject was invited into the experimental room and at a table which had an open wooden box, a device and a postage stamp on it. Next the subject was asked to have a look in the box and see whether it was empty, and then to take the postage stamp, examine it, place it into the box and close the lid.

After this the experimenter switched the device on for 3 seconds, switched it off again and asked the subject whether he or she thought the postage stamp in the box was still the same or if it had changed, and if it did change, then in what way. The subject was then asked to open the lid and remove the stamp from the box. On opening the box the subject found a partially destroyed postage stamp and was asked to explain what had happened. On having the subject's spontaneous explanation the experimenter asked whether he or she thought it was the device that had made part of the object disintegrate.

Next the child was given a new and nice postage stamp and told that it was a present for him or her for the participation. Then the experimenter put the child's present (the postage stamp) into the box, closed the lid and said "Now listen to me carefully. If I don't switch this device on now, I promise that nothing is going to happen to your postage stamp. However, if I do switch the device on, I cannot be sure that nothing would happen to your postage stamp. Now, I am going to do exactly as you tell me: do you want me to switch this device on for some time, or don't you want me to switch it on?". After the answer the experimenter followed the child's instruction, then opened the box and allowed the child to leave with the postage stamp.

Condition 2 (connected device) of this experiment was the same as Condition 1, but the device was now connected to the box by a wire. In this condition the context in which the phenomenon was presented was still a scientific one but it was more likely that subjects would explain the phenomenon in terms of physical causality in this condition than in Condition 1, because the device now had an obvious physical link to the phenomenon.

However, in Condition 3 (parapsychological context), instead of using the physical device after the postage stamp has been placed in a closed box, the experimenter moved her hands towards the box and, keeping them at a distance of 15cm away from each side of the box demonstrated a strong psychic 'effort of will' (trembling hands, a tense facial expression). After the subject's spontaneous explanation was given, the experimenter asked "If I say that I possess a special power that enables me to destroy physical objects at a distance with my sheer 'will power', and I did this now with this postage stamp, would you believe me or not?" Subjects' actual behaviour was tested as in Condition 1.

Another non-scientific causal context was used in Condition 4 (magical context). The procedure was as in Condition 1, however, instead of using the device the experimenter said "Now, I am going to put a magic spell on the box". After this the experimenter closed his/her eyes and whispered some words with his/her lips. The explanation which was suggested to subjects after their spontaneous explanation was asked for was "If I tell you that I can do magic with objects, not just tricks, but real magic and that I destroyed half of this postage stamp by means of magic, would you believe me or not?". The subjects' actual behaviour was tested as in Condition 1. The aims of the experiment were to establish:

(1) to what extent subjects were prepared to invent spontaneously or accept 'ready-made' scientific and non-scientific explanations of the phenomenon

if the phenomenon was accompanied (a) by the action of an unknown physical device under various conditions, (b) by a demonstration of a 'will power',
and (c) by a magic spell;

(2) to what extent these explanations were used by the subjects to guide their
real actions in tackling the non-permanence phenomena.

It can be seen from Table 16.1 that not only did 80 to 100% of 6-year-old
children verbally acknowledge the possibility of magical and parapsychological
causal effects, but the majority of 9-year-olds (i.e. the children who were at the
stage of concrete operations by Piaget) did so as well. As for the children's
actual behaviour, the data showed no differences across conditions between
judgements and behaviours in 6-year-old children. However, 9-year-old children
showed credulity towards the effect of the device (but not towards the effect of
parapsychological or magical manipulations) in their actions to a lesser extent
than in their judgements (one tailed z-test for Condition 1, $z = 2.18$, $P < .05$, and
for Condition 2, $z = 2.12$, $P = .05$). (See Glass & Stanley, 1970.) Contrary to the
expectation which would follow from the linear model (i.e. that children's
verbal credulity towards physical causal explanations increases with age, while
their credulity towards non-scientific causal explanations decreases), the results
showed a decrease in 9-year-old children's credulity towards physical effect if
compared to the one shown by 6-year-old children. This 'nonlinear' pattern of
results finds further support in the fact that 9-year-old children were significantly
more willing to allow the experimenter to reproduce the manipulation over their
valuable object in Conditions 1 and 2 (and, therefore, showed a lesser degree of
credulity towards the effect of the device) than were 6-year-old children. This
age-related decrease in children's credulity towards the experimenter's manipulation did not happen with regard to non-scientific causal explanations. More
than that, 9-year-old children (but not 6-year-olds) prohibited the experimenter's
manipulations in Condition 4 (magic) significantly more often than in Condition
2 (connected device) ($z = 2.13$, $P < .05$), thus revealing in their actions stronger

TABLE 16.1

Percentages of subjects who agreed that the phenomenon had been caused
by the experimenter's manipulation (verbal) and asked the experimenter
not to reproduce (actual) the manipulation

Age	Condition 1 Disconnected		Condition 2 Connected		Condition 3 Will power effect		Condition 4 Magic	
	Verb.	Act.	Verb.	Act.	Verb.	Act.	Verb.	Act.
6	87	81	81	87	93	75	100	87
9	81	43	75	31	56	56	75	68

Sixteen subjects in each age group.
Verb., verbal; Act., actual.

credulity towards the effect of magic than towards the effect of the connected device.

Summing up the results, it is evident that if questions about physical versus non-physical types of causality are put not about some imaginative situations but about the phenomena that children can observe, children as old as 9 years of age are prepared to accept non-scientific modes of causal explanation to the same extent as scientific ones in their verbal judgements. In their real behaviours, the children proved credulous towards magic even to a greater extent than towards natural physical causal explanations.

But if the belief in magical causality is so strong that it does not disappear from judgements and actions in children as old as 9 years old, then the possibility exists that it can be found even in adults. To explore this possibility, 64 adult subjects, students of Lancaster University, participated in four modified conditions of this experiment, 16 subjects (8 men and 8 women) in each condition.

In Condition 1 (scientific) of this experiment the procedure was generally the same as it was in Condition 2 (connected device) in the experiment with children. However, instead of a postage stamp being half destroyed in the box, subjects observed the phenomenon of a solid plastic card being cut in three places. The second difference was that, instead of rewarding subjects with postage stamps, the experimenter asked them to put their driving licences into the box, close the box and then gave the instruction from which it was clear that the experimenter could not guarantee that the driving licence would remain intact if the experimenter reproduced the manipulation. Condition 2 (parapsychological) of this experiment was the same as in Condition 1, but the accompanying manipulation was an 'effort of will'. The procedure of Condition 3 (magic, low risk) of this experiment also followed that of Condition 1, with the manipulation being 'a magic spell' put on the box.

However, in Condition 4 (magic high risk) of this experiment the cost of disregarding a magical explanation was increased. The procedure generally was the same as in Condition 3, with two exceptions: (1) instead of observing a plastic card being 'miraculously' destroyed in the box, the subjects observed a piece of plastic becoming badly scratched after it had been put in the box; (2) instead of putting into the box their driving licences (which are easily replaceable) the subjects were asked to put their hands in the box. To meet the requirements of the BPS Code of Conduct for Psychologists (1991), the subjects were explicitly warned that they had the right to withdraw from the experiment at any time and did not have to do anything they did not want to, even if asked by the experimenter. This made the subjects feel that if they accepted a certain risk, then they did this voluntarily and not because they were forced to. At the same time, it was clear to the subjects that they could avoid any risk at all if they asked the experimenter not to reproduce his actions; in this case, however, it would be clear that the subjects do believe in the possibility of the experimenter's actions causally affecting their hand. The situation did not involve

TABLE 16.2
Numbers of subjects ($n = 16$) who agreed that the phenomenon had been caused
by the experimenter's manipulation (verbal) and asked the experimenter not to
reproduce the manipulation (actual) in Experiment 2

Condition 1 Device		Condition 2 Will effort		Condition 3 Magic, low risk		Condition 4 Magic, high risk	
Verb.	Act.	Verb.	Act.	Verb.	Act.	Verb.	Act.
9	3	3	1	3	2	3	8

Verb., verbal; Act., actual

deception or misleading of participants, and the subjects were debriefed after
the experiment. All subjects found the risk taken in the experiment mild and
justified for the research purposes. The results of this experiment are shown in
Table 16.2.

As is evident from Table 16.2, half of the subjects revealed verbal credulity
towards the effect of a connected device, yet only a few subjects asked the
experimenter not to reproduce the manipulation with the device. In Conditions 2
and 3 subjects showed low credulity towards the possible effect of 'will power
effort' and 'magic spell'. In Condition 4 subjects' verbal credulity was at the
same low level as in Condition 3, yet the number of subjects who asked the
experimenter not to reproduce the manipulation was significantly larger than in
Condition 3 (magic, low risk) (z-test, two tailed, $z = 2.37$, $P < .05$).

The results show that adult subjects' verbal credulity towards the effect of the
connected physical device is still comparable with that of 6-year-old children
(50% and 81%, respectively), yet adults' verbal credulity towards magic (19%
versus 100%) and to the effort of will (19% versus 93%) was significantly lower
than in 6-year-old children; the results are quite in concordance with the
'replacement model'.

Yet, as far as they concern actual behaviour in the high risk condition, the
experiments with adults undermine the replacement model showing that adults'
beliefs in the possibility of magical causality recover their strength as soon as
the cost of disregarding these beliefs becomes high enough.

CONCLUDING REMARKS

Summing up the data of the studies, it can be seen that children as old as 6 years
of age showed strong beliefs in the effect of a magic spell and in the possibility
of inanimate physical objects coming to life as soon as they were put in the
context in which those beliefs could bring either positive or negative outcomes.
It has to be noted here that these beliefs, which are supposed to have disappeared
in children of this age with regard to sensorimotor objects, were not directly
reinforced in this study (i.e. approved or disapproved of by the experimenter).

Rather, it looked like these beliefs simply 'came up' to the surface and showed themselves in children's behaviours, if not in their verbal judgements.

The results of the subsequent experiments strongly supported the view that children's verbal scepticism towards magic and animism was an artifact of the experimental procedures adopted by many researchers. In these procedures children were asked about the possibility of magic and animism regarding imaginative, rather than everyday, phenomena. In experiments reported in this chapter, both 6- and 9-year-old children showed strong verbal credulity towards the possibility of both scientifically and non-scientifically based explanations if they were confronted with an unusual phenomenon (the partial destruction of a physical object in an empty box). However, in their actual behaviour 9-year-old children demonstrated a significantly stronger belief that a magic spell can destroy the postage stamp than that a connected physical device can. There was no such discrepancy in 6-year-old children, who believed that the effect was produced by the device and by non-scientifically based manipulations ('will power' and 'magic spell') to an equal extent.

This may suggest that older children (at least in their actual behaviour) acquire some scepticism about the possibility of one physical object (a device) affecting another physical object (a postage stamp) which has no physical link to it, which is quite in concordance with the data demonstrating children's growing capacity to apply the 'rule of generative transmission' in their causal judgements (Shultz, Fisher, Pratt, & Rulf, 1986). Curiously, this scepticism does not extent to magic which is still viewed by many 9-year-olds as a real threat to the safety of a valuable object. The result runs against the linear 'replacement model' of the development of causal thinking (Piaget, 1930) according to which early beliefs in magic causality are replaced by natural physical causal thinking in the end of the concrete operational period, and in favour of the 'coexistence model' (Subbotsky, 1992). These data suggest that the development of physical causal thinking and thinking alternative to scientific reasoning (such as magical and animistic thinking) is far from being a simple replacement of the latter forms by a former one.

First of all, as children advance in age, magical and animistic beliefs retain their power in children's judgements about social behaviour, such as their causal attribution of human actions. Second, magical thinking is typical and normal as far as it concerns fairy tales, dreams, art and other unusual realities. Even adults conventionally use animistic language when making causal judgements about objects of art, social relations, animal behaviour and other domains alternative to the domain of physical objects. Third, even physical objects are not completely safe from being attributed magical and animistic properties in the area of everyday reality, provided that such attribution can bring certain benefits to a person who engages in this kind of thinking (Edwards, 1994; Scheibe & Erwin, 1979).

Understanding the development of causal thinking in terms of the 'coexistence model' also has obvious implications for the 'theory of mind' studies. It shows that older children and even adults, under certain circumstances, are prepared to view the human mind as possessing the ability to influence physical objects directly (magical causality); they also view physical objects as capable of manifesting some kind of mental activity (animism). This supports some recent evidence coming from the 'theory of mind' approach. The data showed that the so called 'realistic errors', which are supposed to be typical for children, can also occur in adults (Mitchell et al., 1996). The 'coexistence model' view would encourage further search for similar cases of the recurrence of the 'early theories of mind' (like the lack of understanding of false belief) in adults, as well as looking in the opposite direction and searching for the advanced capacities in children of much earlier ages than those in which finding these capacities is usually expected (like the capacity of young and autistic children to reason from false premises—see Harris & Leevers, Chapter 4, this volume).

In particular, it was suggested within the Theory theory approach that the development of representational thinking goes through stages, from an earlier stage (in 2-year-old children), when children judge about characters' actions on the basis of the characters' desires and perceptions only, to the more advanced stage (in 5-year-old children), when children understand that the characters' actions are mediated by representations (Gopnik & Wellman, 1992). While plenty of empirical evidence exists in favour of this view, there is also evidence that some prototypes of representational thinking can exist at much earlier ages (like the capacity of 18-month-old infants to cope with the classical Piagetian task on invisible object displacement) (Butterworth, 1994). There is also evidence that children of advanced ages and even adults, under certain circumstances, react as if they don't have a representational 'theory of mind' (Mitchell et al., 1996). This would suggest that the development of 'beliefs about beliefs' is not a 'stage by stage' replacement process, but rather involves differentiation and cognitive sophistication of some 'prototheories' about other peoples' minds, which coexist in the minds of infants, as well as adults.

If applied to the development of causal reasoning, this would mean that the relations between scientific and non-scientific causal thinking is a kind of 'competition for dominance', in which one or other side experiences occasional victories or defeats depending on the circumstances. It is true that the belief in physical causality as a universal law of nature is dominant in the verbal judgements of an average Western individual, but this belief is not something which is 'taken for granted'. Indeed, in order to exist in the individual's mind, this belief has to be constantly reinforced and supported by the social environment. The experiments with adults reported in this chapter have shown that as soon as subjects are deprived of such a support (i.e. the experimenter suggests that it is entirely on the subject's responsibility whether to allow or not the experimenter to reproduce his magic spell, with the subject's hand being in the box), they become hesitant and inclined to prohibit the repetition of the magic spell.

The question arises whether this prohibition means that the subjects who made it did indeed retreat to beliefs in magical causality. An alternative explanation may be that they simply thought that, when putting a 'magic spell' on the box, the experimenter was, in fact, performing some trick which could affect their licences or hands even if there was no any obvious physical contact between the experimenter and the box. These contrasting interpretations reflect a real problem of studying magical thinking in individuals living in technologically advanced societies.

Indeed, according to the definition of magical causality given in the beginning of this chapter, this type of causation occurs when an initiator (a cause) of a certain event in the world of inanimate physical objects is the subject's psychological activity (thinking or making certain symbolic actions, like a magic spell). However, in contemporary industrial societies technology has become so advanced that it is possible to create all sorts of imitations and fake phenomena that look like magic yet are based on the work of some physical processes (radio and magnetic waves, optical illusions, etc.). The box that was employed in the experiment described was constructed with the purpose to minimise (if not completely avoid) this 'technological interpretation' of the magical effect demonstrated to subjects. It looked like an ordinary wooden box, with no hidden compartments in it, and the experimenter was at a considerable distance from the box throughout the experiment. So, even if the subjects openly denied that magic was involved in the production of the phenomenon in the 'magic' condition, they were unable to offer any plausible technological (scientific) explanation, which made it more likely that the prohibition of the magic spell was based on the subjects' hidden belief that 'real magic' was still possible.

This 'retreat' of adult subjects to magical thinking, which happens only under special circumstances whenever it concerns conscious actions, occurs with greater ease at the level of subconscious functioning of the mind (see Rozin et al., 1986; Rozin, Markwith, & Ross, 1990). In this case, however, as in similar types of behaviour observed in mental patients, the type of causality involved in subjects' accounts about the events is rather more phenomenalistic than magical. The reason for this conclusion is that, according to the definition of magical thinking, it is based on certain theoretical or mythological traditions, i.e. on a certain 'culture of magic'. Therefore, magical thinking in the proper sense of the word can only be displayed on a conscious level of functioning.

Coming back to the fact that superstitions, astrology and beliefs in various mysterious phenomena are widespread in modern Western societies, it can be suggested that this fact has its roots in the nature of the human mind, rather than in the 'naivete' or lack of education in certain individuals. It is under circumstances that are similar to those employed in the experiment described (i.e. lack of the 'social backup' and the presence of a certain risk) that observations of various mysterious phenomena (like ghosts or flying saucers) occur in everyday life, and it is these circumstances which enhance non-scientific thinking. As a distinguished Russian scientist said once in a broadcast interview, "I am 70 years old and—t'fu-t'fu-t'fu—still enjoying good health". ('T'fu-t'fu-t'fu'— spitting three times over your shoulder—is a popular Russian superstition, an equivalent of crossing your fingers.)

NOTES

1. This was exactly the way Piaget (and most post-Piagetian researchers) used to study children's magical and animistic beliefs.
2. This experiment was performed by Joy Cameron in her BSc research project (Cameron, 1996).

ACKNOWLEDGMENTS

The author thanks Joy Cameron for collecting and analysing part of the data reported in this study, and Charlie Lewis, Peter Mitchell and Kevin Riggs for their careful reading of the manuscript and valuable suggestions.

REFERENCES

Beveridge, M., & Davis, M. (1983). A picture-sorting approach to the study of child animism. *Genetic Psychology Monographs, 107,* 211–231.

Bower, T.G.R. (1974). *Development in infancy.* San Francisco: Freeman.

Bullock, M. (1985). Animism in childhood thinking: A new look at an old question. *Developmental Psychology, 21,* 217–225.

Bullock, M., & Gelman, R. (1979). Preschool children's assumptions about cause and effect: Temporal ordering. *Child Development, 50,* 89–96.

Butterworth, G. (1994). Theory of mind and the facts of embodiment. In C. Lewis & P. Mitchell (Eds.), *Children's early understanding of mind. Origins and development* (pp. 115–132). Hove, UK: Lawrence Erlbaum Associates Ltd.

Cameron, J. (1996). *Interpreting unusual phenomena. Judgements and behaviours regarding nonpermanence phenomena presented in scientific and nonscientific contexts in children.* BSc research project, Lancaster University.

Edwards, D. (1994). Imitation and artifice in apes, humans, and machines. *American Behavioral Scientist, 37,* 754–771.

Frazer, J.G. (1922). *The golden bough. A study in magic and religion* (3rd ed.). London: Macmillan & Co. Ltd.

Gelman, R., & Baillargeon, R. (1983). A review of some Piagetian concepts. In J.H. Flavell & E.M. Markman (Eds.), *Handbook of child psychology,* (Vol. III, pp. 166–230). New York: John Wiley, & Sons.

Glass, G.K., & Stanley, J.C. (1970). *Statistical methods in education and psychology.* Englewood Cliffs, New Jersey: Prentice Hall.

Golinkoff, R.M., Barding, C.G., Carlson, V., & Sexton, M.E. (1984). The infant's perception of causal events: the distinction between animate and inanimate objects. In L.P. Lipsitt & C. Rovee-Collier (Eds.), *Advances in infancy research,* (Vol. 3, pp. 145–165). Norwood, NY: Ablex Publishing Corporation.

Gopnik, A., & Astington, J.W. (1988). Children's understanding of representational change and its relation to the understanding of false-belief and the appearance-reality distinction. *Child Development, 62,* 98–110.

Gopnik, A., & Wellman, H.M. (1992). Why the child's theory of mind really is a theory. *Mind and Language, 7*, 145–171.

Hagleitner, L. (1983). Der sogenannte Animismus beim Kind. *Praxis & Kinderpsychologie, 32*, 261–266.

Harris, P.L., Brown, E., Marriott, C., Whittall, S., & Harmer, S. (1991). Monsters, ghosts and witches: Testing the limits of the fantasy-reality distinction in young children. *British Journal of Developmental Psychology, 9*, 105–123.

Huang, I. (1930). Children's explanations of strange phenomena. *Psychologische Forschung, 14*, 63–183.

Inagaki, K., & Sugiyama, K. (1988). Attributing human characteristics: Developmental changes in over- and underattribution. *Cognitive Development, 3*, 55–70.

Jahoda, G. (1969). *The psychology of superstition.* London: Penguin.

Jersild, A.T. (1943). Studies of childrens' fears. In R.G. Barker, J.S. Kounin, & H.F. Wright (Eds.), *Child behavior and development.* New York: McGraw Hill.

Johnson, C., & Harris, P.L. (1994). Magic: Special but not excluded. *British Journal of Developmental Psychology, 12*, 35–52.

Kaku, M. (1994). *Hyperspace. A scientific odyssey through parallel universes, time warps and the tenth dimension.* Oxford: Oxford University Press.

Karniol, R., & Ross, M. (1979). Children's use of a causal attribution schema and the inference of manipulative intentions. *Child Development, 50*, 463–468.

Kassin, S.M., & Gibbons, F.X. (1981). Children's use of the discounting principle in their perceptions of exertion. *Child Development, 52*, 741–744.

Kelley, H.H. (1972). Causal schemata and the attribution process. In E.E. Jones, D.E. Kanouse, H.H. Kelley, R.E. Nisbett, S. Valins, & B. Weiner (Eds.), *Attribution: Perceiving the causes of behavior.* Morristown, NJ: General Learning Press.

Laurendeau, M., & Pinard, A. (1962). *Causal thinking in the child.* Montreal: International University Press.

Lehmann, A.C., & Mayers, J.E. (1985). *Magic, witchcraft, and religion.* Palo Alto: Mayfield Publishing Company.

Lewis, C., & Mitchell, P. (1994). *Children's early understanding of mind. Origins and development.* Hove, UK: Lawrence Erlbaum Associates Ltd.

Mauss, M. (1972). *A general theory of magic.* New York: W.W. Norton.

Mitchell, P., Robinson, E.J., Isaacs, J.E., & Nye, R.M. (1996). Contamination in reasoning about false belief: An instance of realist bias in adults but not children. *Cognition, 59*, 1–26.

Perner, J. (1991). *Understanding the representational mind.* Cambridge, MA: MIT Press.

Piaget, J. (1930). *The child's conception of physical causality.* London: Routledge & Kegan Paul.

Piaget, J. (1986). *The construction of reality in the child.* New York: Ballantine Books.

Raspe, C. (1924). Kindliche Selbstbeobachtung und Theorienbildung. *Zeitschrift für Angewandte Psychologie, 23*, 302–328.

Rosengren, K.S., & Hickling, A.K. (1994). Seeing is believing: Children's explanations of commonplace, magical, and extraordinary transformations. *Child Development, 65*, 1605–1626.

Rosengren, K.S., Kalish, E.W., Hickling, A.K., & Gelman, S.A. (1994). Explaining the relations between preschool children's magical beliefs and causal thinking. *British Journal of Developmental Psychology, 12*, 69–82.

Rozin, P., Markwith, M., & Ross, B. (1990). The sympathetic magical law of similarity, nominal realism, and neglect of negatives in response to negative labels. *Psychological Science, 1*, 383–384.

Rozin, P., Millman, L., & Nemeroff, C. (1986). Operation of laws of sympathetic magic in disgust and other domains. *Journal of Personality and Social Psychology, 50*, 703–712.

Rucker, R. (1984). *The fourth dimension.* Boston: Houghton Mifflin.

Schwartz, R.G. (1980). Presuppositions and children's metalinguistic judgments: concepts of life and the awareness of animacy restrictions. *Child Development, 51*, 364–371.

Sheaffer, R. (1986). *The UFO verdict: Examining the evidence*. Buffalo, NY: Prometheus.

Scheibe, K.E., & Erwin, M. (1979). The computer as alter. *Journal of Social Psychology*, *108*, 103–109.

Schultz, T.R., Fisher, G.W., Pratt, C.C., & Rulf, S. (1986). Selection of causal rules. *Child Development*, *57*, 143–152.

Smith, C.L., Gelfand, D.M., Hartmann, D.P., & Partlow, M.E. (1979). Children's causal attributions regarding help giving. *Child Development*, *50*, 203–210.

Springer, K., & Keil, E.C. (1991). Early differentiation of causal mechanisms appropriate to biological and nonbiological kinds. *Child Development*, *62*, 4, 767–781.

Subbotsky, E.V. (1985). Preschool children's perception of unusual phenomena. *Soviet Psychology*, *23*, 91–114.

Subbotsky, E.V. (1992). *Foundations of the mind. Children's understanding of reality*, New York: Harvester.

Subbotsky, E.V. (1997). Causal judgements and behaviours by children and adults in scientific and nonscientific contexts (submitted).

Venger, A.A. (1958). Razvitije ponimanija prichinnosti u detej doshkol'nogo vozrasta (The development of the understanding of causality in preschool-age children). *Voprosy Psikhologii*, *2*.

White, P.A. (1995). *The understanding of causation and the production of action. From infancy to adulthood*. Hove, UK: Lawrence Erlbaum Associates Ltd.

Williamson, P.A., Kelley, M.F., & Waters, B. (1982). Animistic thought in young children: effects of probing. *Perceptual and Motor Skills*, *54*, 463–466.

Wimmer, H., & Perner, J. (1983). Beliefs about beliefs: Representation and constraining function of wrong beliefs in young children's understanding of deception. *Cognition*, *13*, 103–128.

Zaporojetz, A.V., & Lukov, F.L. (1941). Pro rozvitok mirkuvannija u ditiny molodshego viku (On the development of thinking in a young child). *Scientific Reports of Charkov's Pedagogical Institute*, *5*.

CHAPTER SEVENTEEN

Communication and representation: Why mentalistic reasoning is a lifelong endeavour

Norman H. Freeman
Department of Psychology, University of Bristol, UK

INTRODUCTION

The premise underlying the argument in this chapter is that our acquisition of reasoning about the relation of mind to reality is a special case of the fact that we are a species that is innately impelled to invest heavily in symbolic communication. The need to be explicit about assumptions concerning communication has been made clear in the work of some researchers in the acquisition of reasoning about the mind (Dunn, 1994; Hobson, 1993; Shatz, 1994). Accounts of conceptual change have to explain the learnability problem of reasoning about communicable mental realities. In this chapter, three points are put together to provide a perspective on the learnability problem.

One point is that research in the domain is not well served by theoretically divorcing a concept of representation from a concept of communication. I shall use an analysis of one of the simplest standard cases of communication failure, where someone representationally misleads an agent by being economical with the truth, to show that there are six communicative assumptions to be checked by the agent. That is a large number of assumptions; so a second point is that the demands of coordinating them explains something about the learnability problem. Mentalistic reasoning is a life-span task, in which it is possible for adolescents and adults, as well as young children, to lapse into naïve realism whereby what is taken to be external reality is used to simplify mentalistic reasoning. The third point is that communication is not confined to exchanging utterances or gestures; instead there is a variety of cultural devices whereby we try to bridge the gap between minds and between physical and mental reality. For example, photographs can make the look of things portable, communicating to a viewer how the agent felt about a scene, or what she remembers about it, maybe even inviting the viewer to compare her memory of the scene with that of the agent. All such public symbolic devices are treated as inter-mental realities enabling protagonists to stage-manage a meeting of minds. It is worth noting that such a view has long formed a staple of the Vygotskyan tradition, a tradition that has been canvassed by Astington (1995) as a source of formulations for setting reasoning about the mind in communicative context. We shall, however, not use Vygotskyan terminology in this chapter, because there are more cogent formulations from the literature on representation and intentionality.

In sum, the argument will be that communicative constraints determine both the forms of mentalistic reasoning we develop and the artefacts we generate as representational mediators to communicate between minds. There is a lifelong learnability problem because interpretation of others' communications is an open-ended enterprise. There is, in principle, no specifiable point at which it is possible to say that someone has become a completely skilled interpreter of mental reality (any more than there is a point at which photography can be packed in because the ultimate visual truth has been definitively revealed). This chapter, then, is devoted to exploring something of the life-span implication of mentalistic reasoning being both communicatively constrained and communicatively generative. Any account of children's mentalistic reasoning that is divorced from communicative theory is bound to have only a partial grip on issues in lifespan development of symbolic interpretation.

VARIETIES OF REPRESENTATIONAL INTEREST

The issue of life-span representational development needs a brief general note. It has been reported that whilst 8-year-olds understand that pretenders bear in mind a representation of a pretence when they *decide* to pretend, many of the children do not extend that insight to the question of what is in the pretender's mind *during* a pretend episode (see Lillard, 1996). Why should an initial insight break down when it has to be extended a bit? Fabricius and Imbens-Bailey (Chapter 13, this volume) discuss the phenomenon amongst others, and evaluate the significance of errors and reorganisations of mentalistic concepts up to age 8 years or so. They conclude that representational reasoning is not acquired rather suddenly in or just after the pre-school years, but involves prolonged learning. Their chapter thus invites researchers to consider reformulating the learnability issue of representational reasoning. The representational approach to the learnability problem is to assume that mental representations serve the requisite mediating functions between mind and reality. The theorist's task is to understand how it is possible for mental symbols to be grounded in reality (see Hobson, Chapter 2, this volume). The child's task is to understand the nature of those mental representational mediators. That suggests that the learnability problem centres on the difficulty of understanding how representations work. Mentalistic reasoning is hard-won through the interpretation of people's actions and utterances in the contexts of occurrence. We learn to be on the lookout for what people are trying to do, and what meanings they try to convey through their utterances. We learn to look for the manifestations of mind in all forms of human activity, paying special attention to any communicative acts, whether those be utterances or simply someone waving to attract our attention. It is comprehensible that theory of mind research with young children has focused almost exclusively on ephemera, on what people say and do on the spot. But such a focus has its limitation.

The problem with concentrating on ephemera in context, is that with development we come increasingly to spend our time interpreting the marks of human mentality outside their contexts of initial occurrence. Once children learn to read, they may immerse themselves in storybooks, thus acquiring narrative insight into the complexities of human beings and their relations to possible scenarios. Some children become deeply interested in maps as models of regions and the routes that people may choose for one purpose or another. Other children become involved in investigating pictorial representations in terms of whether one person can ever really show another what she sees. Karmiloff-Smith (1992) summed up the distinctively human competence to be theorised: "Many species generate internal representations, but there is something about the architecture of the human mind that enables children and adults also to produce external notations, that is to use cultural tools for leaving an intentional trace of their communicative and cognitive acts" (Karmiloff-Smith, 1992, p. 139). Research on children's reasoning about the mind has to encompass all manifestations of the functional 'architecture of the human mind'. It is, of course, possible to do valuable research on theory of mind without considering external notations, particularly for the pre-school period where few systems of notation have been systematically encountered. Yet to perpetuate such an emphasis into older ages would yield a lopsided account of development, somewhat as if a text on psycholinguistics were to pretend that development in our society were not bound up with reading and writing as well as speaking and hearing.

The term 'external notations' covers drawing, sculpting, map-making, writing, number-symbolising etc. Notations are organised into representational systems, which can be characterised, as stated by Dretske (1988, p. 52), as systems "whose function it is to indicate how things stand with respect to some other object, condition, or magnitude". We do not confine our mentalistic competence to making direct judgements on people's invisible minds; we make also mentalistic judgements on the external notations that are physical mediators between mental reality and some other object, condition, or magnitude. If we can understand people, we can understand that they produce artefacts non-arbitrarily, to fit their conception of other people's minds and dispositions. In sum, our mentalistic reasoning becomes highly *diversified* as we master notational systems. The question then is what can be learned about children's mentalistic reasoning through studying symbolic diversification?

One answer is that nothing can be learned. I think that that is wrong. Perner (1991) took pains to relate abstract statements about representation to concrete instances of picturing and modelling, as well as of speaking. We shall later examine one of the classic examples he used, and show that there is another way of putting the example to use in exposing a complexity in children's reasoning that common language obscures. The deeper issue is that the kind of reasoning we develop about agents is naturally connected to reasoning about the physical objects that agents produce for communicative purposes. Why that should be so is not hard to explain. Let us concentrate on picturing. As Lopes (1997, p. 144) stated, pictures can be termed "visual prostheses; they extend the informational system by gathering, storing, and transmitting visual information about their subjects". One cannot understand any prosthesis if one considers it in isolation from the minds of agents who produce and use it, and conversely, we cannot understand human actions if we exclude the tools that humans use from their system of activity (Nunes, 1997). We learn about people and their variety of communicative prostheses together. I suggest that drawing the domain of men- talistic reasoning so narrowly so as to exclude representational prostheses misses not only a common source whence children practice mentalistic reasoning but also misses an opportunity to deploy models of communication to the benefit of explaining the possibility of life-span development.

PROSTHETIC REPRESENTATIONAL REASONING

In the course of learning to use representational pictures as a notational tool, children encounter the learnability problems that are involved in reasoning dir- ectly about the minds of the makers and users of the tool. Just as people have intentional states, such as beliefs and memories, states defined by the fact that they are directed towards things other than themselves, so people make artefacts that are instruments of intentionality. Someone who carries a political pamphlet and a filofax in her handbag is carrying mediators of beliefs and memory. We might always need to be taught how a particular type of artefact fits particular social purposes, but we do not doubt the generality of the fit between minds and their instruments. Thus, pre-school children are often taught that family snapshots (Edwards & Middleton, 1988, p. 9) are "a direct route between past and present, a mediator of memory". The children readily seem to accept that photographs enable viewers to re-represent memories and beliefs about states of affairs. Emotions too are invested in snapshots. Wolf (1990, p. 189) reported a young 3-year-old viewing a weekend snapshot, referring to the people in it, including himself, by their proper names, then shifting to the pronoun 'I' in commenting on his emotions at that time, thus "constructing the continuity between his present and his weekend experiential selves". Exactly how pre-school children initially come to understand how a photograph enables representation to be done is still a tantalising question (see Perner, 1991). Understanding cameras as the means of production is extremely hard: Wellman and Hickling (1994) reported that a quarter of their 10-year-olds were still talking of cameras as though they had minds of their own (e.g. "The camera gets the idea of it and draws the picture" from one child, details of age not specified in the report). Maybe it takes a large step from such a conception to realising that the agency is invested by people in using a camera.

One way of phrasing the learnability issue is to say that it is necessary to show what aspects of mentalistic reasoning are easy to acquire and what aspects pose problems that are grave enough to take years in their acquisition. The first two monographs on mentalistic reasoning summed up a trend towards giving two perspectives; and research since then has often endeavoured either to reconcile them, to pit them against one another, or to challenge restrictions that the answers impose. Let us briefly note just the main focus of the two perspectives, which will shortly be shown to be indissolubly linked.

One perspective respects domain specificity. Roughly, the content of *what* is being thought about by the child is bound up with *how* thinking is organised. It was natural for researchers to identify the reasoning that may be peculiar to the mentalistic domain. If the domain demanded that the child make an ontological commitment to the reality of beliefs, desires and intentions, then research did well to focus on the peculiar demands of combining them into belief-desire reasoning. Wellman (1990) accurately represented the strength of that trend, along with building in some assumptions about the learnability of particular aspects of the reasoning. He focused on the problem of diversity. The particular aspect that was taken as central was the diversity of concepts that have to be integrated in mentalistic reasoning. The child has to learn how to take agents' beliefs, desires, emotions and intentions into account in an appropriate way in particular contexts. Those four categories cover diverse manifestations of mind.

The other perspective is to start with some concept of 'representation' as a way of getting at the learnability problem. Roughly, the greater the representational complexity of an acquisition is, the later the target acquisition tends to appear. If the target acquisition appears unpredictably early, one testable supposition is that children are pre-adapted by some constraint that had channelled them in the right direction. Principles of representation provide a potential metric for ordering developmental advances in grasping the contents of reasoning. Perner (1991) represented the strength of that trend very well. No-one maintains that representational complexity is the sole determinant of learnability; but it certainly puts a powerful theoretical tool into a researcher's hands. Perner (1991) argued that reasoning about the mind involves learning to respect the operation of the principles of representation. Those principles set constraints on epistemic states: thus, there are both salient and subtle principled distinctions between pretending, wishing, hoping, remembering, recognising, guessing, or knowing that something is the case. Some of the distinctions take years for a child to sort out (an interesting representational error in adults has been documented by Mitchell, Robinson, Isaacs, & Nye, 1996).

Each perspective leads to a researcher grappling with problems of the other: the perspectives are just different ways of grasping the ends of the same stick. Children are held to acquire a theory *of* mind. If the mind is the target, the theory has to be mentalistic; and if the mind is structured by mental representations, the theory has to be representational. The close-knit package is particularly satisfying. What theoretical reconstruction is necessary to assess patterns of reasoning and learnability for non-natural kinds? It is remarkable that both of the perspectives were anticipated by one philosopher some years before theory of mind research began in psychology. Goodman (1976) tried to reconcile statements on mentalistic diversity with an analysis of representation. Let us defer considering what ideas Goodman formulated, and ask what forced him to theorise the relations between diversity and representation. Goodman was taking a mentalistic approach to explaining how pictures can determine viewers' interpretations. As stated by Wollheim (1993, p. 134), any focus on interpretation is ". . . an appropriate response to the central fact about art: that it is an intentional manifestation of mind". The term 'intentional' is crucial. Consider the informal opening statement of Searle (1983, p. 1): "Intentionality is that property of many mental states and events by which they are directed at or about or of objects and states of affairs in the world". A fear may be a fear of spiders, or about spiders, or focused towards spiders. That is all satisfactorily directed. But as a communicative artefact, a representational picture *of* Charles I *as* Caesar may simultaneously be a portrait *of* Charles, be *about* the artist's conception of kingship, and be *directed towards* viewers whom the artist hopes to influence. That diversity may be termed *intentional dispersion*. The claim in this chapter is that a capacity to integrate intentional dispersion is a central topic for theory of mind. The method used to demonstrate that in the next section is to take a key formulation from Goodman that was appropriately used by Perner (1991) to make a point about a principle of representation, and to show that the case *necessarily* involves a formulation of intentional dispersion.

The above example about a portrayal of kingship might appear to be peculiar to representational pictures, too complex to serve as a pointer to theory, and irrelevant to any model of how children reason about the mind. It is none of those. It is not peculiar to pictures. We look for the manifestations of mind in all types of artefact whose significance lies in the information they transfer between agents. We also look for intentional diversity in what people say and do, as when you find out later that someone who had said something flattering to you had done so in a loud voice that was simultaneously directed to her gang as an expressive signal that she had fulfilled her briefing to be sarcastic. That is a mundane type of playground experience. Such events can make children reflect on states of mind, on communication, and on devices that agents use to regulate relations between mind and reality (see Waksler, 1996, for autobiographical memories of coping with a variety of tribulations and puzzles). The kingship example is not too complex to serve as a guide to theory about children. It was chosen to be decomposable into aspects that one can test children on. For example, it is an empirical question when children learn (1) the most profound principle of representation that representation is necessarily aspectual (which is why misrepresentation is possible); (2) a single picture may have multiple interpretations; and (3) that interpretations are non-arbitrarily related to the varying mind-set of different viewers. Let us take the aspectual problem. In a standard unexpected-change test for misrepresentation, a protagonist mentally (mis)represents an object that is at location B under the aspect of it being at location A. In the pictorial analogue of Zaitchik (1990) a photograph of the object shows the object as it was at A. Pre-schoolers err on both inferring where the protagonist thinks the object is and where the photograph shows it as being. But they generally solve the pictorial problem earlier (Leslie & Thaiss, 1992). However, when children are tested on the insight that a single picture may have multiple interpretations, and on relating interpretation to mind-set, they struggle with the problem as they do with the problem of false belief (see Gopnik & Astington, 1988).

We evaluate a photograph on display by its communicative clarity, and such a judgement involves making assumptions about the social significance of the artefact. You would miss the point about the photographs of the members of staff in the reception area if you thought that they were there to no purpose, or for the purpose of giving you an aesthetic thrill. You assume that one function of the photographs is to communicate how their sitters might look to other people who want to identify them. It is a striking fact that we keep trying to talk as though artefacts actually did the work that people do: we speak of a picture as faithfully representing a scene, for instance. But as Gombrich (1982, p. 172) simply put it: "We represent or describe something to someone". We keep reducing such four-term, agent-scene-picture-agent formulations, to two-term, picture-scene formulations. It is handy shorthand, but it serves to obscure the intentional dispersion that enables us to use shorthand at all. Sometimes we need to reflect on that dispersion. There is just enough empirical evidence to be reviewed in a later section to suggest that young children rely on such shorthand when doing simple pictorial reasoning, and that older people keep lapsing back into shorthand when confronted with difficult pictorial reasoning (Freeman & Parsons, in press). We next conduct a thought-experiment on Goodman's pioneering account, to expose intentional dispersion, imagining someone not just passing a speedy two-term representational judgement, but trying to argue with a picture-producer. Let us concentrate on the concept of representation, because there is always something reassuring about the way that a technical philosophical concept unravels into familiar patterns when one makes a thought experiment of imagining a dialogue.

MENTALISTIC REASONING WITH PICTURES
Truth-testing on the back of Goodman's Horse

Perner (1991, pp. 16–19) argued that a representation should not be thought of as a thing but as a relation that a medium makes possible. What representing relations can be contracted using a pictorial medium? There will be medium-specific constraints on what can be represented, misrepresented, or has to remain non-represented. You cannot represent conditional propositions, for example. There is no way of depicting the immensely useful proposition 'If some men are mortal, Socrates might be mortal on Tuesday'. In fact, only agents make propositions or ask questions; depictions are merely the instrument by which one agent might try to convey information to another agent. In that strict sense, there is no such thing as a 'representational picture', and the term 'representational picture' is indeed shorthand for some impossibly clumsy four-term phrase like 'representing relation contracted between agents about a referent via the pictorial medium'. An immediate prediction may be made. Learners will keep trying to reduce the four-term concept to a two-term concept, so they will err when making propositions about pictures by directly comparing a picture to its referent, forgetting that the picture mediates between the picture-producer and the viewer. Let us go straight to a traditional example that was propounded to lie on the borders of representation, non-representation and misrepresentation.

Goodman (1976, p. 29) wrote: "If I tell you I have a certain black horse, and then I produce a snapshot in which he has come out a light speck in the distance, you can hardly convict me of lying; but you may well feel that I misled you". How would you formulate your complaint? You might focus straight on the production of the snapshot and complain that the camera had been too far from the horse. That is, you start with a two-term formulation, snapshot and horse, and move to a three-term formulation, snapshot, camera, and horse. Maybe you would even expand it a bit if you blamed Goodman for being a poor photographer, thus yielding snapshot, agent-plus-camera, and horse. That gives the rationale for a traditional empirical complaint and its solution in such a situation. But even the expansion obscures *why* you are enabled to suggest an empirical solution. The important fact that has been taken for granted is that the snapshot did not give *you* as viewer a horse-impression. Goodman here talked of the snapshot failing to represent the horse *as* a horse (as did Perner). But that essential re-naming of a function is still only a two-term shorthand between picture and horse. What is interesting about your negotiations with Goodman is the way in which you articulated your demands to bring your recognitional capacities concerning real horses into line with your scrutiny of the photo. You were in accord with the functional analysis of Schier (1986). A marked surface iconifies a referent if and only if (a) the picture triggers a recognition of the referent in (b) a non-privileged viewer who has (c) the disposition to recognise the referent itself. That is the way you do truth-testing about the picture. You may well have been consciously focusing your mind on the distance between camera and horse, but you were actually putting *yourself* centre-stage.

But what enabled you to put yourself centre-stage? It seems to be some conception of how the agent (artist) should have made it possible for you to regulate the relations between your two recognitions. Your disappointment with Goodman may be traced to a feeling that he did indeed mislead you by taking liberties with some sort of artist-viewer 'communicative contract'. His promise to show you a picture of his black horse was *too much* in the sense that it licensed you to fill in the default expectation of seeing a picture that looked horselike. Goodman had simultaneously said *too little* in that he had not explained that you would be seeing a photo taken in his huge paddock that could dwarf a black horse glinting in the sunlight. His utterance had profoundly *underspecified* how the viewer was to view the picture. A traditional formulation is to say that the viewer's response critically depended on the indeterminacy of the artist's caption. At the very least, pictorial naturalism becomes a matter of the relation between viewer and picture in the light of the viewer's attempt at recognition of the artist's beliefs about how a referent's appearance might be displayed. Naturalism, here, rests on the viewer's assumptions about what the artist could and couldn't communicate via the medium as well as assumptions about what the artist wanted and did not want to communicate. Acts of communication are governed by conversational conventions; and it is at that level of convention that iconification is to be judged (Schier, 1986, called it 'Convention C'). The conclusion is that a concept of iconic representation, if it is to be theorised, must be recognised as embedded in a shared human intentionality.

It is no accident that Schier labelled the role of convention 'conversational'. The paragraph above could easily be rewritten as a statement about any problems of meaning-transfer. Here, for instance, is Heal (1978, p. 367) on language: 'When noises have meaning they do not only have distinctive relations with human beings who use them or respond to them but also distinctive connections with some . . . states of affairs . . . in the world'. A meaningful utterance contracts particular relations with speaker, listener and world. It is reassuring that our working of the black horse problem ended up with depiction in an analogous net of two agents, an artefact, and a state of affairs. In sum, your representational theory of pictorial display was a four-term theory encompassing Artist, Viewer, Picture, and World. The discussion has run from a two-term relation, Picture–World, to a four-term network of relations. The four terms actually contract six relations: Artist–World, Artist–Picture, Picture–World, Viewer–World, Viewer–Picture, and Viewer–Artist.

The six-relation net immediately defines a crucial aspect of the learnability problem in acquiring a mentalistic theory of pictures: it is not easy to coordinate six relations. For example, artists have to bear in mind the fact that what they see in their pictures might not be the same as what viewers will see: Golomb (1995) suggested that it is not until the age of seven or so years that children normally conceptualise the viewer–picture relation as entering into the artist–picture relation. The black horse problem is an example of the truth-testing class of pictorial problems, and is actually one of the simplest to be encountered in pictorial reasoning. In addition to the traditional representational problem, there are other problems which define the contents of the domain. Contents will be construed in functional terms, terms that specify what we can do with depiction and what depiction can do for us.

The traditional pictorial functions

It was pointed out above that the net of relations for pictorial representation mapped onto the net for linguistic representation. The traditional pictorial functions also map onto some linguistic functions. The linguistic formulations of Buhler (1934) prefigured the distinctions which Gombrich (1960) brought to the question of what viewers get out of pictures (see Lepsky, 1996). The first of Buhler's functions supports truth-testing: as a 'symbol', a picture serves a representational function. As a 'symptom', a picture serves to preserve something of the desires and intentions of the producer. As a 'signal', a picture elicits particular reactions in a viewer. These functions map onto the standard trio of questions that has dominated theorising pictures: how does it come about that pictures can conserve pictorial representational truth, be expressive of the picture-producer, and strike viewers as paradigmatically beautiful? The black horse problem centres on a question of beliefs, and it is hard to discern how to bring statements about pictorial expressive qualities into the account. Can a picture literally express a producer's pain or serenity? Again one can look to Goodman (1976) for a striking prescience. Goodman argued that the ontological assumption that representation and expression were different kinds of 'things' that had somehow to be welded together to characterise depiction was the wrong place in which to start. Goodman's idea was to start with relations. The initial distinction should be drawn in terms of a contrast in the direction of relation. The picture denotes what it represents, so a picture is of its referent and not vice versa. Goodman argued that the reverse direction applies to expression. That formulation roused resistance at the time, but has since become familiar. Instead of 'direction of denotation' the more usual formulation is 'direction of fit', deployed within the philosophy of mind by Searle (1983) and Dancy (1993). *Believing, seeing* and *remembering* have a mind-to-world direction of fit: a false belief, or a misperception, or a recall-failure, are cases where the mind has failed to fit the world, and you would do well to change your state of mind. *Desiring* and *intending* have a world-to-mind direction of fit: an unfulfilled desire or a thwarted intention are cases where one needs the world to change to fit to oneself. It is rather straightforward to think of artists working along one direction of fit in getting a picture to realise their visual beliefs about a scene in the world, at the same time as trying to express desires by shaping the picture to their will.

In sum, pictures are realisations of belief-desire reasoning and practice, and by that token they are fitting artefacts upon which to exercise belief-desire reasoning. That poses an immense learnability problem, because not only does one have to reckon with six relations in the pictorial net, but with bi-directional relations. The concept of 'direction of fit' gives a way of talking about diverse mental states within the same framework. The net of relations that defines a picture is predicted to constrain the acquisition of a mentalistic theory of pictures for all three traditional contents of the domain. Let us look at some developmental evidence.

ACQUISITION OF AN INTENTIONAL
THEORY OF PICTURES

It is impossible to review all the evidence on children's acquisition of a grasp of how each relation in the intentional net relates to each other. But it is possible to pick out some findings that bear on the most basic conceptions. We begin with the first manifestations of a grasp of the representational potential of the *relation of production* between artist and picture. A picture-producer is an intentional agent. A conception of agency is integral to the development of mentalistic reasoning (Russell, 1996). There are four manifestations of entry into a conception of pictorial representational agency that researchers have noted.

Pre-school children may use a marker as a pretend rabbit, say, and make it hop across the paper, leaving traces that are a *record* of the hopping, rather like footprints in the sand (Freeman, 1993; Gardner & Wolf, 1987). So three things become united in the medium: (1) the activity involved in the relation of production, (2) the referent, which is directly transferred to the medium as (3) the instrument that makes marks.

Children may stipulate in advance what they are going to draw, even though an independent observer could not possibly know what the resulting scribbles represent. Here, pretence is recruited to stand in for a representational function. Pretence has been a key concept in theory of mind research, and serves a proto-representational function in depiction. Pretence might be a royal route into representational depiction for very young children, bypassing some of the key complexities. The natural intentional stance of pretence, with its suspension of truth conditions, enables children to produce scribbles in despite of the recognisability criterion that dogged Goodman's Horse.

Freeman (1980) gave a 2-year-old scribbler incomplete drawings to scribble over on condition that he said what he was going to 'draw' before he started. The resulting scribbles were uninterpretable; but the pen hit at the start precisely where it should to complete the drawing. The child was using his viewer's relation to the picture to organise his relation to the picture as an artist.

Adi-Japha, Levin, and Solomon (1997) elicited many representational interpretations from 2-year-olds by a new technique of pointing to *parts* of a free scribble and asking what that bit was. Smooth lines were largely ineffectual as stimuli, but inflected and broken lines were powerful stimuli. Filming showed how the speed of the child's hand slowed in changing direction on the page according to a rather elegant psychophysical function. The suggestion is that the act of making an inflection in a line involves some investment of attention. Crucially, there was no inflection-advantage when the children were asked about parts of other people's scribbles, or about parts of their own scribbles after a delay. Attention to the act of production itself had primed up a transient willingness to make a representational interpretation.

To sum up, there are indices of 2-year-olds' readiness to engage with a production-centred conception of depiction. Children are constructing some fundamental conceptions. One such conception is that of producing something finished to be looked at, perhaps to be put on display for other viewers. Another conception is that the marks on the paper depict something. A third conception is that one's own actions are crucial in the emerging configuration. This is the beginning of a conception of one's own agency being conserved in the production of meaningful artefacts.

It is less easy to trace what conceptions are acquired early when a child acts as a *viewer of other people's pictures*. The prime question is whether there is a grasp of the picture being an instrument of representation of a referent. It should be easy to track the origins because it seems likely that a capacity to interpret pictures arose in evolution before we did. But it is difficult to ascertain just what non-human animals get out of pictures. A chimpanzee, Vicky, made food-vocalisations when touching a photograph of a bar of chocolate, and would hold photographs of watches to her ear (Hayes & Hayes, 1953). But that might mean that she regarded the photographs as (perhaps disappointing) tokens of the referent types, rather than as representations. A similar worry applies to some behaviours of very young children (Perner, 1991; Woolley & Wellman, 1990). On the other hand, if a depiction is highly recognisable, and non-arbitrarily looks something like the referent, there is no real reason why prepotent responses should be *completely* inhibited. After all, some adults have been known to drool a bit over pictures of food. Three criteria for assessing children's representational comprehension of pictures have been laid out by Nye, Thomas, and Robinson (1995) in a review of the evidence. I shall cast the criteria into the terminology used in the earlier sections of this chapter.

One criterion is that the child should discriminate between visual and non-visual properties of the referent, and understand that non-visual properties cannot be transported from a referent to a viewer via a picture. The outline shape of an ice-cream might be transported, but not the coldness or edibility or taste. Beilin and Pearlman (1991) questioned 3-year-olds about properties, and found intriguing errors. Some errors were resistant to counter-suggestion and deeper post-test questioning, while other errors readily gave way. It is conceivable that a decisive step from realism-correspondence to representation was being struggled with in that age range. Yet we have to be careful about all such data. A picture may be highly *informative* about the coldness, edibility and taste of the referent, and one needs very strict reassurance that no semantic confusion was occurring in the way the child received the adult's questions about how the picture looked, and what it was really. It may be that confusions occur not because the children lack a representational concept of pictures, but because they are still learning some brute facts about the medium. Certainly, increasing experience of medium-specific constraints is a part of learning about medium-specific representation; but at present such research has not yet become analytic enough to license confident performance-competence conclusions. The traditional solution to such a problem is to take such data in conjunction with the following data on confusions about entirely visual properties.

A second criterion for a representational concept is that the visual properties of a picture do not automatically alter if the visual properties of the referent alter, and vice versa, without the intervention of some agent. That is precisely the logic of the unexpected-change false belief test in which an agent's belief about the location of an object does not automatically update if the object moves without the agent acting as viewer and seeing the movement. Even some 4-year-olds claim that a picture will update if the referent does so, and that a changed picture will backdate if their attention is drawn to the unchanged referent (Robinson, Nye, & Thomas, 1994). So the children respond in terms of the direction of fit running from world to picture. That is the correct representational direction. So it seems that even the errors attest to assigning a picture an appropriate status in terms of fit. The error of some children is to make the fit too close. There are two ways of construing the error. One is to focus on the relation of production in the net, and say that the children sometimes fail to take into account that an agent of production is needed to alter the picture if fit is to be maintained. The other construal focuses on the relation of viewer to picture, and say that children sometimes fail to take into account that a picture serves the function for the viewer of being a 'mediator of memory' of how the referent once looked. The suggestions need not be mutually exclusive. The most general formulation is that even 4-year-olds can break down in coordinating different relations in the net. Intentional dispersion over the relations in the net poses a great learnability problem.

Finally, some 4-year-olds make errors when talking about the prime function of depiction, which is to trigger in a viewer the visual appearance of something else that the viewer is capable of recognising (Schier, 1986). Before noting the errors, it is important to remember that adult speech persistently collapses distinctions: we might well refer to a picture of a horse by the shorthand 'horse' when talking about the picture. Similarly, when discussing snapshots as mediators of memory, we might say "look at uncle Abraham there". We do the same with fake models of things: we might well refer to a realistic-looking plastic biscuit as "a biscuit" if there is no real biscuit that it is necessary to disambiguate.

All that is part of the routine of referring expressions in everyday language. It makes it a bit difficult to be sure of the following data. When pre-school children are questioned whether a fake biscuit looks like a biscuit and really is a biscuit, they often make 'appearance-reality' errors, sometimes swinging between appearance and reality as a criterion for answering (see Perner, 1991). One gets analogous errors with pictures, though it is unclear whether the errors are always more strong than with fake objects or less strong (Thomas, Nye, & Robinson, 1994). It is certainly possible to argue the traditional case that the errors show that the children are still acquiring a concept of representation. But for present purposes, the more important point is that our everyday habit of collapsing complexities of the intentional net into simpler referring expressions might be an integral part of the learnability problem with acquiring a mentalistic theory of depiction.

Parsons (1987) argued that a concept of expressivity was much later acquired than a concept of representation of a referent; and that the viewer as an active agent in interpretation of pictorial quality (including beauty) was later still. We would do well here to start with adults' theory, and work back down to children. Parsons' evidence came from semi-structured interview of viewers on their reactions to particular pictures (such as Picasso's *Guernica* and Klee's *Head of a Man*) rather than on their general theory of pictures. It is possible that the respondents became rather trapped by their reactions to the pictures and thus blocked from reflecting deeply on their general conceptions of what is pictorially possible. Still, the data are most interesting. Let us just note two undergraduates' interviews. Dorothy registered that in *Head of a Man*, despite its title, Klee was not investing an unequivocal expressivity in masculinity or femininity, and went on to speculate about whether individual differences in viewers' experience would lead them to focus on the masculinity or the femininity. Dorothy did not assimilate the problem to that of Goodman's Horse, and blame the caption for being misleading. She categorised the interpretative problem along the direction of fit of expressivity, and thought about viewers' uptake. The agency of the viewer was incorporated into Dorothy's theory of depiction. Lewis took a further step by speculating on whether viewers' interpretation of what the artist was trying to say might be radically different from what Klee himself had intended, and ended up by asserting that the viewer's point of view was just as valid as that of the artist. That deep matter of whether an artist and a viewer should be assigned matching status as regards interpretation is a convenient way to start looking at simpler examples of reasoning in children.

We shall consider an extract from a study by Freeman and Sanger (1995), who questioned children, in the absence of pictures, on whether an artist's feelings determine picture-quality, and whether a viewer's feelings determine evaluation of a picture. There was a difference in opinion between 11-year-olds and 14-year-olds about the *artist's* feelings. Of the younger children, 9/12 maintained that the artist's feelings did determine picture-quality, while 9/12 older children maintained the opposite. The explanations were most informative. The younger children treated expressivity as though there were a direct projective link to the picture: a happy artist would produce a happy picture. The relation between artist and picture was treated as though it were a transparent relation instead of an opaque relation. The older children thought that the artist's skills were far more important than feelings, suggesting that they had grasped that the productive resource at the artist's disposal is the key to picture quality. Did the same age-related difference appear when the children were questioned about the feelings that a *viewer* brings to a picture? The pattern of answers reversed, with 9/12 younger children maintaining that a viewer's feelings were irrelevant and 8/12 older children maintaining the opposite. The results had reversed because an underlying mode of reasoning had *not* changed. The younger children regarded a viewer's feelings as irrelevant because they treated the viewer-picture relation as transparent, so that you see what there is really to be seen; but the older children were coming to construe the viewer as an agent in control, as they had with an artist. What would one predict would be the children's assumption about where pictorial beauty comes from? We asked children whether an ugly thing would make a worse picture than a pretty thing. Of the younger children, 10/12 accepted the question and asserted that how pretty a referent was would directly determine how pretty the picture of it would be and only a pretty picture would be a good picture. The older children spontaneously appealed to the artist: 9/12 of them maintained that it was the artist who determined the outcome. That is a useful finding, because it shows the older children spontaneously converting a two-term question into a three-term consideration. Maybe the younger ones could have done that with appropriate scaffolding? That is a separate matter: the important point is that one can be confident about children mastering something of the problem of intentional dispersion when there is evidence of spontaneous recruitment of an unmentioned relation in the net. One crucial point is that none of the children asserted that beauty is in the eye of the beholder.

It might seem somewhat surprising that such old children as 11-year-olds should have stuck with naïve-realist answers. Maybe there was something amiss in the questioning? It may be so. However, those particular children had been selected for a purpose. They were living in a rural part of a remote island, with no tuition in art apart from a short production-centred weekly activity in Sunday school. We have since worked with children in different cities where art is part of the curriculum. The full data remain to be fully scored up, but we obtained essentially the same pattern of change as above, only with the typical age of transition lying somewhere around 9 years of age. The evidence suggests that somewhere in middle childhood, some theoretical re-organisation occurs by which children achieve some dexterity in making inferences over the span of the intentional net.

In sum, from the age of 2 years or even before, children start to acquire a basic conception of each relation in the intentional net. They encounter problems of truth-testable representation and expressivity, which are aspects of how agents invest symbolic significance in the artefacts. Faced with such complexity, a useful simplifying assumption to make is that the separate relations are transparent and unidirectional. Such an assumption helps children represent the relations in common format, and enables them to engage in discussion of pictures where we usually condense the net into simpler terms. To adapt distinctions made by Wellman (1990) for the child's theory of mind, the children thus acquire a framework theory of pictures (Berti & Freeman, 1997; Freeman, 1995) which represents for them interpretative possibilities. Their task is then to develop specific theories that will enable them to integrate different relations in the net by treating each relation as an opaque relation, which thus becomes necessarily tied to each other relation somewhat as we saw with the thought experiment on Goodman's Horse. The major work of integration seems to be a task for middle childhood. That directs us to look at whether a middle childhood acquisition of a constructivist view of mind is empirically associated with a mentalistic theory of depiction.

OVERALL CONCLUSIONS

Research on the learnability of reasoning about the mind has relied heavily on representational analysis, to the relative neglect of communication analysis. Pictorial communication was taken as a focus in the chapter, because the cognate field of philosophy had anticipated some of the conceptual issues that theory of mind research was to encounter. The case of Goodman's horse has been traditionally used to make the point that representation is always aspectual. It takes only a little simulation of an agent's part in the case to discover that six assumptions specify the communicative problem. It is straightforward to discern how the six assumptions operate when one considers external notations that agents use as prosthetic transmitters of information about their mental states. The six assumptions are identical to those that underlie linguistic communication. No-one would seriously rule out language as a consideration in the acquisition of mentalistic reasoning; by that token, no-one should rule out the other communicative media.

The consideration of pictures is particularly useful in forcing to attention the problem of intentional dispersion as a key to the learnability problem. Our common language habit of reducing the dispersion to two-term expressions ("a picture of Goodman's horse") or one-term expressions ("a serene picture") obscures the roles of the two agents, artist and viewer, that we appeal to when reasoning about pictures. Young children may narrow their reasoning to the picture-referent relation in inferring what referent properties map between referent and picture, failing to coordinate that correct direction of fit with those appropriate to the two agents involved. The failure results in errors that some pictorial theorists term 'naïve realism' and some theory of mind researchers term 'reality bias' (see Mitchell & Kikuno, chapter 14, this volume). A sustained attempt to theorise the insight that pictorial prostheses are an intentional manifestation of mind seems to await middle or late childhood. I suggest that that period tends to mark a shift from (a) reasoning about the mind in two-term representational attempts, to (b) discovering the communicative constraints on representation. If that is true, we could characterise that period as one in which the child theorises communication as the framework for reasoning about the mind. It seems likely that the interesting research questions concern the late period of relating an interpretation of mind to an interpretation of representational prostheses.

REFERENCES

Adi-Japha, E., Levin, I., & Solomon, S. (1997). Emergence of representation in drawing: The relation between kinematic and referential aspects. *Cognitive Development*, *13*, 23–49.

Astington, J.W. (1995). What is theoretical about the child's theory of mind?: a Vygotskyan view of its development. In P. Carruthers & P.K. Smith (Eds.), *Theories of theories of mind* (pp. 184–299). Cambridge: Cambridge University Press.

Beilin, H., & Pearlman, E.G. (1991). Children's iconic realism: Object versus property realism. In H.W. Reese (Ed.), *Advances in Child Development and Behaviour*, *23*, 73–112. San Diego, CA: Academic Press.

Berti, A.E., & Freeman, N.H. (1997). Representational change in resources for pictorial innovation: a three-component analysis. *Cognitive Development*, *12*, 501–522.

Buhler, K. (1934). *Sprachtheorie: Die Darstellungsfunktion der Sprache*. Jena: Gustav Fischer Verlag.

Dancy, J. (1993). *Moral reasons*. Oxford: Blackwell.

Dretske, F. (1988). *Explaining behavior: Reasons in a world of causes*. Cambridge, MA: MIT Press.

Dunn, J. (1994). Changing minds and changing relationships. In C. Lewis & P. Mitchell (Eds.), *Children's early understanding of mind* (pp. 297–310). Hove, UK: Lawrence Erlbaum Associates Ltd.

Edwards, D., & Middleton, D. (1988). Conversational remembering and family relationships: How children learn to remember. *Journal of Social and Personal Relationships*, *5*, 3–25.

Freeman, N.H. (1980). *Strategies of representation in young children: Analysis of spatial skills and drawing processes*. London: Academic Press.

Freeman, N.H. (1993). Drawing: public instruments of representation. In C. Pratt & A.F. Garton (Eds.), *Systems of representation in children: development and use* (pp. 113–132). Chichester, UK: John Wiley & Sons.

Freeman, N.H. (1995). The emergence of a framework theory of pictorial reasoning. In C. Lange-Kuttner & G.V. Thomas (Eds.), *Drawing and looking: Theoretical approaches to pictorial representation in children* (pp. 135–146). Hemel Hempstead, UK: Harvester Wheatsheaf.

Freeman, N.H., & Parsons, M.J. (in press). Putting a theory of pictures to work. In B. Torff & R.J. Sternberg (Eds.), *Understanding and teaching the intuitive mind*. Mahwah, NJ: Lawrence Erlbaum Associates Inc.

Freeman, N.H., & Sanger, D. (1995). Commonsense aesthetics of rural children. *Visual Arts Research*, *21*, 1–10.

Gardner, H., & Wolf, D. (1987). The symbolic products of early childhood. In D. Gorlitz & J.F. Wohlwill (Eds.), *Curiosity, imagination and play* (pp. 305–325). Hillsdale, NJ: Lawrence Erlbaum Associates Inc.

Golomb, C. (1995). *The development of artistically gifted children: Selected case studies*. Hillsdale, NJ: Lawrence Erlbaum Associates Inc.

Goodman, N. (1976). *Languages of art*. Indianapolis, IN: Hackett.

Gombrich, E.H. (1960). *Art and illusion: A study in the psychology of pictorial representation*. Oxford: Phaidon.

Gombrich, E.H. (1982). *The image and the eye*. Oxford: Phaidon.

Gopnik, A., & Astington, J. (1988). Children's understanding of representational change and its relation to the understanding of false belief and the appearance-reality distinction. *Child Development*, *59*, 26–37.

Hayes, K., & Hayes, C. (1953). Picture perception in a home-raised chimpanzee. *Journal of Comparative and Physiological Psychology*, *46*, 470–474.

Heal, J. (1978). On the phrase 'theory of meaning'. *Mind*, *87*, 359–375.

Hobson, R.P. (1993). *Autism and the development of mind*. Hove, UK: Lawrence Erlbaum Associates Ltd.

Karmiloff-Smith, A. (1992). *Beyond modularity: A developmental perspective on cognitive science*. Cambridge, MA: MIT Press.

Lepsky, K. (1996). Art and language: Ernst H. Gombrich and Karl Buhler's theory of language. In R. Woodfield (Ed.), *Gombrich on art and psychology* (pp. 27–42). Manchester: Manchester University Press.

Leslie, A.M., & Thaiss, L. (1992). Domain specificity in conceptual development: Neuropsychological evidence from autism. *Cognition*, *43*, 225–251.

Lillard, A.S. (1996). Body or mind: Children's categorizing of pretense. *Child Development*, *67*, 1717–1734.

Lopes, D. (1997). *Understanding pictures*. Oxford: Clarendon Press.

Mitchell, P., Robinson, E.J., Isaacs, J.E., & Nye, R.M. (1996). Contamination in reasoning about false belief: An instance of a realist bias in adults but not children. *Cognition*, *59*, 1–21.

Nunes, T. (1997). Systems of signs and mathematical reasoning. In T. Nunes & P. Bryant (Eds.), *Learning and teaching mathematics* (pp. 29–44). Hove, UK: Psychology Press.

Nye, R., Thomas, G.V., & Robinson, E.J. (1995). Children's understanding about pictures. In C. Lange-Kuttner & G.V. Thomas (Eds.), *Drawing and looking: Theoretical approaches to pictorial representation in children*. Hemel Hempstead, UK: Harvester Wheatsheaf.

Parsons, M.J. (1987). *How we understand art*. Cambridge, UK: Cambridge University Press.

Perner, J. (1991). *Understanding the representational mind*. Cambridge, MA: MIT Press.

Robinson, E.J, Nye, R., & Thomas, G.V. (1994). Children's conceptions of the relationship between pictures and their referents. *Cognitive Development*, *9*, 165–191.

Russell, J. (1996). *Agency: Its role in mental development*. Hove, UK: Lawrence Erlbaum Associates Ltd.

Schier, F. (1986). *Deeper into pictures*. Cambridge: Cambridge University Press.

Searle, J.R. (1983). *Intentionality: An essay in the philosophy of mind*. Cambridge: Cambridge University Press.

Shatz, M. (1994). Theory of mind and the development of social-linguistic intelligence in early childhood. In C. Lewis & P. Mitchell (Eds.), *Children's early understanding of mind* (pp. 311–330). Hove, UK: Lawrence Erlbaum Associates Ltd.

Thomas, G.V., Nye, R., & Robinson, E.J. (1994). How children view pictures: Children's responses to pictures as things in themselves and as representations of something else. *Cognitive Development*, *9*, 141–144.

Waksler, F.C. (1996). *The little trials of childhood and children's strategies for dealing with them*. London: Falmer Press.

Wellman, H.M. (1990). *The child's theory of mind*. Cambridge, MA: MIT Press.

Wellman, H.M., & Hickling, A.K. (1994). The mind's "I": Children's conception of the mind as an active agent. *Child Development*, *65*, 1564–1580.

Wolf, D.P. (1990). Being of several minds: Voices and versions of the self in early childhood. In D. Cicchetti & M. Beeghly (Eds.), *The self in transition: Infancy to early childhood* (pp. 183–212). Chicago. IL: Chicago University Press.

Wollheim, R. (1993). *The mind and its depths*. Cambridge, MA: Harvard University Press.

Woolley, J.D., & Wellman, H.M. (1990). Young children's understanding of realities, nonrealities, and appearances. *Child Development*, *61*, 946–961.

Zaitchik, D. (1990). When representations conflict with reality: The preschooler's problem with false beliefs and "false" photographs. *Cognition*, *35*, 41–68.

CHAPTER EIGHTEEN

About + Belief + Counterfactual

Josef Perner
University of Salzburg, Austria

Most of the contributions to this volume reflect the fact that between 3 and 5 years various intellectual changes take place that are related to children's mastery of the false belief task. This reinforces my impression that the false belief task does index some important intellectual acquisition. Needless to say, just what that intellectual achievement is, is hotly contested. I will try to formulate my position on this issue and, thereby, relate to as many of the other chapters as possible, although, in some cases this will not be possible.

One clear exception to the predominant theme is the chapter by Deanna Kuhn (Chapter 15). She argues that the understanding of the relationship between theory and evidence is not achieved with understanding false beliefs. As someone who has taught research methods to psychology students for many years I am strongly inclined to side with her on that. There are also the voices—the *no interesting development camp*—that deny any marked, interesting intellectual change. They attribute the mastery of the false belief task to the continuous increase in processing capacity (German & Leslie, Chapter 11) or the decrease of some cognitive bias (P. Mitchell & H. Kikuno, Chapter 14). By concluding that the observed development must reflect some deeper intellectual change I present my own position integrating understanding of aboutness, representation and mental causation. The latter of these factors is also central to the position by Wimmer and Gschaider (Chapter 12). Subbotsky (Chapter 16), too, raises the issue of mental causation. I then discuss the several camps that report specific developmental correlations with other abilities and who tend to interpret these in terms of their favourite theory. The *language camp*, Jill and Peter de Villiers (Chapter 10) argue that it is the grammatical apparatus dealing with complement structures that enables children to mentally represent false beliefs. Doug Frye

(Chapter 8) and Phil Zelazo (Chapter 9), the *CCC camp*—named after their theory 'cognitive complexity and control'—found correlations between the false belief task and tasks assessing children's ability to reason with embedded conditionals that also requires executive control. Then there is the largest, the *counterfactual camp* led by Riggs and Peterson (Chapter 5) supported by data from Robinson and Beck (Chapter 6), followed by interesting extensions by Harris and Leevers (Chapter 4) and by Amsel and Smalley (Chapter 7). Why precisely should understanding counterfactuality underlie an understanding of false belief? Riggs and Peterson see the link via simulation. There are others who display sympathy for the *simulation camp*: Harris and Leevers (Chapter 4), Fabricius and Imbens-Bailey (Chapter 13), and R. Mitchell (Chapter 3).

I will try and take issue with all these camps. This, however, leaves one very important issue untouched. It is the question addressed by Freeman (Chapter 17), Hobson (Chapter 2) and R. Mitchell (Chapter 3) of what is mental representation and how it is acquired. With much regret I had to leave this important issue aside.

CAMP 1: NO INTERESTING DEVELOPMENT

There has been a veritable onslaught on the finding that children below a certain age of about 4 years do not understand false belief (Perner, Leekam, & Wimmer, 1987; Wimmer & Perner, 1983). There were many claims that changes in the testing procedure show earlier competence than when the original, 'standard' test is used. I am not denying that some of these procedural changes are effective. However, one could characterise the results of this kind of research in the following points.

Replicability

Some published demonstrations of earlier competence are simply not replicable, e.g. the demonstration by Lewis and Osborne (1990) that a more explicit temporal marker makes the deceptive content task easier. Or the alleged finding by Chandler, Fritz, and Hala (1989) and Hala, Chandler, and Fritz (1991) that could not be replicated with the necessary control conditions by two quite independently working research groups (Sodian, Taylor, Harris, & Perner, 1991).

Volatility

Some of these findings proved to be rather volatile. Although they have been replicated in some studies, others showed a null result. For instance, the claim by Siegal and Beattie (1990) that by asking "Where will Maxi look *first* for his chocolate?" yields earlier competence was originally demonstrated for one of the story vignettes used by Wellman and Bartsch (1988). It was replicated by Surian and Leslie (1995) for the standard false belief story. They found a hefty

difference of 50% but Clements and Perner (1994) found only a 2.5% advantage. Now, I hasten to add, that we in fact did anticipate a large effect because
we intended to show that the "first" cue only works within Vygotsky's zone of
proximal development, whose onset might be indicated by an earlier implicit
understanding of false belief (as argued by Goldin-Meadow, Alibali, & Church,
1993, for a different domain of knowledge) that we had found in children's
visual orienting responses. I emphasise this, since I am aware of the existence of
the well known experimenter effects (Rosenthal, 1986) that one tends to find
what one wants to find.

Alternative interpretations

To the degree that changes in procedure succeed in demonstrating allegedly
earlier competence these changes open the results to alternative interpretations.
There are many. I have reviewed several in my response (Perner, 1995) to Fodor
(1992). I concentrate here on some of the more interesting ones.

Immature concepts.   Bartsch and Wellman (1989) claimed that children can
use false belief to explain mistaken actions before they can predict mistaken
actions on the basis of false belief as required in the standard false belief task.
Moses and Flavell (1990) found this difficult to replicate. Eventually, they did
succeed in getting more children to answer the questions "Why did Sam (in
search of bandaids) go to the empty bandaid box? What did he think?" correctly
with "bandaids there". However, they found that this improvement was a rather
questionable sign of genuine understanding of belief because these children
started to make errors on a subsequent question. When asked what Sam, after
finding out that the box was empty, *now* thought was in the box, they still
answered "bandaids". I attributed this to an immature concept of "prelief" (Perner,
Baker, & Hutton, 1994) where children do not differentiate between similar states
like believing and pretending. Going to an empty bandaid box for bandaids
indicates that Sam is believing/pretending that the bandaids are in there. If the
"think" in the test question is assimilated to this undifferentiated understanding
of pretending/believing (i.e. "prelieve") then it makes sense that Sam after looking inside the empty box can still be prelieving that it has bandaids in it.

Baseline differences.   In their very elegant "identical twin" version of contrasting explanation with prediction Robinson and Mitchell (1995) were able to
provide some support for Bartsch and Wellman's contention. They showed that
more children gave the correct answer to "Which twin (one going to the old, the
other to the object's new location) was in the room when the object was moved?"
than were able to predict where the twin who was absent during the transfer
would look for the object. However, the difference can be almost completely
accounted for by a baseline difference in "correct" responses by those children

who understand nothing (Perner, 1995, p. 253). These children tend to have a naïve theory that people look for an object where the object is. Hence, they tend to give 100% wrong answers in the prediction task. They have no such wrong theory about why people go to wrong places. The worst they can do is guess, which means they are on the average 50% correct. Once one is aware of this baseline difference it is a very obvious mistake to be avoided. However, I have to admit, it took me years to realise that some of our own data were afflicted: The alleged developmental lag between understanding knowledge vs. ignorance and understanding false belief (Hogrefe, Wimmer, & Perner, 1986; Perner & Wimmer, 1988) can be entirely reduced to this baseline effect.

Pragmatic pressures.   German and Leslie (this volume, Chapter 11) cite the finding that false belief based action predictions improve greatly when the object has disappeared. One problem with this finding is pragmatic pressures. From the young child's point of view the question where someone will look for an object that has gone out of existence may be absurd and require the answer "nowhere". Yet the question puts some pressure on the listener to answer with a definite location. In the absence of any clear understanding they use that location that happens to come to mind first. Now we know from the research by Clements and Perner that an implicit understanding of belief emerges fairly sharply at the age of about 2 years and 11 months. Since this implicit knowledge of "he'll look in the original location" exists that may determine children's explicit responses in the disappear condition due to a clear alternative. It would now be interesting whether the explicit response in the disappear condition is due to pragmatic pressure to come up with a definite location or whether it reflects some earlier explicit understanding (in the absence of tempting alternative theories) of belief. This could be tested with the knowledge control condition, i.e. where Max sees that his chocolate disappears. Where will he look for the chocolate? German and Leslie argue that they didn't run this control since it was pragmatically awkward. Yes, but for a young child who does not understand belief, this question is equally awkward in the false belief condition. Pragmatically awkward or not, children's answers in this control condition would shed light on the theoretical alternatives. If they still answer with the original location then the reported finding is difficult to interpret as an indication of understanding false belief. If they say "nowhere" then the reported finding is a clear sign of early explicit understanding of false belief. If they now answer with any of the possible locations then this attests to the presence of pragmatic pressure to pick a definite location and suggests that their choice of the correct location in the false belief condition may be governed by their implicit understanding of false belief.

Content, attitude and spatio-referential confusion.   Peter Mitchell and Haruo Kikuno (Chapter 14) capitalise heavily on the findings by Saltmarsh, Mitchell, and Robinson (1995) using the deceptive container paradigm (Hogrefe, Wimmer,

& Perner, 1986; Perner et al., 1987): children are shown a Smarties box, they say there are Smarties in there. They are shown that they were wrong; there is a pencil in it. Closed up again, with pencil inside, children are then asked either what another naïve person would think is in that box, or what they themselves had earlier thought was inside (Gopnik & Astington, 1988).

Although it is nice to know that children find this task about as difficult as the traditional (unexpected transfer) task and it correlates reasonably with it (e.g. Gopnik & Astington, 1988; Holmes, Black, & Miller, 1996) I have had my problems knowing what to conclude purely on the basis of performance on this task. To see my problems we need to draw a clear distinction between the *content* and the *attitude* of belief (see Perner et al., 1994). The content is the proposition "There are Smarties in the box". The attitude is given by what role this proposition plays in my mind, i.e. whether I hold it as a belief, as a mere thought, as pretence or as a desire, etc. For our interest in when children understand belief, it is critical to be able to infer from test results that children understand the *attitude* of belief. The Smarties task, however, relies heavily on getting the content right. The problem, thus, is that children might render the content correctly without fully understanding that the person holds this content as a belief (i.e. has the attitude of belief towards this content). Unlike in the traditional (unexpected transfer) task, in the Smarties task the content of the belief is highlighted and brought to attention by the looks of the box. Had we found that this task was much easier for children, we would have immediately concluded that it was artificially easy: they just say Smarties because they are looking at a Smarties box. As it turned out, it isn't easier, but one needs to always keep that possibility in mind when investigating new variants of this task.

Similarly, in Gopnik and Astington's memory version, by having the false belief "Smarties in the box" that content registers in children's mind. Now when they answer with this content to the question, "What did you think was in the box", it is not clear that they understand that they *held this content as a belief.* They might come up with it because it is in their mind and because the word "think" suggests that the answer requires something different than what was really in the box (i.e. the pencil). By emphasising the content of the false belief (Mitchell & Lacohée, 1991) this content may be more prevalent in their minds and this raises the probability that they answer with this content.

This paradigm is fraught with another complication: proliferation of temporal × mental spaces. And this leads to a serious problem of knowing which space the experimenter is talking about. To some degree this is even a problem with temporal spaces alone. In a long time unpublished study (Perner et al., 1993) we had two puppets, Blondie and Curly. Blondie printed a star on his tee shirt. Then either Curly printed the same pattern on his tee shirt, or we made a picture of Blondie with the star on his tee shirt. Then Blondie washed off his print and printed a fish. In both cases we have two contexts: t_1 and t_2. In t_1 Blondie had a star on his shirt, in t_2 he had a fish on his shirt. Children had no memory problem, provided one used a unique description of the earlier shape: "which shape did Blondie wash off?" All children remembered that it was a star. However, if one used an initially ambiguous reference: "Which was the shape on Blondie's tee shirt . . ." and then disambiguated by marking which context one is referring to: ". . . before he changed", then children had "memory problems". It seemed that children had difficulty understanding disambiguating context markers like "now", "before", etc. That they have such a problem was also confirmed when we look at the question about the picture of Blondie: "What shape does Blondie have . . . in the picture?" Again, the initial reference is ambiguous, "the shape on Blondie's tee shirt"—in reality or in the picture? In contrast, when the question was about Curly (who had the same shape on his tee shirt as Blondie in the picture) there was no problem because the referential expression was unique: "What shape does Curly have on his tee shirt?" (he only ever had one shape, the star, on his shirt).

This problem of referential confusion with time spaces becomes more severe if it is compounded by reference to mental spaces. One reason is that the problem is being aggravated simply because with two dimensions (time and mind) spaces multiply as can be seen from the following development of the deceptive contents task. In the traditional version two spaces (or contexts) have to be distinguished: what is really in the box and what is in the box according to the naïve person's view. In the memory version two temporal spaces have to be added: what was in the box before the box was opened (at t_1) and what is in the box now (at t_2). This then interacts with one's belief, creating more different spaces: What I now (at t_2) believe was in the box (at t_1), what I now (t_2) believe is in the box now (t_2), what I then (t_1) believed was in the box (t_1) and what I then (t_1) believed would be now (t_2) in the box. Although not all of them are relevant and have to be kept apart, there is a serious problem of knowing which context the test question is referring to. As de Villiers (1995) noted, children of this age have a particular problem keeping apart the time of the mental (or speech) act (e.g. the time of the thinking) and the time of the content event (e.g. the time of the event thought about).

Moreover, this compounding of temporal and mental spaces may become a specially serious and unpredictable problem when a word like "think" is used, because this word can be used with quite different meaning depending on context (e.g. Perner, 1991, ch. 8) ranging from wanting, to entertaining a thought, to believing. And young children have been shown to have problems finding the intended interpretation. For instance, they inappropriately also interpret it as wanting when it was intended as believing (Wellman & Bartsch, 1988, Experiment 1).

Now, I mention all this because in some of the Smarties task variations in the study by Saltmarsh et al. (1995) contexts proliferate. There are not only the ones listed above but in Experiment 2 there is also Duffy as a second observer and what he thinks now, thought then was/is in the box. The critical finding was the contrast between two conditions. In one condition the child observed how the expected content (Smarties) was removed and replaced by an atypical content (pencil). In the other the child discovered the atypical content in the box. Both conditions then continued with the introduction of Duffy being confronted with the Smarties box and children are asked what Duffy thinks is in the box now. The finding was that children answered more often with "Smarties" when there had been Smarties in the box initially than when there had always been a pencil inside. This finding can be expected if children are not quite certain what the "think" refers to and it makes them answer with any thought about what is or was in the box (content). The likelihood of the thought "Smarties in box" coming to mind is greater in the condition where there were actually Smarties in the box than when there never had been any Smarties in the box. This may account for the 24% higher incident of "Smarties" responses in this condition.

Peter Mitchell tries to argue from data like these that there is no substantive developmental change. The young children are just somewhat more strongly subject to cognitive biases. The tendency to answer questions about an earlier belief wrongly can be explained by the hindsight bias (Fischhoff, 1975). Once one knows the truth one tends to remember one's original assumptions as having conformed to the truth. The information that the British won the battle against the Gurkhas, tends to increase the probability of (mis)remembering one's original guess about the outcome as a British victory. By analogy, once the children know that the box contained a pencil they tend to remember the content of their original belief as what was really in the box. I find this rather implausible. Unlike in the case of uncertain knowledge about historical events, in the Smarties task older children or adults show no hindsight bias. The change seems fairly abrupt and 100%. The reason probably has to do with what Wimmer and Gschaider (Chapter 12) emphasised: the older child understands the reason for why one was misled by the deceptive appearance of the box. One's false belief with a particular content (Smarties in the Smarties box) makes good sense, whereas whether the Gurkhas or the British won remains arbitrary.

Moreover, there is Experiment 4 by Saltmarsh et al. (1995). The child thinks there are Smarties in the tube, discovers that there was a pencil inside and then sees how it is replaced by another atypical content, a spoon. Now there are three temporal contexts and a distinction between belief and reality. When asked, "When I first showed you the box, what did you think was inside it?" all types of answers occur: "Smarties", "pencil", with "spoon" as the slight favourite. If errors were due to hindsight bias this should not happen. The child first expresses a belief about the contents at time t_1 and then at t_2 discovers that at t_1 there was a pencil inside. With hindsight they should remember their belief about the contents at time t_1 as having been a pencil (the real content at that time). Why should the content at time t_3 (spoon) influence a belief about t_1? With hindsight, I suspect there was a good dosage of spatio-referential confusion at work in this experiment.

ZPD (Zone of Proximal Development)

Successful demonstrations of earlier competence that can be reliably replicated are typically restricted to a period of at most a year before the traditional age mark. Alibali et al. (1993) used Vygotsky's (1978) concept of the *zone of proximal development* to argue for different domains of knowledge that teaching new concepts and procedural facilitation is successful only within that zone. Importantly, the beginning of this zone can be detected by the onset of implicit understanding of these concepts. Wendy Clements and I (1994) may have identified this point in children's understanding of false belief at the age of about 2 years and 11 months, administering the traditional false belief test but so that children can't see Sam the Mouse in search of his cheese. Sam only becomes visible when he either pops out of the hole at the location where he thinks the cheese is (location A, where he originally put the cheese) or out of the hole where the cheese now is (location B). This made it possible to look at children's eyes as an indicator where the child anticipates Sam to reappear. There was also a knowledge control story in which Sam sees the cheese being moved. The finding was striking: The upper line in Fig. 18.1 shows the number of children who looked to A in the false belief condition but not in the true belief condition. As one can see, although there was no sign of such 'implicit' understanding of belief in the youngest group, after a sharp developmental onset almost 80% of children at the age of 3 years (2;11–3;2) did show implicit knowledge. And there was a large gap at this age between visually orienting to A and answering with "A" the

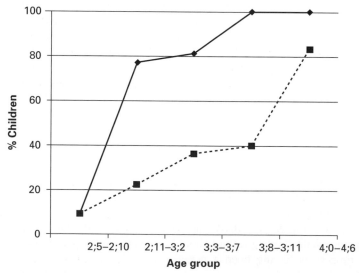

FIG 18.1   Percentage of children responding with location A in false belief story and with location B in true belief control story (after Clements & Perner, 1994). ──◆── implicit: looking; --■-- explicit: answers to questions.

explicit question where Sam will go to look for his cheese, as the lower line in Fig. 18.1 shows.

We have since replicated this using video animations in order to exclude unintentional clues by the experimenter telling the stories (Clements, Perner, Stubbs, & Import, 1998). The observed age trends were very similar. In a series of further studies Clements and Perner (1996) found similar levels of precociously correct responses in children's spontaneous action. Children had to move a mat to where they anticipated Sam to go. Clements, Rustin, and McCallum (1997) also confirmed the contention by Alibali et al. (1993) in that training children to give correct explicit answers to the test question was only successful within the ZPD of implicit understanding.

My main purpose of mentioning this research is that in all these studies there was always a group of children younger than 2 years 10 months with never any systematic sign that they anticipated Sam's reappearance either in their visual orienting responses or in their spontaneous mat movings at location A, where Sam thinks the cheese is. Importantly, this lack of correct anticipation cannot easily be attributed to these young children's failure to understand the story since most of them did well on a battery of three memory questions: Where was the cheese in the beginning? Who put it into the other location? Could Sam see the cheese being moved? Surely at this very young age some children had problems. However in a typical experiment with 10 children in this age group about 6 answered all three memory questions correctly.

In sum, the difficulty of bringing down the age substantially by which children can answer the explicit test questions and the abrupt onset of implicit understanding suggest to me that there is more at stake than a gradual getting better with age. There is an important change taking place between 3 and 5 years: at first in children's implicit understanding, then explicit. Of course, what that change is is the topic of many of the other contributions to this volume. Before delving into these accounts I want to briefly describe my own view of the relevant developmental change.

CAMP 2: ABOUTNESS, REPRESENTATION AND MENTAL CAUSATION

My position on what children need in order to understand false belief developed as a reaction to Leslie's analysis of pretence. I presented a first version of this theory at the first theory of mind conference in Toronto (June, 1986). The difficulty with belief is to understand that the content of a false belief is more than just a false proposition (or possible world, or non-actual situation). It is a false proposition held to be true of the real world. In other words, the child needs not just differentiate between true and false propositions (or real and not real situations) but entertain the idea that something false can be taken for true (Perner et al., 1987). Since the core distinction is also at the core of the notion of representation, I characterised the child who understands false belief as a "representation" theorist (Perner, 1988, 1991). Furthermore, since understanding the mind as representation provides a causal understanding of the mind I also characterised the older child as one with a proper (causal) theory of mind (Perner, 1991). I give here a brief characterisation of how these different notions hang together.

Mental state terms like "believe" are characterised as propositional attitudes that relate an organism (person) to a proposition as in the top part of Fig. 18.2. The fact that the relation between organism and proposition is labelled "believes" indicates what role the proposition plays in the organism's mental economy, i.e. that the proposition functions as a reflection of reality. For instance, "Maxi believes that the chocolate is in the original cupboard", indicates that the proposition "the chocolate is in the original cupboard" is taken by Maxi as reflecting where the chocolate is (rather than where he wants it to be). What this picture hides is the fact that propositions are *about* some world against which they are to be evaluated as true or false. And believing is not just a two place relation between organism and proposition but is a three place relation (as shown in the lower part of Fig. 18.2) that relates the organism to the proposition and the world against which the proposition is to be evaluated. In other words, the believer conceives of the world as being a certain way (as specified by the proposition). This distinction is related to Frege's distinction between sense and reference as components of linguistic meaning, where the proposition would be the sense of a sentence and the world the referent.

My developmental claim about the intellectual change around 4 years is that the younger children have procedural knowledge of evaluating propositions against the world. They can assign truth values; they can decide whether the proposition is true or false but they do not understand that propositions are being evaluated. Consequently, they cannot conceive of the possibility that a proposition could be evaluated differently, e.g. a false proposition being evaluated as true as in the case of a false belief. The children who pass the false belief task have achieved this level of understanding.[1] For brevity's sake, let me refer to it as "understanding of *aboutness*" (hence the word "about" in the title).

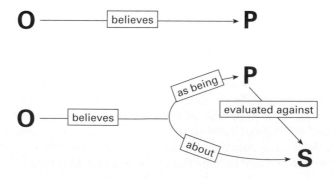

Now, what can the younger child understand? With the ability to represent propositions and evaluate them against reality the child can think in terms of possible worlds or situations[2] (real and non-real). The child can, therefore, understand the actions of organisms in terms of pursuing a goal not just within the real but also within a hypothetical world (e.g. a pretend scenario). Given a certain goal the world gives reasons for carrying out the actions that lead to that goal. For instance, if Maxi wants to get close to his chocolate then the real world gives him reason to approach cupboard B where the chocolate is. If, however, Maxi is pretending that the chocolate is in cupboard A then within that pretend world there is reason to approach cupboard A. That is, the child can understand the reality inappropriate pretend action of going to cupboard A since the child can understand Maxi acting within this pretend world. What the child cannot understand is the inappropriate real world actions resulting from a false belief because there is no good reason within the real world for looking in the empty cupboard A (I have referred to this as the "puzzle of false belief", Perner, 1988).

In order to solve this puzzle the child has to come to grips with the distinction shown in the lower part of Fig. 18.2: that propositions are *about* a world and are evaluated against it. With this understanding, belief can be understood as something that relates the believer to the world as conceiving of (about) the world as being a certain way (as rendered by the proposition). However, this is not enough. The child has to also realise that how the belief shows the world to be takes precedence in determining action over the reasons the world itself gives for action. That is where representation and mental causation come in.

As Goodman (1976) has emphasised, the notion of representation is also based on the distinction between what the representation is about and how it shows that thing as being. So understanding aboutness is a prerequisite for understanding mental states as representations of the world. Moreover, understanding mental states as representations—as Fodor (1978) and Field (1978) have pointed out in their Representational Theory of Mind—makes them amenable to understanding their causal role. Unlike propositional attitudes which link organisms to non-existing, abstract propositions, representations of these propositions are real things with causal properties. So, the second part of my claim is that with understanding aboutness children also understand mental states as representations with causal power. Thus they can understand that a false belief about the chocolate's location makes Maxi look in the wrong place even though the world within which Maxi acts does not give good reasons for doing so. It also enables children to understand that beliefs and knowledge need to be caused by information as Leslie (1988) and Wimmer, Hogrefe, and Sodian (1988) have emphasised.

As an aside I should mention that the causal connection to behaviour is more central to belief than the question of how belief has been caused. A person can have the belief that the chocolate is in cupboard A without concern for where this belief comes from. In contrast, a person who has this belief and then looks for the chocolate somewhere else is a thoroughly irrational being. Of course, the causal origin of beliefs is critical for beliefs to qualify as knowledge. But for knowledge, the causal connection to behaviour is equally critical. And, to notice, our mental ontology does not provide for a mental state for which it would be crucial to be properly caused (like knowledge) without serving a causal role in determining behaviour.

In the later sections of this Chapter I will show how these postulated intellectual changes underlying mastery of the false belief task can also account for concurrent changes in executive control and the ability to engage in counterfactual reasoning.

CAMP 3: LANGUAGE

Jill and Peter de Villiers (Chapter 10) argue that language competence reflects the development of certain grammatical mechanisms that also govern the internal language of thought which is required for thinking about someone's false belief and related mental states. Their evidence for this claim comes from normal development and the development of orally taught deaf children. In both cases mastery of embedded complements (which are used with mental or communication verbs) was the best predictor for the false belief test. It was a better predictor than mastery of other complex sentences. And this is not a developmental coincidence in the normal case since the 3-year delay in mastery of the belief test in deaf children shows the same correlation. Moreover, in a longitudinal study memory for the content of complement sentences at the earlier test point correlated with false belief performance at the later point more strongly than earlier false belief performance did with later ability to remember complements. This indicates that the language ability to deal with complements precedes and is perhaps a prerequisite for false belief understanding.

Although this claim strikes me as a particularly interesting proposal, since the underlying linguistic theory about the grammar of complements would provide a more precise specification of the mechanism that underlies the developing conceptual competence of belief understanding. However, the cited evidence still leaves other more mundane possibilities viable. In particular, it is compatible with the position that language is a very or even the most important data base for working out a theory of mind. The delay in the orally taught deaf children is some of the best evidence that something has to be worked out and that it is closely linked to language. Language may serve this function as data base in two ways: (1) directly as a system that can represent and misrepresent, and (2) as the most precise and easiest access to people's minds, what they want and what they think. Building a theory of mind from just observing people's behaviour would be a tough order. This can explain: (1) why competence in use and comprehension of linguistic aspects that are centrally involved in talking about the mind and communication should correlate and precede other more elaborate measures of understanding the mind (like the false belief task), and (2) why children who are language deprived (orally taught deaf) are delayed in their mastery of the false belief task.

CAMP 4: EXECUTIVE FUNCTIONS AND COGNITIVE COMPLEXITY

Jim Russell (Hughes & Russell, 1993; Russell, Mauthner, Sharpe, & Tidswell, 1991) noticed that children who fail the false belief task have problems pointing deceptively to an empty container to avoid a competitor getting the reward. Although it was originally thought that this reflects the expected difficulty with deception, it soon became clear that the problem goes deeper. The younger children's inability was even resistant to training. This gave rise to an explanation in terms of executive control, in particular in terms of an inability to inhibit a prevalent response tendency. The prevalent tendency in this case is to respond to the question, "Where is X", by pointing to where X is. There is supporting evidence for this explanation. When the pointing is made less automatic by requiring a pointer (instead of their finger) then children's ability to deceptively point improves (Carlson, Moses, & Hix, 1998).

We now know that mastery of the false belief task tends to occur with the mastery of typical executive function tasks (Carlson, 1997; Frye, Zelazo, & Palfai, 1995; Hughes, 1998; Hughes, White, & Dunn, in press; Perner, Lang, & Stummer, 1998). These executive tasks are of a particular kind which I would like to characterise as *executive inhibition* tasks. In line with the model of control proposed by Norman and Shallice (1986) there is first of all automatic inhibition (they call this level of control contention scheduling). Concentrating on performing an action activates the relevant action schema which in turn inhibits incompatible schemata. The tasks that require executive inhibition (Norman and Shallice's Supervisory Attentional System, or for short SAS) have the particularly nasty feature that by concentrating on the intended action an old action tendency, too, gets activated and, thus, becomes likely to interfere with the intended action (Perner, Stummer, & Lang, 1999). Hence, the usual automatic control does not suffice, conscious inhibition from the supervisory attentional system (SAS) is required.

Luria's (Luria, Pribram, & Homskaya, 1964) hand game can serve as an illustration. The easy task is first for the child (C) to imitate what the experimenter (E) does:

E: flat hand → fist → flat hand → . . .
C: flat hand → fist → flat hand → . . .

Then the game changes to doing the opposite, i.e.

E: flat hand → fist → flat hand → . . .
C: fist → flat hand → fist → . . .

The natural tendency is to imitate. Hence, that tendency is likely to interfere with what one is supposed to do. In order to inhibit this natural tendency it is not sufficient to just concentrate more on one's proper task because that task involves concentrating on what the experimenter does and that enhances the interfering natural tendency to imitate. That is, automatic inhibition is thwarted and executive inhibition is needed. Executive inhibition consists of representing the existence of the interfering action tendency in order to inhibit that tendency. There are at least five theories in the literature (Perner & Lang, in press) that contend to explain why the false belief task and executive inhibition tasks are mastered at the same time.

The false belief task requires executive inhibition

Russell et al. (1991), Hughes and Russell (1993) and Harris (1993) noted that there is a strong tendency to answer false belief questions (Where does he think X is? Where will he look for X?) with the real state of affairs (where X really is). Although the younger children might know what the person believes, it won't show in their responses to the belief question because they cannot inhibit this strong tendency to answer in terms of reality. Obviously, if the false belief test itself requires executive inhibition, it correlates developmentally with other tasks that require executive inhibition. There are, however, several findings that speak against this possibility.

Modified belief tasks with the executive component removed.   Several modifications of the false belief task that do not share the potential executive component are not easier and still correlate with executive inhibition tasks. The first example of such a task is the false belief explanation task (Bartsch & Wellman, 1989). Children are shown that the mistaken protagonist looks for the object in the empty place and they are asked to explain why he looked there. Children who do not understand belief simply do not know what to say. Evidently there is no strong but wrong existing answer tendency. Bartsch and Wellman's original claim that explanation is easier for children than action prediction in the traditional belief paradigm has come under repeated methodological criticism (Moses & Flavell, 1990; Wimmer & Mayringer, 1998) and also the identical twin version by Robinson and Mitchell (1995) leaves no difference in difficulty once the data are adjusted for correct guesses (Perner, 1995, p. 253, also see earlier discussion "Camp 1").

Perhaps most relevant for present purposes is that Hughes (1998) not only found no difference between the traditional prediction version of the false belief task and Bartsch and Wellman's explanation version but also found that the explanation version correlated as strongly as the prediction version with inhibitory control tasks (such as Luria's hand game). This makes it unlikely that the alleged inhibitory control requirement of the prediction version of the false belief task accounts for the observed correlations with executive function tasks.

Russell (1996) describes another modification of the false belief task that should, at least, strongly reduce any need for executive inhibition. Children are told that the object was being removed from the original container and being put into one of two other containers without seeing in which one. This should reduce wrong answers, since there is no obvious, well established wrong, reality oriented answer to the belief question. Russell noted no great improvement, and Robinson and Beck (Chapter 6) compared a counterfactual reasoning version of this new condition to the normal counterfactual task and report a zero difference.

Implicit understanding of false belief before explicit understanding. The finding by Clements and Perner (1994, 1996) mentioned earlier also provides a problem for the argument that children's problem with the false belief task resides in an executive problem. The finding is that children in their anticipatory looking behaviour and in their spontaneous actions (moving a mat to where the protagonist will reappear) are more often correct than in their verbal responses or in their hesitant actions. Inhibitory control, however, manifests itself first in deliberate action and verbal descriptions. It is the automatic behaviour of eyes and unreflected action that tends to escape it.

The CCC theory

CCC stands for Cognitive complexity and Control (Zelazo & Frye, 1996; Chapters 8 and 9). The developmental claim is that by the age of about 4 years children become able to apply pairs of antecedent–consequent rules ($a_1 \rightarrow c_1$, $a_2 \rightarrow c_2$) under one setting condition (s_1) and then switch the antecedent–consequent combinations ($a_1 \rightarrow c_2$, $a_2 \rightarrow c_1$) under another setting condition (s_2). For instance in the Dimensional Change Card Sorting (DCCS) children are first to play the shape game (s_1) where they have to put the red car (a_1) to the green car target (c_1) and the green flower (a_2) to the red flower target (c_2). Then the setting is switched to the colour game (s_2) and now the red car (a_1) has to be put to the red flower target (c_2) and the green flower (a_2) to the green car target (c_1). Frye, Zelazo, and Palfai (1995, Frye, Chapter 8) claim that the same logical analysis (at least partially) can be applied to the false belief task:

IF me (s_1),   THEN IF looking for chocolate (a_1) THEN indicate location B (c_1),
IF Max (s_2)   THEN IF looking for chocolate (a_1) THEN indicate location A (c_2).

It is for this reason—according to theory—that the false belief task requires the same logical structure as the particular executive function tasks that they are mastered at the same point in development.

There are several reasons that make me doubt this claim (see Perner et al., 1999):

(i)   The rules identified in Frye's analysis of the false belief task cannot be the rules that children bring to bear on the task, because these rules could only be known after a practice run or as a result of the child having figured out the problem. Hence, it remains a mystery why the structure of these rules should determine the developmental difficulty.

(ii)   Frye's analysis seems arbitrary. There are equally, if not more, plausible analyses, e.g.:

> IF I am looking for chocolate (a1)   THEN answer with location B (c1),
> IF Maxi is looking for chocolate (a2)   THEN answer with location A (c2).

According to this analysis the false belief task reduces to a pair of simple conditionals (without setting conditions) which ought to be within the ability of children one year younger, i.e. 3-year-olds (Zelazo & Frye, 1996).

(iii)   If one accepts Frye's analysis of the false belief task then the same analysis applies to the food preference task used by Repacholi and Gopnik (1997). Unfortunately for CCC theory, there is a very sharp onset of mastering that task at 18 months, well before the age of 4 years. Similarly, but less spectacularly in terms of age differences, we (Perner & Stummer, 1998) found that children find it difficult to not repeat the name or the colour of an object just used by someone else (a modification of the tasks used by Doherty & Perner, 1998). This task is of equal difficulty as and correlates highly with the false belief task and with executive inhibition tasks. However, we also ran a slight modification in which children had to name the colour of the object if the other person had named it, or vice versa. This version also fits the logical specifications of Zelazo and Frye's analysis of embedded conditionals but it is considerably easier than the original versions and the false belief task.

(iv)   Luria's go/no-go task, in which children on presentation of one stimulus (a1) are to press a bulb (c1) and on presentation of another stimulus (a2) are to refrain from pressing (c2), requires but a simple pair of rules. Nevertheless, according to the review by Zelazo and Jacques (1996) it is mastered around 4 years and is as difficult as the other executive inhibition tasks.

Maturation of a common brain region

Ozonoff, Pennington, and Rogers (1991), and Pennington et al. (1998) suggested that the observed association of theory of mind and executive function problems in autism could be due to the fact that both abilities depend on the same or closely interrelated brain structures. Late maturation of these structures could then also explain why executive function and theory of mind performance are related in normal development. One region indicated by brain imaging studies and lesion studies are Brodmann areas 8 and 9. These areas have been recently found to be actlivated in theory of mind tasks (Baron-Cohen et al., 1998; Fletcher et al., 1995; Goel, Grafman, Sadato, & Hallett, 1995; Happé et al., 1996; Mazoyer et al., 1993). And this region has long been known to be involved in executive control (Passingham, 1993), in particular for conditional tasks (Petrides, 1982). I can see at least two (potential) problems with this theory.

(i)   It is not task/age specific. It predicts that theory of mind tasks should developmentally relate to executive control, but there is nothing that predicts that the false belief task should be mastered at the same time as executive inhibition tasks.

(ii)   We know that environmental factors can make a large difference to the timing of false belief task mastery and such factors are unlikely to correlate with brain maturation. In particular the number of older siblings plays a crucial role (Lewis et al., 1996; Perner, Ruffman, & Leekam, 1994; Ruffman et al., 1998). Two older siblings are worth about a year of chronological age. Of course, this is a problem to be tested, because it is possible that the correlation between false belief task and executive control tasks is independent of the correlation between false belief task and number of older siblings. The same issue should also be investigated with the vastly delayed onset of false belief mastery in orally educated deaf children (Chapter 10) and in blind children (Minter, Hobson, & Bishop, 1998).

Self-monitoring and motor images as prerequisites for a theory of mind

Russell (1996, 1998) argued that "the monitoring of actions and the ability to act at will are necessary ingredients to the development of a 'pretheoretical' form of self-awareness [and] . . . that this form of self-awareness must be in place if the individual is to gain an adequate grasp of mental concepts" (1998, p. 295). His theory was designed to explain the problems in autism. An assumed original deficiency in action monitoring and in initiating action would, therefore, explain why people with autism suffer theory of mind and executive problems. However, the theory is not apt to predict why in normal development the mastery of the false belief test coincides with the mastery of executive inhibition tasks. In a similar vein Pacherie (1998) sees the autistic theory of mind deficit as a result of the failure to generate motor images (Jeannerod, 1997). Motor images are a higher level of self-monitoring; they are consciously accessible images of the motor representations that govern our actions. The details have to be worked out, but this might provide a way of making Russell's basic theory specific to false belief tasks and executive inhibition tasks. Apart from this need for greater specificity there is no firm evidence against this theory.

Theory of mind as a constitutive part of executive control

The first insight that gave rise to this theory was Heinz Wimmer's (1989): The better we come to understand our mind the better we can control it and our behaviour. Chris Frith (1992) has used this idea to explain why people with schizophrenia have theory of mind and executive problems. I have tried to make it more specific so that one can predict which level of theory of mind development enables which form of self-control (Perner, 1998). I only concentrate here on the question why the false belief task should relate to executive inhibition tasks.

The theory identifies automatic control (contention scheduling) with control at the level of action schemas as representational vehicles, e.g. inhibit other schemas with which you have inhibitory links. It identifies executive control (SAS) with control at the level of the representational content of action schemas, e.g. boost the schema that is responsible for putting the red car with the red flower. In other words, it is needed for following verbal instructions, because they only specify the content of the action schema to be activated.

Executive inhibition is also directed at schemas with a certain content, e.g. inhibit the schema that made you put the red car with the green car. However, and that is the critical point for why it should emerge with mastery of the false belief task, to see the need for this inhibition one has to understand (represent) that one has action schemas as representational vehicles that (have the causal power to) make one act whether one wants to act that way or not. The action schema has to be understood as a representational vehicle (with causal power) and a representational content (by which it is identified). This is what I have been claiming about how belief needs to be understood in the false belief task: a mental state representing the world (content) and with causal powers (representational vehicle) that makes me do things, e.g. look in the empty cupboard, even though I do not want to look in the empty cupboard (see 'Camp 2').

In sum, executive inhibition requires understanding of action schemas as representational vehicles with representational content and causal efficacy, just as the false belief task requires understanding of beliefs as representational vehicles with a certain content and causal efficacy. This is understood at about 4 years and is responsible for the correlation between the false belief task (and other theory of mind tasks requiring this understanding of mental states) and executive inhibition tasks.

A prediction made from the early version of this theory (Perner, 1991) was that children should understand the involuntary nature of their knee-jerk reflex (Shultz, Wells, & Sarda, 1980) at the same time as false belief. We now can add that it should also correlate with mastery of executive inhibition tasks. Those predictions are fully confirmed (Perner, Stummer, & Lang, 1999).

Our review of available data (Perner & Lang, in press) showed that none of the existing evidence on theory of mind and executive function performance allowed to reject either this theory or the proposal by Russell/Pacherie. In fact, the two theories may describe complementary processes. Self-monitoring and the ability to initiate action may be an integral part of developing a theory of mind which then has to be developed in order to achieve the higher levels of executive control. If the two parts are separable then the best evidence for one theory over the other would be a clinical group that had a clear deficit in one area but no deficit in the other. Existing evidence, however, tends to suggest that groups known for their theory of mind deficit (autism) also suffer from executive dysfunction (Ozonoff et al., 1991) and groups known for their executive problems (e.g. ADHD) seem to be impaired in their theory of mind as well (Hughes, White, & Dunn, in press).

Although the discovery of the link between theory of mind and executive control was first interpreted as showing that theory of mind tasks are hidden executive function tasks, it now appears that executive control and theory of mind are intricately interwoven abilities. In my view, executive function tasks are applied theory of mind problems.

CAMP 5: COUNTERFACTUALITY

Riggs, Peterson, Robinson, and Mitchell (1998) compared children's ability to understand false belief with their ability to reason counterfactually. For this, they changed the false belief task slightly. For instance, Max who had put his chocolate into location A didn't see how his mother used some of the chocolate for baking a cake and then putting the rest of the chocolate into location B. Children's ability to answer the false belief question, "Where will Max look for his chocolate?" correctly with A correlated highly with their ability to answer the counterfactual conditional, "If mother hadn't baked a cake, where would the chocolate now be?" correctly with A.

This finding came as a surprise to me because we (Wimmer & Perner, 1983) had considered that children's difficulty with false belief resides in an inability to represent incompatible, in particular counterfactual states of affairs. However, at that time Alan Leslie (1987) presented a theoretical analysis of pretence at a BPS conference in 1983, which made clear that in pretend play you represent the world as it isn't, i.e. entertaining a counterfactual representation. For instance, when pretending that a banana is a telephone the child has to represent that the object is really a banana and that it is a telephone in pretence. Since the first signs of knowingly pretending occur at the age of $1^1/_2$ years, a good 2 years earlier than an understanding of false belief, an inability to represent counterfactual state of affairs could not be a very good explanation for 3-year-olds' failure on the belief task. My reaction to this at the first theory of mind conference in Toronto 1986 was to argue that the difficulty with belief is to understand that the content of a false belief is more than a false proposition (or possible world, or non-actual situation) but a false proposition held to be true of the real world (Perner et al., 1987; see "Camp 2").

My position would be salvaged by the claim that early pretence falls short of any mentalistic or counterfactual sophistication and requires only understanding of acting like a particular person or animal (Lillard, 1993). For instance, Lillard found that even 5-year-old children do not understand that someone who does not know what a kangaroo is cannot be pretending to be one even when hopping around like one. For them, anyone who behaves like a kangaroo is pretending to be one. If that were all that children below the age of 4 years can do, then their pretence would not show any understanding of counterfactuality. However, in light of data by Harris and Kavanaugh (1993) and Leslie (1994) this seems hard to accept. For instance, in a pretend tea party 2- to 3-year-old children watch how naughty Teddy "pours" pretend tea over a piece of chocolate and they are asked a series of (admittedly) helpful questions (Harris & Kavanaugh, 1993):

(1) What happened—what did Teddy do?
(2) What did Teddy pour?
(3) Where did Teddy pour it?
(4) Teddy made the chocolate all . . . ?
(5) Is the chocolate wet or dry?

By $2\frac{1}{2}$ years most children answer these questions correctly. Now, how could children give correct answers to some of these questions if in their view Teddy just acted like a person pouring tea. Why should the chocolate then be wet? To make this inference, it seems to me, children must represent a counterfactual scenario within which these consequences of Teddy's actions are computed. This also implies that children understand that Teddy's actions are governed by something non-existent. Then more must be involved than purely physical relations. On Brentano's criterion of the mental, children understand pretence as something mental contrary to Lillard's (1993; see Harris, Lillard, & Perner, 1994 for discussion) claim. Moreover, although there is no subjunctive question asked in these pretend scenarios, the required inferences do look very much like counterfactual reasoning: "If there had been tea in the cup what would the chocolate be, wet or dry?"

Another reason why I found the results by Riggs et al. (1998) surprising was that Harris, German, and Mills (1996) reported that 3-year-olds were about as good as 4-year-olds in answering counterfactual questions. As the chapters by Riggs and Peterson (Chapter 5) and Robinson and Beck (Chapter 6) show, the result by Riggs et al. (1998) is reliably difficult for 3-year-old children. And I will present our own data below showing that counterfactual reasoning is as difficult as and correlates highly with the false belief task. Hence, at this point there are at least three interesting questions to be answered:

Q1: Why does understanding counterfactuals develop with false belief understanding?
Q2: Why are counterfactuals so much more difficult to understand than pretence?
Q3: Are the counterfactual tasks used by Harris et al. (1996) substantially easier than the ones used by Riggs et al. (1998), and if so, why?

Here are several attempts to answer some of these questions.

Negative events stimulate counterfactual considerations

Harris and Leevers (Chapter 4) make a plausible suggestion for how to answer Q3. In their stories the real outcome was always negative. Since negative outcomes are to be avoided they stimulate (as found in adult research, Roese, 1997) a search for counterfactual conditions that would have helped avoid the result. This is a particularly plausible explanation for why 3-year-olds are so good at giving counterfactual explanations of how the result could have been avoided (Harris et al., 1996; Experiment 3) but is less plausible for the tasks in which the counterfactual conditions are directly specified as in Riggs et al. (1998). Some of the variations mentioned by Robinson and Beck (Chapter 6) should speak to the issue but show no clear picture. In their Study 2, the wind blew the letter into the tree. Although this is a negative outcome, children did not perform noticeably better than in any of the other tasks with neutral outcomes. Similarly, the pre-schoolers in the studies by Amsel and Smalley (Chapter 7) were equally good whether the counterfactual event was better (sticker) or worse (block) than reality (toy figurine). However, Study 6 by Robinson and Beck does provide some support for Harris and Leevers' contention. Forgetting to put the card into the envelope (a bad outcome to be avoided) and putting the card into the envelope showed a non-significant difference in the direction predicted by Harris and Leevers.

Harris and Leevers's answer to Q1 simply is that the difficulty with false beliefs is to understand their counterfactual nature (counterfactuality hypothesis). However, in order to preserve this hypothesis in light of the negative events hypothesis, an interesting prediction for belief tasks, as Harris and Leevers realised, needs to come out right: False beliefs about negative events—in particular ones that put the negative event right—should be easier to understand. Initial evidence (Paul Harris, personal communication) points that way but—as in the case of counterfactuals (see Robinson & Beck's Study 6)—only with minor effects. So, it looks to me that, perhaps, the use of negative outcomes may be part of the answer, but it does not seem strong enough to be the complete answer.

In any case, even if it is part of the answer to Q3 (and together with the counterfactuality hypothesis) to Q1, I do not see an answer to Q2. Why is pretend play with its obvious counterfactual features so much easier to understand even though no negative real events have to be remedied pretendingly?

Simulation and interpretation

Riggs and Peterson (Chapter 5) address Q1 and Q2. As an answer to Q1 why counterfactual reasoning relates to false belief understanding, Peterson and Riggs (1999) suggest that children are "simulating" Maxi's belief. They suggest this, because conceived as a theory understanding false belief has no obvious counterfactual elements. A "theorist" would, for instance, reason like this: "If one doesn't see an object translocated then one believes that it stays where it was.

Hence Maxi believes that the chocolate is still in the old location. Furthermore, people look for objects where they think they are. Hence, Maxi will look for the chocolate in the old location". This reasoning does not make direct counterfactual statements. The counterfactuality, as it were is hidden in the contents of belief statements. For that reason Peterson and Riggs suggest that children solve belief problems by simulation. As a simulator of Maxi's mind one has to represent a counterfactual claim: "The chocolate stays in the original location while I am out on the playground. When I come back *it is still in there* (counterfactual). So I will look in its original location". But that solution just highlights the urgency of answering Q2, since such counterfactual simulation seems exactly what one needs for pretence, i.e. I imagine the world to be different than it is.

To answer Q2 Peterson and Riggs (1999) suggest that pretence assumptions are not really counterfactual but symbolic interpretations: "The 'is' in pretence statements is not one of predication but of interpretation". This Piagetian suggestion (the position that pretence is "symbolic play") makes sense in the case of "This banana *is* a telephone" (i.e. the banana symbolises the telephone, or the banana plays the role of the telephone), but needs some elaboration in case of Harris and Kavanaugh's pretend scenarios: "this (empty) cup *is* full of tea. The cup is tilted over the chocolate (so that tea *is* being poured over the chocolate). The chocolate *is* now wet." By $2\frac{1}{2}$ years children tend to be quite proficient in keeping track of these counter to fact pretend events and can answer the question whether the chocolate is now wet or dry in terms of the pretence (Harris & Kavanaugh, 1993, Exp. 7).

If instead, we had enacted the tilting of the empty cup and then asked "If there had been tea in the cup, would the chocolate be wet or dry?" then we could expect 3- and even 4-year-old children who do not solve the false belief task to give wrong answers (by extrapolation from Riggs et al.'s 1998, data). I find it difficult to see how Riggs and Peterson's (Chapter 5) 3-point analysis of the difference between pretence and counterfactual reasoning applies here: (Re: 1) In what sense is the relation between the imagined (antecedent) proposition, "There is water in this cup," and the test question, "Is the chocolate now wet or dry?" more arbitrary in the pretend case than in the counterfactual case? (Re: 2) In what sense is the statement, "There is water in the cup", in the pretend case less counterfactual and, thus (Re: 3), less in conflict with other facts in the knowledge base than in the counterfactual reasoning case?

Relating the counterfactual world to reality

Andreas Gschaider and I noticed another difference between the counterfactual tasks used by Harris et al. (1996) and those used by Riggs et al. (1998). Most problems used by Harris et al. (1996) are stereotypical situations where correct answers could be found purely on the basis of the counterfactual condition without knowing the actual event. For instance, when asked, "What if the wind had not come, would the tree be standing up?" one can give the plausible answer, "still standing up" without having heard the story of the wind blowing down the tree[3]. In contrast, in the stories used by Riggs et al. (1998) and the stories used by Robinson and Beck (Chapter 6) this is not possible. For instance, if simply asked, "If there had been no fire, where would Peter now be?" I have no idea what I should answer. This indicates that the specific difficulty in counterfactual reasoning may lie not in having to set reality aside but to combine the counterfactual conditional with what one knows about reality. Amsel and Smalley (Chapter 7) make a similar suggestion but for explaining the later development of understanding regret.

Explicit mental models and working memory overload

Robinson and Beck (Chapter 6) suggest two explanations for why counterfactual reasoning is more difficult than hypothetical reasoning. Using mental model theory of conditional reasoning (Byrne, 1997; Johnson-Laird & Byrne, 1991, ch. 4) the suggestion is that counterfactual statements elicit an explicit representation of the assumed and the real conditions, whereas in hypothetical reasoning the real conditions remain implicit. Explicit representation of alternative models is costly in working memory capacity. The same load is required for understanding false belief on the assumption that it, too, requires explicit representation of where the chocolate is really and where Maxi thinks it is. The required capacity is available at about 4 years. If, in addition, one assumes that pretend play does not require explicit representation of reality while one is pretending, then this can explain why it occurs earlier in development. The critical assumption about working memory capacity is empirically backed up with the finding by Gordon and Olson (1998) that false belief understanding correlates with a measure of working memory capacity and with Robinson and Beck's own study showing that a similar correlation holds between a counterfactual task and the working memory capacity measure.

This starts to look like a coherent story. Let me just propose an alternative explanation (they are always good for sharpening future experimental investigations) and raise a few doubts about the coherence of Robinson and Beck's explanation. An alternative for the finding by Gordon and Olson (1998) was developed in Perner and Lang (in press). It takes into account the finding by Davis and Pratt (1995) that, after partialling out age, false belief understanding correlates with backward digit span, a measure of the central executive function of working memory, and not with forward span, a measure of pure working space capacity. The alternative explanation, therefore, is that it is not growth in work space capacity that is the critical development but understanding the mind that yields better executive control. In fact the task used by Gordon and Olson is a dual task problem (naming and counting 3 objects) which requires executive inhibition. As I have argued earlier, executive inhibition is acquired with false belief understanding.

What is not yet completely convincing in Robinson and Beck's explanation is why the false belief task and the counterfactual task require explicit representation of reality whereas pretence leaves reality implicit. Johnson-Laird and Byrne's (1991) approach is tuned to explaining purely hypothetically posed logic problems where no visible reality is shown. So the simple conditional "If there is a circle then there is a triangle" elicits a single corresponding model with circles and triangles. In contrast, the counterfactual conditional "If there had been a circle there would have been a triangle" generates two explicit models: the counterfactual model of circles and triangles, and a model of the implied reality with an absence of circles and triangles. In pretend play reality is visible and ever present, why should it stay implicit as a model?

Assigning truth-values

Robinson and Beck's other suggestion was that false belief and counterfactual tasks are mastered at the same time since, as we (Perner et al., 1987) had suggested for the false belief task, these tasks require an understanding that one and the same proposition can be assigned different truth values. For the false belief task that means an understanding that Maxi takes the proposition, "the chocolate is in its original place" as true of the real world when the child knows that this proposition is false. The explanation of why pretence is easier to understand is that in pretence the child only needs to assign the correct truth value to each proposition and understand that in pretend play actions can be governed by true and false propositions. No understanding is required that the false pretend propositions are taken as true of the world. In this vein one could equate normal (indicative) conditionals with pretence as descriptions of some possible world, but counterfactual (subjunctive) conditionals as propositions which are temporarily (under the assumption of the antecedent) taken to be true of the actual world.

In fact, this was my first thought of how to explain the results by Riggs et al. (1998) when I had first heard of them. However, I found it hard to make a convincing case for this explanation. My problem is: Why can't I draw my counterfactual conclusions within a possible world specified by the counterfactual antecedent if I can understand pretence as the unfolding of counterfactual consequences of a counterfactual stipulation?

Summary of explanation attempts

All these attempts to explain why counterfactual reasoning is as difficult as false belief understanding and more difficult to understand than pretence pick up some correct insights. However, none seems to provide a complete explanation. I will try to do justice to all these insights and give a more complete answer later. Before I can do this I need to present some more relevant data of our own and some observation about the nature of pretence.

Some data: Counterfactual antecedents with future hypothetical consequents

Sabine Feichtinger and I (ongoing research) have devised the following travel setup (vaguely reminiscent of Frye et al.'s 1995, ramp task): In Peter's village there is his house and two stations (A and B). From Station A a bus goes to the mountains (M) and a train to the lake (L). From station B a bus goes to L and a train to M. Children were first given training on understanding of how to get where. After this initiation, formal tests of three kinds were given (in counterbalanced order). For instance, for *future hypotheticals* (a standardised version of the training problems) they were asked: "If Peter goes to station A and takes the train, where will he arrive?" Complete *counterfactual conditionals* involved problems like, "Peter goes to station A and takes the bus to M. If he had taken the train, where would he have arrived?" The new task was one with a *counterfactual antecedent*: "Peter goes to station A. If he were at station B and takes the bus from there, where will he arrive?"

The findings were very clear. Few of the 29 children aged 3 to 5 years had problems with the future hypotheticals (85% correct). The counterfactual antecedent tasks were as easy (88% correct). Only the complete counterfactual conditionals posed real problems (45% correct) and they were as difficult as the false belief task (48% correct) with a substantial correlation of $\Phi = .51$. Many of the hypotheses discussed so far do not attempt to explain why reasoning with counterfactual antecedents should be substantially easier than reasoning with complete counterfactual conditionals (Harris and Leevers's "negative events"; Riggs and Peterson's "interpretation" hypothesis), and I can't see an obvious way of how they could. The mental models proposal by Robinson and Beck might explain this finding, but the finding would pinpoint more precisely the source of the difficulty. The mentioning of the counterfactual antecedent, "If Peter had gone from home to station B" should elicit an explicit model of reality: Peter has gone from home to station A. The complete counterfactual conditional then differs not by an additional model but by greater complexity of the reality model. That shows, complexity within a model is as important. This should help design a critical test between internal model complexity and alternative explanations. Our data pose a problem for the suggestion that children's difficulty with counterfactuality hinges on their inability to understand truth-value assignment. Why is such an understanding required for the complete counterfactual conditional but not for the conditional with a counterfactual antecedent?

An observation: Pretence rides piggyback on reality

As we have seen the Harris and Kavanaugh pretend sequence ("Teddy pretends there is tea in the pot. He tilts the pot over the chocolate. Is the chocolate now wet or dry?") can be rephrased as a counterfactual conditional: "If Teddy had tea in the pot and if he had tilted the pot over the chocolate, would the chocolate now be wet or dry?". However, the converse is far from true. Not every counterfactual conditional can be turned into pretend play. Take our travel set up. "Peter goes to station A. He takes the bus to the mountains. If he had taken the train from A where would he now be?" One cannot turn this into a pretend scenario: "Peter goes to A. Teddy pretends Peter is at B. Peter takes bus from A to M. Where is he now? (Or: 'Where does Teddy pretend Peter is now?')" The pretend assumption "Peter at B" just doesn't link to the ensuing real actions. The pretence is left behind in station B while reality carries on from A to M. The final question, therefore, has a sensible answer only in terms of reality.

The upshot of this observation is that in successful pretend scenarios a counterfactual pretend world is created as a mixture of real world events and stipulated deviations from that world and the real world changes must be such that their impact on the stipulated deviations remains clear. For instance, in the Harris and Kavanaugh scenario the pot is empty. By stipulation there is tea in it. The pot is tilted above the chocolate. This makes it clear that the pretended tea is pouring out and wetting the chocolate below. In other words, the unfolding of the pretend world is strictly tied to the unfolding of the real world. The pretend world piggybacks in perfect temporal synchrony on the real world changes so that any temporal reference to the pretend world, e.g. "is the chocolate *now* wet or dry?" has the same temporal reference as in reality.

An explanation: Referencing times and possible worlds

I now try to show why children have problems with counterfactual conditionals when they are so adept at future hypotheticals, antecedent counterfactual conditionals and pretence. And I try to show that the mastery of the counterfactual conditionals comes with the understanding of aboutness, i.e. that counterfactual propositions take reference to (are about) the real world but describe it as it isn't. I will take temporal reference to highlight the specific problems posed by counterfactual conditionals.

Three-year olds can think in possible worlds and answer questions about it. However, they can do so only if the question references the right time and world. Children of that age tend to have problems with finding the intended time-world referent as my earlier discussion about referential confusion has shown. In the case of future hypotheticals one possible future development is envisaged (e.g. if he takes the train from A where will he arrive?) and the question has a clear time-world referent: the real world in the future, the later time point in a hypothetical world. In case of a counterfactual antecedent (if he had gone to B and if he takes the bus from there, where will he arrive?) the starting point is in a newly constructed counterfactual world which then develops into later stages that have no competing correspondence in any real future. Hence, the critical question has again a clear referent: a later point in this counterfactual world.

In pretend play (Teddy pretends there is tea in the pot. He tilts the pot over the chocolate. Is the chocolate now wet or dry?), there are two conflicting states at the end: the chocolate is now dry/ it is now wet. Since the counterfactual pretend world rides piggyback on reality it has a present and the temporal reference can point to the present in both worlds. Possible referential confusion exists only between reality and pretend world. The trick in Harris and Kavanaugh's procedure is to keep the child engrossed in the pretend world so that the natural interpretation of the critical question is within the pretence. The child's ability to keep reference within the pretence is, indeed, volatile. Harris and Kavanaugh (1993) had to let the child get actively involved in spelling out the pretend consequences (e.g. "Teddy made the chocolate all ... ?") so that the critical contrast question (Is the chocolate now wet or dry?) appears to be asked and is answered within the pretend world. It is not easy to get such clear performance by such young children but it is possible, as long as one manages to make the children interpret the question within the pretence and avoid temporal reference confusion. The temporal problems are solved in the Harris and Kavanaugh scenario because the pretend world is so closely synchronised with reality.

In contrast, consider Sue Leekam's and my early attempt to show counterfactual reasoning within pretence (which I reported at the first theory of mind conference in Toronto, June 1986). We had a toy dog that was so fluffy that one could not tell head from tail until one searched for its eyes under the hair. Children loved that dog and we told them a story about some boy who is pretending (or was made to believe) that the head was where the tail is. He goes out to get milk: Where will he put the bowl? The child has to indicate the head or tail end of the dog. Children found this as difficult as the false belief version. No wonder! The initial pretend stipulation gets detached from reality as real events unfold. By the time the question is asked about where the boy will put the milk when he returns the pretend world does not really extend to that point in time, only the real world. Similar volatility of reference to pretend stipulations has also been reported by Lillard and Flavell (1992) who found that when first a pretend assumption was given (he pretends there is juice in the cupboard) and then children found out about reality (teddy in cupboard), few $3\frac{1}{2}$ year-olds were able to produce the pretend assumption at the end. Performance improved if the pretence was supported by the character's actions (getting a glass for the juice).

Now let us consider counterfactual conditionals. "Peter takes the train from station A to the lake (L). If he had taken the bus, where would he now be?" You first have to think back to a past state of the real world: Peter at station A. Construct a counterfactual world of him taking the train instead of the bus. This gets you to a different point at some time in some other world. Then comes the question, referring to Peter's present location. How does the child know that it is the counterfactual location? Peter has a location in each world (real: L, counterfactual: M) and the temporal reference is to the real world because the present is a time in the real world. Possible worlds have their own time course (unless they ride piggy back on the real world). Consequently, for someone who thinks in possible worlds and can interpret counterfactual statements only in terms of counterfactual worlds there is great referential pressure to answer in terms of Peter's present (real) location.

That is where a different interpretation of counterfactuals in terms of alternative description of the real world helps. With the statement, "If he had taken the bus . . ." not a possible world with its own time points is opened, but an alternative state of the actual action (taking the train) is given which results in being at the mountains as an alternative end state of the real end state (being at the lake) that resulted from the real action (having taken the train). By thinking of counterfactual conditionals as alternative descriptions of real events at real time points, the temporal synchrony can be explicitly established which in pretence implicitly results from piggybacking on reality. Now the use of the present tense paired with the subjunctive mood makes perfect sense. It describes an alternative state of the present state of affairs.

If one thinks in possible worlds then the subjunctive remains an incomprehensible adjunct. The indicative conditional, "If he takes the train from A then he'll arrive at the lake" describes a possible world. Similarly, if the subjunctive conditional, "If he had taken the bus he would be at the mountains," describes a possible world then why do I need the subjunctive if it is just a possibility? It only starts to make sense if it is seen not just as a possibility but as a point for point alternative to real events. In other words the counterfactual conditional takes reference to points in the real world but shows the events at these points as being different than they really are. And to think this way requires the same intellectual ability that I have claimed necessary for understanding false belief: to understand a proposition (the content of the belief; the counterfactual conditional) as referring to (be about) the real world. That explains the developmental synchrony between understanding false belief and counterfactual reasoning discovered by Riggs et al. (1998).

CAMP 6: SIMULATION

Riggs and Peterson (Chapter 5) appeal to simulation in their account of why understanding false belief relates to counterfactual reasoning. Fabricius and Imbens-Bailey (Chapter 13), and R. Mitchell (Chapter 3) also rely in their theoretical accounts on simulation. Harris (1989) was, I think, the first who introduced simulation as a counterpoint to theory development in children's acquisition of mental concepts. Although I have expressed my doubts about simulation underlying the mastery of the false belief task (Perner, 1991) and had a hand in collecting data against it, I am not against the use of simulation. In fact, I even tried (Perner, 1999) to elaborate on Gordon's (1995) non-introspectionist version of simulation in order to make it compatible with our developmental data

(Perner, 1994; Perner & Howes, 1992) which do speak against the introspectionist variety. Without introspection simulation needs *ascent routines* in order to ascend from descriptions of external facts (e.g. X is a fact) to mental states (I know X). By example of the stories we used to test children's ability to differentiate between belief, pretence and knowledge (Perner, Baker, & Hutton, 1994) I was able to specify ascent routines for these concepts that yield the correct result for each story. This success made me believe that there is more to simulation than I had hitherto thought. Moreover, I became aware that I am not committed to theory theory. In fact, the right combinations of perspective change and ascent routines might provide the subconceptual mechanism embodying the under-standing that false propositions can be held true, as German and Leslie (Chapter 11) remonstrate against my overly conceptually expressed analysis.

I also realised (Perner, 1996) that some parts of our understanding must be based on simulation, other parts on theory. This now seems to be the consensus in the philosophical literature (Heal, 1996; Stich & Nichols, 1997). The question is how we can tell which parts are being simulated and which ones grasped by theory. To answer this question we developed a method to decide (Perner, Gschaider, Schrofner, & Kühberger, 1999). In brief, the method starts with two *target* conditions (TC)—using an example from our recent developmental investigation—the child her/himself plays the role of Maxi in a false belief condi-tion (TC1: does not see the transfer) or in a knowledge control (TC2: sees the transfer). Strictly speaking one would have to test whether children indeed look in the old place in C1 and in the new one in C2. We just assumed that they would. The interesting part comes in the remaining three *prediction* conditions (PC). In the two *independent prediction* conditions children are told either the story of Maxi in the belief condition (PC1) or with Susi in the knowledge con-dition (PC2), and they have to make predictions about Maxi's/Susi's behaviour, where he or she will go to look for the chocolate. In the *juxtaposed predictions* condition children are told stories with both a knowledgeable (Susi) and an ignorant character (Maxi) and then have to make predictions for each one (PC1+2). If predictions are based on theory then the juxtaposed condition might be help-ful, since it highlights the critical feature (seeing vs. not seeing the transfer) and this should help theory application—at least this condition should not be worse than the independent conditions where many different aspects, relevant and irrelevant, might water down the application of the theory. In contrast, if predic-tions are based on simulation then the independent conditions might yield more accurate predictions because one might be better able to empathically identify with a character in a single condition then when both conditions are mentally present. In fact, the basic idea for this method was inspired by Paul Harris's (1992) defence of simulation theory against the alleged counter-examples from attribution theory used by Stich and Nichols (1992). Harris argued that the simultaneous presentation of both experimental conditions might interfere with predicting the results of these conditions by simulation.

Andreas Gschaider, Birgit Lang and I tried to use this method for the follow-ing problem in the Maxi story. The problem is how a simulator knows that the events in Maxi's absence do not register in Maxi's world. Simulationists might argue that this simply falls out of imagining Maxi's situation: "I (as Maxi) put the chocolate in cupboard A. I go out to play. (While I am out mother transfers the chocolate to cupboard B.) When I get hungry I go back to A to get my chocolate". However, it is far from clear that the critical parenthesised story passage is omitted just because one is imagining to be Maxi. The suspicion is that it is omitted on the basis of some theoretical knowledge that events that are not perceived are to be omitted from Maxi's world. If this suspicion is right then children's prediction whether Maxi has or has not seen the critical event might come out as "theoretical knowledge" by our method. Pilot results seemed to confirm this: children were better in the juxtaposed conditions than in the inde-pendent conditions.

In contrast to establishing which facts are to be included or omitted from Maxi's world the predictions of how Maxi will act on the basis of his world can be simulated. And if simulation is to play any role then they should be simu-lated. That is, predictions where Maxi will look for the chocolate should be better in the independent prediction condition than in the juxtaposed prediction condition. Data by Robinson and Mitchell (1995) point in the opposite direction. Predictions are better under juxtaposed than under independent conditions. How-ever, this could be a knock on effect of the earlier "theoretical" problem of knowing which facts to include in Maxi's world. To control for this possibility we looked at just those children who gave perfect judgements on all the "Has Maxi/Susi seen . . . ?" questions. Yet, there was still a (non-significant) advan-tage of the juxtaposed condition when a significant advantage of the independent condition is needed for providing positive evidence for simulation.

In sum, although I have much sympathy for simulation as—at least—an important part of how we understand the mind, I have not been able to find any convincing evidence that imputation of our basic mental categories is based on simulation.

CAMP 2000: CONCLUSION

I have tried—and hope successfully—to defend my view of an important intel-lectual change at about 4 years indexed by children's mastery of the false belief task. The change hinges on an understanding of aboutness, that propositions or representations are about the world (situations). I first defended this view against claims that the observed developmental course of mastering the false belief task is due to mere surface information processing characteristics. Henry Wellman (personal communication) is just writing up a large meta-analysis of 591 false belief conditions. There are several methodological changes that make some difference to when the false belief task is mastered but, overall, the developmental trend between 3 and 5 years persists. My conviction that the false belief task reflects an important change is reinforced by the recent findings that its mastery appears at the same time as a host of other—on the surface often seemingly unrelated—abilities emerge, in particular strengthened self-control and counterfactual reasoning. I have argued that the emergence of these abilities can be related to the same basic intellectual advance of understanding aboutness. At least I have provided a viable alternative explanation for why these different tasks emerge at the same time and given a focus for future experiments to decide between the alternative proposals for how to explain these developmental synchronies.

NOTES

1. German and Leslie (Chapter 11) raise the objection that it is implausible that children have the concepts of propositions and truth evaluation which such an understanding would require. Such concepts are, however, only necessary for a completely explicit conceptual understanding of these matters. The necessary distinctions may remain part of a subconceptual and implicit—German and Leslie suggest the term—"mechanism", as long as this mechanism allows the thought that something (a statement, a belief) is taken as true of the world, or the difference between searching in an empty cupboard because one is pretending vs. believing that an object is in there.
2. For my purposes I use situation and world interchangeably. A situation is simply a relevant part of a possible world.
3. One possible exception is the question "What if Henry had not dropped the chocolate—where would the chocolate be?" In this case one has to know that Henry had the chocolate in his mouth. Perhaps this task, dropped for the second experiment, was more difficult than the other tasks.

REFERENCES

Baron-Cohen, S., Ring, H.A., Wheelwright, S., Bullmore, E.T., Brammer, M.J., Simmons, A., & Williams, S.C. (1998). *Social intelligence in the male, female and autistic brain: An fMRI study*. Unpublished manuscript.

Bartsch, K., & Wellman, H.M. (1989). Young children's attribution of action to beliefs and desires. *Child Development, 60,* 946–964.

Byrne, R.M. (1997). Cognitive processes in counterfactual thinking about what might have been. *The Psychology of Learning and Motivation, 31,* 105–154.

Carlson, S.M. (1997). *Individual differences in inhibitory control and children's theory of mind.* Poster presented at the biennial meeting of the Society for Research in Child Development. April, 1997, Washington, DC.

Carlson, S.M., Moses, L.J., & Hix, H.R. (1998). The role of inhibitory processes in young children's difficulties with deception and false belief. *Child Development, 69,* 672–691.

Chandler, M.J., Fritz, A.S., & Hala, S.M. (1989). Small scale deceit: Deception as a marker of 2-, 3- and 4-year-olds' early theories of mind. *Child Development, 60,* 1263–1227.

Clements, W.A., & Perner, J. (1994). Implicit understanding of belief. *Cognitive Development, 9,* 377–397.

Clements, W.A., & Perner, J. (1996). *Implicit understanding of belief at three in action.* Unpublished manuscript.

Clements, W.A., Perner, J., Stubbs, K., & Import, A. (1998). *Looking for implicit understanding of belief in children with autism*. Unpublished manuscript.

Clements, W.A., Rustin, C., & McCallum, S. (1997). *Promoting the transition from implicit to explicit understanding: A training study of false belief*. Unpublished manuscript, University of Sussex.

Davis, H.L., & Pratt, C. (1995). The development of children's theory of mind: The working memory explanation. Special Issue: Cognitive development. *Australian Journal of Psychology*, *47*, 25–31.

Doherty, M.J., & Perner, J. (1998). Metalinguistic awareness and theory of mind: Just two words for the same thing? *Cognitive Development*, *13*, 279–305.

De Villiers, J.G. (1995). Questioning and answering machines. In D. MacLaughlin & S. McEwen (Eds.), *Proceedings of the 19th Boston University Conference on Language Development*. Cascadilla Press.

Field, H. (1978). Mental representation. *Erkenntnis*, *13*, 9–61.

Fischhoff, B. (1975). Hindsight ≠ foresight: The effect of outcome knowledge on judgement under uncertainty. *Journal of Experimental Psychology: Human Perception and Performance*, *1*, 288–299.

Fletcher, P.A., Happé, F., Frith, U., Baker, S., Dolan, R., & Frakowiak, R.S. (1995). Other minds in the brain: A functional imaging study of the 'theory of mind'. *Cognition*, *57*, 109–128.

Fodor, J.A. (1978). Propositional attitudes. *The Monist*, *61*, 501–523.

Fodor, J.A. (1992). A theory of the child's theory of mind. *Cognition*, *44*, 283–296.

Frith, C.D. (1992). *The cognitive neuropsychology of schizophrenia*. Hillsdale, NJ: Lawrence Erlbaum Associates Inc.

Frye, D., Zelazo, P.D., & Palfai, T. (1995). Theory of mind and rule-based reasoning. *Cognitive Development*, *10*, 483–527.

Goel, V., Grafman, J., Sadato, N., & Hallett, M. (1995). Modelling other minds. *NeuroReport*, *6*, 1741–1746.

Goldin-Meadow, S., Alibali, M.W., & Church, R.B. (1993). Transitions in concept acquisition: Using the hand to read the mind. *Psychological Review*, *100*, 279–297.

Goodman, N. (1976). *Languages of art*. Indianapolis, IN: Hackett Publishing Co.

Gopnik, A., & Astington, J.W. (1988). Children's understanding of representational change and its relation to the understanding of false belief and the appearance-reality distinction. *Child Development*, *59*, 26–37.

Gordon, A.C., & Olson, D.R. (1998). The relation between acquisition of a theory of mind and the capacity to hold in mind. *Journal of Experimental Child Psychology*, *68*, 70–83.

Gordon, R.M. (1995). Simulation without introspection or inference from me to you. In M. Davies & T. Stone (Eds.), *Mental Simulation: Evaluations and applications* (pp. 53–67). Oxford: Blackwell.

Hala, S., Chandler, M., & Fritz, A.S. (1991). Fledgling theories of mind: Deception as a marker of 3-year-olds' understanding of false belief. *Child Development*, *62*, 83–97.

Happé, F., Ehlers, S., Fletcher, P., Frith, U., Johansson, M., Gillberg, C., Dolan, R., Frackowiak, R., & Frith, C. (1996). 'Theory of mind' in the brain: Evidence from a PET scan study of asperger syndrome. *NeuroReport*, *8*, 197–201.

Harris, P.L. (1989). *Children and emotion: The development of psychological understanding*. Oxford: Basil Blackwell.

Harris, P.L. (1992). From simulation to folk psychology: The case for development. *Mind & Language*, *7*, 120–144.

Harris, P.L. (1993). Pretending and planning. In S. Baron-Cohen, H. Tager-Flusberg, & D.J. Cohen (Eds.), *Understanding other minds: Perspectives from autism* (pp. 283–304). Oxford, UK: Oxford University Press.

Harris, P.L., German, T., & Mills, P. (1996). Children's use of counterfactual thinking in causal reasoning. *Cognition*, *61*, 233–259.

Harris, P.L., & Kavanaugh, R.D. (1993). Young children's understanding of pretence. *Society for Research in Child Development Monographs (Serial No. 237)*.

Harris, P.L., Lillard, A.S., & Perner, J. (1994). Commentary: Triangulating pretence and belief. In C. Lewis & P. Mitchell (Eds.), *Children's early understanding of mind* (pp. 287–293). Hove, UK: Psychology Press.

Heal, J. (1996). Simulation and cognitive penetrability. *Mind & Language, 11*, 44–67.

Hogrefe, J., Wimmer, H., & Perner, J. (1986). Ignorance versus false belief: A developmental lag in attribution of epistemic states. *Child Development, 57*, 567–582.

Holmes, H.A., Black, C., & Miller, S.A. (1996). A cross-task comparison of false belief understanding in a head start population. *Journal of Experimental Child Psychology, 63*, 263–285.

Hughes, C. (1998). Executive function in preschoolers: Links with theory of mind and verbal ability. *British Journal of Developmental Psychology, 16*, 233–253.

Hughes, C., & Russell, J. (1993). Autistic children's difficulty with mental disengagement from an object: Its implication for theories of autism. *Developmental Psychology, 29*, 498–510.

Hughes, C., White, A., & Dunn, J. (in press). Trick or treat?: Uneven understanding of mind and emotion and executive dysfunction in 'hard to manage' preschoolers. *Journal of Child Psychology and Psychiatry*.

Jeannerod, M. (1997). *The cognitive neuroscience in action*. Oxford: Blackwell Publishers Ltd.

Johnson-Laird, P.N., & Byrne, R.M. (1991). *Deduction*. Hove, UK: Psychology Press.

Leslie, A.M. (1987). Pretense and representation: The origins of "Theory of Mind". *Psychological Review, 94*, 412–426.

Leslie, A.M. (1988). Some implications of pretense for mechanisms underlying the child's theory of mind. In J.W. Astington, P.L. Harris, & D.R. Olson (Eds.), *Developing theories of mind* (pp. 19–46). New York: Cambridge University Press.

Leslie, A.M. (1994). Pretending and believing: Issues in the theory of ToM. *Cognition, 50*, 211–238.

Lewis, C., Freemann, N.H., Kyriakidou, C., Maridaki-Kassotaki, K., & Berridge, D.M. (1996). Social influences on false belief access: Specific sibling influences or general apprenticeship? *Child Development, 67*, 2930–2947.

Lewis, C., & Osborne, A. (1990). Three-year-olds' problems with false belief: Conceptual deficit or linguistic artefact? *Child Development, 61*, 1514–1519.

Lillard, A.S. (1993). Young children's conceptualization of pretense: Action of mental representational state? *Child Development, 64*, 372–386.

Lillard, A.S., & Flavell, J.H. (1992). Young children's understanding of different mental states. *Developmental Psychology, 28*, 626–634.

Luria, A., Pribram, K.H., & Homskaya, E.D. (1964). An experimental analysis of the behavioural disturbance produced by a left frontal arachnoidal endothelioma (meningioma). *Neuropsychologia, 2*, 257–280.

Mazoyer, B.M., Tzourio, N., Frak, V., Syrota, A., Murayama, N., & Levier, O. (1993). The cortical representation of speech. *Journal of Cognitive Neuroscience, 5*, 467–479.

Minter, M., Hobson, R.P., & Bishop, M. (1998). Congenital visual impairment and 'theory of mind'. *British Journal of Developmental Psychology, 16*, 183–196.

Mitchell, P., & Lacohée, R. (1991). Children's early understanding of false belief. *Cognition, 39*, 107–127.

Moses, L.J., & Flavell, J.H. (1990). Inferring false beliefs from actions and reactions. *Child Development, 61*, 929–945.

Norman, D.A., & Shallice, T. (1986). Attention to Action: Willed and automatic control of behavior. Center for Human Information Processing Technical Report No. 99. Reprinted in revised form. In R.J. Davidson, G.E. Schwartz, & D. Shapiro (Eds.), *Consciousness and self-regulation* (*Vol. 4*, pp. 1–18). New York: Plenum Press.

Ozonoff, S., Pennington, B.F., & Rogers, S.J. (1991). Executive function deficits in high-functioning autistic children: Relationship to theory of mind. *Journal of Child Psychology and Psychiatry, 32*, 1081–1105.

Pacherie, E. (1998). Motor-images, self consciousness and autism. In J. Russell (Ed.), *Autism as an executive disorder* (pp. 215–255). Oxford: Oxford University Press.

Passingham, R. (1993). *The frontal lobes and voluntary action*. New York: Oxford University Press.

Pennington, B.F., Rogers, S., Bennetto, L., Griffith, E.M., Reed, D.T., & Shyu, V. (1998). Validity tests of the executive dysfunction hypothesis of autism. In J. Russell (Ed.), *Autism as an executive disorder* (pp. 143–178). Oxford: Oxford University Press.

Perner, J. (1988). Developing semantics for theories of mind: From propositional attitudes to mental representation. In J.W. Astington, P.L. Harris, & D.R. Olson (Eds.), *Developing theories of mind* (pp. 141–172). New York: Cambridge University Press.

Perner, J. (1991). *Understanding the representational mind*. Cambridge, MA: MIT Press.

Perner, J. (1994). The necessity and impossibility of simulation. *Proceedings of the British Academy, 83*, 129–144.

Perner, J. (1995). The many faces of belief: Reflections on Fodor's and the child's theory of mind. *Cognition, 57*, 241–269.

Perner, J. (1996). Simulation as explicitation of predication-implicit knowledge about the mind: Arguments for a simulation-theory mix. In P. Carruthers & P.K. Smith (Eds.), *Theories of theories of mind* (pp. 90–104). Cambridge: Cambridge University Press.

Perner, J. (1998). The meta-intentional nature of executive functions and theory of mind. In P. Carruthers & J. Boucher (Eds.), *Language and thought* (pp. 270–283). Cambridge: Cambridge University Press.

Perner, J. (1999). Metakognition und Introspektion in entwicklungspsychologischer Sicht: Studien zur "theory of mind". In W. Janke & W. Schneider (Eds.), *100 Jahre Würzburger Schule der Denkpsychologie und Institut für Psychologie* (pp. 411–431). [English Version: Developmental Perspectives on Metacognition and Introspection: Studies in "Theory of Mind" and Simulation.]

Perner, J., Gschaider, A., Schrofner, S., & Kühberger, A. (1999). Predicting others through simulation or by theory? A method to decide. *Mind & Language, 14*.

Perner, J., & Howes, D. (1992). "He thinks he knows"; and more developmental evidence against the simulation (role-taking) theory. *Mind & Language, 7*, 72–86.

Perner, J., & Lang, B. (in press). Theory of mind and executive function: Is there a developmental relationship? In S. Baron-Cohen, H. Tager-Flusberg, & D. Cohen (Eds.), *Understanding other minds: Perspectives from autism and developmental cognitive neuroscience*. Oxford: Oxford University Press.

Perner, J., Lang, B., & Stummer, S. (1998). *Theory of mind and executive function: Which depends on which*. Unpublished manuscript, University of Salzburg.

Perner, J., Leekam, S.R., Myers, D., Davis, S., & Odgers, N. (1993). *Misrepresentation and referential confusion: Children's difficulty with false beliefs and outdated photographs*. Unpublished manuscript.

Perner, J., Leekam, S.R., & Wimmer, H. (1987). Three-year olds' difficulty with false belief: The case for a conceptual deficit. *British Journal of Developmental Psychology, 5*, 125–137.

Perner, J., Ruffman, T., & Leekam, S.R. (1994). Theory of mind is contagious: You catch it from your sibs. *Child Development, 65*, 1228–1238.

Perner, J., & Stummer, S. (1998). *Say something different ToM! Understanding representations, embedded conditionals or executive function?* Unpublished manuscript, University of Salzburg.

Perner, J., Stummer, S., & Lang, B. (1999). Executive functions and theory of mind: Cognitive complexity or functional dependence? In P.D. Zelazo, J.W. Astington, & D.R. Olson (Eds.), *Developing theories of intention: Social understanding and self-control*. Mahwah, NJ: Lawrence Erlbaum Associates Inc.

Perner, J., & Wimmer, H. (1988). Misinformation and unexpected change: Testing the development of epistemic-state attribution. *Psychological Research, 50*, 191–197.

Peterson, D., & Riggs, K.J. (1999). Adaptive modelling and mindreading. *Mind & Language, 14*, 80–112.

Petrides, M. (1982). Motor conditional associative-learning after selective prefrontal lesion in the monkey. *Behavioral Brain Research*, *5*, 407–413.

Repacholi, B.M., & Gopnik, A. (1997). Early reasoning about desires: Evidence from 14- and 18-month-olds. *Developmental Psychology*, *33*, 12–21.

Riggs, K.J., Peterson, D.M., Robinson, E.J., & Mitchell, P. (1998). Are errors in false belief tasks symptomatic of a broader difficulty with counterfactuality? *Cognitive Development*, *13*, 73–90.

Robinson, E.J., & Mitchell, P. (1995). Masking of children's early understanding of the representational mind: Backwards explanation versus prediction. *Child Development*, *66*, 1022–1039.

Roese, N.J. (1997). Counterfactual thinking. *Psychological Bulletin*, *121*, 133–148.

Rosenthal, D.M. (1986). Two concepts of consciousness. *Philosophical Studies*, *49*, 329–359.

Ruffman, T., Perner, J., Naito, M., Parkin, L., & Clements, W.A. (1998). Older (but not younger) siblings facilitate false belief understanding. *Developmental Psychology*, *34*, 161–174.

Russell, J. (1996). *Agency: Its role in mental development*. Hove, UK: Psychology Press.

Russell, J. (1998). How executive disorders can bring about an inadequate 'theory of mind'. In J. Russell (Ed.), *Autism as an executive disorder* (pp. 256–299). Oxford: Oxford University Press.

Russell, J., Mauthner, N., Sharpe, S., & Tidswell, T. (1991). The 'windows task' as a measure of strategic deception in preschoolers and autistic subjects. *British Journal of Developmental Psychology*, *9*, 331–349.

Saltmarsh, R., Mitchell, P., & Robinson, E.J. (1995). Realism and children's early grasp of mental representation: Belief-based judgements in the state change task. *Cognition*, *57*, 297–325.

Shultz, T.R., Wells, D., & Sarda, M. (1980). The development of the ability to distinguish intended actions from mistakes, reflexes, and passive movements. *British Journal of Social and Clinical Psychology*, *19*, 301–310.

Siegal, M., & Beattie, K. (1990). Where to look first for children's knowledge of false belief. *Cognition*, *38*, 1–12.

Sodian, B., Taylor, C., Harris, P.L., & Perner, J. (1991). Early deception and the child's theory of mind: False trails and genuine markers. *Child Development*, *62*, 468–483.

Stich, S., & Nichols, S. (1992). Folk psychology: The case for development. *Mind & Language*, *7*, 35–71.

Stich, S., & Nichols, S. (1997). Cognitive penetrability, rationality and restricted simulation. *Mind & Language*, *12*, 297–326.

Surian, L., & Leslie, A.M. (1995). *Competence and performance in false belief understanding*. Poster presented at the Meeting of the Society for Research in Child Development, Indianapolis, March.

Vygotsky, L.S. (1978). *Mind in society*. Cambridge, MA: Harvard University Press.

Wellman, H.M., & Bartsch, K. (1988). Young children's reasoning about beliefs. *Cognition*, *30*, 239–277.

Wimmer, H. (1989). Common-Sense Mentalismus und Emotion: Einige entwicklungspsychologische Implikationen. In Roth (Ed.), *Denken und Fühlen* (pp. 56–66). Berlin: Springer Verlag.

Wimmer, H., Hogrefe, G.-J., & Sodian, B. (1988). A second stage in children's conception of mental life: Understanding sources of information. In J.W. Astington, P.L. Harris, & D.R. Olson (Eds.), *Developing theories of mind* (pp. 173–192). New York: Cambridge University Press.

Wimmer, H., & Mayringer, H. (1998). False belief understanding in young children: Explanations do not develop before predictions. *International Journal of Behavioral Development*, *22*, 403–422.

Wimmer, H., & Perner, J. (1983). Beliefs about beliefs: Representation and constraining function of wrong beliefs in young children's understanding of deception. *Cognition*, *13*, 103–128.

Zelazo, P.D., & Frye, D. (1996). Cognitive complexity and control: A theory of the development of deliberate reasoning and intentional action. In M. Stamenov (Ed.), *Language structure, discourse and access to consciousness* (pp. 113–153). Amsterdam & Philadelphia: John Benjamins.

Zelazo, P.D., & Jacques, S. (1996). Children's rule use: representation, reflection and cognitive control. In R. Vasta (Ed.), *Annals of child development* (*Vol. 12*, pp. 119–176). London: Jessica Kingsley Publishers Ltd.

Author index

Adams, R.J. 62
Adelson, E. 30
Adi-Jalpa, E. 359
Amsel, E. 7, 123, 125, 126, 132, 133, 136, 137, 139, 140, 141, 157, 310, 368, 387, 389
Andersen, C. 310
Andersen, E.S. 30
Anisfield, M. 62
Armstrong, D.M. 176, 180
Aronson, J.N. 129
Asquith, P.J. 47
Astington, J. 48, 89, 96, 151, 156, 183, 185, 192, 200, 223, 246, 247, 254, 256, 268, 281, 295
Austin, J.L. 47
Avis, J. 222
Ayer, A.J. 46

Baddeley, A.D. 179
Baillargeon, R. 327
Baker, S. 23, 101, 124, 130, 159, 199, 231, 369, 382, 395
Baldwin, J.M. 177
Ball, L. 317
Baltaxe, C.A.M. 27
Barding, C.G. 333

Baron-Cohen, S. 28, 29, 149, 151, 231, 240, 382
Bartlett, F.C. 56
Bartsch, K. 49, 52, 53, 57, 96, 154, 155, 159, 160, 192, 195, 201, 209, 211, 236, 241, 244, 245, 259, 263, 269, 270, 290, 291, 368, 369, 372, 380
Barwise, J. 249
Baumgartner, P. 28
Beardsall, L. 53
Beattie, K. 194, 368
Beck, S. 94, 98, 368, 386, 387, 389, 390
Beeghly, M. 123, 192
Beilin, H. 360
Bennett, R. 306
Bennett, W.L. 49, 50
Berger, S. 161
Berry, D.C. 176
Berti, A.E. 364
Beveridge, M. 333
Bibeau, L. 206
Bickerton, D. 224
Bishop, M. 30, 383
Black, C. 371
Block, N. 169, 185
Bloom, L. 141, 199

Subject index